# The Ultimate Scene Study Series
## Volume I

# *101 Scenes for Groups*

**Smith and Kraus** *Books for Actors*
## THE MONOLOGUE SERIES
The Best Men's / Women's Stage Monologues of 1998
The Best Men's / Women's Stage Monologues of 1997
The Best Men's / Women's Stage Monologues of 1996
The Best Men's / Women's Stage Monologues of 1995
The Best Men's / Women's Stage Monologues of 1994
The Best Men's / Women's Stage Monologues of 1993
The Best Men's / Women's Stage Monologues of 1992
The Best Men's / Women's Stage Monologues of 1991
The Best Men's / Women's Stage Monologues of 1990
One Hundred Men's / Women's Stage Monologues from the 1980s
2 Minutes and Under: Character Monologues for Actors
Street Talk: Character Monologues for Actors
Uptown: Character Monologues for Actors
Ice Babies in Oz: Character Monologues for Actors
Monologues from Contemporary Literature: Volume I
Monologues from Classic Plays 468 B.C. to 1960 A.D.
100 Great Monologues from the Renaissance Theatre
100 Great Monologues from the Neo-Classical Theatre
100 Great Monologues from the 19th C. Romantic and Realistic Theatres
A Brave and Violent Theatre: 20th C. Irish Monologues, Scenes & Hist. Context
Kiss and Tell: Restoration Monologues, Scenes and Historical Context
The Great Monologues from the Humana Festival
The Great Monologues from the EST Marathon
The Great Monologues from the Women's Project
The Great Monologues from the Mark Taper Forum
## SCENE STUDY SERIES
The Ultimate Scene Study Series Vol.I: 101 Scenes for Groups
The Ultimate Scene Study Series Vol.III: 103 Scenes for Three Actors
The Ultimate Scene Study Series Vol.IV: 104 Scenes for Four Actors
Scenes From Classic Plays 468 B.C. to 1970 A.D.
The Best Stage Scenes of 1998
The Best Stage Scenes of 1997
The Best Stage Scenes of 1996
The Best Stage Scenes of 1995
The Best Stage Scenes of 1994
The Best Stage Scenes of 1993
The Best Stage Scenes of 1992
The Best Stage Scenes for Men / Women from the 1980s

If you require prepublication information about upcoming Smith and Kraus books, you may receive our semi-annual catalogue, free of charge, by sending your name and address to *Smith and Kraus Catalogue, 4 Lower Mill Road, North Stratford, NH 03590. Or call us at (800) 895-4331, fax (603) 643-1831.*

# The Ultimate Scene Study Series Volume I

## *101 Scenes for Groups*

edited by Wilma Marcus Chandler

SCENE STUDY SERIES

A SMITH AND KRAUS BOOK

Published by Smith and Kraus, Inc.
177 Lyme Road, Hanover, NH 03755
www.SmithKraus.com

First Edition: June 2001
10 9 8 7 6 5 4 3 2 1

Library of Congress cataloguing in publication data
The ultimate scene study series / edited by Jocelyn A. Beard
p. cm. — (Scene study series)
Includes bibliographical references.
Contents: v.1. 101 scenes for groups — v.2. 102 short scenes for two actors —
v.3. 103 scenes for three actors — v.4. 104 scenes for four actors.
ISBN 1-57525-153-1 (v.2)
1. Acting. 2. English drama. 3. American drama. 4. Drama—Translations into English.
I. Beard, Jocelyn. II. Series.

PN2080.U49 1999
808.82—dc21 99-089197

**NOTE: These scenes are intended to be used for audition and class study; per-
mission is not required to use the material for those purposes. However, if
there is a paid performance of any of the scenes included in this book, please
refer to Permission Acknowledgments to locate the source that can grant permission for public performance.**

# Contents

## PART TWO: SCENES FOR MEN

### SMALL GROUP SCENES

### LARGE GROUP SCENES

### SMALL GROUPS WITH A MAJORITY OF MEN

## LARGE GROUPS WITH A MAJORITY OF MEN

## PART THREE: SCENES FOR MIXED GROUPS

### SMALL GROUP SCENES (5–10 ACTORS)

### LARGE GROUP SCENES (11+ ACTORS)

To the Monday night writing group
and to the creative community of Santa Cruz—
the art spirit abounds.

"I don't know what talent is, and frankly, I don't care.
I do not think it is the actor's job to be interesting.
I think that is the job of the script.
I think it is the actor's job to be truthful and brave—
both qualities which can be developed and exercised
through the will."

David Mamet, *True and False*

# Foreword

Every person in a group or crowd is important. Whether you are the king or the soldier guarding the king you are vital to the scene.

I use the word *group* in this volume to denote scenes with up to ten characters. *Crowd* scenes seem to start at about eleven characters. Some scenes in this book are specific in their requirements: scenes for men, scenes for women, etc. Other scenes are nonspecific and you can be imaginative in combining not only men and women but people of various ages and appearances.

To the actors: In large scenes it is important to understand your own character fully. Give your character a complete life and a history. In doing so you will determine whether your character blends with others in the crowd or takes specific focus. Some questions to ask might be, "Why am I in the crowd?" "What do I want?" What am I willing to do to achieve what I want?" "What energy is required?" "What obstacles are present?" "What period of history is it?" "What is my status in society?" "What would be appropriate behavior for my character?" "What restrictions are being imposed by the situation, by the text, by the time of day, the weather, my health?" Determine when you will merge into the mass and when you will stand out.

To directors who are learning to work with large groups: Begin with your space. How many bodies must you fit into the space provided? Who must have primary focus? Who must be heard? Ask yourself about the dynamics of the scene. Where are the high points? Where do silences occur? What has to happen during the course of the scene? Is the movement within the scene fluid or static? Do you want everyone seen and heard individually or do you wish to create a sense of babble and hubbub? What emotions do you wish to evoke in your audience? Experiment with the geometrics of space, levels, diagonals, and depth perspective. Experiment with the rise and fall of sound, the cacophony of voices or a smooth, unified chorale.

Experiment with the counterpoint of characters who are singled out and those who are immersed within the group.

Think of these scenes as having a unique music and each actor as playing an integral part in the orchestra. Success is dependent on all the players performing harmoniously.

Good luck and have fun.

# PART ONE

# SCENES FOR WOMEN

# SMALL GROUP SCENES

# The Suppliants

Aeschylus
Translated by John Stuart Blackie
490 B.C.

**Dramatic**
**Setting:** a sacred grove in Argos, Greece.
**Scene:** The fifty chaste daughters of Danaus have fled with their
father to their ancestral homeland, Greece, as their fifty male
cousins, sons of Danaus' twin brother Aegyptus wish to marry
them. The two brothers have quarreled bitterly and Danaus and
his children have escaped to Argos. Now they have come to a
sacred grove filled with statues of the Gods and they seek sanctuary.

**Of Note:** Lines can be divided appropriately. This can be performed
as a large and lyrical chorus, or with just a few voices as needed.

**Many Women 5–50**
The Danaides, the daughters of Danaus, various ages

Jove, the suppliant's high protector,
Look from Heaven, benignly favouring
Us the suppliant band, swift-oared
Hither sailing, from the seven mouths
Of the fat fine-sanded Nile!
From the land that fringes Syria,
Land divine, in flight we came,
Not by public vote forth-driven,
Not by taint of blood divorced
From our native state, but chastely
Our abhorrent foot withdrawing
From impure ungodly wedlock
With Ægyptus' sons, too nearly
Cousined with ourselves. For wisely,
This our threatened harm well-weighing,
Danaus, our sire, prime counsellor,
And leader of our sistered band,
Timely chose this least of sorrows
O'er the salt-sea wave to flee;

And here on Argive soil to plant us,
Whence our race its vaunted spring
Drew divinely, when great Jove
Gently thrilled the brize-stung heifer
With his procreant touch, and breathed
Godlike virtue on her womb.
Where on Earth should we hope refuge
On more friendly ground than this,
In our hands these green boughs bearing
Wreathed with precatory wool?
Ye blissful gods supremely swaying
Land and city, and lucid streams;
And ye in sepulchres dark, severely
Worshipped 'neath the sunless ground;
And thou, the third, great Jove the Saviour,
Guardian of all holy homes,
With your spirit gracious-wafted,
Breathe fair welcome on this band
Of suppliant maids. But in the depth
Of whirling waves engulph the swarm
Of insolent youths, Ægyptus' sons,
Them, and their sea-cars swiftly oared,
Ere this slimy shore receive
Their hated footprint. Let them labour,
With wrath-spitting seas confronted:
By the wild storm wintry-beating,
Thunder-crashing, lightning flashing,
By the tyrannous blast shower-laden
Let them perish, ere they mount
Marriage beds which right refuses,
Us, their father's brother's daughters
To their lawless yoke enthralling!

> (The Chorus assemble in a band round the centre of the
> Orchestra, and sing the Choral Hymn.)

STROPHE I
Give ear to our prayer, we implore thee,
Thou son, and the mother that bore thee—

The calf and the heifer divine!
From afar be thine offspring's avenger,
Even thou, once a beautiful ranger
O'er these meads with the grass-cropping kine!
And thou, whom she bore to her honor,
When the breath of the Highest was on her,
And the touch of the finger divine;
Thine ear, mighty god, we implore thee
To the prayer of thine offspring incline!

ANTISTROPHE II
O Thou who with blessing anointed,
Wert born when by Fate 'twas appointed,
With thy name to all ages a sign!
In this land of the mother that bore thee,
Her toils we remember before thee,
Where she cropped the green mead with the kine.
O strange were her fortunes, and stranger
The fate that hath chased me from danger
To the home of the heifer divine.
0 son, with the mother that bore thee,
Stamp my tale with thy truth for a sign!

STROPHE AND ANTISTROPHE II
While we cry, should there haply be near us
An Argive, an augur, to hear us,
When our shrill-piercing wail
His ear shall assail,
'Tis the cry he will deem, and none other,
Of Procne, the woe-wedded mother,
The hawk-hunted nightingale;
Sad bird, when its known streams it leaveth,
And with fresh-bleeding grief lonely grieveth,
And telleth the tale,
With a shrill-voiced wail,
How the son that she loved, and none other,
Was slain by his fell-purposed mother,
The woe-wedded nightingale!

## STROPHE III

Even so from the Nile summer-tinted,
With Ionian wailings unstinted,
My check with the keen nail I tear;
And I pluck, where it bloweth,
Grief's blossom that groweth
In this heart first acquainted with care;
And I fear the fierce band,
From the far misty land,
Whom the swift ships to Argos may bear.

## ANTISTROPHE III

Ye gods of my race, seeing clearly
The right which ye cherish so dearly,
To the haughty your hatred declare
'Gainst the right ye will never
Chaste virgins deliver,
The bed of the lawless to share;
From the god-fenced altar
Each awe-struck assaulter
Back shrinks. Our sure bulwark is there.

## STROPHE IV

0 would that Jove might show to men
His counsel as he planned it;
But ah! he darky weaves the scheme,
No mortal eye hath scanned it.
It burns through darkness brightly clear
To whom the god shall show it;
But mortal man, through cloudy fear,
Shall search in vain to know it.

## ANTISTROPHE IV

Firm to the goal his purpose treads,
His will knows no frustration;
When with his brow the mighty god
Hath nodded consummation.
But strangely, strangely weave their maze
His counsels, dusky wending,

Concealed in densely-tangled ways
From human comprehending.

STROPHE V
From their high-towering hopes the proud
In wretched rout he casteth.
No force he wields; his simple will,
His quiet sentence blasteth.
All godlike power is calm; and high
On thrones of glory seated,
Jove looks from Heaven with tranquil eye,
And sees his will completed.

ANTISTROPHE V
Look down, O mighty god, and see
How this harsh wedlock planning,
That dry old tree in saplings green,
The insolent lust is fanning
Madly he hugs the frenzied plan
With perverse heart unbending,
Hot-spurred, till Ruin seize the man,
Too late to think of mending.


STROPHE VI
Ah! well-a-day! ah! well-a-day!
Thus sadly I hymn the sorrowful lay,
With a shrill-voiced cry,
With a sorrow-streaming eye,
Well-a-day, woe's me!
Thus I grace my own tomb with the wail pouring free,
Thus I sing my own dirge, ah me!
Ye Apian hills, be kind to me,
And throw not back the stranger's note,
But know the Libyan wail.
Behold how, rent to sorrow's note,
My linen robes all loosely float,
And my Sidonian veil.

## ANTISTROPHE VI

Ah! well-a-day! ah! well-a-day!
My plighted vows I'll duly pay,
Ye gods, if ye will save
From the foe, and from the grave
My trembling life set free!
Surges high, surges high, sorrow's many-billowed sea,
And woe towers on woe. Ah me!
Ye Apian hills, be kind to me,
And throw not back the stranger's note
But know the Libyan wail!
Behold how, rent to sorrow's note,
My linen robes all loosely float,
And my Sidonian veil!

## STROPHE VII

And yet, in that slight timbered house, well-armed
With frequent-plashing oar,
Stiff sail and cordage straining, all unharmed
By winter's stormy roar,
We reached this Argive shore.
Safely so far. May Jove, the all-seeing, send
As the beginning, so the prosperous end.
And may he grant, indeed,
That we, a gracious mother's gracious seed,
By no harsh kindred wooed,
May live on Apian ground unyoked and unsubdued!

# Lysistrata

Aristophanes
Translated by Carl R. Mueller
411 B.C.

**Comic**
**Setting:** Athens, A public square
**Scene:** Lysistrata has called a meeting of all the women of Greece.
   She has thought of a way to end war once and for all.

Lysistrata
Kalonikê
Myrrhinê
Lampito
Women of Athens
Women of Sparta

KALONIKÊ: Morning, Lysistrata!
   Gracious, dear, what's the problem?
   Such a frown! Watch it, wrinkles come
   Soon enough by themselves!
LYSISTRATA: Forget the face, Kalonikê.
   It's women I'm worried about.
   You can't trust them. No wonder men say
   The things about us they do.
KALONIKÊ: And they're probably right.
LYSISTRATA: I mean, really! Here I call a meeting,
   Stressing with everything I've got
   That it's of the utmost importance—
   And what do you think!
   Where do you think they are?
   At home! Catching a few more winks!
KALONIKÊ: Easy does it, dear. They'll be along.
   Being a woman's no easy matter. First,
   You rouse the slaves with a well-aimed
   Kick to the butt, then there's little hubby
   Who needs tending to, and the cook,
   And bathing a bawling baby—it never ends!
LYSISTRATA: I know, but there are

Things more pressing!

KALONIKÊ: Pressing? Like what? What's up?

LYSISTRATA: Something big, girl!

KALONIKÊ: Huge?

LYSISTRATA: Huge enough for us all!

KALONIKÊ: God, Lysistrata, then why aren't they *here?*

LYSISTRATA: No, Kalonikê, not that!
Well, not strictly speaking, that is.
But if it were—ah, *if*—they
Couldn't get here fast enough!
No, but there's something I've been
Toying around with in bed
These last sleepless nights—

KALONIKÊ: It must be worn to a frazzle by now, dear—

LYSISTRATA: Kalonikê, the fate of all of Greece
Lies right square in our hands!
Only we women can save it!

KALONIKÊ: Some last ditch resort *that* is!
Poor Greece!

LYSISTRATA: The future of Athens
Rests in our hands, girl! First off,
We have to wipe out the Peloponnesians—

KALONIKÊ: Good! Let's do it!

LYSISTRATA: And then the Boiotians—

KALONIKÊ: Oh, but just not the eels, dear!
They make such luscious—

LYSISTRATA: Don't worry, it's not
The eels I have in mind. As for Athens,
Well, I really have a hard time saying it—
But you know what just might happen
As well as I do,
Now, if we could get all the women
From Thebes and Sparta
And god know where else
To meet with us here—
We could end up the saviors
Of the entire country!

KALONIKÊ: Oh, come on, girl! Talk sense!
Women aren't political animals.

We're good for keeping around the house
Like pets. Sitting around all day
Getting the make-up just right.
Slinking through the house
In our best saffron gowns—and, oh,
Those precious little Persian slippers!

LYSISTRATA: There! You've got it! That's it!
See-through dresses, scents and blushes,
Naughty little negligées, and, oh,
Those precious little Persian slippers!
That's how we'll do it! That's it!

KALONIKÊ: What?

LYSISTRATA: Keep out men busy
From ever hoisting another spear—

KALONIKÊ: I'll send out a little nothing
For dyeing tomorrow—

LYSISTRATA: —or shouldering another shield—

KALONIKÊ: —and then there's this sexy—

LYSISTRATA: —or hauling out another sword.

KALONIKÊ: —and I saw the most dreamy slippers the other—

LYSISTRATA: So where are they, these women
Who should be here by now?

KALONIKÊ: They should have *flown!*
They should have sprouted *wings,*
Taken *flight!*

LYSISTRATA: No mistaking an Athenian.
They're always late. But that doesn't excuse
Those from the Shore or Salamis—

KALONIKÊ: They've probably been coming
Since the crack of dawn,

LYSISTRATA: And no one from Acharnai.
I expected them here hours ago.

KALONIKÊ: I passed Theagenês' wife having her
Fortune told; so she's bound to show.
But here come some of them now!
Who are they, can you see?
*(Enter Myrrhinê and a group of other women.)*

LYSISTRATA: They're from Anagyros.

KALONIKÊ: Wouldn't you know it!

You can smell their cheap scent a mile off!

MYRRHINÊ: Oh, golly, Lysistrata, I hope I'm not late!
—Well, least ways you could say something
Instead of just scowling.

LYSISTRATA: Don't you ever take anything
Seriously, Myrrhinê I mean, not even
Something this important?

MYRRHINÊ: Sorry—it was all I could do
To find my girdle in the dark.
*(Looking around at the others.)* Well, if it's so important,
Why are we waiting? Tell us!

LYSISTRATA: The girls from Thebes and Sparta
Should get here first.

KALONIKÊ: Good idea. Ah, and here come some now.
*(Enter Lampito, a particularly sturdy woman in a particularly out-
landish costume, and other women from Sparta.)*

LYSISTRATA: Lampito, dear!
What a ravishing sight!
How are things in Sparta?
And the colors! My! How absolutely
Out-of-doors you look!
Muscles and all!
You look ready to strangle a bull!

LAMPITO: Sure could, you know.
Work out ever' day in the gym.
And then the fanny-kick dance we do?
Like this? *(She demonstrates.)*

KALONIKÊ: And look at the tits!

LAMPITO: Sure'd be nice if you'd
Keep your hands to yourself.
Makes me feel like a heifer bein'
Led to the slaughter.

LYSISTRATA: And this lovely young lady here?
Where's she from?

LAMPITO: Boiotia. Regular blue-blood type.

LYSISTRATA: Ah, yes, Boiotia—
Spacious skies and amber waves of grain,
And all that!

KALONIKÊ: Look close enough, you'll see the grain

Has just been freshly mown.

LYSISTRATA: And who do we have here?

LAMPITO: Korinth girl. Real special.

KALONIKÊ: Oh, no doubt!

LAMPITO: So, tell us, whose idea was this little meetin'?

LYSISTRATA: Mine, as a matter of fact.

LAMPITO: So, then, what's up?

MYRRHINÊ: Right, dear, tell us what's so urgent it can't wait.

LYSISTRATA: Yes, well. But first a small question.

MYRRHINÊ: So *ask!*

LYSISTRATA: Well, it's has to do with your husbands—
    The fathers of your children.
    Wouldn't you rather have them at home
    Than off somewhere fighting?
    I'll bet you not one of you
    Has a husband in the house.

KALONIKÊ: Mine's been up in Thrace
    For the last five months! Imagine!
    Five months! Keeping an eye
    On that General Eukrates!

MYRRHINÊ: And mine's been in Pylos for seven!

LAMPITO: Mine no sooner gets a discharge
    Than he just plugs himself right back in.

KALONIKÊ: And lovers are about as scare
    As balls on a capon! Ever since those
    Beastly Milesians revolted on Athens
    And cut off the leather trade,
    There hasn't been a decent dildo to be bought!

LYSISTRATA: All right! That's how it is!
    Now! If I can come up with a plan
    To stop this war, who's with me?

MYRRHINÊ: Count *me* in! I'd pawn
    The shift off my back if I had to,
    Though I might buy a few drinks
    With the proceeds if I got the chance.

KALONIKÊ: Me, too! And they can
    Split me up the middle like a flounder
    If they have to—for the cause.

LAMPITO: And me! I'd climb on up Mount Taygetos

On my hands and knees to get at some peace.

LYSISTRATA: All right! Then here it is!

If we women want our men to give up war,
If that's what we *really want*—
I mean if we're serious—
Then we'll simply have to—

MYRRHINÊ: Have to—?

KALONIKÊ: Have to what?

LYSISTRATA: You'll do as I say?

MYRRHINÊ: Damn straight!

We'd die for peace!

LYSISTRATA: Then we must give up getting laid by our men.

*(Long silence among the women.)*

LYSISTRATA: So what's the matter? Second thoughts?

Chickening out so soon?
Why the long faces, girls? Tears?
Pale as ghosts? All weepy?
—Will you or won't you?
I'm waiting! Yes or no!

MYRRHINÊ: I-I-I don't think so.

Maybe it's better the war should just go on—

KALONIKÊ: Me either. The—the war should—

Should just better—go on—

LYSISTRATA: Aha! The little flounder,

Ready to be sliced up the middle for the cause!

KALONIKÊ: Lysistrata, no! You know

I'd walk through fire for you!
I would! But not *that*, dear—
Not *that*—not *sex!*
No! Never!
Lysistrata dear, there's nothing like it!
Nothing!

LYSISTRATA: And you?

MYRRHINÊ: I'd rather walk through *fire*,

Than give up *that!*

LYSISTRATA: Than *what*, dear?

MYRRHINÊ: Fucking!

LYSISTRATA: *Women!* You're all alike!

The entire sex! No wonder the poets

Write tragedies about us! We're raw material!
Out for a hot tumble and then get rid of the baby!
But you, Lampito, dear Lampito,
You and the women of Sparta,
If you all stand by me, we can still win.
What's it going to be?

LAMPITO: Well, you're no fool, girl,
An' I guess you know it's no fun for a girl
To sleep alone all night in a big bed
With no prick around to keep her company.
A little humpin' and pumpin' goes a long way.
But I'm with you, girl! Thick or thin!
I want peace just like ever'body else!

LYSISTRATA: Oh, Lampito, you're a dear!
The only woman here who deserves the name!

KALONIKÊ: No, now just a minute here, Lysistrata!
It's all very well and good for you to say!
What if we *did*—what you said?
I mean—what if we *did* hold out—
*You* know—give it up?
How would *that* bring us peace any sooner?

LYSISTRATA: It can't fail.
Here's what we do. First,
We rub ourselves down
With the sweetest smelling oil
We can lay our hands on, then
We deck ourselves out in our
Sexiest saffron see-through nighties
With nothing underneath and our pussies
Plucked to perfection.
I guarantee you, girls, our men
Will be so horny they won't be able to walk—
At least not farther than the bed,
Which is all they'll have on *their* minds.
And we? We refuse. Simple as that.
There'll be treaties signed in a flash!
Honey, they'll be like *dogs*
On the scent for peace!

LAMPITO: It might work, you know?

I seem to remember that Menelaus,
When he was out to run Helen through with his
Sword, ditched it when he caught sight of her
Naked titties. Worth a try.

KALONIKÊ: Yes, but what if they
Leave us, just flat-out?

LYSISTRATA: We'd do the best we can in a pinch.

KALONIKÊ: And when they rape us!
Drag us by the hair?

LYSISTRATA: Hang on to the doorknob.

KALONIKÊ: What if they beat us?

LYSISTRATA: Lay there cold as a fish.
They'll wise up. Men don't like it
When women don't enjoy it.
Give them a hard time,
Make them suffer,

KALONIKÊ: Well—if you really think it'll work.

LAMPITO: Our Spartan men'll be pushovers;
But I don't know about those
Warmongerin' Athenians of yours.

LYSISTRATA: Leave that to us—you'll see.

LAMPITO: I don't know, girl. I mean,
As long as they got all them ships,
Not to mention a bottomless stash
Of cash up there on the Akropolis.

LYSISTRATA: Darling, forget the Akropolis!
That's all been seen to. While we're down here
Settling sexual politics,
Our Senior Citizen Women's Coalition
Is up there pretending to sacrifice,
But really to take over the Treasury.
And once in, we don't budge.

LAMPITO: Sweetheart, you just make ever'thing
Come out honey!

LYSISTRATA: In that case, I say let's take the oath!

LAMPITO: You say it, we'll swear.

LYSISTRATA: OK, now, here's a shield.
I'll lay it hollow-side up. Like this.
Now bring me the lamb guts.

KALONIKÊ: Really, Lysistrata!
   What *is* this oath you're giving us?
LYSISTRATA: Aeschylus. You know?
   *Seven Against Thebes.* You slaughter a lamb
   Then swear on the shield.
KALONIKÊ: But how can we swear
   An oath to peace on a *shield?*
LYSISTRATA: You have a better suggestion?
KALONIKÊ: How about we cut the head off
   An adult male cock—?
LYSISTRATA: Redundant, Kalonikê,
   And you have a one-track mind.
KALONIKÊ: Well, if *you're* so smart,
   How *do* we do it?
MYRRHINÊ: I have an idea!
   First we get a large black bowl.
   Then we fill it to the top
   With Thrasian wine. And then
   We take an oath on it—
   Not to water it down with a single drop!
LAMPITO: Oh, I *do* like that oath!
LYSISTRATA: Bring us a bowl! And wine!
   *(Two female Attendants enter, one with a large black bowl, the other with a large jar of wine.)*
KALONIKÊ: Oh, my! And such a big one!
LYSISTRATA: Just don't turn size-queen on me, dear.
KALONIKÊ: A girl could get a glow just smelling it!
LYSISTRATA: All right, girls,
   Let's help me butcher this boar!
   Kalonikê, the jar!
   *(The Attendant hands the bowl to Lysistrata and exits. The remaining Attendant hands the wine jar to Kalonikê and exits.)*
LYSISTRATA: Holy Goddess Persuasion!
   Lady of the Loving-cup!
   Receive this offering with favor!
   Grant our wish!
   *(Kalonikê tips the Jar and pours the wine into the bowl as Lysistrata speaks the invocation.)*
MYRRHINÊ: What a lovely red!

LAMPITO: Spurts just like blood!

MYRRHINÊ: Let me be the first to swear!

KALONIKÊ: Not a chance! We'll draw lots!

LYSISTRATA: Right! Lampito,
    You and the rest of the girls
    Put your right hands on the bowl.
    Now, I'll need a spokesgirl
    To repeat the oath after me,
    And at the end all of you will ascent together.
    *(Kalonikê raises her hand and steps forward. The women place
    their right hands on the bowl.)*

LYSISTRATA: Repeat after me.
    From this time forward,
    No husband, lover or pickup—

KALONIKÊ: *From this time forward,
    No husband, lover or pickup—*

LYSISTRATA: Will have access or entrance
    To me for any reason—

KALONIKÊ: *Will have access or entrance
    To me for any reason—*

LYSISTRATA: I will dress to the nines in my
    Sexiest saffron see-through—

KALONIKÊ: *I will dress to the nines in my
    Sexiest saffron see-through—*

LYSISTRATA: Made up to look like
    Venus on the make—

KALONIKÊ: *Made up to look like
    Venus on the make—*

LYSISTRATA: So when he comes with his
    Wildly wiggling willy—

KALONIKÊ: *So when he comes with his—
    Oh, Lysistrata—what a—what a—*

LYSISTRATA: Say it!

KALONIKÊ: -What a terrible thing to say—
    I'm going all—
    All weak in the—
    Knees—

LYSISTRATA: Kalonikê!

KALONIKÊ: *—Wildly—wiggling—willy—*

LYSISTRATA: Tight as a drum
  And ready to be flogged—
KALONIKÊ: *Tight as a drum*
  *And ready to be—flogged—*
LYSISTRATA: I will purse my lips and smile
  And sashay past—
KALONIKÊ: *I will purse my lips and smile*
  *And sashay past—*
LYSISTRATA: Driving him up a creek
  Without a paddle—
KALONIKÊ: *Driving him up a creek*
  *Without a paddle—*
LYSISTRATA: Hearing him pant and moan
  And squeal with longing—
KALONIKÊ: *Hearing him pant and moan*
  *And squeal with longing—*
LYSISTRATA: And if he batters my gate
  Against my wishes—
KALONIKÊ: *And if he batters my gate*
  *Against my wishes—*
LYSISTRATA: With his bouncing rammer,
  I'll twist my legs like pretzels—
KALONIKÊ: *With his bouncing rammer,*
  *I'll twist my legs like pretzels—*
LYSISTRATA: And lay there limp as a rag
  Or a gutted flounder—
KALONIKÊ: *And lay there limp as a rag*
  *Or a gutted flounder—*
LYSISTRATA: Passive as a passion
  Out the door—
KALONIKÊ: *Passive as a passion*
  *Out the door—*
LYSISTRATA: I now swear by this oath that,
  If I break it—
KALONIKÊ: *I now swear by this oath that,*
  *If I break it—*
LYSISTRATA: May none of my drinks henceforth
  Be more than water—
KALONIKÊ: *May none of my drinks henceforth*

*Be more than water—*
LYSISTRATA: Swear!
ALL: We swear!
LYSISTRATA: And so I sacrifice the victim— *(Lysistrata takes a long drink from the bowl.)*
KALONIKÊ: Well, don't drink it all, dear!
Let's share. I mean, we *are* friends—
  *(As Kalonikê and the other women take a drink, women's voices are heard from offstage in a cry of triumph.)*
LAMPITO: What was that?
LYSISTRATA: It's what I said was going to happen!
  The older women have taken the Citadel!
  The Akropolis is ours!
  And with it the Treasury!
  Time you went back, Lampito,
  And get to work on your Spartan men.
  You can leave your friends here.
  We can use the help.
  *(Lampito hurries off.)*
LYSISTRATA: The rest of us, up to the Akropolis
  And lock the doors!
KALONIKÊ: What about the men?
  Won't they be sending
  Reinforcements to run us out?
LYSISTRATA: The men are my department.
  They can threaten all they like!
  Let them set fire to the place—
  We won't budge!
KALONIKÊ: That's the spirit, girl!
  Let's live up to our reputation!
  *(All go off.)*

# Diana of Dobson's

Cicely Hamilton
1908

**Dramatic**
**Scene:** one of the assistant's dormitories at Dobson's Drapery Emporium

Miss Smithers
Kitty Brant
Miss Jay
Diana Massingberd
Miss Morton
Miss Pringle

*(Miss Smithers shaking skirt outside door. An awkward silence—Miss Jay frizzles her hair hurriedly—then Kitty lays a hand on Diana's shoulder.)*

KITTY: Di, what's come over you lately? You usen't to be like this—not so bad. It's only the last fortnight that you've been so dreadfully discontented.

DIANA: Oh, it has been coming on a great deal longer than that—coming on for years.

KITTY: For years?

DIANA: I have fits of this sort of thing, every now and then. I can't help myself. They come and take hold of you—and you realise what your life might be—and what it is—I'm about at the end of my tether, Kit.

KITTY: But why? What is the matter just now, in particular?

DIANA: There isn't anything particular the matter. That's just it.

KITTY: What do you mean, dear?

DIANA: Everything's going on the same as usual—the same old grind. As it was in the beginning, is now, and ever shall be: world without end. Amen.

MISS JAY: *(With a shock.)* Oh, Miss Massingberd—that's in the prayer book.

DIANA: *(Imitating her.)* Ow, Miss Jay, you do surprise me—
*(Kitty sits on edge of bed.)*

DIANA: Is it really?
*(Miss Jay turns back to bureau annoyed.)*

DIANA: You're going to have done with it, Kitty. In three months' time you'll be married. However your marriage turns out, it will be a change for you—a change from the hosiery department of Dobson's.

KITTY: *(Hurt.)* Di—

DIANA: *(Still seated, her arm round Kitty's waist.)* Oh, I didn't mean to be unkind, Kit. You're a dear, and if I'm nasty to you it's only because I envy you. You're going to get out of all this: in three months' time you'll have turned your back on it for good—you'll have done with the nagging and the standing and this horrible bare room—and the dining-room with the sloppy tea on the table and Pringle's sour face at the end of it. Lucky girl! But I haven't any prospect of turning my back on it, and it doesn't seem to me I ever shall.

SMITHERS: *(Significantly.)* You will, and before very long too, if you don't look out. *(Crosses to bed, sits up on middle of bed with her back to audience, combing hair.)*

DIANA: Oh, I shan't be here much longer—I can quite see that. But when I am fired out I shall only start the same old grind some-where else—all over again. The delectable atmosphere of Dobson's will follow me about wherever I go. I shall crawl round to similar establishments, cringing to be taken on at the same starvation salary—and then settle down in the same stuffy dor-mitory, with the same mean little rules to obey—I shall serve the same stream of intelligent customers—and bolt my dinner off the same tough meat in the same gloomy dining-room with the same mustard-coloured paper on the walls. And that's life. Kit! *(Clapping Kitty on the shoulder.)* That's what I was born for. *(Rises.)* Hurrah for life! *(Tosses Miss Smithers's puffs and switch in the air.)*

MISS JAY: *(With grease pot, greasing her face.)* Well, I never, you do— *(Checks herself.)*

*(Miss Smithers retrieves her hair with indignation.)*

DIANA: Say funny things—yes, I know.

SMITHERS: Look here, girls, it's only five minutes now till we have to turn the light out. Instead of listening to Miss Massingberd's nonsense, we'd better—

*(Enter hurriedly Miss Morton—she wears dark—not black—skirt, jacket and hat and white shirt waist. She is unbuttoning jacket as*

*she runs in—the others are beginning to undress, plaiting hair, etc., with the exception of Diana.)*

MISS MORTON: Hallo, girls! Gas not out yet. *(Closes door, hangs hat on peg.)* That's a blessing.

SMITHERS: Had a nice evening out, Miss Morton?

MISS MORTON: Tip-top, thanks. *(Removes jacket.)* Been at my cousin's at Balham. I hurried back though.
*(Miss Jay crosses with skirt, etc., and stands.)*

MISS MORTON: I was afraid I shouldn't get in till after eleven—and I do so hate having to go to bed in the dark. *(Hangs jacket on a peg.)* *(When Miss Morton goes up—Miss Jay crosses to bed with things. As she does so she sees a letter sticking out of pocket.)*

MISS MORTON: Oh, Miss Massingberd, I brought this up for you. *(Gives letter to Diana.)* It was in the hall. I suppose it came by the last post. *(Goes to box foot of bed, sits and unlaces shoes.)*

DIANA: *(Rises and goes to gas, surprised.)* A letter for me? *(Moves a few steps, looking at envelope.)*

MISS MORTON: *(Unlacing boots.)* My cousin Albert sent his kind regards to you, Miss Jay. Said I was to be sure not to forget 'em.

MISS JAY: *(Has hung skirt on peg and is now rolling up waist, etc.; giggling.)* Ah! Did he?

MISS MORTON: He asked most particular which department you was in.

MISS JAY: Whatever did you say? You never went and told him it was corsets?

MISS MORTON: Didn't I just? *(Getting into slippers.)*

MISS JAY: Well, I never—you are a caution. What did he say when you told him?

MISS MORTON: Said he was downright disappointed, and he wished you'd been in the tie department—then he could have dropped in now and again to buy a new tie and have a chat.

MISS JAY: Oh, go on!

MISS MORTON: He was afraid he'd be too shy to ask to look at a pair of corsets even for the pleasure of seeing you.

MISS JAY: *(Giggling more than ever.)* Well, I must say, he has got a nerve. Did you ever—

DIANA: *(Who has been standing under the gas reading her letter—then staring at it incredulously.)* Girls—girls—
*(Smithers comes down to below bed.)*

KITTY: *(On bed—foot of it.)* Di, what is it?

SMITHERS: What's the matter, Miss Massingberd?

DIANA: *(Hysterically.)* The letter—it says— *(Holding it out.)* Read it—oh no, let me read it again first.

KITTY: It's not bad news, is it?

DIANA: Bad news—bad news. *(She laughs.)*

MISS JAY: She's got hysterics.

MISS MORTON: *(Moves to and picks up glass of water from washstand.)* Have a glass of water, Miss Massingberd, dear.

DIANA: No, no—I'm all right.

*(Miss Morton returns glass of water to washstand. Diana pulls herself together.)*

KITTY: Tell us what it is?

DIANA: It's this letter—the letter Miss Morton brought up.

MISS MORTON: Yes.

DIANA: It comes from a lawyer—a solicitor in Manchester—

KITTY: Yes?

DIANA: It seems that a cousin of my father's used to live in Manchester— a distant cousin whom I never knew, and who was in some sort of business there. He died suddenly a while ago, without leaving a will. His money is all to be divided up among the next of kin— and I'm one of them—one of the next of kin—and I get three hundred pounds!

*(Chorus of 'Oh! Three hundred pounds! Oh, you lucky girl!')*

KITTY: Di, I'm so glad—so glad, dear.

DIANA: I can't believe it yet—I can't get myself to believe it. Read the letter, some one. *(Gives letter to Smithers.)* Read it aloud to me— and tell me if it is really true.

*(Business of dropping letter and picking it up, etc. They hoist Smithers on the chair under the gas.)*

SMITHERS: *(Reading.)* 'Madam, re R. C. Cooper, deceased. I beg to inform you that, by the recent death of my client, Mr. Edward Chamberlain Cooper, you, as one of his next of kin, are entitled to a share in his estates—'

DIANA: *(Snatching letter from her.)* It's true then—it is really true.

*(The girls crowd round her.)*

KITTY: Of course it is.

DIANA: Girls, I'm not a pauper any more. I've got three hundred pounds of my own. Think of it—three hundred golden sovereigns.

MISS JAY: What are you going to do with it?

DIANA: I don't know—I haven't had time to think yet. I'll stand you all a treat on Sunday, for one thing.
(The girls cheer.)
DIANA: And Kitty shall have a wedding present—what shall it be, Kit?
KITTY: (Shaking her head.) You mustn't be extravagant and waste your money. You ought to put it straight in the bank.
DIANA: Put it in the bank—not me. What's the good of that?
SMITHERS: You should invest it in something really safe. (Sits.)
DIANA: And get nine or ten pounds a year for it at the outside. No, thank you—not good enough. Now I've got three hundred pounds—
(Diana sits on box, Kitty sits on bed, Miss Morton sits on floor at Diana's feet and Miss Jay on box.)
DIANA: —three hundred pounds to do as I like with—I intend to have some fun out of it.
MISS MORTON: You'll chuck Dobson's, I suppose?
DIANA: (Scornfully.) What do you think?
MISS MORTON: (Sitting on floor in front of Diana.) Tomorrow?
DIANA: (Nods.) I can get an advance tomorrow—the solicitor—Mr. Crampton says so. So this is my last night here, girls. You don't suppose I'll stay in this beastly den a moment longer than I can help! Dobson's hosiery department has seen the last of me. I'd clear out of the place tonight if it wasn't so late. No, I wouldn't, though—if I went tonight I shouldn't be able to have an interview with Mr. Septimus Dobson—to tell him what I think of him.
(Chorus of 'OH!')
MISS JAY: You're not really going to?
DIANA: Not going to—you wait and see. Why, it'll be glorious—glorious. Girls, have you ever grasped what money really is? It's power! Power to do what you like, to go where you like, to say what you like. Because I have three hundred pounds in my pocket, I shall be able tomorrow morning to enjoy the priceless luxury of telling Dobson to his fat white face, what we all whisper behind his mean old back—
MISS MORTON: Shall you dare?
DIANA: Dare? With three hundred pounds in my pocket I'd dare any mortal thing on earth.
SMITHERS: I think you're forgetting, Miss Massingberd, that three hundred pounds won't last for ever.

DIANA: Oh, no, I'm not. But while it does last, I mean to have everything I want—everything.

KITTY: Oh Di, don't do anything silly—

SMITHERS: It won't last you very long at that rate.

DIANA: I know—but I don't care. Who was it said something about a crowded hour of glorious life? Well, that's just what I'm going to have—a crowded hour, and it *shall* be crowded. For once in my life I'll know what it is to have a royal time—I'll deny myself nothing. I have had six years of scrape and starve—now I'll have a month of everything that money can buy me—and there are very few things that money can't buy me—precious few.

SMITHERS: *(Sarcastically.)* And when it's all spent? *(Combing her hair.)*

DIANA: *(Defiantly.)* When it is all spent—

SMITHERS: Yes?

DIANA: I shall go back, I suppose—back to the treadmill grind. But I shall have something to remember—I shall be able to look back at my crossing hour—my one little bit of life. For one month I shall have done what I chose—not what I was forced to. For one month I shall have had my freedom—and that will be something to remember. But I'm not going to think of the afterwards yet—I'm going to think of the now. What shall I do, Kit? For one thing, I shall travel—I've always longed and craved to see something of the world besides one narrow little piece of it.

MISS MORTON: Where shall you go?

DIANA: Haven't thought yet, but of course I shall begin with Paris.

MISS MORTON: Paris?

DIANA: To buy my clothes. I'll know what it is to wear a decently cut frock before I die.

MISS JAY: I say, you are going it.

DIANA: Also boots that cost more than seven and elevenpence a pair. I'm going to have the best of everything, I tell you, and I'll start with Paris for clothes. *(Rises.)* Then I shall go on—move about—Switzerland, Italy, where I feel inclined—

KITTY: It will be lovely—but—Diana—

DIANA: *(Goes to Kitty.)* No buts—Kitty—for the next month I am not going to have any buts. For part of the time I think I shall go somewhere in the mountains—I've always longed to see real mountains—I shall stay at the best hotels—I shall call myself Mrs.

Massingberd, I think. You're ever so much freer when you're married. I shall be a widow. *(Sits on box.)*

KITTY: A widow!

*(All laugh.)*

SMITHERS: Mrs. Massingberd! Hush, the Pringle!

*(The door is suddenly flung open, and Miss Pringle enters, middle-aged, sour-faced, and wearing a palpable transformation. All except Diana rush to their beds. Diana whistles.)*

MISS PRINGLE: What is all this noise about? It's past eleven, and the gas ought to have been out long ago. Miss Massingberd— *(One step down, on line with Diana.)* —was it your voice I heard?

DIANA: Miss Pringle, it was.

MISS PRINGLE: Then—

DIANA: *(Interrupting.)* The usual thing, I suppose? We're all of us fined. Gas burning after eleven o'clock at night—unbusinesslike conduct—sixpence all round. Never mind, girls, don't you worry. I'm standing treat for this lot.

MISS PRINGLE: Miss Massingberd!

DIANA: Miss Pringle!

MISS PRINGLE: Do you wish me to report you?

DIANA: For more unbusinesslike conduct? Certainly, if you like. Please yourself about it—I don't really care a row of brass pins.

MISS PRINGLE: Are you out of your senses?

DIANA: Now you mention it, I do feel rather like it.

MISS PRINGLE: You'll be sorry for your impertinence tomorrow.

DIANA: I assure you, you are entirely mistaken.

*(Miss Jay rises in bed.)*

DIANA: The combination of fury and astonishment in your face will always remain with me as a pleasing memory—grateful and comforting. I may add that the effect is singularly unbecoming.

*(Miss Jay giggles audibly—then chokes as Miss Pringle turns round.)*

MISS PRINGLE: *(Viciously.)* Miss Massingberd—

DIANA: Allow me to remind you that you have made that remark before. If you have nothing to add to it, we need not detain you any longer. I'll turn out the gas when I've done with it—which won't be for a few minutes yet. *(Rises.)*

MISS PRINGLE: *(Beside herself with fury.)* Miss Massingberd— *(Makes a step towards Diana.)* —I believe you're drunk.

GIRLS: Oh!

DIANA: *(Coming back towards box.)* You are quite at liberty to believe any mortal thing you like—you are quite at liberty to say any mortal thing you like. What you choose to think and what you choose to say are matters of perfect indifference to me now. It has ceased to matter to me in the very least whether you are satisfied with me or whether you are not—whether you fine me or whether you don't. This morning the stony glare in your eye would have made me shiver—tonight, it merely makes me smile. In short— *(Takes belt from foot of bed.)* —Miss Pringle, you are no longer in a position to bully me, so take my advice and don't try it on. *(She sits on box and faces Miss Pringle.)*

MISS PRINGLE: Miss Massingberd, the first thing in the morning—the *very* first thing in the morning—I shall make it my business to inform Mr. Dobson—

DIANA: *(Composedly.) Damn* Mr. Dobson.
*(Quick curtain.)*

# Yerma

Federico Garcia Lorca
Translated by Caridad Svich
1934

**Dramatic**

**Scene:** a fast flowing mountain stream where the village women
gather to wash clothes. The women are singing and chatting.

Five Laundresses, with the appearance of a Sixth Laundress

FIRST LAUNDRESS: I don't like to talk.

THIRD LAUNDRESS: We talk here.

FOURTH LAUNDRESS: And there's no harm in it.

FIFTH LAUNDRESS: Whoever wants a good name, let her earn it.

FOURTH LAUNDRESS: I planted thyme,
I watched it grow.
Whoever wants a good name
Must behave just so.
*(They laugh.)*

FIFTH LAUNDRESS: That's the way to talk.

FIRST LAUNDRESS: But we never really know anything.

FOURTH LAUNDRESS: What we do know is that her husband has brought
his two sisters to live with them.

FIFTH LAUNDRESS: The old maids?

FOURTH LAUNDRESS: Yes. They were in charge of taking care of the church
and now they will take care of their sister-in-law. I wouldn't be able
to live with them.

FIRST LAUNDRESS: Why not?

FOURTH LAUNDRESS: Because they give me the creeps. They're like those
big leaves that spring up over graves all of a sudden. They're
smeared with wax. They're turned inward. They must fry their
food with lamp oil.

THIRD LAUNDRESS: And they're in the house already?

FOURTH LAUNDRESS: As of yesterday. Her husband's going back to his
fields now.

FIRST LAUNDRESS: But what exactly has happened?

FIFTH LAUNDRESS: Night before last, she spent the whole night sitting on
her doorstep, in spite of the cold.

FIRST LAUNDRESS: But why?

FOURTH LAUNDRESS: It's hard for her to stay at home.

FIFTH LAUNDRESS: Those tomboys are all like that: when they could be making lace or apple cakes, they climb up on the roof and walk barefoot along the river instead.

FIRST LAUNDRESS: Who are you to say such things? She doesn't have children, but it is not through any fault of hers.

FOURTH LAUNDRESS: A woman who wants children, has them. These spoiled, lazy, pampered girls don't have them so as not to wrinkle their bellies.

*(They laugh.)*

THIRD LAUNDRESS: And they dust their faces with powder and put on rouge, and they pin sprigs of oleander on themselves to go looking for someone other than their husband.

FIFTH LAUNDRESS: Nothing could be more true!

FIRST LAUNDRESS: But, have you seen her with someone else?

FOURTH LAUNDRESS: We haven't, but other people have.

FIRST LAUNDRESS: It's always other people…

FIFTH LAUNDRESS: On two separate occasions, they say.

SECOND LAUNDRESS: And what were they doing?

FOURTH LAUNDRESS: They were talking.

FIRST LAUNDRESS: Talking is not a sin.

FOURTH LAUNDRESS: In this world, even a glance is something. My mother used to say that. A woman looking at roses is not the same as a woman looking at a man's thighs. She looks at him.

FIRST LAUNDRESS: But at whom?

FOURTH LAUNDRESS: Someone. Haven't you heard? Find out for yourself. Shall I say it even louder?

*(Laughter.)*

FOURTH LAUNDRESS: And when she doesn't look at him, because she's alone, because she doesn't have him in front of her, she carries his picture in her eyes.

FIRST LAUNDRESS: That's a lie!

*(Much shouting.)*

FIFTH LAUNDRESS: And the husband?

THIRD LAUNDRESS: The husband acts like he is deaf. He stands around like a lizard in the sun.

*(They laugh.)*

FIRST LAUNDRESS: Everything would be taken care of if they only had children.

SECOND LAUNDRESS: Everything comes down to a question of people who are not content with their lot in life.

FOURTH LAUNDRESS: Every passing hour increases the feeling of hell in that house. She and her sisters-in-law, with their pursed lips, scrub the walls all day, polish the copper, clean the windows with steam, and oil the floors: the more the house shines, the more it seethes inside.

FIRST LAUNDRESS: It's his fault; his: when a man can't have children, he should take care of his wife.

FOURTH LAUNDRESS: It's her fault because she has a tongue as hard as flint.

FIRST LAUNDRESS: What devil has gotten into your hair for you to talk that way?

FOURTH LAUNDRESS: And who has given your mouth permission to give me advice?

SECOND LAUNDRESS: Be quiet!

FIRST LAUNDRESS: I'd like to string all the murmuring tongues on a knitting needle.

SECOND LAUNDRESS: Quiet!

FOURTH LAUNDRESS: And I the nipples of all the hypocrites.

SECOND LAUNDRESS: Silence. Can't you see the sisters-in-law are coming? *(They murmur. Yerma's two sisters-in-law enter. They are dressed in mourning. In the silence, they begin their washing. Sheep bells are heard.)*

FIRST LAUNDRESS: Are the shepherds leaving already?

THIRD LAUNDRESS: Yes, all the flocks leave today.

FOURTH LAUNDRESS: I like the smell of sheep.

THIRD LAUNDRESS: You do?

FOURTH LAUNDRESS: And why not? It's a smell we carry inside of us. Just as I like the smell of red mud the river carries in the winter.

THIRD LAUNDRESS: Whims.

FIFTH LAUNDRESS: *(Looking.)* All the flocks are leaving together.

FOURTH LAUNDRESS: It's a flood of wool. They sweep everything along. If the green wheat had eyes, it would tremble to see them coming.

THIRD LAUNDRESS: Look how they run! What a band of devils!

FIRST LAUNDRESS: They're all out now, not a flock is missing.

FOURTH LAUNDRESS: Let's see…, no…yes, yes, one is missing.

FIFTH LAUNDRESS: Which one?

FOURTH LAUNDRESS: Victor's.

> *(The two sisters-in-law turn and look.)*

FOURTH LAUNDRESS: In the cold river
> I wash your ribbon.
> Like a burning jasmine
> Is your smile.
> I want to live
> In the small blizzard
> This jasmine puts out.

FIRST LAUNDRESS: Alas for the barren wife!
> Alas for the one whose breasts are sand!

FIFTH LAUNDRESS: Tell me if your husband
> Has fertile seed
> So that the water may sing
> Through your chemise.

FOURTH LAUNDRESS: Your chemise is a boat
> of silver and breeze
> along the banks of the river.

FIRST LAUNDRESS: I come to wash
> My son's clothes
> To teach the stream
> Lessons in transparency.

SECOND LAUNDRESS: From the hillside comes
> My husband to eat.
> He brings me a rose
> And I give him three.

FIFTH LAUNDRESS: From the valley comes
> My husband to eat.
> The live coals he brings me
> I cover with myrtle sweet.

FOURTH LAUNDRESS: Through the sky comes
> my husband to sleep.
> I, violet red.
> And he, red violet.

FIRST LAUNDRESS: Flower with flower must be wed
> When the summer dries the reaper's blood so red.

FOURTH LAUNDRESS: And open the wombs of birds without sleep
> When winter calls trembling on the door.

FIRST LAUNDRESS: One must weep on the sheets.

FOURTH LAUNDRESS: And sing!

FIFTH LAUNDRESS: When the man brings
The bread and the wreath.

FOURTH LAUNDRESS: Because our arms intertwine.

SECOND LAUNDRESS: Because light breaks in our throats.

FOURTH LAUNDRESS: Because the stem of the branches grows weak.

FIRST LAUNDRESS: And the wind's tents cover the mountains.

SIXTH LAUNDRESS: *(Appearing at the topmost part of the swiftly flowing stream.)* So that a child may weld
White crystals in the dawn.

FIRST LAUNDRESS: And our bodies hold
Raging coral branches.

SIXTH LAUNDRESS: So that there will be oarsmen
In the waters of the sea.

FIRST LAUNDRESS: A small child, a child.

SECOND LAUNDRESS: And the doves open their wings and beaks.

THIRD LAUNDRESS: A child weeps, a child.

FOURTH LAUNDRESS: And the men advance
Like wounded deer.

FIFTH LAUNDRESS: Joy, joy, joy,
Of broken wombs under the chemise!

SECOND LAUNDRESS: A navel, a tender cup of happiness.

FIRST LAUNDRESS: But, alas for the barren wife!
Alas for the one whose breasts are sand!

THIRD LAUNDRESS: Let her shine resplendent!

SECOND LAUNDRESS: Let her run!

FIFTH LAUNDRESS: And shine again!

FIRST LAUNDRESS: Let her sing!

SECOND LAUNDRESS: Let her hide!

FIRST LAUNDRESS: And let her sing again!

SIXTH LAUNDRESS: The dawn of my child
Is in this apron.

SECOND LAUNDRESS: *(They all sing together.)* In the cold river
I wash your ribbon
Like a burning jasmine
Is your smile.
Ha! Ha! Ha!
*(They move the clothes in rhythm and beat them.)*

# Medea

Robinson Jeffers
1947

**Dramatic**
**Scene:** before the palace

Medea
Nurse
First Corinthian Woman
Second Corinthian Woman
Third Corinthian Woman

MEDEA: This is it. I did not surely know it: loathing is all. This flesh
He has touched and fouled. These hands that wrought for him, these knees
That ran his errands. This body that took his…what they call love and made children of it. If I could peel off
The flesh, the children, the memory…
*(Again she scarifies one hand with the other. She looks at her hand.)*
Poor misused hand: poor defiled arm: your bones
Are not unshapely. If I could tear off the flesh and be bones; naked bones;
Salt-scoured bones on the shore
At home in Colchis…
*(She stands staring, thinking of home perhaps.)*
FIRST CORINTHIAN WOMAN: God keep me from fire and the hunger of the sword,
Save me from the hateful sea and the jagged lighting,
And the violence of love.
SECOND WOMAN: A little love is a joy in the house,
A little fire is a jewel against frost and darkness.
FIRST WOMAN: A great love is a fire
That burns the beams of the roof.
The doorposts are flaming and the house falls.
A great love is a lion in the cattle-pen,
The herd goes mad, the heifers run bawling
And the claws are in their flanks.
Too much love is an armed robber in the treasury,

He has killed the guards and he walks in blood.

SECOND WOMAN: And now I see the black end,
　　The end of great love, and God save me from it:
　　The unburied horror, the unbridled hatred,
　　The vultures tearing a corpse:
　　God keep me clean of those evil beaks.

THIRD WOMAN: What is she doing, that woman,
　　Staring like stone, staring?
　　Oh, she has moved now.

MEDEA: Annihilation. The word is pure music: annihilation.
　　To annihilate the past—
　　Is not possible: but its fruit in the present...
　　Can be nipped off. Am I to look in my sons' eyes
　　And see Jason's forever? How could I endure the endless defile-
　　ment, those lives
　　That mix Jason and me? Better to be clean
　　Bones on the shore. Bones have no eyes at all, how could they
　　weep? White bones
　　On the Black Sea shore...
　　Oh, but that's far. Not yet. Corinth must howl first. *(She stands
　　meditating.)*

FIRST WOMAN: The holy fountains flow up from the earth.
　　The smoke of sacrifice flows up from the earth,
　　The eagle and the wild swan fly up from the earth,
　　Righteousness also
　　Has flown up from the earth to the feet of God.
　　It is not here, but up there; peace and pity are departed;
　　Hatred is here; hatred is heavy, it clings to the earth.
　　Love blows away, hatred remains.

SECOND WOMAN: Women hate war, but men will wage it again.
　　Women may hate their husbands, and sons their fathers,
　　But women will never hate their own children.

FIRST WOMAN: But as for me, I will do good to my husband,
　　I will love my sons and daughters, and adore the gods.

MEDEA: If I should go into the house with a sharp knife
　　To the man and his bride...
　　Or if I could fire the room they sleep in, and hear them
　　Wake in the white of the fire, and cry to each other, and
　　howl like dogs,

And howl and die...
But I might fail; I might be cut down first;
The knife might turn in my hand, or the fire not burn, and my
enemies could laugh at me.
No: I have subtler means, and more deadly cruel; I have
my dark art
That fools call witchcraft. Not for nothing I have worshipped the
wild gray goddess that walks in the dark, the wise one,
The terrible one, the sweet huntress, flower of night, Hecate,
In my house at my hearth.

THE NURSE: *(Has entered, and hurries toward Medea.)* My lady: he was
leaving Creon's door: he is coming.
*(Medea pays no attention; The Nurse kneels, catches her hand.)*

THE NURSE: Aegeus is coming!
The power of Athens.

MEDEA: I will not see him. Go back and tell him so.
*(The Nurse retreats behind chorus. Medea prays.)*

MEDEA: Ancient Goddess to whom I and my people
Make the sacrifice of black lambs and black female hounds,
Holy one, haunter of cross-roads, queen of night, Hecate,
Help me now: to remember in my mind the use of the venomous
fire, the magic song,
And the sharp gems.
*(She sits on the steps in deep thought.)*

# The Cretan Woman

Robinson Jeffers
1954

**Dramatic**
**Scene:** in front of the palace of Theseus. Troezene. At left an altar to Aphrodite.

First Woman
Second Woman
Third Woman
Phaedra
Selene—her nurse
Aphrodite—the goddess of love

FIRST WOMAN: We have never quite starved, thanks to some god or other: but my husband has had no work since New Year's.

SECOND WOMAN: Don't be troubled, darling. You are still young enough to attract a lover from time to time. Some kindly old gentleman...

FIRST WOMAN: How you talk!

SECOND WOMAN: A piece of fish or a pound of olives, if not a copper coin.

THIRD WOMAN: My husband has plenty of work, and well-paid too; but he drinks every penny. I don't think we could live without these hand-outs from the palace.
*(They are approaching the altar.)*

FIRST WOMAN: We have still a handful of meal in the bin... *(She throws her hand to her heart, staring at the altar, and steps backward.)* Oh—hush!

THIRD WOMAN: *(Staring and retreating.)* I feel it too!

FIRST WOMAN: Something divine is here. There was such a dizziness at my heart suddenly...

THIRD WOMAN: I feel my eyes dazzle and my knees tremble.

SECOND WOMAN: Did you feel something? It is the great Goddess— Aphrodite—*her* altar.

FIRST WOMAN: *(Her hand at her throat.)* Walk wide of it! She is angry. There is a divine anger in this place: like the glaring eyes
Of a wild beast. Yet she is kind, we know...

SECOND WOMAN: What I felt—like an earthquake. Something has roused her.

*(They tiptoe at a distance around the altar and approach the door of the house.)*

FIRST WOMAN: *(Speaking low.)* I hope all's well in this great house. The Goddess doesn't waste wrath on poor people.

THIRD WOMAN: I am still afraid. Terribly. I feel the power…

SECOND WOMAN: If this great house ever falls—I wish it no evil— I wish my boy had the looting of it.

FIRST WOMAN: The door is tight shut, and I dare not knock. Make a little music on that zither of yours, Cleone. But softly.

*(Third Woman plucks the strings of her instrument; a low music is heard. The door opens partially; Selene speaks through the opening.)*

SELENE: *(Intensely whispers.)* Go away. Be quiet.

FIRST WOMAN: Our children are hungry. Have you nothing for us today?

SELENE: Be off. Let my lady sleep.

FIRST WOMAN: Not even a spoiled cake or a stale crust?

SELENE: *(Slips through the doorway and stands on the threshold, closing the door carefully behind her.)* Will you worry me to death?
Be quiet, women.
My lady is ill; she never closed her eyes all night long,
And has just fallen asleep. She has been delirious, I think.
I have been beaten like a fluttering bird, all night and day,
In the storm of her mind.

FIRST WOMAN: What is it, a fever?

SELENE: And for three days she has not tasted food.
Oh, I am weary!

SECOND WOMAN: You mean there was food and she wouldn't eat it!

SELENE: She is like someone possessed
By an angry god.

THE WOMEN: *(Startled, look significantly at each other, and back toward the altar.)* Oh!

FIRST WOMAN: What goddess?

SELENE: A divine power—how could I know?
There is a mystery…
In the delirium, in all the wild rush of her mind
There is something she avoids, something she hides. Like the mad waves of the sea, moulding but hiding

A sunken reef.

FIRST WOMAN: I will tell you. We felt the anger—we all felt it—of a—certain Divine Person

When we approached this house.

SELENE: What Person?

*(First Woman shakes her head, finger to lips, afraid to speak.)*

SELENE: I say what god, or what goddess?

*(First Woman shakes her head; Second Woman points stealthily toward the altar.)*

SELENE: There? Aphrodite? That's out. Or it has nothing to do with my lady Phaedra.

She is loving and good, and she neglects no divinity.

And faithful to her dear husband, my lord Theseus: almost *too* faithful

To be a woman. Oh, what a time I've had

Trying to make her eat, cooking things…

SECOND WOMAN: *(Hungrily.)* What kind of things?

SELENE: Little Cretan cakes, for instance. Brown spice, golden honey, a whipped egg…

SECOND AND THIRD WOMEN: Oh! Oh!

SELENE: I thought perhaps she was homesick for the dear island

Where she was born. That's what they eat there.

She poured the dish on the floor when it came in…

SECOND WOMAN: Oh!

SELENE: And the slaves had them. Worse than that:

Once she called for raw meat, flesh with the blood, like a northern barbarian: she, royal-born,

Of the most highly cultured family in Europe! and naturally

Shrieked when the mere smell… *(Listening.)* Oh dear! Is she calling me?

Is she awake?

*(The door opens as she turns to it. Phaedra stands in the doorway; a beautiful woman wound carelessly in a cloak, haggard but royal. Selene steps back from her.)*

SELENE: My lady!

*(Phaedra stands bewildered, gazing at the women and the scene. Her lips move, but without a voice. Finally she speaks aloud, slowly and clearly.)*

PHAEDRA: I will not shame myself. I will not defile this house.

SELENE: What are you saying?

PHAEDRA: I *will* not.

And you, be silent. You are my servant, I think. What's your name? Selene? My poor Selene.

*(She gazes from one to other of the women.)*

Who are all these women, Selene? So many and so very many and such proud faces?

Are you the queens of the East that have come to comfort me? I will die sooner.

SELENE: You are ill, my lady. You are weak, trembling with fever: come back, dear,

Into the house.

PHAEDRA: *(Stepping down from the doorway.)* Not at all: I will walk in my lovely garden: up and down: and feel the warm sun…

*(She shudders violently.)*

They say death's bitter cold. Ah? You beautiful haughty queens, I shall soon know.

*(Selene supports her as she moves forward. The women follow.)*

PHAEDRA: *(To herself.)* I'll tear it out of me. Tear. *Tear,* you know: like a barbed spearhead

Out of my bitter heart. *(She shudders.)* Bitter cold: bitter heart: my bitter longing. The bitter end.

What a queer word!

FIRST WOMAN: She is going straight toward the goddess.

SECOND WOMAN: The altar: see? Like a gray moth

To candle flame. Like a sleepwalker.

FIRST WOMAN: Let us go back to the great door, Cleone,

And see if we can get something.

*(They return to the door, but often looking back to see what happens. Third Woman plays her zither. Presently the door half opens, the basket is passed through it. Meanwhile Phaedra moves helplessly toward the altar.)*

SELENE: *(Trying to draw her aside.)* This way, my lady: the path is better.

PHAEDRA: Let me alone, woman.

I will pray here: it seems to be a religious place. I cannot well remember…

There are so many gods in so many places…

SELENE: Do not go near it!

*(She reaches out her arms in vain; Phaedra blindly moves on. But suddenly jerks and stiffens, throwing her head back.)*

PHAEDRA: *(In a strangled voice.)* This is the one! *(Retreating.)* The awful power

That has me in hand. The goddess of love and longing, cruel, cruel and beautiful. I may as well confess now.

The crime is not great if I will not yield.—It is my husband's son by that Amazon woman.

It is Hippolytus.

I have long loved his beauty: but now the goddess has thrown stark madness

Into my heart: *I want. I want*...I will never yield to it.

SELENE: You—are in love with—Hippolytus?

PHAEDRA: If you call it love!

This loathsomeness in me. This disease. This burning shame. *(Dazed, looks around.)* Why, where have my great queens of the East gone to? *(Laughing.)*

They thought I meant it! They thought I didn't know a beggar-woman

From a great queen!

SELENE: *(Pointing.)* They are at their trade yonder. *(Thoughtfully.)* Hippolytus...

Is not the kind of young man for any woman to love.

PHAEDRA: What?

SELENE: *(With slow emphasis.)* He does not care for women.

PHAEDRA: I am glad of that. Why should he waste himself? Cold, proud and pure.—I'm going in, Selene.

Oh, I am tired of the light. I have a cold edge in me

That thinks it is worse than evil; it is ridiculous.—Like all our miseries!—Will you come?

—And of course you understand that this is secret, and we'll never, never, speak of it again. I shall not live long.

SELENE: You are better for having told me, dear. You walk more firmly; you have faced the truth...

PHAEDRA: Be silent, will you!

I have not faced the truth but an idiot deception, a great false fire in the fog

On a phantom coast.—If decency and common shame were out of the question—For I love his father,

My husband Theseus. It is not even *possible* to love two men. I know how my heart lighted up
When I came down the plank from the Cretan ship and saw him—tall, fierce and tender, there waiting for me,
In the dirty-cluttered Athenian harbor among the sailors—like the temple of a god
On a high rock. For I *love* him, you know! Theseus I love. I have been fighting myself…
He is—not young—if any person he loves should betray him…When anyone's very young he can slide
From one lust to another, nothing is mortal: but a fierce man of war growing grizzle
Under the helmet: I know him: if anyone should betray him even in thought
He'd hate the world.—And when I look at…his son…my eyes
Scald with the stupid tears.—Die…ah! No choice. *(Quietly.)* I am going in to hide myself
From the great eye of the sun; I have only one god
To pray to now. Not Love, not Light, not Fortune. Death, tall and silent,
Has a flower in his hand; its name is Forgetfulness.
Its name—we hope—is Peace.
*(They approach the door.)*

PHAEDRA: Why, look: here are my gay-colored East-queens!
Have you had good fortune, majesties?
*(Second Woman hides the basket behind her.)*

PHAEDRA: No: show me.
*(It is shown.)*

PHAEDRA: Poor women: it is not much. May I take a crust from it?
I do not think I have eaten since dawn.

SELENE: My lady!

PHAEDRA: One little crumb. I have been too proud in my lifetime:
That's a great sin. But now I will beg of beggars, a bit of bread to eat. You are kind, women.
I am truly grateful.
*(She goes into the house; Selene follows, weeping. The stage is gradually growing darker.)*

FIRST WOMAN: The goddess has unraveled her mind. As if she were struck by sudden lightning

When she went near the altar.

SECOND WOMAN: *(Terrified.)* The altar! Look!

*(The women cower and shield their eyes. The Goddess Aphrodite has glided from behind a flowering bush, and leans her hand on the altar, her spot of light increasing. She is tall and very beautiful, marble white and marble-polished, but perhaps pale gold hair. She has a spray of fruit-blossom in her hand, and plays with it. She speaks as if she were alone, thinking aloud.)*

APHRODITE: ...So I have come down to this place,
And will work my will. I am not the least clever of the powers of heaven.

*(She smiles, fondling the blossom-spray.)*

I am the goddess the Greeks call Aphrodite; and the Romans will call me Venus; the Goddess of Love. I make the orchard-trees
Flower, and bear their sweet fruit. I make the joyful birds to mate in the branches. I make the man
Lean to the woman. I make the huge blue tides of the ocean follow the moon; I make the multitude
Of the stars in the sky to love each other, and love the earth. Without my saving power
They would fly apart into the horror of night. And even the atoms of things, the hot whirling atoms,
Would split apart: the whole world would burst apart into smoking dust, chaos and darkness; all life
Would gasp and perish. But love supports and preserves them: *my saving power.*

This is my altar,
Where men worship me. Sometimes I grant the prayers of those that worship me: but those who reject me
I will certainly punish. Not because I am angry: love is my nature: the man who rejects love
Will be certainly punished.

There is a young man here,
Hippolytus, the son of Theseus, who rejects love and disdains to worship me. Horses, hounds and keen hunting,
And the dear friendship of the young men, his comrades, are all he cares for.

*(Bitterly.)* A chaste young athlete. He boasts of it:
That he will never make love to a woman nor worship
The Queen of Love. *(Pauses and smiles, admiring the blossom spray.)* Well...I shall have my will of him. The young man
Will be taken care of. It is not right—nor safe—to be insolent
To a great goddess.

I am a little sorry for the lady Phaedra, his old father's young wife,
Who must go down into shame and madness to make his ruin; and I am sorry for the old hero,
Theseus, his father: but to suffer is man's fate, and they have to bear it. We gods and goddesses
Must not be very scrupulous; we are forces of nature, vast and inflexible, and neither mercy
Nor fear can move us. Men and women are the pawns we play with; we work our games out on a wide chess board,
The great brown-and-green earth. *(She pauses, lifts her head and smiles frankly at the audience.)* You are gathered here
To see the game?

Watch, then. I have planted the agony of love in that woman's flesh, like a poisoned sword
In her beautiful body: and I shall watch unseen, from my altar here, the sudden accomplishment
Of my planned purpose. The day will be
Today. *This* day. Look: the dark night is passing;
The beautiful feet of dawn come over the mountain, the pale bright feet sandaled with music,
Driving the gentle stars, like a man frightening
A flock of birds.
*(Light increases on the sky and background, and comes slowly downward onto the stage. Pastoral music of flutes, increasing with the light. Meanwhile the spot of light fades from the altar; the goddess vanishes. She leaves her blossom-spray on the altar. The women, who have been crouching by the door of the house, are seen clearly again. They move like persons awaking from a night's sleep.)*
FIRST WOMAN: *(Pushing back her hair.)* I had a terrible dream.
SECOND WOMAN: A dream? I too!

FIRST WOMAN: I dreamed that a strong flame burned on the stone...
*(Furtively pointing.)* The altar there...a white-hot column of fire,
Whirling and smoking: and little men and women were struggling in it,
Burning alive. Frightful...

SECOND WOMAN: I dreamed that a great white cat—a snow-leopard—
With pitiless glaring eyes and fierce claws unsheathed
Crouched on the altar, ready to pounce...on me I thought...
Oh, how foolish it is to tell our dreams!
They bring bad luck.

THIRD WOMAN: Not mine, dear. I too had a dream, a pleasant one.
I dreamed that a pure-white dove came down from heaven
And perched on the altar; she had a spray of
white apple blossom
In her beak...Why, look, look! There it *is!*
Was my dream true?

# Beautiful Bodies

Laura Cunningham
1987

**Serio-comic**
**Scene:** a baby shower for Claire

Martha
Jessie
Sue Carol
Claire
Nina
Lisbeth

MARTHA: ...drinking this rotgut wine that will cause a furry baby. And *I* try to be sympathetic and helpful...I won't even mention how much money I spent! And to add insult to injury, *you* all treat me as if I'm a fool!

JESSIE: Martha, you are over the line.

MARTHA: No, lets clear the air! All night long, you've all been talking about me behind my back!

SUE CAROL: Uh-oh. The grass. Some people get paranoid.

*(Martha strikes, moving on the tippy-toes of paranoia: fast and furious.)*

MARTHA: Some people! Not me! What're you trying to pull? Talking and giggling about me behind my back? I've felt it underneath for years. Through all the phonecalls and the lunches, the dinners, and the movies. You only see me because it would be harder to stop seeing me than just see me once in awhile...

JESSIE: It's not like that!

MARTHA: It is so! So! Fine! Fine! It's been making me sick for years, but I know what's behind it...

NINA: What?

MARTHA: My mother told me not to even bother to come tonight. She said—"They're all jealous of you. Because of your obvious advantages." And I told her, "No, Mommy, you're *wrong*...They don't begrudge me the apartment, Donald, my success." But you *do*!

JESSIE: We don't want what you have!

MARTHA: Hahahahahahaha. I'm not stupid. Even I knew enough to

**46 SCENES FOR WOMEN**

downplay my achievements. Last year, I didn't even tell you, because I worried how it would affect you…that's only human…that I reached the top: I was voted *"Realtor of the Year!"*

*(The others collapse, laughing in shock.)*

MARTHA: *(Continued.)* See! You can't stand it! Can you? You want to vomit when you see me in my apartment, don't you?

NINA, SUE CAROL: *(Cracking up.)* Yes!

MARTHA: Does anyone ever say anything about *my* clothes? And I'm so careful to compliment you all, no matter what you have on. And does anyone ever have a nice word for Donald? No, you treat him like furniture. You should have seen your faces when I talked about my wedding, the honeymoon trip. When I said "Lago Maggiore," you all looked like you wanted to throw me in it!

LISBETH: That's not true!

MARTHA: Oh, you're so sick with jealousy you won't even be maid of honor, you won't wear a dress and…a bonnet! Huh? What's that?

NINA: Martha: Cool it.

MARTHA: Oh, I should cool it? How long do you think you can go your hotsy-totsy way? In a couple of years, men won't even be interested enough to abuse you. You'll be lucky if you can make love with the exterminator.

JESSIE: Martha! That's enough!

SUE CAROL: You got a mean streak in you, Martha!

MARTHA: *(To Jessie.)* And you won't have anyone to take care of you in your old age, you'll just get weirder and weirder and weirder!

JESSIE: I'd rather be weird than what you are!

MARTHA: Oh, go on. Get it over with…Buy the chihuahua! Knit dog booties! You'll need something. I'll have a family. I'll be happy, and none of you want to see it!

SUE CAROL: It would make anyone want to puke!

MARTHA: Woooo! Finally! It's coming out! Admit it. Admit it—*You're sorry you invited me!*

*(Group profound silence: an admission.)*

MARTHA: *(Continued. Marching to her gift pile.)* Look at these gifts! You all talk a good game. But who actually does the most?

*(Claire is now in a silent panic, noticeably shaken.)*

MARTHA: *(Continued.)* Who does the most for Claire! I put my money where my mouth is!

*(Martha's mouth opens wider, as Claire bolts for the door.)*

CLAIRE: *(To Jessie.)* I can't stay. I'm sorry. I have to go.

OTHERS: No! *(They pursue Claire toward the door.)*

SUE CAROL: Don't let Martha push you out!

NINA: This party is for you!

*(Claire squeezes eyes shut, bites her fist against the tears. She picks up her detached front bike wheel, flees.)*

CLAIRE: I want to go home! I just want to go home!

MARTHA: Don't you dare go!

*(Claire exits through elevator door, door slams shut.)*

MARTHA: *(Continued.)* …Its too late.

*(Group shock. Others stare at the door, then turn on Martha and one another.)*

JESSIE: How could you?

SUE CAROL: I've never seen a mouth go meaner… *(To Jessie.)* Why'd you invite her?

LISBETH: You gave her such ugly gifts…You didn't consider…the aesthetic effect. I thought and thought about what to give Claire… something beautiful, permanent…with emotional meaning…You wanted to depress her!

NINA: At least the doll I gave her was *cute!*

JESSIE: I'm really glad I had this in my house…I'm so thrilled I spent over three hundred dollars at Dean and DeLuca…

MARTHA: I would never have had that rotgut wine if it was at my place. It should have been at my place.

SUE CAROL: Your place looks like the lobby of a Ramada Inn!

MARTHA: A Ramada! That shows what *you* know…It should have been at my place…It's bigger and more conveniently located…I would have had it catered…

JESSIE: *(Whisper to Lisbeth.)* I want to kill her.

*(Lisbeth, Jessie huddle, conspiring, and Nina and Sue Carol join them—a team is forming, with Martha on the "other side.")*

LISBETH: *(Whisper to Jessie.)* Tell her off, tell her off…

NINA: *(Also to Jessie, whisper.)* Let her have it…

SUE CAROL: When I think how I rushed to get here…On a night when my own life was falling apart all around me…But I thought "Oh, we'll have a good time, we'll be happy, we'll forget…"

MARTHA: That your lives are shit.

*(Jessie has been building, trying to get a word in edgewise.)*

JESSIE: Stop it...Stop it...Stop it...All of you...

*(They ignore her, overlapping accusations to one another.)*

MARTHA: *(To Sue Carol.)* All you ever think about is yourself...You're so cheap...When was the last time you picked up a check?

SUE CAROL: I'd rather pick up a check than eat with you...

MARTHA: You'd split the tax...

NINA: *(To Martha.)* Don't ever call me...Next Tuesday is off...

LISBETH: The whole world is disintegrating...I want to die, I want to die. *(To Jessie.)* When I came in here tonight and saw all the decorations I wanted to take an overdose of something...anything...

NINA: I could have stayed in bed with Stan...I didn't need this...

*(Jessie grabs the dinner platter, bangs it down.)*

JESSIE: *(Peak.)* Look at me! I'm exhausted! I was up at dawn to peel radishes into rosebuds! I was on line for groceries for three hours! I couldn't wait for delivery so I *pushed* a cart for ten blocks, and rode up in the elevator...I carried those wine jugs! Do you know how much they weigh? My cleaning lady didn't show up, and I had to vacuum...and my vacuum broke...I breathed in dust! I didn't have time to take a shower! I didn't have time to pee!

NINA: *(Nodding to the war drum beat.)* She busted her hump...

JESSIE: And I'm sorry! I'm sorry! I'm sorry I bothered! I feel like a real jerk for even...making *the effort!* I wanted tonight... *(She trashes the rest of her party display.)* to be *perfect!* And nobody has showed the least bit of consideration *for me!* I was the hostess here! I'm always the hostess! And nobody cares about me! I shouldn't have bothered!

NINA: I brought the cake.

MARTHA: And you ate it.

NINA: *(To Martha.)* Oh why don't you shut your trap and get out of here?

SUE CAROL: I brought all those vegetables...

MARTHA: That was a new low, even for you...

SUE CAROL: I hate you, I hate you...When you call me and I'm home...I leave my machine on...

LISBETH: I do too...

SUE CAROL: Just get the hell out!

MARTHA: It's Jessie's house!

JESSIE: Oh, you can all go: I'm going to bed…

LISBETH: *(To Martha.)* And take all your presents with you! *(She roots through pile, selects her own christening dress. Low, to herself.)* I might as well take this…

NINA: *(Picking up baby boy doll. To Jessie.)* I sensed you resented having this at your place.

JESSIE: I do *now!*

*(Everyone scrambles, selecting their gifts, coats, heading for the door. They are giving up, leaving: Martha, as usual, leads. She is almost at the door. Jessie is on the verge of tears.)*

JESSIE: *(A near sob: choking grief.)* Tonight was about kindness!

*(Simultaneously, the door swings open: Claire reappears, holding a vandalized parking meter pole, like a spear, her bike lock dangling from it. She stamps the meter pole: She looks fiery, determined.)*

EVERYONE: Claire!

*(Claire confronts Martha.)*

NINA: Don't even talk to her. I wouldn't even talk to her…

CLAIRE: No! I'm not taking this! You have a lot of nerve coming down here…like a SAC missile: You hit every weak spot! You're unerring!

MARTHA: I just want you to face reality!

CLAIRE: No! Reality will have to face me! I haven't been so mad since my folks told me to forget medieval music and teach math! Well, I fought them, and I *fight* you…

MARTHA: What's wrong with being a math teacher? At certain points in life, you must make certain compromises…

CLAIRE: Well, I don't intend to end up looking mine in the eye! Keep it up Martha…Keep droning on about orthodontia and IRAs! You only make me fight harder! I sense a miracle upon me, and I refuse to let you make it…*mundane.* Don't infect me with your fear…I have my own!

MARTHA: It's not enough!

CLAIRE: Oh, yes it is! I'm the one who has to go through with this! I'm the one who wakes up at four A.M.…I hear *two* pounding hearts! I sleep all day, and lie awake all night! I go grocery shopping at four A.M.…

MARTHA: That's foolish…

CLAIRE: No! This is the way it is now…It's getting stranger and stranger out there…A trip to the Safeway is like a visit to Mars…It's crazy and new, and it's not going to defeat me...I don't care if you think I'm unfit; I don't care if I'm broke...I have new life in me! And only a child can lead any of us, out of this...Children are our guides to this future...This is a world they will explain to us! They know how to play, to bring joy to this terrible place...I saw a little boy, in a subway arcade...and he was laughing, and winning a war at a machine that led him into outer space...

MARTHA: You're having a baby so you can know how to play video games!

CLAIRE: *(Thrown for a moment, then regaining her momentum.)* Yes! Yes! In a sense! Because, otherwise, it will get worse! There's a bad wind blowing...and a new cold is creeping toward us...Each day, something new and awful happens... *(Rattling the meter.)* We have worse enemies than ourselves...

MARTHA: Your bike was stolen...I'll buy you a new one.

NINA: That's the least you can do...

CLAIRE: I don't want what you can buy me.

*(Martha is shaken, in distraction, finishes packing her gifts in the stroller.)*

MARTHA: *(Weakened by Claire's strength.)* I guess I should go. *(Martha works blindly in the confusion of her emotion. She is literally losing it: Her purse drops, spilling keys, money. She is on the brink of breaking down.)* What do you want me to do? I'll do it. *(Desperate, looking up from the floor.)* Do you want me to have a brunch? My treat. At a nice restaurant...

*(The others look at her stonily.)*

MARTHA: *(Continued.)* I was having a good time.

NINA: You were having a ball.

MARTHA: I thought it was a wonderful party...considering the location.

JESSIE: Thank you. So glad you could come.

MARTHA: I haven't had so much fun in years. Since we all lived in the same building.

SUE CAROL: Oh, go home to Donald, that pussy-whipped wimp...

MARTHA: I wish he was pussy-whipped... *(She decides to offer her real gift: an honest admission.)* I didn't want to go out with him tonight...I wanted to stay here...

LISBETH: You missed a great dinner.

MARTHA: And who do you think would have had to pick up the check?

SUE CAROL: *(Elated.)* You have to pay with him too!

JESSIE: *(Hushing Sue Carol.)* Sssssh.

*(The others lean in, needing to hear Martha's ultimate truth.)*

MARTHA: You'll be happy to hear I pay all the bills, make all the reservations...He doesn't even speak to me at meals. He just lowers his head into a bowl and makes sounds...

JESSIE: You support Donald!

SUE CAROL: I suspected it, I suspected it...

CLAIRE: *(Restraining Sue Carol's glee.)* Hold on...

MARTHA: Ask him to "contribute" and he says his money is all tied up...huh...in his sock! He won't even open a *joint account.*

SUE CAROL: And how's his joint?

NINA: Yeah, how is it?

MARTHA: *(Laughing on the verge of tears.)* Ha Ha...you don't know the half of it. He only makes love to me on my birthday. August 7th. I have to get on top and do all the work. Things are slipping fast...His doo-hickey isn't as strong as it used to be. It has a pleat. It folds...like an accordion. I don't know that I can fix it in time for the wedding... *(She makes a helpless gesture, as if repairing an accordion.)* Oh, God, I'm getting tired of trying...

LISBETH: Do you love him?

MARTHA: Sweetie, his pupils don't even focus. There's no one home.

SUE CAROL: So why all the bullshit with the QE II, and the earrings?

MARTHA: I decided to marry him, anyway.

OTHERS: Why?

MARTHA: *(Defeated.)* It's easier. I can still go to a good restaurant.

JESSIE: That may not be the pinnacle of human experience...

NINA: It can be pretty close...

MARTHA: Well, I love lobster places. Can you imagine me, alone in a bib? I'd feel absurd. Where am I supposed to go? To the coffee shops, where the plates are chipped, and the glasses are all spotty? So some waitress can plunk down my dinner, and say, "There you go?"

SUE CAROL: Hey, I'm on the other end of that. There *I* go!

MARTHA: You all hate me...and you're my best friends!

*(Martha is crying, has scooped up most of her belongings, and is wheeling next to the door. She presses the elevator. Claire takes pity on her, takes her hand from the elevator button, holds it.)*

CLAIRE: Oh look...All friends have arguments, little ripples...undercurrents...It doesn't mean we don't *care*...Listen, some of what you said made sense...I've grown old, but I haven't grown up...

MARTHA: *(Weeping.)* I didn't mean that personally. We belong to the first generation that refused to give up sneakers. We're still young but we've been young for so long...

CLAIRE: God, you just put things the wrong way...But in a way, I ought to thank you...

*(Martha perks up.)*

CLAIRE: You made me so mad...it cleared my head...

MARTHA: *(Apologizing.)* Maybe I was a little outspoken.

CLAIRE: Well, you lit a fire under me. Running out and running back up here is the most action I've seen since the fruit store...God, there may not be a right way, or a wrong way to do this... *(She touches her belly.)* We each have to find our own way. Our children are our choices, and this is mine. I'd rather have the child of that night than the offspring of some lifelong "accommodation"...I don't want my life to be some long shlep to the finish...

MARTHA: *(Sarcastic but resigned.)* Thanks.

CLAIRE: I think it's just as scary to play it safe. If I lose out, at least I lose *big!*

MARTHA: I envy you...and believe me, I wish you well...

CLAIRE: I know you do...We don't hate you.

MARTHA: I'm sorry, I'm sorry! I'd never hurt you!

*(They collapse into a weeping, group huddle.)*

NINA: Don't cry...

LISBETH: I can't stand to see you cry...

MARTHA: I should never have opened my mouth!

SUE CAROL: I'm sorry I said you had a mean streak...

MARTHA: That hurt.

JESSIE: I'm glad I had this here...This is what I wanted.

CLAIRE: Oh, God, I love you all.

OTHERS: We love you. *(They are crying, laughing, clinging.)*

CLAIRE: You've all given me so much. Let's face it. This may be as good as it gets...

LISBETH: You mean we won't get to meet new people?

*(They close in, laughing at themselves, as dawn seeps into the loft, bleaching away the cityscape, and leaving the women, exposed to one another.)*

# Tea

Velina Hasu Houston
1987

**Dramatic**
**Scene:** in the closed-off home of the deceased Himiko.
**Of Note:** Himiko—a ghost, narrates the scene from a separate play-
ing area.

Himiko
Atsuko
Teruko
Chiz
Setsuko

HIMIKO: I was the *best* wife.

TERUKO: He never let her out of the house and hardly let her have
guests. Remember during the big snow storm? The phone lines
were down and—

HIMIKO: —I didn't have any tea or rice left. Billy had gone to Oklahoma
to visit his family. He said, "Don't leave the house" and took my
daughter, Mieko, with him. So there I was, starving to death,
standing behind—

TERUKO: *(Overlapping with Himiko's last two words.)* —Standing
behind the frosty glass. She looked like she was made of wax.

HIMIKO: *(Smiles at herself.)* I asked him once. I said, "Why did you
marry me?" And he said he wanted a good maid, for free.

ATSUKO: Maybe she wanted too much.

HIMIKO: I never asked for anything. Except soy sauce and good rice.
And dreams...for Mieko. *(Himiko glows with love for her child,
turns around and seems to see her as a tot, and beckons to her.)*
Mieko-chan! My little girl! *(Himiko exits as if chasing "Mieko.")*

ATSUKO: Teruko, I saw your daughter last week. *(A compliment.)* She
looks Japanese. That's nice. Too bad she isn't friends with my girl.
My girl's always with Setsuko-san's daughter. Have you seen her?
Looks Indonesian, not Japanese at all. Shame, ne.

TERUKO: But Setsuko's daughter is the only one who cooks Japanese
food My daughter likes hamburger sandwich and yellow-haired
boys.

ATSUKO: My daughter always goes to Setsuko-san's house. I've never been invited.

TERUKO: Setsuko likes her privacy.

ATSUKO: She invited you to tea.

TERUKO: Well, if you're not willing to be genuine with her, how can you share the honor of tea together?

ATSUKO: She invited Himiko, too!

TERUKO: Yes, even after the incident. Even though everyone was afraid.

*(A siren wails as a deafening gunshot echoes in the air and all lights blackout. Atsuko and Teruko exit to the kitchen in the darkness. Himiko, without sunglasses drifts from the darkness and stops center stage. The siren fades out and a spotlight fades up immediately on Himiko, who crouches as if shooting a pistol. She smiles and rises gracefully. She speaks matter-of-factly to the audience.)*

HIMIKO: *(Imitates the sound of shots, pronounced "bahn" like in bonfire.)* Ban! Ban! Ban! Yes. I am Himiko Hamilton. The murderess. I married and murdered a gentleman from Oklahoma. And they let me go on self-defense. It took one shot—right through the heart I never knew he had. Now that he's gone, I can speak freely. Please listen. I wasted my life in Kansas. The state—of mind. Not Kansas City, but *Junction City,* a stupid hick town that rests like a pimple on an army base called Fort Riley. Where the Army's resettlement policy exiled our husbands because they were married to "Japs."

*(Himiko indicates her own face as Chiz and Setsuko enter from opposite corners carrying food in a basket and furoshiki, respectively.)*

HIMIKO: They won't tell you that because they're real *Japaneezy* Japanese.

*(Chiz and Setsuko smile and bow formally to each other in greeting; Setsuko bows a second time.)*

HIMIKO: See what I mean? Well...I'm about as Japanese as corn flakes, or so they say, and I killed my husband because he laughed at my soy sauce just one time too many. *(Himiko smiles whimsically and turns away from the audience.)*

*(Chiz and Setsuko drift downstage. They are unaware of Himiko's presence. Setsuko and Chiz stand outside of the house.)*

SETSUKO: Oh, Chizuye-san, I wish Himiko-san could have seen all the Japanese women at her funeral.

HIMIKO: *(To the audience.)* All the Japanese women who were too ashamed to say hello to me in public because I was "no good."

CHIZ: *(Adamant with characteristic exuberance.)* Ever since she shot her husband two years ago, she's kind of haunted me. It made me remember that underneath my comfortable American clothes, I am, after all, Japanese. *(A quick smile.)* But don't tell anybody.

SETSUKO: Well, after all, you were the one who went looking for her.

CHIZ: Someone had to. The rest of you were too afraid of what you would find. *(Looks into space as she recalls.)* I forced her door open and, there she was, paler and bluer than the sky over Hiroshima that strange August. She had pulled her kimono over her American dress, as if it might make her journey into the next life a little easier. But I took one look at her and I knew nothing was ever going to be easy for her, not in life or in death.

HIMIKO: I would have given anything to have tea with Japanese girls. I drank alone.

*(Setsuko and Chiz approach the house and remove their shoes. Setsuko straightens hers and Chiz's.)*

CHIZ: What'd you bring?

SETSUKO: Maki-zushi.

CHIZ: *(Smiles to poke fun at her friend.)* Figures. I brought spinach quiche, Sue.

SETSUKO: My name is not Sue. My name is Setsuko. Chizuye-san, I tell you many times not to call me by this nickname you made up.

CHIZ: But it's easier.

SETSUKO: Like Chiz. *(Pronounces it "cheese.)*

CHIZ: *(Laughs; pronounces it with a short "i.")* No, Setsuko, like "Chiz." That's what my customers at my restaurant call me, but you can call me anything you like.

*(The enter the house and Chiz looks toward the kitchen.)*

CHIZ: Hello? Hello? Ah, Teruko! Hello.

*(Teruko appears from the kitchen with food including fruit. Setsuko scurries to help her.)*

TERUKO: Hello! Hello! Look, Atsuko-san is here, too.

CHIZ: *(Much surprise and a touch of contempt.)* Atsuko?!

SETSUKO: Well, what an unexpected pleasure.

ATSUKO: Setsuko-san! I rarely see you, but you look younger every time I do. I was sorry to hear about your husband.

SETSUKO: Yes, well, it was his time to…to move on.

ATSUKO: Negroes don't live very long. The food they eat, you know.

SETSUKO: My husband ate almost entirely Japanese food.

TERUKO: Atsuko-san's husband hates Japanese food. *(Giggles.)* And he's Japanese Amerikan!

ATSUKO: He does *not* hate Japanese food! *(To Setsuko and Chiz.)* Why are you both so late? We cleaned the kitchen already. And, of course, we must have tea.

SETSUKO: Oh, yes, tea sounds very good to me now.

TERUKO: Why, yes. Everything must start with tea.

CHIZ: *(Laughs.)* Tea is just a drink.

SETSUKO: Oh, it's much more than that.

ATSUKO: I couldn't live without tea.

HIMIKO: Yes…it brings everything into balance.

ATSUKO: I think it improves my eyesight.

SETSUKO: *(Laughing.)* And my insight.

*(Teruko, Setsuko, and Atsuko have a good laugh over this as Chiz looks on deadpan. Finally she smiles and lights up a cigarette.)*

CHIZ: Hey, enough about tea. Who else is coming?

TERUKO: More than four would be too many. I stopped asking for volunteers after Atsuko-san spoke up.

CHIZ: How many were there?

TERUKO: At least fifty Japanese women!

CHIZ: Fifty? Jesus. You'd think it was a blue-light special.

SETSUKO: Chizuye-san! Shame, ne! After all, this is a difficult occasion for us: the first time a member of our Japanese community has passed on.

CHIZ: What "community"?

HIMIKO: *(Again, to audience.)* Yes, what community? We knew each other, but not really…We didn't care enough to know.

CHIZ: Who's got time to chit-chat, right, "Ats"? *(Pronounced with a short "a," like "ahts".)* Now that I'm finally having tea with the great Atsuko Yamamoto, you get a nickname.

ATSUKO: Thank you, but you can keep your…gift. *(A beat.)* It's obvious we're all from different neighborhoods.

SETSUKO: But we are all Army wives—and we are all Japanese.

CHIZ: So what? That won't buy us a ticket to Nirvana. Let's face it, girls, after we get through dealing with our jobs and our families, we're ready to go to sleep. And, if any of us are willing to drive across town and have tea, we don't even talk about what's really on our minds—whether coming to Amerika was such a good idea. *(She smiles.)* Countries last; love is mortal.

SETSUKO: But we're here today because we're Japanese.

CHIZ: We're here today because we're scared.

HIMIKO: Scared they will be next to die or their souls will be left in limbo like mine.

*(Atsuko can hardly contain her excitement at finally being able to ask a question she's pondered for years.)*

ATSUKO: Tell us, Setsuko-san. Is it true about Himiko being a dance hall girl in Japan?

SETSUKO: If that's what she said. I never really knew her until after her husband died. I would see her walking in the middle of a humid summer day in a heavy coat and the yellow haired wig.

HIMIKO: *(Reliving that day.)* "Hello. I am Mrs. William Hamilton. May I have a glass of water? Oh, thank you, thank you. You are so kind."

ATSUKO: *(Gesticulating that Himiko was crazy.)* Kichigai, ne...

CHIZ: She was *not* crazy.

TERUKO: It is the Japanese way to carry everything inside.

HIMIKO: Yes. And that is where I hid myself.

ATSUKO: She came from Japan, but the way she dressed, the way she walked. Mah, I remember the district church meeting. She came in a low-cut dress and that yellow-haired wig, *(Mocks how she thinks a Korean walks.)* walking like a Korean.

SETSUKO: Atsuko-san, ne, we have something in common with all the Oriental women here, even the Vietnamese. We all left behind our countries to come and live here with the men we loved.

ATSUKO: Okay, okay. It's not that I didn't like Himiko-san. So many things she did were not acceptable. If she acted like that in Japan, people would think she was...well, a prostitute. Something was not right inside her head. I mean, who ever heard of a Japanese shooting her husband with a rifle? I told you that day at the cemetery.

*(Himiko, having had enough, rushes forward and the women freeze.)*

HIMIKO: *(Defiantly calls them back into the past with a roll call, stamp-*

*ing her foot as she calls out each name.)* Teruko. Setsuko. Atsuko. Chizuye.

*(Himiko exists through the kitchen as the music for "Taps" sets the mood. The women drift from the house as if answering the roll call. The lights fade out on house and fade up downstage. They stand as if around a headstone at a cemetery as Himiko enters. A black-veiled hat, black coat and black pumps complete her widow ensemble. She carries a black bag out of which she pulls a can of beer. The women watch in shock as Himiko opens the beer and pours it over the "grave" by which they stand. Setsuko runs to her and takes the beer.)*

HIMIKO: Mah, there must be a thousand graves here!

SETSUKO: Shame on you, Himiko-san! Pouring beer on your husband's grave!

HIMIKO: I am celebrating. First Memorial Day since he "left me." He liked beer when he was alive. Why shouldn't he like it when he's dead?

CHIZ: Sounds pretty fair to me.

ATSUKO: Teruko-san, come. We've seen enough.

*(Atsuko pulls away a reluctant Teruko, who beckons to Chiz. All three exit. Setsuko, concerned, lingers as Himiko suddenly looks up at an invisible object in great shock.)*

HIMIKO: I'm sorry, Billy. That's right. I forgot. You like Budweiser beer. This is cheap kind, brand X. See? *(Points at the can.)* Just B-E-E-R. Billy, what are you doing here? I believe in reincarnation, but this is a little soon. I planned on being gone before you came back. I'm sorry I didn't bury you in your favorite shirt. I couldn't fix the hole in it from when I shot you. No, no. I don't want to go with you. *(Fighting.)* No, I want to stay here with our daughter. She's not mad at me for what I did. She says you deserved it. No, I don't want to be alone with you anymore. I don't want to kiss and make up. *(Pushes away at unseen presence.)* Setchan! Help me! Billy's going to take me away.

*(The presence knocks her off her feet.)*

SETSUKO: *(An antithetical picture of solitude, she draws near.)* Himiko-san. Let's go home now. We'll make tea and talk.

HIMIKO: Help me, Setchan. He's going to beat me up again.

SETSUKO: Come, Himi-chan. You must go home and rest.

HIMIKO: There is only unrest. It is like the war never ended.

SETSUKO: *(Sympathetically.)* Oh, Himi-san. *(Not knowing what else to do, she releases Himiko and bows her head sorrowfully.)*

HIMIKO: *(Enervated, to herself.)* I wish I would have died in World War II. It was an easier war than this one.

# Alice in Bed

Susan Sontag
1993

**Serio-comic**
**Scene:** a tea party

Margaret
Emily
Kundry
Mother
Alice
Myrtha

ALICE: I must be calm. When I crossed the Atlantic it was November. The sea was calm. But I never left my cabin. Shortly after the ship sailed I had what Father called on of my nervous attacks. I never left my cabin. Miss Loring was with me. Harry met the boat at Liverpool. Two stout sailors carried me ashore and I spent a week recuperating in a Liverpool hotel, attended by a maid Harry had brought and a nurse and Miss Loring. Then Harry took me to London and installed me in lodgings near Piccadilly near his own rooms.

MARGARET: You crossed the Atlantic and never left your cabin?

ALICE: Recumbent.

MARGARET: The sea was, there was no, the sea—

ALICE: Calm.

MARGARET: You didn't want to see anything.

ALICE: Don't reproach me.

*(Lights change. Emily enters with flowers. She distributes them.)*

ALICE: You left us Emily. We waited for you. That doesn't seem fair.

EMILY: The pain deserved a blank.

ALICE: I did think this was a party you were giving for me. And so I thought no doubt mistakenly that I could count on a minimum of— *(She sees Emily at the table reaching for the teapot.)* You know there isn't any tea.

*(Emily pours herself tea, stands sipping it.)*

MARGARET: (To Alice.) I'm beginning to worry about you. Truly worry.

ALICE: What do you mean.

*(Emily sits demurely on a mattress.)*

MARGARET: I do question the need, I suppose I mean the wisdom, but of course it's in the end a matter of common sense, when, by asking Emily as well, you—

ALICE: What have you got against Emily, Margaret. *(To Emily.)* You don't mind if I ask Margaret to say what she means.

EMILY: No.

ALICE: Be blunt.

MARGARET: I always am. But now I wonder—

ALICE: No please.

EMILY: Yes.

MARGARET: *(After a pause.)* You're not I think giving life a chance.

ALICE: Because I invited Emily.

EMILY: One can't think about death steadily any more than one can stare at the sun. I think about it slant.

MARGARET: You like that tone don't you.

ALICE: *(To Margaret.)* I suppose I do. *(To Emily.)* I think your interest in death is more interesting than mine.

MARGARET: I thought we were here to talk about life.

EMILY: Death is the lining. The lines.

ALICE: I remember when my mother died—

*(Mother enters; all in white. White full coat, carries white umbrella, wears white gloves.)*

ALICE: Oh my god. I didn't invite her. I never invited her.

*(Mother moves toward table.)*

MARGARET: Alice.

EMILY: Alice.

KUNDRY: *(Lifts head, eyes closed.)* Who called.

ALICE: *(Air of terror.)* She'll stay and then we can't talk.

MARGARET: You can talk. *(Moves to stand protectively near Alice.)*

EMILY: You are talking.

ALICE: I'm going to pretend that I don't mind. Then perhaps she'll go away.

MOTHER: Oh your poor mother.

*(Stands behind chair next to Kundry, whose head rests on the table.)*

ALICE: *(Whispering.)* It's my mother. She's dead too.

MARGARET: You didn't invite her.

ALICE: *(Whispering.)* Certainly not. *(Pauses.)* Mother.

MOTHER: Oh your poor mother.

ALICE: Sit down, Mother. *(Whispering, to Margaret and Emily.)* I have to invite her now. It would be rude not to.

MOTHER: I can't say I'm observing it but I'm not ignoring it either.

MARGARET: *(Loud whisper.)* What's she talking about.

ALICE: Me. I suppose. *(To Mother.)* Sit down please. *(To Margaret and Emily.)* You see. I don't mean anything I say. *(Pauses.)* She was always out of range.
*(Mother attempts to sit. Crowds Kundry, who whimpers, flails about; won't let her sit.)*

KUNDRY: What day is it. What year is it. How dare she.

MARGARET: Couldn't you just turn it upside down. Throw it down a hole. Tip it sideways. And let all those hard griefs slither away like curds turned out of their dish.

MOTHER: I can't say I'm walking but I'm not limping either. *(She has stopped trying to wrest a chair from Kundry. Opens umbrella. Looks up.)*

KUNDRY: At this table there's no room.

MOTHER: I never insisted. *(Mother exits.)*

KUNDRY: *(Eyes still shut.)* I think Kundry has saved you. *(Rocks back and forth.)*

MARGARET: A chastening apparition.

ALICE: I remember when my mother died my youngest brother said that we had all been educated by Father to feel that death was the only reality and that life was simply an experimental thing.

MARGARET: An experiment. An experiment. An experiment.

ALICE: Are you making fun of me.
*(Margaret sighs, shakes her head.)*

KUNDRY: *(Still rocking.)* It is hard to save anyone. But that is all we desire.

ALICE: He said, my brother said, that we feel we are more near to her now than ever before, simply because she is already at the goal to which we all cheerfully bend our steps.

EMILY: *Cheerfully* is a lovely, lethal word.

ALICE: He said, my youngest brother said, after our mother died: "The last two weeks have been the happiest I have known." *(Looks at Margaret and Emily, then starts to laugh.)* Yes it is mad isn't it. But you see how difficult it was for us. Father had high standards. We were not supposed to be, well, like the others.

MARGARET: Lived. Lived. Lived. Yes I lived, and yes I did not find it so difficult. I went out on the deck. Nothing could have made me renounce standing on the deck, feeling the wind on my face, pushing through my clothes.

EMILY: I've never been on a boat.

KUNDRY: *(Still rocking.)* My horse. My legs.

MARGARET: *(To Emily, in a kindly tone.)* I know this can't mean much to *you.* But I think—at least I said, I did say—They have not lived who have not seen Rome.

ALICE: Ah travel.

KUNDRY: *(Rocking.)* The Pope. He can bless, but can he save, but can he damn. No.

EMILY: It's a question of scale. To me it was an adventure to cross the village lane.
*(Myrtha enters. Long white dress, chiffon veil, baby wings, headband with flowers, etc. A kind of dervish twirling step. Music from Giselle.)*

ALICE: Did I invite her. Who is it. It's not—Ah Myrtha. Come and join us.
*(Myrtha stops.)*

ALICE: What's wrong.

MYRTHA: I'd rather not lie down.

MARGARET: No one will force you.

ALICE: Do you want to stand.

MYRTHA: Actually I'm not supposed to lie down. *(Resumes twirling.)* In the forest. In the glade. I live in the forest. That's where the graves are. He brings flowers. *(Stops again.)* What beautiful flowers.

MARGARET: We were talking about unhappiness. *(Sits at the table, opposite Kundry.)*

MYRTHA: *(To Alice.)* I think there is a man who has broken your heart.

ALICE: My father perhaps.

MYRTHA: We could kill him. Then you would have to kill yourself. Beautiful flowers. *(Resumes twirling.)*

ALICE: I always thought a man would crush me. He would put a pillow over my face. I wanted a man's weight on my body. But then I couldn't move.
*(Emily stands, helps Alice to stand; Margaret leaves table to help. Together they bring Alice to her seat at the table.)*

MARGARET: I can understand your not wanting it. Of course you feel pinned down. It's good. And then you get up afterward.

*(M I and M II have entered. M I sets a pot of tea on the table.)*

MYRTHA: He can't atone. You shouldn't forgive him.

*(M I and M II gather up and remove most of the mattresses and the hookahs.)*

ALICE: I remember a young man, Julian, he was a music student, a friend of my brother, of Harry I mean. He and Harry were always together. But he liked me. I used to imagine that we could go swimming together. I used to imagine his body.

MYRTHA: Flowers. Revenge.

EMILY: It's a winsome longing.

MARGARET: My idea is this. Want what you are capable of, and what you are capable of wanting, and be *completely* clear on the matter, and live according to it.

ALICE: Life is not just a question of courage.

MARGARET: But it is.

EMILY: *(To Alice.)* I think you are quite brave.

MYRTHA: How can you stand to be inside. In a room.

ALICE: You don't know the fearful things I see when I close my eyes. I have to die so I don't see the monstrous things.

MARGARET: I see terrible things when I open my eyes.

MYRTHA: In a room. In a tomb.

KUNDRY: *(To Alice, reaching convulsively across the table.)* Give me your hand.

ALICE: What do you see?

*(Extends her hand. Kundry takes it, brings it to her forehead, kisses it, then flings it back.)*

KUNDRY: Kundry's visions are the most terrible. Most terrible. I must be punished. My body wants—but I don't. It wants, it's so big, I can't I don't want, he wants, he makes me, but I want to, I want to first... *(Starting to fall asleep.)* First I'll want, if they let me, when I don't feel...

ALICE: Poor soul.

KUNDRY: *(Waking again.)* Why have I been awakened. I want to sleep.

ALICE: Please don't become, well...crazed. We mean you no harm. We have the most sisterly respect for your suffering.

MARGARET: However retrograde.

EMILY: I trust that my flowers have the good grace to be seared by our shouts.

KUNDRY: Why did you wake me.

ALICE: I told you.

*(Kundry stares uncomprehendingly.)*

MARGARET: She told you. But there may have been a mistake.

ALICE: Please don't be angry. You needn't have come if you really didn't want to.

EMILY: It wasn't an order, that's what she's saying. But it was a wind.

KUNDRY: Oh, oh.

MARGARET: There's a mattress. Lie down.

ALICE: Do you want anything to drink or eat. We did not offer before because we thought you preferred—

*(Kundry is very agitated. Margaret and Emily help her lie down on a mattress.)*

EMILY: Let her sleep.

MARGARET: Here. Some tea.

*(Kundry groans, refuses the tea.)*

ALICE: I was, we are, wrong to have disturbed her.

KUNDRY: Sleep, sleep... *(She sleeps, or seems to.)*

MARGARET: She'll be of no more use now.

EMILY: Shhhh...

MARGARET: Is this sleep different from when she was at the table. I don't see why we have to whisper. It's not I think that she sleeps so soundly.

ALICE: Yes she wakes when she wants to.

MYRTHA: I like being aware. *(Picks up sheaf off flowers and dances with them.)*

KUNDRY: *(Opening her eyes.)* There's an answer. Which is... *(Her eyes start to close; she makes an effort.)* There's a question.

ALICE: We've decided to ask you straight out why you sleep.

KUNDRY: Because my body is heavy. The innocent boy came and I tried to corrupt him. To make him desire me. He did desire me, but more as a mother than as a lover. And, still, he resisted me. So I felt ashamed. I fell down a bottomless well of shame. I'm still falling. How tiring. Oblivion.

MYRTHA: Exact your revenge. Men making women into whores and angels, how can you believe that. Have you no self-respect.

MARGARET: My husband was a boy and, unlike me, an exceedingly delicate person. I felt safe with him. And we had a child. I think he would have proved an excellent father, though he could not speculate about it, or indeed about anything.

EMILY: I stayed home and wrote. My brother fornicated. I was in a room with blue trim. I could see an orchard from my window. He came in, he had a goatee. Death. The frogs were singing. They have such pretty lazy times. How nice to be a frog! When the best is gone I know that other things are not of consequence. The heart wants what it wants or else it does not care.

# White Chocolate for My Father

Laurie Carlos
1994

**Dramatic**
**Scene:** in the house by the radio, 1959

Lore, a young girl
Tony, her younger sister
Tiny, her youngest sister
Mickey, their mother
Mama, Mickey's mother
Emilyn, Mama's grandmother
Deola, Emilyn's great-grandmother
Radio, The Spirit of the Red Light (a live character)

> *(Radio plays "Why Do Fools Fall in Love." The children sing "My Name Is Jimmy Durante." They sing and move to their own places. The White Light Spirit comes up across the red light in drums and movement, in grace. Lore gets caught up in drums and other children dance to what they can hear.)*

LORE: You dont know him do you? They wont let us see no pictures.

DEOLA: Fill yourself up girl. Its this thing they call the classics.

LORE: Every time we think we are gonna see his picture they take everything away. Have you seen his picture. What does he look like? Is he like Jackie Wilson? Is he like George Johnson? I want to marry him.

DEOLA: I can fly. I learned how to in the hole. In the hole like a bird I flew. Ears first. I tore open my thighs when the back of my head was chewed away. My beautiful breast lost in the hole in the earth. Buried up to the neck. My hands became my head and the legs bleed. Their dogs eat my head.

TINY: We want him to send kisses thru the phone.

DEOLA: I am old and I fight the men. They have seen his picture and rewrite his name. They feed my nose to the dog. My thighs are torn by my own hands. The breath of dogs against my teeth.

MICKEY: All these mistakes are mine.

EMILYN: Cotton and flax dont need to be boiled. Spoons. Vinegar, alum. Getting closer to my joy. Nettle, black alder, tansy. Forget thunder and leaves. Every little neatly combed head is counted as profit for my father and his wife. We all been sold two times.

TINY: Third person. Past tense.

EMILYN: First person. Present tense. I have no white mans children. Raw wool or silk must be washed to take out the grease. I have no white mans children, sister has nine. Mama has us. Yes I am taken by the same man who is the father of my sisters children. Dyers all of us. We know the ways to get color. Red? Alkanet, barberry, cranberry. He can only take me like this. *(She places the bag over her head and loosens her dress.)* Can't look at my face.

LORE, TONY, AND TINY: Clap hands clap hands till daddy comes home daddy has money and mommy has none!

DEOLA: My father was tender and smiled at me and welcomed me with music his hands made music from air.

LORE: Who are you?

EMILYN: I am his sister.

*(The red lights take over. The children dance to the radio.)*

RADIO: Sam Cooke, Dion, Ruth Brown. "Mama He Treats Your Daughter Mean," Frankie Limon.

MICKEY: We got out just in time. The truck was coming to evict us. Memphis was hard to live in, everything was high. Rent, meal, fatback, ribbon. We got out before they could get us. Mama would roll up newspaper to stick in the holes to keep the wind out. So eat those goddamn peas. Eat em and be glad there aint no Mr. Chissolm.

TINY: Who?

MICKEY: Yes!

MAMA: Sho as you born!

ALL: Sho as you born!

LORE: I come here with nothing. My mothers face my grandmothers hips my fathers nose and pudgy hands, his heels.

MAMA: Your nose is too wide too big too flat. *(She repeats line four more times.)* You need to teach those girls to play piano. They need to learn to sew. That dancing wont get em nowhere.

*(This is a moving photograph.)*

MICKEY: I dream of Sweden and Paris in your eyes.

MAMA: Looking at your face I see what the race will come to.

TONY: The face moves over to cry in crowds.

MAMA: Your face lives like belching on ice cream.

TINY: This face is Sharon and Walter dreaming.

MICKEY: This face is always a photo and music.

MAMA: Your face is remembered and ruined.

MICKEY: My face is unimagined and forgotten.

EMILYN: Rain water, copper kettle or an iron pot can be used for darker colors. Ammonia, lime.

TONY: *(Sings.)* I got a girlfriend and her name is lore lore lip lip.
She is my girlfriend and her name is lore lore lip lip.

MAMA: Only men would talk to me even in the church was them niggers in them cloth caps. I aint never want no nigger in a cloth cap, and old sports coat. These folks in New York dont care nothin bout a good-looking well-dressed cultured colored woman.

MICKEY: My great-grandmother was a white woman.

EMILYN: Looked just like a white woman.

MICKEY: And she brought a good price.

EMILYN: First person. Present tense. Brings a good price.

MICKEY: We picked cotton till I was twelve and came to New York. Where I met your father and made my mistakes. Yes sir they can dance.

*(Mickey sings "Blueberry Hill," the children do back-up.)*

MAMA: Chicken feet onions salt black pepper Do Re Mi Fa So La Tee Do and 947-7947 lx" 902? "91? 17 71-71Q4-v

TONY: And what does Ching Chow have to say today?

MAMA: Ching Chow say sixteen whites horses does not secure future make.

TONY: Ching Chow say anything else?

MAMA: He say if I had hair like my sister I would never have to pay my rent!

LORE: You look at his hat, at his ear, and you dont see nothing.

LORE, TONY, AND TINY: Clap hands clap hands till daddy comes home daddy has money and mama has none.

*(They create and play hand games—everyone spirit and slave.)*

TONY: Avenue C Friday 4:30.

TINY: For you ten cents off a yard. You take six yards eleven cents. Just for you!

LORE: I am closing! Sorry closed!

TINY: Before Shabbat Shabbat Shabbat.

TONY: Buy the best fish heads anyplace you could find better? Impossible.

LORE: Come over here rings, lace, shirts, I got for you towels.

TONY: One day your people will be free.

TINY: For you I give an extra half-pound.

TONY: Just for you.

LORE: Run before sundown catch them before sundown run catch them before sun—

TONY: Are you a smart girl you look like a smart girl.

LORE: So if you want a bargain? You got a bargain here. I got it for you.

TONY: We got colored work here.

LORE: Sorry. Sorry. We are closed. Closed at 4:30.

TONY: Amidst the clash of laughing and pennys-worth of swatches I was loved, patted and cherished. I was expected, planned for. Hands moved over my head and marked my growing with tears.

TINY: Memories for so many no longer here.

TONY: My back gave refuge to hugs too full for strangers.

TINY: Strong arms helped me ascend to giggles.

LORE: A half-size was put away till I got there. A licorice. A half-yard of white lace and velvet ribbon stored under the heaps till I got there.

TINY: Essex Street pickle man waiting to lift me by my head with two hands up so I could see my great-grandfather.

LORE, TONY AND TINY: Can you see? Can you see him?

TINY: Yes.

TONY: Up so he could guide me careful over the top of the pickle barrel to hold me awkward. Pickle juice so are up my arm.

LORE, TONY AND TINY: My laughter expected.

TINY: My joy welcomed on Essex Street.

LORE: Sometime I gave way to believing my being was justified. Known to be a valuable whimsy. I grew up in a love zone with a reputation for tough endings.

EMILYN: No white mans children. Put every one of those in the ground bloody with no hands.

MAMA: Second person. Present tense.

EMILYN: We make the best cloth in Legrange and all around. My mama know the roots for dyeing the cloth. She showed us the flowers for gold and red and death. No white mans children. The dogs chewed away my great-grandmothers lips she was still in Africa. We carry that picture in our heart when giving birth. Mama birth us with that in her and it helps us fetch a good price. (She places bag over her head and sings and loosens her clothes.)

TONY: I need new shoes.

TINY: My ponytail and my tight skirt and my Aunt Anna and my new train and my castor oil and my dog Billy and my frankfurters and my boy bug and my playground and my daddy.

TONY: Lets Speak Chinese.

*(They make language.)*

TONY: Lets Speak Spanish.

*(They make language.)*

LORE: I think we might be Spanish.

TINY: I want to be Catholic. But I think we're Indian first.

MAMA: You aint nothin but some ignorant niggers?

TONY: Forever ever ever ever forever. Ida digs them up over there. When they tear down the buildings. We put all the rats in our pockets and in Pitt Street Park we bury our friends. Tiny sings them away from the devil. Ida and me we kiss them.

# LARGE GROUP SCENES

# Hippolytus

Euripides
Translated by Carl R. Mueller

**Dramatic**

**Setting:** outside Phaidra's palace. At one side of the stage is a statue of Aphroditê and one of Artemis on the other.

**Scene:** An old servant apologizes to Aphroditê, goddess of love, for Hippolytus' failure to pay homage, having paid homage instead to Artemis, goddess of the hunt and of chastity. The chorus of the women of Troizen enters preceding the entrance of the love-sick Queen Phaidra and her nurse.

**Of Note:** The lines of the Chorus should be divided up among its members and spoken individually.

Hippolytus: (early 20s) step-son of Phaidra and King Thêseus
Phaidra: (30s–40s) wife of King Thêseus
Nurse: (50s–60s) Phaidra's servant
Servant: (60s) attendant to Hippolytus
Women's Chorus and Chorus Leader: women of Troizen (at least five)
Men's Chorus: male hunting attendants of Hippolytus

SERVANT: She's proud, too—Aphroditê.
  Men do her great honor.
HIPPOLYTUS: Gods have their likes and dislikes
  The same as men.
SERVANT: Well, then, good luck—
  And the good sense you'll need!
HIPPOLYTUS: Gods who work wonders at night
  Don't interest me.
SERVANT: My boy, we all must honor the gods.
  *(Hippolytus turns to his Huntsmen.)*
HIPPOLYTUS: Let's get on in there, men!
  There's no better end to a hunt
  Than a table groaning with meat and drink.
  *(To one of his men.)* And, you, see to my colts.
  A good rub down and lots of pampering.
  When I've finished, I'll hitch them to my chariot
  And take them for a proper workout.

*(To the old Servant.)* As for your Aphroditê—
Good riddance!
*(Hippolytus and the Chorus of Huntsmen enter the palace. The old Servant remains behind.)*

SERVANT: How foolish the young are.
Their heads so filled with crazy ideas.
Not to imitate them is best.
And so, goddess, Aphroditê,
I speak to you, as a slave should speak,
With reverence. Forgive this young fool.
It's his youth talking. His heart
Is stiff with pride. Be gracious—
Pretend not to hear.
Gods should always be wiser
Than mere mortals.
*(The old Servant enters the palace as the Chorus of the Women of Troizen enters from the right.)*

CHORUS: Mountain
    cliff, mountain
        stream, flowing,
  dripping,
      flowing, water from
        Ocean, they
  say, spouting,
      lunging, from
        sheer
  cliff
    face,
      where
  pitchers
    plunge in the
      running
  stream, there,
    there, a
      friend steeped
  crimson robes
    in the
      stream's
  flood, and

lay them,
          lay them
out, lay them,
     on a rock's
               warm
back,
     full in the
               sun.
There I heard,
     there,
          for the first
time,
     news,
          word of my
queen's,
     word of my
               mistress'
illness.
     She lies, they
          tell me, lies there,
on a bed of
     sickness,
          inside the house,
never
     leaving, never,
          wasting,
wasting away,
     wasting, on a
          bed of sickness,
sickness,
     sorely afflicted, her
          fair head shaded,
shadowed,
     by fine-spun
          fabrics, delicate
cloths.
     Three days now,
          they say,
three days,

                she has
                        fasted,
        kept herself
                pure from
                        Dêmêter's
        grain, no
                bread,
                        pure, no
        bread, passing her
                lips, wishing,
                        wishing,
        longing, wishing,
                in her secret
                        sorrow,
        secret
                grief, unspoken
                        grief, to
        ground the
                craft of her
                        life on death's
        unhappy
                shore.
                        Is your mind
        wandering, lady,
                wandering
                        wildly, because
        Pan,
                Pan, has
                        possessed you,
        Pan, or
                Hekate,
                        Hekate, or the
        holy
                Korybantes,
                        holy, or the
        mountain mother,
                great mountain
                        mother, Kybêlê,
        great mother?

Or has Artemis,
        huntress,
Artemis of wild
        beasts, has
                Artemis been
slighted by
        unoffered
                offerings,
unoffered, and
        now wastes you,
                wastes you
away for
        offerings not
                poured, offerings
unpoured on her
        holy
                altar?
For she has
        power to
                range the
march, range the
        sea's dry
                land that
stands in the salt
        eddies of the sea.
                Or is it your
husband, is it,
        is it Thêseus,
                Thêseus,
king of Athens,
        Thêseus,
                nobly
born, who has
        taken another
                woman, a
woman in the
        palace, a
                woman who
tends to him

far from your
        bed, from your
sight?
        Or has a
            sailor from Krete
sailed into our
        harbor, our
            welcoming
harbor, with
        news for the
            queen, news of
misfortune that
        binds her, binds her
            fast to her
bed, powerless,
        helpless,
            helpless, unable to
act in her
        sorrow?
            Woman's
nature is an
        uneasy
            accord, uneasy
harmony, and a
        terrible weary
            helplessness
overtakes her,
        robbing her of
            reason, when the
pangs of
        childbirth lay on.
            I, too,
I, too, have
        felt it's breath
            dart through my
womb. But I
        called to her,
            called, called to the
heavenly one, Artemis of the

arrows, Artemis,
        called, when
labor
        approached, and she
                always,
always,
        by the gods'
                grace, gods'
grace,
        eases my
                pain.

*(Phaidra, supported by several female Servants, enters after the Nurse from the palace. They are followed by other Servants bearing a pallet for her to lie on.)*

CHORUS LEADER: But look,
Here's her old nurse in the doorway.
And Phaidra just behind,
Helped by her slaves.
How troubled the nurse looks.
Perhaps now we'll learn the nature
Of our queen's illness—
What eats away at her body
And steals her color.

NURSE: Ah, what a blight of troubles this life is!
What am I to do with you, child? What?
These awful, hateful illnesses! All your
Thought was getting out into the sunlight,
Bringing out your bed, your sickbed,
And that's here, too, now.
And now what? Mm?
As if I didn't know! There it is!
There! Right on cue. The wrinkle of a frown
That tells me a complaint's on the way.
All you talked of was coming outside;
And now you're here, you'll
Soon want to hurry back in,
Back into your bedchamber to hide.
Nothing pleases you. Nothing.
At least not for long. What you have,

You're unhappy with; what you don't have
Is what you want most.
*(To the Chorus.)* I'd rather be sick as a dog myself
Than have to tend the sick,
Being sick is a simple proposition.
Tending the sick is not only trouble,
But a grief to the heart as well.
What a mess of pain life is.
Never rest for the weary.

PHAIDRA: Help me—please—
Raise me up—hold my head straight…
—My poor arms are so weak,
No strength in them anymore—
As if the strings had all loosened—
My delicate arms…Raise me…
And undo my hair, dear Nurse, won't you?
It's so heavy right now. Let it
Flow to my shoulders…let it free…
*(The Nurse undoes her hair.)*

NURSE: Easy does it, my darling.
The less tossing the better, you know.
Relax now, be calm. It will
Help you to bear up better if you're calm.
Show us a little of that grand nobility of yours.
Everyone has to suffer—
That's what life is.

PHAIDRA: Ohhhh, I want to drink pure water
From a crystal spring, and lie beneath
Black poplars in the uncut meadows!

NURSE: Child, child! What are you saying!
Such crazy words, too! And all these
People here to hear your rantings!
What will they think!

PHAIDRA: The mountains! Oh, the mountains!
Take me there! To the woods,
The pine woods, the hounds and huntsmen,
Oh, dear gods, tracking down their wild prey,
Closing in on the dappled deer, the cries,
The shouting, shouting to the hounds, tossing,

Tossing a spear of Thessaly past my ear,
Clutching the barbed missile in my hand,
Tossing—!

NURSE: My dear, you're delirious!
What's all this hunting and crystal springs?
There's a well-watered hillside
Just by the city walls.
You could drink there.

PHAIDRA: Artemis, mistress of the salt lake,
Mistress of the flats where horses thunder,
How I long to be in your sacred sanctuary
Taming Venetian colts!

NURSE: You're out of your mind!
Chattering nonsense in your madness!
Once you're off to the hills all afire for the hunt,
And now you fancy horses on the waveless sands
Of the seashore! What god
Is making your mind swerve from its course?

PHAIDRA: Oh, no! What have I done!
Lost my senses! What god did this?
I'm ashamed! Ashamed for what I've said!
Nurse, dear Nurse, cover my face again.
Hide me, please. Cover it. Hide my
Tears of shame.
Sanity is pain, but madness is worse.
It's better to die aware of nothing.

NURSE: All right. I'll cover it. There.
But when will death come to cover *my* body?
I haven't lived long to learn little,
And one thing I've learned is this:
That we humans love far too hard.
There should be a limit to our love.
Moderation. Love must never
Pierce to the depths of our souls.
It should be as easily unbound as bound.
*(To the Chorus.)* What can be worse than suffering pain for two?
Ask me. I know. The grief I suffer
For this woman is almost unbearable, My advice
Is that principles should go only so far

And then give way to reason. Otherwise
You're headed straight for a breakdown.
Satisfaction seldom comes from too rigid a standard.
Besides, it's bad for the health.
—I have little praise for excess,
And much for moderation.
I think the wise will agree.
CHORUS LEADER: Old woman, your faithful care
    For our queen is touching. It's clear to us
    How sick she really is, what we don't know
    Is it's cause. What can you tell us?
NURSE: I question her,
    But she tells me nothing.
CHORUS LEADER: Not even how it first began?
NURSE: Nothing. She refuses to speak.
CHORUS LEADER: How feeble she is,
    How wasted, poor thing.
NURSE: She hasn't eaten in three days.
CHORUS LEADER: Her madness?
    Or does she want to die?
NURSE: I don't know;
    But this fast will kill her.
CHORUS LEADER: Yes, but her husband?
    Why doesn't he help?
NURSE: She hides her troubles—
    Refuses to admit them.
CHORUS LEADER: But can't he see?
    Can't he look at her face?
NURSE: He's away from home—
    Out of the city.
CHORUS LEADER: But then it's your duty to force her.
    Someone has to discover the truth.
NURSE: I've tried it all, everything,
    With no luck. But I won't give up.
    I'm a faithful slave and loyal to my mistress.
    You'll see how loyal I can be.
    You'll see.
    (Turning back to Phaidra.) All right now, child,
    What say we start again?

But you need to help a little.
Now stop your frowning;
It does no good, do you hear?
Relax, try to relax, dear. There.
And I'll try, too.
—So we had our differences.
Nothing so terrible there.
We didn't agree is all.
We'll try again. You'll see.
It will all be different. And if your
Problem is one only women can discuss—
Well, then, look, we're all women here, aren't we?
We'll help you with it.
Of course we will.
We can speak freely. You'll see.
We'll put it all right. But if it's
A subject that men can discuss,
You have only to tell us
And doctors will be brought.
*(Phaidra does not respond.)*

NURSE: My baby, you're so silent! Why?
Tell me.
Silence helps nothing, my dear.
If I've said something, anything,
To upset you, anything out of place—
Correct me. If not—why, then,
Agree that I've said something right,
That I've hit the mark with my
Rambling old nurse's chatter!
*(Phaidra continues her silence.)*

NURSE: Say something, won't you!
Look at me!
*(To the Chorus.)* Women—well, you can see—
We're no farther than before.
Wasting our time.
Words wouldn't move her then,
And won't now.
*(To Phaidra.)* All right, now, mistress, listen to this—
And then you can be as stubborn as you like,

Stubborn as the sea in a gale!
Are you ready?
Now! If you die, my lady—
If you die, you'll have betrayed your own sons!
That's right! Betrayed them!
Cast them out! Because they will have
No part of their father's house!
No part of their inheritance! None,
Do you hear? I say this
In the name of that horse-loving Amazon queen
Who bore a master to rule over your sons—
A bastard—but a bastard with the ambition
Worthy of a legitimate son!
And you know who I mean!
Hippolytus—

PHAIDRA: Aiiiiiii!

NURSE: Aha, so I've hit home, have I?

PHAIDRA: Nurse, you're destroying me!
I won't hear that name again!

NURSE: You're sane enough all right, dearie,
Just not sane enough
To save your life and your children's!

PHAIDRA: I *love* my children!
Another fate destroys me!

NURSE: Surely your hands aren't
Stained with pollution?

PHAIDRA: No, not my hands,
It's my heart that's polluted!

NURSE: A spell, then,
From someone who hates you!

PHAIDRA: No! Someone dear!
Neither of us wills it!

NURSE: Thêseus?
Has he done you a wrong?

PHAIDRA: No! And I would rather
Die than harm him!

NURSE: What terrible thing
Is driving you to death?

PHAIDRA: Leave me to my wrong!

It's not *you* who are wronged!

NURSE: No, I won't!
    And it's *your* fault if I fail!

PHAIDRA: What are you doing?
    You're grasping my hand!

NURSE: *And* your knees!
    I'll never let go!

PHAIDRA: You're mad, poor woman!
    The truth will destroy you!

NURSE: Can destruction be worse
    Than losing you, child?

PHAIDRA: But what I'm doing
    Brings me honor!

NURSE: And still you won't tell?
    When I'm trying to help you?

PHAIDRA: I can't! I *will* turn
    Shame into honor!

NURSE: Then *say* it!
    Let everyone *know* your honor!

PHAIDRA: Leave me alone!
    Leave me! Let go!

NURSE: Not till you give me
    The gift you owe me.

PHAIDRA: Yes. I respect
    The hand of a suppliant.

NURSE: It's for you to speak now;
    Me to be silent. *(The Nurse releases her grasp.)*

PHAIDRA: Oh, my poor mother!
    The horror of your passion!

NURSE: Her lust for the bull—
    Is that what you mean, child?

PHAIDRA: And my wretched sister!
    Bride of Dionysos!

NURSE: Has your madness returned?
    Why are you doing this?

PHAIDRA: And now it's my turn
    To be destroyed!

NURSE: You frighten me, dear.
    What are you saying?

PHAIDRA: The women of my family
   Have suffered calamity—
NURSE: You'll have to speak clearer, dear—
   Just say it.
PHAIDRA: If only you could
   Say the words *for* me!
NURSE: I'm no prophet
   To see into secrets.
PHAIDRA: What is meant when they say
   That people are—in love?
NURSE: Something, my dear, that's both
   Sweet and painful.
PHAIDRA: And that's the pain
   I'm suffering now,
NURSE: Love? So it's love, then?
   Tell me? The man?
PHAIDRA: The man—the man—his name—
   The—the Amazon's—
NURSE: Hippolytus!?
PHAIDRA: The words are yours, not mine.
NURSE: What more can you say, child?
   It's over with me! Over!
   It can't be, women, it can't!
   Not possible! The good, the virtuous, the pure—
   In love with the vilest lechery!
   Want it? No. And still they do it.
   I hate the day! Hate the day's light!
   Hate it! Hate my life I can no longer bear!
   Hate it! Life! Let it go! Let it not be!
   *(To the statue of Aphroditê.)*
   Aphroditê, you are no goddess.
   But something greater, far greater.
   You have destroyed my lady, destroyed me,
   Destroyed the royal house.
   *(She falls to the floor as the Chorus assembles.)*
CHORUS: Did you hear,
      did you
         hear our
   queen cry,

cry out her
         dreadful sorrow,
terrible, past
         hearing?
              Dear Lady,
dear mistress, let
         death take me
              before I
conceive, before I
         share, ever
              fall prey to a
passion like
         yours. Your
              pain, your
pain, how
         piteous your
              pain. Piteous the
troubles
         mortals must
              bear,
piteous. It's
         you who must
              pay. You who have
spoken. Spoken what
         must not be
              spoken. Spoken
calamity
         in the
              light of
day. Spoken what
         pulls you
              down to your
end, What
         awaits you in the
              long
hours of this
         day? What
              horror does it
hold? A change is

coming,
        unknown before,
coming, a
    change for this
        house. No
question
    now, no
        more, where your
star of fortune
    leads, to what
        end, Unhappy
child, how
    love has
        deserted you. The
goddess'
    pawn. Poor
        daughter of
Krete.
    Victim of
        Aphroditê.

# O Virga Ac Diadema—
# Praise for the Mother

Hildegard of Bingen
12th Century

**A choral reading for twelve women**
**Scene:** a sequence in praise of the Virgin Mary


1a. O branch and diadem
of the king's purple,
strong in your enclosure
like a breastplate:

1b. Burgeoning, you blossomed
after another fashion
than Adam gave rise
to the whole human race.

2a. Hail, hail! from your womb
came another life
of which Adam
had stripped his sons.

2b. O flower, you did not spring from the dew
nor from drops of rain,
nor did the air sweep over you,
but the divine radiance
brought you forth on a most noble branch.

3a. O branch, God had foreseen your flowering
on the first day
of His creation.

3b. And He made you for His Word
as a golden matrix,
O praiseworthy Virgin.

4a. O how great
in its powers is the side of man
from which God brought forth the form of woman,
which He made the mirror
of all His beauty
and the embrace
of His whole creation.

4b. Thence celestial voices chime in harmony
and the whole earth marvels,
O praiseworthy Mary,
for God has greatly loved you.

5a. O how greatly we must lament and mourn
because sadness flowed in guilt
through the serpent's counsel
into woman.

5b. For the very woman
whom God made to be mother of all
plucked at her womb
with the wombs of ignorance
and brought forth consummate pain
for her kind.

6a. But, O dawn,
from your womb
a new sun has come forth,
which has cleansed all the guilt of Eve
and through you brought a blessing greater
than the harm Eve did to mankind.

6b. Hence, O saving Lady,
you who bore the new light
for humankind:
gather the members of your Son
into celestial harmony.

# Riders to the Sea

John Millington Synge
1904

**Dramatic**

**Scene:** the small cottage of Maurya and her children, Aran Islands

Maurya
Nora
Cathleen
Neighbor women, dressed for mourning
(Plus two coffin-bearers) , male, who stand aside or exit

CATHLEEN AND NORA: Uah. *(They crouch down in front of the old woman at the fire.)*

NORA: Tell us what it is you seen.

MAURYA: I went down to the spring well, and I stood there saying a prayer to myself. Then Bartley came along, and he riding on the red mare with the grey pony behind him. *(She puts up her hands, as if to hide something from her eyes.)* The Son of God spare us, Nora!

CATHLEEN: What is it you seen?

MAURYA: I seen Michael himself.

CATHLEEN: *(Speaking softly.)* You did not, mother. It wasn't Michael you seen, for his body is after being found in the far north, and he's got a clean burial, by the grace of God.

MAURYA: *(A little defiantly.)* I'm after seeing him this day, and he riding and galloping. Bartley came first on the red mare, and I tried to say "God speed you," but something choked the words in my throat. He went by quickly; and "The blessing of God on you," says he, and I could say nothing. I looked up then, and I crying, at the grey pony, and there was Michael upon it—with fine clothes on him, and new shoes on his feet.

CATHLEEN: *(Begins to keen.)* It's destroyed we are from this day. It's destroyed, surely.

NORA: Didn't the young priest say the Almighty God won't leave her destitute with no son living?

MAURYA: *(In a low voice, but clearly.)* It's little the like of him knows of the Sea…Bartley will be lost now, and let you call in Eamon and make me a good coffin out of the white boards, for I won't live after them. I've had a husband, and a husband's father, and six sons in this house—six fine men, though it was a hard birth I had with every one of them and they coming into the world—and some of them were found and some of them were not found, but they're gone now the lot of them...There were Stephen and Shawn were lost in the great wind, and found after in the Bay of Gregory of the Golden Mouth, and carried up the two of them on one plank, and in by that door.

*(She pauses for a moment; the girls start as if they heard something through the door that is half open behind them.)*

NORA: *(In a whisper.)* Did you hear that, Cathleen? Did you hear a noise in the north-east?

CATHLEEN: *(In a whisper.)* There's someone after crying out by the seashore.

MAURYA: *(Continues without hearing anything.)* There was Sheamus and his father, and his own father again, were lost in a dark night, and not a stick or sign was seen of them when the sun went up. There was Patch after was drowned out of a curragh that turned over. I was sitting here with Bartley, and he a baby lying on my two knees, and I seen two women, and three women, and four women coming in, and they crossing themselves and not saying a word. I looked out then, and there were men coming after them, and they holding a thing in the half of a red sail, and water dripping out of it—it was a dry day, Nora—and leaving a track to the door.

*(She pauses again with her hand stretched out towards the door. It opens softly and old women begin to come in, crossing themselves on the threshold, and kneeling down in front of the stage with red petticoats over their heads.)*

MAURYA: *(Half in a dream, to Cathleen.)* Is it Patch, or Michael, or what is it at all?

CATHLEEN: Michael is after being found in the far north, and when he is found there how could he be here in this place?

MAURYA: There does be a power of young men floating round in the sea, and what way would they know if it was Michael they had, or another man like him, for when a man is nine days in the sea, and the wind blowing, it's hard set his own mother would be to say what man was in it.

CATHLEEN: It's Michael, God spare him, for they're after sending us a bit of his clothes from the far north.

*(She reaches out and hands Maurya the clothes that belonged to Michael. Maurya stands up slowly, and takes them in her hands. Nora looks out.)*

NORA: They're carrying a thing among them, and there's water dripping out of it and leaving a track by the big stones.

CATHLEEN: *(In a whisper to the women who have come in.)* Is it Bartley it is?

ONE OF THE WOMEN: It is, surely, God rest his soul.

*(Two younger women come in and pull out the table. Then men carry in the body of Bartley, laid on a plank, with a bit of a sail over it, and lay it on the table.)*

CATHLEEN: *(To the women as they are doing so.)* What way was he drowned?

ONE OF THE WOMEN: The grey pony knocked him over into the sea, and he was washed out where there is a great surf on the white rocks. *(Maurya has gone over and knelt down at the head of the table. The women are keening softly and swaying themselves with a slow movement. Cathleen and Nora kneel at the other end of the table. The men kneel near the door.)*

MAURYA: *(Raising her head and speaking as if she did not see the people around her.)* They're all gone now, and there isn't anything more the sea can do to me...I'll have no call now to be up crying and praying when the wind breaks from the south, and you can hear the surf is in the east, and the surf is in the west, making a great stir with the two noises, and they hitting one on the other. I'll have no call now to be going down and getting Holy Water in the dark nights after Samhain, and I won't care what way the sea is when the other women will be keening. *(To Nora.)* Give me the Holy Water, Nora; there's a small sup still on the dresser.
*(Nora gives it to her.)*

MAURYA: *(Drops Michael's clothes across Bartley's feet, and sprinkles the Holy Water over him.)* It isn't that I haven't prayed for you, Bartley, to the Almighty God. It isn't that I haven't said prayers in the dark night till you wouldn't know what I'd be saying; but it's a great rest I'll have now, and it's time, surely. It's a great rest I'll have now, and great sleeping in the long nights after Samhain, if it's only a bit of wet flour we do have to eat, and maybe a fish that would be stinking. *(She kneels down again, crossing herself, and saying prayers under her breath.)*

# The House of Bernarda Alba

Federico Garcia Lorca
Translated by Caridad Svich
1936

**Dramatic**
**Scene:** a white room in Bernarda Alba's house, a wake

Angustias
Martirio
Magdalena
Amelia
Poncia
Servant, brief entrance
And many other women

BERNARDA: Let them leave the way they came. I don't want them walking through here.

GIRL: *(To Angustias.)* Pepe el Romano was with the men during the funeral service.

ANGUSTIAS: There he was.

BERNARDA: His mother was there. She saw his mother. Neither she nor I saw Pepe.

GIRL: I thought…

BERNARDA: Who *was* there was Darajali, the widower. He was sitting very close to your aunt. We all saw him.

SECOND WOMAN: *(Aside, in a low voice.)* Wicked, she is worse than wicked!

THIRD WOMAN: *(Aside.)* A tongue like a knife!

BERNARDA: When women are in a church, they shouldn't look at any man, save for the priest, and only because he wears a skirt. To turn your head is to look for corduroy's heat.

FIRST WOMAN: *(Aside.)* Dried-up old lizard!

PONCIA: *(Between her teeth.)* Itching for a man's heat!

BERNARDA: Blessed be God!

ALL: *(Crossing themselves.)* May He be praised and blessed forever!

BERNARDA: Rest in peace with the Holy Trinity at your head!

ALL: Rest in peace!

BERNARDA: With Saint Michael the Archangel and his sword of justice.

ALL: Rest in peace!

BERNARDA: With the key that opens all doors and the hand that closes them.

ALL: Rest in peace!

BERNARDA: With those blessed with good fortune, and the small lights that can be seen in the fields.

ALL: Rest in peace!

BERNARDA: With our holy charity and all the souls on land and sea.

ALL: Rest in peace!

BERNARDA: Grant your servant Antonio Maria Benavides eternal rest and crown him with your blessed glory.

ALL: Amen.

MAID: *(Breaking into a wail.)* Oh, Antonio Maria Benavides, you will no longer see these walls nor break bread in this house! Of all your servants, I was the one who most loved you. *(Pulling her hair.)* And how must I live now that you've gone? Must I go on living? *(Two hundred women finish coming into the house. Bernarda and her five daughters appear.)*

BERNARDA: *(To the Maid.)* Silence!

MAID: *(Weeping.)* Bernarda!

BERNARDA: Less shrieking and more work. You should have made sure everything was much cleaner for the wake. Get out. This is not your place.

*(The Maid exits, crying.)*

BERNARDA: The poor are like animals; it's as if they're made of different stuff.

FIRST WOMAN: The poor feel their sorrows too.

BERNARDA: But they forget them when a plateful of peas is placed before them.

GIRL: *(Timidly.)* Eating is necessary to live.

BERNARDA: At your age you shouldn't talk in front of your elders.

FIRST WOMAN: Be quiet, child.

BERNARDA: I've never let anyone preach to me. Sit down.

*(They sit. Pause.)*

BERNARDA: *(Loudly.)* Magdalena, don't cry; if you want to cry, go under your bed. Do you hear me?

SECOND WOMAN: *(To Bernarda.)* Have you started to work the fields?

BERNARDA: Yesterday.

THIRD WOMAN: The sun comes down like lead.

FIRST WOMAN: It's been years since I've known such heat.

*(Pause. They all fan themselves.)*

BERNARDA: Is the lemonade ready?

PONCIA: Yes, Bernarda.

*(She brings a large tray full of little white jars, which she distributes.)*

BERNARDA: Give the men some.

PONCIA: They're already drinking in the patio.

BERNARDA: *(She rises and chants.)* "Requiem aeternam donat eis Domine."

ALL: *(Standing and chanting in Gregorian fashion.)* "Et lux perpetua, luccat eis." *(They cross themselves.)*

FIRST WOMAN: May you have health to pray for his soul.

*(They start filing out.)*

THIRD WOMAN: You won't lack for loaves of hot bread.

SECOND WOMAN: Nor a roof for your daughters.

*(They all file in front of Bernarda and exit. Angustias leaves through a door that leads to the patio.)*

FOURTH WOMAN: May you continue enjoying the same wheat as the one you had at your wedding.

PONCIA: *(Enters with a bag.)* From the men: a bag of money for the Masses.

BERNARDA: Thank them and give them a glass of brandy.

GIRL: *(To Magdalena.)* Magdalena…

BERNARDA: *(To Magdalena who is starting to cry.)* Shh.

*(All the women have left.)*

BERNARDA: *(Calling out to them.)* Go back to your houses and criticize everything you have seen! I hope many years will pass before you come into my house again!

PONCIA: You've nothing to complain about. The whole town showed up.

BERNARDA: Yes, to fill my house with the sweat from their slips and the poison of their tongues.

AMELIA: Mother, don't talk like that!

BERNARDA: That is the way I must talk in this cursed town without a river, this town of wells, where you always drink water afraid it will be poisoned.

PONCIA: Look what they've done to the floor!

BERNARDA: As though a herd of goats had passed through.

*(Poncia cleans the floor.)*

BERNARDA: Child, give me a fan.

ADELA: Here you are. *(She hands her a round fan with green and red flowers.)*

BERNARDA: *(Throwing the fan to the floor.)* Is this the fan you give to a widow? Give me a black one and learn how to respect your father's memory.

MARTIRIO: Take mine.

BERNARDA: And you?

MARTIRIO: I'm not hot.

BERNARDA: Well, find another, because you will need one. In the eight years of mourning to come, not a breath of air from the street will enter this house. We'll act as if the doors and windows were sealed up with bricks. That's what we did in my father's house, and in my grandfather's house as well. Meanwhile, you can all start embroidering the linens of your hope-chests. I have twenty bolts of linen with which you can cut sheets and coverlets. Magdalena can embroider them.

MAGDALENA: It's all the same to me.

ADELA: *(Sourly.)* If you don't want to embroider them, then we'll do without. That way yours will look so much better.

MAGDALENA: Neither mine nor yours. I know I won't get married. I'd rather carry sacks to the mill. Anything but to sit here day after day inside this dark room.

BERNARDA: That's what a woman is for.

MAGDALENA: Cursed be all women.

BERNARDA: In this house, we do what I say. You can't go crying to your father anymore. Needle and thread for the girls. A whip and a mule for the boys. That's what people with means are born with. *(Adela exits.)*

VOICE: Bernarda! Let me out!

BERNARDA: *(Calling.)* Let her out now!
*(The Maid appears.)*

MAID: I had a hard time keeping her down. Your mother is as strong as an oak, in spite of her eighty years.

BERNARDA: It runs in the family. My grandfather was the same.

MAID: Several times during the wake I had to gag her with an empty sack because she wanted to ask you to give her some dishwater to drink, and some dog-meat to eat, which she says is what you give her.

MARTIRIO: She wishes us harm!

BERNARDA: *(To the Maid.)* Let her get some fresh air in the patio.

MAID: She's taken all her rings and the amethyst earrings out of the box; she's put them on, and has told me she wants to get married.

*(The daughters laugh.)*

BERNARDA: Go to her and be careful she doesn't go near the well.

MAID: You needn't be afraid she'll jump in.

BERNARDA: It's not that...But from there the neighbors can see her from their windows.

*(The Maid exits.)*

MARTIRIO: We'll go change our clothes.

BERNARDA: Yes, but don't take the kerchiefs off your heads.

*(Adela enters.)*

BERNARDA: And Angustias?

ADELA: *(With malice.)* I saw her looking through the cracks of the back door. The men had just left.

BERNARDA: And what you were doing at the door?

ADELA: I went to see if the hens had laid.

BERNARDA: But the men had already left!

ADELA: *(With malice.)* A group of them were still standing outside.

BERNARDA: *(Furiously.)* Angustias! Angustias!

ANGUSTIAS: *(Entering.)* Did you want something?

BERNARDA: What were you looking at, and at whom?

ANGUSTIAS: No one.

BERNARDA: Is it decent for a woman of your class to be running after a man the very day of her father's funeral? Answer me! Who were you looking at?

*(Pause.)*

ANGUSTIAS: I...

BERNARDA: Yes, you!

ANGUSTIAS: No one!

BERNARDA: *(Striking her.)* Soft! Honeytongue!

PONCIA: *(Running to her.)* Bernarda, calm down!

*(She holds her. Angustias weeps.)*

BERNARDA: Get out of here. All of you!

*(They exit.)*

PONCIA: She didn't know what she was doing, although it's wrong, of course. It disgusted me to see her sneaking off toward the patio. Then she stood at the window listening to the men talk, which, as usual, is not the sort of conversation one should listen to.

BERNARDA: That's what they come to funerals for. *(With curiosity.)* What were they talking about?

PONCIA: They were talking about Paca la Roseta. Last night they tied her husband up in a stall, and they threw her onto the back of a horse and carried her off to the depths of the olive grove.

BERNARDA: And what did she do?

PONCIA: She? She was happy as could be. They say her breasts were exposed and Maximiliano held onto her as if he were playing a guitar. Shocking!

BERNARDA: And then what happened?

PONCIA: What would happen. They came back at daybreak. Paca la Roseta had her hair down and a crown of flowers on her head.

BERNARDA: She is the only bad woman we have in this town.

PONCIA: That's because she's not from here. She's from far away. And those who went with her are also sons of outsiders. The men from this town would never do such a thing.

BERNARDA: No, but they like to see it and talk about it and they lick their fingers when something like this happens.

PONCIA: They were saying a lot more things.

BERNARDA: *(Looking about, fearfully.)* What things?

PONCIA: I'm ashamed to repeat them.

BERNARDA: And my daughter heard them?

PONCIA: Naturally!

BERNARDA: She takes after her aunts: white and mealy-mouthed, and then they would cast kittenish eyes at any little barber's compliment. How one has to fight and suffer so that people can be decent and not be too wild!

PONCIA: It's just that your daughters are of an age when they ought to have husbands! Little trouble they give you. Angustias must be more than thirty years old by now.

BERNARDA: Thirty-nine exactly.

PONCIA: Imagine. And she's never had a beau…

BERNARDA: *(Furiously.)* None of them have ever had a beau and they don't need one! They get along just fine.

PONCIA: I didn't mean to offend you.

BERNARDA: There's no one good enough for them, not for a hundred miles around. The men in this town are not of their station. Do you want me to hand them over to any field-hand?

PONCIA: You should have moved to another town.

BERNARDA: Exactly. To sell them!

PONCIA: No, Bernarda, to change...Of course, any place else, they'd be the poor ones.

BERNARDA: Hold your tormenting tongue!

PONCIA: One can't even talk to you. Are we, or are we not familiar with each other?

BERNARDA: We are not. You're my servant, and I pay you. Nothing more!

# Electra

Hugo von Hofmansthal
Translated by Carl Richard Mueller

**Dramatic**
Electra
First woman servant
Second woman servant
Third woman servant
Fourth woman servant
Fifth woman servant
Woman overseer
Chrysothemis, Electra's younger sister

FIRST WOMAN SERVANT: *(Lifting her water jug.)* Where is Electra?
SECOND WOMAN SERVANT: Time has come again,
    the hour when she howls out for her father,
    till all the walls resound.
    *(Electra enters running from the already darkened hallway. They*
    *all turn toward her. Electra recoils like an animal into its lair, one*
    *arm covering her face.)*
FIRST WOMAN SERVANT: Did you see the look she gave us?
SECOND WOMAN SERVANT: Furious
    as any wildcat.
THIRD WOMAN SERVANT: A moment past I saw her
    lie and moan—
FIRST WOMAN SERVANT: She always lies and moans
    when the sun is low.
THIRD WOMAN SERVANT: The two of us went towards her,
    but came too close—
FIRST WOMAN SERVANT: One thing she'll not endure
    is to be looked at.
THIRD WOMAN SERVANT: Yes, we came too close.
    And then she screeched out at us like a cat:
    "Away with you, you flies!" she cried, "Away!"
FOURTH WOMAN SERVANT: "Blow-flies, away!"
THIRD WOMAN SERVANT: "Must you eat at my wounds!"
    And struck out at us with a straw.
FOURTH WOMAN SERVANT: "Away,

blow-flies, away!"

THIRD WOMAN SERVANT: "You shall not feed upon
the sweetness of my agony nor smack
your lips to lick the foam from off my madness."

FOURTH WOMAN SERVANT: Go on, crawl to your beds," she screamed at us.
"Eat sweets and fats and sneak to bed with your men,"
she screamed, and you—

THIRD WOMAN SERVANT: I was not idle—

FOURTH WOMAN SERVANT: —answered her!

THIRD WOMAN SERVANT: Yes: "If you are hungry," I answered her,
"then you eat, too." She sprang up then and shot
horrible glances at me, stretched her fingers
claw-like towards me and cried out: "I am feeding
a vulture here within my body," she cried.

SECOND WOMAN SERVANT: And you?

THIRD WOMAN SERVANT: I said to her: "And that is why
you're always crouching where there's smell of carrion,
and scratching the ground for a body long since dead!"

SECOND WOMAN SERVANT: What did she say to that?

THIRD WOMAN SERVANT: She howled and cast herself
back to her corner.
*(They have finished drawing the water.)*

FIRST WOMAN SERVANT: I can't but be amazed
that the queen should let this demon run about
freely in house and court to do her mischief.

THIRD WOMAN SERVANT: Her own child, too!

SECOND WOMAN SERVANT: If she were mine, by God,
I'd keep her under lock and key.

FOURTH WOMAN SERVANT: Don't you feel
they're hard enough on her now? Don't they place
her bowl so she eats with the dogs?
*(Softly.)* Haven't you seen
the master strike her?

FIFTH WOMAN SERVANT: *(Young, with a tremulous, excited voice.)* I will
throw myself
down before her feet and kiss those feet.
Is she not the daughter of a king, and
made to endure such outrage! I will anoint
her feet with oil and wipe them with my hair.

WOMAN OVERSEER: Get on with you! *(Pushes her.)*

FIFTH WOMAN SERVANT: There's nothing to be found
in all the world more royal than she. She lies
in rags upon the threshold, but not one *(Crying out.)*
not one in all this house can look in her eyes!

WOMAN OVERSEER: Get on! *(Pushes her through the low open doorway
downstage left.)*

FIFTH WOMAN SERVANT: *(Jammed in the doorway.)* Not any one of you is
worthy
to breathe the air that she breathes! O if only
I could see all of you, all, hanged by the neck,
see you strung up in some dark granary,
for all that you have done against Electra!

WOMAN OVERSEER: *(Shuts the door, stands with her back against it.)* Did
you hear that? What we've done against Electra!
When told to eat with us, she knocked her bowl
clear off the table and spat at us and called us
dirty female dogs.

FIRST WOMAN SERVANT: What? What she said was,
there's no dog can be humiliated,
and that's why they broke us in like animals
to wash away with water, with fresh water,
the everlasting blood of murder from the floor—

THIRD WOMAN SERVANT: —and to sweep, said she, the outrage in the corner,
the outrage that renews itself day and night—

FIRST WOMAN SERVANT: —and our bodies, she cried out, are stiffening
with the dirt that we are bound in bondage to!
*(They carry their jugs into the house left.)*

WOMAN OVERSEER: *(Who has opened the door for them.)* And screams
out when she sees us with our children,
that there is nothing, nothing, so accursed
as children that we've littered in this house,
slipping upon the stairs in blood like dogs.
Did she say that or not?

THE WOMEN SERVANTS: *(Already inside.)* Yes! Yes!

FIFTH WOMAN SERVANT: They're beating me!
*(The Woman Overseer goes in. The door falls shut. Electra steps
from the house. She is alone with the splashes of red light which*

*fall obliquely from the branches of the fig trees upon the ground*
*and upon the walls like splashes of blood.)*

ELECTRA: Alone! All, all alone. My father gone,
held prisoner in the coldness of the grave.
*(Toward the ground.)* Father, where are you? Have you not the strength
to make your way to earth again and me?
The hour is come, the hour that is our own!
The same cold hour in which they slaughtered you,
your wife and the thing that shares her bed with her,
who sleeps with her in your once royal bed.
They slew you in your bath, your blood ran red
down across your eyes, and all the bath
steamed with your blood; this coward took you then
and lugged you by the shoulders from the chamber,
head first, your legs trailing on behind you;
your eyes, staring, open, saw into the house.
And so you'll come again, and set one foot
in front of the other, and suddenly appear,
your eyes wide open, and a royal round
of purple placed upon your brows that eats
upon the open wound it finds there.
Father!
I must see you, don't leave me here alone!
Show me yourself, if only as a shadow,
there, in the wall's niche, like yesterday!
Father! Your time will come! The stars decree
our times, and so a time will come when blood
from a hundred throats will gush upon your grave,
will flow as from a hundred upset jugs,
stream from the throats of shackled murderers,
and round the naked bodies of their helpers,
like marble jugs, from men and women both,
and in a single flood, one swollen stream,
shall all of their life's life gush out of them;
and we shall slaughter the horses of your house,
and drive them to your grave, and they shall snuff
death, and neigh in the air laden with death,
and die; and we shall slaughter for you the hounds,

because they are the litter of the litter
of that same pack you hunted with, and who
would lick your feet, to whom you threw the morsels,
their blood must flow to serve you, and we, we,
your blood, your son Orestes and your daughters,
we three, when all is done and purple canopies
are raised high by the steam of your royal blood,
which the sun sucks to itself, then shall we dance,
then shall your blood dance round about your grave:
and over every corpse my knee shall rise
higher with every step, and they who see me,
dancing thus, yea, they who see from afar
only my shadow dancing, they shall say:
How great must be this king whose flesh and blood
would celebrate so grand a feast for him;
happy that king with children who would dance
so royal a dance of victory round his tomb!
*(Chrysothemis, the younger sister, stands in the doorway of the house. She looks anxiously at Electra, then calls softly.)*
CHRYSOTHEMIS: Electra!
*(Electra starts like a sleep-walker who hears his name called out, She staggers. She looks about as though not quite able to find her way. Her face becomes distorted as she sees the anxious features of her sister. Chrysothemis stands depressed in the doorway.)*
ELECTRA: Ah, that face!
CHRYSOTHEMIS: Is it so hateful?
ELECTRA: What is it? Tell me, speak, what do you want?
Then go away and leave me!
*(Chrysothemis raises her hands as though warding off a blow.)*
ELECTRA: You raise your hands?
Our father once raised both his hands that way
and then the axe struck down cleaving his flesh.
What is it you want, daughter of my mother?
CHRYSOTHEMIS: They're planning something terrible, I know it.
ELECTRA: *Both* the women?
CHRYSOTHEMIS: Who?
ELECTRA: Why, my mother, of course,
and then that other woman, the cowardly one,
Aegisthus, yes, Aegisthus, the brave assassin,

whose only hero's deeds are done in bed.
What have they in mind?

CHRYSOTHEMIS: They mean to throw you
in a dark tower where neither sun nor moon
will visit you again.
*(Electra laughs.)*

CHRYSOTHEMIS: They will, I know,
I've heard them.

ELECTRA: Yes, I think I've heard it, too.
At table, wasn't it? just before finishing?
He loves to raise his voice then and brag about,
I think it helps his digestion.

CHRYSOTHEMIS: No, not at table,
nor was he boasting. He and she together
discussed it secretly.

ELECTRA: Oh, secretly?
How did you hear them then?

CHRYSOTHEMIS: I heard at the door.

ELECTRA: Let no doors ever be opened in this house!
There's nothing in these rooms but gasping for air
and the death-rattle of strangulation. Never
open a door that stifles a groan behind it:
for surely they cannot always be in there killing,
at times they are alone in there together!
Open no doors! Do not prowl about.
Sit on the ground like me and wish for death
and for judgment upon her and him.

CHRYSOTHEMIS: I cannot sit and stare into the dark
like you. O there's a burning in my heart
that makes me rove the house incessantly.
There's not a room to comfort me, and so
I wander up the stairs and down the stairs,
from one place to another; O it seems a
room will call to me, and once I'm there,
there's nothing but an empty, staring room.
I'm so afraid, my knees tremble beneath me
day and night; it seems as if two hands
are here at my throat; I can't even cry;
I've turned to stone! Sister, pity, pity!

# Electra

Hugo von Hofmansthal
Translated by Carl Richard Mueller

**Dramatic**
Electra
Chrysothemis, Electra's younger sister
Crowd of women
Clytemnestra
Woman servant
Trainbearer to Clytemnestra
Women carrying torches

CHRYSOTHEMIS: O stop!
ELECTRA: May your children, when you have them,
    do unto you as you do to our father!
    *(Chrysothemis cries out.)*
ELECTRA: Why must you howl so? Get in! That's your place.
    There's a noise broken out. Are they preparing
    your wedding? I hear running. Everyone's up.
    Either they are in birthpangs or at murder.
    Should there be corpses lacking, they must make some,
    or else they'll not sleep soundly in their beds!
CHRYSOTHEMIS: Stop, O stop! That's past and done, it's done!
ELECTRA: Past and done? They're up to some new crime now!
    Do you think I don't know the sound of bodies
    as they drag them down the stairs, whispering
    and wringing out cloths sopped in blood!
CHRYSOTHEMIS: Sister!
    You must not stay.
ELECTRA: This time I *will* be here!
    Not as before. This time I will be strong.
    I'll throw myself upon her, I'll tear the axe
    out of her hands and swing it over her head—
CHRYSOTHEMIS: You must not stay here, hide before she sees you.
    Don't cross her path today, she scatters death
    Wherever she looks. She's had terrible dreams.
    *(The noise of people approaching draws nearer.)*
CHRYSOTHEMIS: You must not stay. They're coming through the passage.

They'll come by here. She's had terrible dreams;
I don't know what, I heard it from her women,
I don't know if it's true, sister, but they say
she has had terrible dreams of Orestes,
and that she cried out in the middle of night
like one about to be strangled.

ELECTRA: I! I!
I sent it to her. I sent her this dream
from my own breast! I lie in bed and hear
the footsteps of the spectre haunting her.
I hear him make his way from room to room
and lift the curtain from her bed: screaming
she leaps from the bed, but he is always there,
close behind her on the stairs, the chase continues
from one vault to another and another.
It is far darker now than any night,
far quieter and darker than the grave,
she gasps and staggers in darkness, but he is there:
he swings the torch to right and left of the axe.
And I like a hunting-hound am at her heels:
should she hide in a hollow, I spring after,
sideways, upon her trail, and drive her on
till a wall end her flight, and there in darkness,
there in deepest darkness—I see him still,
his shadow, and his limbs, the light of his eyes—
there sits our father, who neither sees nor hears,
and yet, it must happen: we drive her to his feet,
and the axe falls!
*(Torches and figures fill the passage, left of the door.)*

CHRYSOTHEMIS: They're coming now. She's driving her women on
with torches. Look, they're dragging animals
and sacrificial knives. O sister, Electra,
she is most dreadful when she is afraid;
you must not cross her path today, not now!

ELECTRA: I have a mind to speak with my mother now
as I have never spoken!
*(A noisy and shuffling procession hurries past the glaringly lighted
windows. There is a tugging and hauling of animals, a subdued*

*chiding, a quickly stifled cry, the swish of a whip, a pulling back and a staggering forward again.)*

CHRYSOTHEMIS: I will not hear it. *(She rushes off through the door of the court.)*

*(The figure of Clytemnestra appears in the wide window. Her sallow, bloated face, in the light thrown from the glaring torches, appears even more pale above her scarlet dress. She supports herself upon one of her women, dressed in dark violet, and upon an ivory staff embellished with precious jewels. Her train is carried by a yellow figure, whose black hair is combed back like an Egyptian, and whose sleek face resembles a poised snake. The Queen is almost completely covered with precious stones and talismans. Her arms are full of bracelets, her fingers almost rigid with rings. The lids of her eyes seem excessively large, and it appears to be a great effort for her to hold them open. Electra stands rigid, her face toward the window. Clytemnestra suddenly opens her eyes and trembling with anger goes towards the window and points at Electra with her staff.)*

CLYTEMNESTRA: *(At the window.)* What do you want? Look there! Look at it there!
See how it rears its swollen neck at me
and hisses! And this thing I let run free
in my own house!
O how she'd like to kill me with those eyes!
Gods, why must you weigh so heavy on me?
Why must you send destruction on me? Why
do you cripple all the strength within me, why am
I, a living being, like a wasteland,
covered with weeds and nettles that grow on me,
and I have not the strength to root them out!
Why must I suffer this, immortal gods?

ELECTRA: Gods? The gods? But you are a goddess yourself!
The same as they.

CLYTEMNESTRA: What? What was that she said?
Did you understand what she said?

THE WOMAN: That you, too
stem from the gods.

TRAIN BEARER: *(Hissingly.)* But she means it only in spite.

CLYTEMNESTRA: *(As her heavy eyelids fall shut.)* How familiar it sounds,
like a thing forgotten
long, long ago. How well she knows me.
Yet no one ever knows what she will do.
*(The women and the Train Bearer whisper together.)*

ELECTRA: You are yourself no longer. Reptiles hang
from your body. What they hiss into your ear
severs your thoughts forever; you go about
in a frenzy, as though living in a dream,

CLYTEMNESTRA: I will go down to her. I will speak to her.
She is no beast today—talks like a doctor.
The hours hold our fate firm in their hands.
Nothing is so unbearable but once
must show a pleasant aspect in its nature.
*(She walks from the window and appears at the doorway, her
woman at her side, the Train Bearer behind her, and torches
bringing up the rear.)*

CLYTEMNESTRA: *(From the threshold.)* You call me a goddess.
Did you say it
in malice? Then take care. For this may be
the last time you will see the light of day
and breathe the free air.

ELECTRA: If you are not
a goddess, tell me, then, where are the gods!
There's nothing in this world makes me tremble so
than to think your body was the dark door
through which I crept into the light of the world.
Have I lain here naked upon this lap?
Have you lifted me up to reach these breasts?
Well, then, I must have crept from my father's grave
and played about in swaddling-clothes upon
the place where my father was murdered. Then you must be
a colossus whose brazen hand I never escaped.
You have me by the bridle and can tie me
to what you will. You have cast up like the sea
a living being, a father, and a sister.
I do not know how I should ever die—
unless you died before me.

CLYTEMNESTRA: Is this how you honor me? Is there so little

respect in you?

ELECTRA: I lack not of respect!
>    What troubles me troubles you as well.
>    I grow ill to see Aegisthus, your husband,
>    wear the robes of my father, who's dead, as you know,
>    he was the former king. It makes me ill,
>    believe me, for they do not fit him well.
>    I think they are too broad across the chest,

THE WOMAN: What she says is not what she means.

TRAIN BEARER: Every word a lie.

# Aztec Definitions

Anonymous—traditional Aztec
16th Century
From Fray Bernardino de Sahagun
Translated by Charles Dibble and Arthur J. O. Anderson

**Scene:** a readers' theater/performance piece for women's voices

*Ruby-Throated Hummingbird*
It is ashen, ash-colored. At the top of its head and the throat, its feathers are flaming, like fire. They glisten, they glow.

*Amoyotl (a water strider)*
It is like a fly, small and round. It has legs, it has wings; it is dry. It goes on the surface of the water; it is a flyer. It buzzes, it sings.

*Bitumen (a shellfish)*
It falls out on the ocean shore; it falls out like mud.

*Little Blue Heron*
It resembles the brown crane in color; it is ashen, gray. It smells like fish, rotten fish, stinking fish. It smells of fish, rotten fish.

*Seashell*
It is white. One is large, one is small. It is spiraled, marvelous. It is that which can be blown, which resounds. I blow the seashell. I improve, I polish the seashell.

*A Mushroom*
It is round, large, like a severed head.

*The Avocado Tree*
The leaves, the foliage are brown. Its fruit is black, dark; it shines. Within, it is herb-green. Its base is thin, the top rounded, round. It is oily; it has moisture; it has a center.

*Elocpulin (a tree)*
Its foliage, its leaves, its fruit: broad, thick, fat, ball-like; each one

ball-like, large, pulpy, breakable into small pieces, watery...They fill one's mouth, satisfy one, taste good to one, make one covet them, make one want them, are constantly required. The center is fat; they fill one's mouth; they satisfy one.

Pine

The pine tree is tender, verdant, very verdant. It has particles of (dried) pine (resin). It has cones—pine cones; it has a bark, a thick skin. It has pine resin, a resin. (The wood) can be broken, shattered. The pine is embracing. It is a provider of light, a means of seeing, a resinous torch. It is spongy, porous, soft. It forms a resin; drops stand formed; they stand sputtering. They sputter. It burns, it illuminates things, it makes a resin; a resin exudes. It turns into a resin. Resin is required.

A Mountain

High, pointed; pointed on top, pointed at the summit, towering; wide, cylindrical, round; a round mountain, low, low-ridged; rocky, with many rocks; craggy with many crags; rough with rocks; of earth; with trees; grassy; with herbs; with shrubs; with water; dry; white; jagged; with a sloping plain, with gorges, with caves; precipitous, having gorges; canyon land, precipitous land with boulders.

I climb the mountain; I scale the mountain. I live on the mountain. I am born on the mountain. No one becomes a mountain— no one turns himself into a mountain. The mountain crumbles.

Another Mountain

It is wooded; it spreads green.

Forest

It is a place of verdure, of fresh green; of wind—windy places, in wind, windy; a place of cold: it becomes cold; there is much frost; it is a place which freezes. It is a place from which misery comes, where it exists; a place where there is affliction—a place of affliction, of lamentation, a place of affliction, of weeping; a place where there is sadness, a place of compassion, of sighing; a place which arouses sorrow, which spreads misery.

It is a place of gorges, gorge places; a place of crags, craggy places; a place of stony soil, stony-soiled places; in hard soil, in clayey soil, in moist and fertile soil. It is a place among moist and fertile lands, a place of moist and fertile soil, in yellow soil.

It is a place with cuestas, cuesta places; a place with peaks, peaked places; a place which is grassy, with grassy places; a place of forests, forested places; a place of thin forest, thinly forested places; a place of thick forest, thickly forested places; a place of jungle, of dry tree stumps, of underbrush, of dense forest.

It is a place of stony soil, stony-soiled places; a place of round stones, round-stoned places; a place of sharp stones, of rough stones; a place of crags, craggy places; a place of *tepetate;* a place with clearings, cleared places; a place of valleys, of coves, of places with coves, of cove places; a place of boulders, bouldered places; a place of hollows.

It is a disturbing place, fearful, frightful; home of the savage beast, dwelling-place of the serpent, the rabbit, the deer; a place from which nothing departs, nothing leaves, nothing emerges. It is a place of dry rocks, of boulders; bouldered places; boulder land, a land of bouldered places. It is a place of caves, cave places, having caves—a place having caves.

It is a place of wild beasts; a place of wild beasts of the ocelot, the *cuitlachtli,* the bobcat, the serpent, the spider, the rabbit, the deer; of stalks, grass, prickly shrubs: of the mesquite, of the pine. It is a place where wood is owned. Trees are felled. It is a place where trees are cut, where wood is gathered, where there is chopping, where there is logging: a place of beams.

It becomes verdant, a fresh green. It becomes cold, icy. Ice forms and spreads; ice lies forming a surface. There is wind, a crashing wind; the wind crashes, spreads whistling, forms whirlwinds. Ice is blown by the wind; the wind glides.

There is no one; there are no people. It is desolate; it lies desolate. There is nothing edible. Misery abounds, misery emerges, misery spreads. There is no joy, no pleasure. It lies sprouting; herbs lie sprouting; nothing lies emerging; the earth is pressed down. All die of thirst. The grasses lie sprouting. Nothing lies cast about. There is hunger; all hunger. It is the home of hunger; there is death from hunger. All die of cold; there is freezing; there is trembling; there is the clattering, the chattering of teeth. There are cramps, the stiffening of the body, the constant stiffening, the stretching out prone.

There is fright, there is constant fright. One is devoured; one is slain by stealth; one is abused; one is brutally put to death; one is tormented. Misery abounds. There is calm, constant calm, continuing calm.

*Mirror Stone*

Its name comes from nowhere. This can be excavated in mines; it can be broken off. Of these mirror stones, one is white, one black. The white one—this is a good one to look into: the mirror, the clear, transparent one. They named it mirror of the noblemen, the mirror of the ruler.

The black one—this one is not good. It is not to look into; it does not make one appear good. It is one (so they say) which contends with one's face. When someone uses such a mirror, from it is to be seen a distorted mouth, swollen eyelids, thick lips, a large mouth. They say it is an ugly mirror, a mirror which contends with one's face.

Of these mirrors, one is round; one is long: they call it *acaltezcatl*. These mirror stones can be excavated in mines, can be polished, can be worked.

I make a mirror. I work it. I shatter it. I form it. I grind it. I polish it with sand. I work it with fine abrasive sand. I apply to it a glue of bat shit. I prepare it. I polish it with a fine cane. I make it shiny. I regard myself in the mirror. I appear from there in my looking-mirror; from it I admire myself.

*Secret Road*

Its name is secret road, the one which few people know, which not all people are aware of, which few people go along. It is good, fine; a good place, a fine place. It is where one is harmed, a place of harm. It is known as a safe place; it is a difficult place, a dangerous place. One is frightened. It is a place of fear.

There are trees, crags, gorges, rivers, precipitous places, places of precipitous land, various places of precipitous land, various precipitous places, gorges, various gorges. It is a place of wild animals, a place of wild beasts, full of wild beasts. It is a place where one is put to death by stealth; a place where one is put to death in the jaws of the wild beasts of the land of the dead.

I take the secret road. I follow along, I encounter the secret road. He goes following along, he goes joining that which is bad, the corner, the darkness, the secret road. He goes to seek, to find, that which is bad.

*The Cave*

It becomes long, deep; it widens, extends, narrows. It is a constricted place, a narrowed place, one of the hollowed-out places. It forms hollowed-out places. There are roughened places; there are asperous places. It is frightening, a fearful place, a place of death. It is called a place of death because there is dying. It is a place of darkness; it darkens; it stands ever-dark. It stands wide-mouthed, it is wide-mouthed. It is wide-mouthed; it is narrow-mouthed. It has mouths which pass through.

I place myself in the cave. I enter the cave.

*The Precipice*

It is deep—a difficult, a dangerous place, a deathly place. It is dark, it is light. It is an abyss.

# Who Will Carry the Word?

Charlotte Delbo

**Dramatic**

**Scene:** in the women's sleeping barracks, French Catholic women in an unmanned concentration camp, WW II, winter

Large number of women prisoners
Claire
Françoise
Mounette
Yvonne
Gina
Réine

CLAIRE: Come here. I want to talk to you.

FRANÇOISE: Who, me?

CLAIRE: Yes, you.

FRANÇOISE: And who are you?

CLAIRE: Claire. Don't you recognize me?

FRANÇOISE: Now I recognize your voice. Voices are difficult to recognize. Even the voices have changed. Are they muffled or is it my ears?

MOUNETTE: It's the air here. It's the air that changes the sounds, the snow that blots our sounds.

FRANÇOISE: It's even more strange when you don't recognize those who are close to you. The hair, the walk, the silhouette. Is it enough to have your hair shorn to no longer be yourself?

YVONNE: If the men who loved us could see what has become of us…Let's be happy that on the morning of their death they could say goodbye to us when still we had the faces they loved.

GINA: We'll soon get used to these others that we have become and we'll recognize each other.

MOUNETTE: When is soon?

GINA: A few days.

YVONNE: A few days, that's too long.

FRANÇOISE: And what did you want with me, Claire?

CLAIRE: Come over here.

FRANÇOISE: Talk. Here, we think out loud.

CLAIRE: What have I heard?

FRANÇOISE: What have you heard?

CLAIRE: That you wanted to commit suicide.

FRANÇOISE: Yes, so what?

CLAIRE: You have no right to.

FRANÇOISE: Oh, that'll do, Claire. Forget your formulas; here they aren't worth anything. It's the only right I have left, the only choice. The last free act.

CLAIRE: There are no free acts here. No choices like that.

FRANÇOISE: Oh yes. I have a choice. I have a choice, between becoming a cadaver which will have suffered for only eight days, which will still be clean enough to look at, and one which will have suffered fifteen days, which will be horrible to look at.

CLAIRE: You have nothing left. No such choices, nothing. You are not free to do it. You don't have the right to take your life.

FRANÇOISE: And why don't I have the right?

CLAIRE: A fighter doesn't commit suicide.

FRANÇOISE: Claire, please. Forget your affirmations, forget your certitudes. None of them fit here. Don't you see that truth has changed, that truth is no longer the same?

CLAIRE: I am asking you why you decided to commit suicide.

FRANÇOISE: You ask me!…Ask those who are lying rigid in the snow; ask their faces which are no longer faces; ask the sockets of their eyes which the rats have widened; ask their limbs which resemble dead wood; ask their skin which is a color no one has ever seen before. Don't you know all that a human being can withstand before dying? Don't you believe that to become so scrawny, so ugly, so convulsed, so trapped in what remains of skin and flesh, you have to have suffered to the limit, a limit which no one reached before us? I don't want to suffer to that limit.

CLAIRE: Can't you see further than yourself and your own death? Can't you see…

FRANÇOISE: I see. I am lucid. I am logical. I've never been more reasonable.

CLAIRE: You don't want to fight.

FRANÇOISE: I'm willing to fight, to try, but with a chance, even a little one, however small, but a chance. And I don't see any. No one will survive. If it's to be death for death's sake, then better right away, before having suffered that suffering you see written on the dead there in the snow, over there on the pile where the ravens and the rats get together, those naked dead bodies, entangled in a pile, even on top of those still alive, who arrived a week before us. I prefer to die before becoming a corpse as ugly as those.

CLAIRE: Coquetry is out of place here.

FRANÇOISE: I have no gift for lost courage.

CLAIRE: Will you listen to me?

FRANÇOISE: You must wait until my eyes do not see what they see, for my ears to listen to you.

CLAIRE: My eyes see as well as yours. You're afraid. You're a coward.

FRANÇOISE: Afraid to suffer, yes. A coward—another word that is meaningless here.

CLAIRE: I'll tell you again that you don't have the right to take your life. You don't have the right because you're not alone. There are the others. And above all, there are the little ones. Mounette, Denise, and her sister, all the little ones whom you taught to recite poetry, whom you had perform in plays before we left, when we invented pastimes while we waited for departure. They admired you because you were grown up. They listen to you, they follow you. If you commit suicide, they may imitate you. Suppose that among them, there is one who has a chance to come back, just one, and that because of you, she loses that chance. Even if you were to die in fifteen days and become as tortured a cadaver as those, you have to stand it.

FRANÇOISE: What good will it do? None of us has a chance. No one knows we're here. We're fighters off the battlefield, useless. If we fight to get out, it's no use to anyone, not even to ourselves. We are cut off from everything, cut off from ourselves.

CLAIRE: There must be one who returns, you or another, it doesn't matter. Each of us expects to die here. She is ready. She knows her life doesn't matter any more. Every one of us looks to the others. There must be one who comes back, one who will tell. Would you want millions of people to have been destroyed here and all those cadavers to remain mute for all eternity, all those lives to have been sacrificed for nothing?

FRANÇOISE: It's exactly that. For nothing. To die here, in this place, whose name we don't even know—perhaps it has no name.

CLAIRE: There must be one who comes back, who will give it its name.

FRANÇOISE: Here, at the frontiers of the inhabited world, yes, it's to die for nothing. It's already as if we were dead.

CLAIRE: If the world never knows anything about it. But there will be one who will return and who will talk and who will tell, and who will make known, because it is no longer we who are at stake, it's history—and people want to know their history. Haven't you heard them, the dying, who all say, "If you return, you'll tell?" Why do they say that? They say that because none of us is alone and each must render an account to all the others.

FRANÇOISE: The others...Other people in other places. To us, here, *they* have lost their reality. All that is left is the amount of time we must suffer before dying.

CLAIRE: Yes, the others, the people you know, your friends—this one or that particular one—have lost their reality. But I speak of the whole world, those who are now and those who will come after-wards. To them you must render an account.

FRANÇOISE: Why me? One more, one less...Choose someone else for your mission.

CLAIRE: We arrived two hundred, two hundred women from all the provinces, from all classes, who were thrown here into this pop-ulation of fifteen thousand women. Fifteen thousand women who are never the same. They die by the hundreds each day, they arrive by the hundreds each day. Of these fifteen thousand women from all countries of all the languages of Europe, how many will survive? Fifteen thousand women more or less, two hundred women more or less, what difference does it make? You, me; it doesn't matter who—no one matters. They will only matter if there is one who returns.

FRANÇOISE: It won't be me.

CLAIRE: Don't you really want to understand anything? Even if you hold out for only fifteen days...

FRANÇOISE: I won't hold out for fifteen days because I don't want to, because I don't believe it matters, because I prefer to finish it off right away and skip those fifteen days.

CLAIRE: Suppose you hold out fifteen days during which you will have helped others to hold out? Even if you give up then, fifteen days will have been gained. Another will take your place, then another, then another, so that there will be one who makes it until the end.

FRANÇOISE: Until the end…When do you see it arriving?

CLAIRE: I don't see it any more than you. Even if there is no hope, even if all is lost, you still have to try.

GINA: I'm ready to hold out for as long as it takes. Who knows the future? There may be a surprise, something may happen which would change all the calculations.

FRANÇOISE: The Allies will drop from the sky suddenly, tear out the barbed wire, pull down the watchtowers, and we'll be free? Do you believe in miracles?

GINA: Whatever way we get out, getting out of here will be a miracle.

MADELEINE: You have to believe in miracles. My father used to say that in all battles, in all shipwrecks, there's always one survivor.

YVONNE: Is it a rule? No rules stand here. I know we'll win, but the war will last another two years and I won't last two months.

CLAIRE: You'll last two months if you want to.

YVONNE: No, Claire. Until we came here, I believed that a person could be stripped of everything, could lose everything, but could still keep her pride. When I joined my resistance group, I thought of torture, I thought of it a lot, so as not to be caught unaware, to get used to resisting it, and I acquired a certain strength the certainty of resisting torture. Before, I was afraid. I was especially afraid of myself, afraid of weakness. That's why until we came here, I believed that nothing could divest a human being of his pride. Nothing except dysentery. You can no longer look at yourself when you gradually dissolve, turning into dirty water, when diarrhea is dripping from you night and day without being able to do anything to stop it, to hide yourself, to wash. I am turning into dirty water. My strength is ebbing, stinking, it flows, right here, right now, while I stand still because if I move it will be worse. My strength and my will are going. I am emptying. It is normal for life to expire through the lips. When it goes through the intestines—that's complete humiliation.

FRANÇOISE: We've been here for eight days. We've already lost ten of our group.

MOUNETTE: What did they die from, so quickly?

FRANÇOISE: What their eyes saw made their hearts burst.

CLAIRE: The old ones. You're young. You too, Yvonne.

YVONNE: Death will be coming more and more quickly. There are some who no longer have the strength to stand on their feet. Every morning, at roll call, they fall. We help them stand up again. Today. Tomorrow, we won't have the strength to help them.

FRANÇOISE: You see, Claire, I'm not rambling.

*(Enter Réine, who listens.)*

CLAIRE: Since you've decided to die, a little sooner or a little later doesn't matter. Make it a little later, for the sake of the one who has to return.

FRANÇOISE: None of us shall return.

CLAIRE: How do you know?

FRANÇOISE: I know. And you know just as well.

CLAIRE: Reasonable knowledge isn't necessarily right. I know it's easier to die than to live. You tear your dress lengthways, you twist it and attach it to a beam in the roof. You tie the knot and jump into the middle of the aisle between the bunks.

FRANÇOISE: Or you run into the barbed wire, you touch the wire...

MOUNETTE: Electrocuted...I wouldn't choose that, it's horrible.

FRANÇOISE: Here, there are only horrible versions of death.

CLAIRE: And you think you can do that? You aren't free. Even if you are nothing but the smallest link, you are part of a chain that links all men—that links them far into the future. No matter what you do, you are part of the human chain. You cannot exclude yourself.

RÉINE: Claire is right. If there is only one chance to get out of here and for only one of us, we must force that chance and help the one among us who will have it. There must be one who returns.

FRANÇOISE: You're lucky, Claire, and you too Réine, to always know what ought to be done.

*(Claire and Réine move away to return to their group.)*

# SMALL GROUP SCENES
# WITH A MAJORITY
# OF WOMEN

# The Eumenides

Aeschylus
Translated by Paul Roche

**Dramatic**
**Scene:** at the shrine of Apollo at Delphi

The Chorus of Eumenides (the Furies)
Clytemnestra, her ghost, the deceased Queen of Argos
Apollo, patron of the Delphic Shrine
The Pythia, an old woman, priestess of Apollo
Orestes, son and murderer of Clytemnestra
Hermes, accompanies Orestes, silent, a messenger of the gods

THE PYTHIA: Prime in this address before the gods
    I praise the Earth, primordial prophetess.
    And Themis next, the Right:
    second from her mother so tradition says
    to be seated on this sybil's chair
    Third in line, another Titan:
    Earth's daughter Phoebe,
    who in peaceable succession without force
    sat this seat and as a birthday present gave it
    to Phoebus named from Phoebe:
    who left the lake on Delos with its nub of land
    and beached upon these ship-trailed shores of Pallas,
    coming to this country and these purlieus of Parnassus
    where the children of Hephaestus
    (roadbuilding breed)
    cheered him on with pomp—
    paving the lawless wilderness with law.
    Oh, how his advent made the people sing
    his praises. Delphus, too,
    the steerer of their state and king.
    And Zeus breathed into Phoebus' soul the art;
    sat him down as fourth upon this seer's throne.
    So Zeus it is, his father,
    for whom Loxias the prophet speaks.

These are the gods fixed in the prelude of my prayer;
with words of praise for Pallas-of-the-Holies too,
and worship for the nymphs where the hollow rock
of Corycis is bird-loud, loved
by deities that haunt.
Bromius invests the spot (he's not forgotten)
ever since the time as god he marshaled his Bacchants
and trapped poor Pentheus to a hunted hare's demise.
The springs of Pleistus too, and all Poseidon's power:
I call upon, with Zeus—perfector and most high.

And so I take my throne: the prophetess.
Now may these excel every blessing that my introit won.
Let any Greeks, by lot, here enter in
according to the law;
and I shall prophesy as the god leads on.
*(She goes into the temple but almost immediately comes out
again—distraught.)*
THE PYTHIA: Oh, horrible to tell about—horrible to see!
Things that hurl me back again from Loxias' domain,
too weak to walk or stand;
scurrying on my hands with legs gone dumb.
An old woman in a panic is nothing but a child.

I was on my way
to the deep and garland-heavy shrine,
when there I see a man in God's disgrace
upon the center stone:
sitting where the contrite sit,
so you can make this fool of me among the other dead—
among the shades where I (because of those I killed)
am a reproach that never stops wandering in my shame.
Oh, I tell you, in their eyes—most heinously—
I am the one to blame.
Yet even this absurd suffering from my own
makes not a single deity excite himself for me,
cut down though I am by a mother-killing son.

See these gashes here—into my heart—from where?
Surely in sleep your eyes can see it plain,
where the daylight blaze is dark for man's concern.
You've sucked up quite a goodly deal from me:
with your wineless oblations, thin appeasements,
and those dead-of-nightly dinners
grilled by me in fire and sacrifice
at an hour no god shared.
All under foot now, I see.
All trodden down;
while *he* skips off, is gone, just like a fawn:
yes, leaps out lightly from your midst
with a merry bleat of laughter.

Listen to me pleading for my soul.
Awake and think, you goddesses of deep below;
for only in your dreams now is Clytemnestra calling.
*(The Chorus stirs, whimpering and muttering in sleep.)*
THE PYTHIA: Oh, whine away! The man is gone, fled far.
His friends are not at all like mine.
*(The Chorus continues to whimper and whine.)*
THE PYTHIA: You're too drugged with sleep. No sympathy at all.
And Orestes gone! This poor mother's murderer.
*(The Chorus moans desultorily.)*
THE PYTHIA: You moan and sleep…Why won't you wake?
What else have you to do but stir up trouble?
*(They moan again.)*
THE PYTHIA: Hands oozing blood,
sword fresh-drawn, long olive branch
piously, enormously, bedecked with wool
as white as fleece and piercing as I saw it.
And before that man:
the weirdest troupe of women
lolling on their seats asleep—
oh no, not women, Gorgons, surely!
or not Gorgons even but shapes like…
like once I saw in pictures—
carrying off the feast of Phineus—
only, these I saw were wingless, black,

absolute in their mephitic deadliness:
snoring and blowing disgustingly,
with cess of droppings leaking from their eyes; their dress
not fit to wear before the idols of the gods
nor any human home.
I have not seen what race could spawn
such clots as these, nor any earth
that could be proud of such a breed
and not groan out in hurt and sorrow.

But let the rest now fall to his domain:
the lord himself of here, great Loxias the strong.
For he is health diviner, marvel reader,
and of others' homes the healing purger.
*(The Pythia retires and the doors of the temple open to disclose Orestes sitting on the center stone near the sacred tripod, surrounded by the nodding Furies. Near him stands Apollo, with Hermes in the background.)*

APOLLO: No—I'll not desert you, no!
Your guardian to the end—
from a distance,
at your side:
never weak or meek towards your enemies.
See them overcome now, these fiendish crones:
stilled into sleep, these damsels of disgust,
hoary urchin hags with whom no god can mix,
nor man nor beast—ever.
For, issued out of vice in vicious night they live
in Tartarus beneath:
a blotch of hate for both Olympian gods and men.

But you must still go fleeing
and not grow faint of heart;
for they will chase your roaming footfall far
over the steppes and constant
across the oceans even
to sea-enswirling cities.
So leave the thought behind
or tire before your time;
but when you touch upon the town of Pallas,

sit down and hug in your hands her ancient effigy.
For there'll be judges there of this
and words to charm; and we shall find a means—
an absolute release for you from all this strife:
for *I* it was who told you to take your mother's life.

ORESTES: Apollo, Lord—
so well aware of avoiding wrong—
add to your intent the not-avoiding care;
so's your power for good your testimonial.

APOLLO: Remember: let no fear unseat your soul...
and you my brother Hermes, of my very father's blood,
look after him, true to your name: escort him,
be shepherd to my suppliant
(for God regards the outcast's rights)
into the mortal round, with happy auspices.
*(Apollo disappears. Orestes departs led by Hermes. The Ghost of Clytemnestra rises from the ground.)*

CLYTEMNESTRA: Go on! Go sleeping on! We just need sleepers, eh?
Sleep and suffering—oh, so brilliantly conspiring!—
have altogether dimmed you down, you fiery dragoness.
*(The Furies start from sleep, crying out.)*

CHORUS: At him! At him! At him! At him!—Get him!

CLYTEMNESTRA: Yelping after game like silly dogs in sleep
which never can stop thinking they are on the chase.
What are you *doing?* Get up and don't give in to toil
or let yourselves go soft with sleep and leave me in my pain.
Whip up your livers with the lashes they deserve.
For people in the right, reproaches can be spurs.
Oh, breathe upon him with that butchery breath of yours.
Shrivel him to ash from your smoking burning bowels.
Off at him again. Pursue him to the bone.
*(The Ghost of Clytemnestra sweeps away. The Furies begin to waken one by one.)*

PARODOS: Wake up! Wake up! Wake her
As I have woken *you.*
Asleep? Get on your feet
And let your slumbers go.
For we must see if we
Must sing an empty show.

STROPHE 1

Oh, curse it! Curse it, sisters:
    We have been betrayed.
    And after all I've suffered,
    All of it in vain.
    Oh, yes! oh, yes, we've suffered
    Through a deal of pain,
    Of hellish pain.
    He's slipped out from our noose,
    Our beast he's got away.
    We lost ourselves in sleep,
    And lost our prey.

ANTISTROPHE 1

    Shame! you son of Zeus
    To turn a sneak
    And ride us down—us gray
    Divinities—a youth.
    You cherish *him,* a beggar:
    A man God hates,
    A parent-hurter.
    You snatch a matricide
    Away, and you a god.
    Can anyone at all
    Call this fair?

STROPHE 2

    In the middle of my dreams
    I felt a scolding smite
    Me hard like a horseman's goad
    Right in the midriff, right
    Under the heart.
    And I am made for someone
    To beat and to benight,
    Sting and benumb:
    Ah! made to smart.

ANTISTROPHE 2

    So this is how the younger

Gods behave and rule:
Beyond all right!
Beads of blood on a throne
From head to foot;
And I am made to see
Earth's center stone
Crudely, bloodily blotched:
Ah! made to hurt.

STROPHE 3

Seer though he is he has smeared
His very hearth himself,
Sullied his own recess:
To flout the gods' behests,
Promoted things of man—
Upsetting old establishments.

ANTISTROPHE 3

Annoy me though he will
*Him* I'll not unloose.
Though he flee beneath the earth
Outlet there'll be none.
Contrite and accursed
He shall repeat his family doom.
(*Apollo appears from the inner sanctuary and confronts the furies.*)
APOLLO: Out, I say from here.
Leave this edifice at once.
Get off and gone from my prophetic holy place,
or feel the strike of a winged and coruscating snake
whipped from my golden bow,
to make you froth away your life in spasms
of black and man-drawn bile—
spewing out your clotted human suckings.

This is no fitting residence for you to board.
Yours is a place of sentences:
where heads are chopped, eyes gouged, throats cut,
and seed is crushed from striplings spoiled in flower.

Yes, a place of mutilations, stonings—
helpless wailings long drawn out
from men pinned through the spine.

Do you want to know what turns the stomachs of the Gods?
Those feasts you find so charming.
Your whole shape and mien give you away.
Freaks like you should make their hole
deep in some blood-beslobbered lion's den
and not come rubbing off their filth
on those beside these sacred mantic spots.

Get gone, you goatish rabble with no goatherd:
No god's love is lost on such a flock.
CHORUS: My lord Apollo,
    you must take your turn to listen too:
    for no mere accessory of this
    but perpetrator absolute, arch-criminal, are you.
    *(Chorus and Apollo.)*
APOLLO: How's that? Explain exactly what you say.
CHORUS: It was you arranged this traveling matricide.
APOLLO: Arrangement for a vengeance of a father: yes—what then?
CHORUS: And then you made yourself receiver of spilt blood.
APOLLO: I sent him for his purging to this very house.
CHORUS: While we who spurred him on, we are the ones abused.
APOLLO: You took the liberty of coming near my home.
CHORUS: But that precisely is the part we were assigned.
APOLLO: Your part and special privilege, eh? Oh, boast it out.
CHORUS: Murderers of mothers we harry from their homes.
APOLLO: Then what about a woman who undermines her man?
CHORUS: Such a killing does not count as blood of kin.
APOLLO: How you heap contempt upon—make cheap—
    Hera's consummated pact with Zeus.
    Aphrodite too such logic brushes off, condemns—
    the source of mankind's sweetest joys.
    Love in marriage is a holy state between a man and woman:
    stronger than an oath, sentineled by Right.
    And if one slays the other and you be lax,
    not flash in anger on them,

I'll never for a moment say you are not wrong
to hunt Orestes down.
Your passion for the one is all too plain,
as slackness and remiss are blazoned in the other.
But Pallas shall preside in this: the goddess, judge.
*(Chorus and Apollo.)*

CHORUS: Never shall I leave that man alone.

APOLLO: Go on then, chase—and pile your troubles up.

CHORUS: You shan't lop short my privileges with talk.

APOLLO: Your privileges! I would not take them as a gift.

CHORUS: No: for you are altogether perfect, so they say,
    at Zeus's throne.
    But I'll pursue my suit,
    and I am on the scent
    of mother's blood
    with justice for this man.

APOLLO: And I shall hurry to his side and save my client.
    For under heaven and earth no anger is so deep
    as a postulant's who's spurned—
    if from him I let myself be turned.

# The Braggart Warrior

Plautus
Translated by George E. Duckworth
circa 180 B.C.

**Comic**

**Scene:** a street in Ephesus. Pyrgopolynices has abducted Philocomasium and has been holding her at his home in Ephesus. Her true love, Pleusicles, with the aide of Palaestrio has staged an elaborate ruse to bring her home, claiming her mother and twin sister need her desperately. They have also hired a prostitute to win the heart of the vain Pyrgopolynices so he will release Philocomasium. Here, she pretends to be grief-stricken about having to leave the vain warrior whom she really hates.

Pyrgopolynices, a soldier, a braggart, and a showoff
Philocomasium, a young woman abducted by Pyrgopolynices
Palaestrio, a slave belonging to Pleusicles but in the power of Pyrgo-
    polynices
Pleusicles, a young Athenian gentleman in love with Philocomasium
Cario, a cook
Slave Boy
Periplectomen, an elderly citizen of Ephesus
Other Servants, young men

> (Enter Palaestrio and Philocomasium from the house of Pyrgo-
> polynices.)

PALAESTRIO: *(To Philocomasium.)* When in the world will you stop weeping, I want to know?

PHILOCOMASIUM: *(Sobbing.)* How can I help weeping? I've had such a
happy life here, and—and now I'm going away.

PALAESTRIO: *(Pointing to Pleusicles.)* See! There's the man who has come
from your mother and sister.

PHILOCOMASIUM: *(Without interest.)* I see him.

PYRGOPOLYNICES: Listen, Palaestrio, will you?

PALAESTRIO: What do you wish?

PYRGOPOLYNICES: Go and order those things I gave her to be brought out.
    *(Palaestrio goes to the door and gives the orders to the slaves.)*

PLEUSICLES: Good day, Philocomasium.

PHILOCOMASIUM: Good day to you, sir.

PLEUSICLES: Both your mother and your sister asked me to give you their greetings.

PHILOCOMASIUM: I hope they're well.

PLEUSICLES: They beg you to come so that they can set sail, while the breeze is favourable. They would have come along with me, if your mother had not been suffering from sore eyes.

PHILOCOMASIUM: I'll go. But I do it against my will; my devotion to the soldier—

PLEUSICLES: I understand; you're sensible.

PYRGOPOLYNICES: But she'd still be stupid today, if she hadn't been spending her life with me.

PHILOCOMASIUM: That's just what tortures me, that I'm being separated from such a man; why, you can make anyone at all overflow with cleverness; and I was so elated at heart when I was with you. This distinction I see I must give up. (She sobs bitterly.)

PYRGOPOLYNICES: Ah! Don't cry.

PHILOCOMASIUM: I—I can't help it when I look at you.

PYRGOPOLYNICES: Be of good cheer.

PHILOCOMASIUM: No one but myself knows the anguish I feel.

PALAESTRIO: Well, I don't at all wonder that you were happy here, Philocomasium, and that his beauty, his manners, his valour touched your heart with tenderness; for, when I, a mere slave, look at him, I weep that we are being parted. (He turns away, pretending to cry.)

PHILOCOMASIUM: Please may I embrace you once before I go?

PYRGOPOLYNICES: You may.

PHILOCOMASIUM: (Embracing him.) Oh, my darling! Oh, my life!

PALAESTRIO: (Leading her to Pleusicles.) Hold the woman, I beg of you, or she'll dash herself to the ground.
(Pleusicles holds her tenderly, as she pretends to faint.)

PYRGOPOLYNICES: (Looking at them suspiciously.) Hey! What the devil does this mean?

PALAESTRIO: The poor girl has suddenly fallen into a faint at the thought of leaving you.

PYRGOPOLYNICES: Run inside and bring out some water.

PALAESTRIO: I don't want any water; I'd rather have her rest a bit. Don't interfere, please, while she's recovering.

PYRGOPOLYNICES: *(Watching Pleusicles and Philocomasium.)* These two have their heads too close together; I don't like it.

*(As Pleusicles forgets himself and kisses her.)*

PYRGOPOLYNICES: Sailor, get your lips away from her lips; look out for trouble!

PLEUSICLES: I was trying to find out whether she was breathing or not.

PYRGOPOLYNICES: Then you should have used your ear.

PLEUSICLES: If you prefer, I'll let her go.

PYRGOPOLYNICES: *(Hastily.)* I don't want that. Keep holding her.

PALAESTRIO: *(As a hint to the lovers.)* I'm unhappy.

PYRGOPOLYNICES: *(To the slaves inside.)* Come out and bring out here all the things I gave her.

*(Enter the slaves with the luggage.)*

PALAESTRIO: *(Solemnly.)* And now, Household God, before I go, I bid you farewell! And all my fellow slaves, both male and female, good-bye and a happy life to you! And in your conversations I hope that you will speak well of me, even though I am absent. *(He pretends to weep.)*

PYRGOPOLYNICES: Come, come, Palaestrio! Cheer up!

PALAESTRIO: Oh! Oh! I just can't keep from weeping at leaving you.

PYRGOPOLYNICES: Endure it calmly.

PALAESTRIO: No one but myself knows the anguish I feel.

PHILOCOMASIUM: *(Pretending to regain consciousness.)* But what's this? What has happened? What do I see? Greetings, O light of day!

PLEUSICLES: Have you recovered now?

PHILOCOMASIUM: *(Looking at Pleusicles in feigned horror.)* Heavens! What man have I embraced? I'm ruined! Am I in my senses? *(She sinks back again into Pleusicles' arms.)*

PLEUSICLES: Have no fear, *(In a lower tone.)* my darling!

PYRGOPOLYNICES: What does this mean?

PALAESTRIO: The girl has just fainted away. *(Aside to Pleusicles.)* I'm fearfully afraid that this business will become too public.

*(Philocomasium revives again.)*

PYRGOPOLYNICES: *(Overhearing.)* What's that you say?

PALAESTRIO: I mean, sir, if all this stuff is carried through the city behind us; I fear that people may criticise you for it.

PYRGOPOLYNICES: I gave away my own property, not theirs; it's damned little I care for what they think. Come, go now with the blessings of the gods.

PALAESTRIO: I mention this for your sake.

PYRGOPOLYNICES: I believe you.

PALAESTRIO: And now good-bye, sir.

PYRGOPOLYNICES: Good-bye to you.

PALAESTRIO: *(To the others.)* You go on quickly; I'll follow you in a moment. I want a few words with my master.

*(Philocomasium and Pleusicles depart, followed by the slaves with the luggage.)*

PALAESTRIO: I am most grateful to you for everything, sir, in spite of the fact that you have always considered other slaves more faithful than me to you. If it were your wish, I should prefer to be your slave than another person's freedman. *(Pretending to weep.)*

PYRGOPOLYNICES: Be of good courage!

PALAESTRIO: Ah me! When I consider how I must change my way of life, learn the ways of women and set aside the soldiers' ways!

PYRGOPOLYNICES: Come now, be a worthy fellow.

PALAESTRIO: I can't now; I've lost all my desire.

PYRGOPOLYNICES: Go, follow them, don't delay!

PALAESTRIO: *(Tearfully.)* Good-bye.

PYRGOPOLYNICES: Good-bye to you.

PALAESTRIO: *(Stopping.)* If I happen to find myself a free man, I'll send you a message; remember, I beg of you, not to desert me.

PYRGOPOLYNICES: That's not the way I do things.

PALAESTRIO: *(Trying to keep a straight face.)* And every now and then just consider how faithful I've been to you. If you do this, you'll know finally who is a good servant and who is a bad servant.

PYRGOPOLYNICES: I do know; I've often thought about it.

PALAESTRIO: But you'll know it particularly today, even though you've realised it before this. Why, today you'll speak even more of my achievements, I'll guarantee.

PYRGOPOLYNICES: *(Impressed.)* I can hardly refrain from bidding you to stay.

PALAESTRIO: *(In alarm.)* Oh, don't do that, sir. People would say that you were deceitful and untruthful and faithless; and they would say that I was the only faithful slave you had. If I thought you could do it with honour, I'd urge you to; but it just can't be. Don't do it.

PYRGOPOLYNICES: Be off, then.

PALAESTRIO: *(Sadly.)* I'll endure whatever happens.

PYRGOPOLYNICES: Well, good-bye.

PALAESTRIO: *(Apparently at the point of breaking down.)* It's better to go quickly. *(He hastens off towards the harbour.)*

PYRGOPOLYNICES: *(Calling after him.)* Once more, good-bye. *(To himself.)* Before this affair came up, I always thought he was the greatest rascal among the slaves; now I find that he is devoted to me. Now that I think it over, I've been very stupid to let him go. Well, I'll go in now to my beloved. *(He turns towards the door of Periplectomenus' house.)* But the door has made a noise, I perceive. *(He pauses.)*

*(Enter a Slave Boy from the house of Periplectomenus.)*

BOY: *(To those within.)* Don't be giving me orders; I remember my duty. I'll find him, no matter where he is. I'll track him down; I won't spare any labour.

PYRGOPOLYNICES: *(Aside.)* He's looking for me. I'll go to meet the lad.

BOY: Oho! You're the person I'm looking for. Greetings to you, you most delightful man, abounding in opportuneness, the one mortal beloved beyond all others by the two deities.

PYRGOPOLYNICES: Which two?

BOY: Mars and Venus.

PYRGOPOLYNICES: *(Approvingly.)* Smart boy!

BOY: She begs you to come inside, she wants you, she desires you, she anxiously awaits you. Do help the lovesick lady. Why do you stand there? Why don't you go inside?

PYRGOPOLYNICES: I'm going. *(He enters the house of Periplectomenus.)*

BOY: *(Elated.)* Now he's entangled himself in the toils; the trap is all ready. The old man is at his post ready to plunge at this adulterer, who boasts of his beauty, who thinks that every woman that sees him falls in love with him. Everyone despises him, men and women both. Now I'll go in and join the uproar. I hear them shouting inside. *(He returns to the house.)*

*(Enter Periplectomenus from his house, followed by Cario and other slaves who are holding the struggling Pyrgopolynices.)*

PERIPLECTOMENUS: Drag him along! If he won't follow, pick him up and throw him out! Lift him up between heaven and earth! Tear him to pieces!

PYRGOPOLYNICES: Oh, God! Periplectomenus, I beg you to have mercy.

PERIPLECTOMENUS: You beg in vain. *(To Cario.)* See that that knife of yours is well sharpened, Cario.

CARIO: *(Testing his knife.)* Why, it's been anxious for a long time to rip open the abdomen of this adulterer, so that I can hang trinkets around his neck the way they hang from a baby's neck.

PYRGOPOLYNICES: *(In terror.)* I'm killed!

PERIPLECTOMENUS: Not yet. You speak too soon.

CARIO: *(Waving the knife.)* Can I fly at the man now?

PERIPLECTOMENUS: No. I want him clubbed with cudgels first.

CARIO: With lots of them, I hope.

PERIPLECTOMENUS: How did you dare to seduce another man's wife, you lecher?

PYRGOPOLYNICES: As the gods love me, she came to me of her own accord.

PERIPLECTOMENUS: He lies. Strike him!

*(They raise their clubs.)*

PYRGOPOLYNICES: Wait, while I explain.

PERIPLECTOMENUS: *(To the slaves.)* Why do you hesitate?

PYRGOPOLYNICES: Won't you let me speak?

PERIPLECTOMENUS: Speak.

PYRGOPOLYNICES: I was urged to come to her.

PERIPLECTOMENUS: But how did you dare? There, take that!

*(He strikes him, the slaves joining in.)*

PYRGOPOLYNICES: Ow! Ow! I've had enough. Oh, heavens!

CARIO: *(Eagerly.)* How soon am I to begin cutting?

PERIPLECTOMENUS: As soon as you wish. Spread the fellow apart; stretch him out.

PYRGOPOLYNICES: Oh, God! I beseech you, listen to me before he starts cutting.

PERIPLECTOMENUS: Speak.

PYRGOPOLYNICES: I had some justification; damn it, I thought she was divorced! That's what her maid, the go-between, told me.

PERIPLECTOMENUS: Swear that you won't injure a living soul because of this—that you've had a thrashing here today or that you will have a thrashing—if we send you away from here alive, you darling little grandson of Venus!

PYRGOPOLYNICES: I swear by Jupiter and Mars that I won't injure a soul because I've had a thrashing here today, and I think I deserved it. If I go away from here as a man, I'm being well treated for my offence.

PERIPLECTOMENUS: And if you don't keep your word?

PYRGOPOLYNICES: Then may I always live unmanned.

CARIO: *(To Periplectomenus.)* Let's beat him once more; then I move we let him go.

PYRGOPOLYNICES: May the gods bless you forever, since you plead so well in my behalf.

CARIO: Well, give us *(Pointing to the slaves.)* a mina of gold, then.

PYRGOPOLYNICES: What for?

CARIO: So that we'll let you go away from here today with your manhood intact, you darling little grandson of Venus! Otherwise you shan't get away from here; don't deceive yourself about that.

PYRGOPOLYNICES: *(In haste.)* You'll get it.

CARIO: Now you show more sense. But don't count on your tunic and your cloak and your sword; you won't get them back.

A SLAVE: Shall I hit him again, or are you going to let him beat it?

PYRGOPOLYNICES: I've been beaten to a jelly already. Please have mercy.

PERIPLECTOMENUS: *(To slaves.)* Let him loose.

*(They do so.)*

PYRGOPOLYNICES: I am grateful to you.

PERIPLECTOMENUS: *(Sternly.)* If I ever catch you here again, you will lose your manhood.

PYRGOPOLYNICES: I accept your terms.

PERIPLECTOMENUS: Let's go inside, Cario.

*(Periplectomenus goes into his house, followed by Cario and the other slaves.)*

PYRGOPOLYNICES: *(Looking down the street.)* Well, I see my slaves!
*(Enter Sceledrus and other slaves from the harbour.)*

PYRGOPOLYNICES: Has Philocomasium departed already? Tell me.

SCELEDRUS: A long time ago.

PYRGOPOLYNICES: Oh, damn it!

SCELEDRUS: You'd damn it still more, if you knew what I know. That fellow with the woollen patch over his eye was no sailor.

PYRGOPOLYNICES: Who was he, then?

SCELEDRUS: Philocomasium's lover,

PYRGOPOLYNICES: How do you know?

SCELEDRUS: I know, all right. Why, from the time they left the city gate, they never stopped kissing and hugging each other.

PYRGOPOLYNICES: What a confounded fool I am! I've been deceived; I see that now. That rogue of a fellow, Palaestrio! He's the one that lured me into this trap. *(Reflecting.)* Well, I believe I've deserved it. If the same treatment were given to other adulterers, there would be fewer adulterers about; they would have greater fear of punishment, and less desire for such pursuits. *(To the slaves.)* Let's go home. *(To the audience.)* Give us your applause.

# Alan's Wife

Florence Bell and Elizabeth Robins
1893

**Dramatic**
**Scene:** a village street in the north of England

Mrs. Holroyd
Mrs. Ridley
Jean
Warren
First Woman
Second Woman
Woman and two Men—brief entrances

WOMAN: *(As she passes to Mrs. Holroyd.)* A fine day!
MRS. HOLROYD: *(Nodding.)* Ay, it's a fine day.
*(The woman passes on.)*
MRS. RIDLEY: *(Comes along with a basket on her arm—she stops.)* Good morning, Mrs Holroyd!
MRS. HOLROYD: Good morning to you, Mrs Ridley: it's a warm day!
MRS. RIDLEY: And you look very comfortable there.
MRS. HOLROYD: Yes, it's nice out here—sit you down and rest a bit; you'll be tired after your marketing.
MRS. RIDLEY: *(Sitting down by her on the seat.)* Well, I don't say I won't be glad of a rest. It's fine to see you settled in your daughter's house for a bit, like this.
MRS. HOLROYD: It's the only place I do feel settled in, now she's married. I just feel lost in my own house without her.
MRS. RIDLEY: Ay, you will that. It's bad when lassies take up with their husbands and leave their mothers alone.
MRS. HOLROYD: Ay, you may well say so! And Jean is all I have. I never had a lad of my own, or another lass either, and it's hard to be left when one is getting into years.
MRS. RIDLEY: Still, you must be glad she has got a good husband, that can work hard and give her all she wants.
MRS. HOLROYD: Ay, Alan Creyke's a fine fellow, no doubt, and they say he'll soon be foreman. I did think my Jean would have looked higher. I always thought she would marry a schoolmaster, as I did,

or even a minister—seeing all the book-learning she got from her poor father. She knows as much as any lady, I do believe.

MRS. RIDLEY: Ay, it's wonderful what the books'll do. They say young Mr. Warren, that's just come to the chapel here, has got more book-learning than the schoolmaster himself, and can talk about it so as no one can understand him. Eh, but it's fine to know as much as that!

MRS. HOLROYD: *(With a sigh.)* It is indeed! And, Mrs Ridley, as sure as you see me sitting here beside you, there was a time when that young man was after our Jean, and she might have been the mistress of yon pretty house near the chapel, instead of living in a cottage like this.

MRS. RIDLEY: Dear, dear! To think of that! Ah well, it's no wonder you're put about at the way she chose.

MRS. HOLROYD: I don't say that Alan isn't a good husband, mind you, and a good worker too—only I did hope to see my girl a bit grander than she is, as mothers will.

MRS. RIDLEY: Ah well, young people will do their own way. You must just make up your mind to it, Mrs Holroyd. I fear the book-learning doesn't go for much with the lassies, where a fine fellow like Creyke is concerned—and after all, as to the cottage, it's a nice little place, and she keeps it beautiful!

MRS. HOLROYD: She does that—and she wouldn't be her mother's daughter if she didn't. And the pleasure she takes in it, too! keeping it as bright and shining as if there were five or six pair of hands to do it! She and Alan are nobbut two children about it, and their house is just like a new toy.

MRS. RIDLEY: Well, that's right! let them be happy now, poor things; they'll leave it off soon enough.

MRS. HOLROYD: Eh, yes, I doubt they will, like other folk.

MRS. RIDLEY: Where is Jean? I should like to wish her good morning. Is she in?

MRS. HOLROYD: Yes, she's in the kitchen, I believe. *(Calls.)* Jean, Jean! What are you doing, honey? Here's a neighbour come to see you.

JEAN: *(From within room to the left.)* I'll come directly. I'm getting Alan's dinner ready. I can't leave the saucepan.

MRS. RIDLEY: *(Smiling.)* Ay, getting Alan's dinner ready! That's the way of it.

MRS. HOLROYD: Yes, it's always Alan's dinner, or Alan's tea, or Alan's supper, or Alan's pipe. There isn't another man in the North gets waited on as he does.

MRS. RIDLEY: Eh, but that's what he'll want to keep him in his home; they're bad to please, is the men, unless you spoil them. *(Bell begins to ring outside.)*

MRS. RIDLEY: There's the mid-day bell from the works. Creyke'll soon be here now—I must be getting home too.

MRS. HOLROYD: Eh, now, but Jean would have liked to shake hands with ye. *(Calls.)* Jean! Jean! Be quick, child!

JEAN: *(From within.)* Just ready, Mother—I'm lifting it off the fire.

MRS. RIDLEY: *(Looking along the street.)* And in the nick of time too, for here are the men.

*(Two or three men walk past.)*

MRS. RIDLEY: Yes, hurry up, Jean, or your man will be here before his dinner's ready.

JEAN: *(From within.)* No, no he won't. *(Appears in doorway of cottage.)* Here it is! *(Comes out carrying a large smoking dish in her hand, which she puts on the table.)* There! How are you, Mrs Ridley? *(Shakes hands with her.)*

MRS. RIDLEY: Nicely, thank you. And are you going to get your dinner outside then?

JEAN: Yes, indeed; let's be in the air while we can—it's not often we have it as fine as this.

MRS. HOLROYD: I never saw such a lass for fresh air! and Alan is just as bad.

MRS. RIDLEY: Well, they'll take no harm with it, I daresay; fresh air is bad for nowt but cobwebs, as the saying is.

JEAN: *(Laughs.)* Ah, that's true enough! *(Arranging table.)* Now then, if that isn't a dinner fit for a king!

MRS. RIDLEY: And I'll be bound, if it is, you won't be thinking it too good for your husband.

JEAN: Too good! I should think not! Is anything too good for him? Is anything good enough?

MRS. HOLROYD: *(Smiling.)* Ah, Jean, Jean!

JEAN: Well, Mother, you know quite well it's true! Isn't he the best husband a girl ever had? And the handsomest, and the strongest?

MRS. HOLROYD: Ah, yes, he's all that, I daresay.

JEAN: *(Vigorously wiping tumblers.)* Well, what more do you want?

MRS. HOLROYD: Ah, my dear, as I've often told you, I should like you to have looked higher.

JEAN: Looked higher! How could I have looked higher than Alan?

MRS. HOLROYD: I wanted to see you marry a scholar.

JEAN: We can't all marry scholars, Mother dear—some of us prefer marrying men instead. *(Goes into house.)*

MRS. RIDLEY: The lass is right—there must be some of that sort that there may be some of all sorts, as the saying is; and, neighbour, you must just make the best of it, and be pleased with the man that's made her look so happy. *(Getting up.)*

MRS. HOLROYD: *(Smiling.)* Ay she looks bright enough, in all conscience. *(Jean comes back with cheese and butter on a dish.)*

MRS. RIDLEY: *(Smiling at Jean.)* She does that, indeed! Well, you won't have to wait long for him now, honey. Here they come down the road, and I must get back to my two lads. Good day to you both. *(Exit through garden gate and up street to the left exchanging greetings with passing workmen.)*

JEAN: *(Cutting bread.)* Scholar, indeed! Mother, how can you say such things before folks? I know what you mean when you say scholar—yon minister, poor little Jamie Warren.

MRS. HOLROYD: Ah, Jean, how can you speak so! He's a man who is looked up to by everybody. Didn't he go up to the big house last Christmastide, to dinner with the gentry, just like one of themselves?

JEAN: Well, that's right enough if it pleased him, but I shouldn't care to go among folk who thought themselves my betters.
*(Look from Mrs Holroyd.)*

JEAN: No, I shouldn't. I like Jamie, and have done ever since we were boy and girl together; but it's a far cry to think of taking him for my master! no, Mother, that's not my kind. *(Goes to tub under the window, wrings out tea cloths and hangs them on picket fence.)*

MRS. HOLROYD: Ah, Jean, what would your poor father have said! When you and Jamie used to play together on the village green and go to school together, and Jamie was minding his books and getting all the prizes, your father used to say, "When that lad grows up, he'll be the husband for Jean—he's a good lad, he never gets into mischief; he's never without a book in his hand."

JEAN: Ah, poor father! but what would *I* have done with a good boy who never got into mischief! *(Laughs.)* No, I always knew it wasn't to be Jamie. Why, I remember as far back as when Jamie and I used to come from school, and I'd rush on before and go flying up on the moors, to find the stagshorn moss, with the heathery wind in my face, and hear the whirring summer sounds around us, I used to want to shout aloud, just for the pleasure of being alive—and Jamie, poor little creature, used to come toiling up after me, and call out, "Not so fast, Jean, I'm out of breath, wait for me!" And *I* used to have to help *him* up!

MRS. HOLROYD: Well, perhaps he couldn't run and jump as well as you, but he had read all about the flowers and plants in his book, and could tell you the names of every one of them.

JEAN: Ay, their names, perhaps; but he couldn't swing himself up to the steep places where they grew to pull them for me. He was afraid—afraid! while *I*, a girl, didn't know what it was like to be afraid. I don't know now.

MRS. HOLROYD: Maybe—but he would have been a good husband for all that!

JEAN: Not for me. I want a husband who is brave and strong, a man who is my master as well as other folks'; who loves the hills and the heather, and loves to feel the strong wind blowing in his face and the blood rushing through his veins! Ah! to be happy—to be alive!

MRS. HOLROYD: Oh, Jean, you always were a strange girl!
*(Two men pass.)*

JEAN: Ah, Mother, can't you see how fine it is to have life, and health, and strength! Jamie Warren, indeed! Think of the way he comes along, poor fellow, as though he were scared of coming into bits if he moved faster! And the way Alan comes striding and swinging down the street, with his head up, looking as if the world belonged to him! Ah! it's good to be as happy as I am!

MRS. HOLROYD: Well, you silly fondy! In the meantime, I wonder what Alan is doing this morning? Yon fine dinner of his will be getting cold.

JEAN: Indeed it will. I wonder where he is!
*(Men pass.)*

JEAN: All the men seem to have passed.
*(Stands just outside the door and looks down the street to the*

right, sheltering her eyes from the sun. Hutton, a workman, passes, and stops to speak to her.)

HUTTON: Good morning, Mrs Creyke: a fine day again!

JEAN: It is indeed, Mr. Hutton. What's got my husband this morning, do you know? Why is he so long after the rest?

HUTTON: He's stayed behind to see about something that's gone wrong with the machinery. It's the new saw, I believe—that's what happens when folks try to improve on the old ways. I don't believe in improvements myself, and in trying these new-fangled things no one can understand.

JEAN: No one? I'll be bound Alan understands them well enough.

HUTTON: Well, happen he does, more than most, and that's why the manager called him back to fettle it up—but I doubt he won't be much longer now.

JEAN: Ah, well, that's all right, as long as I know what keeps him. Good morning.

(Hutton moves on.)

JEAN: You see, Mother, how they turn to Alan before all the rest!

MRS. HOLROYD: Ah, well, when a lass is in love she must needs know better than her mother, I suppose.

JEAN: Ah, Mother dear, wasn't there a time when you were a girl—when you knew better too?

MRS. HOLROYD: (Shaking her head.) Eh, but that's a long time ago.

JEAN: But you remember it, I'll be bound! I think I'd best be setting that dish in the oven again; it will be getting cold. (Exit with dish.)

MRS. HOLROYD: (Alone.) Well— (Shakes her head with a little smile as she goes on knitting.) there's nowt so queer as folk! (Shakes her head again.)

JEAN: (Coming back.) I wonder what makes him bide so long?

MRS. HOLROYD: You had far better give over tewing, and sit quietly down with a bit of work in your hands till he comes.

JEAN: No, Mother, I can't! (Smiling.) I'm too busy—watching for him! (Leans over railing and looks along road to the right.)

MRS. HOLROYD: That'll be Jamie coming along. (Looking off to the left.)

JEAN: (Looking round.) So it is. (Indifferently.) Well, Jamie, good morning. (Warren, a small delicate man, wearing a wide-awake hat and carrying a stick in his hand comes along the road from the left.)

WARREN: Good morning, Jean. Well, Mrs Holroyd, how are you?

*(Jean stands and leans against the railing to the right, looking down the road and listening to what the others are saying.)*

MRS. HOLROYD: Good morning, my lad: sit down a bit. And what have you been doing the day? You look tired.

WARREN: *(Takes off his hat wearily passing his hand over his brow.)* I've been doing my work—giving the Word to those who can hear it.

MRS. HOLROYD: And yon will have been edifying, that it will! And ye'll have done them good with it, for ye always were a beautiful speaker, Jamie!

JEAN: *(From the back.)* Mother, I doubt you should call him Mr. Warren now he's a minister.

MRS. HOLROYD: Eh, not I! I mind him since he was a bit of a lad running barefoot about the village at home.

JEAN: And do you mind, Jamie, that when you had a book in your hand I'd snatch it from you and throw it over the hedge? *(Laughs.)*

WARREN: Yes, you always pretended you didn't like books, Jean—but you used to learn quicker than anybody else when you chose.

MRS. HOLROYD: And so she does still, I'm sure. She likes her book as well as any one, though she will have it that she doesn't. She'll sit and read to Alan, when he's smoking his pipe, for half an hour at a time.

WARREN: And what does he think of it?

MRS. HOLROYD: *(Smiling.)* Between you and me, Jamie, I don't think he minds much for what she reads.

JEAN: *(Hotly.)* Indeed, but he does! Alan can understand what I read just as well as me.

MRS. HOLROYD: Eh, lass, it isn't the strongest in the arm that's the best at the books!

WARREN: Yes, it's rather hard upon the rest of us poor fellows if a fellow like Creyke is to have everything—if we mayn't have a little more book-learning to make up for not being a Hercules, like him.

JEAN: Why, Jamie, you wouldn't care to be a Hercules, as you call it— you never did.

WARREN: That's what you say.

JEAN: *(Lightly, still watching road to the right.)* Well, I say what I think, as honest folk do! *(Sheltering her eyes with her hand.)* Where can he be? His dinner will be burnt to a cinder directly.

MRS. HOLROYD: I wish he'd come and be done with it. She can't mind for anything else but yon dinner while she's waiting for him.

WARREN: Well, well, that's how it should be, I daresay.

MRS. HOLROYD: And have you got settled in your new house against the chapel?

WARREN: Pretty well, yes.

MRS. HOLROYD: Ah, I doubt you find it hard. A man's a poor creature at siding up, and getting things straight.

WARREN: He is indeed!

MRS. HOLROYD: *(Sympathetically.)* You'll be lonesome at times, my lad, isn't it so?

WARREN: *(Shakes his head.)* Indeed I am!

MRS. HOLROYD: Come, you must get yourself a little wife, and she'll make it nice and homely for you.

WARREN: *(Shakes his head.)* No, I don't think I shall be taking a wife yet a bit, somehow. *(Gets up.)* Well, I must be going. *(Looks at watch.)* I said I would look in at the school for a bit after dinner, and the children go in again at half-past one.

JEAN: Yes, I always see them bustling past—some of them so little that if they didn't take hold of each other's hands they'd be tumbling down! *(She laughs.)*

WARREN: Yes, there are some very weeny ones in the infant school. Canny little bairns! Good-bye, Jean—good-bye, Mrs Creyke.

JEAN: Good-bye, Jamie!

*(Exit Warren.)*

MRS. HOLROYD: Eh, but he has a tender heart. I like a man that can speak about the little ones that way.

JEAN: So do I. Oh, Mother, I like to watch Alan with a child—the way he looks at it and the way he speaks to it! Do you know, with those strong arms of his he can hold a baby as well as you, Mother? He picked up a little mite that was sobbing on the road the other day, and carried it home, and before a minute was over the bairn had left off crying, and nestled itself to sleep on his shoulder.

MRS. HOLROYD: Ah, yes, he'll make a good father some day!

JEAN: A good father and a happy one, too! Yes, we shall be happier then than we are now even. Oh, Mother, is that possible?—shall I be happier when I have my baby in my arms?

MRS. HOLROYD: Ah, my child, yes, you will that, in truth. People talk of happiness and the things that bring it, and the young people talk about it and dream of it—but there's one happiness in the world that's better and bigger when it comes than one ever thinks for beforehand—and that is the moment when a woman's first child lies in her arms.

JEAN: Is it, is it really? Oh, Mother, to think that this is coming to me! I shall have that too, besides all the rest! Isn't it wonderful?

MRS. HOLROYD: *(Moved.)* God keep you, honey!

JEAN: Yes, when I think of the moment when my child will lie in my arms, how he will look at me—

MRS. HOLROYD: *(Smiling.)* He! It's going to be a boy then, is it?

JEAN: Of course it is! Like his father. He shall be called Alan, too, and he will be just like him. He will have the same honest blue eyes, that make you believe in them, and the same yellow hair and a straight nose, and a firm, sweet mouth. But that's what he'll be like when he grows up a little; at first he'll be nothing but a pink, soft, round, little baby, and we will sit before the fire—it will be the winter, you know, when he comes—and he'll lie across my knee, and stretch out his little pink feet to the blaze, and all the neighbours will come in and see his sturdy little limbs, and say, 'My word, what a fine boy!' He'll be just such another as his father. Oh, Mother, it's too good to be true!

MRS. HOLROYD: No, no, honey, it isn't! It will all come true some day.

JEAN: Oh, Mother, Mother, what a good world it is! *(Kisses her.)* Ah, I see some more people coming—he'll soon be here now! *(Goes in to right.)*

MRS. HOLROYD: *(Looking along road.)* Yes, there they come. *(Gets up, puts her knitting down, begins straightening table, then goes in as though to fetch something.)*
*(Gradual signs of commotion two boys rush along stage from right to left, then return with two more, and go off, right. Two children rush past; then two women enter at back, left, and stand a little to the right of cottage, shading their eyes. Mrs Holroyd comes out of door with a brown jug in her hand.)*

. MRS. HOLROYD: What is it? Anything happened?

FIRST WOMAN: Ay, it's an accident, they say, at the works.

MRS. HOLROYD: *(Alarmed.)* An accident?

SECOND WOMAN: Yes, yes, look there! *(She points off to the right.)*

JEAN: *(Leaning out of room to the left, with her arms crossed on win-*

*dow sill.)* And, Mother, I've been thinking we shall have to call him wee Alan, to tell him from his father, you know. Mother! *(Looks.)* Mother, what has happened?

MRS. HOLROYD: *(Hurriedly.)* Nothing, honey, nothing.

*(Jean comes hurriedly out of room and down passage.)*

JEAN: No, Mother, I am sure there is something! What is it? *(To woman.)* Do you know?

FIRST WOMAN: It will be an accident, they say, at the works.

JEAN: At the works! Any one hurt?

SECOND WOMAN: Eh, with yon machines, ye never know but there'll be something.

JEAN: With the machines! *(Sees Warren coming hurriedly past, right.)* Jamie, Jamie, what is it? What has happened?

WARREN: Jean, dear Jean, you must be prepared.

JEAN: Prepared? For what?

WARREN: There has been an accident.

JEAN: Not to Alan? Ah, do you mean he has been hurt?

*(Warren is silent.)*

JEAN: But he's so strong it will be nothing! I'll make him well again. Where is he? We must bring him back!

WARREN: No, no! *(He looks back at something approaching.)*

JEAN: What is that?

*(Pause.)*

WARREN: God's will be done, Jean; His hand is heavy on ye.

*(A moment of silence. Jean is seen to look aghast at something coming Hutton and two more, carrying a covered litter, come to the gate, followed by a little crowd of men, women and children.)*

JEAN: Oh, they're coming here! *(Rushes to them.)* Hutton, tell me what has happened?

HUTTON: Best not look, missis—it's a sore sight!

*(Mrs. Holroyd holds Jean back.)*

JEAN: Let me be, Mother—I *must* go to him!

FIRST WOMAN: Na, na, my lass—best keep back!

MRS. HOLROYD: Keep back, honey! you're not the one to bear the sight!

JEAN: I must—let me go! *(Struggles, breaks away, and rushes forward—lifts up cover.)* Alan! *(She falls back with a cry into Mrs Holroyd's arms.)*

# Playboy of the Western World

John Millington Synge
1907

**Serio-comic**
**Scene:** the public-house bar in County Mayo, Ireland

Christy Mahon
Susan
Nelly
Honor
Sara
Widow Quin
Pegeen

CHRISTY: *(To himself, counting jugs on dresser.)* Half a hundred beyond.
Ten there. A score that's above. Eighty jugs. Six cups and a broken one. Two plates. A power of glasses. Bottles, a school-master'd
be hard set to count, and enough in them, I'm thinking, to
drunken all the wealth and wisdom of the County Clare. *(He puts
down the boot carefully.)* There's her boots now, nice and decent
for her evening use, and isn't it grand brushes she has? *(He puts
them down and goes by degrees to the looking-glass.)* Well,
this'd be a fine place to be my whole life talking out with swear-
ing Christians, in place of my old dogs and cat, and I stalking
around, smoking my pipe and drinking my fill, and never a day's
work but drawing a cork an odd time, or wiping a glass, or rins-
ing out a shiny tumbler for a decent man. *(He takes the looking-
glass from the wall and puts it on the back of a chair; then sits
down in front of it and begins washing his face.)* Didn't I know
rightly I was handsome, though it was the divil's own mirror we
had beyond, would twist a squint across an angel's brow; and I'll
be growing fine from this day, the way I'll have a soft lovely skin
on me and won't be the like of the clumsy young fellows do be
ploughing all times in the earth and dung. *(He starts.)* Is she coming again? *(He looks out.)* Stranger girls. God help me, where'll I
hide myself away and my long neck naked to the world? *(He
looks out.)* I'd best go to the room maybe till I'm dressed again.
*(He gathers up his coat and the looking-glass, and runs into the*

inner room. The door is pushed open, and Susan Brady looks in, and knocks on door.)

SUSAN: There's nobody in it. (Knocks again.)

NELLY: (Pushing her in and following her, with Honor Blake and Sara Tansey.) It'd be early for them both to be out walking the hill.

SUSAN: I'm thinking Shawn Keogh was making, game of us and there's no such man in it at all.

HONOR: (Pointing to straw and quilt.) Look at that. He's been sleeping there in the night. Well, it'll be a hard case if he's gone off now, the way we'll never set our eyes on a man killed his father, and we after rising early and destroying ourselves running fast on the hill.

NELLY: Are you thinking them's his boots?

SARA: (Taking them up.) If they are, there should be his father's track on them. Did you never read in the papers the way murdered men do bleed and drip?

SUSAN: Is that blood there, Sara Tansey?

SARA: (Smelling it.) That's bog water, I'm thinking, but it's his own they are surely, for I never seen the like of them for whity mud, and red mud, and turf on them, and the fine sands of the sea. That man's been walking, I'm telling you. (She goes down right, putting on one of his boots.)

SUSAN: (Going to window.) Maybe he's stolen off to Belmullet with the boots of Michael James, and you'd have a right so to follow after him, Sara Tansey, and you the one yoked the ass cart and drove ten miles to set your eyes on the man bit the yellow lady's nostril on the northern shore. (She looks out.)

SARA: (Running to window with one boot on.) Don't be talking, and we fooled today. (Putting on other boot.) There's a pair do fit me well, and I'll be keeping them for walking to the priest, when you'd be ashamed this place, going up winter and summer with nothing worth while to confess at all.

HONOR: (Who has been listening at the door.) Whisht! there's someone inside the room. (She pushes door a chink open.) It's a man.
(Sara kicks off boots and puts them where they were. They all stand in a line looking through chink.)

SARA: I'll call him. Mister! Mister!
(He puts in his head.)

SARA: Is Pegeen within?

CHRISTY: *(Coming in as meek as a mouse with the looking-glass held behind his back.)* She's above on the enuceen, seeking the nanny goats, the way she'd have a sup of goat's milk for to color my tea.

SARA: And asking your pardon, is it you's the man killed his father?

CHRISTY: *(Sidling toward the nail where the glass was hanging.)* I am, God help me!

SARA: *(Taking eggs she has brought.)* Then my thousand welcomes to you, and I've run up with a brace of duck's eggs for your food today. Pegeen's ducks is no use, but these are the real rich sort. Hold out your hand and you'll see it's no lie I'm telling you.

CHRISTY: *(Coming forward shyly, and holding out his left hand.)* They're a great and weighty size.

SUSAN: And I run up with a pat of butter, for it'd be a poor thing to have you eating your spuds dry, and you after running a great way since you did destroy your da.

CHRISTY: Thank you kindly.

HONOR: And I brought you a little cut of cake, for you should have a thin stomach on you, and you that length walking the world.

NELLY: And I brought you a little laying pullet—boiled and all she is— was crushed at the fall of night by the curate's car. Feel the fat of that breast, mister.

CHRISTY: It's bursting, surely. *(He feels it with the back of his hand, in which he holds the presents.)*

SARA: Will you pinch it? Is your right hand too sacred for to use at all? *(She slips round behind him.)* It's a glass he has. Well, I never seen to this day a man with a looking-glass held to his back. Them that kills their fathers is a vain lot surely.
*(Girls giggle.)*

CHRISTY: *(Smiling innocently and piling presents on glass.)* I'm very thankful to you all today...

WIDOW QUIN: *(Coming in quickly, at door.)* Sara Tansey, Susan Brady, Honor Blake! What in glory has you here at this hour of day?

GIRLS: *(Giggling.)* That's the man killed his father.

WIDOW QUIN: *(Coming to them.)* I know well it's the man; and I'm after putting him down in the sports below for racing, leaping, pitching, and the Lord knows what.

SARA: *(Exuberantly.)* That's right, Widow Quin. I'll bet my dowry that he'll lick the world.

WIDOW QUIN: If you will, you'd have a right to have him fresh and nourished in place of nursing a feast. *(Taking presents.)* Are you fasting or fed, young fellow?

CHRISTY: Fasting, if you please.

WIDOW QUIN: *(Loudly.)* Well, you're the lot. Stir up now and give him his breakfast. *(To Christy.)* Come here to me...
*(She puts him on bench beside her while the girls make tea and get his breakfast.)*

WIDOW QUIN: ...and let you tell us your story before Pegeen will come, in place of grinning your ears off like the moon of May.

CHRISTY: *(Beginning to be pleased.)* It's a long story; you'd be destroyed listening.

WIDOW QUIN: Don't be letting, on to be shy, a fine, gamey, treacherous lad the like of you. Was it in your house beyond you cracked his skull?

CHRISTY: *(Shy but flattered.)* It was not. We were digging spuds in his cold, sloping, stony, divil's patch of a field.

WIDOW QUIN: And you went asking money of him, or making talk of getting a wife would drive him from his farm?

CHRISTY: I did not, then; but there I was, digging and digging, and "You squinting idiot," says he, "let you walk down now and tell the priest you'll wed the Widow Casey in a score of days."

WIDOW QUIN: And what kind was she?

CHRISTY: *(With horror.)* A walking terror from beyond the hills, and she two score and two hundredweights and five pounds in the weighing scales, with a limping leg on her, and a blinded eye, and she a woman of noted misbehavior with the old and young.

GIRLS: *(Clustering round him, serving him.)* Glory be.

WIDOW QUIN: And what did he want driving you to wed with her? *(She takes a bit of the chicken.)*

CHRISTY: *(Eating with growing satisfaction.)* He was letting on I was wanting a protector from the harshness of the world, and he without a thought the whole while but how he'd have her hut to live in and her gold to drink.

WIDOW QUIN: There's maybe worse than a dry hearth and a widow woman and your glass at night. So you hit him then?

CHRISTY: *(Getting almost excited.)* I did not. "I won't wed her," says I, "when all know she did suckle me for six weeks when I came into the world, and she a hag this day with a tongue on her has the crows and seabirds scattered, the way they wouldn't cast a shadow on her garden with the dread of her curse."

WIDOW QUIN: *(Teasingly.)* That one should be right company.

SARA: *(Eagerly.)* Don't mind her. Did you kill him then?

CHRISTY: "She's too good for the like of you," says he, "and go on now or I'll flatten you out like a crawling beast has passed under a dray." "You will not if I can help it," says I. "Go on," says he, "or I'll have the divil making garters of your limbs tonight." "You will not if I can help it," says I. *(He sits up, brandishing his mug.)*

SARA: You were right surely.

CHRISTY: *(Impressively.)* With that the sun came out between the cloud and the hill, and it shining green in my face. "God have mercy on your soul," says he, lifting a scythe; "or on your own," says I, raising the loy.

SUSAN: That's a grand story.

HONOR: He tells it lovely.

CHRISTY: *(Flattered and confident, waving bone.)* He gave a drive with the scythe, and I gave a lep to the east. Then I turned around with my back to the north, and I hit a blow on the ridge of his skull, laid him stretched out, and he split to the knob of his gullet. *(He raises the chicken bone to his Adam's apple.)*

GIRLS: *(Together.)* Well, you're a marvel! Oh, God bless you! You're the lad surely!

SUSAN: I'm thinking the Lord God sent him this road to make a second husband to the Widow Quin, and she with a great yearning to be wedded, though all dread her here. Lift him on her knee, Sara Tansey.

WIDOW QUIN: Don't tease him.

SARA: *(Going over to dresser and counter very quickly, and getting two glasses and porter.)* You're heroes surely, and let you drink a supeen with your arms linked like the outlandish lovers in the sailor's song. *(She links their arms and gives them the glasses.)* There now. Drink a health to the wonders of the western world, the pirates, preachers, poteen-makers, with the jobbing jockies; parching peelers, and the juries fill their stomachs selling judgments of the English law. *(Brandishing the bottle.)*

WIDOW QUIN: That's a right toast, Sara Tansey. Now Christy.

*(They drink with their arms linked, he drinking with his left hand, she with her right. As they are drinking, Pegeen Mike comes in with a milk can and stands aghast. They all spring away from Christy. He goes down left. Widow Quin remains seated.)*

PEGEEN: *(Angrily, to Sara.)* What is it you're wanting?

SARA: *(Twisting her apron.)* A ounce of tobacco.

PEGEEN: Have you tuppence?

SARA: I've forgotten my purse.

PEGEEN: Then you'd best be getting it and not fooling us here. *(To the Widow Quin, with more elaborate scorn.)* And what is it you're wanting, Widow Quin?

WIDOW QUIN: *(Insolently.)* A penn'orth of starch.

PEGEEN: *(Breaking out.)* And you without a white shift or a shirt in your whole family since the drying of the flood. I've no starch for the like of you, and let you walk on now to Killamuck.

WIDOW QUIN: *(Turning to Christy, as she goes out with the girls.)* Well, you're mighty huffy this day, Pegeen Mike, and, you young fellow, let you not forget the sports and racing when the noon is by. *(They go out.)*

PEGEEN: *(Imperiously.)* Fling out that rubbish and put them cups away. *(Christy tidies away in great haste.)*

PEGEEN: Shove in the bench by the wall.
*(He does so.)*

PEGEEN: And hang that glass on the nail. What disturbed it at all?

CHRISTY: *(Very meekly.)* I was making myself decent only, and this a fine country for young lovely girls.

PEGEEN: *(Sharply.)* Whisht your talking of girls. *(Goes to counter—right.)*

CHRISTY: Wouldn't any wish to be decent in a place...

PEGEEN: Whisht I'm saying.

CHRISTY: *(Looks at her face for a moment with great misgivings, then as a last effort, takes up a loy, and goes towards her, with feigned assurance.)* It was with a loy the like of that I killed my father.

PEGEEN: *(Still sharply.)* You've told me that story six times since the dawn of day.

CHRISTY: *(Reproachfully.)* It's a queer thing you wouldn't care to be hearing it and them girls after walking four miles to be listening to me now.

PEGEEN: *(Turning round astonished.)* Four miles.

CHRISTY: *(Apologetically.)* Didn't himself say there were only four bona fides living in this place?

PEGEEN: It's bona fides by the road they are, but that lot came over the river lepping the stones. It's not three perches when you go like that, and I was down this morning looking on the papers the post-boy does have in his bag. *(With meaning and emphasis.)* For there was great news this day, Christopher Mahon. *(She goes into room left.)*

CHRISTY: *(Suspiciously.)* Is it news of my murder?

PEGEEN: *(Inside.)* Murder, indeed.

CHRISTY: *(Loudly.)* A murdered da?

PEGEEN: *(Coming in again and crossing right.)* There was not, but a story filled half a page of the hanging of a man. Ah, that should be a fearful end, young fellow, and it worst of all for a man who destroyed his da, for the like of him would get small mercies, and when it's dead he is, they'd put him in a narrow grave, with cheap sacking wrapping him round, and pour down quicklime on his head, the way you'd see a woman pouring any frish-frash from a cup.

CHRISTY: *(Very miserably.)* Oh, God help me. Are you thinking I'm safe? You were saying at the fall of night, I was shut of jeopardy and I here with yourselves.

PEGEEN: *(Severely.)* You'll be shut of jeopardy no place if you go talking with a pack of wild girls the like of them to be walking abroad with the peelers, talking whispers at the fall of night.

CHRISTY: *(With terror.)* And you're thinking they'd tell?

PEGEEN: *(With mock sympathy.)* Who knows, God help you.

CHRISTY: *(Loudly.)* What joy would they have to bring hanging to the likes of me?

PEGEEN: It's queer joys they have, and who knows the thing they'd do, if it'd make the green stones cry itself to think of you swaying and swiggling at the butt of a rope, and you with a fine, stout neck, God bless you! the way you'd be a half an hour, in great anguish, getting your death.

CHRISTY: *(Getting his boots and putting them on.)* If there's that terror of them, it'd be best, maybe, I went on wandering like Esau or Cain and Abel on the sides of Neifin or the Erris plain.

PEGEEN: *(Beginning to play with him.)* It would, maybe, for I've heard the Circuit Judges this place is a heartless crew.

CHRISTY: *(Bitterly.)* It's more than Judges this place is a heartless crew. *(Looking up at her.)* And isn't it a poor thing to be starting again and I a lonesome fellow will be looking out on women and girls the way the needy fallen spirits do be looking on the Lord?

# The Weavers

Gerhardt Hauptmann
1898

**Dramatic**

Mother Baumert
Emma
Bertha
Fritz
Ansorge
Frau Heinrich

MOTHER BAUMERT: *(In a pitiful, exhausted voice as the girls leave off their weaving and lean over their looms.)* Do you have to make knots again?

EMMA: *(The elder of the two girls, twenty-two years old; while knotting threads.)* This is sure some yarn!

BERTHA: *(Fifteen years old.)* This warp is giving us trouble, too.

EMMA: Where is he? he left at nine o'clock.

MOTHER BAUMERT: Yes, I know, I know! Don't you know where he could be?

BERTHA: Don't you worry, mother.

MOTHER BAUMERT: It's always a worry to me.

*(Emma goes on with her weaving.)*

BERTHA: Wait a minute, Emma!

EMMA: What's the matter?

BERTHA: I thought I heard a noise like somebody coming.

EMMA: More likely Ansorge coming home.

FRITZ: *(A small barefoot, ragged little boy of four comes in crying.)* Mother, I'm hungry.

EMMA: Wait a while, Fritzy, wait a while! Grandpa'll be here soon. He'll bring some bread with him and some grain.

FRITZ: I'm still hungry, mother!

EMMA: I just told you. Don't be so stupid. He'll be here right away. He'll bring some nice bread with him and some coffee beans.—When work's over, mother'll take the potato peelings and she'll go to the farmer with them, and then he'll give her a nice swallow of milk for her little boy.

FRITZ: Where'd grandpa go?

EMMA: To the factory owner's, to deliver a web, Fritzy.

FRITZ: The factory owner?

EMMA: Yes, Fritzy, yes! Down to Dreissiger's, in Peterswaldau.

FRITZ: That where he gets the bread?

EMMA: Yes, yes, he gets money there, and then he can buy the bread.

FRITZ: Will he get much money?

EMMA: *(Intensely.)* Oh, stop it; boy, with your talking.

*(She goes on weaving like Bertha. Then they both stop again.)*

BERTHA: August, go and ask Ansorge if we could have a little light.

*(August leaves. Fritz goes with him.)*

MOTHER BAUMERT: *(With increasing, childlike fear, almost whining.)* Children, children, where could he be so long?

BERTHA: He probably only dropped in to see Hauffen.

MOTHER BAUMERT: *(Cries.)* I only hope he's not in a tavern.

EMMA: You mustn't cry, mother! Our father's not that kind.

MOTHER BAUMERT: *(Beside herself with a multitude of fears.)* Well, well...well, tell me what will happen if he...if he comes home and...and if he's drunk everything up and don't bring nothing home? There's not a handful of salt in the house, not a piece of bread. We need a shovel of fuel...

BERTHA: Don't worry, mother! The moon's out tonight. We'll take August with us and gather some wood for the fire.

MOTHER BAUMERT: So you can be caught by the forester?

ANSORGE: *(An old weaver with a gigantic body frame, who must bend low to enter the room, sticks his head and upper body through the doorway. His hair and beard are quite unkempt.)* What's the matter here?

BERTHA: You *could* give us some *light!*

ANSORGE: *(In a subdued voice, as though speaking in the presence of a sick person.)* It's light enough here.

MOTHER BAUMERT: Now you even make us sit in the dark.

ANSORGE: I do the best I can. *(He pulls himself out through the door-way.)*

BERTHA: You see there how stingy he is?

EMMA: So now we sit here and wait till he's ready.

FRAU HEINRICH: *(Enters. She is a woman of thirty and pregnant. Her tired face expresses tortuous anxieties and fearful tensions.)* Good evening, everyone.

MOTHER BAUMERT: Well, Mother Heinrich, any news?

FRAU HEINRICH: *(Limping.)* I stepped on a piece of glass.

BERTHA: Come here, then, sit down. I'll see if I can get it out for you. *(Frau Heinrich sits down, while Bertha kneels in front of her and works with the sole of the woman's foot.)*

MOTHER BAUMERT: How are you at home, Mother Heinrich?

FRAU HEINRICH: *(Breaks out in despair.)* It can't go on like this. *(She fights in vain against a torrent of tears. Then she cries silently.)*

MOTHER BAUMERT: It would be better for our kind, Mother Heinrich, if the Good Lord had a little understanding and took us from the world altogether.

FRAU HEINRICH: *(Her self-control gone, she cries out, weeping.)* My poor children are starving! *(She sobs and moans.)* I don't know what to do. You can do what you want, but all you ever do is chase around till you drop. I'm more dead than alive, and still there's no one. Nine hungry mouths I've got to feed, and how will I do it? Last evening I had a little piece of bread, it wasn't even enough for the two littlest. Which one was I to give it to? They all cried out to me: Me, mama, me, mama...No, no! This is what happens when I can still get about. What'll happen the day I can't get up out of bed no more? The flood's washed away the couple potatoes we had. We haven't got bread nor food to eat.

BERTHA: *(Has removed the piece of glass and washed the wound.)* We'll tie a rag around it now. *(To Emma.)* See if you can find one.

MOTHER BAUMERT: It's no better here with us, Mother Heinrich.

FRAU HEINRICH: You still got your girls at least. You got a husband who can work, too. Last week my husband just broke down. He had such a fit and I was so scared to Heaven I didn't know what to do with him. Whenever he has an attack like that he just has to lay in bed for a good eight days.

MOTHER BAUMERT: Mine's not so much better either anymore. He's about to give out, too. It's in his chest and his back. And there's not a pfennig in the house now. If he don't bring a couple of groschen home tonight, I don't know what'll happen.

EMMA: You can believe her, Mother Heinrich. We're so hard up, father had to take Ami along with him. He had to let them butcher him so we could have something solid in our bellies again.

FRAU HEINRICH: Don't you have a handful of flour left over, maybe?

MOTHER BAUMERT: Not even that much, Mother Heinrich; not even a grain of salt left in the house.

FRAU HEINRICH: Well, then, I don't know! *(She rises, remains standing and broods.)* Then I just don't know!—I just can't help it. *(Crying out in rage and fear.)* I'd be happy if we only had pig-swill! But I can't go home with empty hands. I just can't. God forgive me. I just don't know what else there is to do. *(She limps out quickly, stepping on the heel of her left foot.)*

MOTHER BAUMERT: *(Calls after her, warningly.)* Mother Heinrich, Mother Heinrich, you mustn't go and do nothing foolish.

BERTHA: She won't do no harm to herself. Don't you worry.

EMMA: She's always like that. *(She sits down and weaves again for a few seconds.)*

# Medea

Robinson Jeffers
1947

**Scene:** outside the palace

**Dramatic**
Creon
Medea
Nurse
First Woman
Second Woman —Chorus
Third Woman

CREON: I will tell you frankly: because you nourish rancorous ill will toward persons
　　Whom I intend to protect: I send you out before you've time to do harm here. And you are notorious
　　For occult knowledge: sorcery, poisons, magic. Men say you can even sing down the moon from heaven,
　　And make the holy stars to falter and run backward, against the purpose
　　And current of nature. Ha? As to that I know not: I know you are dangerous. You threaten my daughter: you have to go.
MEDEA: But I wish her well, my lord! I wish her all happiness. I hope that Jason may be as kind to her
　　As...to me.
CREON: *(Fiercely.)* That is your wish?
MEDEA: I misspoke. I thought of...old days... *(She seems to weep.)*
CREON: I acknowledge, Medea,
　　That you have some cause for grief. I all the more must guard against your dark wisdom and bitter heart.
MEDEA: You misjudge me cruelly. It is true that I have some knowledge of drugs and medicines: I can sometimes cure sickness:
　　Is that a crime? These dark rumors, my lord,
　　Are only the noise of popular gratitude. You must have observed it often: if any person
　　Knows a little more than the common man, the people suspect him. If he brings a new talent,

How promptly the hateful whispers begin. But you are not a common man, lord of Corinth, you

Will not fear knowledge.

CREON: No. Nor change my decision. I am here to see you leave this
house and the city:

And not much time. Move quickly, gather your things and go. I
pity you, Medea,

But you must go.

MEDEA: You pity me? You...pity me?

*(She comes close to him, wild with rage.)*

I will endure a dog's pity or a wart-grown toad's. May God who
hears me...We shall see in the end

Who's to be pitied.

CREON: *(Shocked, recovering his dignity.)* This is good. This is what I
desire. Unmask the livid face of your hatred

And I see whom I deal with, Serpent and wolf: a wolf from Asia:
I'd rather have you rage now

Than do harm later. Now. Medea: out of here.

Before my men drive you out.

MEDEA: *(Controls her fury, then speaks.)* You see a woman driven half
mad with sorrow, laboring to save

Her little children. No wolf, my lord. And though I was born in
far-off Asia: call that misfortune

Not vice. The races of Asia are human too,

As the bright Greeks are. And our hearts are as brittle: if you hurt
us we cry.

And we have children and love them,

As Greeks do. You have a daughter, sir—

CREON: Yes, and I'll keep her safe of your female hatred: therefore
I send you

Out of this land.

MEDEA: It is not true, I am not jealous, I never hated her.

Jealous for the sake of Jason? I am far past wanting Jason, my
lord. You took him and gave him to her,

And I will say you did well, perhaps wisely. Your daughter is loved
by all: she is beautiful: if I were near her

I should soon love her.

CREON: You can speak sweetly enough, you can make honey in your
mouth like a brown bee

When it serves your turn.

MEDEA: Not honey: the truth.

CREON: Trust you or not, you are going out of this country, Medea.
   What I decide is fixed; it is like the firm rocks of Acrocorinth,
      which neither earthquake can move
   Nor a flood of tears melt. Make ready quickly: I have a guest in
      my house. I should return to him.

THE NURSE: (Comes beside Medea and speaks to her.) What guest? O
      my lady, ask him
   Who is the guest? If powerful and friendly
   He might be a refuge to us in bitter exile...

MEDEA: (Pays no attention to her. Kneels to Creon.)
      I know that your will is granite. But even on the harsh face of
         a granite mountain some flowers of mercy
   May grow in season. Have mercy on my little sons, Creon,
   Though there is none for me.
   (She reaches to embrace his knees. He steps backward from her.)

CREON: How long, woman? This is
   decided; done; finished.

MEDEA: (Rising from her knees, turns half away from him.)
      I am not a beggar.
   I will not trouble you. I shall not live long.
   (She turns to him again.)
   Sire: grant me a few hours yet, one day to prepare in, one little day
   Before I go out of Corinth forever.

CREON: What? No! I told you. The day is today, Medea, this day.
   And the hour is now.

MEDEA: There are no flowers on this mountain: not one violet, not one
      anemone.
   Your face, my lord, is like flint.—If I could find the right words, if
      some god would lend me a touch of eloquence,
   I'd show you my heart. I'd lift it out of my breast and turn it over
      in my hands, you'd see how pure it is
   Of any harm or malice toward you or your household. (She holds
      out her hands to him.) Look at it: not a speck: look, my lord.
      They call mercy
   The jewel of kings. I am praying
   To you as to one of the gods: destroy us not utterly. To go out
      with no refuge, nothing prepared,

Is plain death: I would rather kill myself quickly and here.
    If I had time but to ask the slaves
And strolling beggars where to go, how to live: and I must gather
    some means: one or two jewels
And small gold things I have, to trade them for bread and goat's
    milk. Wretched, wretched, wretched I am,
I and my boys. *(She kneels again.)* I beseech you Creon,
By the soft yellow hair and cool smooth forehead and the
    white knees
Of that young girl who is now Jason's bride: lend me this inch of
    time: one day—half a day,
For this one is now half gone—and I will go my sad course and
    vanish in the morning quietly as dew
That drops on the stones at dawn and is dry as sunrise. You will
    never again be troubled by any word
Or act of mine. And this I pray you for your dear child's sake.
    Oh Creon, what is half a day
In all the rich years of Corinth?
CREON: I will think of it. I am no tyrant.
    I have been merciful to my own hurt, many times. Even to myself
    I seem to be foolish
If I grant you this thing…No, Medea,
I will not grant it.
*(She has been kneeling with bowed head. Silently she raises her
    imploring face toward him.)*
CREON: Well…We shall watch you: as a hawk does a viper. What harm
    could she do
In the tail of one day? A ruler ought to be ruthless, but I am not.
    I am a fool
In my own eyes, whatever the world may think. I can be gruff
    with warriors, a woman weeping
Floods me off course.—Take it, then. Make your preparations.
But if tomorrow's sun shines on you here—Medea, you die…
    Enough words. Thank me not. I want my hands
Washed of this business.
*(He departs quickly, followed by his men. Medea rises from her
    knees.)*
MEDEA: I will thank you.
    And the whole world will hear of it.

FIRST WOMAN: I have seen this man's arrogance, I watched and heard him.
　　I am of Corinth, and I say that Corinth
　　Is not well ruled.
SECOND WOMAN: The city where even a woman, even a foreigner,
　　Suffers unjustly the rods of power
　　Is not well ruled.
FIRST WOMAN: Unhappy Medea, what haven, what sanctuary, where will you wander?
　　Which of the gods, Medea,
　　Drives you through waves of woe, the mooring broken, the hawsers and the anchor-head,
　　Hopeless from harbor?
MEDEA: ...This man...this barking dog...this gulled fool...gods of my father's country,
　　You saw me low on my knees before the great dog of Corinth; humble, holding my heart in my hands
　　For a dog to bite—break this dog's teeth!
　　Women: it is a bitter thing to be a woman
　　A woman is weak for warfare, she must use cunning. Men boast their battles: I tell you this, and we know it:
　　It is easier to stand in battle three times, in the front line, in the stabbing fury, than to bear one child.
　　And a woman, they say, can do no good but in childbirth. It may be so. She can do evil, she can do evil.
　　I wept before that tall dog, I wept my tears before him, I degraded my knees to him, I gulled and flattered him:
　　O triple fool, he has given me all that I needed: a little time, a space of time. Death is dearer to me
　　Than what I am now; and if today by sunset the world has not turned, and turned sharp too—let your dog Creon
　　Send two or three slaves to kill me and a cord to strangle me: I will stretch out
　　My throat to it. But I have a bitter hope, women I begin to see light
　　Through the dark wood, between the monstrous trunks of the trees, at the end of the tangled forest an eyehole,
　　A pin-point of light: I shall not die perhaps.

As a pigeon dies. Nor like an innocent lamb, that feels a hand on
    its head and looks up from the knife
To the man's face and dies.—No, like some yellow-eyed beast
    that has killed its hunters let me lie down
On the hounds' bodies and the broken spears.—Then how to
    strike them? What means to use? There are so many
Doors through which painful death may glide in and catch...
    Which one, which one?

*(She stands meditating. The Nurse comes from behind her and
speaks to the First Woman of the chorus.)*

THE NURSE: Tell me: do you know what guest
    Is in Creon's house?

FIRST WOMAN: What?—Oh. An Athenian ship came from the north last
    night: it is Aegeus,
    The lord of Athens.

THE NURSE: Aegeus! My lady knows him: I believe he will help us. Some
    god has brought him here,
    Some savior god.

FIRST WOMAN: He is leaving, I think, today.

THE NURSE: *(Hobbling back toward Medea.)* My lady! Lord Aegeus
    Is here in Corinth, Creon's guest. Aegeus of Athens.

    *(Medea looks at her silently without attention.)*

THE NURSE: If you will see him and speak him fairly,
    We have a refuge.

MEDEA: I have things in my hand to do. Be quiet.

THE NURSE: Oh, listen to me!
    You are driven out of Corinth, you must find shelter. Aegeus of
    Athens is here.

    *(Medea turns from her and moves to re-enter the house. The
    Nurse catches at her clothing, servile but eager, slave and
    mother at the same time.)*

MEDEA: *(Angrily turning on her.)* What's that to me?

THE NURSE: I lifted you in my arms when you were...this long. I gave
    you milk from these breasts, that are now dead leaves.
    I saw the little beautiful body straighten and grow tall:
    Oh...child...almost my child...how can I
    Not try to save you? Life is better than death—

MEDEA: Not now.

THE NURSE: Time's running out!

MEDEA: I have time.

    Oh, I have time.

    It would be good to sit here a thousand years and think of nothing

    But the deaths of three persons.

THE NURSE: Ai! There's no hope then.

    Ai, child, if you could do this red thing you dream of, all Corinth

    Would pour against you.

MEDEA: After my enemies are punished and

    I have heard the last broken moan—Corinth?

    What's that? I'll sleep. I'll sleep well. I am alone against all; and
        so weary

    That it is pitiful.

    *(The Nurse stands wringing her hands. Medea goes slowly up to
        the door of the house. Some of the Corinthian women are
        watching her; others gaze into the distance.)*

FIRST WOMAN: Look: who is coming? I see the sunlight glitter on
        lanceheads.

SECOND WOMAN: Oh, it is Jason!

THIRD WOMAN: Jason! Medea's worst enemy, who should have been
    Her dearest protector.

# Ondine

Jean Giraudoux
Translated by Maurice Valency
1951

**Dramatic**
**Scene:** a guest house deep in the woods

Eugenie
Hans
Auguste
The Ondine
Second Ondine
Third Ondine

HANS: Good night. Good night.
> (*Auguste and Eugenie go out. Hans sits down by the fire and closes his eyes for a moment. The wall of the hut slowly becomes transparent and through it appear the lake and the forest. In the half-light there rises the figure of an Ondine, blonde and nude.*)

THE ONDINE: Take me, handsome knight.
HANS: (*Looking up with a start.*) What?
THE ONDINE: Kiss me.
HANS: I beg pardon?
THE ONDINE: Take me. Kiss me.
HANS: What are you talking about?
THE ONDINE: Am I too bold, handsome knight? Do I frighten you?
HANS: Not in the least.
THE ONDINE: Would you rather I were clothed? Shall I put on a dress?
HANS: A dress? What for?
THE ONDINE: Come to me. Take me. I am yours. (*She vanishes.*)
> (*Another Ondine appears. She is dark and clothed.*)

THE SECOND ONDINE: Don't look at me, handsome knight.
HANS: Why not?
THE SECOND ONDINE: Don't come near me. I'm not that sort. If you touch me, I'll scream.
HANS: Don't worry.
THE SECOND ONDINE: If you touch my hair, if you touch my breasts, if you kiss my lips, I swear, I'll kill myself. I will not take off my dress!

HANS: As you please.

THE SECOND ONDINE: Don't come out, handsome knight. Don't come near me. I am not for you, handsome knight. *(She vanishes.)* *(Hans shrugs his shoulders. The two Ondines appear together at opposite sides of the room.)*

THE FIRST ONDINE: Take me.

THE SECOND ONDINE: Don't touch me.

THE FIRST ONDINE: I am yours.

THE SECOND ONDINE: Keep your distance.

THE FIRST ONDINE: I want you.

THE SECOND ONDINE: You frighten me.—

THE ONDINE: *(Appears suddenly.)* Oh how silly you look, both of you! *(The two Ondines vanish.)*

HANS: *(Takes Ondine in his arms.)* Little Ondine! What is this nonsense? Who are those women?

THE ONDINE: My friends. They don't want me to love you. They say anyone can have you for the asking. But they're wrong.

HANS: They're very nice, your friends. Are those the prettiest?

THE ONDINE: The cleverest. Kiss me, Hans.

THE FIRST ONDINE: *(Reappears.)* Kiss me, Hans—

THE ONDINE: Look at that fool! Oh, how silly a woman looks when she offers herself! Go away! Don't you know when you've lost? Hans—

THE SECOND ONDINE: *(Appears again next to the first.)* Hans—

THE ONDINE: Go away, I say! Hans—

A THIRD ONDINE: *(Appears next to the others.)* Hans—

THE ONDINE: It's not fair! No!

HANS: Let them speak, Ondine.

THE ONDINE: No. It's the Song of the Three Sisters. I'm afraid.

HANS: Afraid? Of them?

THE ONDINE: Cover your ears, Hans.

HANS: But I love music.

THE FIRST ONDINE: *(Sings.)* Hans Wittenstein zu Wittenstein,
Without you life is but a fever.
Alles was ist mein ist dein,
Love me always, leave me never.

HANS: Bravo! That's charming.

THE ONDINE: In what way is that charming?

HANS: It's simple. It's direct. It's charming. The song of the sirens must have been about like that.

THE ONDINE: It was exactly like that. They copied it. They're going to sing again. Don't listen.

THE THREE ONDINES: *(Sing.)* Heed no more the west wind's urging,
Slack your sail and rest your oar.
Drift upon the current surging
Powerfully toward our shore.

HANS: The tune is not bad.

THE ONDINE: Don't listen, Hans.

THE THREE ONDINES: *(Sing.)* Sorrow once for all forsaking,
Take our laughter for your sighs.
These are yours but for the taking,
Tender breasts and wanton thighs.

THE ONDINE: If you think it's pleasant to hear others singing the things one feels and can't express…

THE THREE ONDINES: *(Sing.)* Come and take your fill of pleasure,
Taste delight and drink it deep.
We shall give you beyond measure
Joy and rest and love and sleep.

HANS: That's wonderful! Sing it again! Sing it again!

THE ONDINE: Don't you understand? They don't mean a word of it. They're just trying to take you away from me.

THE FIRST ONDINE: You've lost, Ondine, you've lost!

HANS: What have you lost?

THE ONDINE: Your song means nothing to him!

THE FIRST ONDINE: He holds you in his arms, Ondine, but he looks at me!

THE SECOND ONDINE: He speaks your name, Ondine, but he thinks of me!

THE THIRD ONDINE: He kisses your lips, Ondine, but he smiles at me!

THE THREE ONDINES: He deceives you! He deceives you! He deceives you!

HANS: What are they talking about?

THE ONDINE: He may look at you and smile at you and think of you as much as he pleases. He loves me. And I shall marry him.

THE FIRST ONDINE: Then you agree? You make the pact?

HANS: What pact?

THE ONDINE: Yes. I agree. I make the pact.
*(The words are taken up mysteriously. They echo and re-echo from every quarter.)*

THE FIRST ONDINE: I am to tell them?

THE ONDINE: Yes. Tell them. Tell them all. Those who sit and those who swim, those who float in the sunlight and those who crawl in darkness on the ocean floor.

HANS: What the devil are you saying?

THE ONDINE: Tell them I said yes.

*(The word* yes *is taken up by a thousand whispering voices.)*

THE FIRST ONDINE: And the Old One? Shall we tell him also?

THE ONDINE: Tell him I hate him! Tell him he lies!

THE FIRST ONDINE: Yes?

THE ONDINE: Yes! Yes! Yes!

*(Again the sound is taken up. The mysterious voices whisper through the darkness until the air is filled with echoes. There is a climax of sound, then silence. The Ondines vanish. The walls of the hut regain their solidity.)*

HANS: What a fuss! What a racket!

THE ONDINE: Naturally. It's the family.

*(Hans sits in the arm chair. Ondine sits at his feet.)*

THE ONDINE: You're caught, my little Hans?

HANS: Body and soul.

THE ONDINE: You don't wish to struggle a little more? Just a little more?

HANS: I'm too happy to struggle.

THE ONDINE: So it takes twenty minutes to catch a man. It takes longer to catch a bass.

HANS: Don't flatter yourself. It took thirty years to catch me. All my life. Ever since I was a child, I've felt something drawing me toward this forest and this lake. It was you?

THE ONDINE: Yes. And now after thirty years, would it be too much if you told me at last that you love me?

HANS: I love you.

THE ONDINE: You say it easily. You've said it before.

HANS: I've said something like it that meant something else.

THE ONDINE: You've said it often?

HANS: I've said it to every woman I didn't love. And now at last I know what it means.

THE ONDINE: Why didn't you love them? Were they ugly?

HANS: No. They were beautiful. But they no longer exist.

THE ONDINE: Oh, Hans, I meant to give you everything in the world, and I begin by taking everything away. Some day you will hate me for it.

HANS: Never, Ondine.

THE ONDINE: Shall I ever see them, these women you don't love?

HANS: Of course.

THE ONDINE: Where?

HANS: Everywhere. In their castles. In their gardens. At the court.

THE ONDINE: At the court? I?

HANS: Of course. We leave in the morning.

THE ONDINE: Oh, Hans, am I to leave my lake so soon?

HANS: I want to show the world the most perfect thing it possesses. Did you know you were the most perfect thing the world possessed?

THE ONDINE: I suspected it. But will the world have eyes to see it?

HANS: When the world sees you, it will know. It's really very nice, Ondine, the world.

THE ONDINE: Tell me, Hans. In this world of yours, do lovers live together always?

HANS: Together? Of course.

THE ONDINE: No. You don't understand. When a man and a woman love each other are they ever separate?

HANS: Separate? Of course.

THE ONDINE: No, you still don't understand. Take the dogfish, for instance. Not that I'm especially fond of dogfish, mind you. But, once the dogfish couples with its mate, he never leaves her, never as long as he lives, did you know that? Through storm and calm they swim together, thousands and thousands of miles, side by side, two fingers apart, as if an invisible link held them together. They are no longer two. They become one.

HANS: Well?

THE ONDINE: Do lovers live like that in your world?

HANS: It would be a little difficult for lovers to live like that in our world, Ondine. In our world, each has his own life, his own room, his own friends—

THE ONDINE: What a horrible word that is, each.

HANS: Each has his work—his play—

THE ONDINE: But the dogfish too have their work and their play. They have to hunt, you know, in order to live. And sometimes they come upon a school of herrings which scatter before them in a thousand flashes, and they have a thousand reasons to lose each other, to swerve one to the right, the other to the left. But they never do. As long as they live, not even a sardine can come between them.

HANS: In our world, Ondine, a whale can come between a husband and wife twenty times a day, no matter how much they love each other.

THE ONDINE: I was afraid of that.

HANS: The man looks to his affairs, the woman to hers. They swim in different currents.

THE ONDINE: But the dogfish have to swim through different currents also. There are cold currents and warm currents. And sometimes the one likes the cold and the other the warm. And sometimes they swim into currents so powerful that they can divide a fleet, and yet they cannot divide these fish by the breadth of a nail.

HANS: That merely proves that men and fish are not the same.

THE ONDINE: And you and I, we are the same?

HANS: Oh yes, Ondine.

THE ONDINE: And you swear that you will never leave me, not even for a moment?

HANS: Yes, Ondine.

THE ONDINE: Because now that I love you, two steps away from you my loneliness begins.

HANS: I will never leave you, Ondine.

THE ONDINE: Hans, listen to me seriously. I know someone who can join us forever, someone very powerful. And if I ask him, he will solder us together with a band of flesh so that nothing but death can separate us. Would you like me to call him?

HANS: No, Ondine.

THE ONDINE: But, Hans, the more I think of it, the more I see there is no other way to keep lovers together in your world.

HANS: And your dogfish? Do they need to be soldered like that?

THE ONDINE: It's true. But they don't live among men. Let me call him. You'll see. It's a very practical arrangement.

HANS: No. Let's try this way first. Later, we'll see.

THE ONDINE: I know what you're thinking. Of course, she's right, you're thinking, the little Ondine, and naturally I shall be with her always, but once in a while, for just a little moment perhaps I shall go and take a turn by myself, I shall go and visit my friend.

HANS: Or my horse.

THE ONDINE: Or your horse. When this angel falls asleep, you're thinking, this angel whom I shall never leave not even for a moment, then, at last, I shall have a chance to go and spend a good half hour with my horse.

HANS: As a matter of fact, I had better go and have a look at him now, don't you think? We're leaving at dawn, you know, and I ought to see if he's bedded properly. Besides I always tell him every-thing.

THE ONDINE: Ah yes. Well, tonight you shall tell him nothing.

HANS: But why, Ondine?

THE ONDINE: Because tonight you're going to sleep, my little Hans. *(And with a gesture, she throws sleep into his eyes.)* Good night, my love. *(He falls asleep.)*

THE FIRST ONDINE: *(Her voice seems very far away.)* Good-bye, Ondine.

THE ONDINE: Look after my lake!

THE SECOND ONDINE: Good-bye, Ondine.

# The Wedding Band
Alice Childress
1973

**Dramatic**
**Scene:** Summer 1918, South Carolina. In the yard (and then the bungalow) of Julia, mutually shared with several other bungalows... dirt...a porch

Julia
Herman's mother
Lula
Fanny
Annabelle
Herman
Nelson

JULIA: Oh, Miss Lula.
LULA: Anyway, he didn't say nothin'.
  *(Herman's mother enters the yard. She is a "poor white" about fifty-seven years old. She has risen above her poor farm background and tries to assume the airs of "quality." Her clothes are well-kept-shabby. She wears white shoes, a shirtwaist and skirt, drop earrings, a cameo brooch, a faded blue straw hat with a limp bit of veiling. She carries a heavy black oilcloth bag. All in the yard give a step backward as she enters. She assumes an air of calm well-being. Almost as though visiting friends, but anxiety shows around the edges and underneath. Julia approaches and Herman's Mother abruptly turns to Mattie.)*
HERMAN'S MOTHER: How do.
  *(Mattie, Teeta and Princess look at Herman's Mother. Herman's Mother is also curious about them.)*
MATTIE: *(In answer to a penetrating stare from the old woman.)* She's mine. I take care-a her. *(Speaking her defiance by ordering the children.)* Stay inside 'fore y'all catch the flu!
HERMAN'S MOTHER: *(To Lula.)* You were very kind to bring word...er...
LULA: Lula, ma'am.
HERMAN'S MOTHER: The woman who nursed my second cousin's children...she had a name like that...Lulu we called her.

LULA: My son, Nelson.

HERMAN'S MOTHER: Can see that.

*(Mattie and the children exit. Fanny hurries in from the front entry. Is most eager to establish herself on the good side of Herman's Mother. With a slight bow. She is carrying the silver tea service.)*

FANNY: Beg pardon, if I may be so bold, I'm Fanny, the owner of all this property.

HERMAN'S MOTHER: *(Definitely approving of Fanny.)* I'm...er...Miss Annabelle's mother.

FANNY: My humble pleasure...er...Miss...er...

HERMAN'S MOTHER: *(After a brief, thoughtful pause.)* Miss Thelma.

*(They move aside, but Fanny makes sure others hear.)*

FANNY: Miss Thelma, this is not Squeeze-gut Alley. We're just poor, humble, colored people...and everybody knows how to keep their mouth shut.

HERMAN'S MOTHER: I thank you.

FANNY: She wanted to get a doctor. I put my foot down.

HERMAN'S MOTHER: You did right. *(Shaking her head, confiding her troubles.)* Ohhhh, you don't know.

FANNY: *(With deep understanding.)* Ohhhh, yes, I do. She moved in on me yesterday.

HERMAN'S MOTHER: Friend Fanny, help me to get through this.

FANNY: I will. Now this is Julia, she's the one...

*(Herman's Mother starts toward the house without looking at Julia. Fanny decides to let the matter drop.)*

HERMAN'S MOTHER: *(To Lula.)* Tell Uncle Greenlee not to worry. He's holdin' the horse and buggy.

NELSON: *(Bars Lula's way.)* Mama. I'll do it.

*(Lula exits into her house. Fanny leads Herman's Mother to the chair near Herman's bed.)*

ANNABELLE: Mama, if we don't call a doctor Herman's gonna die.

HERMAN'S MOTHER: Everybody's gon' die. Just a matter of when, where and how. A pretty silver service.

FANNY: English china. Belgian linen. Have a cup-a tea?

HERMAN'S MOTHER: *(As a studied pronouncement.)* My son comes to deliver baked goods and the influenza strikes him down. Sickness, it's the war.

FANNY: *(Admiring her cleverness.)* Yes, ma'am, I'm a witness. I saw him with the packages.

JULIA: Now please call the doctor.

ANNABELLE: Yes, please, Mama. No way for him to move 'less we pick him up bodily.

HERMAN'S MOTHER: Then we'll pick him up.

HERMAN: About Walter...your Walter...I'm sorry...

*(Julia tries to give Herman some water.)*

HERMAN'S MOTHER: Annabelle, help your brother.

*(Annabelle gingerly takes glass from Julia.)*

HERMAN'S MOTHER: Get that boy to help us. I'll give him a dollar. Now gather his things.

ANNABELLE: What things?

HERMAN'S MOTHER: His possessions, anything he owns, whatever is his. What you been doin' in here all this time?

*(Fanny notices Julia is about to speak, so she hurries her through the motions of going through dresser drawers and throwing articles into a pillowcase.)*

FANNY: Come on, sugar, make haste.

JULIA: Don't go through my belongings.

*(She tears through the drawers, flinging things around as she tries to find his articles. Fanny neatly piles them together.)*

FANNY: *(Taking inventory.)* Three shirts...one is kinda soiled.

HERMAN'S MOTHER: That's all right, I'll burn 'em.

FANNY: Some new undershirts.

HERMAN'S MOTHER: I'll burn them too.

JULIA: *(To Fanny.)* Put 'em down. I bought 'em and they're not for burnin'.

HERMAN'S MOTHER: *(Struggling to hold her anger in check.)* Fanny, go get that boy. I'll give him fifty cents.

FANNY: You said a dollar.

HERMAN'S MOTHER: All right, dollar it is.

*(Fanny exits toward the front entry. In tense, hushed, excited tones, they argue back and forth.)*

HERMAN'S MOTHER: Now where's the billfold...there's papers...identity...

*(Looks in Herman's coat pockets.)*

ANNABELLE: Don't make such a to-do.

HERMAN'S MOTHER: You got any money of your own? Yes, I wanta know where's his money.

JULIA: I'm gettin' it.

HERMAN'S MOTHER: In her pocketbook. This is why the bakery can't make it.

HERMAN: I gave her the Gawd-damned money!

JULIA: And I know what Herman wants me to do…

HERMAN'S MOTHER: (With a wry smile.) I'm sure you know what he wants.

JULIA: I'm not gonna match words with you. Furthermore, I'm too much of a lady.

HERMAN'S MOTHER: A lady oughta learn how to keep her dress down.

ANNABELLE: Mama, you makin' a spectacle outta yourself.

HERMAN'S MOTHER: You a big simpleton. Men have nasty natures, they can't help it. A man would go with a snake if he only knew how. They cleaned out your wallet.

HERMAN: (Shivering with a chill.) I gave her the damn money.
(Julia takes it from her purse.)

HERMAN'S MOTHER: Where's your pocket-watch, or did you give that too? Annabelle, get another lock put on that bakery door.

HERMAN: I gave her the money to go—to go to New York.
(Julia drops the money in Herman's Mother lap. She is silent for a moment.)

HERMAN'S MOTHER: All right. Take it and go. It's never too late to undo a mistake. I'll add more to it. (She puts the money on the dresser.)

JULIA: I'm not goin' anywhere.

HERMAN'S MOTHER: Look here, girl, you leave him 'lone.

ANNABELLE: Oh, Mama, all he has to do is stay away.

HERMAN'S MOTHER: But he can't do it. Been years and he can't do it.

JULIA: I got him hoo-dooed, I sprinkle red pepper on his shirttail.

HERMAN'S MOTHER: I believe you.

HERMAN: I have a black woman…and I'm gon' marry her. I'm gon' marry her…got that? Pride needs a paper, for…for the sake of herself…that's dignity—tell me, what is dignity—Higher than the dirt it is…dignity is…
Oh, Mama, all he has to do is stay away.
Let's take him to the doctor, Mama.

HERMAN'S MOTHER: When it's dark.

JULIA: Please!

HERMAN'S MOTHER: Nightfall.

*(Julia steps out on the porch but hears every word said in the room.)*

HERMAN'S MOTHER: I had such high hopes for him. *(As if Herman is dead.)* All my high hopes. When he wasn't but five years old I had to whip him so he'd study his John C. Calhoun speech. Oh, Calhoun knew 'bout niggers. He said, *"Men* are not born...equal, or any other kinda way...MEN are *made"*...Yes, indeed, for recitin' that John C. Calhoun speech...Herman won first mention and a twenty-dollar gold piece...at the Knights of The Gold Carnation picnic.

ANNABELLE: Papa changed his mind about the Klan. I'm glad.

HERMAN'S MOTHER: Yes, he was always changin' his mind about somethin'. But I was proud-a my menfolk that day. He spoke that speech...The officers shook my hand. They honored me..."That boy a-yours gonna be somebody." A poor baker-son layin' up with a nigger woman, a overgrown daughter in heat over a common sailor. I must be payin' for somethin' I did. Yesiree, do a wrong, God'll whip you.

ANNABELLE: I wish it was dark.

HERMAN'S MOTHER: I put up with a man breathin' stale whiskey in my face every night ... pullin' and pawin' at me...always tired, inside and out... *(Deepest confidence she has ever shared.)* Gave birth to seven...five-a them babies couldn't draw breath.

ANNABELLE: *(Suddenly wanting to know more about her.)* Did you love Papa, Mama? Did you ever love him?...

HERMAN'S MOTHER: Don't ask me 'bout love...I don't know nothin' about it. Never mind love. This is my harvest.

HERMAN: Go home. I'm better.

*(Herman's mother's strategy is to enlighten Herman and also wear him down. Out on the porch, Julia can hear what is being said in the house.)*

HERMAN'S MOTHER: There's something wrong 'bout mismatched things, be they shoes, socks, or people.

HERMAN: Go away, don't look at us.

HERMAN'S MOTHER: People don't like it. They're not gonna letcha do it in peace.

HERMAN: We'll go North.

HERMAN'S MOTHER: Not a thing will change except her last name.

HERMAN: She's not like others...she's not like that...

HERMAN'S MOTHER: All right, sell out to Schumann. I want my cash-money… You got no feelin' for me, I got none for you.

HERMAN: I feel…I feel what I feel…I don't know what I feel…

HERMAN'S MOTHER: Don't need to feel. Live by the law. Follow the law—law, law of the land. Obey the law!

ANNABELLE: We're not obeyin' the law. He should be quarantined right here. The city's tryin' to stop an epidemic.

HERMAN'S MOTHER: Let the city drop dead and you long with it. Rather be dead than disgraced. Your papa gimme the house and little money…I want my money back. *(She tries to drag Herman up in the bed.)* I ain't payin' for this. *(Shoves Annabelle aside.)* Let Schumann take over. A man who knows what he's doin'. Go with her… Take the last step against your own! Kill us all. Jesus, Gawd, save us or take us—

HERMAN: *(Screams.)* No! No! No! No!

HERMAN'S MOTHER: Thank Gawd, the truth is the light. Oh, Blessed Savior…
*(Herman screams out, starting low and ever going higher. She tries to cover his mouth. Annabelle pulls her hand away.)* Thank you, Gawd, let the fire go out…this awful fire.
*(Lulu and Nelson enter the yard.)*

ANNABELLE: You chokin' him. Mama…

JULIA: *(From the porch.)* It's dark! It's dark. Now it's very dark.

HERMAN: One ticket on the Clyde Line…Julia…where are you? Keep singing…count…one, two…three. Over there, over there…send the word, send the word…

HERMAN'S MOTHER: Soon be home, son.
*(Herman breaks away from the men, staggers to Mattie's porch and holds on. Mattie smothers a scream and gets the children out of the way. Fanny enters.)*

HERMAN: Shut the door…don't go out…the enemy…the enemy… *(Recites the Calhoun speech.)* Men are not born infants are born! They grow to all the freedom of which the condition in which they were born permits. It is a great and dangerous error to suppose that all people are equally entitled to liberty.

JULIA: Go home— Please be still.

HERMAN: It is a reward to be earned, a reward reserved for the intelligent, the patriotic, the virtuous and deserving; and not a boon to be bestowed on a poeple too ignorant, degraded and vicious…

JULIA: You be stil now, shut up.

HERMAN: ...to be capable either of appreciating or of enjoying it.

JULIA: *(Covers her ears.)* Take him...

HERMAN: A black woman...not like the others...

JULIA: ...outta my sight...

HERMAN: Julia, the ship is sinking...

*(Herman's mother and Nelson help Herman up and out.)*

ANNABELLE: *(To Julia on the porch.)* I'm sorry...so sorry it had to be this way. I can't leave with you thinkin' I uphold Herman, and blame you.

HERMAN'S MOTHER: *(Returning.)* You the biggest fool.

ANNABELLE: I say a man is responsible for his own behavior.

HERMAN'S MOTHER: And you, you oughta be locked up...workhouse... jail! Who you think you are!?

JULIA: I'm your damn daughter-in-law, you old bitch! The Battleship Bitch! The bitch who destroys with her filthy mouth. They could win the war with your killin' mouth. The son-killer, man-killer-bitch... She's killin' him 'cause he loved me more than anybody in the world.

*(Fanny returns.)*

HERMAN'S MOTHER: Better off... He's better off dead in his coffin than live with the likes-a you...black thing! *(She is almost backing into Julia's house.)*

JULIA: The black thing who bought a hot-water bottle to put on your sick, white self when rheumatism threw you flat on your back... who bought flannel gowns to warm your pale, mean body. He never ran up and down King Street shoppin' for you...I bought what he took home to you...

HERMAN'S MOTHER: Lies... tear outcha lyin' tongue.

JULIA: ...the lace curtains in your parlor...the shirtwaist you wearin' — I made them.

FANNY: Go on...I got her. *(Holds Julia.)*

HERMAN'S MOTHER: Leave 'er go! The undertaker will have-ta unlock my hands off her black throat!

FANNY: Go on, Miss Thelma.

JULIA: Miss Thelma my ass! Her first name is Frieda. The Germans are here...in purple paint!

HERMAN'S MOTHER: Black, sassy nigger!

JULIA: Kraut, knuckle-eater, redneck...

HERMAN'S MOTHER: Nigger whore…he used you for a garbage pail…

JULIA: White trash! Sharecropper! Let him die…let 'em all die…Kill him with your murderin' mouth—sharecropper bitch!

HERMAN'S MOTHER: Dirty black nigger…

JULIA: …If I wasn't black with all-a Carolina 'gainst me I'd be mistress of your house! *(To Annabelle.)* Annabelle, you'd be married livin' in Brooklyn, New York… *(To Herman's mother.)* …and I'd be waitin' on Frieda…cookin' your meals…waterin' that damn red, white, and blue garden!

HERMAN'S MOTHER: Dirty black bitch.

JULIA: Daughter of a bitch!

ANNABELLE: Leave my mother alone! She's old…and sick.

JULIA: But never sick enough to die…dirty ever-lasting woman.

HERMAN'S MOTHER: *(Clinging to Annabelle, she moves toward the front entry.)* I'm as high over you as Mount Everest over the sea. White reigns supreme…I'm white, you can't change that.
*(They exit. Fanny goes with them.)*

JULIA: Out! Out! Out! And take the last ten years-a my life with you and…when he gets better…keep him home. Killers, murderers…Kinsmen! Klansmen! Keep him home. *(To Mattie.)* Name and protection… he can't gimme either one. *(To Lulu.)* I'm gon' get down on my knees and scrub where they walked…what they touched… *(To Mattie.)* …with brown soap…hot lye-water… scaldin' hot… *(She dashes into the house and collects an armful of bedding.)* Clean!… Clean the whiteness outta my house… clean everything…even the memory…no more love… Free… free to hate-cha for the rest-a my life. *(Back to the porch with her arms full.)* When I die I"m gonna keep on hatin'…I don't want any whiteness in my house. Stay out…out… *(Dumps the things in the yard.)*…out…out…out…and leave me to my black self! *(Blackout.)*

# Twelve Dreams

James Lapine
1982

**Dramatic**
**Scene:** the study, and then a dream state

Jenny
Emma
Ms. Banton
Rindy
Professor
Putnam
Hatrick

*(Jenny enters the study carrying a silver tray and teapot. She notices Hatrick reading in the dark and turns on his reading light. She then pours him a cup of tea and exits.)*

PROFESSOR: The decoration of lights symbolizes the lighting up of darkness. I like to think that I make a profession of lighting up the darkness...in a manner of speaking, of course. *(Pause. With amusement.)* Well, yes of course, men and women are different in America than in my country, or for that matter all of Europe and the rest of the world. It seems, though, here, if my perceptions are correct, that men and women are directing their greatest energies everywhere except toward their relationships with one another.

*(Jenny reappears on the second floor. She tiptoes into Emma's bedroom and tucks her in. She rearranges a few objects and exits.)*

PROFESSOR: Everyone is always running, here, hardly leaving time to catch one's breath, which of course allows for little introspection and intercourse. *(Pause.)* Why the titters? *(Pause.)* Oh. *(Annoyed.)* Intercourse as in the exchange of ideas. I'm not certain of the other.

*(Music. The back wall of Emma's bedroom is of a scrim material. Slowly lights rise behind it, revealing a ballerina [Banton] on toe. She mechanically dances, as a ballerina in a music box might,*

*twisting back and forth. The Professor pauses to gaze up at her, then turns to respond to the next question.)*

PROFESSOR: Indeed, I do think we give short shrift to our intuitive selves. Like the sedimentary layers of the earth we stand on, so does the human mind contain layers that date back far beyond our own experiences. None of us knows what we really know!

*(Music fades, as do lights, and the ballerina disappears.)*

PROFESSOR: We must shut off our overly trained intellects and get in touch with our other parts. My experiences with the American Indians have been a great factor in my theoretical formulations.

*(Emma rises from her bed, grabs her bird book, and slowly walks from her room, down the stairs, directly to the Professor. She gets to him just as he completes his speech.)*

PROFESSOR: The Indian knows to think with the heart not the head. When the Pueblo Indian meets a stranger, for instance, they ask, "What animal is this?" There was great difficulty in their deciding which animal to assign me. One day I had to climb a ladder to enter one of their structures. Well, I did so—but while the Indians climb up backward, I climbed up in the normal European fashion, facing the ladder. When I did this a great shout came forth. A bear! A bear! *(He laughs.)* They thought I was a bear.

*(He turns and lets out a loud bear roar in Emma's direction. Startled, she backs off, but he continues growling and advances toward her. His noise is joined by the other characters, each of whom enters taking on the likeness and sounds of an animal; Jenny, a billy goat; Banton, a horse. Hatrick remains in his seat as the group converges around Emma. Their animal noises grow in volume and intensity, then suddenly break into a peal of laughter. Hatrick has grabbed a tray with a bottle and glasses and has come behind the group. Trowbridge, Banton, and Rindy make a speedy exit. As the lights come up slowly, Hatrick pours Professor and Putnam drinks. Jenny takes the tray from him and goes to the side with Emma. There is simultaneous conversation that approximates the following.)*

| | |
|---|---|
| HATRICK: Well, I've been saving this sherry for you. | JENNY: It's getting awfully late, young lady. |
| PUTNAM: This is very good sherry, Charles. | EMMA: Oh, Jenny, can't I sit and visit for a little while? |

PROFESSOR: I am flattered, Charles.

HATRICK: This visit of yours has been much too long in the coming.

PUTNAM: This is a rare sight, Professor.

PROFESSOR: Well, I hope I haven't intruded on your holidays in any way.

HATRICK: On the contrary, you're making it a more festive occasion.

JENNY: Emma, you've been up late every night this week.

EMMA: But I'm not tired.

JENNY: All right, but just for a little while longer. And no story, either.

EMMA: Okay, but I really wish I could have a story too.

JENNY: Maybe tomorrow night.

PUTNAM: *(To Jenny.)* Excuse me. Another glass, please. *(Professor and Hatrick sit.)*

PROFESSOR: Well, Charles, this house of yours is certainly decked in the Christmas spirit.

HATRICK: Emma and Jenny manage to escalate our celebration from year to year.

EMMA: *(Goes and sits on Hatrick's lap.)* Daddy doesn't believe in Christmas.

HATRICK: Not exactly, Emma…

PROFESSOR: Well, Christmas seems to be doing wonders for the economy.

HATRICK: Not mine.

*(Professor laughs, perhaps too loudly. Jenny shakes her head and exits.)*

PUTNAM: How did you feel about today's lectures, Professor?

HATRICK: Sanford…

PROFESSOR: Why, Mr. Putnam, I thought they went very well.

PUTNAM: You mean you're not disturbed by the resistance to some of your new thinking? *(He pours himself another drink, then positions himself between the two.)*

PROFESSOR: Not at all, my boy, not at all. It is difficult for some to hear contrary opinions—I guess you might say that a new idea upsets them.

HATRICK: *(Apologetic.)* I just don't think it was quite what the committee had in mind when they invited you.

PUTNAM: Well, how do you respond when some of the doctors at the university suggest your ideas are not within the realm of science?

HATRICK: *(Annoyed.)* Sanford, this is a social visit. Let's not grill the doctor anymore.

PROFESSOR: Hogwash! My ideas and theories are documented from experience. I have never claimed that they came to me by divine revelation. Tell me again your position, Mr. Putnam.

PUTNAM: I am the youngest resident in psychiatry at the clinic and Charles is my adviser.

PROFESSOR: Ah-hah!

PUTNAM: Charles and I were both very interested in your early theories.

HATRICK: And we're still interested in your theories.

# Pressure Defense

Jon Jory
1980s

**Dramatic**
**Scene:** the player's bench of a women's basketball team

Michelle
Sandra
Mary Lou
Jessy
Andrea
'Becca
Coach
Mark


*(The game is in progress and the coach is agitated.)*

MICHELLE: Hubba-hubba! Stick tight! Hubba-hubba!

SANDRA: You mind me asking a question?

MICHELLE: That's two! Way to go! Hubba-hubba!

SANDRA: What does hubba-hubba mean?

MICHELLE: It is a cry of triumph emitted by Berber tribesmen when they catch a chicken buried up to its neck in the sand as they gallop by.

COACH: Don't come out! Stay back. Stay in the zone! Collapse! Collapse!

MARY LOU: He's very excitable for a seminarian.

SANDRA: He can't believe God wants us to have a five and eighteen record.

COACH: Outlet pass, c'mon! What are you doing? Will someone tell me what you're doing?

CAROL: Pretty amazing we're only seven points down.

COACH: Drive the lane, Suzanne!

SANDRA: Did you ever think that when you were nineteen a hunky-looking young minister would be screaming at you to "drive the lane?"

COACH: Way to go. In their face! Way to go.

ANDREA: Wish they'd pull away so I could get in the game.

MICHELLE: What, are you crazy? You rootin' against the team?

ANDREA: I'm not rooting against the team. I would just like to get out on the floor so I don't have to hear you yelling hubba-hubba.

COACH: Stay in her face, Martine. Watch the back door. Zone. Zone! No, on the other side!

MICHELLE: Rebound! Get up in the air! Nuts!

COACH: This is driving me crazy! Watch the press!

MARY LOU: *(To Jessy who sits next to her.)* How's the nose bleed?

JESSY: I think it's broken.

MARY LOU: Really?

JESSY: That's the third time this season.

MARY LOU: You've come a long way, baby.

JESSY: Yeah, I'm very Eighties, but I look like Joe Frazier.

MICHELLE: Hubba-hubba! Turnover! Way to go!

COACH: Set it up. Thirty-six.

ANDREA: *(To the only male player, Mark, next to her.)* So what're you reading?

MARK: *Square Dancing in the Ice Age* by Abbie Hoffman.

ANDREA: Who's he?

MARK: I'm doing a paper on the Sixties.

ANDREA: He'll never put you in. You read on the bench.

MARK: He'll never put me in anyway.

*(Another basket is made by the other team.)*

MICHELLE: Come on. Get hot! Get it back.

*(The Coach sits on the bench, his head in his hands.)*

MARK: I made my point. Anyway, it's the last game.

COACH: *(Despairing.)* Who was that to? What play was that?

ANDREA: How have you made your point if you've never been in a game?

MARK: I integrated the team.

ANDREA: Baloney.

MARK: What baloney?

ANDREA: You're just taking up space. You're not a player. You're taking up space a woman athlete should have.

MICHELLE: Foul her. Foul her! That's right! Three minutes left.

MARK: Let her play on the men's team.

ANDREA: Let her play on the men's team! Get serious. There is nobody on the squad, including 'Becca out there, who could even make the squad.

MARK: That's exactly the kind of sexist attitude that made me do this.

ANDREA: There is a difference between sexism and facts which is eternally lost on you knee-jerk liberals.

SANDRA: No fighting, no biting, kids.

ANDREA: *(Speaking to Mark.)* Sport, in case you hadn't noticed, is based on competition. The administration forced you on us to cool out the idiot controversy you started, which is patronizing and double reverse sexism.

SANDRA: Double reverse sexism? This is a serious charge.

MICHELLE: Will you guys shut up and get into the game?

ANDREA: What game? We're down fourteen points as usual.

MICHELLE: Come on, Coach, tell 'em to knock it off.

COACH: Coaching this team is the psychological equivalent of suicide.

MARK: *(Pointing to Coach.)* What about him? He's taking up space a woman athlete should have.

ANDREA: There were no women applicants.

MARK: Mrs. Hodges.

MARY LOU: Mrs. Hodges is the house mother for the Tri Delts. She is seventy-one years old.

MARK: That's ageism.

ANDREA: She wasn't a real applicant. The girls put her up to it.

MARK: Her application was received.

ANDREA: He knows basketball, she knows hors d'oeuvres. It should be based on quality. And that, my radical friend, would let you out.

COACH: If it's completely based on quality, there should only be one basketball team.

MARY LOU: There's a physiological difference between women and men.

SANDRA: God, Mary Lou. Don't let your fiancé find out.

MARK: So, you're admitting at least a physical male superiority.

MARY LOU: I said difference.

ANDREA: And based on that difference, there should be two teams, and within each of those teams quality should be the measuring stick.

MARK: You know what this is? It's *apartheid!*

SANDRA: Interesting. I started out today in a three-two zone, and I ended up in South Africa.

ANDREA: We cannot have a sport without relatively equal competition. Is it apartheid that welterweights do not fight heavyweights?

MARK: That's not the point. There are no women boxers.

JESSY: Yes there are. I saw them on cable.

MARK: There are no *good* women boxers.

ANDREA: They are perfectly good if they are boxing women!

COACH: *(Unable to bear this.)* Jordan, get over to the timer's table.

MARK: The timer's table?

COACH: You're in for 'Becca.

MARK: I can't play basketball. I'm a Political Science major.

SANDRA: Fidel Castro plays basketball. He's got a great jump-shot.

    *(A buzzer sounds. The Coach slaps Mark on the butt.)*

COACH: The basic idea is to put the little ball through the metal hoop.

    *(Mark runs off.)*

MICHELLE: Hubba-hubba.

    *('Becca, exhausted, enters, runs over to the bench and sits.)*

SANDRA: This is an historic moment. For the first time in Missouri, women and nerds are playing on the same court.

MICHELLE: Good goin', 'Becca baby.

    *(The buzzer sounds.)*

COACH: Times in.

ANDREA: Twenty-three seconds left.

MICHELLE: Defense, get your hands up!

MARY LOU: Stay on her.

ANDREA: Machopower!

COACH: Can you believe that?

MICHELLE: He stole it! Drive.

COACH: That's unbelievable.

ANDREA: Drive, don't look behind you!

    *(A loud ringing sound as a human being collides with a metal pole.)*

MICHELLE: Oh, man!

SANDRA: Idealist meets reality.

COACH: You're supposed to shoot the ball, not run into the pole.

    *(The buzzer sounds.)*

MARY LOU: Is he all right?

JESSY: He's apologizing to the pole.

MICHELLE: Is that a photographer? I think that's a photographer.

SANDRA: Where? Right. Now that's really depressing.

MARY LOU: Why?

SANDRA: We play twenty-four games, like a thousand minutes of basketball, a billion potential images, and the only reporter who ever shows up takes a picture of the one man on the floor running into a basket support.

ANDREA: Poor baby. Is he looking for a contact?

MARY LOU: Actually, I think he's looking for his tooth.

ANDREA: Ouch. Maybe I'll take him out for a coke. Well, we lose by twenty-two. Another day at the office.

COACH: I am the laughing stock of Marymount College. *(He sits on the bench.)*

SANDRA: I wonder if, historically, moments of social significance have always felt this silly to the participants at the time.

MICHELLE: Hubba-hubba, Jordan. Hubba-hubba, Jordan!

ANDREA: You know what, I think on this campus that will always be his name.

*(The lights fade out.)*

# LARGE GROUP SCENES
# WITH A MAJORITY
# OF WOMEN

# The Eumenides

Aeschylus
Translated by John Stuart Blackie
458 B.C.

**Dramatic**

**Scene:** At the shrine of Apollo at Delphi. The priestess of the shrine pays homage to the Earth and the Gods and sets forth the premise of the situation. She has witnessed Orestes surrounded by the sleeping Furies—hideous female creatures in black robes, and they and Apollo are brought forth and paraded before Orestes to exemplify the opposing forces at work within him. The Furies are born of evil and exist to track down evil in the world. and are sometimes described as "the repulsive maidens."

The Chorus Of Eumenides (the Furies), black-robed female creatures who follow Orestes
Clytemnestra, her ghost, the deceased Queen of Argos who murdered Agamemnon, her husband and Orestes' father
Apollo, patron of the Delphic Shrine
The Pythia, an old woman, priestess of Apollo
Orestes, son and murderer of Clytemnestra, in revenge for the murder of his father, King Agamemnon
Hermes accompanies Orestes, silent, a messenger of the gods

THE PYTHONESS: Old Earth, primeval prophetess, I first
    With these my prayers invoke; and Themis next,
    Who doth her mother's throne and temple both
    Inherit, as the legend runs; and third
    In lot's due course, another Earth-born maid
    The unforced homage of the land received,
    Titanian Phoebe; she in natal gift
    With her own name her hoary right bequeathed
    To Phoebus: he from rocky Delos' lake
    To Attica's ship—cruised bays was wafted, whence
    He in Parnassus fixed his sure abode.
    Hither with pious escort they attend him:
    The Sons of Vulcan pioneer his path,
    Smoothing the rugged desert where he comes:

The thronging people own him, and king Delphos,
The land's high helmsman, flings his portals wide.
Jove with divinest skill his heart inspires,
And now the fourth on this dread seat enthroned
Sits Loxias, prophet of his father Jove.
These be the gods, whom chiefly I invoke:
But thee, likewise, who 'fore this temple dwellest,
Pallas, I pray, and you, ye Nymphs that love
The hollow Corycian rock, the frequent haunt
Of pleasant birds, the home of awful gods.
Thee, Bromius, too, I worship, not unweeting
How, led by thee, the furious Thyads rushed
To seize the godless Pentheus, ev'n as a hare
Is dogged to death. And you, the fountains pure
Of Pleistus, and Poseidon's mighty power
I pray, and Jove most high, that crowns all things
With consummation. These the gods that lead me
To the prophetic seat, and may they grant me
Best-omened entrance; may consulting Greeks,
If any be, by custom'd lot approach;
For as the gods my bosom stir, I pour
The fateful answer.
(She goes into the Temple, but suddenly returns.)
O horrid tale to tell! O sight to see
Most horrible! that drives me from the halls
Of Loxias, so that I nor stand nor run,
But, like a beast fourfooted stumble on,
Losing the gait and station of my kind,
A gray-haired woman, weaker than a child!
Up to the garlanded recess I walked,
And on the navel-stone behold! a man
With crime polluted to the altar clinging,
And in his bloody hand he held a sword
Dripping with recent murder, and a branch
Of breezy olive, with flocks of fleecy wool
All nicely tipt. Even thus I saw the man;
And stretched before him an unearthly host
Of strangest women, on the sacred seats
Sleeping—not women, but a Gorgon brood,

And worse than Gorgons, or the ravenous crew
That filched the feast of Phineus (such I've seen
In painted terror); but these are wingless, black,
Incarnate horrors, and with breathings dire
Snort unapproachable, and from their eyes
Pestiferous beads of poison they distil.
Such uncouth sisterhood, apparel'd so,
From all affinity of gods or men
Divorced, from me and from the gods be far,
And from all human homes! Nor can the land,
That lends these unblest hags a home, remain
Uncursed by fearful scourges. But the god,
Thrice-potent Loxias himself will ward
His holiest shrine from lawless outrage. Him
Physician, prophet, soothsayer, we call,
Cleansing from guilt the blood-polluted hall. *(Exit.)*
*(The interior of the Delphic Temple is now presented to view.*
*Orestes is seen clinging to the navel-stone; the Eumenides lie*
*sleeping on the seats around. In the background Hermes beside*
*Orestes. Enter Apollo.)*

APOLLO: *(To Orestes.)* Trust me, I'll not betray thee. Far or near,
Thy guardian I, and to thine every foe
No gentle god. Thy madded persecutors
Sleep-captured lie: the hideous host is bound.
Primeval virgins, hoary maids, with whom
Nor god, nor man, nor beast hath known communion.
For evil's sake they are: in evil depth
Of rayless Tartarus, underneath the ground,
They dwell, of men and of Olympian gods
Abhorred. But hence! nor faint thy heart, though they
Are mighty to pursue from land to land
O'er measureless tracks, from rolling sea to sea,
And sea-swept cities. A bitter pasture truly
Was thine from Fate; but bear all stoutly. Hie thee
Away to Pallas' city, and embrace
Her ancient image with close-clinging arms.
Just judges there we will appoint to judge
Thy cause, and with soft-soothing pleas will pluck
The sting from thy offence, and free thee quite

From all thy troubles. Thou know'st that I, the god,
When thou didst strike, myself the blow directed.

ORESTES: Liege lord Apollo, justice to the gods
Belongs; in justice, O remember me.
Thy power divine assurance gives that thou
Can'st make thy will a deed.

APOLLO: Fear nought. Trust me.
*(To Hermes.)* And thou, true brother's blood, true father's son,
Hermes, attend, and to this mission gird thee.
Fulfil the happy omen of thy name,
The GUIDE, and guide this suppliant on his way.
For Jove respects thy function and thy pride,
The prosperous convoy, and the faithful guide.
*(Exit Hermes, leading Orestes. Apollo retires. Enter The Shade of Clytemnestra.)*

CLYTEMNESTRA: Sleeping? All sleeping! Ho! What need of sleepers?
While I roam restless, of my fellow-dead
Dishonoured and reproached, by fault of you,
That when I slew swift vengeance overtook me.
But being slain myself, my avengers sleep
And leave my cause to drift! Hear me, sleepers!
Such taunts I bear, such contumelious gibes,
Yet not one god is touched with wrath to avenge
My death, who died by matricidal hands.
Behold these wounds! look through thy sleep, and see!
Read with thy heart; some things the soul may scan
More clearly, when the sensuous lid hath dropt,
Nor garish day confounds. Full oft have ye
Of my libations sipped the wineless streams,
The soothings of my sober sacrifice,
The silent supper from the solemn altar,
At midnight hour when only ye are worshipped.
But now all this beneath your feet lies trampled.
The man is gone; fled like a hind! he snaps
The meshes of your toils, and makes—O shame!
Your Deity a mark for scoffers' eyes
To wink at! Hear me, ye infernal hags,
Unhoused from hell! For my soul's peace I plead,
Once Clytemnestra famous, now a dream

*(The Chorus moans.)*

CLYTEMNESTRA: Ye moan! the while the man hath fled, and seeks
    For help from those that are no friends to me.

*(The Chorus moans again.)*

CLYTEMNESTRA: Sleep-bound art thou. Hast thou no bowels for me?
    My Furies sleep, and let my murderer flee.

*(The Chorus groans.)*

CLYTEMNESTRA: Groaning and sleeping! Up! What work hast thou
    To do, but thine own work of sorrow? Rouse thee!

*(The Chorus groans again.)*

CLYTEMNESTRA: Sleep and fatigue have sworn a league to bind
    The fearful dragon with strong mastery.

CHORUS: *(With redoubled groans and shrill cries.)* Hold! Seize him!
    Seize him! Seize there! There! There! Hold!

CLYTEMNESTRA: Thy dream scents blood; and, Like a dog that doth
    In dreams pursue the chase, even so dost thou
    At phantasms bark and howl. To work! To work!
    Let not fatigue o'ermaster thus thy strength,
    Nor slumber soothe the sense of sharpest wrong.
    Torture thy liver with reproachful thoughts;
    Reproaches are the pricks that goad the wise.
    Up! blow a blast of bloody breath behind him!
    Dry up his marrow with the fiery vengeance!
    Follow! give chase! pursue him to the death!

*(Chorus starting up in hurry and confusion.)*

VOICE ONE: Awake! awake! rouse her as I rouse thee!

VOICE TWO: Dost sleep? arise! dash drowsy sleep away!
    Brave dreams be prelude to brave deed! Ho, sisters!

## STROPHE I

VOICE ONE: Shame, sisters, shame!
    Insult and injury!
    Shame, O shame!

VOICE TWO: Shame on me, too: a bootless, fruitless shame!

VOICE ONE: Insult and injury,
    Sorrow and shame!
    Burden unbearable,
    Shame! O shame!

VOICE TWO: The snare hath sprung: flown is the goodly game,

VOICE THREE: I slept, and when sleeping
        He sprang from my keeping;
        Shame, O shame!

ANTISTROPHE I
VOICE ONE: O son of Jove, in sooth,
        If thou wilt hear the truth,
        Robber's thy name!
VOICE TWO: Thou being young dost overleap the old.
VOICE ONE: A suppliant, godless,
        And bloodstained, I see,
        And bitter to parents,
        Harboured by thee.
VOICE TWO: Apollo's shrine a mother-murderer's hold!
VOICE THREE: Apollo rewardeth
        Whom justice discardeth,
        And robber's his name!

STROPHE II
VOICE ONE: A voice of reproach
        Came through my sleeping,
        Like a charioteer
        With his swift lash sweeping.
VOICE TWO: Thorough my heart,
        Thorough my liver,
        Keen as the cold ice
        Shot through the river.
VOICE THREE: Harsh as the headsman,
        Ruthless exacter,
        When tearless he scourges
        The doomed malefactor.

ANTISTROPHE II
VOICE ONE: All blushless and bold
        The gods that are younger
        Would rule o'er the old,
        With the right of the stronger.
VOICE TWO: The Earth's navel-stone
        So holy reputed,

All gouted with blood,
With fresh murder polluted,
Behold, O behold!
VOICE THREE: By the fault of the younger,
The holiest holy
Is holy no longer.


STROPHE III
VOICE ONE: Thyself thy hearth with this pollution stained
Thyself, a prophet, free and unconstrained
VOICE TWO: O'er the laws of the gods
Thou hast recklessly ridden,
Dispensing to men
Gifts to mortals forbidden.
VOICE THREE: Us thou hast reft
Of our name and our glory,
Us and the Fates,
The primeval, the hoary.


ANTISTROPHE III
VOICE ONE: I hate the god. Though underneath the ground
He hide my prey, there, too, he shall be found.
VOICE TWO: I at each shrine
Where the mortal shall bend him,
Will jealously watch,
That no god may defend him.
VOICE THREE: Go where he will,
A blood-guilty ranger
Hotly will hound him still
I, the Avenger!
APOLLO: Begone! I charge thee, leave these sacred halls!
From this prophetic cell avaunt! lest thou
A feathered serpent in thy breast receive,
Shot from my golden bow; and, inly pained,
Thou vomit forth black froth of murdered men,
Belching the clotted slaughter by thy maw
Insatiate sucked. These halls suit not for thee;
But where beheading, eye-out-digging dooms,
Abortions, butcheries, barrenness abound,

Where mutilations, flayings, torturings,
Make wretches groan, on pointed stakes impaled,
There fix your seats; there hold the horrid feasts,
In which your savage hearts exultant revel,
Of gods abominate—maids whose features foul
Speak your foul tempers plainly. Find a home
In some grim lion's den sanguinolent, not
In holy temples which your breath pollutes.
Depart, ye sheep unshepherded, whom none
Of all the gods may own!

CHORUS: Liege lord, Apollo,
   Ours now to speak, and thine to hear: thyself
   Not aided only, but the single cause
   Wert thou of all thou blamest.

APOLLO: How so? Speak!

CHORUS: Thine was the voice that bade him kill his mother.

APOLLO: Mine was the voice bade him avenge his father.

CHORUS: All reeking red with gore thou didst receive him.

APOLLO: Not uninvited to these halls he came.

CHORUS: And we come with him. Wheresoe'er he goes,
   His convoy we. Our function is to follow.

APOLLO: Follow! but from this holy threshold keep
   Unholy feet.

CHORUS: We, where we must go, go
   By virtue of our office.

APOLLO: A goodly vaunt!
   Your office what?

CHORUS: From hearth and home we chase
   All mother-murderers.

APOLLO: She was murdered here,
   That murdered first her husband.

CHORUS: Yet should she
   By her own body's fruitage have been slain?

APOLLO: Thus speaking, ye mispraise the sacred rites
   Of matrimonial Hera and of Jove,
   Unvalued make fair Aphrodite's grace,
   Whence dearest joys to mortal man descend.
   The nuptial bed, to man and woman fated,
   Hath obligation stronger than an oath,

And Justice guards it. Ye who watch our crimes,
If that loose reins to nuptial sins ye yield,
Offend, and grossly. If the murtherous wife
Escape your sharp-set vengeance, how can ye
Pursue Orestes justly? I can read
No even judgment in your partial scales,
In this more wrathful, and in that more mild.
She who is wise shall judge between us, Pallas.

CHORUS: The man is mine already. I will keep him.

APOLLO: He's gone; and thou'lt but waste thy toil to follow.

CHORUS: Thy words shall not be swords, to cut my honors.

APOLLO: Crowned with such honors, I would tear them from me!

CHORUS: A mighty god beside thy father's throne
Art thou, Apollo. Me this mother's blood
Goads on to hound this culprit to his doom.

APOLLO: And I will help this man, champion and save him,
My suppliant, my client; should I not,
Both gods and men would brand the treachery.

# The Witlings

Fanny Burney
1779

**Comedy**
**Scene:** a milliner's shop

Young women milliners
Miss Jenny
Mrs. Wheedle
Miss Sally
Miss Polly
A Footman
Young Woman
Mrs. Voluble
Beaufort
Censor

MRS. WHEEDLE: So, young ladies! pray what have you done today? *(She examines their work.)* Has anybody been in yet?

MISS JENNY: No, ma'am, nobody to signify;—only some people afoot.

MRS. WHEEDLE: Why, Miss Sally, who is this cap for?

MISS SALLY: Lady Mary Megrim, ma'am.

MRS. WHEEDLE: Lady Mary Megrim, Child? Lord, she'll no more wear it than I shall! why how have you done the lappets? they'll never set while it's a cap;—One would think you had never worked in a Christian land before. Pray, Miss Jenny, set about a cap for Lady Mary yourself.

MISS JENNY: Ma'am, I can't; I'm working for Miss Stanley.

MRS. WHEEDLE: O, ay, for the wedding.

MISS SALLY: Am I to go on with this cap, ma'am?

MRS. WHEEDLE: Yes, to be sure, and let it be sent with the other things to Mrs. Apeall in the Minories; it will do well enough for the City. *(Enter a Footman.)*

FOOTMAN: Is Lady Whirligig's cloak ready?

MRS. WHEEDLE: Not quite, Sir, but I'll send it in five minutes.

FOOTMAN: My lady wants it immediately; it was bespoke a week ago, and My Lady says you promised to let her have it last Friday.

MRS. WHEEDLE: Sir, it's just done, and I'll take care to let her Ladyship have it directly.

*(Exit Footman.)*

MISS JENNY: I don't think it's cut out yet.

MRS. WHEEDLE: I know it i'n't. Miss Sally, you shall set about it when you've done with that cap. Why Miss Polly, for goodness' sake, what are you doing?

MISS POLLY: Making a tippet, ma'am, for Miss Lollop.

MRS. WHEEDLE: Miss Lollop would as soon wear a halter: 'twill be fit for nothing but the window, and there the Miss Notables, who work for themselves, may look at it for a pattern.

*(Enter a Young Woman.)*

YOUNG WOMAN: If you please, ma'am, I should be glad to look at some ribbons.

MRS. WHEEDLE: We'll show you some presently.

*(Enter Mrs. Voluble.)*

MRS. VOLUBLE: Mrs. Wheedle, how do do? I'm vastly glad to see you. I hope all the young ladies are well. Miss Jenny, my dear, you look pale; I hope you a'n't in love, Child? Miss Sally, your servant. I saw your uncle the other day, and he's very well, and so are all the children; except, indeed, poor Tommy, and they're afraid he's going to have the whooping cough. I don't think I know that other young lady? O Lord yes, I do,—it's Miss Polly Dyson! I beg your pardon, my dear, but I declare I did not recollect you at first.

MRS. WHEEDLE: Won't you take a chair, Mrs. Voluble?

MRS. VOLUBLE: Why yes, thank you, ma'am; but there are so many pretty things to look at in your shop, that one does not know which way to turn oneself. I declare it's the greatest treat in the world to me to spend a hour or two here in a morning; one sees so many fine things, and so many fine folks,—Lord, who are all these sweet things here for?

MRS. WHEEDLE: Miss Stanley, ma'am, a young lady just going to be married.

MRS. VOLUBLE: Miss Stanley? why I can tell you all about her. Mr. Dabbler, who lives in my house, makes verses upon her.

MISS JENNY: Dear me! is that gentleman who dresses so smart poet?

MRS. VOLUBLE: A poet? yes, my dear, he's one of the first wits of the age. He can make verses as fast as I can talk.

MISS JENNY: Dear me! Why he's quite a fine gentleman; I thought poets were always as poor as Job.

MRS. VOLUBLE: Why so they are, my dear, in common; your *real* poet is all rags and atoms: but Mr. Dabbler is quite another thing; he's what you may call a poet of fashion. He studies, sometimes, by the hour together. O he's quite one of the great geniuses, I assure you! I listened at his door, once, when he was at it,—for he talks so loud when he's by himself, that we can hear him quite downstairs: but I could make nothing out, only a heap of words all in a chime, as one may say,—mean, lean, dean, wean—Lord, I can't remember half of them! At first when he came, I used to run in his room, and ask what was the matter? but he told me I must not mind him, for it was only the *fit* was on him, I think he called it, and so—

YOUNG WOMAN: I wish somebody would show me some ribbons, I have waited this half hour.

MRS. WHEEDLE: O, ay, I forgot; do show this young gentlewoman some ribbons. *(In a low voice.)* Take last year's. You shall see some just out of the loom.

MRS. VOLUBLE: Well but, Mrs. Wheedle, I was going to tell you about Miss Stanley; you must know she's a young lady with a fortune all in her own hands, for she's just come of age, and she's got neither Papa nor Mama, and so—
*(Enter a Footman.)*

FOOTMAN: Lady Bab Vertigo desires Mrs. Wheedle will come to the coach door. *(Exit.)*
*(Mrs. Wheedle goes out.)*

MRS. VOLUBLE: *(Turning to Miss Jenny.)* And so, Miss Jenny, as I was saying, this young lady came to spend the winter in town with Lady Smatter, and so she fell in love with my lady's nephew, Mr. Beaufort, and Mr. Beaufort fell in love with her, and so—
*(Reenter Mrs. Wheedle.)*

MRS. WHEEDLE: Miss Jenny, take Lady Bab the new trimming.

MRS VOLUBLE: *(Turning to Miss Sally.)* And so, Miss Sally, the match is all agreed upon, and they are to be married next week, and so, as soon as the ceremony is over—

MRS. WHEEDLE: Miss Sally, put away those ribbons.

MRS. VOLUBLE: *(Turning to Miss Polly.)* And so, Miss Polly, as soon as the ceremony's over, the bride and bridegroom—

CENSOR: *(Within.)* No, faith, not I! Do you think I want to study the fashion of a lady's topknot?

BEAUFORT: Nay, prithee, Censor, in compassion to me—
(Enter Beaufort and Censor struggling.)

CENSOR: Why how now, Beaufort? Is not a man's person his own property? Do you conclude that, because you take the liberty to expose your own to a ridiculous and unmanly situation, you may use the same freedom with your friend's?

BEAUFORT: Pho, prithee don't be so churlish. Pray, ma'am (Advancing to Mrs. Wheedle.) has Miss Stanley been here this morning?

MRS. WHEEDLE: No, sir; but I expect her every moment.

BEAUFORT: Then, if you'll give me leave, I'll wait till she comes.

CENSOR: Do as you list, but for my part, I am gone.

BEAUFORT: How! Will you not stay with me?

CENSOR: No Sir; I'm a very stupid fellow—I take no manner of delight in tapes and ribbons. I leave you, therefore, to the unmolested contemplation of this valuable collection of dainties: and I doubt not but you will be equally charmed and edified by the various curiosities you will behold, and the sagacious observations you will hear. Sir, I heartily with you well entertained. (Going.)

BEAUFORT: (Holding him.) Have you no bowels, man?

CENSOR: Yes, for myself—and therefore it is I leave you.

BEAUFORT: You sha'n't go, I swear!

CENSOR: With what weapons will you stay me? Will you tie me to your little finger with a piece of ribbon, like a lady's sparrow? Or will you enthrall me in a net of Brussels lace? Will you raise a fortification of caps? Or barricade me with furbelows? Will you fire at me a broadside of pompons? or will you stop my retreat with a fan?

MISS JENNY: Dear, how odd the gentleman talks!

MRS. WHEEDLE: I wonder they don't ask to look at something.

MRS. VOLUBLE: I fancy I know who they are.
(Whispers.)

BEAUFORT: Are you not as able to bear the place as I am? if you had any grace, you would blush to be thus outdone in forbearance.

CENSOR: But, my good friend, do you not consider that there is some little difference in our situations? I, for which I bless my stars! am a *free* man, and therefore may be allowed to have an opinion of my own, to act with consistency, and to be guided by the light of Reason: you, for which I most heartily pity you, are a lover, and, consequently, can have no pretensions to similar privileges. With you, therefore, the practice of patience, the toleration of impertinence, and the study of nonsense, are become duties indispensable; and where can you find more ample occasion to display these acquirements, than in this region of foppery, extravagance, and folly?

BEAUFORT: Ought you not, in justice, to acknowledge some obligation to me for introducing you to a place which abounds in such copious materials to gratify your splenetic humor?

CENSOR: Obligation? what, for showing me new scenes of the absurdities of my fellow creatures?

BEAUFORT: Yes, since those new scenes give fresh occasion to exert that spirit of railing which makes the whole happiness of your life.

CENSOR: Do you imagine, then, that, like Spenser's Strife, I *seek* Occasion? Have I not eyes? and can I open them without becoming a spectator of dissipation, idleness, luxury, and disorder? Have I not ears? and can I use them without becoming an auditor of malevolence, envy, futility, and detraction? O Beaufort, take me where I can *avoid* occasion of railing, and then, indeed, I will confess my obligation to you!

MRS. VOLUBLE: *(Whispering to Mrs. Wheedle.)* It's the youngest that's the bridegroom, that is to be; but I'm pretty sure I know the other too, for he comes to see Mr. Dabbler; I'll speak to him. *(Advances to Censor.)* Sir, your humble servant.

CENSOR: Madam!

MRS. VOLUBLE: I beg your pardon, Sir, but I think I've had the pleasure of seeing you at my house, Sir, when you've called upon Mr. Dabbler.

CENSOR: Mr. Dabbler?—O, yes, I recollect.—Why, Beaufort, what do you mean? did you bring me hither to be food to this magpie?

BEAUFORT: Not I, upon my honor; I never saw the woman before. Who is she?

CENSOR: A fool, a prating, intolerable fool. Dabbler lodges at her house, and whoever passes through her hall to visit him, she claims for her acquaintance. She will consume more words in an hour than ten men will in a year; she is infected with a rage for talking, yet has nothing to say, which is a disease of all others the most pernicious to her fellow creatures, since the method she takes for her own relief proves their bane. Her tongue is as restless as scandal, and, like that, feeds upon nothing, yet attacks and tortures everything; and it vies, in rapidity of motion, with the circulation of the blood in a frog's foot.

MISS JENNY: *(To Mrs. Volable.)* I think the gentleman's very proud, ma'am, to answer you so short.

MRS. VOLUBLE: O, but he won't get off so, I can tell him! I'll speak to him again. Poor Mr. Dabbler, Sir, *(To Censor.)* has been troubled with a very bad headache lately; I tell him he studies too much, but he says he can't help it; however, I think it's a friend's part to advise him against it, for a little caution can do no harm, you know, Sir, if it does no good, and Mr. Dabbler's such a worthy, agreeable gentleman, and so much the scholar, 'twould be a thousand pities he should come to any ill. Pray, Sir, do you think he'll ever make a match of it with Mrs. Sapient? She's ready enough, we all know, and to be sure, for the matter of that, she's no chicken. Pray, Sir, how old do you reckon she may be?

CENSOR: Really, madam, I have no talents for calculating the age of a lady. What a torrent of impertinence! Upon my honor, Beaufort, if you don't draw this woman off, I shall decamp.

# A Dream Play

August Strindberg
Translated by Carl R. Mueller
1901

**Dramatic**

**Scene:** Daughter has come to Earth to more fully understand its ways
and its people. The Officer is travelling with her through the
world. Here they arrive at Foulstrand and Fairhaven, two sites
across the water, covered in snow. They are resorts in the country. Foulstrand is deep in shadow, and Fairhaven is bathed in
glowing lights. All that happens is as in a dream, free-floating
with characters and situations that move swiftly across the stage
and seen through the eyes of The Daughter.

Three Couples
Two Children (Male or Female)
Six women
Schoolboys (and girls)
Five men
The Daughter of a goddess, young and innocent, romantic, and opti-
mistic
The God Indra
The Officer, a young career soldier
Ugly Edith, a forlorn, disheveled young lady sitting at a piano
Three Girls, young women watching the dance in Fairhaven
Two Children, dressed in summer clothing, playing ball

*(All cry out as before.—For a moment the stage grows com-
pletely black, during which everyone either exits or changes
places. When the lights come on again, Foulstrand can be seen
upstage in shadow. Center stage is the water. Downstage is
Fairhaven, bathed in light. To the right is a corner of the casino.
The windows are open and dancing couples are seen inside.
Three Girls stand outside on an empty box, their arms wrapped
around one another's waists as they watch the dance. On the terrace is a bench on which Ugly Edith sits sadly, without a hat and
with long disheveled hair. In front of her is an open piano, and to
the left a yellow wooden house. Outside, two Children dressed in*

summer clothes are playing ball. In the foreground, near the strait, is a dock with white boats and flagpoles with flags waving. Farther out on the strait a white warship, a brig with gunports, is anchored. The entire landscape appears in winter dress; snow lies upon bare trees and on the ground. The Daughter and the Officer enter.)

DAUGHTER: There's peace and happiness here in this holiday resort. Nobody works. Parties every day. People dressed in holiday clothes. Even music and dancing before noon. (To the Three Girls.) Children, why aren't you in there dancing?

MAID: Us?

OFFICER: But they're servants!

DAUGHTER: That's true. But why is Edith sitting here instead of dancing? (Edith hides her face in her hands.)

OFFICER: Don't ask her! She's sat there for three whole hours and not a soul asked her to dance. (He goes into the yellow house to the left.)

DAUGHTER: What cruel pleasure!

EDITH'S MOTHER: (Enters in a low-cut dress and goes to Edith.) Why don't you go on in, like I told you?

EDITH: Because—because I can't dance with myself. I know I'm ugly, and that's why no one will dance with me, but I wish you'd stop reminding me!
(She begins to play Bach's Toccata and Fugue No. 10 on the piano. The waltz, heard very faintly at first from inside the hall, grows louder as though to compete with the Bach Toccata. But Edith's playing overcomes and silences it. The Dancers appear at the door and listen to her in rapt silence as she plays.)

A NAVAL OFFICER: (Takes Alice, one of the girls at the ball, by the waist and leads her down to the dock.) Come on! Hurry!
(Edith breaks off suddenly, stands, and looks after them in despair. She remains standing there as if turned to stone. The wall of the yellow house is drawn aside. Three school benches come into view with Schoolboys sitting on them. The Officer is among them, looking restless and worried. A bespectacled Schoolmaster stands in front of them holding chalk and a cane.)

SCHOOLMASTER: (To the Officer.) Now, my boy, Can you tell how much two times two is?

*(The Officer remains seated, trying painfully to remember, but fails to find the answer.)*

SCHOOLMASTER: You are to stand when you are asked a question!

OFFICER: *(Rises, depressed.)* Two—times two—just a minute—makes two—twos.

SCHOOLMASTER: Hm! I see you haven't studied your lesson!

OFFICER: *(Embarrassed.)* No, I did, I learned it, but—I know it but I just can't say it.

SCHOOLMASTER: You're making excuses! You know it but can't say it! Perhaps I can be of some help. *(He pulls the Officer's hair.)*

OFFICER: This is terrible! Terrible!

SCHOOLMASTER: Yes, terrible that a big boy like you has no ambition!

OFFICER: *(Humiliated.)* Big boy! Yes, I'm bigger than these others! I'm a grown man! I've finished school— *(As though awakening.)* Why—why, I even have my degree!—Then why am I sitting here? Wasn't I awarded a degree?

SCHOOLMASTER: Certainly! Of course! But you still must sit here and mature, mustn't you? You must mature. Is that or is that not correct?

OFFICER: *(Hand at his forehead.)* Of course that's right. One must mature. Two times two—is two. And I can prove that by analogy, the highest form of proof! Listen!—One times one is one, therefore two times two is two. For what applies to one must apply to the other!

SCHOOLMASTER: According to the rules of logic your proof is quite correct, but the answer is wrong!

OFFICER: What is right according to the rules of logic *cannot* be wrong! Let's prove it. One goes into one one time, therefore two goes into two two times.

SCHOOLMASTER: Correct—according to the rules of analogy. But then how much is one times three?

OFFICER: Three!

SCHOOLMASTER: Consequently two times three is also three.

OFFICER: *(Considering.)* No, that can't be right—or is it? *(Sits down in despair.)* No, I'm not mature yet.

SCHOOLMASTER: No, not by a long shot—

OFFICER: But how long do I have to sit here?

SCHOOLMASTER: How long? Do you believe in time and space?—Well, assuming that time exists, you must be able to tell me what time is. What is time?

OFFICER: Time? *(Reflects.)* I can't say it, but I know. And therefore I can also know how much two times two is without being able to say it! Can *you* tell me what time is?

SCHOOLMASTER: Certainly!

SCHOOLBOYS: Then tell us!

SCHOOLMASTER: Time—let me see— *(Stands there unmoving, finger aside his nose.)* While we're talking, time runs on. Therefore time is something that runs on while I talk.

A SCHOOL BOY: *(Gets up.)* Since you're talking, sir, and while you're talking, I run, I must be time. *(And he runs on out.)*

SCHOOLMASTER: According to the rules of logic that is quite correct.

OFFICER: But then the rules of logic are insane, because Nils, who fled, can't be time.

SCHOOLMASTER: That, too, is quite correct according to the rules of logic, even though it's insane.

OFFICER: Then logic is insane.

SCHOOLMASTER: It would certainly seem so. But if logic is insane, then the whole world is insane, and why in hell should I sit here teaching you insanities! How about it! If anyone wants to treat us to a drink, we'll go for a swim!

OFFICER: That's a *posterus prius,* the world turned backward! The custom is first to have a swim and *then* a drink! You old idiot!

SCHOOLMASTER: You needn't be so conceited, Doctor!

OFFICER: Colonel, if you please! I am an officer, and I fail to understand why I sit here being scolded among schoolboys!

SCHOOLMASTER: *(Raises his finger.)* We must mature!

QUARANTINE MASTER: *(Enters.)* The quarantine's beginning!

OFFICER: Oh, there you are! Imagine, this fellow making me sit here on a school bench, and I have my degree!

QUARANTINE MASTER: Then leave, why don't you?

OFFICER: Do you mean that? Leave? That's not as simple as it sounds.

QUARANTINE MASTER: I know. But try.

OFFICER: *(To the Quarantine Master.)* Save me! Save me from his eyes!

QUARANTINE MASTER: Come along. Come to our dance. We have to dance before the plague breaks out. We do!

OFFICER: Will the ship sail then?

QUARANTINE MASTER: The ship will sail first. And that will cause many tears.

OFFICER: Tears, always tears—when it comes and when it goes! Let's go.
*(They go off. The Schoolmaster continues his instruction. The*

*three girls who were standing at the window of the hall now go sadly toward the dock, Edith, who stood stonelike by the piano, follows them.)*

DAUGHTER: *(To the Officer.)* Are there no happy people in this Paradise?

OFFICER: Of course. The two newlyweds over there. Just listen to them. *(The Newlyweds enter.)*

HUSBAND: *(To the Wife.)* I'm so happy, I wish I could die!

WIFE: But why die?

HUSBAND: Because no happiness is without its seed of unhappiness. It consumes itself in its own flame. It can't burn forever, so it has to die. And knowing what's to come destroys my love when it burns most brightly.

WIFE: Then let's die together—now.

HUSBAND: Die! Yes! I'm afraid of happiness—happiness only betrays. *(They go toward the sea.)*

DAUGHTER: *(To the Officer.)* Life is evil! Alas for mankind!

# Job

Oskar Kokoschka
Translated by Walter H Sokel and Jacquelin Sokel
1917

**Dramatic**
**Scene:** a bench outside Job's house

Nine young ladies
Job
Anima

FIRST YOUNG LADY: *(Softly, emerges with her curly head from the bed of roses, tries to awaken Job and to seize his dangling hand.)* Quite as you please! My God! In the wilderness the strong eat the weak. At home it's just the other way! Consequently one often has the face of a little lamb, the phlegmatic temper of a capon and…

JOB: *(Softly, in his sleep.)* …and you the brain of a chicken.

SECOND YOUNG LADY: *(Softly laughing behind a tree.)* Indeed, yes, when an ardent young man visits her, she goes to roost at once. She begs his pardon—does he have his red comb?

THIRD YOUNG LADY: *(Who has been squatting under the bench, looking up at him, softly.)* You'll never again make that one lose his equilibrium! That's him all right, Homo anthropos! Just feel his calves! *(Job, tickled, kicks in his sleep, so that the Young Lady tumbles over backward.)*

THIRD YOUNG LADY: Accursed frog's perspective! I'll be limping from this for the rest of my life!

FOURTH YOUNG LADY: *(Tickling Job's ear with a flower stem, drops an apple, hiding all the while in a bush behind him.)* Adam lives on in posterity because he bowed before Eve in Paradise!

JOB: *(Dreaming.)* When one rejects how posterity is made by such worthless dalliances, he must lose faith in a better future!

FIFTH YOUNG LADY: *(Reaching out from the draperies of the house door for his shock of hair, softly.)* 'Tis Fortune. Grab a hold! Or else she'll pull you 'round!

SIXTH YOUNG LADY: *(Administering him a gentle slap on the back.)* As a man of the world, let him consider now which side of himself he wishes to show!

JOB: *(Sleepy.)* Fortune is a gypsy who leads us by the nose! She wants her behind to be the object of our attention. When she performs her striptease there, beware the horn of plenty with which she might surprise you!

SEVENTH YOUNG LADY: *(Mockingly, from a tree.)* Oh, for floating forth to meet furtive confessions and for uniting the warring sexes with the rainbow of forgiveness!

JOB: *(Dreaming, overcome by nostalgia.)* My feelings are descending meteors hurtling down through the night of my heart and burning themselves out in it! My word, that transcends my self like the gesture of an invisible hand, remains for you mere stage effect!

ALL YOUNG LADIES: *(Singing softly.)* Oh, how we love effects, farces and tragedies at midnight, when they hold sleep at bay...

JOB: *(Mumbling.)* Is this no demon towering in the sky who sets her heel upon me in the mud—but yet gentle angel who cools my head?

EIGHTH YOUNG LADY: Look about you, Sunday's child! Ghosts wear no clothes. What then can flesh and blood have on? *(She comes from the path of the now dimly illuminated garden, the sun rises, she kisses his brow.)* Good day, my friend! Life smiles upon you!

JOB: *(Snarls at her, wipes off her kiss.)* I have lumbago, the witches' dart...

EIGHTH YOUNG LADY: *(Giving him up as hopeless.)* That thought at once makes love freeze stiff...

*(Job, touching himself in front and back to see if some new misfortune has not befallen him, staggers into the light the better to see.)*

NINTH YOUNG LADY: Uprooted plants wither in the sun no less than in the shade.

JOB: *(Disgruntled.)* To your health, Dame Fortune! The morning crows and not the cock, the game shoots the hunter down—a weary man curses the carnival and now shuts shop.

*(Goes into the house. Brings a bottle of poison, a skull, and two human bones to the window, contemplates the skull, lifts the bottle to his lips. The Tenth Young Lady reaches down from her tree for it and then drums gaily with the bones on the skull.)*

JOB: *(Throws the poison bottle after the Young Lady, who retaliates with the skull and bones, which Job wraps in paper.)* Women, get going, out with you!

ALL YOUNG LADIES: *(Singing softly to the tune of the folk song, departing. Job closes the store.)* "Now I lay me down to sleep," etc. *(Brief pause.)*

JOB: *(Behind closed window shutters.)* The soul of man or magic lantern…Times were when it projected God and Devil into the world; these days it casts women on the wall! *(Humbly.)* Oh, to laugh a little, to laugh…And not to run after these nurses who tease us children; from out there the witch looks in and can't be overlooked. *(He smiles wanly.)*

*(A silvery many-voiced choir echoes—cascading laughter, a hurricane—an inundation of laughter. Job jumps out the window, pulls his pants tighter, stops short. In the upper story, above Job, a window lights up in rosy illumination. The Parrot flies down from the opened window, flutters after the fugitive, opens wide her eyes, assails him, during the subsequent scene does not permit him to leave the protective wall of the house along which Job runs to and fro.)*

JOB: *(Sprouts horns which develop into antlers. Whenever he rushes past the lit window, two shadows toss garments upon them so that the antlers soon become a clothes tree. Cuffs, collar, jackets, night- and under-garments of a gentleman and a lady. Job grabs the doorbell and rings the house phone in deathly terror.)* For pity's sake! I'm getting frightened! Anima, help! Salvation! What are they doing to me?

ANIMA: *(From the window.)* Conjuring spirits—do you see the plan? It's been the custom since time began.

ADAM: *(The gardener, comes from the garden.)* A woman, having turned his head, now makes a fool of him.

ANIMA: Mother's wit inspired me to this! An enlightened spirit has taken me to wife today, he disenchants me and now I aid him in his task!

JOB: That devil! A true enchanter he! Who bravely with kisses and fervid oaths conjures Anima up for his use. Oh, gaping Hell! Most fugitive witch! Treaties she signs, herself to surrender; confused, she blushes on bosom and neck; she opens her heart; airs secrets and skirts; and then shares in bed, in housewifely fashion, the power of the male...What is it I feel? I am not like him, my opposite, that I could settle there and start begetting just like that!... *(Anima drops like a ripe apple down from the window, scantily clothed, to land with her buttocks on Job's head. He collapses under Anima's weight and dies.)*

# Alkibiades Saved

Georg Kaiser
Translated by Bayard Quincy Morgan
1920

**Dramatic**
**Scene:** a cramped and hectic fishmarket, cobblestones, carts, smells

Sokrates
Forerunner
Fifteen Fishwives

FIRST FISHWIFE: *(Stopping before Sokrates.)* Shall I make a detour around
    your hunchback?
SOKRATES: My hump is a detour in my back, so that the blood won't
    rise too fast into my head and flood my reason.
FIRST FISHWIFE: What is your hump to me?
SOKRATES: Just now you found it in your way.
    *(First Fishwife goes around him.)*
SECOND FISHWIFE: *(Behind Sokrates.)* Watch out, honey, you'll get your
    toes flattened!
SOKRATES: Why do you tell me in advance that you're going to run over
    me? I'll feel it all right when your cart rolls over my feet.
SECOND FISHWIFE: You—to one side!
SOKRATES: Or did you want to prepare me for the pain which I shall
    now encounter with self-control?
    *(Second Fishwife goes around him in a curve.)*
THIRD FISHWIFE: *(At a vat in the rear—spraying Sokrates from her dipper.)*
    Has that lump taken root in the cobblestones? That's a fearfully
    hard ground—you got to soften it up!
    *(The Fishwives shriek.)*
SOKRATES: *(Knocks the water off his coat.)* You hit too high—one doesn't
    water a tree trunk, it's the base one soaks.
FOURTH FISHWIFE: *(At a vat in the rear—to the Third Fishwife.)* Whose
    hide got washed by your spray, ha?
SECOND FISHWIFE: *(Replying shrilly.)* I'll collect haddock bones for your
    mattress—that'll make you lively, you stockfish!
FOURTH FISHWIFE: *(Bursts out laughing.)* Put sticklebacks into your bed—
    otherwise nothing is going to stick you, you piddock!

FIFTH FISHWIFE: *(In front of Sokrates with her cart and tub.)* This is a thor-
oughfare—gangway!

SIXTH FISHWIFE: *(Behind Sokrates with her cart and tub.)* Truck coming—
step aside!

SOKRATES: *(Turns his head to left—to right.)* I can't move a foot.

FIFTH FISHWIFE: I'll teach you to run!

SIXTH FISHWIFE: I'll make you jump!

SOKRATES: I stand fast between you.

FIFTH FISHWIFE: Now—I'll shove!

SIXTH FISHWIFE: Now—I'll push!

SOKRATES: How will this end? I give way—all right—: you'll push your
carts ahead and knock them together so that the tubs will burst
and their contents be poured out. Did your men pull the fish out
of the sea to be thrown on the pavement? I'm preventing your
irretrievable loss if I stick to the spot I stand on.

SEVENTH FISHWIFE: *(At a vat to the right.)* He'll make you roll your carts
across the moon to get to your vats!

FIFTH FISHWIFE: *(Curving to the front around Sokrates—to the Sixth
Fishwife.)* Do you have to trundle your cart when I come along?

SIXTH FISHWIFE: *(Around Sokrates to the rear—retorting.)* Did you lease
the fish market for your finger-length herrings?

FIFTH FISHWIFE: *(Shrilly.)* I smell a stink from your tub—why don't you
bring your dead flounders to market in a basket?

SIXTH FISHWIFE: You got water in your tub? Nope, it's vinegar—or your
carrion would rot on the way!

FIFTH FISHWIFE: *(Hurling water at her with the dipper.)* Vinegar —see
how it stings!

SIXTH FISHWIFE: *(Spraying water back.)* Rotten water—try the taste of it!

EIGHTH FISHWIFE: *(At a vat.)* Give that fellow a bath—till he floats off like
a limp perch!

NINTH FISHWIFE: *(Advancing with her cart toward Sokrates.)* Forward
straight ahead to the vat!

SOKRATES: *(Stopping the cart with both hands—bending forward.)*
What have you, smelts?

NINTH FISHWIFE: Whales!

SOKRATES: Do you say "whales" in order to make my ignorance of the
kinds of fish clear to me with particular emphasis?

FIFTH FISHWIFE: I say—straight ahead to the vat!

SOKRATES: *(Bracing himself against the cart.)* If a purchaser stepped up to your fish vat and asked you what you have to sell, would you reply with the same exaggeration if he took your pikes to be smelts?

NINTH FISHWIFE: Pikes!

SOKRATES: You would make the gullible person perplexed and injure your business.

NINTH FISHWIFE: *(Letting go her pushcart and clasping her hands over her head.)* Now this good-for-nothing is giving me advice how to carry on my business!

SOKRATES: I am inexperienced and am using the opportunity to instruct myself.

NINTH FISHWIFE: *(Rudely.)* You want to buy fish?

SOKRATES: How can I buy a commodity when I don't know what it is?

NINTH FISHWIFE: You'll tell by the taste!

SOKRATES: Granted that I like your fish—and by all appearances they have come to the fish market fresh out of the net—how, if the appetite for just such fish comes over me again, can I get them anew, if I lack any more precise designation for the coveted object?

NINTH FISHWIFE: Come to the fish market and look in the vats! *(Taking hold again.)* Onward!

SOKRATES: *(Stopping her.)* I may be prevented from leaving the house myself. How can I make clear to a messenger I send what he is to bring?

NINTH FISHWIFE: *(Letting go again—angry.)* I'll serve the booby all right!

SOKRATES: Now, are they smelts or pikes or whales?

NINTH FISHWIFE: *(Swinging her arms.)* Whales!!

SOKRATES: Now I know that they are whales—and every day, without taking the trouble to go to the fish market myself, I'll have whales brought from your vat. You see that your business looks up as soon as you have imparted some of your knowledge to the ignorant.

NINTH FISHWIFE: Smelts—pikes—whales—!—the head of a smelt—the fins of a pike—the tail of a whale—!—: the fish market is turning around!

TENTH FISHWIFE: *(Behind the Ninth Fishwife with her pushcart.)* Go ahead—don't block the road!

NINTH FISHWIFE: *(Abusively.)* Did anybody ever hear the like? It's enough to make you grow ears as big as a whale's gills! Here she comes along and takes over——imagine a whale in my pushcart that I'm shoving in front of me with two hands!

TENTH FISHWIFE: *(Shoving the Ninth Fishwife from behind with her push-cart.)* If you've got time—I've got to make two more trips down to the wharf!

NINTH FISHWIFE: *(Turning around.)* Are you blind, you wall-eyed pike, that you don't see where I'm standing?

TENTH FISHWIFE: I'd hear your croaking, you squawking old rook!

NINTH FISHWIFE: You tootle sweetly—just open your gullet good and wide—there's pay for you! *(Dips water and throws it in her face.)*

TENTH FISHWIFE: *(Pouring water over her from the dipper.)* Don't swallow it the wrong way!

NINTH FISHWIFE: *(Again.)* Dirt tastes bitter!

TENTH FISHWIFE: *(Again.)* Then my tub water must taste sweet to you!

ELEVENTH FISHWIFE: *(Bringing her cart up behind the Tenth Fishwife.)* Watch your step. Wash your scabs at home!

TENTH FISHWIFE: *(Turning around.)* Who's got scabs?—Look, you're gray around the muzzle! *(Gives her a dipperful.)*

NINTH FISHWIFE: *(Likewise aiming at the Eleventh Fishwife.)* Where's a scab?—You wait, you and your talk both need a washing! *(Dipperful.)*

ELEVENTH FISHWIFE: *(Briskly spraying them both.)* I can dip twice—before you bend your stiff frames once!

TWELFTH FISHWIFE: *(Spraying the Ninth and Tenth Fishwife.)* Got hot, eh?—I'll cool your behinds!

THIRTEENTH FISHWIFE: *(Spraying the Twelfth Fishwife.)* Who called you into this quarrel?

TWELFTH FISHWIFE: *(Spraying back.)* Must I ask your lousy whiskers for permission?

FOURTEENTH FISHWIFE: *(Spraying the Thirteenth Fishwife.)* Is somebody meddling who wants a dipperful of fish water?

FIFTEENTH FISHWIFE: *(Spraying blindly.)* There's a dousing for you out of the vat!

SIXTEENTH FISHWIFE: *(Spraying and shrieking.)* Now fish are flying with the water!!

SEVENTEENTH FISHWIFE: Anybody who sprays—gets splashed!!

EIGHTEENTH FISHWIFE: Fishes—water!!

*(The fight has become general: from tubs and vats water is eagerly dipped and hurled from the dippers. Amid the noise the words: "Dishes!" "Water!" From the left alley the Forerunner— half nude, resplendent trousers. He motions back into the alley defensively.)*

FORERUNNER: Make way for Alkibiades!!

*(The Fishwives lower their dippers.)*

# Kantan

Yukio Mishima
Translated by Donald Keene
1973

**Dramatic**
**Scene:** Jiro's dream

Jiro
Beauty
Three Dancers
Chorus of women, any number

JIRO: *(Turning away.)* A baby is born. Into this dark, gloomy world. His mother's womb was more cheerful. Why should he ever have wanted to leave it for a gloomier place? Little idiot. I can't understand him at all.

BEAUTY: He's winking! He's laughed.

JIRO: The bones have already learned to laugh. Don't you think it's frightening? Don't you?

BEAUTY: Peek-a-boo!

JIRO: I hope and pray this is only a dream.

BEAUTY: Peek-a-boo! I see you!

JIRO: Only a dream...

BEAUTY: He's looking at Papa and smiling.

JIRO: Is he? Do you think he looks like me or like you?

BEAUTY: You may say what you will, but I know deep at heart you're interested in him.

JIRO: Huh? Which of us does he look like?

BEAUTY: If you make such a frightening face he'll start crying. Now that you ask, I regret to say he looks more like his father than he does me.

JIRO: Does he?

BEAUTY: The eyebrows, the nose, the mouth...I can see your face faintly traced behind his.

JIRO: Then he looks like me.

BEAUTY: It should make you happier.

JIRO: I don't like it, for him to look like me.

BEAUTY: You're so modest.

JIRO: How disgusting, a brat who resembles me has been born.

BEAUTY: *(Wailing.)* Stop it!

JIRO: *(Picking up an ashtray from his bedside and furiously banging the inside of the cradle with it.)* I'll show him!

BEAUTY: Stop it! What are you doing? Stop it!

JIRO: He's dead.

BEAUTY: My little son! How dreadful! How dreadful!

JIRO: He's better off this way. If he had lived to grow up he would sooner or later have suffered because of his resemblance to his father. That's the experience everybody goes through.

BEAUTY: You horrible man! You're jealous even of your own child.

JIRO: That's right. I won't allow anybody to look like me.

BEAUTY: *(Weeping.)* Monster...dreadful monster...

JIRO: Look, the bones are laughing.

BEAUTY: I suppose I love you all the same.

JIRO: I should hope so.

BEAUTY: Now I understand! You killed the baby because you love me. You were afraid that someone might come between us. That was it, wasn't it? I love you. I love you so much. At last I understand! You're a very passionate man. I didn't realize how passionate you are. It was silly of me. The baby is already a thing of the past— I forgive you. I forgive you everything, every last thing.

JIRO: I wonder how a woman's self-conceit can be so conveniently arranged?

BEAUTY: Jiro, in exchange, don't leave me.

JIRO: If you will be a faithful wife to me.

BEAUTY: I will! I'll do anything. I'll scrub the floors, sweep, mend your clothes, anything. If you tell me to walk naked through the streets, I'll do that too.

JIRO: A splendid resolution. First of all, you must never be jealous.

BEAUTY: Yes. I'll put up with anything, anything.

JIRO: *(Stretching.)* Let me see. Oh, yes. I am a father who's lost his child. I need some sort of consolation. Something to cheer me up. A distraction, like other men have.

BEAUTY: That's right, enjoy yourself all you like. I'll just watch. No matter what you do, I'll just watch and never once get jealous. I'll be patient and watch. Just to be able to look at you will be all the satisfaction I ask for. I'm happy.

*(A strange, sensuous music is heard.)*

BEAUTY: I shall be silent and look at you, like a lily.

JIRO: What a lily! Well, you can look at me all you like. It doesn't cost anything to look.

*(The Beauty sits in a child's chair to stage-right. Three half-naked Dancing Girls enter. They wear masks. They form a circle and dance.)*

CHORUS: The pillow is blameless

If you dance the sun shines, the clouds grow bright

If you dance your life is not the same

The dance is blameless

If you dance your shadow is not the same.

FIRST DANCER: Jiro...Jiro...

CHORUS: Dance! Dance! Dance!

SECOND DANCER: Dance! Dance! Dance!

THIRD DANCER: Jiro...Jiro...

CHORUS: Dance! Dance! Dance!

*(The three Dancers unsuccessfully attempt to draw Jiro into the dance. He remains obdurate. He lies in bed, his head propped on his elbows, watching them. The Dancers finally give up and sit on the bed around him.)*

FIRST DANCER: What beautiful eyes! I've never seen a man with such divine eyes.

JIRO: You say that because you see your own face reflected in them. Isn't that it?

FIRST DANCER: That's not a very nice answer.

SECOND DANCER: What beautiful teeth you have!

JIRO: I brush them every morning in sulfuric acid.

SECOND DANCER: Oh, how ferocious! Isn't he wonderful!

JIRO: You have a nice fat hand. It looks good enough to eat.

SECOND DANCER: Eat all you like. Another one will grow back.

*(Dancers laugh.)*

JIRO: Can't you say anything without laughing? There's nothing more boring than when a woman starts to laugh. You never know how long it's going to last.

DANCERS: Doesn't he say the most amusing things?

THIRD DANCER: It's my turn now. I love Jiro's forehead. It's white and broad, like an airplane runway.

JIRO: It'd be a pity to leave it as a runway. One of you ought to culti-vate it and grow something there.

FIRST DANCER: I'll do it…

SECOND DANCER: No, I will.

THIRD DANCER: Let me !

FIRST DANCER: Let's *all* cultivate it.

JIRO: All right, all right…Just supposing you cultivate it. You plant seeds—carrots and turnips, say. Before you know it, the carrots grow. The turnips grow. You pull the carrots and turnips from my forehead. You boil them to a pulp. Then you pile them on a plate…

FIRST DANCER: Yes, and then?

JIRO: You eat them up.

FIRST DANCER: Oh-h.

JIRO: You polish them off completely.

SECOND DANCER: What a wonderful story! What happens next?

JIRO: That's all there is to it. That's what life is like. You get it, don't you? If you do, go away, and quickly.

FIRST DANCER: No, Jiro. I don't want to go.

JIRO: What a nuisance! Get out of here, quick!

SECOND DANCER: How rude he is! But I must say, there's something charming about his coldness.

JIRO: I said you're all nuisances. Go! Leave me!

THIRD DANCER: We'll do as you say, then, but give us a big tip, won't you?

FIRST DANCER: Next time we must spend a lot longer together.

SECOND DANCER: Jiro, I could tell you were generous from the first moment I laid eyes on you. I adore people with open faces.

# Success

Arthur Kopit

**Comic**
**Scene:** a banquet room in a hotel. Lectern and two chairs on the dias

Mrs. Hoffensberg
Eliot Krum, author
An audience full of mostly women

HOFFENSBERG: I had the great honor of meeting Eliot Krum two weeks ago at San Francisco State College where he was delivering a... *(Her words grow indistinct. The sound of the surf returns. Over this sound, the sound of thunderous applause at whatever Mrs. Hoffensberg is now saying. Presently, the sound of applause grows distant; then it and the sound of surf disappear.)*

HOFFENSBERG: I found Mr. Krum at that time to be a man of both subtle... *(And again her words disappear behind the sound of surf. Mrs. Hoffensberg holds up her book and, smiling, glances toward Krum. Then, looking back to her audience, opens the book to its last page, looks soberly out at her audience, then back at the book, and reads what is obviously to her a very moving last paragraph. Finished, she closes the book and looks up at the audience. Not a sound. Not a movement. Then...applause. Mrs. Hoffensberg looks over at Krum, who does not move. Apparently, she has just introduced him. She says his name again. This time, it is barely audible. Then it comes through louder. He stirs. He has recognized the sound of his name. She smiles at him and he rises. As he does, she says—)*

HOFFENSBERG: Eliot Krum!

*(Wild applause as Krum assumes the lectern, spreads out his notes, arranges them, then looks over his audience. Smiles. Clears his throat. Opens his mouth. Nothing. Closes his mouth. Frowning, he reaches for a glass of water. Takes a sip. Puts down the glass. Ponders. Opens his mouth. Studies his audience for clues. Finds none.)*

KRUM: Would someone be so kind...as to tell me...what...city...this is? *(Laughter.)*

VARIOUS WOMEN: *(Together.)* Santa Monica!

KRUM: Santa Monica! Well, well—
(Laughter from audience.)
KRUM: And what...organization...might this be?
(Louder laughter, wild applause.)
HOFFENSBERG: (To the audience, laughing.) Mr. Krum has been in such recent demand on the lecture circuit that it seems he no longer knows whereof he speaks!
(Laughter and applause.)
KRUM: Actually, it doesn't really matter. No one seems surprised that I'm here, so apparently I'm in the right place.
(Again, more laughter and applause. He shuffles his notes.)
KRUM: ...I thought I'd just ramble on a bit this afternoon, explore a few areas suggested by my book, then open up the floor to relevant and exciting questions, if that meets with the approval of you ladies and— (He peers around his audience for men; finds one.) ...gentleman. First, however, I'd like to thank my gracious host, the lovely Miss, umm—
HOFFENSBERG: (Sotto voce.) Mrs.
KRUM: Mrs., ummm—
HOFFENSBERG: Hoffensberg.
KRUM: Hoffensberg, yes, for bringing me to this delightful spot, wherever it is, and...all of you,...whoever...you are. Indeed, had I not had the great fortune to meet Mrs., uh...let me write that down.
HOFFENSBERG: Hoffensberg.
KRUM: "Hoffensberg." Indeed, had I not had the great fortune to meet Mrs.— (He glances at his note.) —Hoffensberg some...while ago at...some...place or other, who knows where I'd be today? (Pause.) To Mrs....H then, my heartfelt thanks and solid reassurance that in the scrapbook of my mind, she will live forever. Certainly, I shall always cherish the memory of our first conversation. As I recall, immediately, upon taking me aside, she unbuttoned her blouse—
HOFFENSBERG: What?
(Long pause.)
KRUM: Ladies,...as the former president of a well-known West Coast university once aptly said—sometime, I believe, in the sixties: "It appears I am no longer in possession of my faculties."...Now, I am not particularly *pleased* with this condition. Nor, obviously, are you. Certainly, when you invited me here today, as a leading lit-

erary light, you surely did not expect to find the light quite so flickering, if not dim. How has it come about, this dismal state? Well, frankly, it's none of your business. Nonetheless, I will tell you, it has definitely not been helped by my recent madcap schedule, set up at the behest of my fiendish publisher, a relentlessly charming man, whom I shall try my very best to strangle the next time we meet. You see, for the past several months—six, seven, eight, who can say?—it seems I have been doing nothing but going from one strange place to another talking about this goddamn book of mine—a book I could hardly bear when I was writing, so imagine how I like it now! Which is why, today, I thought I would discuss football. *(He clears his throat.)* Football, as I see it, is one of our most— *(Pause.)* ...Or is it? *(Pause.)* No! It's not at all, *not at all!* Why would I think it *was? Question! Yes!* No? Thought I saw a hand, clutching, upwards. Ladies, for God's sake, I will give you back my fee, assuming you had planned to give me one, but let me out of this! It is an embarrassment to us all!...Except, of course, to Mrs. H, who's shown herself to be beyond embarrassment and whose bizarre bosom has, these last few weeks, played such a vital role in the continuation of my thought processes.

HOFFENSBERG: *What?*

KRUM: Sorry. Slipped out. Didn't mean to mention it. Forget I ever said a word. So, what shall we talk about? *My book!* Yes. Why not? Ladies, in all candor, the extraordinary popular success of my book has not only taken me completely by surprise, but apparently has taken my mind along with it. Surely, ladies, *surely,* an eight-hundred-and-fifty-page book about suicide— *(He has a sudden and terrible coughing fit; reaches for some water; gains control; takes out a pill, pops it in his mouth, sips some water, puts the glass back down.)* —about...suicide...would not seem, at first glance, a likely candidate for the best-seller list. And yet!— unless there is some enormous and rather peculiar hoax going on—there it is! Top o' the list! Thirty-fourth straight week! And I am rich. And getting laid like crazy. Mind you, not that sex means that much to me, but in my seven years as a rabbi in Bridgeport and my three as a priest in New Rochelle, I would say I got laid no more than ten, twelve times maximum, and that includes four nuns and a mother superior I ravaged on my last official day, which, as those of you who've read my little volume know, was the first day of Lent, yes, question.

WOMAN IN AUDIENCE: Do you really expect us to sit here and listen to this crap?

KRUM: I'm sorry, I am *very sorry,* but I have not come all this way just to be insulted! To continue. After serving my three years as a priest in a mostly Jewish neighborhood, right on the heels of having served seven as a rabbi in a mostly Catholic, I made the first of my many suicide attempts. Ate seventeen of Mrs. Smith's jumbo apple pies, followed by twelve Sarah Lee pound cakes. When this failed to finish me, I became a psychiatrist. In Mamaroneck.

SAME WOMAN: Mr. Krum!

KRUM: *Question!*

SAME WOMAN: You don't seem to understand: we have all *read* your book. Which means we know your background. And your background is *not this.*

KRUM: ...It's not?

SAME WOMAN: No.

(*Silence.*)

KRUM: Are you...sure we're talking about...the *same book?*

SAME WOMAN: *The Gods of War,* by E. E. Krum.

KRUM: Or *"Eeeek,"* as they used to call me in kindergarten!

SAME WOMAN: This *is* your book, then.

KRUM: Definitely. But please, feel free to keep it. To continue! As a psychiatrist, in Mamaroneck—

SAME WOMAN: Mr. *Krum!*

KRUM: Heavens, you're a pest.

SAME WOMAN: According to this book, you never were a rabbi. Never a priest. And never a psychiatrist.

KRUM: *Just what are you trying to say?*

(*Pause.*)

SAME WOMAN: That...you never were a rabbi. Never a priest. And never a psychiatrist.

KRUM: I see. (*Pause.*) Well, this is certainly a very startling piece of news.

SAME WOMAN: To us, especially.

KRUM: Was I a...*baseball* player?

SAME WOMAN: No. Sorry.

KRUM: Dentist?

SAME WOMAN: Perhaps you should read your book.

SAME WOMAN: What, eight hundred pages, about suicide? You must think I'm mad!

SAME WOMAN: Mr. Krum, frankly, I was very moved by your book. It is really a most astonishing account of a man's constant battle against despair.

KRUM: Sounds amusing.

SAME WOMAN: It isn't.

KRUM: Was it illustrated?

SAME WOMAN: Not *my* copy.

KRUM: Well, why'd you read it, then?
(*Silence.*)

KRUM: Why'd any of you read it?
(*Silence.*)

KRUM: I don't understand this. Have you all nothing better to do with your time?
(*Silence.*)

KRUM: All right, come now, truthfully, game's over. How many of you actually read it, raise your hands. Let's go. Hands. Hands. (*He looks at what would appear to be a sea of hands.*) Well, this makes no sense. No sense at all. And it's been the same everywhere. *What are you people doing?* I'd *never* buy a book like that. It's the most lugubrious thing imaginable. You should be home, fucking. Not reading. You'll ruin your eyes! You wanna go blind? What's wrong with you people? *I can't take this anymore!* Yes. Question. Sorry. Thought you had a question. Oh, God, this isn't right, isn't right. I'm fading, fading… (*Pause.*) Fading… (*Very long pause.*) Faded. (*Pause.*) Ladies…Gentleman. Forgive me. But I find I just can't speak any more today. (*He turns, goes to one of the windows, and opens it.*)
(*Sound of surf. He leaps. Lights to original position, with only the iridescent sky lit, all else in silhouette. No movement.*)

PART TWO

# SCENES FOR MEN

# SMALL GROUP SCENES

# The Captives

Plautus
Translated by E. H. Sugden
circa 180 B.C.

**Comic**
**Scene:** outside the house of Hegio. Ergasilus sets the scene—a war is
   on and Hegio's son has been taken prisoner. Now, the loving
   father wants to arrange a trade.

Ergasilus, a parasite
Guard
Hegio, middle-aged, buys prisoners of war to try to arrange an exchange
   for his captured son
Assistants
Several Prisoners of War
Tyndarus and Philocrates, two prisoners

ERGASILUS: My patron has been captured by the foe—
   The Ætolians and the Elians are at war,
   (This is Ætolia); Philopolemus,
   The son of Hegio here, whose house this is,
   In Elis lies a prisoner; so this house
   A house of lamentation is to me;
   As oft as I behold it, I must weep.
   Now for his son's sake, he's begun a trade,
   Dishonorable, hateful to himself;
   He's buying prisoners, if perchance he may
   Find any to exchange against his son.
   O how I pray that he may gain his wish!
   Till he's recovered, I am past recovery.
   The other youths are selfish, hopelessly,
   And only he keeps up the ancient style.
   I've never flattered him without reward;
   And the good father takes after his son!
   Now I'll go see him. Ha! the door is opening,
   Whence I have often come, just drunk with gorging.
   *(Enter from the house Hegio and an Overseer.)*
HEGIO: Attend to me; those prisoners that I bought

A day ago from the Commissioners
Out of the spoil, put lighter fetters on them;
Take off these heavier ones with which they're bound,
And let them walk indoors or out at will;
But watch them with the utmost carefulness.
For when a free man's taken prisoner,
He's just like a wild bird; if once he gets
A chance of running off, it's quite enough;
You needn't hope to catch your man again.

OVERSEER: Why, all of us would rather far be free
Than slaves.

HEGIO: Why not take steps, then, to be free?

OVERSEER: Shall I give *leg-bail?* I've naught else to give!

HEGIO: I fancy that in that case you would *catch it!*

OVERSEER: I'll be like that wild bird you spoke about.

HEGIO: All right; then I will clap you in a cage.
Enough of this; do what I said, and go.
*(Exit Overseer into the house.)*

HEGIO: I'll to my brother's, to my other captives,
To see how they've behaved themselves last night,
And then I'll come back home again straightway.

ERGASILUS: *(Aside.)* It grieves me that the poor old man should ply
This gaoler's trade to save his hapless son.
But if perchance the son can be brought back,
The father may turn hangman: what care I?

HEGIO: Who speaks there?

ERGASILUS: One who suffers in your grief.
I'm growing daily thinner, older, weaker!
See, I'm all skin and bones, as lean as lean!
All that I eat at home does me no good;
Only a bite at a friend's agrees with me.

HEGIO: Ergasilus! hail!

ERGASILUS: Heav'n bless you, Hegio!

HEGIO: Don't weep!

ERGASILUS: Not weep for him? What, not bewail
That excellent young man?

HEGIO: I always knew
You and my son to be the beat of friends.

ERGASILUS: Alas! we don't appreciate our blessings

Till we have lost the gifts we once enjoyed.
Now that your son is in the foeman's bands,
I realize how much he was to me!

HEGIO: Ah, if a stranger feels his loss so much,
What must *I* feel? He was my only joy.

ERGASILUS: A stranger? I a stranger? Hegio,
Never say that nor cherish such a thought!
Your only joy he was, but oh! to me
Far dearer than a thousand only joys.

HEGIO: You're right to make your friend's distress your own;
But come, cheer up!

ERGASILUS: Alas! it pains me here,
That now the feaster's army is discharged.

HEGIO: And can't you meantime find another general
To call to arms this army that's discharged?

ERGASILUS: No fear! since Philopolemus was taken,
Who filled that post, they all refuse to act.

HEGIO: And it's no wonder they refuse to act.
You need so many men of divers races
To work for you; first, those of Bakerton;
And several tribes inhabit Bakerton;
Then men of Breadport and of Biscuitville,
Of Thrushborough and Ortolania,
And all the various soldiers of the sea.

ERGASILUS: How oft the noblest talents lie concealed!
O what a splendid general you would make,
Though now you're serving as a private merely,

HEGIO: Be of good cheer; in a few days, I trust,
I shall receive my dear son home again.
I've got a youthful Elian prisoner,
Whom I am hoping to exchange for him,
One of the highest rank and greatest wealth.

ERGASILUS: May Heaven grant it!

HEGIO: Where've you been invited
To dine to-day?

ERGASILUS: Why, nowhere that I know of.
Why do you ask?

HEGIO: Because it is my birthday;
And so, I pray you, come and dine with me.

ERGASILUS: Well said indeed!

HEGIO: That is if you're content
    With frugal fare.

ERGASILUS: Well, if it's not *too* frugal;
    I get enough of that, you know, at home.

HEGIO: Well, name your figure!

ERGASILUS: Done! unless I get
    A better offer, and on such conditions
    As better suit my partners and myself.
    As I am selling you my whole estate,
    It's only fair that I should make my terms.

HEGIO: I fear that this estate you're selling me
    Has got a bottomless abyss within't!
    But if you come, come early.

ERGASILUS: Now, if you like!

HEGIO: Go hunt a hare; you've only caught a weasel.
    The path my guest must tread is full of stones.

ERGASILUS: You won't dissuade me, Hegio; don't think it!
    I'll get my teeth well shod before I come.

HEGIO: My table's really coarse.

ERGASILUS: Do you eat brambles?

HEGIO: My dinner's from the soil.

ERGASILUS: So is good pork.

HEGIO: Plenty of cabbage!

ERGASILUS: Food for invalids!
    What more?

HEGIO: Be there in time.

ERGASILUS: I'll not forget. *(Exit Ergasilus to the marketplace.)*

HEGIO: Now I'll go in and look up my accounts,
    To see what I have lying at my banker's;
    Then to my brother's, as I said just now. *(Exit Hegio into the house.)*
    *(Enter Overseers, Philocrates and Tyndarus, each in the other's clothes, and other slaves.)*

OVERSEER: Since Heaven has willed it should be so,
    That you must drink this cup of woe,
    Why, bear it with a patient mind,
    And so your pain you'll lighter find.
    At home, I dare say, you were free;

Now that your lot is slavery,
Just take it as a thing of course,
Instead of making matters worse;
Behave yourselves and don't be queasy
About your lord's commands; 't is easy.

PRISONERS: Oh, oh!

OVERSEER: No need for howls and cries!
I see your sorrow in your eyes.
Be brave in your adversities.

TYNDARUS: But we're ashamed to wear these chains.

OVERSEER: My lord would suffer far worse pains,
Should he leave you to range at large out of his custody,
Or set you at liberty whom he bought yesterday.

TYNDARUS: Oh, he needn't fear that he'll lose his gains;
Should he release us, we know what's our duty, sir.

OVERSEER: Yes, you'll run off; I know *that.* You're a beauty, sir!

TYNDARUS: Run off? run off where?

OVERSEER: To the land of your birth.

TYNDARUS: Nay, truly, it never would answer
to imitate runaway slaves.

OVERSEER: Well, by Jove!
I'd advise you, if you get a chance, sir.

TYNDARUS: One thing I beg of you.

OVERSEER: What's your petition, sir?

TYNDARUS: Give us a chance of exchanging a word,
Where there's no fear that we'll be overheard.

OVERSEER: Granted! Go, leave them.
We'll take our position there.
See that your talk doesn't last too long!

TYNDARUS: Oh, that's my intention.
So, now, come along!

OVERSEER: Go, leave them alone.

TYNDARUS: We ever shall own
We're in your debt for the kindness you've shown to us;
You have the power, and you've proved yourself bounteous.

PHILOCRATES: Come away farther, as far as we can from them;
We must contrive to conceal our fine plan from them,
Never disclose any trace of our trickery,
Else we shall find all our dodges a mockery.

Once they get wind of it,
There'll be an end of it;
For if you are my master brave,
And I pretend to be your slave,
Then we must watch with greatest care;
Of eavesdroppers we must beware.
With Caution and skill keep your senses all waking;
There's no time to sleep; it's a big undertaking.

TYNDARUS: So I'm to be master?

PHILOCRATES: Yes, that is the notion.

TYNDARUS: And so for your head (I would pray you remark it),
You want me to carry my own head to market!

PHILOCRATES: I know.

TYNDARUS: Well, when You've gained your wish, remember my devotion.
This is the way that you'll find most men treating you;
Until they have
The boon they crave,
They're kind as can be; but success makes the knave!
When they have got it, they set to work cheating you.
Now I have told you the treatment you owe to me.
You I regard as a father, you know, to me.

PHILOCRATES: Nay, let us say,—no conventions shall hinder us,—
Next to my own, you're my father, dear Tyndarus.

TYNDARUS: That will do!

PHILOCRATES: Now then, I warn you always to remember this;
I no longer am your master but your slave; don't be remiss.
Since kind Heav'n has shown us plainly that the way
      ourselves to save
Is for me, who was your master, now to turn into your slave,
Where before I gave you orders, now I beg of you in prayer,
By the changes in our fortune, by my father's kindly care,
By the common fetters fastened on us by the enemy,
Think of who you were and are, and pay no more respect to me
Than I used to pay to you, when you were slave and I was free.

TYNDARUS: Well, I know that I am you and you are me!

PHILOCRATES: Yes, stick to that!
Then I hope that by your shrewdness we shall gain what we are at.

# The Jew of Malta

Christopher Marlowe
1594

**Dramatic**
**Scene:** in Barabas' counting house, heaps of gold all around

Barabas, the jew
Merchant
Second merchant
First Jew
Second Jew
Third Jew

BARABAS: So that of thus much that return was made:
    And of the third part of the Persian ships,
    There was the venture summed and satisfied.
    As for those Samnites, and the men of Uz,
    That bought my Spanish oils, and wines of Greece,
    Here have I pursed their paltry silverlings.
    Fie; what a trouble 'tis to count this trash!
    Well fare the Arabians, who so richly pay
    The things they traffic for with wedge of gold,
    Whereof a man may easily in a day
    Tell that which may maintain him all his life.
    The needy groom that never fingered groat,
    Would make a miracle of thus much coin:
    But he whose steel-barred coffers are crammed full,
    And all his life-time hath been tired,
    Wearying his fingers' ends with telling it,
    Would in his age be loath to labour so,
    And for a pound to sweat himself to death:
    Give me the merchants of the Indian mines,
    That trade in metal of the purest mould;
    The wealthy Moor, that in the Eastern rocks

    Without control can pick his riches up,
    And in his house heap pearl like pibble-stones,
    Receive them free, and sell them by the weight;

Bags of fiery opals, sapphires, amethysts,
Jacinths, hard topaz, grass-green emeralds,
Beauteous rubies, sparkling diamonds,
And seld-seen costly stones of so great price,
As one of them indifferently rated,
And of a caract of this quantity,
May serve in peril of calamity
To ransom great kings from captivity.
This is the ware wherein consists my wealth:
And thus methinks should men of judgement frame
Their means of traffic from the vulgar trade,
And as their wealth increaseth, so inclose
Infinite riches in a little room.
But now how stands the wind?
Into what corner peers my halcyon's bill?
Ha, to the East? Yes. See how stands the vanes?
East and by South: why then I hope my ships
I sent for Egypt and the bordering isles
Are gotten up by Nilus' winding banks:
Mine argosy from Alexandria,
Loaden with spice and silks, now under sail,
Are smoothly gliding down by Candy shore
To Malta, through our Mediterranean sea.
But who comes here? How now.
*(Enter a Merchant.)*
MERCHANT: Barabas, thy ships are safe,
Riding in Malta road: and all the merchants
With all their merchandise are safe arrived,
And have sent me to know whether yourself
Will come and custom them.
BARABAS: The ships are safe thou say'st, and richly fraught?
MERCHANT: They are.
BARABAS: Why then go bid them come ashore,
And bring with them their bills of entry:
I hope our credit in the custom-house
Will serve as well as I were present there.
Go send 'em threescore camels, thirty mules,
And twenty waggons to bring up the ware.
But art thou master in a ship of mine,

And is thy credit not enough for that?

MERCHANT: The very custom barely comes to more
Than many merchants of the town are worth,
And therefore far exceeds my credit, sir.

BARABAS: Go tell 'em the Jew of Malta sent thee, man:
Tush, who amongst 'em knows not Barabas?

MERCHANT: I go.

BARABAS: So then, there's somewhat come.
Sirrah, which of my ships art thou master of?

MERCHANT: Of the Speranza, sir.

BARABAS: And saw'st thou not
Mine argosy at Alexandria?
Thou couldst not come from Egypt, or by Caire,
But at the entry there into the sea,
Where Nilus pays his tribute to the main,
Thou needs must sail by Alexandria.

MERCHANT: I neither saw them, nor inquired of them.
But this we heard some of our seamen say,
They wondered how you durst with so much wealth
Trust such a crazed vessel, and so far.

BARABAS: Tush; they are wise, I know her and her strength:
But go, go thou thy ways, discharge thy ship,
And bid my factor bring his loading in.
(Exit Merchant.)

BARABAS: And yet I wonder at this argosy.
(Enter a Second Merchant.)

SECOND MERCHANT: Thine argosy from Alexandria,
Know Barabas doth ride in Malta road,
Laden with riches, and exceeding store
Of Persian silks, of gold, and orient pearl.

BARABAS: How chance you came not with those other ships
That sailed by Egypt?

SECOND MERCHANT: Sir we saw 'em not.

BARABAS: Belike they coasted round by Candy shore
About their oils, or other businesses.
But 'twas ill done of you to come so far
Without the aid or conduct of their ships.

SECOND MERCHANT: Sir, we were wafted by a Spanish fleet
That never left us till within a league,

That had the galleys of the Turk in chase.
BARABAS: Oh they were going up to Sicily: well, go
    And bid the merchants and my men dispatch
    And come ashore, and see the fraught discharged.
SECOND MERCHANT: I go.
BARABAS: Thus trowls our fortune in by land and sea,
    And thus are we on every side enriched:
    These are the blessings promised to the Jews,
    And herein was old Abram's happiness:
    What more may heaven do for earthly man
    Than thus to pour out plenty in their laps,
    Ripping the bowels of the earth for them,
    Making the sea their servant, and the winds
    To drive their substance with successful blasts?
    Who hateth me but for my happiness?
    Or who is honoured now but for his wealth?
    Rather had I a Jew be hated thus,
    Than pitied in a Christian poverty:
    For I can see no fruits in all their faith,
    But malice, falsehood, and excessive pride,
    Which methinks fits not their profession.
    Haply some hapless man hath conscience,
    And for his conscience lives in beggary.
    They say we are a scattered nation:
    I cannot tell, but we have scambled up
    More wealth by far than those that brag of faith.
    There's Kirriah Jairim, the great Jew of Greece,
    Obed in Bairseth, Nones in Portugal,
    Myself in Malta, some in Italy,
    Many in France, and wealthy every one:
    Ay, wealthier far than any Christian.
    I must confess we come not to be kings:
    That's not our fault: alas, our number's few,
    And crowns come either by succession
    Or urged by force; and nothing violent,
    Oft have I heard tell, can be permanent.
    Give us a peaceful rule, make Christians kings,
    That thirst so much for principality.
    I have no charge, nor many children,

But one sole daughter, whom I hold as dear
As Agamemnon did his Iphigen:
And all I have is hers. But who comes here?
*(Enter three Jews.)*

FIRST JEW: Tush, tell not me, 'twas done of policy.

SECOND JEW: Come therefore let us go to Barabas;
For he can counsel best in these affairs;
And here he comes.

BARABAS: Why how now countrymen?
Why flock you thus to me in multitudes?
What accident's betided to the Jews?

FIRST JEW: A fleet of warlike galleys, Barabas,
Are come from Turkey, and lie in our road:
And they this day sit in the council-house
To entertain them and their embassy.

BARABAS: Why let 'em come, so they come not to war;
Or let 'em war, so we be conquerors:
*(Aside.)* Nay, let 'em combat, conquer, and kill all,
So they spare me, my daughter, and my wealth.

FIRST JEW: Were it for confirmation of a league,
They would not come in warlike manner thus.
Come therefore let us go to Barabas;
I fear their coming will afflict us all.

BARABAS: Fond men, what dream you of their multitudes?
What need they treat of peace that are in league?
The Turks and those of Malta are in league.
Tut, tut, there is some other matter in't.

FIRST JEW: Why, Barabas, they come for peace or war.

BARABAS: Haply for neither, but to pass along
Towards Venice by the Adriatic Sea;
With whom they have attempted many times,
But never could effect their stratagem.

THIRD JEW: And very wisely said, it may be so.

SECOND JEW: But there's a meeting in the senate-house,
And all the Jews in Malta must be there.

BARABAS: Umh; all the Jews in Malta must be there?
Ay, like enough, why then let every man
Provide him, and be there for fashion-sake.
If any thing shall there concern our state

Assure yourselves I'll look unto *(Aside.)* myself

FIRST JEW: I know you will; well brethren let us go.

SECOND JEW: Let's take our leaves; farewell good Barabas.

BARABAS: Do so: farewell Zaareth, farewell Temainte.

*(Exeunt the Jews.)*

BARABAS: And Barabas now search this secret out.
Summon thy senses, call thy wits together:
These silly men mistake the matter clean.
Long to the Turk did Malta contribute;
Which tribute all in policy, I fear,
The Turks have let increase to such a sum
As all the wealth of Malta cannot pay;
And now by that advantage thinks, belike,
To seize upon the town: ay, that he seeks:

Howe'er the world go, I'll make sure for
And seek in time to intercept the worst,
Warily guarding that which I ha' got.
*Ego mihimet sum semper proximus.*
Why let 'em enter, let 'em take the town. *(Exit.)*

# The Taming of the Shrew

William Shakespeare
1594

**Comic**
**Scene:** Padua, a public place

Lucentio
Tranio
Baptista
Bianca
Katharina
Gremio
Hortensio

LUCENTIO: Tranio, since for the great desire I had
    To see fair Padua, nursery of arts,
    I am arriv'd for fruitful Lombardy,
    The pleasant garden of great Italy;
    And by my father's love and leave am arm'd
    With his good will and thy good company,
    My trusty servant well approv'd in all,
    Here let us breathe, and haply institute
    A course of learning and ingenious studies.
    Pisa, renowned for grave citizens,
    Gave me my being and my father first,
    A merchant of great traffic through the world,
    Vincentio, come of the Bentivolii.
    Vincentio's son, brought up in Florence,
    It shall become to serve all hopes conceiv'd,
    To deck his fortune with his virtuous deeds:
    And therefore, Tranio, for the time I study,
    Virtue and that part of philosophy
    Will I apply that treats of happiness
    By virtue specially to be achiev'd.
    Tell me thy mind; for I have Pisa left
    And am to Padua come, as he that leaves
    A shallow plash to plunge him in the deep,
    And with satiety seeks to quench his thirst.

TRANIO: Mi perdonate, gentle master mine,
 I am in all affected as yourself
 Glad that you thus continue your resolve
 To suck the sweets of sweet philosophy.
 Only, good master, while we do admire
 This virtue and this moral discipline,
 Let 's be no stoics nor no stocks, I pray;
 Or so devote to Aristotle's checks
 As Ovid be an outcast quite abjur'd.
 Balk logic with acquaintance that you have,
 And practise rhetoric in your common talk;
 Music and poesy use to quicken you;
 The mathematics and the metaphysics,
 Fall to them as you find your stomach serves you:
 No profit grows where is no pleasure ta'en;
 In brief, sir, study what you most affect.
LUCENTIO: Gramercies, Tranio, well dost thou advise.
 If, Biondello, thou wert come ashore,
 We could at once put us in readiness,
 And take a lodging fit to entertain
 Such friends as time in Padua shall beget.
 But stay awhile: what company is this?
TRANIO: Master, some show to welcome us to town.
 *(Enter Baptista, Katharina, Bianca, Gremio, and Hortensio. Lucentio and Tranio stand aside.)*
BAPTISTA: Gentlemen, importune me no further,
 For how I firmly am resolv'd you know;
 That is, not to bestow my youngest daughter
 Before I have a husband for the elder.
 If either of you both love Katharina,
 Because I know you well and love you well,
 Leave shall you have to court her at your pleasure.
GREMIO: To cart her rather: she 's too rough for me.
 There, there, Hortensio, will you any wife?
KATHARINA: *(To Baptista.)* I pray you, sir, is it your will
 To make a stale of me amongst these mates?
HORTENSIO: Mates, maid! how mean you that? no mates for you
 Unless you were of gentler, milder mould.
KATHARINA: I' faith, sir, you shall never need to fear:

I wis it is not half way to her heart;
But if it were, doubt not her care should be
To comb your noddle with a three-legg'd stool,
And paint your face, and use you like a fool.

HORTENSIO: From all such devils, good Lord deliver us!

GREMIO: And me too, good Lord!

TRANIO: Hush, master! here is some good pastime toward:
That wench is stark mad or wonderful froward.

LUCENTIO: But in the other's silence do I see
Maid's mild behaviour and sobriety.
Peace, Tranio!

TRANIO: Well said, master; mum! and gaze your fill.

BAPTISTA: Gentlemen, that I may soon make good
What I have said,—Bianca, get you in:
And let it not displease thee, good Bianca,
For I will love thee ne'er the less, my girl.

KATHARINA: A pretty peat! it is best
Put finger in the eye, an she knew why.

BIANCA: Sister, content you in my discontent.
Sir, to your pleasure humbly I subscribe:
My books and instruments shall be my company,
On them to look and practise by myself.

LUCENTIO: Hark, Tranio! thou mayst hear Minerva speak.

HORTENSIO: Signior Baptista, will you be so strange?
Sorry am I that our good will effects
Bianca's grief.

GREMIO: Why will you mew her up,
Signior Baptista, for this fiend of hell,
And make her bear the penance of her tongue?

BAPTISTA: Gentlemen, content ye; I am resolv'd.
Go in, Bianca.
*(Exit Bianca.)*

BAPTISTA: And for I know she taketh most delight
In music, instruments, and poetry,
Schoolmasters will I keep within my house,
Fit to instruct her youth. If you, Hortensio,
Or Signior Gremio, you, know any such,
Prefer them hither; for to cunning men
I will be very kind, and liberal

To mine own children in good bringing up;
And so, farewell. Katharina, you may stay;
For I have more to commune with Bianca. *(Exit.)*

KATHARINA: Why, and I trust I may go too; may I not?
What! shall I be appointed hours, as though, belike,
I knew not what to take, and what to leave? Ha! *(Exit.)*

GREMIO: You may go to the devil's dam: your gifts are so good, here's none will hold you. Their love is not so great, Hortensio, but we may blow our nails together, and fast it fairly out: our cake's dough on both sides. Farewell: yet, for the love I bear my sweet Bianca, if I can by any means light on a fit man to teach her that wherein she delights, I will wish him to her father.

HORTENSIO: So will I, Signior Gremio: but a word, I pray. Though the nature of our quarrel yet never brooked parle, know now, upon advice, it toucheth us both,—that we may yet again have access to our fair mistress and be happy rivals in Bianca's love,—to labour and effect one thing specially.

GREMIO: What 's that, I pray?

HORTENSIO: Marry, sir, to get a husband for her sister.

GREMIO: A husband! a devil.

HORTENSIO: I say, a husband.

GREMIO: I say, a devil. Thinkest thou, Hortensio, though her father be very rich, any man is so very a fool to be married to hell?

HORTENSIO: Tush, Gremio! though it pass your patience and mine to endure her loud alarums, why, man, there be good fellows in the world, an a man could light on them, would take her with all faults, and money enough.

GREMIO: I cannot tell; but I had as lief take her dowry with this condition, to be whipped at the high-cross every morning.

HORTENSIO: Faith, as you say, there 's small choice in rotten apples. But, come; since this bar in law makes us friends, it shall be so far forth friendly maintained, till by helping Baptista's eldest daughter to a husband, we set his youngest free for a husband, and then have to 't afresh. Sweet Bianca! Happy man be his dole! He that runs fastest gets the ring. How say you, Signior Gremio?

GREMIO: I am agreed: and would I had given him the best horse in Padua to begin his wooing, that would thoroughly woo her, wed her, and bed her, and rid the house of her. Come on.
*(Exeunt Gremio and Hortensio.)*

TRANIO: I pray, sir, tell me, is it possible
    That love should of a sudden take such hold?
LUCENTIO: O Tranio! till I found it to be true,
    I never thought it possible or likely;
    But see, while idly I stood looking on,
    I found the effect of love in idleness;
    And now in plainness do confess to thee,
    That art to me as secret and as dear
    As Anna to the Queen of Carthage was,
    Tranio, I burn, I pine, I perish, Tranio,
    If I achieve not this young modest girl.
    Counsel me, Tranio, for I know thou canst:
    Assist me, Tranio, for I know thou wilt.
TRANIO: Master, it is no time to chide you now;
    Affection is not rated from the heart:
    If love have touch'd you, nought remains but so,
    Redime te captum, quam queas minimo.
LUCENTIO: Gramercies, lad; go forward: this contents:
    The rest will comfort, for thy counsel's sound.
TRANIO: Master, you look'd so longly on the maid,
    Perhaps you mark'd not what's the pith of all.
LUCENTIO: O yes, I saw sweet beauty in her face,
    Such as the daughter of Agenor had,
    That made great Jove to humble him to her hand,
    When with his knees he kiss'd the Cretan strand.
TRANIO: Saw you no more? Mark'd you not how her sister
    Began to scold and raise up such a storm
    That mortal ears might hardly endure the din?
LUCENTIO: Tranio, I saw her coral lips to move,
    And with her breath she did perfume the air;
    Sacred and sweet was all I saw in her.
TRANIO: Nay, then, 'tis time to stir him from his trance.
    I pray, awake, sir: if you love the maid,
    Bend thoughts and wits to achieve her. Thus it stands:
    Her elder sister is so curst and shrewd,
    That till the father rid his hands of her,
    Master, your love must live a maid at home;
    And therefore has he closely mew'd her up,
    Because she will not be annoy'd with suitors.
LUCENTIO: Ah, Tranio, what a cruel father's he!

But art thou not advis'd he took some care
To get her cunning schoolmasters to instruct her?
TRANIO: Ay, marry, am I, sir; and now 'tis plotted.
LUCENTIO: I have it, Tranio.
TRANIO: Master, for my hand,
   Both our inventions meet and jump in one.
LUCENTIO: Tell me thine first.
TRANIO: You will be schoolmaster,
   And undertake the teaching of the maid:
   That's your device.
LUCENTIO: It is: may it be done?
TRANIO: Not possible; for who shall bear your part,
   And be in Padua here Vincentio's son?
   Keep house and ply his book, welcome his friends;
   Visit his countrymen, and banquet them?
LUCENTIO: Basta; content thee; for I have it full.
   We have not yet been seen in any house,
   Nor can we be distinguish'd by our faces
   For man, or master: then, it follows thus:
   Thou shalt be master, Tranio, in my stead,
   Keep house, and port, and servants, as I should:
   I will some other be; some Florentine,
   Some Neapolitan, or meaner man of Pisa.
   'Tis hatch'd and shall be so: Tranio, at once
   Uncase thee, take my colour'd hat and cloak:
   When Biondello comes, he waits on thee;
   But I will charm him first to keep his tongue.
   *(They exchange habits.)*
TRANIO: So had you need.
   In brief then, sir, sith it your pleasure is,
   And I am tied to be obedient;
   For so your father charg'd me at our parting,
   'Be serviceable to my son,' quoth he,
   Although I think 'twas in another sense:
   I am content to be Lucentio,
   Because so well I love Lucentio.
LUCENTIO: Tranio, be so, because Lucentio loves;
   And let me be a slave, to achieve that maid
   Whose sudden sight hath thrall'd my wounded eye.
   Here comes the rogue.

# Peer Gynt

Henrik Ibsen
Translated by Kai Jurgensen, Robert Schenkkan
1867

**Dramatic**
**Scene:** the southwest coast of Morocco, a dinner table set under a
  grove of palm trees

Peer Gynt
Mr. Cotton
M. Ballon
Herr von Eberkopf
Herr Trumpeterstraale

PEER: Gentlemen, drink! If man is made for pleasure,
  He may as well enjoy himself.
  You know the saying. "Lost is lost,"
  "What's done is done."—What will you have?
TRUMPETERSTRAALE: You play the role of host superbly.
PEER: I share the honor with my cash,
  My cook and steward.
COTTON: Very well;
  Let's toast all four, and wish them luck!
BALOON: Monsieur, you have a *goût,* a *ton,*
  One seldom meets with nowadays
  Among men living *en garçon,*—
  A certain—what's the word—?
VON EBERKOPF: A whiff,
  A touch of liberal *geistesanschauung,*
  An ecumenical autochthony,
  A fleeting glance through drifting clouds
  Unbound by narrow prejudice,
  A stamp of higher inspiration,
  An *Ur-Natur,* sophisticated,
  United in a trinity.
  I think that's what you meant, monsieur?
BALOON: Yes, possibly; it doesn't sound
  Quite that magnificent in French.

VON EBERKOPF: *Ei was!* That language is so stiff.—
  But if we want to find the source
  Of the phenomenon—
PEER: It's found.
  It's just because I haven't married.
  Yes, gentlemen, it's clear as day.
  What it is a man should be?
  My answer's very brief: *Himself.*
  Should only love himself and his.
  But can he if he, like a camel,
  Is burdened down with others' woes?
VON EBERKOPF: Ah, but this in-and-for-yourselfness,
  I'm sure it's cost you many struggles—
PEER: Oh, yes, perhaps; in former days;
  But I have always won the honors;
  Though once I very nearly fell
  Into the trap against my will.
  I was a handsome, dashing fellow,
  The girl with whom I was in love,—
  She was of royal family—
BALOON: Of royal—?
PEER: *(Casually.)* One of those old lines,
  You know—
TRUMPETERSTRAALE: *(Strikes the table.)* Aristocrats! The trolls!
PEER: *(Shrugs.)* Forgotten Highnesses, whose pride
  It is to keep their coats of arms
  Unstained by anything plebeian.
BALOON: The family objected to it?
PEER: No, not at all.
BALOON: Ah!
PEER: Well, you see,
  For certain reasons it seemed urgent
  That we should marry right away.
  But to be frank, the whole affair,
  From first to last, did not attract me.
  In certain things I'm rather choosy,
  And, too, prefer my independence.
  And when the lady's father came
  With veiled requests and hints that I

Should change my name and place in life,
And get aristocratic papers,
Plus more demands that were distasteful,—
Conditions that I couldn't stomach,—
I then withdrew with dignity,
Refused the father's ultimatum,
And so gave up my youthful blide.
*(He drums his fingers on the table and appears to be in a reverie.)*
Oh, yes, there is a Guiding Hand.
We mortals can depend on that;
And it's a comfort, too, to know it.

BALOON: And that's the way it ended, eh?

PEER: No, I ran into something else.
Some busybodies jumped in, too,
With shouts and cries, and joined the fray.
The youngest brothers were the worst.
I had to duel seven of them.
I never will forget that time,
Though I came through with flying colors.
It cost some blood; but still, that blood
Attests my stature as a person,
And points with reassurance to
The Wise and Guiding Hand I mentioned.

VON EBERKOPF: You have a view of life's affairs
That lifts you up among the thinkers.
For, while the ordinary burgher
Sees only unconnected scenes
And never stops his helpless groping,
You grasp the whole of it at once.
With just one norm, you measure all.
You point each single observation
Till all of them project like rays
Of light from your philosophy.—
And yet, you haven't been to college?

PEER: I am, as I have said before,
A self-taught man from start to finish.
There's been no method in my learning.
But I have thought and meditated,
And picked up this and that by reading.

I didn't start till I was older,
And then, you know, it's difficult
To plow through reams of heavy books
And take in everything you read.
I've skipped around in history;
I never did have time for more.
And since it seems, in times of trial,
A man needs faith in something certain,
I took small doses of religion.
It goes down easier that way.
You shouldn't read to—simply swallow,
But only see what you can use.

COTTON: That's practical enough!

PEER: *(Lights a cigar.)* My friends,
Just give a thought to my career.
What was I when I first went west?
Young, penniless, and empty-handed.
I had to slave away for bread;
Believe me, it was often thorny.
But life, my friends, is very dear,
And death is bitter, as they say.
Well! Luck, you see, was with me then;
And good old fate smiled on me, too.
I got along; since I'm elastic,
My fortune went from good to better.
In ten years' time I'd earned the name
Of Croesus of the Charleston shippers;
My fame had spread from port to port,
And fortune sailed aboard my ships—

COTTON: What did you sell?

PEER: I traded mostly
In Negroes for the Carolinas,
And idol images for China.

BALOON: *Fi donc!*

TRUMPETERSTRAALE: Good heavens! *Uncle* Gynt!

PEER: No doubt you think my business stretched beyond
The point of what's permissible!
I often felt the same myself.
I even found it odious.

But, please believe me, once you start,
It seems impossible to stop.
At any rate, it's very hard
In businesses as big as that,
Affecting people by the thousands,
To put an end to it completely.
I can't abide that word, "completely,"
But, on the other hand, confess
I've always had a sound respect
For what is called "the consequences."
And when I overstepped the line,
It always worried me a little.
Besides, the years were catching up;
Why, I was getting close to fifty.—
My hair was slowly turning gray;
Although my health was always good,
This thought kept rising up to plague me:
"Who knows how soon the hour will come,
That brings the jury's verdict in
And separates us, sheep from goats?"
Well, what to do? To end the trade
With China was impossible.
I thought of something. Opened up
A second traffic to that country.
I sent them idols every spring,
And missionaries in the fall.
Fitted them out with all they needed,
As stockings, Bibles, rum, and rice—

COTTON: But, at a profit?
PEER: Naturally.

It worked. They went on undiscouraged.
For every god a Chinese bought,
They got a coolie well converted.
So, the effect was neutralized.
The missions' field was never fallow,
Because the missionaries held
In check the idols we exported.

COTTON: But then, the trade in Africans?
PEER: There, too, my morals won the field.

I realized the trade was wrong
For any man who's getting old.
You never know when you'll drop off.
And add to that the thousand traps
Set by the philanthropic camp;
That's not to mention privateers,
And constant risks from wind and weather.
All that together finally won.
I thought, "Now Peter, reef your sails;
And see that you correct your faults."
I bought myself some land down south,
And kept the last imported meat—
Which was of first-class quality.
They throve; they got so sleek and fat
It was a pleasure for us both.
Yes, I dare say, and I'm not bragging,
I treated them just like a father,—
Which brought me very good returns.
I built them schools in order to
Inculcate virtue and maintain
It at a standardized *niveau,*
And strictly watched the mercury
To see it didn't drop below it.
Now, furthermore, I've gotten out
Of such transactions altogether;—
I've sold the whole plantation, plus
Its livestock, sold it hide and hair.
The day I left, I even gave free drinks,
Free drinks to them, both young and old,
So all of them were drunk and happy.
The widows got some snuff besides.
And that's the reason I can hope—
In case it isn't just a proverb:
"Whoever does no harm, does good,—"
My old mistakes will be forgotten,
And I, much more than many others,
Can cover up my sins with virtues.

VON EBERKOPF: *(Clinking his glass against Peer's.)* It's most encouraging
   to hear.

A principle of life enacted,
Released from theoretic night,
Unmoved by any outside forces!

PEER: *(Who has been drinking freely.)* We Northern men know how to see
Our battles through! The key to life's
Affairs, its art, is simply this:
To keep your ears closed tight against
The entrance of one fearful viper.

COTTON: What sort of viper, my dear friend?

PEER: A tiny one that would seduce you
To take irrevocable steps.
*(He drinks again.)*
The backbone of the art of daring,
The art of having nerve to act,
Depends on this: To keep free choice
Among the cunning snares of life,—
To know for sure on every day
That *it is not* the last of battle,—
To know you always have a bridge
Behind you that will take you back.
This theory has brought me forward,
Has colored my entire career;
And I inherited the thought,—
A race-peculiarity.

BALOON: You're a Norwegian?

PEER: Yes, by birth;
But cosmopolitan in spirit.
For such good luck as I've enjoyed
I have to thank America.
My well-filled bookshelves,—those I owe
To later German schools of thought.
From France I get my handsome waistcoats,
My bearing and my touch of wit;—
From England came my industry,
And sense of what's to my advantage;
The Jew has taught me how to wait;
A taste for *dolce far niente*
Has been my gift from Italy.—
And once, when I was in a spot,

I stretched the measure of my days
By calling on good Swedish steel.
TRUMPETERSTRAALE: *(Lifts his glass.)* Yes, Swedish steel—!
VON EBERKOPF: But, first of all,
We toast the wielder of the steel!
*(They clink glasses and drink with Peer. The drink is beginning to go to his head.)*
COTTON: Well, all of this is very fine,—
But, sir, I'd like to know what you
Intend to do with all your gold.
PEER: Hm, do? Well...
ALL FOUR: *(Move closer.)* Yes, come on and tell us!
PEER: Well, first of all, I want to travel.
That's why I took you four aboard,
As drinking cronies in Gibraltar.
I needed such a dancing-chorus
Of friends around my gold-calf-altar—
VON EBERKOPF: How witty!
COTTON: Yes, but no one hoists
His sails in order just to sail.
You have a goal; I'm sure you do;
And what's the goal?
PEER: To be a Caesar.
ALL FOUR: What?
PEER: *(Nods.)* Caesar!
ALL FOUR: Where?
PEER: Of all the world.
BALOON: But how, my friend?
PEER: By means of gold!
It's not the least a new idea;
It's been the soul of all I've done.
In boyhood dreams, I flew across
The ocean, riding on a cloud.
I soared aloft in golden armor
And flopped to earth on hands and knees.
But I've held steadfast to my purpose.—
They say, or it is written down
Someplace,—I don't remember where,—
That if you were to win the world

But lost *yourself,* you'd only gain
A wreath around a broken skull.
That's how it goes—or something like it.
And take my word, it's true enough.

VON EBERKOPF: But then, what is this Gyntish self?

PEER: That private world behind my brow
Which makes me *me*—and no one else,—
No more than God could be the Devil.

TRUMPETERSTRAALE: Ah, now I see where this is leading.

BALOON: Divine philosopher!

VON EBERKOPF: High poet!

PEER: *(His spirits still rising.)* The Gyntish self,—a multitude
Of wishes, appetites and lusts,—
The Gyntish self,—a mighty ocean
Of impulse, greed and high demands.
In short, it's all that fills my breast
And makes of me the one I am.
But just as God has need of dirt
If he's to last as God of earth,
So, also, I have need of gold
If I'm to make a handsome Caesar.

BALOON: You have your gold!

PEER: But not enough.
Yes, maybe for a little show
As Caesar of a county, say.
But I must be *myself—en bloc.*
Must be a Gynt for all the world,—
Sir Gynt, complete, from crown to root!

BALOON: *(Carried away.)* Possess the world's most stunning beauty!

VON EBERKOPF: And all the oldest Rhenish wines!

TRUMPETERSTRAALE: And all the swords of Charles the Twelfth!

COTTON: But first a profitable chance.
For money-making.

PEER: Found already,
By virtue of our landing here.
This very night we're sailing north!
The papers that were brought aboard
Informed me of important news—!
*(He stands and lifts his glass.)*

It seems that Fortune still bestows
Her favors on the one who's bold—

ALL FOUR: Well! Tell us—!

PEER: Greece is in revolt.

ALL FOUR: *(Leaping up.)* What! Greece—

PEER: Is torn by revolution.

ALL FOUR: Hurray!

PEER: The Turks are up a tree! *(He empties his glass.)*

BALOON: To Greece! The open door to glory!
I'll help them with a Frenchman's sword!

VON EBERKOPF: And I with cheering—from a distance.

COTTON: Me, too!—I'll sell them their supplies!

TRUMPETERSTRAALE: Let's go! I'll find again in Bender
The famous spurs of Charles the Twelfth!

BALOON: *(Throws his arms around Peer's neck.)* Forgive me, friend,
if I misjudged
You for a while!

VON EBERKOPF: *(Pressing both Peer's hands.)* Oh, what an ass
I am! I thought you were a scoundrel!

COTTON: No, that's too strong; let's just say "fool"—

TRUMPETERSTRAALE: *(Wants to kiss him.)* I thought you were a good example
Of what is worst among the Yankees.
Forgive me—

VON EBERKOPF: We have all been wrong—

PEER: What's this about?

VON EBERKOPF: But now we see
In all their glory, the multitudes
Of Gyntish impulse, lust and wish—!

BALOON: *(Admiringly.)* So this is being *Monsieur* Gynt!

VON EBERKOPF: *(The same.)* Yes, this is being Gynt with honor!

PEER: But tell me—?

BALOON: Don't you understand?

PEER: No, hang me, I have no idea!

BALOON: What's this? You mean you aren't heading
To join the Greeks with ship and money—?

PEER: *(Snorts.)* No, many thanks! I'm for the stronger!
I'll lend my money to the Turks.

BALOON: Impossible!

VON EBERKOPF: A witty joke!

# The Emperor
Luigi Pirandello
1922

**Serio-comic**
**Scene:** in the hall of a villa decorated to resemble the German Emperor
Henry the Fourth's throne room

Landolf
Bertold
Harald
Ordulf
First Valet
Second Valet
Giovanni

LANDOLF: *(To Bertold as if following up an explanation.)* And this is the throne room!

HARALD: At Goslar!

ORDULF: Or, if you'd prefer that, in his castle in the Hartz Mountains!

HARALD: Or at Worms.

LANDOLF: It jumps around a bit. According to the scene we're acting out. Now here, now there—

ORDULF: Now in Saxony—

HARALD: Now in Lombardy—

LANDOLF: Now on the Rhine.

FIRST VALET: *(Holding his position, hardly moving his lips.)* Sss, Sss!

HARALD: *(Hearing and turning.)* What's the matter?

FIRST VALET: *(Still like a statue in an undertone.)* Well, is he coming or isn't he?
*(The allusion is to the Emperor.)*

ORDULF: He isn't. He's sleeping. Take it easy.

SECOND VALET: *(Dropping the pose as his partner does so, taking a long breath, and going to lie down again on the ledge.)* Well, for God's sake, why didn't you say so before?

BERTOLD: *(Who has been observing everything in mixed amazement and perplexity walking round the room and looking at it then looking at his clothes and his companions' clothes.)* But, look...this room...these clothes...What Henry the Fourth?...I don't quite get it.—Is it Henry the Fourth of France or Henry the Fourth of England?

*(At this demand Landolf, Harald and Ordulf burst into a roar of laughter.)*

LANDOLF: *(Laughing all the time and pointing at Bertold as if inviting the others—who also go on laughing—to continue making fun of him.)* Is it Henry the Fourth of France?

ORDULF: Or Henry the Fourth of England?

HARALD: Why, my dear child, its Henry the Fourth of *Germany!*

ORDULF: The great and tragic Emperor—

LANDOLF: —who repented and knelt in the snow before the Pope at Canossa! And day by day in this room we keep the war going—the terrible war between Church and State—

ORDULF: —between Pope and Emperor!

BERTOLD: *(Covering his head with his hands to protect himself against this avalanche of information.)* I see, I see!—I just didn't get it. Clothes like this. A room like this. I was right: these are *not* sixteenth century clothes!

HARALD: Sixteenth century indeed!

ORDULF: We're between the year 1000 and the year 1100.

LANDOLF: Count it up yourself: if we're in the snow at Canossa on January 25, 1077...

BERTOLD: *(More distressed than ever.)* God, this is a disaster!

ORDULF: It certainly is, if you thought it was the *French* court.

BERTOLD: The *English* court, I studied up on *English* history, I was reading Shakespeare and everything...

LANDOLF: My dear man, *where* were you educated? Still, you're only a couple of centuries out.

BERTOLD: *(Getting angry.)* But why in God's name couldn't they have told me it was Henry the Fourth of Germany! I had two weeks to study the thing up—I can't tell you the number of books I've had my nose in!

HARALD: Look, dear boy. Didn't you know that poor Tony was called Adalbert, Bishop of Bremen, in this house?

BERTOLD: Adalbert, Bishop of...? How'd I know that?!

LANDOLF: Well, you see how it was: when Tony died, the Marquis...

BERTOLD: Ah, so it *was* the marquis. The why on earth didn't he tell me...

HARALD: Maybe he thought you knew, dear boy.

LANDOLF: He wasn't going to take anyone else on. There were three of us left, and he thought we'd be enough. But then *he* took to shouting: "Adalbert driven out, Adalbert driven out!" Poor Tony, you see, it didn't seem to *him* Tony had died, it seemed to him the bishops of Mainz and Cologne had driven Adalbert out!

BERTOLD: *(Taking his head in his two hands and keeping it there.)* But I never heard a word of all this!

ORDULF: Then you're in a fix, my dear fellow.

HARALD: And the trouble is that we don't know who *you* are either, dear boy!

BERTOLD: Even you don't know? You don't know what part I'm to play?

ORDULF: Well, um—Bertold.

BERTOLD: Bertold? Who's he? *Why* Bertold?

LANDOLF: "They've driven Adalbert away from me? Then *I want* Bertold, I want Bertold!"—He took to shouting *that.*

HARALD: The three of us just stared at each other. Who the devil could this Bertold be?

ORDULF: So here you are, my dear fellow,—Bertold.

LANDOLF: And what a wonderful job you'll make of it.

BERTOLD: *(Rebelling and starting to go.)* Oh, no! Not for me, thank you! I'm going, I'm going.

HARALD: *(While he and Ordulf hold him back, amid laughter.)* Calm down, deal boy, calm down!

ORDULF: You won't be the Bertold of the story.

LANDOLF: Comfort yourself with the thought that even we don't really know who we are. He's Harald, he's Ordulf, I'm Landolf...That's what we are *called,* and by now we've got used to it, but who *are* we? Names. Names of the period.—And that's what you'll be—a name—of the period: Bertold. Only one of us, the late lamented Tony, ever had a good part, a part out of the story—the Bishop of Bremen. He looked like a real bishop, he was marvelous, poor Tony!

HARALD: God how the dear boy would study: read, read read!

LANDOLF: And he gave orders. Even to His Majesty. Oh yes, he knew how to put himself over. Guided him. Was a tutor. An adviser in effect. We're Privy Councillors for that matter. But with us it's just for appearances: because the history books say the Emperor was hated by the *higher* aristocracy for surrounding himself at court with young men of the *lower* aristocracy.

ORDULF: That's us my dear fellow.

LANDOLF: It really is a shame, because, well, with these clothes we could make a sensational appearance on the stage. In a costume play. They go over big these days. The Life and Loves of Henry the Fourth—what a story! Material not for one but for half a dozen tragedies! And now look at us! Just look at the four of us—and those two unfortunates standing by the throne like stuck pigs. *(He points at the two valets.)* —No one—no one puts us on stage, no one gives us scenes to act. We've got the—what do you call it?—we've got the *form*—but we don't have the *content!*—We're worse off than the Emperor's real Privy Councillors because, well, it's true no one had given *them* a part to play either, but they didn't know they *had* to play one, they played it because they played it, it wasn't a part, it was their life, see what I mean? They acted in their own interests, they fought their rivals, they sold investitures, and so forth, while we…here are we in this beautiful court, dressed up as you see, and for what? To do what? To do nothing…Six puppets hanging on the greenroom wall.

HARALD: No, no, dear boy, pardon me, but our replies do have to be in character.

LANDOLF: Yes, as far as that goes—

BERTOLD: And you said we do nothing! How'm *I* going to reply in character? I've got myself all prepared for Henry of England, and now someone calling himself Henry of Germany comes…comes butting in!

*(Landolf, Ordulf, Harald start laughing again.)*

HARALD: You'd better attend to it, dear boy—

ORDULF: —and we'll help you, my dear fellow—

HARALD: —we've lots of books in there, my dear man—but first we'll just run through the main points—

ORDULF: —so you'll have a general idea—

HARALD: Look, at this! *(Turns him round and shows him the Countess Matilda's portrait on the back wall.)* —Who's that for example?

BERTOLD: *(Looking.)* That? Well, in the first place, if you don't mind my saying so, it's out of place. Two modern paintings in the midst of all this medieval stuff?

HARALD: You're right dear boy. And as a matter of fact they weren't there originally. Behind the pictures, there are two niches—for two statues they were going to put in—in the style of the period.

The niches stayed empty—then they were covered by these two canvases—

LANDOLF: *(Interrupting and continuing.)* —which would certainly be out of place—if they really were paintings!

BERTOLD: They're not paintings? What are they then?

LANDOLF: If you go and touch them, yes, they're paintings. But for *him* *(He points mysteriously out right, alluding to the Emperor.)* — since he does *not* touch them...

BERTOLD: He doesn't? What are they then—for him?

LANDOLF: Well, this is just my interpretation, don't forget. All the same, I think it's pretty good. They're—images. Images—like, um, like images in a mirror, you see? That one there is him *(Pointing.)*, the living image of him, like in this throne room—which is also—as it should be—in the style of the period. What are you so amazed about, may I ask? If we place you in front of a mirror, won't you see *your* living image? Won't you see the you of today in the trappings of yesteryear? Well then, it's as if we had two mirrors here—two living images—in the midst of a world which...Well, you'll see for yourself, now you live with us, you'll see how this world too, every part or it, will come to life.

BERTOLD: Now, really, I didn't come here to go mad.

HARALD: Go mad, dear boy? Ts, ts. You're going to have fun.

BERTOLD: *(To Landolf.)* You certainly have quite a line in philosophy!

LANDOLF: My dear man, you can't go behind the scenes of history— eight hundred years of it—and not bring back a bit of experience!

HARALD: Let's be going, dear boy. We'll fix you up in no time—

LANDOLF: We'll fasten the wires on and have you in full working order: the perfect marionette!

ORDULF: Let's go. *(Takes him by the arm, to lead him off.)*

BERTOLD: *(Stopping and looking toward the other portrait.)* Just a minute. You haven't told me who *she* is. Emperor's wife?

HARALD: No, dear boy. The Emperors wife is called Bertha of Susa.

ORDULF: The Emperor can't stand her. He wants to be young like us. He's planning to get rid of her.

LANDOLF: That's his fiercest enemy: Countess Matilda Of Tuscany.

BERTOLD: Wait. Wasn't she the Pope's hostess at...

LANDOLF: At Canossa.

ORDULF: Precisely.

HARALD: Now *do* let's get going!

*(They are all moving over toward the door on the right by which they had entered when the old butler Giovanni, in modern cutaway, comes in at the left.)*

GIOVANNI: *(In a great hurry and worked up.)* Sss, ss! Franco! Lolo!

HARALD: *(Stopping and turning.)* Hey! What do *you* want?

BERTOLD: *(Amazed to see him come into the throne room in his modern coat.)* What's this? He comes in here?

LANDOLF: At visitor from the twentieth century! Away!
*(He and his two comprades make a joke of running over to threaten him and drive him out.)*

ORDULF: The Pope's ambassador—away with him!

HARALD: Away with the rogue!

GIOVANNI: *(Defending himself, annoyed.)* O come on, stop this!

ORDULF: No, you're not allowed in here!

HARALD: Get away, old man!

LANDOLF: *(To Bertold.)* It's witchcraft! He's a demon conjured up by the Great Magician of Rome! Out with your sword! *(And he reaches for his own.)*

GIOVANNI: *(Shouting.)* Stop this, I say! This is no time for fooling, the Marquis is here, and there's company with him...

LANDOLF: *(Rubbing his hands.)* Oh, wonderful! Ladies?

ORDULF: *(Doing the same.)* Old? Young?

GIOVANNI: Two gentlemen.

HARALD: But the ladies, who are they?

GIOVANNI: Countess Matilda and her daughter.

LANDOLF: *(Amazed.)* What? *(Pause.)* What's that?

ORDULF: *(Also amazed.)* The Countess, you say?

GIOVANNI: Yes, yes, the Countess!

HARALD: And the two men?

GIOVANNI: I don't know.

HARALD: *(To Bertold.)* Landolf told you we have form without content here, but keep your eyes open!

ORDULF: The Pope has sent a whole *bevy* of ambassadors! We'll have fun all right.

GIOVANNI: Will you let me speak?

HARALD: Speak! *(Pause.)* Speak!

GIOVANNI: Well, one of the two men seems to be a doctor.

LANDOLF: Oh, sure, we're used to *them*.

HARALD: Many thanks, Bertold, you bring us luck!

LANDOLF: You'll see how we'll manage *him.*

BERTOLD: I'm walking into a fine old mess, I can see that.

GIOVANNI: Now listen. They'll be coming into this room.

LANDOLF: *(In amazement and consternation.)* What? Is that true? Even she? The Countess will come in here?

HARALD: This is content—with a vengeance!

LANDOLF: This'll be a real tragedy!

BERTOLD: *(His curiosity aroused.)* But why? What are you talking about?

ORDULF: *(Pointing to the portrait.)* The Countess is the woman in the portrait.

LANDOLF: Her daughter is engaged to the Marquis.

HARALD: But what have they come for? That's the question.

ORDULF: If *he* sees her, there'll be fireworks.

ORDULF: Maybe he won't recognize her anymore.

GIOVANNI: If he wakes up, you'll just have to keep him in there.

ORDULF: Are you joking? How'd we do that?

HARALD: You know what he's like, dear boy!

GIOVANNI: Good heavens, use force if need be!—Those are the Marquis's orders. Now get going! Get going!

HARALD: Yes, we'd better go, he may be awake already.

ORDULF: Let's go.

LANDOLF: *(Leaving with the others, to Giovanni.)* You must explain it all later!

GIOVANNI: *(Shouting after them.)* Lock the door on that side and hide the key! This other door too. *(He points to the other door at right.)*

*(Landolf, Harald and Ordulf leave by the second door on the right.)*

GIOVANNI: *(To the two valets.)* You must go too, go on, that way! *(He points to the first door on the right.)* Lock the door and take the key out of the lock!

# Marty

Paddy Chayefsky
1950s

**Dramatic**
**Scene:** Marty's neighborhood bar

Critic
Twenty year old
Angie
Forty year old
Marty
Bartender

CRITIC: …So the whole book winds up, Mike Hammer, he's inna room
there with this doll. So he says: "You rat, you are the murderer."
So she begins to con him, you know? She tells him how she loves
him. And then Bam! He shoots her in the stomach. So she's laying there, gasping for breath, and she says: "How could you do
that?" And he says: "It was easy."

TWENTY YEAR OLD: Boy, that Mickey Spillane. Boy, he can write.

ANGIE: *(Leaning out of the booth and looking down the length of the
bar, says with some irritation.)* What's keeping Marty?

CRITIC: What I like about Mickey Spillane is he knows how to handle
women. In one book, he picks up a tomato who gets hit with a
car, and she throws a pass at him. And then he meets two beautiful twins, and they throw passes at him. And then he meets
some beautiful society leader, and she throws a pass at him,
and…

TWENTY YEAR OLD: Boy, that Mickey Spillane, he sure can write…

ANGIE: *(Looking out, down the bar again.)* I don't know watsa matter
with Marty.

FORTY-YEAR-OLD: Boy, Angie, what would you do if Marty ever died?
You'd die right with him. A couple-a old bachelors hanging to
each other like barnacles. There's Marty now.
*(Angie leans out of the booth.)*

ANGIE: *(Calling out.)* Hello, Marty, where you been?
*(Cut to: front end of the bar. Marty has just come in. He waves*

back to Angie, acknowledges another hello from a man by the bar, goes over to the bar, and gets the bartender's attention.)

MARTY: Hello, Lou, gimme change of a half and put a dime in it for a telephone call.

(The bartender takes the half dollar, reaches into his apron pocket for the change.)

BARTENDER: I hear you was at the Waverly Ballroom last night.

MARTY: Yeah, Angie tell you?

BARTENDER: (Picking out change from palm full of silver.) Yeah, I hear you really got stuck with a dog.

(Marty looks at him.)

MARTY: She wasn't so bad.

BARTENDER: (Extending the change.) Angie says she was a real scrawny-looking thing. Well, you can't have good luck alla time.

(Marty takes the change slowly and frowns down at it. He moves down the bar and would make for the telephone booth, but Angie hails him from the booth.)

ANGIE: Who you gonna call, Marty?

MARTY: I was gonna call that girl from last night, take her to a movie tonight.

ANGIE: Are you kidding?

MARTY: She was a nice girl. I kinda liked her.

ANGIE: (Indicating the spot in the booth vacated by the forty year old.) Siddown. You can call her later.

(Marty pauses, frowning, and then shuffles to the booth where Angie and the other two sit. The critic moves over for Marty. There is an exchange of hellos.)

TWENTY YEAR OLD: I gotta girl, she's always asking me to marry her. So I look at that face, and I say to myself: "Could I stand looking at that face for the resta my life?"

CRITIC: Hey, Marty, you ever read a book called I, the Jury, by Mickey Spillane?

MARTY: No.

ANGIE: Listen, Marty, I gotta good place for us to go tonight. The kid here, he says, he was downna bazaar at Our Lady of Angels last night and…

MARTY: I don't feel like going to the bazaar, Angie. I thought I'd take this girl to a movie.

ANGIE: Boy, you really musta made out good last night.

MARTY: We just talked.

ANGIE: Boy, she must be some talker. She musta been about fifty years old.

CRITIC: I always figger a guy oughtta marry a girl who's twenny years younger than he is, so that when he's forty, his wife is a real nice-looking doll.

TWENTY YEAR OLD: That means he'd have to marry the girl when she was one year old.

CRITIC: I never thoughta that.

MARTY: I didn't think she was so bad-looking.

ANGIE: She musta kept you inna shadows all night.

CRITIC: Marty, you don't wanna hang around with dogs. It gives you a bad reputation.

ANGIE: Marty, let's go downna bazaar.

MARTY: I told this dog I was gonna call her today.

ANGIE: Brush her.

*(Marty looks questioningly at Angie.)*

MARTY: You didn't like her at all?

ANGIE: A nothing. A real nothing.

*(Marty looks down at the dime he has been nervously turning between two fingers and then, frowning, he slips it into his jacket pocket. He lowers his face and looks down, scowling at his thoughts. Around him, the voices clip along.)*

CRITIC: What's playing on Fordham Road? I think there's a good picture in the Loew's Paradise.

ANGIE: Let's go down to Forty-second Street and walk around. We're sure to wind up with something.

*(Slowly Marty begins to look up again. He looks from face to face as each speaks.)*

CRITIC: I'll never forgive La Guardia for cutting burlesque outta New York City.

TWENTY YEAR OLD: There's burlesque over in Union City. Let's go to Union City...

ANGIE: Ah, they're always crowded on Sunday night.

CRITIC: So wadda you figure on doing tonight, Angie?

ANGIE: I don't know. Wadda you figure on doing?

CRITIC: I don't know. *(Turns to the twenty year old.)* Wadda you figure on doing?

*(The twenty year old shrugs. Suddenly Marty brings his fist down*

on the booth table with a crash. The others turn, startled, toward him. Marty rises in his seat.)

MARTY: "What are you doing tonight?" "I don't know, what are you doing?" Burlesque! Loew's Paradise! Miserable and lonely! Miserable and lonely and stupid! What am I, crazy or something? I got something good! What am I hanging around with you guys for?! (He has said this in tones so loud that it attracts the attention of everyone in the bar. A little embarrassed, Marty turns and moves quickly to the phone booth, pausing outside the door to find his dime again. Angie is out of his seat immediately and hurries after him.)

ANGIE: (A little shocked at Marty's outburst.) Watsa matter with you?

MARTY: (In a low, intense voice.) You don't like her. My mother don't like her. She's a dog, and I'm a fat, ugly little man. All I know is I had a good time last night I'm gonna have a good time tonight. If we have enough good times together, I'm going down on my knees and beg that girl to marry me. If we make a party again this New Years, I gotta date for the party. You don't like her, that's too bad. (He moves into the booth, sits, turns again to Angie, smiles.) When you gonna get married, Angie? You're thirty-four years old. All your kid brothers are married. You oughtta be ashamed of yourself. (Still smiling at his private joke, he puts the dime into the slot and then—with a determined finger—he begins to dial.)

# Equus

Peter Shaffer
1974

**Dramatic**
**Scene:** inside Alan's mind and memory

Dr. Dysart
Alan
Three men dressed as horse figures
Nugget, the main horse

DYSART: Quietly as possible. Dalton may still be awake. Sssh...
Quietly...Good. Now go in.
*(Alan steps secretly out of the square through the central open-*
*ing on to the circle, now glowing with a warm light. He looks*
*about him. The horses stamp uneasily: their masks turn towards*
*him.)*
DYSART: You are on the inside now. All the horses are staring at you.
Can you see them?
ALAN: *(Excited.)* Yes!
DYSART: Which one are you going to take?
ALAN: Nugget. *(Alan reaches up and mimes leading Nugget carefully*
*round the circle downstage with a rope, past all the horses on the*
*right.*
DYSART: What colour is Nugget?
ALAN: Chestnut.
*(The horse picks his way with care. Alan halts him at the corner*
*of the square.)*
DYSART: What do you do, first thing?
ALAN: Put on his sandals.
DYSART: Sandals? *(He kneels, downstage center.)*
ALAN: Sandals of majesty!...Made of sack. *(He picks up the invisible*
*sandals and kisses them devoutly.)* Tie them round his hooves.
*(He taps Nuggets right leg: the horse raises it, and the boy mimes*
*tying the sack round it.)*
DYSART: All four hooves?
ALAN: Yes.
DYSART: Then?

ALAN: Chinkle-chankle. *(He mimes picking up the bridle and bit.)* He doesn't like it so late, but he takes it for my sake. He bends for me. He stretches forth his neck to it.
*(Nugget bends his head down. Alan first ritually puts the bit into his own mouth, then crosses, and transfers it into Nuggets. He reaches up and buckles on the bridle. Then he leads him by the invisible reins, across the front of the stage and up round the left side of the circle. Nugget follows obediently.)*

ALAN: Buckle and lead out.

DYSART: No saddle?

ALAN: Never.

DYSART: Go on.

ALAN: Walk down the path behind. He's quiet. Always is, this bit. Meek and mild legs. At least till the field. Then there's trouble.
*(The horse jerks back. The mask tosses.)*

DYSART: What kind?

ALAN: Won't go in.

DYSART: Why not?

ALAN: It's his place of Ha Ha.

DYSART: What?

ALAN: Ha Ha.

DYSART: Make him go into it.

ALAN: *(Whispering fiercely.)* Come on!…Come on!…
*(He drags the horse into the square as Dysart steps out of it.)*
*(Nugget comes to a halt staring diagonally down what is now the field. The Equus noise dies away. The boy looks about him.)*

DYSART: *(From the circle.)* Is it a big field?

ALAN: Huge!

DYSART: What's it like?

ALAN: Full of mist. Nettles on your feet. *(He mimes taking off his shoes and the sting.)* Ah!

DYSART: *(Going back to his bench.)* You take your shoes off?

ALAN: Everything.

DYSART: All your clothes?

ALAN: Yes. *(He mimes undressing completely in front of the horse. When he is finished, and obviously quite naked, he throws out his arms and shows himself fully to his God, bowing his head before Nugget.)*

DYSART: Where do you leave them?

ALAN: Tree hole near the gate. No one could find them. *(He walks upstage and crouches by the bench, stuffing the invisible clothes beneath it.)*

*(Dysart sits again on the left bench, downstage beyond the circle.)*

DYSART: How does it feel now?

ALAN: *(Holds himself.)* Burns.

DYSART: Burns?

ALAN: The mist!

DYSART: Go on. Now what?

ALAN: The Manbit. *(He reaches again under the bench and draws out an invisible stick.)*

DYSART: Manbit?

ALAN: The stick for my mouth.

DYSART: Your mouth?

ALAN: To bite on.

DYSART: Why? What for?

ALAN: So's it won't happen too quick.

DYSART: Is it always the same stick?

ALAN: Course. Sacred stick. Keep it in the hole. The Ark of the Manbit.

DYSART: And now what?…What do you do now? *(Pause. He rises and approaches Nugget.)*

ALAN: Touch him!

DYSART: Where?

ALAN: *(In wonder.)* All over. Everywhere. Belly. Ribs. His ribs are of ivory. Of great value!…His flank is cool. His nostrils open for me. His eyes shine. They can see in the dark…*Eyes!*—*(Suddenly he dashes in distress to the farthest corner of the square.)*

DYSART: *Go on!*…Then?

*(Pause.)*

ALAN: Give sugar.

DYSART: A lump of sugar?

*(Alan returns to Nugget.)*

ALAN: His Last Supper.

DYSART: Last before what?

ALAN: Ha Ha. *(He kneels before the horse, palms upward and joined together.)*

DYSART: Do you say anything when you give it to him?

ALAN: *(Offering it.)* Take my sins. Eat them for my sake…He always does.

*(Nugget bows the mask into Alan's palm, then takes a step back to eat.)*

ALAN: And then he's ready.

DYSART: You can get up on him now?

ALAN: Yes!

DYSART: Do it, then. Mount him.

*(Alan, lying before Nugget, stretches out on the square. He grasps the top of the thin metal pole embedded in the wood. He whispers his God's name ceremonially.)*

ALAN: Equus!...Equus!...Equus!

*(He pulls the pole upright. The actor playing Nugget leans forward and grabs it. At the same instant all the other horses lean forward around the circle, each placing a gloved hand on the rail. Alan rises and walks right back to the upstage corner, left.)*

ALAN: *Take me! (He runs and jumps high on to Nugget's back. Crying out.)* Ah!

DYSART: What is it?

ALAN: Hurts!

DYSART: Hurts?

ALAN: Knives in his skin! Little knives—all inside my legs.

*(Nugget mimes restiveness.)*

ALAN: Stay, Equus. No one said Go!...That's it. He's good. Equus the Godslave, Faithful and True. Into my hands he commends himself—naked in his chinkle-chankle. *(He punches.)* Stop it!...He wants to go so badly.

DYSART: Go, then. Leave me behind. Ride away now, Alan. Now!...Now you are alone with Equus.

*(Alan stiffens his body.)*

ALAN: *(Ritually.)* Equus—son of Fleckwus—son of Neckwus—*Walk.*

*(A hum from the Chorus. Very slowly the horses standing on the circle begin to turn the square by gently pushing the wooden rail. Alan and his mount start to revolve. The effect, immediately, is of a statue being slowly turned round on a plinth. During the ride however the speed increases, and the light decreases until it is only a fierce spotlight on horse and rider, with the overspill glinting on the other masks leaning in towards them.)*

ALAN: Here we go. The King rides out on Equus, mightiest of horses. Only I can ride him. He lets me turn him this way and that. His neck comes out of my body. It lifts in the dark. Equus, my

Godslave!…Now the King commands you. Tonight, we ride against them all.

DYSART: Who's all?

ALAN: My foes and His.

DYSART: Who are your foes?

ALAN: The Hosts of Hoover. The Hosts of Philco. The Hosts of Pifco. The House of Remington and all its tribe!

DYSART: Who are His foes?

ALAN: The Hosts of Jodhpur. The Hosts of Bowler and Gymkhana. All those who show him off for their vanity. Tie rosettes on his head for their vanity! Come on, Equus. Let's get them!…*Trot!*
*(The speed of the turning square increases.)*

ALAN: *Stead-y! Stead-y! Stead-y! Stead-y!* Cowboys are watching! Take off their stetsons. They know who we are. They're admiring us! Bowing low unto us! Come on now—show them! *Canter!*…CANTER! *(He whips Nugget.)* And Equus the Mighty rose against All!

His enemies scatter, his enemies fall!

TURN!

Trample them, trample them,

Trample them, trample them,

TURN!

TURN!!

TURN!!!
*(The Equus noise increases in volume.)*

ALAN: *(Shouting.)* WEE!…WAA!…WONDERFUL!…I'm stiff! Stiff in the wind!

*My* mane, stiff in the wind!

*My* flanks! *My* hooves!

Mane on my legs, on my flanks, like whips!

Raw!

Raw!

*I'm raw! Raw!*

Feel me on you! *On* you! *On* you! *On* you!

I want to be *in* you!

I want to BE you forever and ever!—

*Equus, I love you!*

Now!—

Bear me away!

Make us One Person!
*(He rides Equus frantically.)*
*One Person! One Person! One Person! One Person!*
*(He rises up on the horse's back, and calls like a trumpet.)*
Ha-HA!…Ha-HA!…Ha HA!
*(The trumpet turns to great cries.)*
ALAN: HA-HA! HA-HA! HA-HA! HA-HA! HA!…HA!…HAAAAA!
*(He twists like a flame. Silence. The turning square comes to a stop in the same position it occupied at the opening of the Act. Slowly the boy drops off the horse's back on to the ground. He lowers his head and kisses Nugget's hoof. Finally he flings back his head and cries up to him.)*
ALAN: AMEN!
*(Nugget snorts, once.)*

# The Great White Hope

Howard Sackler

**Dramatic**
**Scene:** Brady's farm, Ohio

Brady, the heavyweight champion
Cap'n Dan, a champion of earlier years
Smitty, a well-known sportswriter
Pressmen and photographers
Trainers
Goldie

BRADY: Get Burke, or Kid Foster. Big Bill Brain! I ain't gonna fight no
  dinge.
FRED: Now, Frank—
CAP'N DAN: Listen here to me, Franklin—
BRADY: You wouldn't fight one when you had the belt!
CAP'N DAN: Well, let's say none of them came up to it then. It wasn't
  that I wouldn't, I didn't have to.
FRED: He didn't have to, Frank, but you do.
BRADY: In your hat I do! I know what retired means, and that's what I
  am. All I have to do is dip the sheep and pay taxes.
CAP'N DAN: Hear that, boys? It's old Farmer Brown!
FRED: Sure looks retired, don't he! Look at the arms on him.
PRESSMAN ONE: Three months back on the mill, that's all you need—
SMITTY: How long is it you put away Stankiewiez—
FRED: Not even a year! And if you smoked him in seven—
TRAINER ONE: You'll get this one in five—
PRESSMAN TWO: Four!
FRED: Two! They got glass jaws, right, Cap'n Dan?
BRADY: I ain't gonna fight no dinge.
CAP'N DAN: Now, Franklin, when you retired with that gold belt last
  summer, nobody thought it would work out like this. Everybody
  just thought that Sweeney'd fight Woods, and whoever won that
  would be the new Number One, right? So when the nigger asked
  could he fight Woods first we figured, what the hell, it'll keep up
  the interest—nobody, least of all Woods, thought he would lick
  him. And then when he said he wants to try out Sweeney too,

why Sweeney never puts the gloves or with a nigger, everybody knew that—besides, he was in Australia. Nobody thought the nigger would go all that way to him, and even when he did, who would have thought he could needle old Tommy into taking him on?

SMITTY: I was down in Melbourne for the paper, Mr. Brady, and let me tell you, no paper here could print how bad it really was. He'd say, Hit me now, Tommy, and then he'd let him, grinning all the time, and then cuffing him, jabbing him, making smart-ass remarks to the crowd—wouldn't be a man and just knock him out, no, and then, when they stopped it, with Tommy there bleeding, he's still got that big banjo smile on him—Jesus.

PRESSMAN ONE: You're the White Hope, Mr. Brady!

BRADY: I'm the what?

PRESSMAN TWO: The White Hope! Every paper in the country is calling you that.

FRED: Frank, he lands in San Francisco tomorrow—come on!

BRADY: *(To Cap'n Dan.)* Honest, I don't like this any more than you do.

CAP'N DAN: How're you going to like it when he claims the belt's his because you won't fight him. The heavyweight belt, son, yours and mine. He can say it's his.

SMITTY: Just grin and put it on.

CAP'N DAN: How're you going to like it when the whole damn country says Brady let us down, he wouldn't stick a fist out to teach a loudmouth nigger, stayed home and let him be Champion of the World.

SMITTY: Don't do it, Mr. Brady.

BRADY: I'll tell you the truth, Cap'n Dan. I hate to say it, but I feel too old. I mean it, that's the truth.

FRED: The doc says different and I do too—

TRAINER ONE: He's thinkin old because he's worried what to do—

SMITTY: Shut up. Cap'n Dan, you know what I mean.

CAP'N DAN: I know you trust me and I say you're up to it—and, Franklin, God Almighty hates a quitter! Listen here, I'll confess something to you, I had this lots of times when I was your age, every time I had a fight or a birthday.

BRADY: How'd you get rid of it?

CAP'N DAN: The one way there is: plenty of heat and nice deep massage. Now, Frank, go inside. Mrs. Brady wants to show you a letter I brought for you. I paid a call in Washington on my way out here, and even though I think it'll make you so big-headed you won't be fit to talk to, you read it, then come out here and we'll see where we stand.

*(Exit Brady. Goldie comes forward.)*

GOLDIE: Good, so it's fixed?

CAP'N DAN: Somebody say something?

GOLDIE: Me. I'm asking, Is it settled please, gentlemen? You tell me Yes I can maybe catch the train.

CAP'N DAN: The man's in a hurry, Fred.

FRED: What about terms?

GOLDIE: What, you expect I'm gonna yell about terms? Look, we're no babies here, you know like I know, my Jackie would fight it for a nickel, tomorrow. But it wouldn't look nice for you to take advantage, so you'll offer me low as you can get away with and I'll say OK.

FRED: Eighty-twenty, Goldie.

GOLDIE: What! A world's championship? You can't go twenty-five?

FRED: Eighty-twenty. That's it.

GOLDIE: Well…God bless America.

FRED: And Cap'n Dan to be the referee.

GOLDIE: Fred, you're kidding me?

FRED: Him or forget it. You know how it works.

GOLDIE: I don't mean no disrespect, but—

CAP'N DAN: Who'd you have in mind, friend, Booker T. Washington?

GOLDIE: All right, all right. Boy! What else?

FRED: That's all.

GOLDIE: He don't have to fight with his feet tied together?

FRED: I said that's all.

CAP'N DAN: We better set the place.

GOLDIE: Any place, name it, the Coast, Chicago—

CAP'N DAN: No big towns, Fred. You'll have every nigger and brother jamming in there.

GOLDIE: For my money they could have it in Iceland!

SMITTY: How about Tulsa? Denver? Reno?

PHOTOGRAPHER ONE: Hey, Reno, that's OK!

PRESSMAN ONE: Small.

FRED: No—wait—

TRAINER TWO: Reno—

CAP'N DAN: Why not? The good old Rockies—

FRED: Yeah—

CAP'N DAN: A white man's country!

GOLDIE: Sure, but you can find them?

FRED: They'll come from all over, it's on the main line now—

SMITTY: And it's high and dry. Mr. Brady would like that—

TRAINER TWO: The drier the better! If that nigger gets a sweat up, one good whiff and Frank'll be finished.

*(Enter Brady carrying the gold belt.)*

BRADY: Well, he's not through yet!

CAP'N DAN: There we are—

BRADY: Want some photos, boys?

PHOTOGRAPHER ONE: Sure thing, Mr. Brady—

PHOTOGRAPHER TWO: With it on, OK?

*(Photographers set up cameras. Pressmen ready notebooks.)*

GOLDIE: A deal?

FRED: It's a deal.

*(Fred and Goldie shake hands.)*

BRADY: And it's gonna be a pleasure—tell your nigger I said so!

PRESSMAN ONE: Pour it on, Mr. Brady—

GOLDIE: I should miss a train for this?

BRADY: *(Rolling up his sleeves.)* You tell Mr. Black Boy to give me that smile when he's inside those ropes—

TRAINER ONE: *(To Pressman.)* Get it down, get it down—

BRADY: I'll appreciate it, tell him—my eyes ain't too good these days, you understand, I like something nice and shiny to aim at— *(Puts on belt.)* OK, boys?

PRESSMAN ONE: Ah!

PHOTOGRAPHER TWO: Stance, please, Mr. Brady—

*(Brady takes stance; Photographers' magnesium flares till end of scene.)*

FRED: *(Leading, Goldie off.)* Don't let your boy take this nigger stuff to heart, huh? Explain how it's going to pack em in, that's all.

GOLDIE: He knows how it is. Good luck! *(Exits.)*

FRED: *(Calling after him.)* You're OK, Goldie!

SMITTY: *(To Cap'n Dan, looking at Brady.)* Well, there we are!

CAP'N DAN: Oh, he's the man all right. I just don't like the idea of calling it a Hope, I wish you boys hadn't hung that tag on him.

SMITTY: It's sure caught on, though!

CAP'N DAN: That's what bothers me, I guess.

SMITTY: Can I quote you on that?

CAP'N DAN: No, lend me a comb. I better go stand up with him and get my picture took!

*(Laughter and blackout.)*

# The Poison Tree

Ronald Ribman
1976

**Dramatic**
**Scene:** the Adjustment Center, maximum security area, prison

Officer Di Santis
Rollock
Friezer
Lloyd
Coyne
Lowery
Turner
Other prisoners, no lines

LOWERY: Turner? What's the matter with you? Turner? You hear what I'm saying to you? What are you doing? What's the matter with you? *(The music and dance have built to a crescendo. The Prisoner is totally oblivious to anything outside of himself. The Guard moves forward, placing his head against the bars of the cell.)*

LOWERY: Turner? Turner?

*(Suddenly the Prisoner grabs the Guard around the neck and begins to strangle him. The Guard fights back, clawing at the Prisoner's face. The slide rule falls to the floor. The fight is desperate, furious, filled with anguished cries of pain. For a long time the Guard fights back. He calls "Di Santis, Di Santis," over and over again until, with a final jerk of his arm, the Prisoner breaks his neck. Di Santis enters in time to catch the falling body of the dead Guard. Tuner emits a scream of exaltation and flings himself high up on the bars. The other Prisoner continues to stare straight forward, smoking his cigarette. Lights Out. Officer Rollock enters stage left followed a few paces behind by Officer Friezer. Friezer holds a clipboard with some papers and Rollock a laundry bag filled with personal belongings of the dead guard.)*

ROLLOCK: Hi, Sarge.

FRIEZER: *(Crossing to Officer Lloyd at desk.)* Hey, buddy, how ya doing? Lloyd? You get settled in yet?

LLOYD: No, not yet.

COYNE: Is that it, Rollock?

ROLLOCK: *(Putting down the laundry bag.)* That's it.

FRIEZER: *(Handing a sheet of paper from the clipboard to Sergeant Coyne.)* Here's a checklist.

DI SANTIS: *(At left of Rollock, staring down at the laundry bag.)* What is this?

ROLLOCK: Lowery's stuff.

DI SANTIS: I know it's Lowery's stuff. What did you put it in, a laundry bag?

ROLLOCK: Sure, I put it in a laundry bag. What did ya want me to put it in, a cardboard box? *(Offering up a small laugh.)*

DI SANTIS: *(Suddenly grown even more angry.)* No, not a cardboard box. I expected you to put it into something that shows his wife some respect—a valise, a suitcase. Is this what you want me to dump on his front porch—a laundry bag?

COYNE: Take it easy, Di Santis.

DI SANTIS: No, I don't feel like taking it easy. What is this? Some kind of joke? I ask him why he puts Lowery's belongings in a laundry bag, and he asks me if I want it put in a cardboard box?

ROLLOCK: *(Turning around to the others for support.)* That's what they gave me in supply. I asked them to give me something to put his stuff in and they gave me a laundry bag. That's what they always give me.

DI SANTIS: You got a man's personal belongings in there, Rollock, it's not a load of wash.

FRIEZER: *(Crosses to right of Di Santis.)* Hey, man, take it easy. He knows it's not a load of wash.

DI SANTIS: Does he? *(To Rollock.)* What would you do if they gave you a paper bag from the A&P, put it in that?

FRIEZER: It's just routine, man. What are you getting so excited about?

DI SANTIS: *(Pulling some unfolded clothes out of the bag.)* I'll tell you what I'm getting excited about, Friezer. You didn't even pack it. You just dumped his stuff in here. A man you worked with for five years gets killed and you just dump his stuff in a laundry bag without even packing it.

ROLLOCK: That's the way I put everybody's stuff in.

DI SANTIS: Well, not this time, Rollock. This time you're gonna take everything outa there and pack it. You understand me, Rollock? *(Pointing down at the laundry bag.)* Pack it!

COYNE: You want the truth of it straight, Di Santis? I'll give it to you. Lowery didn't have to get killed. He got himself killed because he was negligent. Sloppy and negligent.

(Lights gradually begin coming up on the entire scene. Sergeant Coyne sits behind a paper-strewn desk at stage right. Seated near the desk, to his left, is Officer Lloyd, a new guard, who is black.)

COYNE: He sat on his behind reading his goddamn college books when he should have been keeping his eyes on his cages. One week on rotation duty in the Adjustment Center and we lose a man who's been in our section five years. For what? For nothing.

DI SANTIS: (Deeply angry.) He did his job.

COYNE: You think so? Well, I'm telling you he didn't do his job.

LLOYD: (Starting to get up.) Maybe I oughtta wait outside, Sergeant Coyne.

COYNE: Just sit where you are, Officer Lloyd. Di Santis here will tell you all about the man you're replacing—Mr. St. Francis of Assisi.

DI SANTIS: You got no call saying that.

COYNE: (Rising and pacing stage right.) Oh, don't I? Lemme tell you something about your buddy. He came to work here in a zoo, a zoo filled with some of the most stinking vicious animals that ever ended up in a cage, and he wouldn't buy it. I told him that, you told him that, everybody he ever worked with in here told him that, but he wouldn't buy it. Oh no, he was gonna be the one guard in here that was gonna be different—Mr. St. Francis of Assisi.

DI SANTIS: What is that? Some kind of dirty word? What are you blaming him for? For trying to be a decent human being? For trying to make something outa his life besides working in here?

COYNE: That's right. You got it right on the button, because you work in here there's no room for college books, or slide rules, or anything else but keeping your eyes on your cages. (Crossing to Di Santis at left of center.) He saw that con was giving him trouble, he should've called as many guards as he needed to subdue that man. He should've fixed it so that man wanted to buck the system, he couldn't even crawl outa that cage. But no, he hadda wing it alone. As far as I'm concerned he wanted to be St. Francis of Assisi, he should've gone to work in a monastery. Somewhere you make a mistake they don't cut your heart out.

DI SANTIS: Is that what you want me to tell his wife?

COYNE: Yeah, you tell her how you're sloppy in this place you end up a pair of broken shoelaces and a badge, you tell her what happens to great human beings in this place. You tell her, tell her what you want, he was your friend. *(Crosses to his desk.)*

# Terra Nova

Ted Tally
1981

**Dramatic**
**Scene:** the expedition to the south geographic pole, 1911–12

Scott
Wilson
Bowers
Oates
Evans

SCOTT: My fellow members of the Society. *(Loudly and firmly.)* We are all engaged, all of us here in this room tonight, in a great scientific race, in which our national pride is at stake. No human footprints have yet appeared at the South Geographic Pole. When they do first appear—and I assure you that day is very close—I intend that they shall be British footprints! My new ship, the *Terra Nova*, will steam down the Thames on the morning of May thirtieth, and her destination is Antarctica. I *am* going back, I am going to try a second time—and this time I shall not return until I've planted the Union Jack on the bottom of the earth!
*(Toward the end of the above, there is the sound of lusty singing approaching. Scotts men—Bowers, Wilson, Oates and Evans are singing a chantey.)*
BOWERS, WILSON, OATES AND EVANS: *(Singing together offstage.)* What shall we do with a drunken sailor?
What shall we do with a drunken sailor?
What shall we do with a drunken sailor?
Ear-ly in the mor-nin'?
Put 'em in the scuppers with a hosepipe on 'em,
Put 'em in the scuppers with a hosepipe on 'em,
Put 'em in the scuppers with a hosepipe on 'em,
Ear-ly in the mor-nin'!
*(By the end of the second stanza of the chantey, Bowers, Wilson, Oates and Evans enter, hauling their sled. Bowers, Wilson and Oates are in the lead, hauling on leather traces. Evans trails, pushing. The sled is very heavy, and awkward to move. It is piled high*

with supply boxes and lashed over with tarpaulin. The Lights cover the entire stage. Bowers spots an obstruction in their path.)

BOWERS: (Breathlessly.) Whoa! Bit of a crack here!

(They stop. All but Evans come forward and kneel to examine the crack which bars their way. Evans sits on the back of the sled, grateful to catch his breath.)

OATES: That's not a crack. That's another bleeding crevasse.

BOWERS: There's a thin crust over it.

WILSON: (To Bowers.) Can you see bottom, Birdie?

BOWERS: (Lordly.) I can see a Chinaman, on his way up.

(As Scott speaks again, they kneel in silence, studying the ground. They are not certain that the ice immediately ahead of them will bear the weight of the sled.)

SCOTT: (Still facing front; continuing his speech.) There is another man who will attempt the race. I mean the Norwegian, Roald Amundsen. Listen to the means by which our Mr. Amundsen thinks fit to achieve the Pole. He intends to take along huge teams of dogs, whip them into hauling his men overland to the Great Barrier Glacier, then slaughter them when he has no further use for them and feed on the fresh dog meat! Well. I leave it to you to decide how sporting that is.

(Oates sighs and gets up.)

OATES: Help me pull us up to the edge. Come on, Birdie, put your scrawny little back to it.

(They pick up the traces again.)

OATES: Together—One! Two! Three!

(They heave at the lines, straining mightily, but the sled will not budge. They collapse, puffing.)

SCOTT: My own men have trained until they're in the peak of condition, and we intend to march it on foot.

OATES: Nothing. Stuck again.

WILSON: The runners are iced up.

(They rest on the sled, catching their breath.)

SCOTT: To the Pole and back—on foot!

WILSON: (Wearily.) There's only one thing for it.

BOWERS: Go back two hundred miles and turn starboard, 'stead of port.

OATES: Build a bridge of ice.

BOWERS: Wait here for the spring thaw—'cept there isn't any.

WILSON: Thank you. No, I mean we'll have to unload again.
   (*The others groan noisily.*)
OATES: Unload! You're off your chump. (*He chops at the ice around the base of the runners.*)
SCOTT: Only we English could so believe in an ideal…
BOWERS: Nothing like the army, is it, Titus?
OATES: Cavalry, not army!
BOWERS: All the same to me, mate.
WILSON: (*Sarcastically.*) Let's just *talk* it across!
SCOTT: Only we will so achieve it…
OATES: Well I say it's bloody stupid to unload if we can yank it!
BOWERS: And I say we just bloody well tried that, didn't we?
OATES: Then let's ask the Captain!
BOWERS: Fine!
WILSON: Yes, Robert—what do you say?
SCOTT: (*Still facing front.*) Not with cheap tricks, or cruelty to brute beasts, but with the pride of English manhood!
WILSON: (*After a slight pause.*) Robert, did you hear me?
   (*Scott turns and stares at them.*)
SCOTT: What?
OATES: The crevasse.
BOWERS: Do we yank or unload, Captain?
SCOTT: (*After a pause.*) Yes, yes, of course. (*He goes to them briskly.*) Wilson, Bowers, slip your traces back along the sides. Foot the back ends of the runners and when I signal, pull like the devil. The rest of us lifting the front corners. Ready? Heave!
   (*They all tug together; the front end of the sled is slowly lifted a few inches and yanked forward, after a tremendous effort. They once again catch their breath, Bowers half-collapsing over the side of the sled.*)
SCOTT: You see how simple it is, Bowers? We've moved it all of eight inches further along, and all it's cost you is the chance ever to have children.
BOWERS: (*Grimacing.*) If you're referring to that ungodly popping noise, that was Mr. Oates, thank you. My last one blew a hundred miles back.
OATES: The footing is better on this side.
WILSON: I hope to God we've seen the last of that soft powder.

BOWERS: Well—let's get on with it, then. *(Passing Scott.)* Ev'nin', Captain. Lovely weather for ducks!
*(They drag the sled rather easily now, over the stage and off. Evans, pushing, must struggle a bit to keep up.)*

EVANS: *(Puffing, as he passes Scott.)* Ev'nin', sir.

SCOTT: Evans.
*(Bowers, Wilson and Evans exit, singing. Oates lingers at the edge of the stage. In the distance we hear the sound of singing again, gradually trailing off.)*

BOWERS, WILSON AND EVANS: *(Offstage.)* Hoo-ray and up he rises!
Hoo-ray and up he rises!
Hoo-ray and up he rises,
Ear-ly in the mor-nin'!
*(Scott looks at Oates curiously.)*

OATES: Captain Scott—may I have a word with you?

SCOTT: Certainly, Oates.

OATES: Its Evans, sir.

SCOTT: What about him?

OATES: *(Reluctantly.)* Well he's not pulling his weight, sir.

SCOTT: *(Surprised.)* Evans?

OATES: Yes, sir. He tires easily for a big man. I don't like it.

SCOTT: Do you mean he's shirking?

OATES: No, but he's slowing the pace, that's certain, and he favors his left hand.

SCOTT: I see. Put him on point so he can rest a bit, but don't let him see he's getting any sort of special attention. If you can, get a look at that hand. I don't like the sound of that. *(Pause.)* I won't have the pace slowed, Oates. We've got to do five more miles this afternoon.

OATES: *(Grinning.)* We'll do five easily enough, Captain. We'll do eight. We're all in good spirits.

SCOTT: I can depend on you, Oates.

OATES: It's not me. All I have to do is mention the Norwegians, and they fairly fly.

SCOTT: Splendid. Well then, that's all, Oates. Carry on.

OATES: Yes, sir. I mean aye aye, sir. *(He starts to go then hesitates.)* Firmer crust here, Captain. Maybe things will start to look up, this side of the glacier.

SCOTT: I hope so, Oates. I sincerely do.

OATES: Yes, sir. *(Pause.)* Well. *(Oates exits.)*

*(The wind is heard softly. The lights fade to a spot on Scott. After a moment of uncertainty he faces out front again. During the following, Amundsen enters upstage, unseen.)*

SCOTT: In—conclusion—ladies and gentlemen. No journey ever made with dogs can approach that glory which is realized when a party of men go forth to face hardships unaided, and by days and weeks of splendid physical excertion, succeed in solving some problem of the great unknown. Our final victory over Norway will be all the sweeter, all the nobler, because we will know we've taken the prize by playing the game as it *ought* to be played!

*(Scott concludes as if expecting a great ovation. Instead we hear only one pair of hands clapping, mockingly. Scott turns, is startled to see Amundsen, revealed upstage behind the scrim. He now wears high boots and a huge dark coat with a bristling fur collar. The spot fades off Scott. Light glows through the cyclorama; an eerie wash of color fills the stage. Amundsen stops clapping, and, after a pause, speaks. All trace of the M.C.'s manner is now gone: he speaks in his own harsh, slightly accented voice.)*

AMUNDSEN: Success is a bitch. Grab her, and have her—but don't stand under her window with a mandolin.

*(Scott turns, his eyes wander over the audience.)*

SCOTT: The explanations I have to go through, the flag-waving, even at the Society! They call themselves scientists, but for three years now their stinginess has frustrated my efforts to open a whole new *continent* for science.

AMUNDSEN: For science? What can that possibly have to do with you? *(He moves down through a slash in the scrim.)* A strange science, to tell you a thousand pound sled can be manhauled across sixteen hundred miles. *(Pause.)* I consult a chart and a caloric table. It tells me that on the eightieth day of my journey, according to precise schedule, the seventeenth animal must be converted to protein. And that is science.

SCOTT: Of a certain kind, perhaps.

AMUNDSEN: *(Shrugging.)* Two methods, one goal. *(Pause.)* Most men squander their chances. Their lives pass as if they slept—at the end a vague sadness, then... *(He makes a little gesture.)* But you—and me. How many in the world like us, eh? We concentrate, we wait—for what? One place, one turning. The pattern revealed. *(Pause.)* Suppose we could stand on another planet, English, and see our whole lives at once?

SCOTT: How like another planet it must feel to stand at the bottom of the earth.

AMUNDSEN: And what a moment to be there first. Oh yes. How many lifetimes would we give for that? *(Pause.)* You and me, we're the same, eh? But you act the fine gentleman, and I'm only a filthy barbarian. A killer of dogs.

SCOTT: I said nothing of the kind.

AMUNDSEN: A foreigner, then. It's the same thing to you.

SCOTT: You don't play the game.

AMUNDSEN: Oh yes, the English game. By which you mean that peculiar love affair between your race and Man's Best Friend. Shall I tell you a little secret? It's only the big ones I shoot. With the puppies I like to snap off the heads and drink the blood.

SCOTT: I don't find you very amusing. And you know precisely what I mean.

AMUNDSEN: Do I? Oh, yes. *(Pause.)* You're angry because I swore to take the North Pole, and leave the South to you.

SCOTT: Yes, damn it. You betrayed my trust for the shabby little advantage of a few weeks' head start. You lied to me in front of the whole world!

AMUNDSEN: It wasn't a lie. I meant what I said, for as long as it was convenient. *(Pause.)* Oh, but I did *want* the North! More than you've ever wanted anything in your life. From the time I sat in the firelight and listened to tales of huge icecaps, where perhaps the gods still walked the earth…But you see—the American beat me there. Do you know what it is to see a dream strangled in newspaper cuttings? No…Well, I can't see the point of being the second man in history to reach the North Pole—can you? *(Pause.)* I'm going South, English.

SCOTT: You're at liberty to try. A decent sense of courtesy toward a brother explorer is more than I have any right to expect.

AMUNDSEN: Think of it as a sporting gesture, Scott! Just a bit of healthy open-air competition. Isn't that part of playing your damned game? As for the dogs, I won't apologize for common sense. A husky is fifty pounds of dinner hauling you along until you need to eat it.

SCOTT: There *are* rules. Codes, standards, among civilized men! One doesn't cease behaving properly simply because one is entering a wilderness. All the more reason to set an example. *(Pause.)* You'll never understand. You're not English.

AMUNDSEN: But I do understand. Playing the game means treating your dogs like gentlemen, and your gentlemen like dogs. You're an infant, tickling yourself with a razor!

# LARGE GROUP SCENES

# Paphnutius

Hrotsvitha
900

**Dramatic**
**Scene:** at Paphnutius' abode

Paphnutius the hermit, a priest
Disciples of Paphnutius (several)

DISCIPLES: Why are you so unhappy, why not the serene countenance
to which we are accustomed, Father Paphnutius?

PAPHNUTIUS: He whose heart is sad wears a sorrowful countenance.

DISCIPLES: Why are you so sad?

PAPHNUTIUS: Because of the ingratitude shown to my Creator.

DISCIPLES: What is this ingratitude of which you speak.

PAPHNUTIUS: That which He suffers from His own creatures, creatures
made to His image and likeness.

DISCIPLES: You frighten us by your words.

PAPHNUTIUS: It is understood that the eternal majesty of God cannot be
injured by any wrong, nevertheless, if it were permitted to trans-
fer by a metaphor the weakness of our frail nature to God, what
greater wrong could be conceived than this—that while the
greater part of the world is subject to His will, one part rebels
against His law?

DISCIPLES: Which part rebels?

PAPHNUTIUS: Man.

DISCIPLES: Man?

PAPHNUTIUS: Yes.

DISCIPLES: What man?

PAPHNUTIUS: All men.

DISCIPLES: How can this be?

PAPHNUTIUS: It so pleases our Creator.

DISCIPLES: We do not understand.

PAPHNUTIUS: All of us do not understand.

DISCIPLES: Do explain it to us.

PAPHNUTIUS: Listen then, to what I say.

DISCIPLES: We are listening.

PAPHNUTIUS: Accordingly, the greater part of the world is made up of four contrary elements, but by the will of the Creator, the contraries are adjusted according to harmonious rule, and man possesses not only these same elements, but has more varying components.

DISCIPLES: And what then is more varying than the elements?

PAPHNUTIUS: The body and the soul, because one can understand that they are contrary, yet they are both in one person; the soul is not mortal like the body, and the body is not spiritual like the soul.

DISCIPLES: So!

PAPHNUTIUS: If, moreover, we follow the logicians, we will not admit these to be contrary.

DISCIPLES: And who can deny it?

PAPHNUTIUS: He who can argue logically; because nothing is contrary to Essence, for she is the receptacle of all contraries.

DISCIPLES: What did you mean when you said "according to harmonious rule"?

PAPHNUTIUS: I meant that, as low and high sounds are joined together harmoniously to make a certain music, thus discordant elements, being brought together harmoniously, make one world.

*(Here follows a lengthy discussion that does not contribute to the dramatic development and is therefore omitted.)*

DISCIPLES: Where did you acquire all this knowledge with which you have just wearied us?

PAPHNUTIUS: I wish to share with you the small drop of knowledge which flowed from the full well of learning; this I found, passing by chance rather than by seeking it.

DISCIPLES: We appreciate your goodness, but we are terrified by the word of the Apostle saying: "God chooses the foolish of the world to confound the wise."

PAPHNUTIUS: Whether a foolish man or a wise man does wrong he deserves punishment from God.

DISCIPLES: Indeed he does.

PAPHNUTIUS: Knowledge does not offend God, but the wrong doing of him who has knowledge offends Him.

DISCIPLES: True, indeed!

PAPHNUTIUS: To whom may the knowledge of the arts be more worthily and rightly referred than to Him who made things which are knowable and gave us the capacity to understand them?

DISCIPLES: To none other.

PAPHNUTIUS: The more man sees by what marvelous law God has arranged all things by number, by measure, and by weight, the more intensely he will love Him.

DISCIPLES: And rightly so!

PAPHNUTIUS: But why do I dwell upon these things which afford so little pleasure?

DISCIPLES: Tell us the cause of your grief, that we may no longer be burdened by the weight of our curiosity.

PAPHNUTIUS: If ever you do find it out, you will not be happy in that knowledge.

DISCIPLES: A man is often sadder when he has satisfied his curiosity, yet he is unable to overcome this fault because it is a part of our weak nature.

PAPHNUTIUS: A certain infamous woman lives in this neighborhood.

DISCIPLES: This is dangerous to the people.

PAPHNUTIUS: Her beauty is unsurpassed, her wickedness is unspeakable.

DISCIPLES: Horrible! What is her name?

PAPHNUTIUS: Thais.

DISCIPLES: That harlot!

PAPHNUTIUS: Yes, that one.

DISCIPLES: Her wickedness is known to everyone.

PAPHNUTIUS: And no wonder, because she is not satisfied to go to destruction with a few, but she is ready to ensnare all men by the enticements of her beauty and to drag them to ruin with her.

DISCIPLES: How tragic!

PAPHNUTIUS: Not only do wastrels squander their substance by wooing her, but even respectable citizens lay their wealth at her feet, enriching her to their own undoing.

DISCIPLES: Terrible to hear!

PAPHNUTIUS: Crowds of lovers flock to her.

DISCIPLES: They destroy themselves.

PAPHNUTIUS: These lovers, in blindness of heart, quarrel and fight for access to her.

DISCIPLES: One vice begets another.

PAPHNUTIUS: When the struggle begins, sometimes fist fights result in broken noses and jaws; other times they attack with weapons so shamelessly that the threshold of the vile house is drenched with blood.

DISCIPLES: O detestable sin!

PAPHNUTIUS: This is the insult to the Creator which I mourn; this is the cause of my grief.

DISCIPLES: We do not doubt that you rightly grieve aloud about this; and that the heavenly citizens mourn with you.

PAPHNUTIUS: What if I were to approach her in the disguise of a lover; might she by chance turn from her wayward life?

DISCIPLES: He Who has inspired you with this idea is able to bring about its fulfillment.

PAPHNUTIUS: Support me, meanwhile, with your fervent prayers that I may not be overcome by the wiles of the wicked serpent.

DISCIPLES: May He Who laid low the king of darkness give you victory against the enemy!

# Paphnutius

Hrotsvitha
900

**Dramatic**
**Scene:** in the marketplace in the city

Paphnutius the hermit, a priest
Young men of the city (several)


PAPHNUTIUS: Look at the young men in the marketplace. I shall go to them first and inquire where I may find the woman for whom I am looking.

YOUTHS: Look, a stranger is coming toward us. Let us find out what he wants.

PAPHNUTIUS: Hello! Young men, who are you?

YOUTHS: We are citizens of this city.

PAPHNUTIUS: Greetings!

YOUNG MEN: And the same to you; whether a native of this country or a stranger.

PAPHNUTIUS: A stranger, for I have just now arrived.

YOUNG MEN: Why do you come? What do you seek?

PAPHNUTIUS: I cannot say.

YOUNG MEN: Why not?

PAPHNUTIUS: Because I cannot reveal it.

YOUNG MEN: It is better that you reveal it, because if you are a stranger, it will be difficult to transact any business with us citizens.

PAPHNUTIUS: What if I did tell you and in the telling I should raise some obstacle for myself?

YOUNG MEN: Not from us.

PAPHNUTIUS: I take you at your word, trusting your loyalty; I'll tell you my secret.

YOUNG MEN: There will be no disloyalty on our part, no harm shall come to you.

PAPHNUTIUS: I have learned from reports of certain persons that a woman, sweet and gracious to all, and loved by all, lives among you.

YOUNG MEN: Do you know her name?

PAPHNUTIUS: Yes, I do know it.

YOUNG MEN: Won't you tell us?

PAPHNUTIUS: Thais.

YOUNG MEN: Thais! She is the harlot.

PAPHNUTIUS: They say she is the most beautiful and most exquisite of all women.

YOUNG MEN: Those who told you this have not deceived you.

PAPHNUTIUS: For her sake, I undertook the difficulty of a long journey; I came to see her.

YOUNG MEN: There is nothing to keep you from seeing her.

PAPHNUTIUS: Where does she stay?

YOUNG MEN: In that house near by.

PAPHNUTIUS: That one to which you are pointing?

YOUNG MEN: Yes, that one.

PAPHNUTIUS: I shall go there.

YOUNG MEN: If you wish, we shall go with you.

PAPHNUTIUS: I prefer to go alone.

YOUNG MEN: As you prefer.

# The Play of St. Nicholas

Jean Bedel
Translated by Oscar Mandel
1200 A.D.

**Comic**
**Scene:** in a village near a tavern

King
Oberon
Innkeeper
Clickett
Emir of Hyrcania
Emir of Olifern
Emir of Arbisek
Emir of Iconium
Christian Warriors (several)
An Angel
An army of heathen soldiers, many, Saracens

KING: Where is Oberon, my messenger?

OBERON: Here I am, your highness, at your command.

KING: Now, Oberon, let me see how nimble you are. Go summon the Giants and the Kennelings. Carry my letters every place, exhibit my royal seal, proclaim to all men that the Christians are spoiling my law. Warn those who hesitate that they and theirs will be slaves to the end of time. On your way! You should have been in the outskirts by now!

OBERON: Trust me, sire. I can leave a galloping camel behind.

*(All leave. Enter the Innkeeper in front of his tavern.)*

INNKEEPER: Welcome one and all! Best lunch in town served here! Welcome! Welcome! Good warm bread, fresh herring, the best wines by the barrel!

*(Enter Oberon.)*

OBERON: Thank God, another inn! *(To the Innkeeper.)* What's to be had in your place?

INNKEEPER: Wine, my friend, thick enough to cut with a knife.

OBERON: Expensive?

INNKEEPER: Regular price, no extras, everything on the level. This is an honest establishment. Sit on the terrace, make yourself comfortable.

OBERON: I'll take a glass, my good man, but standing up. I'm not supposed to dawdle. Official business.

INNKEEPER: Whose?

OBERON: The King's. I'm carrying his message and his seal.

INNKEEPER: Try this. Guaranteed to go to your head. Down the hatch! The best part comes last.

OBERON: This glass has a false bottom. There was just enough to get my lips wet. Anyway, how much do I owe? I must be out of my mind staying this long.

INNKEEPER: You owe me seventy-five cents.

OBERON: All I've got is a dollar bill and a fifty-cent coin.

INNKEEPER: That's all right. I haven't got any change, so why don't you give me the dollar now, and on your way back I'll let you have a glass for fifty cents. As God is my witness, I should have charged you twice what I did. Give me the dollar, or else let me pour you a second glass.

OBERON: Why don't you take the fifty cents now and the dollar when I return?

INNKEEPER: Are you trying to kid me? You owe me seventy-five cents, my friend. And I'll have them before you leave the premises.

OBERON: But this is silly! I'm going to pay you a full dollar on my way back!

INNKEEPER: I get you. The year snow falls in June. It's no use, mister.

OBERON: Well, what am I supposed to do? Cut the fifty-cent piece in two?

*(Enter Clickett.)*

CLICKETT: Who's for killing time with a little game of dice? We'll play for small change.

INNKEEPER: *(To Oberon.)* You heard him. See if you can pay me out of his pocket.

OBERON: All right. Let's roll for a quarter.

CLICKETT: A quarter? Come on—we'll go for the six bits you owe.

OBERON: If it's all right with the boss.

CLICKETT: *(To the Innkeeper.)* All right with you, ain't it?

INNKEEPER: Sure, provided nobody leaves the premises before I'm paid up.

OBERON: *(To Clickett.)* Roll em; one roll, high man wins, and don't load the dice.

CLICKETT: Here they go, they're clean. *(He rolls.)*

OBERON: Not bad. Two threes and a snake eye. Could be worse.

CLICKETT: A lousy seven! My usual bad luck.

OBERON: Be that as it may, it's my roll. Here goes. You count, my friend. Three fours in a row. Too bad!

CLICKETT: God damn these messengers! Slippery bastards!

OBERON: Landlord, this gentleman will settle for me. He has insulted me, but I've got a thick skin.

INNKEEPER: On your way! *(To Clickett.)* You bit off more than you could chew.

*(All leave. Faraway lands. Oberon reappears.)*

OBERON: May Mahomet protect the Emir of Iconium, whom the King is summoning to his aid!

EMIR OF ICONIUM: Oberon, instruct the King on my behalf that I intend to join him with a mighty host. Tell him that nothing on earth will hold me back.

*(Oberon moves on.)*

OBERON: May Mahomet protect and bless you, mighty Emir of Hyrcania! I have been sent by the King to require your help.

EMIR OF HYRCANIA: Mahomet save your soul, Oberon. Go on your way. Since the King demands it, I shall depart this very day.

*(Oberon moves on.)*

OBERON: May our God Mahomet, who reigns over all things, protect you, great Emir of Olifern. The King has sent me to summon you.

EMIR OF OLIFERN: Oberon, assure the King that I will support him with all my forces, and that I would not fail him for the world.

*(Oberon moves on.)*

OBERON: Emir of Arbisek, the King of Africa and Arabia commands you to succor him without delay, for the Christians are waging war against him.

EMIR OF ARBISEK: Oberon, tomorrow at dawn I shall leave at the head of a hundred thousand heathens.

*(All leave. Oberon returns to the palace.)*

OBERON: Your Majesty, may Mahomet save and protect you and yours.

KING: And may he bless you, Oberon. Do you bring good news?

OBERON: Your Highness, I have done so well, scouting through Arabia and every heathen land, that there never was a king who assembled even a tenth of the crowd of pagan counts, kings, princes, and barons that I have mustered for you.

KING: Go take a rest, friend Oberon.
  *(Exit Oberon; enter the Emir of Iconium.)*
EMIR OF ICONIUM: I salute you, sire, in the name of Apollo and Mahomet.
  Behold, I am here to serve you as becomes a faithful vassal.
KING: Wisely done, my dear friend. Always come when I call you.
EMIR OF ICONIUM: Your Majesty, I have sped from the land where the
  grickles grow, far beyond the Neronian field, because of the dan-
  gers which beset you. I have walked thirty days on ice with hob-
  nailed boots. I believe I deserve your love.
  *(Enter the Emir of Hyrcania.)*
KING: What is this army?
EMIR OF HYRCANIA: Sire, these men are from beyond the Gray Wallings,
  where the very turds of dogs are made of gold. Will you bestow
  your love on me? I have ordered a hundred vessels filled with my
  treasures to sail into your harbor.
KING: My good Emir, I am heartily sorry for all the trouble you are taking.
  *(Enter the Emir of Olifern.)*
KING: And where do you come from?
EMIR OF OLIFERN: From beyond Mecca, sire, a vast and hot domain. I am
  not niggardly with you, oh King, for I have brought you thirty
  chariots full of rubies and emeralds.
  *(Enter the Emir of Arbisek.)*
KING: And you, the man who is staring at me, where do you come
  from?
EMIR OF ARBISEK: From beyond Arbisek. I can bring you nothing, sire, for
  in my land millstones are our only coin.
KING: Well, here's a fine gift of poverty for me!
EMIR OF ARBISEK: Your Majesty, in our land—and this is the truth—one
  man can carry a hundred of these coins in his purse.
COUNCILLOR: My liege, since these lords have all answered your sum-
  mons, order them to attack the Christians at once.
KING: I will, by Mahomet! I'll give these Christians a bellyfull of war.
  Every mother's son of them must be killed, caught, or driven out.
  Go tell these lords in my name to take the best possible measures.
COUNCILLOR: My lords, I bid you all in the King's name to confound the
  Christian religion. Your duty, gentlemen, is to slaughter the
  enemy. He must be repaid for the ills he has made us suffer. Go
  at once. The King wills it.

ALL THE EMIRS TOGETHER: Let us go, and may Mahomet help us! *(They leave.)*

*(The Christian Warriors appear on the battlefield.)*

A CHRISTIAN: Forward, by Saint Sepulcher!

ANOTHER: My lords, on to noble deeds!

ANOTHER: The pagans and the Saracens are coming to crush us!

ANOTHER: See how these weapons shine! I'm the happiest man on earth!

ANOTHER: Stun them with our valor!

ANOTHER: They're a hundred to one, my lords!

ONE OF THE CHRISTIANS: My lords, let there be no mistake, this is the last day of our lives. We shall all die doing God's work on earth. But as long as my sword is whole, I intend to sell my life at a high rate and to hack through many a Saracen armor. My lords, we must be ready to lay down our lives in the service of God. It will be paradise for us, and hell for them. See to it, my friends, that they taste our iron.

A NEWLY KNIGHTED CHRISTIAN: I am young, my lords, but don't belittle me! A young body often holds a mighty heart. There is a heathen warrior in the distance, the strongest of them all—I have been watching him, and unless he kills me first I mean to strike him dead.

AN ANGEL: *(T. B. W. Reid suggests that the Angel speaks throughout the play from a rostrum or a pulpit in his own distinct place.)* Lords, be of good cheer. I am a messenger of God. He will soon put an end to your troubles. Trust him. The unbelievers are ready to fling themselves upon you, but do not falter, offer your lives boldly to God, and take here the death of the faithful whose hearts are with the Lord.

A CHRISTIAN: Who are you, bright creature, bringing us words of encouragement and high meaning from God? Though you speak the truth, know that we shall face our mortal enemy with undaunted hearts.

ANGEL: I am an angel sent by God, dear friend, to comfort you. Take heart, for he shall seat you with the elect in heaven. Continue as you have begun. You must be slaughtered, all of you, but a glorious crown awaits you hereafter. Now I must be gone. You, remain with God. *(Exit the Angel.)*

*(The heathens appear.)*

EMIR OF ICONIUM: Lords, as the oldest among you, I have already given you a great deal of excellent advice. We are all experienced fighters. Let us not allow any Christian we meet to escape.

EMIR OF HYRCANIA: Escape? These sons of whores? Watch me strike and see whether I leave a single Christian standing up.

EMIR OF ICONIUM: I too, on my side, intend to cut them down like a reaper in a cornfield.

EMIR OF OLIFERN: My fine cutthroats, aren't you going to leave a couple of Christians to me?

EMIR OF ARBISEK: Here comes the hated race! Soldiers of Mahomet, forward! Strike, strike, all together!

*(Now the Saracens kill all the Christians. This stage direction is in the manuscript. We must imagine an extremely lively and reasonably lengthy fight at this point, not without ad libs and Shakespearean drums, trumpets, and alarums.)*

EMIR OF HYRCANIA: My lords, hurry over here! The marvels we have seen are nothing compared to this prisoner of mine! Take a look at this grizzled villain who is clutching his fetish. Shall we kill him or take him alive? *(This grizzled villain, who will presently speak, is called "Li Preudom" in the original, that is to say the wise, good, reliable, respected man—the perfect elderly gentleman, in short. What is he doing amidst these warriors on a battlefield in heathendom? He is not a reporter or a cook, after all. Oddly enough, scholars have unanimously overlooked this small yet singular problem. Here is a guess: Bodel would have liked to make his Preudom a priest or a monk accompanying the Christian army, but thought—or was advised—that such a figure would be indecorous for the comic stage, either in general or in the particular circumstance for which his play was written. Be that as it may, the Gentleman might well become a priest or monk in a modern production. The fetish that he clutches is called "horned" in the original—a reference to St. Nicholas' miter; but I have dropped the adjective.)*

EMIR OF OLIFERN: Let's not kill him. We'll show him off to the King as an oddity. Get up, you rascal, and come along.

EMIR OF ARBISEK: Hold him, men. I'll take care of his fetish.

GOOD CHRISTIAN: Help, Saint Nicholas! Protect me from these tormentors!

*(All leave.)*

ANGEL: Knights who lie here, how fortunate you are! How justly you now despise the world in which you suffered! And in exchange for your woes, you know, do you not, how precious is the paradise in which God places those he loves. Let all men imitate your death, for God receives into his gentle bosom whoever desires to come to him. As for you, good Christian, though you were led away by traitors, fear nothing, place your trust in God, and after God in Saint Nicholas, who will comfort you in your need when he sees your faith unshaken.

*(In the palace.)*

EMIR OF ICONIUM: King of Africa and Arabia, happier than happy! Through our valor, through our wisdom, your war is concluded. The miserable invaders are dead. Their bodies litter the countryside four leagues in every direction.

KING: Well done, my lords. But tell me, who is that sorry-looking hooded rogue you have brought along? He's the ugliest villain I have ever seen.

EMIR OF ICONIUM: Your Majesty, we kept him alive in order to entertain you with a marvel. We discovered him on his knees, hands clasped, weeping and praying to some kind of wooden puppet he adores.

KING: Come closer. Tell me, wretch, do you really believe in this image?

GOOD CHRISTIAN: I do, your highness, by the holy cross! And so should the entire world.

KING: Tell me why, you dog.

GOOD CHRISTIAN: This is Saint Nicholas. He helps those who are in need. He finds that which is lost. He shows wayfarers the path from which they strayed. He leads unbelievers to the true faith. He restores their vision to the blind. He revives those who have drowned. Nothing he guards can vanish or deteriorate, no matter how forsaken, how neglected.

# Julius Ceasar

William Shakespeare

**Dramatic**
**Scene:** before the Capitol

Julius Ceasar
Artemidorus
The Soothsayer
Brutus
Cassius
Casca
Decius
Metellus
Trebonius
Cinna
Antony
Lepidus
Popilius
Publius
and others

JULIUS CAESAR: The ides of March are come.

SOOTHSAYER: Ay, Caesar; but not gone.

ARTEMIDORUS: Hail, Caesar! read this schedule.

DECIUS BRUTUS: Trebonius doth desire you to o'er-read,
    At your best leisure, this his humble suit.

ARTEMIDORUS: O Caesar, read mine first; for mine's a suit
    That touches Caesar nearer; read it, great Caesar.

JULIUS CAESAR: What touches us ourself, shall be last served.

ARTEMIDORUS: Delay not, Caesar; read it instantly.

JULIUS CAESAR: What, is the fellow mad?

PUBLIUS: Sirrah, give place.

CASSIUS: What, urge you your petitions in the street?
    Come to the Capitol.
    *(Caesar enters the Capitol, the rest following. All the Senators rise.)*

POPILIUS LENA: I wish your enterprise to-day may thrive.

CASSIUS: What enterprise, Popilius?

POPILIUS LENA: Fare you well. *(Advances to Caesar.)*
MARCUS BRUTUS: What said Popilius Lena?
CASSIUS: He wisht to-day our enterprise might thrive.
 I fear our purpose is discovered.
MARCUS BRUTUS: Look, how he makes to Caesar: mark him.
CASSIUS: Casca,
 Be sudden, for we fear prevention.—
 Brutus, what shall be done? If this be known,
 Cassius or Caesar never shall turn back,
 For I will slay myself.
MARCUS BRUTUS: Cassius, be constant:
 Popilius Lena speaks not of our purpose;
 For, look, he smiles, and Caesar doth not change.
CASSIUS: Trebonius knows his time; for, look you, Brutus,
 He draws Mark Antony out of the way.
 *(Exeunt Antony and Trebonius. Caesar and the Senators take their seats.)*
DECIUS BRUTUS: Where is Metellus Cimber? Let him go,
 And presently prefer his suit to Caesar.
MARCUS BRUTUS: He is addrest: press near and second him.
CINNA: Casca, you are the first that rears your hand.
JULIUS CAESAR: Are we all ready? What is now amiss
 That Caesar and his senate must redress?
METELLUS CIMBER: Most high, most mighty, and most puissant Caesar,
 Metellus Cimber throws before thy seat
 An humble heart,— *(Kneeling.)*
JULIUS CAESAR: I must prevent thee, Cimber.
 These couchings and these lowly courtesies
 Might fire the blood of ordinary men,
 And turn pre-ordinance and first decree
 Into the law of children. Be not fond,
 To think that Caesar bears such rebel blood
 That will be thaw'd from the true quality
 With that which melteth fools; I mean, sweet words,
 Low-crooked curt'sies, and base spaniel-fawning.
 Thy brother by decree is banished:
 If thou dost bend, and pray, and fawn for him,
 I spurn thee like a cur out of my way.
 Know, Caesar doth not wrong; nor without cause

Will he be satisfied.

METELLUS CIMBER: Is there no voice more worthy than my own,
    To sound more sweetly in great Caesar's ear
    For the repealing of my banisht brother?

MARCUS BRUTUS: I kiss thy hand, but not in flattery, Caesar;
    Desiring thee that Publius Cimber may
    Have an immediate freedom of repeal.

JULIUS CAESAR: What, Brutus!

CASSIUS: Pardon, Caesar; Caesar, pardon:
    As low as to thy foot doth Cassius fall,
    To beg enfranchisement for Publius Cimber.

JULIUS CAESAR: I could be well moved, if I were as you;
    If I could pray to move, prayers would move me:
    But I am constant as the northern star,
    Of whose true-fixt and resting quality
    There is no fellow in the firmament.
    The skies are painted with unnumber'd sparks,
    They are all fire, and every one doth shine;
    But there's but one in all doth hold his place:
    So in the world,—'tis furnisht well with men,
    And men are flesh and blood, and apprehensive;
    Yet in the number I do know but one
    That unassailable holds on his rank,
    Unshaked of motion: and that I am he,
    Let me a little show it, even in this,—
    That I was constant Cimber should be banisht,
    And constant do remain to keep him so.

CINNA: O Caesar,—

JULIUS CAESAR: Hence! wilt thou lift up Olympus?

DECIUS BRUTUS: Great Caesar,—

JULIUS CAESAR: Doth not Brutus boothless kneel?

CASCA: Speak, hands, for me!
    *(They stab Caesar.)*

JULIUS CAESAR: *Et tu, Brute?*—Then fall, Caesar! *(Dies.)*

CINNA: Liberty! Freedom! Tyranny is dead!—
    Run hence, proclaim, cry it about the streets.

CASSIUS: Some to the common pulpits, and cry out,
    'Liberty, freedom, and enfranchisement!'

MARCUS BRUTUS: People, and senators, be not affrighted;

Fly not; stand still: ambition's debt is paid.

CASCA: Go to the pulpit, Brutus.

DECIUS BRUTUS: And Cassius too.

MARCUS BRUTUS: Where's Publius?

CINNA: Here, quite confounded with this mutiny.

METELLUS CIMBER: Stand fast together, lest some friend of Ceasar's
Should chance—

MARCUS BRUTUS: Talk not of standing.—Publius, good cheer;
There is no harm intended to your person,
Nor to no Roman else: so tell them, Publius.

CASSIUS: And leave us, Publius; lest that the people,
Rushing on us, should do your age some mischief.

MARCUS BRUTUS: Do so:—and let no man abide this deed,
But we the doers.
(Enter Trebonius.)

CASSIUS: Where is Antony?

TREBONIUS: Fled to his house amazed:
Men, wives, and children stare, cry out, and run
As it were doomsday.

MARCUS BRUTUS: Fates, we will know your pleasures:—
That we shall die, we know; 'tis but the time,
And drawing days out, that men stand upon.

CASSIUS: Why, he that cuts off twenty years of life
Cuts off so many years of fearing death.

MARCUS BRUTUS: Grant that, and then is death a benefit:
So are we Caesar's friends, that have abridged
His time of fearing death.—Stoop, Romans, stoop,
And let us bathe our hands in Caesar's blood
Up to the elbows, and besmear our swords:
Then walk we forth, even to the market-place,
And, waving our red weapons o'er our heads,
Let's all cry, 'Peace, freedom, and liberty!'

CASSIUS: Stoop then, and wash.—How many ages hence
Shall this our lofty scene be acted over
In states unborn and accents yet unknown!

MARCUS BRUTUS: How many times shall Caesar bleed in sport,
That now on Pompey's basis lies along
No worthier than the dust!

CASSIUS: So oft as that shall be,

So often shall the knot of us be call'd
The men that gave their country liberty.

DECIUS BRUTUS: What, shall we forth?

CASSIUS: Ay, every man away:
Brutus shall lead; and we will grace his heels
With the most boldest and best hearts of Rome.

MARCUS BRUTUS: Soft! who comes here!

*(Enter a servant.)*

MARCUS BRUTUS: A friend of Antony's.

SERVANT: Thus, Brutus, did my master bid me kneel;
Thus did Mark Antony bid me fall down;
And, being prostrate, thus he bade me say:—
Brutus is noble, wise, valiant, and honest;
Caesar was mighty, bold, royal, and loving:
Say I love Brutus, and I honour him;
Say I fear'd Caesar, honour'd him, and loved him.
If Brutus will vouchsafe that Antony
May safely come to him, and be resolved
How Caesar hath deserved to lie in death,
Mark Antony shall not love Caesar dead
So well as Brutus living; but will follow
The fortunes and affairs of noble Brutus
Thorough the hazards of this untrod state
With all true faith. So says my master Antony.

MARCUS BRUTUS: Thy master is a wise and valiant Roman;
I never thought him worse.
Tell him, so please him come unto this place,
He shall be satisfied; and, by my honour,
Depart untoucht.

SERVANT: I'll fetch him presently. *(Exit.)*

MARCUS BRUTUS: I know that we shall have him well to friend.

CASSIUS: I wish we may: but yet have I a mind
That fears him much; and my misgiving still
Falls shrewdly to the purpose.

MARCUS BRUTUS: But here comes Antony.

*(Enter Antony.)*

MARCUS BRUTUS: Welcome, Mark Antony.

MARCUS ANTONIUS: O mighty Caesar! dost thou lie so low?
Are all thy conquests, glories, triumphs, spoils,

Shrunk to this little measure? Fare thee well.—
I know not, gentlemen, what you intend,
Who else must be let blood, who else is rank:
If I myself, there is no hour so fit
As Caesar's death's hour: nor no instrument
Of half that worth as those your swords, made rich
With the most noble blood of all this world.
I do beseech ye, if you bear me hard,
Now, whilst your purpled hands do reek and smoke,
Fulfil your pleasure. Live a thousand years,
I shall not find myself so apt to die:
No place will please me so, no mean of death
As here by Caesar, and by you cut off,
The choice and master spirits of this age.

MARCUS BRUTUS: O Antony, beg not your death of us.
Though now we must appear bloody and cruel,
As, by our hands and this our present act,
You see we do; yet see you but our hands,
And this the bleeding business they have done:
Our hearts you see not,—they are pitiful;
And pity to the general wrong of Rome—
As fire drives out fire, so pity pity—
Hath done this deed on Caesar. For your part,
To you our swords have leaden points, Mark Antony,
Our arms no strength of malice; and our hearts,
Of brothers' temper, do receive you in
With all kind love, good thoughts, and reverence.

CASSIUS: Your voice shall be as strong as any man's
In the disposing of new dignities.

MARCUS BRUTUS: Only be patient till we have appeased
The multitude, beside themselves with fear,
And then we will deliver you the cause,
Why I, that did love Caesar when I struck him,
Have thus proceeded.

MARCUS ANTONIUS: I doubt not of your wisdom.
Let each man render me his bloody hand:
First, Marcus Brutus, will I shake with you:—
Next, Caius Cassius, do I take your hand;—
Now, Decius Brutus, yours;—now yours, Metellus;

Yours, Cinna;—and, my valiant Casca, yours;—
Though last, not least in love, yours, good Trebonius.
Gentlemen all,—alas, what shall I say?
My credit now stands on such slippery ground,
That one of two bad ways you must conceit me,
Either a coward or a flatterer.—
That I did love thee, Ceasar, O, 'tis true:
If, then, thy spirit look upon us now,
Shall it not grieve thee dearer than thy death,
To see thy Antony making his peace,
Shaking the bloody fingers of thy foes,
Most noble! in the presence of thy corse?
Had I as many eyes as thou hast wounds,
Weeping as fast as they stream forth thy blood,
It would become me better than to close
In terms of friendship with thine enemies.
Pardon me, Julius!—Here wast thou bay'd, brave hart;
Here didst thou fall; and here thy hunters stand,
Sign'd in thy spoil, and crimson'd in thy lethe.—
O world, thou wast the forest to this hart;
And this, indeed, O world, the heart of thee.—
How like a deer, strucken by many princes,
Dost thou here lie!

CASSIUS: Mark Antony,—

MARCUS ANTONIUS: Pardon me, Caius Cassius:
The enemies of Caesar shall say this;
Then, in a friend, it is cold modesty.

CASSIUS: I blame you not for praising Caesar so;
But what compact mean you to have with us?
Will you be prickt in number of our friends;
Or shall we on, and not depend on you?

MARCUS ANTONIUS: Therefore I took your hands; but was, indeed,
Sway'd from the point, by looking down on Caesar.
Friends am I with you all, and love you all;
Upon this hope, that you shall give me reasons
Why and wherein Ceasar was dangerous.

MARCUS BRUTUS: Or else were this a savage spectacle:
Our reasons are so full of good regard,
That were you, Antony, the son of Caesar,

You should be satisfied.

MARCUS ANTONIUS: That's all I seek:
  And am moreover suitor that I may
  Produce his body to the market-place;
  And in the pulpit, as becomes a friend,
  Speak in the order of his funeral.

MARCUS BRUTUS: You shall, Mark Antony.

CASSIUS: Brutus, a word with you.
  *(Aside to Brutus.)* You know not what you do: do not consent
  That Antony speak in his funeral:
  Know you how much the people may be moved
  By that which he will utter?

MARCUS BRUTUS: *(Aside to Cassius.)* By your pardon;—
  I will myself into the pulpit first,
  And show the reason of our Caesar's death:
  What Antony shall speak, I will protest
  He speaks by leave and by permission;
  And that we are contented Caesar shall
  Have all true rites and lawful ceremonies.
  It shall advantage more than do us wrong.

CASSIUS: *(Aside to Marcus Brutus.)* I know not what may fall;
  I like it not.

MARCUS BRUTUS: Mark Antony, here, take you Caesar's body.
  You shall not in your funeral speech blame us,
  But speak all good you can devise of Caesar;
  And say you do't by our permission;
  Else shall you not have any hand at all
  About his funeral: and you shall speak
  In the same pulpit whereto I am going,
  After my speech is ended.

MARCUS ANTONIUS: Be it so; I do desire no more.

MARCUS BRUTUS: Prepare the body, then, and follow us.
  *(Exeunt all but Antony.)*

MARCUS ANTONIUS: O, pardon me, thou bleeding piece of earth,
  That I am meek and gentle with these butchers!
  Thou art the ruins of the noblest man
  That ever lived in the tide of times.
  Woe to the hand that shed this costly blood!
  Over thy wounds now do I prophesy,—

Which, like dumb mouths, do ope their ruby lips,
To beg the voice and utterance of my tongue,—
A curse shall light upon the limbs of men;
Domestic fury and fierce civil strife
Shall cumber all the parts of Italy;
Blood and destruction shall be so in use,

Pray to the gods to intermit the plague
That needs must light on this ingratitude.
FLAVIUS: Go, go, good countrymen, and, for this fault,
Assemble all the poor men of your sort;
Draw them to Tiber banks, and weep your tears
Into the channel, till the lowest stream
Do kiss the most exalted shores of all.
(*Exeunt all the commoners.*)
FLAVIUS: See, whe'r their basest metal be not moved!
They vanish tongue-tied in their guiltiness.
Go you down that way towards the Capitol;
This way will I: disrobe the images,
If you do find them deckt with ceremonies.
MARULLUS: May we do so?
You know it is the feast of Lupercal.
FLAVIUS: It is no matter; let no images
Be hung with Caesar's trophies. I'll about,
And drive away the vulgar from the streets:
So do you too, where you perceive them thick.
These growing feathers pluckt from Caesar's wing
Will make him fly an ordinary pitch;
Who else would soar above the view of men,
And keep us all in servile fearfulness. (*Exeunt.*)

# The Group

Mercy Otis Warren
1775

**Satiric**
**Scene:** a large dining room furnished for drinking and card playing

Lord Chief Justice Hazelrod (offstage)
Scriblerius Fribble
Monsieur de François
Hum Humbug, Esq.
Beau Trumps, a gambler
Collateralis, a new-made judge


SCRIBLERIUS: Thy toast, Monsieur—
    Pray, why that solemn phiz?—
    Art thou, too, balancing 'twixt right and wrong?
    Hast thou a thought so mean as to give up
    Thy present good, for promise in reversion?
    'Tis true hereafter has some feeble terrors,
    But e'er our grizzly heads are wrapped in clay
    We may compound, and make our peace with Heaven.
MONSIEUR: Could I give up the dread of retribution,
    The awful reckoning of some future day,
    Like surly Hateall I might curse mankind,
    And dare the threatened vengeance of the skies.
    Or like yon apostate— *(Pointing to Hazlerod, retired to a corner to read Massachusettensis.)*
    Feel but slight remorse
    To sell my country for a grasp of gold.
    But the impressions of my early youth,
    Infixed by precepts of my pious sire,
    Are stings and scorpions in my goaded breast.
    Oft have I hung upon my parent's knee
    And heard him tell of his escape from France;
    He left the land of slaves and wooden shoes;
    From place to place he sought a safe retreat,
    Till fair Bostonia stretched her friendly arm

And gave the refugee both bread and peace.
(Shall I ungrateful 'rase the sacred bonds,
And help to clank the tyrant's iron chains
O'er these blest shores—once the sure asylum
From all the ills of arbitrary sway?)
With his expiring breath he bade his sons,
If e'er oppression reached the western world,
Resist its force, and break the servile yoke.

SCRIBLERIUS: Well, quit thy post;—Go make thy flattering court
To Freedom's sons, and tell thy baby fears;
Show the soft traces in thy puny heart,
Made by the trembling tongue and quivering lip
Of an old grandsire's superstitious whims.

MONSIEUR: No.—I never can—
So great the itch I feel for titled place,
Some honorary post, some small distinction,
To save my name from dark oblivion's jaws,
I'll hazard all, but ne'er give up my place;
For that I'll see Rome's ancient rites restored,
And flame and faggot blaze in every street.

BEAU TRUMPS: —That's right, Monsieur,
There's nought on earth that has such tempting charms
As rank and show, and pomp, and glittering dress,
Save the dear counters at beloved quadrille.
Viner unsoiled, and Littleton may sleep,
And Coke lie moldering on the dusty shelf,
If I by shuffling draw some lucky card
That wins the livres or lucrative place.

HUM HUMBUG: When sly Rapatio showed his friends the scroll,
I wondered much to see thy patriot name
Among the list of rebels to the state,
I thought thee one of Rusticus's sworn friends.

BEAU TRUMPS: When first I entered on the public stage
My country groaned beneath base Brundo's hand,
Virtue looked fair and beckoned to her lure,
Through Truth's bright mirror I beheld her charms
And wished to tread the patriotic path,
And wear the laurels that adorn his fame;
I walked a while and tasted solid peace

With Cassius, Rusticus, and good Hortensius,
And many more, whose names will be revered
When you and I, and all the venal herd,
Weighed in Nemesis' just, impartial scale,
Are marked with infamy till time blot out
And in oblivion sink our hated names.
But 'twas a poor, unprofitable path—
Naught to be gained, save solid peace of mind.
No pensions, place, or title there I found;
I saw Rapatio's arts had struck so deep
And given his country such a fatal wound,
None but its foes promotion could expect;
I trimmed, and pimped, and veered, and wavering stood,
But half resolved to show myself a knave,
Till the arch Traitor, prowling round for aid,
Saw my suspense and bid me doubt no more;—
He gently bowed, and smiling took my hand,
And whispering softly in my listening ear,
Showed me my name among his chosen band,
And laughed at virtue dignified by fools,
Cleared all my doubts, and bid me persevere
In spite of the restraints or hourly checks
Of wounded friendship, and a goaded mind,
Or all the sacred ties of trust and honor.

COLLATERALIS: Come, 'mongst ourselves we'll e'en speak out the truth.
Can you suppose there yet is such a dupe
As still believes that wretch an honest man?
The latter strokes of his serpentine brain
Outvie the arts of Machiavel himself;
His Borgian model here is realized,
And the stale tricks of politicians played
Beneath a vizard fair—
—Drawn from the heavenly form
Of blest Religion weeping o'er
the land
For virtue fallen, and for freedom lost.

BEAU TRUMPS: I think with you—
—unparalleled his effrontery,
When by chicanery and specious art,

Midst the distress in which he'd brought the city,
He found a few (by artifice and cunning,
By much industry of his wily friend
The false Philanthrop—sly, undermining tool,
Who with the Siren's voice—
Deals daily round the poison of his tongue.)
To speak him fair—and overlook his guilt.
They by reiterated promise made
To stand their friend at Britain's mighty court,
And vindicate his native injured land,
Lent him their names to sanctify his deeds.
But mark the traitor—his high crime glossed o'er
Conceals the tender feelings of the man,
The social ties that bind the human heart;
He strikes a bargain with his country's foes,
And joins to wrap America in flames.
Yet with feigned pity and Satanic grin,
As if more deep to fix the keen insult,
Or make his life a farce still more complete,
He sends a groan across the broad Atlantic,
And with a phiz of crocodilian stamp,
Can weep and wreathe, still hoping to deceive,
He cries, the gathering clouds hang thick about her,
But laughs within—then sobs—
—Alas! my country!
HUM HUMBUG: Why so severe, or why exclaim at all,
Against the man who made thee what thou art?
BEAU TRUMPS: I know his guilt,—I ever knew the man,
Thy father knew him ere we trod the stage;
I only speak to such as know him well;
Abroad I tell the world he is a saint.
But as for interest, I betrayed my own
With the same views, I ranked among his friends;
But my ambition sighs for something more.
What merits has Sir Sparrow of his own,
And yet a feather graces the fool's cap:
Which did he wear for what himself achieved,
'Twould stamp some honor on his latest heir—
But I'll suspend my murmuring care awhile;

Come, t'other glass—and try our luck at loo,
And if before the dawn your gold I win,
Or ere bright Phoebus does his course begin,
The eastern breeze from Britain's hostile shore
Should waft her lofty floating towers o'er,
Whose waving pendants sweep the watery main,
Dip their proud beaks and dance towards the plain,
The destined plains of slaughter and distress,
Laden with troops from Hanover and Hess,
I would invigorate my sinking soul,
For then the continent we might control;
Not all the millions that she vainly boasts
Can cope with veteran barbarian hosts;—
But the brave sons of Albion's warlike race,
Their arms and honors never can disgrace,
Or draw their swords in such a hated cause
In blood to seal a N_____'s oppressive laws.
They'll spurn the service;—Britons must recoil,
And show themselves the natives of an isle
Who fought for freedom, in the worst of times
Produced her Hampdens, Fairfaxes, and Pyms.
But if by carnage we should win the game,
Perhaps by my abilities and fame,
I might attain a splendid, glittering car,
And mount aloft, and sail in liquid air;
Like Phaeton, I'd then outstrip the wind,
And leave my low competitors behind.

# Ruddigore

W.S. Gilbert

**Comic**
**Scene:** the portrait gallery

Robin
Sir Roderic
Chorus of family portraits come to life
First Ghost
Second Ghost
Third Ghost
Fourth Ghost, all Baronets Murgatroyd
Fifth Ghost
Sixth Ghost
Seventh Ghost
Eighth Ghost

ROBIN: For a week I have fulfilled my accursed doom! I have duly committed a crime a day! Not a great crime, I trust, but still, in the eyes of one as strictly regulated as I used to be, a crime. But will my ghostly ancestors be satisfied with what I have done, or will they regard it as an unworthy subterfuge? *(Addressing pictures.)* Oh, my forefathers, wallowers in blood, there came at last a day when, sick of crime, you, each and every, vowed to sin no more, and so, in agony, called welcome Death to free you from your cloying guiltiness. Let the sweet psalm of that repentant hour soften your long-dead hearts, and tune your souls to mercy on your poor posterity! *(Kneeling.)*
*(The stage darkens for a moment. It becomes light again, and the pictures are seen to have become animated.)*
CHORUS OF FAMILY PORTRAITS: Painted emblems of a race,
  All accurst in days of yore,
  Each from his accustomed place
  Steps into the world once more.
  *(The Pictures step from their frames and march round the stage.)*
CHORUS OF FAMILY PORTRAITS: Baronet of Ruddigore,
  Last of our accursèd line,
  Down upon the oaken floor—

Down upon those knees of thine.
Coward, poltroon, shaker, squeamer,
Blockhead, sluggard, dullard, dreamer,
Shirker, shuffler, crawler, creeper,
Sniffler, snuffler, wailer, weeper,
Earthworm, maggot, tadpole, weevil!
Set upon thy course of evil,
Lest the king of Spectre-Land
Set on thee his grisly hand!
*(The Spectre of Sir Roderic descends from his frame.)*

SIR RODERIC: Beware! beware! beware!

ROBIN: Gaunt vision, who are thou
That thus, with icy glare
And stern relentless brow,
Appearest, who knows how?

SIR RODERIC: I am the spectre of the late
Sir Roderic Murgatroyd,
Who comes to warn thee that thy fate
Thou canst not now avoid.

ROBIN: Alas, poor ghost!

SIR RODERIC: The pity you
Express for nothing goes:
We spectres are a jollier crew
Than you, perhaps, suppose!

CHORUS: We spectres are a jollier crew
Than you, perhaps, suppose!

SIR RODERIC: *(Song.)* When the night wind howls in the chimney cowls, and the bat in the moonlight flies,
And inky clouds, like funeral shrouds, sail over the midnight skies—
When the footpads quail at the night-bird's wail, and black dogs bay at the moon,
Then is the spectre's holiday—then is the ghosts' high-noon!

CHORUS: Ha! ha!
Then is the ghosts' high-noon!

SIR RODERIC: As the sob of the breeze sweeps over the trees, and the mists lie low on the fen,
From grey tomb-stones are gathered the bones that once were women and men,

And away they go, with a mop and a mow, to the revel that ends too soon,

For cockcrow limits our holiday—the dead of the night's high-noon!

CHORUS: Ha! ha!

The dead of the night's high-noon!

SIR RODERIC: And then each ghost with his ladye-toast to their church-yard beds takes flight,

With a kiss, perhaps, on her lantern chaps, and a grisly grim "good-night";

Till the welcome knell of the midnight bell rings forth its jolliest tune,

And ushers in our next high holiday—the dead of the night's high-noon!

CHORUS: Ha! ha!

The dead of the night's high-noon!

ROBIN: I recognize you now—you are the picture that hangs at the end of the gallery.

SIR RODERIC: In a bad light. I am.

ROBIN: Are you considered a good likeness?

SIR RODERIC: Pretty well. Flattering.

ROBIN: Because as a work of art you are poor.

SIR RODERIC: I am crude in colour, but I have only been painted ten years. In a couple of centuries I shall be an Old Master, and then you will be sorry you spoke lightly of me.

ROBIN: And may I ask why you have left your frames?

SIR RODERIC: It is our duty to see that our successors commit their daily crimes in a conscientious and workman-like fashion. It is our duty to remind you that you are evading the conditions under which you are permitted to exist.

ROBIN: Really, I don't know what you'd have. I've only been a bad baronet a week, and I've committed a crime punctually every day.

SIR RODERIC: Let us inquire into this. Monday?

ROBIN: Monday was a Bank Holiday.

SIR RODERIC: True. Tuesday?

ROBIN: On Tuesday I made a false income-tax return.

ALL: Ha! ha!

FIRST GHOST: That's nothing.

SECOND GHOST: Nothing at all.

THIRD GHOST: Everybody does that.

FOURTH GHOST: It's expected of you.

SIR RODERIC: Wednesday?

ROBIN: *(Melodramatically.)* On Wednesday I forged a will.

SIR RODERIC: Whose will?

ROBIN: My own.

SIR RODERIC: My good sir, you can't forge your own will!

ROBIN: Can't I, though! I like that! I *did!* Besides, if a man can't forge his own will, whose will can he forge?

FIRST GHOST: There's something in that.

SECOND GHOST: Yes, it seems reasonable.

THIRD GHOST: At first sight it does.

FOURTH GHOST: Fallacy somewhere, I fancy!

ROBIN: A man can do what he likes with his own?

SIR RODERIC: I suppose he can.

ROBIN: Well, then, he can forge his own will, stoopid! On Thursday I shot a fox.

FIRST GHOST: Hear, hear!

SIR RODERIC: That's better. *(Addressing Ghosts.)* Pass the fox, I think? *(They assent.)*

SIR RODERIC: Yes, pass the fox. Friday?

ROBIN: On Friday I forged a cheque.

SIR RODERIC: Whose cheque?

ROBIN: Old Adam's.

SIR RODERIC: But Old Adam hasn't a banker.

ROBIN: I didn't say I forged his banker—I said I forged his cheque. On Saturday I disinherited my only son.

SIR RODERIC: But you haven't got a son.

ROBIN: No—not yet. I disinherited him in advance, to save time. You see—by this arrangement—he'll be born ready disinherited.

SIR RODERIC: I see. But I don't think you can do that.

ROBIN: My good sir, if I can't disinherit my own unborn son, whose unborn son can I disinherit?

SIR RODERIC: Humph! These arguments sound very well, but I can't help thinking that, if they were reduced to syllogistic form, they wouldn't hold water. Now quite understand us. We are foggy, but we don't permit our fogginess to be presumed upon. Unless you undertake to—well, suppose we say, carry off a lady?

*(Addressing Ghosts.)* Those who are in favour of his carrying off a lady?

*(All hold up their hands except a Bishop.)*

SIR RODERIC: Those of the contrary opinion?

*(Bishop holds up his hand.)*

SIR RODERIC: Oh, you're never satisfied! Yes, unless you undertake to carry off a lady at once—I don't care what lady—any lady—choose your lady—you perish in inconceivable agonies.

ROBIN: Carry off a lady? Certainly not, on any account. I've the greatest respect for ladies, and I wouldn't do anything of the kind for worlds! No, no. I'm not that kind of baronet, I assure you! If that's all you've got to say, you'd better go back to your frames.

SIR RODERIC: Very good—then let the agonies commence.

*(Ghosts make passes. Robin begins to writhe in agony.)*

ROBIN: Oh! Oh! Don't do that! I can't stand it!

SIR RODERIC: Painful, isn't it? It gets worse by degrees.

ROBIN: Oh—Oh! Stop a bit! Stop it, will you? I want to speak.

*(Sir Roderic makes signs to Ghosts, who resume their attitudes.)*

SIR RODERIC: Better?

ROBIN: Yes—better now! Whew!

SIR RODERIC: Well, do you consent?

ROBIN: But it's such an ungentlemanly thing to do!

SIR RODERIC: As you please. *(To Ghosts.)* Carry on!

ROBIN: Stop—I can't stand it! I agree! I promise! It shall be done!

SIR RODERIC: To-day?

ROBIN: To-day!

SIR RODERIC: At once?

ROBIN: At once! I retract! I apologize! I had no idea it was anything like that!

ALL: We want your pardon, ere we go.
For having agonized you so—
So pardon us—
So pardon us—
So pardon us—
Or die!

ROBIN: I pardon you!
I pardon you!

ALL: He pardons us—
Hurrah!

*(The Ghosts return to their frames.)*

CHORUS: Painted emblems of a race,
    All accurst in days of yore,
    Each to his accustomed place
    Steps unwillingly once more!
    *(By this time the Ghosts have changed to pictures again. Robin is overcome by emotion.)*

# The Visit
Friedrich Duerenmatt
1956

**Dramatic**
**Scene:** at the Guellen Railway Station

Four Townsmen
Painter
Stationmaster
Guard
Mayor
Priest
Bailiff
III

MAN ONE: The Goodrun. Hamburg-Naples.

MAN TWO: The Racing Roland gets here at eleven twenty-seven. Venice-Stockholm.

MAN THREE: Our last remaining pleasure: watching trains go by.

MAN FOUR: Five years ago the Goodrun and the Racing Roland stopped in Guellen. And the Diplomat. And the Lorelei. All famous express trains.

MAN ONE: World famous.

MAN ONE: Now not even the commuting trains stop. Just two from Kaffigen and the one-thirteen from Kalberstadt.

MAN THREE: Ruined.

MAN FOUR: The Wagner Factory gone crash.

MAN ONE: Bockmann bankrupt.

MAN TWO: The Foundry on Sunshine-Square shut down.

MAN THREE: Living on the dole.

MAN FOUR: On Poor Relief soup.

MAN ONE: Living?

MAN TWO: Vegetating.

MAN THREE: And rotting to death.

MAN FOUR: The entire township.
    *(Bell rings.)*

MAN TWO: It's more than time that millionairess got here. They say she founded a hospital in Kalberstadt.

MAN THREE: And a kindergarten in Kaffigen. And a memorial church in the Capital.

PAINTER: She had Zimt do her portrait. That Naturalistic dauber.

MAN ONE: She and her money. She owns Armenian Oil, Western Railways, North Broadcasting Company and the Hong Kong— uh—Amusement District.

*(Train clatter. Station-Master salutes. Men move heads from right to left after train.)*

MAN FOUR: The Diplomat.

MAN THREE: We were a city of the Arts then.

MAN TWO: One of the foremost in the land.

MAN ONE: In Europe.

MAN FOUR: Goethe spent a night here. In the Golden Apostle.

MAN THREE: Brahms composed a quartet here.

*(Bell rings.)*

MAN TWO: Bertold Schwarz invented gunpowder here.

PAINTER: And I was a brilliant student at the *École des Beaux Arts*. And what am I doing here now? Sign-painting!

*(Train clatter. Guard appears, left, as after jumping off train.)*

GUARD: *(Long-drawn wail.)* Guellen!

MAN ONE: The Kaffigen commuter.

*(One passenger has got off, left. He walks past men on bench, disappears through doorway marked "Gents.")*

MAN TWO: The Bailiff.

MAN THREE: Going to distrain on the Town Hall.

MAN FOUR: We're even ruined politically.

STATION-MASTER: *(Waves green flag, blows whistle.)* Stand clear!

*(Enter from town, Mayor, Schoolmaster, Priest and Ill—a man of near sixty-five; all shabbily dressed.)*

MAYOR: The guest of honor will be arriving on the one-thirteen commuting from Kalberstadt.

SCHOOLMASTER: We'll have the mixed choir singing, the Youth Club.

PRIEST: And the fire bell ringing. It hasn't been pawned.

MAYOR: We'll have the town band playing on Market Square. The Athletics Club will honor the millionairess with a pyramid. Then a meal in the Golden Apostle. Finances unfortunately can't be stretched to illuminating the Cathedral for the evening. Or the Town Hall.

*(Bailiff comes out of little building.)*

BAILIFF: Good morning, Mister Mayor, a very good morning to you.

MAYOR: Why, Mister Glutz, what are you doing here?

BAILIFF: You know my mission, Mister Mayor. It's a colossal undertaking I'm faced with. Just try distraining on an entire town.

MAYOR: You won't find a thing in the Town Hall. Apart from one old typewriter.

BAILIFF: I think you're forgetting something, Mister Mayor. The Guellen History Museum.

MAYOR: Gone three years ago. Sold to America. Our coffers are empty. Not a single soul pays taxes.

BAILIFF: It'll have to be investigated. The country's booming and Guellen has the Sunshine Foundry. But Guellen goes bankrupt.

MAYOR: We're up against a real economic enigma.

MAN ONE: The whole thing's a Free Masons' plot.

MAN TWO: Conspired by the Jews.

MAN THREE: Backed by High Finance.

MAN FOUR: International Communism's showing its colors.
    (Bell rings.)

BAILIFF: I always find something. I've got eyes like a hawk. I think I'll take a look at the Treasury. (Exit.)

MAYOR: Better let him plunder us first. Not after the millionairess's visit.
    (Painter has finished painting his banner.)

ILL: You know, Mister Mayor, that won't do. This banner's too familiar. It ought to read, "Welcome Claire Zachanassian."

MAN ONE: But she's Claire!

MAN TWO: Claire Wascher!

MAN THREE: She was educated here!

MAN FOUR: Her dad was the builder.

PAINTER: O.K., so I'll write "Welcome Claire Zachanassian" on the back. Then if the millionairess seems touched we can turn it round and show her the front.

MAN TWO: It's the Speculator. Zürich-Hamburg.
    (Another express train passes, right to left.)

MAN THREE: Always on time, you can set your watch by it.

MAN FOUR: Tell me who still owns a watch in this place.

MAYOR: Gentlemen, the millionairess is our only hope.

PRIEST: Apart from God.

MAYOR: Apart from God.

SCHOOLMASTER: But God won't pay.

MAYOR: You used to be a friend of hers, Ill, so now it all depends on you.

PAINTER: But their ways parted. I heard some story about it—have you no confession to make to your Priest?

ILL: We were the best of friends. Young and hotheaded. I used to be a bit of a lad, gentlemen, forty-five years ago. And she, Clara, I call see her still: coming towards me through the shadows in Petersens' Barn, all aglow. Or walking barefoot in the Konrad's Village Wood, over the moss and the leaves, with her red hair streaming out, slim and supple as a willow, and tender, ah, what a devilish beautiful little witch. Life tore us apart. Life. That's the way it is.

MAYOR: I ought to have a few details about Madam Zachanassian for my little after-dinner speech in the Golden Apostle. *(Takes a small notebook from pocket.)*

SCHOOLMASTER: I've been going through the old school-reports. Clara Wascher's marks, I'm sorry to say were appalling. So was her conduct. She only passed in botany and zoology.

MAYOR: *(Takes note.)* Good. Botany and zoology. A pass. That's good.

ILL: I can help you here, Mister Mayor. Clara loved justice. Most decidedly. Once when they took a beggar away she flung stones at the police.

MAYOR: Love of justice. Not bad. It always works. But I think we'd better leave out that bit about the police.

ILL: She was generous too. Everything she had she shared. She stole potatoes once for an old widow woman.

MAYOR: Sense of generosity. Gentlemen, I absolutely must bring that in. It's the crucial point. Does anyone here remember a building her father built? That'd sound good in my speech.

ALL: No. No one.

*(Mayor shuts his little notebook.)*

MAYOR: I'm fully prepared for my part. The rest is up to Ill.

ILL: I know. Zachanassian has to cough up her millions.

MAYOR: Millions—that's the idea. Precisely.

SCHOOLMASTER: It won't help us if she only founds a nursery.

MAYOR: My dear Ill, you've been the most popular personality in Guellen for a long while now. In the spring, I shall be retiring. I've sounded out the Opposition: we've agreed to nominate you as my successor.

ILL: But Mister Mayor.

SCHOOLMASTER: I can confirm that.

ILL: Gentlemen, back to business. First of all, I'll tell Clara all about our wretched plight.

PRIEST: But do be careful—do be tactful.

ILL: We've got to be clever. Psychologically acute. If we make a fiasco of the welcome at the station, we could easily wreck everything else. You won't bring it off by relying on the municipal band and the mixed choir.

MAYOR: Ill's right, there. It'll be one of the decisive moments. Madam Zachanassian sets foot on her native soil, she's home again, and how moved she is, there are tears in her eyes, ah, the old familiar places. The old faces. Not that I'll be standing here like this in my shirtsleeves. I'll be wearing my formal black and a top hat. My wife beside me, my two grand children in front of me, all in white. Holding roses. My God, if only it all works out according to plan!

*(Bell rings.)*

MAN ONE: It's the Racing Roland.

MAN TWO: Venice-Stockholm eleven twenty-seven.

PRIEST: Eleven twenty-seven! We still have nearly two hours to get suitably dressed.

MAYOR: Kuhn and Hauser hoist the "Welcome Claire Zachanassian" banner. *(Points at four men.)* You others better wave your hats. But please: no bawling like last year at the Government Mission, it hardly impressed them at all and so far we've had no subsidy. This is no time for wild enthusiasm, the mood you want is an inward, an almost tearful sympathy for one of our children, who was lost, and has been found again. Be relaxed. Sincere. But above all, time it well. The instant the choir stops singing, sound the fire-alarm. And look out…

*(His speech is drowned by the thunder of the oncoming train. Squealing brakes. Dumbfounded astonishment on all faces. The five men spring up from bench.)*

PAINTER: The Express!

MAN ONE: It's stopping!

MAN TWO: In Guellen!

MAN THREE: The lousiest—

MAN FOUR: Most poverty-stricken—

MAN ONE: Desolate dump on the Venice-Stockholm line!

STATION-MASTER: It's against the Laws of Nature. The Racing Roland ought to materialize from around the Leuthenau bend, roar through Guellen, dwindle into a dark dot over at Pückenreid valley and vanish.

# The Royal Hunt of the Sun

Peter Shaffer
1964

**Dramatic**
Pizarro
Rodas
Vasca
Domingo
Juan
Pedro
Young Martin
Soldiers, many
Incas, many

PIZARRO: We are commanded to court by a brown King, more powerful than any you have ever heard of, sole owner of all the gold
we came for. We have three roads. Go back, and he kills us. Stay
here, and he kills us. Go on, and he still may kill us. Who fears to
meet him can stay here with the Veedor and swell a garrison.
He'll have no disgrace, but no gold neither. Who stirs?

RODAS: Well, I hissing stir for one. I'm not going to be chewed up by
no bloody heathen king. What do you say, Vasca lad?

VASCA: I don't know. I reckon if he chews us first, he chews you second. We're the eggs and you're the stew.

RODAS: Ha, ha, day of a hundred jokes!

SALINAS: Come on friend, for God's sake. Who's going to sew us up if
you desert?

RODAS: You can all rot for all I care, breeches and what's bloody in 'em.

SALINAS: Bastard!

RODAS: To hell with the lot of you! *(He walks off.)*

PIZARRO: Anyone else?

DOMINGO: Well, I don't know…Maybe he's right.

JUAN: Hey, Pedro, what do you think?

PEDRO: Hell, no. Vasca's right. It's as safe to go as stay here.

SALINAS: That's right.

VASCA: Anyway, I didn't come to keep no hissing garrison.

PEDRO: Nor me. I'm going on.

JUAN: Right boy.

SALINAS: And me.

DOMINGO: Well, I don't know…

VASCA: Oh, close your mouth. You're like a hissing girl. *(To Pizarro.)* We're coming. Just find us the gold.

PIZARRO: All right then. *(To Young Martin.)* You stay here.

YOUNG MARTIN: No, sir. The place of a squire is at all times by his Knight's side. Laws of Chivalry.

PIZARRO: *(Touched.)* Get them in rank. Move!

YOUNG MARTIN: Company in rank. Move!

*(The soldiers form up in rank.)*

PIZARRO: Stand firm. Firmer!…Look at you, you could be dead already. If he sees you like that you will be. Make no error, he's watching every step you take. You're not men any longer, you're Gods now. Eternal Gods, each one of you. Two can play this immortality game, my lads. I want to see you move over his land like figures from a Lent procession. He must see Gods walk on earth. Indifferent! Uncrushable! No death to be afraid of. I tell you, one shiver dooms the lot of us. One yelp of fright and we'll never be heard of again. He'll serve us like cheeseworms you crush with a knife. So come on you tattered trash—shake out the straw. Forget your village magic: fingers in crosses, saints under your shirts. You can grant prayers now—no need to answer them. Come on! Fix your eyes! Follow the pig-boy to his glory! I'll have an Empire for my farm. A million boys driving in the pigs at night. And each one of you will own a share—juicy black earth a hundred mile apiece—and golden ploughs to cut it! Get up you Godboys—March!

*(Martin bangs his drum. The Spaniards begin to march in slow motion. Above, masked Indians move on to the upper level.)*

MANCO: They move Inca! they come! One hundred and sixty and seven.

ATAHUALLPA: Where?

MANCO: Zaran.

VILLAC UMU: Ware! Ware, Inca!

MANCO: They move all in step. Not fast, not slow. They keep straight on from dark to dark.

VILLAC UMU: Ware! Ware, Inca!

MANCO: They are at Motupe, Inca! They do not look on left or right.

VILLAC UMU: Ware! this is great danger.

ATAHUALLPA: No danger. He is coming to bless me. A god and all his priests. Praise Father Sun!

ALL ABOVE: *(Chanting.)* Virchen Atix!

ATAHUALLPA: Praise Sapa Inca!

ALL ABOVE: Sapa Inca! Inca Capac!

ATAHUALLPA: Praise Inti Cori.

ALL ABOVE: Keild Ya, Inti Cori!

CHALLCUCHIMA: They come to the mountains.

VILLAC UMU: Kill them now.

ATAHUALLPA: Praise Atahuallpa.

VILLAC UMU: Destroy them! Teach them death!

ATAHUALLPA: *Praise Atahuallpa!*

ALL ABOVE: Atahuallpa! Sapa Inca! Hua-car-cu-ya-t!

ATAHUALLPA: *(Crying out.)* Let them see my mountains!

> *(A crash of primitive instruments. The lights snap out and, lit from the side, the rays of the metal sun throw long shadows across the wooden wall. All the Spaniards fall down. A cold blue light fills the stage.)*

DE SOTO: God in heaven!

> *(Enter Old Martin.)*

OLD MARTIN: You call them the Andes. Picture a curtain of stone hung by some giant across your path. Mountains set on mountains: cliffs on cliffs. Hands of rock a hundred yards high, with flashing nails where the snow never moved, scratching the gashed face of the sun. For miles around the jungle lay black in its shadow. A freezing cold fell on us.

PIZARRO: Up, my godlings. Up, my little gods. Take heart, now. He's watching you. *Get to your feet! (To Diego.)* Master, what of the horses?

DIEGO: D'you need them, sir?

PIZARRO: They're vital, boy.

DIEGO: Then you'll have 'em, sir. They'll follow you as we will.

PIZARRO: Up we go, then! We're coming for you, Atahuallpa. Show me the toppest peak-top you can pile—show me the lid of the world—I'll stand tiptoe on it and pull you right out of the sky. I'll grab you by the legs, you Son of the Sun, and smash your flaming crown on the rocks. Bless them, Church!

VALVERDE: God stay you, and stay with you all.

DE NIZZA: Amen.

(Whilst Pizarro is calling his last speech to the Inca, the silent King thrice beckons to him, and retires backwards out of the sun into blackness.)

# The Royal Hunt of the Sun

Peter Shaffer
1964

**Dramatic**
Old Martin
Soldiers of Pizarro's army
Incas, several

The Mime of the Great Ascent

> *(As Old Martin describes their ordeal, the men climb the Andes. It is a terrible progress; a stumbling, tortuous climb into the clouds, over ledges and giant chasms, performed to an eerie, cold music made from the thin whine of huge saws.)*

OLD MARTIN: Have you ever climbed a mountain in full armour? That's what we did, him going first the whole way up a tiny path into the clouds, with drops sheer on both sides into nothing. For hours we crept forward like blind men, the sweat freezing on our faces, lugging skittery leaking horses, and pricked all the time for the ambush that would tip us into death. Each turn of the path it grew colder. The friendly trees of the forest dropped away, and there were only pines. Then they went too, and there were just scrubby little bushes standing up in ice. All round us the rocks began to whine with cold. And always above us, or below us, those filthy condor birds, hanging on the air with great tasselled wings.

> *(It grows darker. The music grows colder yet. The men freeze and hang their heads for a long moment, before resuming their desperate climb.)*

OLD MARTIN: Then night. We lay down twos and threes together on the path, and hugged like lovers for warmth in that burning cold. And most cried. We got up with cold iron for bones and went on. Four days like that; groaning, not speaking; the breath a blade in our lungs. Four days, slowly, like flies on a wall; limping flies, dying flies, up an endless wall of rock. A tiny army lost in the creases of the moon.

INDIANS: *(Off: in echo.)* Stand!

> *(The Spaniards whirl round. Villac umu and his attendants appear,*

*clothed entirely in white fur. The high Priest wears a snow-white llama head on top of his own.)*

VILLAC UMU: You see Villac Umu. Chief Priest of the Sun. Why do you come?

PIZARRO: To see the Great Inca.

VILLAC UMU: Why will you see him?

PIZARRO: To give him blessing.

VILLAC UMU: Why will you bless him?

PIZARRO: He is a God. I am a God.

VALVERDE: *(Sotto voce.)* General!

PIZARRO: Be still.

VILLAC UMU: Below you is the town of Cajamarca. The great Inca orders: rest there. Tomorrow early he will come to you. Do not move from the town. Outside it is his anger.

*(He goes off with his attendants.)*

VALVERDE: What have you done, sir?

PIZARRO: Sent him news to amaze him.

VALVERDE: I cannot approve blasphemy.

PIZARRO: To conquer for Christ, one can surely usurp his name for a night, Father. Set on.

# Indians
Arthur Kopit
1969

**Dramatic**
**Scene:** Spotted Tail is standing on a ledge on a high plains. Night. Moonlight. A rifle shot is heard. ·

Spotted Tail
Buffalo Bill
Members of the Cavalry
The Archduke's Interpreter
The Grand Duke
Ned Buntline

> (*Spotted Tail peers in its direction. Sound, offstage, of wounded bulls. Enter an Indian dressed as a buffalo, wounded in the eye and bellowing with pain. He circles the stage. Enter two more buffaloes, also wounded in the eyes. The first buffalo dies. The two other buffaloes stagger over to his side and die beside him; another buffalo [missing an eye] enters, staggers in a circle, senses the location of the dead buffaloes and heads dizzily toward them—dying en route, halfway there. Spotted Tail crouches and gazes down at them. Then he stares up at the sky. Night creatures screeches in the dark. A pause.*)

BUFFALO BILL: (*Offstage but coming closer.*) Ninety-three, ninety-four, ninety-five…ninety six! *I DID IT!*

> (*Enter, running, a much younger Buffalo Bill, rifle in hand, followed shortly by members of the U.S. Cavalry bearing torches, and the Grand Duke's Interpreter.*)

BUFFALO BILL: I did it, I did it! No one believed I could, but *I did it!* One hundred buffalo—one hundred shots! "You jus' gimme some torches," I said. "I *know* there's buffalo around us. *Here.* Put yer ear t' the ground. Feel it tremblin'? Well. You wanna see somethin' fantastic, you get me some torches. I'll shoot the reflections in their eyes. I'll shoot 'em like they was so many shiny nickels!"

INTERPRETER: I'll tell the Grand Duke you did what you said. I know he'll be pleased.

BUFFALO BILL: Well he oughta be! I don' give exhibitions like this fer just anybody!

*(Exit the Interpreter.)*

BUFFALO BILL: 'Specially as these critters're gettin' so damn hard t' find. *(To the soldiers.)* Not like the ol' days when I was huntin' 'em fer the railroads. *(He laughs, gazes down at one of the buffaloes. Pause. He looks away; squints as if in pain.)*

A SOLDIER: Are you all right, sir?

BUFFALO BILL: Uh...yes. Fine.

*(Exit the Soldiers. Buffalo Bill rubs his head. Spotted Tail hops down from his perch and walks up behind Cody unnoticed; stares at him. Pause. Buffalo Bill senses the Indian's presence and turns, cocking his rifle. The Indian makes no move. Buffalo Bill stares at the Indian. Pause.)*

BUFFALO BILL: *Spotted Tail!* My God. I haven't seen you in years. How...ya been?

*(Slight laugh.)*

SPOTTED TAIL: *What are you doing here?*

*(Pause.)*

BUFFALO BILL: Well, well, what...are *you* doing here? This isn't Sioux territory!

SPOTTED TAIL: It isn't *your* territory either.

*(Pause.)*

BUFFALO BILL: Well I'm with...these *people*. I'm scoutin' for 'em.

SPOTTED TAIL: *These people*...must be very hungry.

BUFFALO BILL: Hm?

SPOTTED TAIL: To need so many buffalo.

BUFFALO BILL: Ah! Of course! You were following the buffalo *also!*...Well listen, I'm sure my friends won't mind you takin' some. 'Tween us, my friends don't 'specially care for the taste o' buffalo meat. *(He laughs.)* My God, but it's good t' see you again!

SPOTTED TAIL: *Your friends:* I have been studying them from the hills. They are very strange. They seem neither men, nor women.

BUFFALO BILL: Well! Actually, they're sort of a new *breed* o' people. Called dudes. *(He chuckles.)*

SPOTTED TAIL: You *like* them?

BUFFALO BILL: Well...sure. Why not? *(Pause.)* I mean, obviously, they ain't the sort I've been used to. But then, things're changin' out here. An' these men are the ones who're changin' 'em. So, if you wanna be part o' these things, an' not left behind somewhere, you jus' plain hafta *get used* to 'em. You —uh—follow...what I mean?

*(Silence.)*

BUFFALO BILL: I mean...you've got to *adjust*. To the times. Make a plan fer yerself. I have one. You should have one, too. Fer yer own good. Believe me.

*(Long pause.)*

SPOTTED TAIL: *What is your plan?*

BUFFALO BILL: Well, my plan is 't help people. Like you, ferinstance. Or these people I'm with. More...even...than that, maybe. And, and, whatever...it is I *do* 't help, for it, these people may some-day jus' possibly name streets after me. Cities. Counties. States! I'll...be as famous as Dan'l Boone!...An' somewhere, on top of a beautiful mountain that overlooks more plains 'n rivers than any other mountain, there might even be a statue of me sittin' on a great white horse, a-wavin' my hat t' everyone down below, thankin' 'em, fer thankin' me, fer havin' done...whatever...it is I'm gonna...*do* fer 'em all. How...come you got such a weird look on yer face?

BUNTLINE: *(Offstage.)* HEY, CODY! *STAY WHERE YA ARE!*

BUFFALO BILL: *DON' WORRY! I AIN'T BUDGIN'!* *(To Spotted Tail.)* That's Mister Ned Buntline, the well-known newspaper reporter. I think he's gonna do an *article* on me! General Custer, who's in charge, an' I think is pushin' fer an article on *himself,* says this may well be the, most important western expedition since Lewis 'n Clark.

BUNTLINE: *(Offstage.) BY THE WAY, WHERE ARE YA?*

BUFFALO BILL: I...AIN'T SURE! JUST HEAD FOR THE LIGHTS! *(He laughs to himself.)*

SPOTTED TAIL: Tell me. Who is the man everyone always bows to?

BUFFALO BILL: Oh! The Gran' Duke! He's from a place called Russia. This whole shindig's in his honor. I'm sure he'd love t' meet you. He's never seen a real Indian.

SPOTTED TAIL: There are no Indians in Russia?

*(Buffalo Bill shakes his head.)*

SPOTTED TAIL: Then I will study him even more carefully than the others. Maybe if he takes me back to Russia with him, I will not end like my people will...end.

BUFFALO BILL: *(Startled.) What?*

SPOTTED TAIL: I mean, like these fools here, on the ground. *(He stares at the buffalo.)*

BUFFALO BILL: Ah...Well, if ya don' mind my sayin', I think you're bein' a bit pessimistic. But you do what ya like. Jus' remember: these people you're studyin'—some folk think *they're* the fools.

SPOTTED TAIL: Oh, no! They are not fools! *No one who is a white man can be a fool.*

*(He smiles coldly at Buffalo Bill; heraldic Russian fanfare offstage. Enter Russian Torchbearers and Trumpeteers. Buffalo Bill and Spotted Tail, in awe, back away. Enter with much pomp and ceremony Grand Duke Alexis on a splendid litter carved like a horse. He is accompanied by his Interpreter, who points out the four buffaloes to the Grand Duke as he majestically circles the clearing. He is followed by Ned Buntline, who carries camera and tripod.)*

BUFFALO BILL: MY God, but that is a beautiful sight!

*(The Grand Duke comes to a halt. Majestic sweep of his arms to those around him.)*

GRAND DUKE: *(Makes a regal Russian speech.)*

INTERPRETER: His Excellency the Grand Duke wishes to express his heartfelt admiration of Buffalo Bill...

*(Music up.)*

INTERPRETER: ...for having done what he has done tonight.

*(The Grand Duke gestures majestically. The Interpreter opens a small velvet box. Airy music. The Interpreter walks toward Buffalo Bill.)*

GRAND DUKE: *(Gesturing for Buffalo Bill to come forward.)* Boofilo Beel!

*(Buffalo Bill walks solemnly forward. The Interpreter takes out a medal. Buffalo Bill, deeply moved, looks around, embarrassed. The Interpreter smiles and holds up the medal, gestures warmly for Buffalo Bill to kneel. He does so. The Interpreter places the medal, which is on a bright ribbon, around his neck. Flashgun goes off.)*

BUNTLINE: Great picture, Cody! FRONT PAGE! My God, what a night! *What* a story! Uh...sorry, yer Highness. Didn't mean t' distoib ya. *(He backs meekly away. Sets up his camera for another shot. The Grand Duke regains his composure.)*

GRAND DUKE: *(Russian speech.)*

INTERPRETER: His Excellency wonders how Buffalo Bill became such a deadly shot.

BUFFALO BILL: Oh, well, you know, just...practice. *(Embarrassed laugh.)*

GRAND DUKE: *(Russian speech.)*

INTERPRETER: His Excellency says he wishes that his stupid army knew how to practice.

GRAND DUKE: *(Russian speech.)*

INTERPRETER: Better yet, he wishes you would come back with him to his palace and protect him yourself.

BUFFALO BILL: Oh. *(Slight laugh.)* Well, I'm sure the Grand Duke's in excellent hands.

*(The Interpreter whispers what Buffalo Bill has just said.)*

GRAND DUKE: Da! *Hands. (He holds out his hands, then turns them and puts them around his throat.)*

BUFFALO BILL: I think His Majesty's exaggeratin'. I can't believe he's not *surrounded* by friends.

GRAND DUKE: FRIENDS! *(He cackles and draws his sword, slashes the air.)* Friends! Friends!...Friends! *(He fights them off.)*

BUFFALO BILL: *(To Buntline.)* I think he's worried 'bout somethin'.

BUNTLINE: Very strange behavior.

GRAND DUKE: *(Nervous Russian speech.)*

INTERPRETER: His Excellency wonders if Buffalo Bill has ever been afraid.

BUFFALO BILL: ...Afraid?

GRAND DUKE: *(Russian word.)*

INTERPRETER: Outnumbered.

BUFFALO BILL: Ah. *(Slight laugh.)* Well, uh—

BUNTLINE: Go on, tell 'm. It'll help what I'm plannin' t' write.

BUFFALO BILL: *(Delighted.)* It *will?*

BUNTLINE: Absolutely. Look: de West is changin'—right? Well, people wanna know about it. Wanna feel...*part* o' things. I think *you're* what dey need. Someone t' listen to, observe, *identify* wid. No, no, really! I been studyin' you.

BUFFALO BILL: ...You have?

BUNTLINE: I think you could be de inspiration o' dis land.

BUFFALO BILL: Now I *know* you're foolin!

BUNTLINE: Not at all...Well go on. Tell ]m what he wants t' hear. T'rough my magic pen, others will hear also...Donmentionit. De nation needs men like me, too.

*(He pats Cody on the shoulder and shoves him off toward the Grand Duke; Cody gathers his courage.)*

BUFFALO BILL: *(To the Grand Duke.)* Well, uh…where can I begin? Certainly it's true that I've been outnumbered. And—uh—many times. Yes.

BUNTLINE: That's the way.

BUFFALO BILL: More times, in fact, than I can count.

BUNTLINE: Terrific.

BUFFALO BILL: *(Warming to the occasion.)* An believe me, I can count pretty high!

BUNTLINE: SENSATIONAL!

BUFFALO BILL: Mind you, 'gainst *me,* twelve's normally an even battle— long's I got my two six shooters that is.

BUNTLINE: Keep it up, keep it up!

BUFFALO BILL: THIRTEEN! If one of 'em's thin enough for a bullet t' go clean through. Fourteen if I got a huntin' knife. Fifteen if there's a hard surface off o' which I can ricochet a few shots.

BUNTLINE: *Go on!*

BUFFALO BILL: Um twenty…if I got a stick o' dynamite. HUNDRED! IF THERE'S ROCKS T' START A AVALANCHE!
*(Buntline applauds.)*

BUFFALO BILL: What I mean is, with *me* it's never say die! Why…I remember once I was ridin' for the Pony Express 'tween Laramie 'n Tombstone. Suddenly, jus' past the Pecos, fifty drunk Comanches attack. Noise like a barroom whoop-di-do, arrows fallin' like hail stones! I mean, they come on me so fast they don' have time t' see my face, notice who I am, realize I'm in fact a very good *friend* o' theirs!

GRAND DUKE: FRIEND! FRIEND!

BUNTLINE: *(Sotto voce.)* Get off de subject!

BUFFALO BILL: Well, there was no alternative but t' fire back. Well I'd knocked off 'bout thirty o' their number when I realized I was *out* o' bullets. Just at that moment, a arrow whizzed past my head. Thinkin' fast, I reached out an' caught it. Then, usin' it like a fly swatter, I knocked away the other nineteen arrows that were headin' fer my heart. Whereupon, I stood up in the stirrups, hurled the arrow sixty yards….An' killed their chief. *(Pause.)* Which…*depressed*…the remainin' Indians. *(Pause.)* And sent 'em scurryin' home. Well! That's sort o' what ya might call a typical day!

(Bravos from everyone except the Grand Duke.)

GRAND DUKE: (Russian speech, quite angry.)

INTERPRETER: His Excellency says he would like to kill a Comanche also.

BUFFALO BILL: Hm?

GRAND DUKE: (With obvious jealousy.) Like Boofilo Beel!

INTERPRETER: Like Buffalo Bill!

GRAND DUKE: (Excited Russian speech.)

INTERPRETER: He will prove he cannot be intimidated!

GRAND DUKE: Rifle, rifle, rifle!

BUFFALO BILL: (To Buntline.) I think my story may've worked a bit too well.

BUNTLINE: Nonsense! This is terrific!

(They duck as the Grand Duke, cackling madly, scans the surrounding darkness over his rifle sight.)

BUNTLINE: Shows you've won the Grand Duke's heart.

GRAND DUKE: (Pounding his chest.) Boofilo Beel!...I am BOOFILO BEEL! (He laughs demonically.)

BUNTLINE: I think you'd better find 'm a Comanche.

BUFFALO BILL: Right! Well. Um... (Slight laugh.) That could be a...problem.

GRAND DUKE: Comanche! Comanche!

BUFFALO BILL: Ya see, fer one thing, the Comanches live in Texas. And we're in Missouri.

GRAND DUKE: COMANCHE! COMANCHE!

BUFFALO BILL: Fer another, I ain't xactly sure what they look like.

GRAND DUKE: Ah! (He fires into the darkness. Spotted Tail stumbles out, collapses and dies. The Grand Duke and his Interpreter delirious with joy. Buntline dumbfounded. Buffalo Bill stunned, but for vastly different reasons.)

BUNTLINE: (Approaching the body cautiously.) My God, will you look at that? Fate must be smiling! (He laughs weakly, stares up at the heavens in awe.)

(Buffalo Bill, almost in a trance, walks over to the body; stares down at it. Weird music heard. The lights change color, grow vague. All movement arrested. Spotted Tail rises slowly and moves just as slowly toward the Grand Duke; stops.)

SPOTTED TAIL: My name is Spotted Tail. My father was a Sioux; my

mother, part Cherokee, part Crow. No matter how you look at it, I'm just not a Comanche. *(He sinks back to the ground.)*
*(Lights return to normal, the music ends.)*

GRAND DUKE: *(Baffled Russian speech.)*

INTERPRETER: His Excellency would like to know what the man he just shot has said.
*(Long pause. Buffalo Bill looks around as if for help; all eyes upon him.)*

BUFFALO BILL: *(Softly.)* He said… *(Pause.)* "I… *(Pause.)* should have…
*(He looks at Buntline, takes a deep breath.)*

BUFFALO BILL: stayed at home in…Texas with the rest of my…Comanche tribe."

BUNTLINE: Fabulous! *(He takes Spotted Tail's picture; the night sky glows from the flash.)* Absolutely fabulous!
*(The scene fades around Buffalo Bill, who stands in the center, dizzily gripping his head.)*

# Failure to Zigzag

John Ferrzaca

**Dramatic**

**Scene:** in the shark-infested waters of the Pacific Ocean as the Indianapolis sinks and the men are tossed overboard to swim until rescue is possible.

Capt. McVay
Sailors of the S.S. Indianapolis, many

MCVAY: The seaman, holding up the dead body of his friend. An old value: friendship. Wouldn't let his buddy go. He was taking him home. We didn't tell him the truth. The dead body of his friend was the only thing keeping that seaman alive. We all need something to hold onto. Not just somebody. Something worth dying for...to live for too. In 1941, we had both.
*(The water.)*

LOFTEN: Fight back; don't give in. You don't die in your mind, you don't die.

SAMUELSON: You ain't wrapped tight.

LOFTEN: Be prepared; next time might be worse.

SAMUELSON: *Next* time?

LOFTEN: Keep your guard up. Who knows what lies ahead?

SAMUELSON: Cowboy, you are dead from the neck up.

LOFTEN: I *was* dead once. War taught me what real living is like.

SAMUELSON: You call this living?

LOFTEN: More here than in Waco.

SAMUELSON: In Waco, you were dry.

LOFTEN: I was dried *up* in Waco. Doing nothing and going nowhere. No dicking around now. It's do or die. Real living guy.

SAMUELSON: You're *real* weird—guy.

LOFTEN: Make fun. I'm alive and gonna stay that way. I got it straight in my head. Do like I do, you can have yourself a hell of a time.

SAMUELSON: *That*—I already got.

MCVAY: *(To Greene.)* One sailor claimed our ship never sank. Said it lay just below the surface. Then dived below to get a glass of milk from the galley. Men swam off to an undersea island built by seabees. Where beautiful bare breasted women waited for them with bowls of tomato juice. We believed any story, our own and others.

BERTELLI: *(Elated.)* One year, nine months, two weeks, three days—just a few more hours—and I'm out.

KINGMAN: We get the purple heart, Sam the man is gonna send his to the Jap who sunk us.

ABERNATHY: That's a fine way to talk.

BERTELLI: Going to write that Nip a letter, Abernathy. Little guy deserves a promotion.

ABERNATHY: There's still a war on, you know.

BERTELLI: That Jap monkey bought us our ticket home. War's over, Ace.

KINGMAN: The minute we took our second hit, Sam starts to sing.

BERTELLI: Minute I get home I'm gonna find me a bottle and some place dry.

KINGMAN: I'm ass over appetite on the top deck wondering what day it is—he's *singing.*

BERTELLI: Get some good loving from a bad woman.

KINGMAN: He fires a kapok at me, then dives in the drink.

ABERNATHY: That ain't funny; it's un-American.

KINGMAN: "Come on in," right, Sam? "The water's great."

ABERNATHY: What did you do?

KINGMAN: I'm here, ain't I?

ABERNATHY: Piss poor attitude.

BERTELLI: *(Sharp.)* It comes from having your ship shot out from under you. People dying all around you. Sitting in the water a million miles from nowhere. With an asshole like you for company.

ABERNATHY: We're supposed to be fighting Japs. Not with each other. Why doesn't everyone shut up?
*(Silence. Kingman starts to sing a popular Christmas carol. Abernathy joins him, then Bertelli. Singing stops. Sound of water.)*

MCVAY: One of the men trapped below managed somehow to fight his way onto the deck. Burned so bad you couldn't tell who he was. He kept screaming: "Don't touch me...Don't touch me." Preferring to die in the water. Half dead, fighting his way to the deck...to die in the water. It's called "irony." I remember the word from school. The use of irony in literature. I saw how irony worked in life. Even more, how it worked in death. The prisoners in the brig, released from their cells to become prisoners of the sea. The man who found fifty packs of Camels in his life raft, but couldn't find a match anywhere. Sitting in an ocean of water with nothing to drink. We ran short of everything those four days in the water. But not irony. We never ran short of that.

(*The water.*)

JOHNSON: I don't want to die.

PULASKI: Don't talk about dying.

JOHNSON: Not like this. Not here.

PULASKI: Don't talk about dying.

JOHNSON: Not like this.

PULASKI: Talk about something else.

JOHNSON: Remember that guy named Ham? The chicken farmer? Called his place "Ham and Eggs?" Nice guy.

PULASKI: He's dead. Change the subject.

JOHNSON: I wanted to save the world. I wanted to die a big hero.

PULASKI: Don't talk about dying.

JOHNSON: Just like in the movies.

PULASKI: In the movies, everyone gets saved.

JOHNSON: Yeah. At the last minute, someone always comes.

PULASKI: And-it-don't-take-forever. I hate the movies.

JOHNSON: What about Betty Grable?

PULASKI: Don't talk about Betty Grable.

MCVAY: Fear was everywhere. The fear of being machine-gunned in the water by the Japanese submarine. The fear of never seeing another day. Of never again seeing land. Afraid of each other. The fear of no longer caring whether you lived or died—that was the worst. Day brought new hope. But not for long. During the night we heard men die. By day we saw them. (*Pause.*) We could see the sharks too.

(*Men in water, huddled together.*)

ABERNATHY: Jesus Christ. Look.

KINGMAN: Sharks!

PULASKI: The oar. Grab something.

LOFTEN: I got a knife.

JOHNSON: I count six. I see six sharks.

BERTELLI: Splash—scare them away.

LOFTEN: Where's my knife?

JOHNSON: What do we do?

KINGMAN: I'm going to be sick.

SAMUELSON: Make noise.

*(Men yell.)*

JOHNSON: Why are they circling?

ABERNATHY: Stay calm. Don't move.

KINGMAN: They're circling us.

ABERNATHY: Nobody move.

*(Silence.)*

SAMUELSON: Make noise.

ABERNATHY: No. Don't make a sound.

*(Silence.)*

BERTELLI: I don't see them.

LOFTEN: Where did they go?

PULASKI: Under us!

KINGMAN: No.

BERTELLI: They're coming up!

# God's Country

Steven Dietz

**Dramatic**
**Scene:** A sacred circle of white supremacy indoctrination ritual

Boy, twelve years old
Actors, number is flexible, male, caucasian, can be of any age. Lines
are divided among the actors.

*(At rise: Darkness. Silence. Lights reveal the cast scattered about
the stage. They watch the boy as he enters, carrying a white candle. The boy arrives at the center bench and stops, facing the
audience. He puts his hand over his heart.)*

BOY: I pledge allegiance. To the flag. Of the United States of America.
*(Actor One, Actor Three, Actor Seven, Actor Eight, Actor Nine
and Actor Ten enter and stand in a circle around the bench,
where the candles are burning. The boy backs away, watching.
The men wear rugged clothing, some in camouflaged fatigues,
some with weapons. Actor Ten places a baby, bundled in a blan-
ket, on the bench.)*

ACTOR TEN: I, as a free Aryan man, hereby swear an unrelenting oath
upon the green graves of our sires—

ACTOR ONE: Upon the children in the wombs of our wives—

ACTOR NINE: Upon the throne of God Almighty—

ALL MEN: *(Except Parmenter.)* Sacred be his name.

ACTOR THREE: To join together in holy union with those brothers in this
circle—

ACTOR EIGHT: And to declare forthright that from this moment on I have
no fear of death—

ACTOR SEVEN: No fear of foe—

ACTOR TEN: That I have a sacred duty to do whatever is necessary to
deliver our people from the Jew—

ACTOR ONE: And bring total victory to the Aryan race.

ACTOR SEVEN: I, as an Aryan warrior, swear myself to complete secrecy
to The Order—

ACTOR THREE: And total loyalty to my comrades.

ALL MEN: Let me bear witness to you, my brothers—

ACTOR NINE: That should one of you fall in battle, I will see to the welfare and well-being of your family.

ALL MEN: Let me bear witness to you, my brothers—

ACTOR TEN: That should one of you be taken prisoner, I will do whatever is necessary to regain your freedom.

ALL MEN: Let me bear witness to you, my brothers—

ACTOR THREE: That should an enemy agent hurt you—

ACTOR ONE: I will chase him to the ends of the earth—

ACTOR EIGHT: And remove his head from his body.

ALL MEN: Let me bear witness to you, my brothers—

ACTOR TEN: That if I break this oath, let me be forever cursed upon the lips of our people as a coward.

ACTOR ONE: My brothers, let us be his battle axe and weapons of war.

ACTOR NINE: Let us go forth by ones and by twos—

ACTOR THREE: By scores and by legions—

ACTOR EIGHT: And as true Aryan men with pure hearts and strong minds—

ACTOR SEVEN: Face the enemies of our faith and our race with courage and determination.

ALL MEN: We hereby invoke the blood covenant, and declare that we are in a full state of war and will not lay down our weapons until we have driven the enemy into the sea, and reclaimed that land which was promised to our fathers of old—And through our blood and His will, becomes the land of our children to be.

ACTOR TEN: *(Holding the baby toward the sky.)* Hail Victory!

# God's Country

Steven Dietz

**Dramatic**

**Scene:** The young man is being interrogated by older members of the
white supremacy group, The Order. He has learned his lessons
well and is prepared to recite the dogma of hate to prove his wor-
thiness to the select group.

Boy, twelve years old
Actors, number is flexible, male, caucasian, can be of any age. Lines
are divided among the actors.

*(The boy runs on, tossing a football in the air. Lights crossfade to
lights on the actors as they question the boy.)*

ACTOR: What should an Order member carry at all times?

BOY: An Order member should carry $500 cash with him at all times.

ACTOR: What number should he know?

BOY: He should know the Bear trap number. He should only call this
number if his cover is blown and he is arrested.

ACTOR: What other numbers should he know?

BOY: He should know the Message Center number. He should only
leave messages for other members between four and five p.m.
Mountain Standard Time.

ACTOR: Who will relay the messages?

BOY: Carlos.

ACTOR: Who is Carlos?

BOY: Robert Mathews.

ACTOR: Where did his name come from?

BOY: From Carlos Sanchez, the man who disposed of the Jew athletes
at the Munich Olympics.

ACTOR: What are phones to an Order member?

BOY: Phones are poison. They are monitored by ZOG.

ACTOR: Should a member give out his phone number?

BOY: Only in code. One digit above the actual number.

ACTOR: What is the number?

BOY: *(Tossing Actor Four the football.)* It is 426-1438.

ACTOR: What words should not be used on the phone?

BOY: Right-wing. Guns. Feds. Money. Dollars. Agents. Warrants.

ACTOR: Why?

BOY: ZOG is listening. THere is always a more discreet word that can be substituted.

ACTOR: How does an Order member confuse ZOG?

BOY: He makes two misleading phone calls each wek to various parts of the country, then hangs up. ZOG will have to use extra man-power to follow these false leads.

ACTOR: Personality conflicts.

BOY: All personality conflicts must come to an immediate end. If you do not have something positive to say about a comrade, then say nothing at all.

ACTOR: Alcohol.

BOY: The over-consumption of alcohol is a security risk, it lowers morale, and it will not be tolerated.

ACTOR: If ZOG launches an offensive against The Order, what should be done?

BOY: Inflict maximum damage. Go for the brain, not the foot. Go for the throat, not the hand. An individual Aryan Warrior is capable of inflicting great harm to ZOG.

ACTOR: How does a man become an Aryan Warrior?

BOY: By earning one full point under the Point System.

ACTOR: How are points earned?

BOY: Assassinating members of Congress: one-fifth; Judges: one-sixth; FBI agents and Federal Marshals: one-tenth; journalists and local politicians: one-twelfth.

ACTOR: Is there a way to earn a full point?

BOY: Yes. By assassinating the President of the United States.

ACTOR: What is the ultimate end of politics?

BOY: The ultimate end of politics is war.

ACTOR: *(Tossing the football back to the Boy.)* And whose country is this?

BOY: This is God's country, which he has given to me.

# SMALL GROUP SCENES WITH A MAJORITY OF MEN

# Hamlet

William Shakespeare

**Dramatic**
**Scene:** a room in the castle

King
Queen
Polonius
Ophelia
Rosencrantz
Guildenstern

KING: And can you, by no drift of circumstance,
    Get from him why he puts on this confusion,
    Grating so harshly all his days of quiet
    With turbulent and dangerous lunacy?
ROSENCRANTZ: He does confess he feels himself distracted;
    But from what cause he will by no means speak.
GUILDENSTERN: Nor do we find him forward to be sounded;
    But, with a crafty madness, keeps aloof,
    When we would bring him on to some confession
    Of his true state.
QUEEN: Did he receive you well?
ROSENCRANTZ: Most like a gentleman.
GUILDENSTERN: But with much forcing of his disposition.
ROSENCRANTZ: Niggard of question; but, of our demands,
    Most free in his reply.
QUEEN: Did you assay him
    To any pastime?
ROSENCRANTZ: Madam, it so fell out, that certain players
    We o'er-raught on the way: of these we told him;
    And there did seem in him a kind of joy
    To hear of it: they are about the court;
    And, as I think, they have already order
    This night to play before him.
POLONIUS: 'Tis most true:
    And he beseecht me to entreat your majesties
    To hear and see the matter.

KING: With all my heart; and it doth much content me
   To hear him so inclined—
   Good gentlemen, give him a further edge,
   And drive his purpose on to these delights.
ROSENCRANTZ: We shall, my lord.
   *(Exeunt Rosencrantz and Guildenstern.)*
KING: Sweet Gertrude, leave us too;
   For we have closely sent for Hamlet hither,
   That he, as 'twere by accident, may here
   Affront Ophelia;
   Her father and myself—lawful espials—
   Will so bestow ourselves that, seeing, unseen,
   We may of their encounter frankly judge;
   And gather by him, as he is behaved,
   If't be th'affliction of his love or no
   That thus he suffers for.
QUEEN: I shall obey you:—
   And for your part, Ophelia, I do wish
   That your good beauties be the happy cause
   Of Hamlet's wildness: so shall I hope your virtues
   Will bring him to his wonted way again,
   To both your honours.
OPHELIA: Madam, I wish it may.
   *(Exit Queen.)*
POLONIUS: Ophelia, walk you here.—Gracious, so please you,
   We will bestow ourselves.— *(To Ophelia.)* Read on this book;
   That show of such an exercise may colour
   Your loneliness.—We are oft to blame in this,—
   'Tis too much proved,—that with devotion's visage
   And pious action we do sugar o'er
   The devil himself.
KING: *(Aside.)* O, 'tis too true!
   How smart a lash that speech doth give my conscience!
   The harlot's cheek, beautied with plastering art,
   Is not more ugly to the thing that helps it
   Than is my deed to my most painted word:
   O heavy burden!
POLONIUS: I hear him coming: let's withdraw, my lord.
   *(Exeunt King and Polonius. Enter Hamlet.)*

HAMLET: To be, or not to be,—that is the question:—
Whether 'tis nobler in the mind to suffer
The slings and arrows of outrageous fortune,
Or to take arms against a sea of troubles,
And by opposing end them?—To die,—to sleep,—
No more; and by a sleep to say we end
The heart-ache, and the thousand natural shocks
That flesh is heir to, 'tis a consummation
Devoutly to be wisht. To die,—to sleep;—
To sleep! perchance to dream: ay, there's the rub;
For in that sleep of death what dreams may come,
When we have shuffled off this mortal coil,
Must give us pause: there's the respect
That makes calamity of so long life;
For who would bear the whips and scorns of time,
The oppressor's wrong, the proud man's contumely,
The pangs of despised love, the law's delay,
The insolence of office, and the spurns
That patient merit of the unworthy takes,
When he himself might his quietus make
With a bare bodkin? who would fardels bear,
To grunt and sweat under a weary life,
But that the dread of something after death,—
The undiscover'd country, from whose bourn
No traveller returns,—puzzles the will,
And makes us rather bear those ills we have
Than fly to others that we know not of?
Thus conscience does make cowards of us all;
And thus the native hue of resolution
Is sicklied o'er with the pale cast of thought;
And enterprises of great pith and moment,
With this regard, their currents turn awry,
And lose the name of action.—Soft you now!
The fair Ophelia!—Nymph, in thy orisons
Be all my sins remember'd.
OPHELIA: Good my lord,
How does your honour for this many a day?
HAMLET: I humbly thank you; well, well, well.
OPHELIA: My lord, I have remembrances of yours,

That I have longed long to re-deliver;
I pray you, now receive them.

HAMLET: No, not I;
I never gave you aught.

OPHELIA: My honour'd lord, you know right well you did;
And, with them, words of so sweet breath composed
As made the things more rich: their perfume lost,
Take these again; for to the noble mind
Rich gifts wax poor when givers prove unkind.
There, my lord.

HAMLET: Ha, ha! are you honest?

OPHELIA: My lord?

HAMLET: Are you fair?

OPHELIA: What means your lordship?

HAMLET: That if you be honest and fair, your honesty should admit no discourse to your beauty.

OPHELIA: Could beauty, my lord, have better commerce than with honesty?

HAMLET: Ay, truly; for the power of beauty will sooner transform honesty from what it is to a bawd than the force of honesty can translate beauty into his likeness: this was sometime a paradox, but now the time gives it proof. I did love you once.

OPHELIA: Indeed, my lord, you made me believe so.

HAMLET: You should not have believed me; for virtue cannot so inoculate our old stock, but we shall relish of it: I loved you not.

OPHELIA: I was the more deceived.

HAMLET: Get thee to a nunnery: why wouldst thou be a breeder of sinners? I am myself indifferent honest: but yet I could accuse me of such things, that it were better my mother had not borne me: I am very proud, revengeful, ambitious; with more offences at my beck than I have thoughts to put them in, imagination to give them shape, or time to act them in. What should such fellows as I do crawling between earth and heaven? We are arrant knaves, all; believe none of us. Go thy ways to a nunnery. Where's your father?

OPHELIA: At home, my lord.

HAMLET: Let the doors be shut upon him, that he may play the fool no where but in's own house. Farewell.

OPHELIA: O, help him, you sweet heavens!

HAMLET: If thou dost marry, I'll give thee this plague for thy dowry,—

be thou as chaste as ice, as pure as snow, thou shalt not escape calumny. Get thee to a nunnery, go: farewell. Or, if thou wilt needs marry, marry a fool; for wise men know well enough what monsters you make of them. To a nunnery, go; and quickly too. Farewell.

OPHELIA: O heavenly powers, restore him!

HAMLET: I have heard of your paintings too, well enough; God has given you one face, and you make yourselves another: you jig, you amble, and you lisp, and nickname God's creatures, and make your wantonness your ignorance. Go to, I'll no more on't; it hath made me mad. I say, we will have no more marriages: those that are married already, all but one, shall live; the rest shall keep as they are. To a nunnery, go. *(Exit.)*

OPHELIA: O, what a noble mind is here o'erthrown!
The courtier's, soldier's, scholar's eye, tongue, sword;
Th'expectancy and rose of the fair state,
The glass of fashion and the mould of form,
Th'observ'd of all observers,—quite, quite down!
And I, of ladies most deject and wretched,
That suckt the honey of his music vows,
Now see that noble and most sovereign reason,
Like sweet bells jangled, out of tune and harsh;
That unmatcht form and feature of blown youth
Blasted with ecstasy: O, woe is me
T'have seen what I have seen, see what I see!
*(Enter King and Polonius.)*

KING: Love! his affections do not that way tend;
Nor what he spake, though it lackt form a little,
Was not like madness. There's something in his soul
O'er which his melancholy sits on brood;
And I do doubt the hatch and the disclose
Will be some danger: which for to prevent,
I have in quick determination
Thus set it down:—he shall with speed to England,
For the demand of our neglected tribute:
Haply, the seas, and countries different,
With variable objects, shall expel
This something-settled matter in his heart;
Whereon his brains still beating puts him thus

From fashion of himself. What think you on't?

POLONIUS: It shall do well: but yet do I believe
   The origin and commencement of his grief
   Sprung from neglected love.—How now, Ophelia!
   You need not tell us what Lord Hamlet said;
   We heard it all.—My lord, do as you please;
   But, if you hold it fit, after the play,
   Let his queen mother all alone entreat him
   To show his grief: let her be round with him;
   And I'll be placed, so please you, in the ear
   Of all their conference. If she find him not,
   To England send him; or confine him where
   Your wisdom best shall think.

KING: It shall be so:
   Madness in great ones must not unwatcht go. *(Exeunt.)*

# The Divorce Court Judge

Miguel de Cervantes
Translated by Dawn L. Smith
1615

**Comic**
**Scene:** in court

Mariana
Old Man
Judge
Notary
Attorney
Guiomar
Soldier
Surgeon
Aldonza

MARIANA: At last the divorce judge has taken his place in court! Enough of this shilly-shallying. This time I am going to be set free—free as a bird!

OLD MAN: For pity's sake, Mariana, there's no need to bellow from the roof-tops. Speak more softly. God's wounds, you're deafening the neighbours with your shouting. The judge is right there, so just lower your voice and tell him what's wrong.

JUDGE: Well, good people, what's your quarrel?

MARIANA: Divorce, divorce, divorce. A thousand times divorce!

JUDGE: Who from, madam? On what grounds?

MARIANA: Who from? From this old crock here.

JUDGE: On what grounds?

MARIANA: I can't abide his peevish demands any longer. I refuse to look after his countless ailments all the time. My parents didn't bring me up to be a nurse and handmaid. A very good dowry I brought this old bag of bones who's consuming my life. When he first got his hands on me, my face was as bright and polished as a mirror, and now it's as crumpled as a widow's veil. Please, your honour, unmarry me or I'll hang myself. Just look at the furrows I've got from the tears I shed every day that I'm married to this walking skeleton.

JUDGE: Cry no more, madam. Cease your bawling and dry your tears. I'll see that justice is done.

MARIANA: Let me cry, your honour. It's such a comfort. In well-ordered societies a marriage should be reviewed every three years, and dissolved or renewed like a rental agreement. It shouldn't have to last a lifetime and bring everlasting misery to both parties.

JUDGE: If that policy were practical, desirable, or financially profitable, it would already be law. But, madam, you must be specific about your reasons for seeking a divorce.

MARIANA: For one thing, my husband is in the winter of life, while I'm in the spring of youth. For another, I lose my sleep getting up in the middle of the night to put hot cloths and poultices on his belly; then I have to fetch him one bandage after another—what I'd give to see him condemned to be bandaged to a post! I have to prop up his pillows at night and bring him cough syrup for the congestion in his lungs. What's more, I have to put up with the stench of his breath—it stinks to high heaven.

NOTARY: He must have a rotten tooth in there.

OLD MAN: That can't be. The devil knows I don't have a tooth in my head!

ATTORNEY: I believe there's a law that recognises bad breath as sufficient cause for a wife to leave her husband, or vice versa.

OLD MAN: The fact is, gentlemen, that the bad breath she complains about doesn't come from my rotten teeth (because I haven't any), or from my stomach (which is in excellent condition). It comes from her ill will. Gentlemen, you don't know what this woman is like. I swear that if you did you'd avoid her like the plague, or else treat her like the devil. She's rude, quarrelsome, and capricious, and I've been an uncomplaining martyr for twenty-two years. For the past two years she's been coaxing and pushing me towards the grave. She's almost deafened me and driven me half mad with her scolding and arguing. If she nurses me, as she claims, it's always with nagging, instead of with the gentle voice and manner that you expect from someone who ministers to the sick. I swear, gentlemen, that, thanks to her, I'm the one who's dying, while she's thriving off me—after all, she has complete control over my estate.

MARIANA: Your estate indeed! Everything you own was bought with my dowry! Like it or not, half the belongings we've acquired since we married are mine! If I die tomorrow I won't leave you a far-thing—that's how much I love you!

JUDGE: Tell me, sir, when you married your wife, weren't you healthy, carefree, and in fine fettle?

OLD MAN: I've told you that I've been married to her for twenty-two years—like a galley slave under the command of a Calabrian renegade. When I met her I could satisfy all her demands.

MARIANA: That was a nine-day wonder!

JUDGE: Silence, woman. Hold your tongue for God's sake! I find no reason to unmarry you. You enjoyed the fruit when it was ripe, now you must put up with the rotting remains. A husband can't be expected to weather the passage of time. Time waits for no man. Forget the ills he causes you today and remember the pleasures he gave you when he was in his prime. I don't want to hear another word from you!

OLD MAN: Your honour, you'd do me a great favour if you'd put an end to my misery and release me from my prison. I'm at breaking point, so if you don't release me now you'll just be handing me back to my torturer. If that's not possible, let's agree on one thing: she can shut herself away in a convent and I'll go to a monastery. We'll divide the estate and live out the rest of our lives in peace and to the glory of God.

MARIANA: To hell with that! A fine idea to shut me away! A convent's for a girl who enjoys life behind bars, with everything passed through a turnstile and visits supervised by the nuns! Try shutting yourself away—it makes no difference to you: you can't see or hear; your feet will hardly carry you and your hands are useless. I'm in good health, in full possession of my senses. I'm not playing my cards close to my chest. I mean to lay them all on the table where they can be seen.

NOTARY: This woman doesn't mince her words!

ATTORNEY: The husband's a sensible man, but there's a limit to his patience.

JUDGE: Well, I can't grant you a divorce. I find no fault at all...

*(Enter a well-groomed soldier with his wife, Guiomar.)*

GUIOMAR: Thank Heaven for this opportunity to speak to your honour. I beseech you with all my heart, be pleased to release me from marriage to this creature.

JUDGE: What do you mean by 'this creature?' Doesn't he have a name? It would be better if you at least referred to him as 'this man.'

GUIOMAR: If he were a man I wouldn't be trying to end the marriage.

JUDGE: What is he, then?

GUIOMAR: A block of wood.

SOLDIER: *(Aside.)* My God, only a block of wood would take what I put up with and never say a word. Perhaps if I don't try to defend myself and let her have her say, the judge will find against me. He'll think he's punishing me, but he'll be setting me free, just as surely as if he released a prisoner from the dungeons of North Africa.

ATTORNEY: Watch your language, madam, and get to the point without insulting your husband. His honour the Judge, whom you see before you, will see that you are treated fairly.

GUIOMAR: Why, sirs, what's wrong with calling a statue a block of wood if it behaves like one?

MARIANA: It sounds as though this woman and I share a common complaint.

GUIOMAR: In short, sir, I'm saying that I was married off to this man (if that's what you insist on calling him), but this man isn't the one I married.

JUDGE: How's that? I don't follow you.

GUIOMAR: I mean that I thought I was marrying a man who was normal—you might say run-of-the-mill—but I soon found out he was a block of wood, just as I said. He can't tell his right hand from his left, and he makes no effort whatsoever to earn anything to support his family. He spends his morning at Mass or hanging around the Guadalajara Gate, gossiping and exchanging lies and hearsay. In the afternoon, and sometimes in the morning too, he does the round of the gaming houses. There he joins the crowd of onlookers who hang around the gamblers in the hope of a tip—though they're heartily disliked by the people in charge. He shows up for dinner around two o'clock without a shilling to show for his pains because they're no longer in a tipping mood. He goes out again, returns at midnight, has supper if he can find any leftovers, and if not, he blesses himself, gives a yawn and goes to bed. Then he can't sleep and tosses all night. I ask him what's wrong. He tells me he's composing a sonnet for a friend who wants an epitaph. He insists on being a poet, as if that weren't the worst-paid job in the world!

SOLDIER: My dear wife, everything you say is perfectly reasonable—just as everything I do is perfectly reasonable. If it were not so, I would have managed to get hold of some small official favour—like many clever wheedlers I know, who land themselves a staff of office and a small bad-tempered mule (the kind you can hire from a livery stable when they have nothing else available, and that comes without a groom). In one saddlebag they carry a clean shirt and collar, in the other a wedge of cheese, a loaf of bread, and a wineskin; they're wearing their city clothes, with leggings and a single spur added for the journey; their commissions are gnawing at them inside their shirts. Out across the Toledo Bridge they clatter, urging on their stubborn mules; a few days later they send home a salted leg of pork and a length of unbleached linen—in short, items that can be bought cheap in the places they've been sent to, and that help to put food on the table at home. However, I enjoy neither job nor patronage. I don't know what to do because no one wants to hire a married man. With the gentry so tight-fisted and my wife so insistent, I've no choice, your honour, but to implore you to grant us a divorce.

GUIOMAR: There's something else, sir. Since I know my husband is so puny and inadequate, I do my best to help, but there's a limit: after all, I'm a respectable woman and I don't have to do anything I'd be ashamed of!

SOLDIER: On that score alone this woman deserves to be loved; but look beneath those scruples and you'll find the most ill-natured creature alive. She turns jealous for no reason at all, starts screaming without provocation, has far too high an opinion of herself, and turns her nose up at me because I'm poor. But the worst part, your honour, is that in return for remaining faithful to me, she expects me to put up with her bad temper and disagreeable ways.

GUIOMAR: Well, why not? Seeing that I'm such a virtuous woman, why shouldn't you treat me with the honour and respect that I deserve?

SOLDIER: Just listen to me, wife—let these gentlemen hear what I have to say to you: why do you keep harping on how virtuous you are, when that's what any self-respecting Christian lady of decent family is expected to be? Just imagine women wanting their husbands to respect them for being faithful and modest! As if that were enough to make them perfect! They don't notice that all their other virtues have fallen through the cracks! What do I care that you're satisfied with your own moral standards? On the other hand, I care a great deal that you ignore your maid's immoral behaviour, that you're a spendthrift, and that you're constantly frowning, complaining, and arguing; that you're angry, jealous, distracted, lazy, idle, and a lot more besides. That's enough to finish off two hundred husbands! Yet when all's said and done, your honour, my wife Mistress Guiomar doesn't have any of these vices and I admit that I'm a block of wood, good for nothing, negligent, a lazybones. So if for no other reason than to uphold the law, sir, you'll have to give us a separation. I make no objection to what my wife has said; I consider the case closed and I'll be glad to accept your judgment.

GUIOMAR: What objection could you possibly make? You provide nothing to eat, either for me or our servant (take note that I said servant, in the singular), and she's as skinny as a baby born before its time—doesn't eat enough to keep a cricket alive.

NOTARY: Order, there. Here come some more plaintiffs.

*(Enter a Barber-Surgeon dressed as a doctor, with his wife, Aldonza de Minjaca.)*

SURGEON: I come to you, your honour, to beg you to grant me a separation from my wife, Aldonza de Minjaca, on four principal counts.

JUDGE: You've made up your mind already. Tell me what the four counts are.

SURGEON: First, because I can no more put up with her than with all the devils in hell. Second, for reasons that she's aware of. Third, for reasons I can't mention. Fourth, to save my soul from the devil. Just see if I'm going to put up with her company for the rest of my life!

ATTORNEY: You've more than stated your case.

ALDONZA: Your honour, listen to me. I'll have you know that if my husband's asking for a divorce on four counts, then I'm asking for one on four hundred. First, because every time I set eyes on him I believe I'm seeing the devil himself. Second, because he deceived me when I married him: he told me he was a qualified doctor and then he turned out to be a mere surgeon—someone who bandages and attends to minor ailments—he's a far cry from a real doctor. Third, because he's jealous of everything, even the sun that shines on me. Fourth, since I can't abide him, I'd like to put a million miles between us.

NOTARY: How the devil can anyone ever make these two clocks chime together? They don't even keep the same time!

ALDONZA: Fifth...

JUDGE: Madam, madam, if you plan to give us every one of your four hundred reasons, I'm not disposed to hear them and, besides, there isn't time. We'll hold your case over pending further evidence—so you can go now, God rest you. We have other cases to consider.

SURGEON: What more evidence do you need, since I refuse to die in her company and she doesn't want to live in mine?

JUDGE: If that were sufficient reason for a divorce, there'd be no end of couples in a hurry to shake off the matrimonial yoke.

# The Relapse: or Virtue in Danger

Sir John Vanbrugh
1697

**Comic**
**Scene:** Lord Foppington's dressing chambers

Lord Foppington
Page
La Vérole
Taylor
Young Fashion
Lory
Shoemaker
Mr. Mend-Legs
Sempstress (female, one line)
Mr. Foretop
Coupler
Waterman


YOUNG FASH: Come, pay the waterman, and take the portmantle.

LORY: Faith, sir, I think the waterman had as good take the portmantle and pay himself.

YOUNG FASH: Why, sure there's something left in't!

LORY: But a solitary old waistcoat, upon honour, sir.

YOUNG FASH: Why, what's become of the blue coat, sirrah?

LORY: Sir, 'twas eaten at Gravesend. The reckoning came to thirty shillings, and your privy purse was worth but two half crowns.

YOUNG FASH: 'Tis very well.

WATER: Pray master, will you please to dispatch me?

YOUNG FASH: Ay, here, a—Canst thou change me a guinea?

LORY: *(Aside.)* Good.

WATER: Change a guinea, master! Ha! ha! Your honour's pleased to compliment.

YOUNG FASH: Egad I don't know how I shall pay thee then, for I have nothin but gold about me.

LORY: *(Aside.)* Hum, hum.

YOUNG FASH: What dost thou expect, friend?

WATER: Why master, so far against wind and tide is richly worth half a piece.

YOUNG FASH: Why, faith, I think thou art a good conscionable fellow. I'gad I begin to have so good an opinion of thy honesty, I care not if I leave my portmantle with thee, till I send thee thy money.

WATER: Ha! God bless your honour! I should be as willing to trust you, master, but that you are, as a man may say, a stranger to me, and these are nimble times. There are a great many sharpers stirring. *(Taking up the portmantle.)* Well master, when your worship sends the money your portmantle shall be forthcoming. My name's Tugg. My wife keeps a brandyshop in Drab Alley at Wapping.

YOUNG FASH: Very well; I'll send for't tomorrow.

*(Exit Waterman.)*

LORY: So.—Now sir, I hope you'll own yourself a happy man. You have out-lived all your cares.

YOUNG FASH: How so, sir?

LORY: Why, you have nothing, left to take care of.

YOUNG FASH: Yes sirrah, I have myself and you to take care of still.

LORY: Sir, if you could but prevail with somebody else to do that for you, I fancy we might both fare the better for't.

PAGE: Sir.

LORD FOP: Sir, pray sir, do me the favour to teach your tongue the title the king has thought fit to honour me with.

PAGE: I ask your lordship's pardon, my lord.

LORD FOP: O, you can pronounce the word then! I thought it would have choked you. D'ye hear?

PAGE: My lord.

LORD FOP: Call La Vérole, I would dress....

*(Exit Page.)*

LORD FOP: *(Solus.)* Well, 'tis an unspeakable pleasure to be a man of quality!...Strike me dumb!...My lord!...Your lordship!...My lord Foppington!...*Ah c'est quelque chose de beau, que le diable m'emporte*...Why, the ladies were ready to puke at me, whilst I had nothing but sir Navelty to recommend me to 'em...Sure whilst I was but a knight, I was a very nauseous fellow...Well, 'tis ten thousand pawnd well given—stap my vitals!

*(Enter La Vérole.)*

LE VÉR: Me lord, de shoemaker, de taylor, de hosier, de semstress, de barber, be all ready, if your lordship please to be dress.

LORD FOP: 'Tis well, admit 'em.

LE VÉR: Hey, *messieurs, entrez!*
*(Enter Taylor, etc.)*

LE VÉR: So gentlemen, I hope you have all taken pains to show your-selves masters in your professions.

TAYLOR: I think I may presume to say, sir….

LE VÉR: My *lord*—you clawn you!

TAYLOR: Why, is he made a lord?—My lord, I ask your lordship's pardon, my lord; I hope, my lord, your lordship will please to own, I have brought your lordship as accomplished a suit of clothes as ever peer of England trod the stage in. My lord, will your lordship please to try 'em now?

LORD FOP: Ay, but let my people dispose the glasses so, that I may see myself before and behind, for I love to see myself all raund.
*(Whilst he puts on his clothes, enter Young Fashion and Lory.)*

YOUNG FASH: Hey-day, what the devil have we here? Sure my gentle-man's grown a favourite at court, he has got so many people at his levee.

LORY: Sir, these people come in order to make him a favourite at court. They are to establish him with the ladies.

YOUNG FASH: Good God, to what an ebb of taste are women fallen, that it should be in the power of a laced coat to recommend a gallant to 'em.

LORY: Sir, taylors and periwig-makers are now become the bawds of the nation. 'Tis they debauch all the women.

YOUNG FASH: Thou say'st true, for there's that fop now, has not by nature wherewithal to move a cook-maid, and by that time these fellows have done with him, egad he shall melt down a count-ess.—But now for my reception. I'll engage it shall be as cold a one as a courtier's to his friend who comes to put him in mind of his promise.

LORD FOP: *(To his Taylor.)* Death and eternal tartures, sir, I say the packet's too high by a foot.

TAYLOR: My lord, if it had been an inch lower, it would not have held your lordship's pocket-handkerchief.

LORD FOP: Rat my packet-handkerchief! Have not I a page to carry it?

You may make him a packet up to his chin a purpose for it. But I will not have mine come so near my face.

TAYLOR: 'Tis not for me to dispute your lordship's fancy.

YOUNG FASH: *(To Lory.)* His lordship! Lory, did you observe that?

LORY: Yes sir, I always thought 'twould end there. Now I hope you'll have a little more respect for him.

YOUNG FASH: Respect! Damn him for a coxcomb! Now has he ruined his estate to buy a title, that he may be a fool of the first rate. But let's accost him. *(To Lord Foppington.)* Brother, I'm your humble servant.

LORD FOP: O lard, Tam, I did not expect you in England! Brother, I am glad to see you. *(Turning to his Taylor.)* Look you, sir, I shall never be reconciled to this nauseous packet, therefore pray get me another suit with all manner of expedition for this is my eternal aversion. *(To the Sempstress.)* Mrs. Calico, are not you of my mind?

SEMP: O, directly, my lord, it can never be too low.

LORD FOP: You are positively in the right on't, for the packet becomes no part of the body but the knee.

SEMP: I hope your lordship is pleased with your steenkirk.

LORD FOP: In love with it, stap my vitals! Bring your bill, you shall be paid tomarrow.

SEMP: I humbly thank your honour. *(Exit Sempstress.)*

LORD FOP: Hark thee, shoemaker, these shoes an't ugly but they don't fit me.

SHOE: My lord, methinks they fit you very well.

LORD FOP: They hurt me just below the instep.

SHOE: *(Feeling his foot.)* My lord, they don't hurt you there.

LORD FOP: I tell thee they pinch me execrably.

SHOE: My lord, if they pinch you, I'll be bound to be hanged, that's all.

LORD FOP: Why, wilt thou undertake to persuade me I cannot feel?

SHOE: Your lordship may please to feel what you think fit, but that shoe does not hurt you. I think I understand my trade!

LORD FOP: Now by all that's Great and Powerful, thou art an incomprehensible coxcomb! But thou makest good shoes, and so I'll bear with thee.

SHOE: My lord, I have worked for half the people of quality in town, these twenty years, and 'twere very hard I should not know when a shoe hurts and when it don't.

LORD FOP: Well, prithee begone about thy business.

*(Exit Shoemaker.)*

LORD FOP: (To the Hosier.) Mr. Mend-legs, a word with you; the calves of these stockings are thickened a little too much. They make my legs look like a chairman's.

MEND: My lord, methinks they look mighty well.

LORD FOP: Ay, but you are not so good a judge of these things as I am— I have studied 'em all my life. Therefore pray let the next be the thickness of a crawn-piece less. *(Aside.)* If the town takes notice my legs are fallen away 'twill be attributed to the violence of some new intrigue— *(To the Periwig-maker.)* Come, Mr. Foretop, let me see what you have done, and then the fatigue of the marning will be over.

FORE: My lord, I have done what I defy any prince in Europe t'outdo; I have made you a periwig so long and so full of hair it will serve you for hat and cloak in all weathers.

LORD FOP: Then thou hast made me thy friend to eternity. Come, comb it out.

YOUNG FASH: Well, Lory, what dost think on't? A very friendly reception from a brother after three years' absence.

LORY: Why, sir, it's your own fault. We seldom care for those that don't love what we love. If you would creep into his heart, you must enter into his pleasures. Here have you stood ever since you came in, and have not commended any one thing that belongs to him.

YOUNG FASH: Nor never shall, whilst they belong to a coxcomb.

LORY: Then, sir, you must be content to pick a hungry bone.

YOUNG FASH: No, sir, I'll crack it, and get to the marrow before I have done.

LORD FOP: Gad's curse! Mr. Foretop, you don't intend to put this upon me for a full periwig?

FORE: Not a full one, my lord? I don't know what your lordship may please to call a full one, but I have crammed twenty ounces of hair into it.

LORD FOP: What it may be by weight, sir, I shall not dispute, but by tale, there are not nine hairs of a side.

FORE: O lord! O lord! O Lord! Why, as God shall judge me, your honour's side-face is reduced to the tip of your nose.

LORD FOP: My side-face may be in eclipse for aught I know, but I'm sure my full-face is like the full-moon.

FORE: Heavens bless my eye-sight! *(Rubbing his eyes.)* Sure I look through the wrong end of the perspective, for by my faith, an't please your honour, the broadest place I see in your face does not seem to me to be two inches [in] diameter.

LORD FOP: If it did, it would be just two inches too broad. Far a periwig to a man should be like a mask to a woman—nothing, should be seen but his eyes.

FORE: My lord, I have done; if you please to have more hair in your wig, I'll put it in.

LORD FOP: Pasitively, yes.

FORE: Shall I take it back now, my lord?

LORD FOP: No! I'll wear it today, though it show such a manstrous pair of cheeks. Stap my vitals, I shall be taken for a trumpeter. *(Exit Foretop.)*

YOUNG FASH: Now your people of business are gone, brother, I hope I may obtain a quarter of an hour's audience of you.

LORD FOP: Faith, Tam, I must beg you'll excuse me at this time, for I must away to the House of Lards immediately. My lady Teaser's case is to come on today, and I would not be absent for the salvation of mankind. Hey page, is the coach at the door?

PAGE: Yes, my lord.

LORD FOP: You'll excuse me, brother. *(Going.)*

YOUNG FASH: Shall you be back at dinner?

LORD FOP: As Gad shall jidge me, I can't tell; for 'tis passible I may dine with some of aur House at Lacket's.

YOUNG FASH: Shall I meet you there? For I must needs talk with you.

LORD FOP: That I'm afraid mayn't be so praper, far the lards I commonly eat with are people of a nice conversation, and you know, Tam, your education has been a little at large. But if you'll stay here, you'll find a family-dinner. Hey fellow! What is there for dinner? There's beef; I suppose, my brother will eat beef. Dear Tam, I'm glad to see thee in England, stap my vitals. *(Exit with his equipage.)*

YOUNG FASH: Hell and furies, is this to be borne?

LORY: Faith, sir, I could almost have given him a knock o'th' pate myself.

YOUNG FASH: 'Tis enough; I will now show thee the excess of my passion by being very calm. Come, Lory, lay your loggerhead to mine, and in cool blood let us contrive his destruction.

LORY: Here comes a head, sir, would contrive it better than us both, if he would but join in the confederacy.
(Enter Coupler.)

YOUNG FASH: By this light, old Coupler alive still! Why, how now, matchmaker, art thou here still to plague the world with matrimony? You old bawd, how have you the impudence to be hobbling out of your grave twenty years after you are rotten!

COUP: When you begin to rot, sirrah, you'll go off like a pippin—one winter will send you to the devil. What mischief brings you home again? Ha! You young lascivious rogue, you. Let me put my hand in your bosom, sirrah.

YOUNG FASH: Stand off, old Sodom.

COUP: Nay, prithee now, don't be so coy.

YOUNG FASH: Keep your hands to yourself, you old dog you, or I'll wring your nose off.

COUP: Hast thou then been a year in Italy, and brought home a fool at last? By my conscience, the young fellows of this age profit no more by their going abroad than they do by their going to church. Sirrah, sirrah, if you are not hanged before you come to my years, you'll know a cock from a hen. But come, I'm still a friend to thy person, though I have a contempt of thy understanding; and therefore I would willingly know thy condition, that I may see whether thou standest in need of my assistance, for widows swarm, my boy, the town's infected with 'em.

YOUNG FASH: I stand in need of anybody's assistance, that will help me to cut my elder brother's throat, without the risk of being hanged for him.

COUP: Egad, sirrah, I could help thee to do him almost as good a turn, without the danger of being burnt in the hand for't.

YOUNG FASH: Sayest thou so, old Satan? Show me but that and my soul is thine.

COUP: Pox o'thy soul, give me thy warm body, sirrah. I shall have a substantial title to't when I tell thee my project.

YOUNG FASH: Out with it then, dear dad, and take possession as soon as thou wilt.

COUP: Say'st thou so my Hephaestion? Why then, thus lies the scene—but hold! Who's that? If we are heard we are undone.

YOUNG FASH: What, have you forgot Lory?

COUP: Who, trusty Lory, is it thee?

LORY: At your service, sir.

COUP: Give me thy hand, old boy. Egad I did not know thee again, but I remember thy honesty, though I did not thy face. I think thou had'st like to have been hanged once or twice for thy master?

LORY: Sir, I was very near once having that honour.

COUP: Well, live and hope, don't be discouraged! Eat with him, and drink with him, and do what he bids thee, and it may be thy reward at last, as well as another's. (To Young Fashion.) Well, sir, you must know I have done you the kindness to make up a match for your brother.

YOUNG FASH: Sir, I am very much beholding to you, truly.

COUP: You may be, sirrah, before the wedding-day yet. The lady is a great heiress—fifteen hundred pound a year, and a great bag of money. The match is concluded, the writings are drawn, and the pipkin's to be cracked in a fortnight.—Now you must know, stripling,—with respect to your mother,—your brother's the son of a whore!

YOUNG FASH: Good.

COUP: He has given me a bond of a thousand pounds for helping him to this fortune, and has promised me as much more in ready money upon the day of marriage, which I understand by a friend, he ne'er designs to pay me! If therefore you will be a generous young dog, and secure me five thousand pounds, I'll be a covetous old rogue and help you to the lady.

YOUNG FASH: Egad, if thou canst bring this about, I'll have thy statue cast in brass. But don't you dote, you old pander you, when you talk at this rate?

COUP: That your youthful parts shall judge of. This plump partridge that I tell you of lives in the country, fifty miles off, with her honoured parents, in a lonely old house which nobody comes near. She never goes abroad, nor sees company at home. To prevent all misfortunes she has her breeding within doors, the parson of the parish teaches her to play upon the bass-viol, the clerk to sing, her nurse to dress, and her father to dance. In short, nobody can give you admittance there but I, nor can I do it any other way than by making you pass for your brother.

YOUNG FASH: And how the devil wilt thou do that?

COUP: Without the devil's aid, I warrant thee! Thy brother's face, not one of the family ever saw; the whole business has been managed by me, and all the letters go through my hands. The last that was writ to sir Tunbelly Clumsy (For that's the old gentleman's name,) was to tell him his lordship would be down in a fortnight to consummate. Now you shall go away immediately, pretend you writ that letter only to have the romantic pleasure of surprising your mistress; fall desperately in love, as soon as you see her; make that your plea, for marrying her immediately, and when the fatigue of the wedding-night's over, you shall send me a swinging purse of gold, you dog you.

YOUNG FASH: Egad, old dad, I'll put my hand in thy bosom now.

COUP: Ah, you young hot lusty thief, let me muzzle you! *(Kissing.)* Sirrah, let me muzzle you!

YOUNG FASH: *(Aside.)* Pshaw, the old leche....

COUP: Well, I'll warrant thou hast not a farthing of money in thy pocket now, no; one may see it in thy face....

YOUNG FASH: Not a souse, by Jupiter.

COUP: Must I advance then? Well sirrah, be at my lodgings in half an hour, and I'll see what may be done. We'll sign and seal, and eat a pullet, and when I have given thee some farther instructions, thou sha't hoist sail and begone. *(Kissing.)* T'other buss and so adieu.

YOUNG FASH: Hum...pshaw....

COUP: Ah, you young warm dog you, what a delicious night will the bride have on't. *(Exit Coupler.)*

YOUNG FASH: So, Lory! Providence, thou see'st at last, takes care of men of merit. We are in a fair way to be great people.

LORY: Ay sir, if the devil don't step between the cup and the lip, as he uses to do.

YOUNG FASH: Why, faith, he has played me many a damned trick to spoil my fortune, and egad I'm almost afraid he's at work about it again now. But if I should tell thee how, thou'dst wonder at me.

LORY: Indeed, sir, I should not.

YOUNG FASH: How dost know?

LORY: Because, sir, I have wondered at you so often, I can wonder at you no more.

YOUNG FASH: No—what wouldst thou say, if a qualm of conscience should spoil my design?

LORY: I would eat my words, and wonder more than ever.

YOUNG FASH: With, faith, Lory, though I am a young rakechell, and have played many a roguish trick, this is so full-grown a cheat, I find I must take pains to come up to't. I have scruples.

LORY: They are strong symptoms of death. If you find they increase, pray, sir, make your will.

# Desire Under the Elms

Eugene O'Neill
1924

**Dramatic**
**Scene:** the Cabot farmhouse, 1850

Ephraim Cabot
His sons:
    Simeon
    Peter
    EbenAbbie Putnam

EBEN: *(Breathlessly.)* Waal—har they be! The old mule an' the bride! I seen 'em from the barn down below at the turnin'.

PETER: How could ye tell that far?

EBEN: Hain't I as far-sight as he's near-sight? Don't I know the mare 'n' buggy, an' two people settin' in it? Who else…? An' I tell ye I kin feel 'em a-comin' too! *(He squirms as if he had the itch.)*

PETER: *(Beginning to be angry.)* Waal—let him do his own unhitchin'!

SIMEON: *(Angry in his turn.)* Let's hustle in an' git our bundles an' be a-goin' as he's a-comin'. I don't want never t'step inside the door agen arter he's back.

*(They both start back around the corner of the house. Eben follows them.)*

EBEN: *(Anxiously.)* Will ye sign it afore ye go?

PETER: Let's see the color o' the old skinflint's money an' we'll sign.

*(They disappear left. The two brothers clump upstairs to get their bundles. Eben appears in the kitchen, runs to window, peers out, comes back and pulls up a strip of flooring in under stove, takes out a canvas bag and puts it on table, then he sets the floorboard back in place. The two brothers appear a moment after. They carry old carpet bags.)*

EBEN: *(Puts his hand on bag guardingly.)* Have ye signed?

SIMEON: *(Shows paper in his hand.)* Ay-eh. *(Greedily.)* Be that the money?

EBEN: *(Opens bag and pours out pile of twenty-dollar gold pieces.)* Twenty-dollar pieces—thirty on 'em. Count 'em.

*(Peter does so, arranging them in stacks of five, biting one or two to test them.)*

PETER: Six hundred. *(He puts them in bag and puts it inside his shirt carefully.)*

SIMEON: *(Handing paper to Eben.)* Har ye be.

EBEN: *(After a glance, folds it carefully and hides it under his shirt—gratefully.)* Thank yew.

PETER: Thank yew fur the ride.

SIMEON: We'll send ye a lump o' gold fur Christmas.

*(A pause. Eben stares at them and they at him.)*

PETER: *(Awkwardly.)* Waal—we're a-goin'.

SIMEON: Comin' out t' the yard?

EBEN: No. I'm waitin' in here a spell.

*(Another silence. The brothers edge awkwardly to door in rear—then turn and stand.)*

SIMEON: Waal—good-bye.

PETER: Good-bye.

EBEN: Good-bye.

*(They go out. He sits down at the table, faces the stove and pulls out the paper. He looks from it to the stove. His face, lighted up by the shaft of sunlight from the window, has an expression of trance. His lips move. The two brothers come out to the gate.)*

PETER: *(Looking off toward barn.)* Thar he be—unhitchin'.

SIMEON: *(With a chuckle.)* I'll bet ye he's riled!

PETER: An thar she be.

SIMEON: Let's wait 'n' see what our new Maw looks like.

PETER: *(With a grin.)* An' give him our partin' cuss!

SIMEON: *(Grinning.)* I feel like raisin' fun. I feel light in my head an' feet.

PETER: Me, too. I feel like laffin' till I'd split up the middle.

SIMEON: Reckon it's the likker?

PETER: No. My feet feel itchin' t' walk an' walk—an' jump high over thin's—an'....

SIMEON: Dance?

*(A pause.)*

PETER: *(Puzzled.)* It's plumb onnateral.

SIMEON: *(A light coming over his face.)* I calc'late it's 'cause school's out. It's holiday. Fur once we're free!

PETER: *(Dazedly.)* Free?

SIMEON: The halter's broke—the harness is busted—the fence bars is down—the stone walls air crumblin' an' tumblin'! We'll be kickin' up an' tearin' away down the road!

PETER: *(Drawing a deep breath—oratorically.)* Anybody that wants this stinkin' old rock-pile of a farm kin hev it. T'ain't our'n, no sirree!

SIMEON: *(Takes the gate off its hinges and puts it under his arm.)* We harby 'bolishes shet gates, an' open gates, an' all gates, by thunder!

PETER: We'll take it with us fur luck an' let 'er sail free down some river.

SIMEON: *(As a sound of voices comes from left, rear.)* Har they comes! *(The two brothers congeal into two stiff, grim-visaged statues. Ephraim Cabot and Abbie Putnam come in. Cabot is seventy-five, tall and gaunt, with great, wiry, concentrated power, but stoop-shouldered from toil. His face is as hard as if it were hewn out of a boulder, yet there is a weakness in it, a petty pride in its own narrow strength. His eyes are small, close together, and extremely near-sighted, blinking continually in the effort to focus on objects, their stare having a straining, ingrowing quality. He is dressed in his dismal black Sunday suit. Abbie is thirty-five, buxom, full of vitality. Her round face is pretty but marred by its rather gross sensuality. There is strength and obstinacy in her jaw, a hard determination in her eyes, and about her whole personality the same unsettled, untamed, desperate quality which is so apparent in Eben.)*

CABOT: *(As they enter—a queer strangled emotion in his dry cracking voice.)* Har we be t' hum, Abbie.

ABBIE: *(With lust for the word.)* Hum! *(Her eyes gloating on the house without seeming to see the two stiff figures at the gate.)* It's purty—purty! I can't b'lieve it's r'ally mine.

CABOT: *(Sharply.)* Yewr'n? Mine!

*(He stares at her penetratingly. She stares back.)*

CABOT: *(He adds relentingly.)* Our'n—mebbe! It was lonesome too long. I was growin' old in the spring. A hum's got t' hev a woman.

ABBIE: *(Her voice taking possession.)* A woman's got t' hev a hum!

CABOT: *(Nodding uncertainly.)* Ay-eh. *(Then irritably.)* Whar be they? Ain't thar nobody about—'r wukin'—'r nothin'?

ABBIE: *(Sees the brothers. She returns their stare of cold appraising contempt with interest—slowly.)* Thar's two men loafin' at the gate an' starin' at me like a couple o' strayed hogs.

CABOT: *(Straining his eyes.)* I kin see 'em—but I can't make out....

SIMEON: It's Simeon.

PETER: It's Peter.

CABOT: *(Exploding.)* Why hain't ye wukin'?

SIMEON: *(Dryly.)* We're waitin' t' welcome ye hum—yew an' the bride!

CABOT: *(Confusedly.)* Huh? Waal—this be yer new Maw, boys.
    *(She stares at them and they at her.)*

SIMEON: *(Turns away and spits contemptuously.)* I see her!

PETER: *(Spits also.)* An I see her!

ABBIE: *(With the conquerors conscious superiority.)* I'll go in an' look at my house. *(She goes slowly around to porch.)*

SIMEON: *(With a snort.)* Her house!

PETER: *(Calls after her.)* Ye'll find Eben inside. Ye better not tell him it's yewr house.

ABBIE: *(Mouthing the name.)* Eben. *(Then quietly.)* I'll tell Eben.

CABOT: *(With a contemptuous sneer.)* Ye needn't heed Eben. Eben's a dumb fool—like his Maw—soft an' simple!

SIMEON: *(With his sardonic burst of laughter.)* Ha! Eben's a chip o' yew—spit 'n' image—hard 'n' bitter's a hickory tree! Dog'll eat dog. He'll eat ye yet, old man!

CABOT: *(Commandingly.)* Ye git t' wuk!

SIMEON: *(As Abbie disappears in house—winks at Peter and says tauntingly.)* So that thar's our new Maw, be it? Whar in hell did ye dig her up?
    *(He and Peter laugh.)*

PETER: Ha! Ye'd better turn her in the pen with the other sows.
    *(They laugh uproariously, slapping their thighs.)*

CABOT: *(So amazed at their effrontery that he stutters in confusion.)* Simeon! Peter! What's come over ye? Air ye drunk?

SIMEON: We're free, old man—free o' yew an' the hull damned farm!
    *(They grow more and more hilarious and excited.)*

PETER: An' we're startin' out fur the gold fields o' Californi-a!

SIMEON: Ye kin take this place an' burn it!

PETER: An' bury it—fur all we cares!

SIMEON: We're free, old man! *(He cuts a caper.)*

PETER: Free! *(He gives a kick in the air.)*

SIMEON: *(In a frenzy.)* Whoop!

PETER: Whoop!
    *(They do an absurd Indian war dance about the old man who is petrified between rage and the fear that they are insane.)*

SIMEON: We're free as Injuns! Lucky we don't skulp ye!

PETER: An' burn yer barn an' kill the stock!

SIMEON: An' rape yer new woman! Whoop!

>*(He and Peter stop their dance, holding their sides, rocking with wild laughter.)*

CABOT: *(Edging away.)* Lust fur gold—fur the sinful, easy gold o' Californi-a! It's made ye mad!

SIMEON: *(Tauntingly.)* Wouldn't ye like us to send ye back some sinful gold, ye old sinner?

PETER: They's gold besides what's in Californi-a! *(He retreats back beyond the vision of the old man and takes the bag of money and flaunts it in the air above his head, laughing.)*

SIMEON: And sinfuller, too!

PETER: We'll be voyagin' on the sea! Whoop! *(He leaps up and down.)*

SIMEON: Livin' free! Whoop! *(He leaps in turn.)*

CABOT: *(Suddenly roaring with rage.)* My cuss on ye!

SIMEON: Take our'n in trade fur it! Whoop!

CABOT: I'll hev ye both chained up in the asylum!

PETER: Ye old skinflint! Good-by!

SIMEON: Ye old blood sucker! Good-by!

CABOT: Go afore I…!

PETER: Whoop! *(He picks a stone from the road.)*

>*(Simeon does the same.)*

SIMEON: Maw'll be in the parlor.

PETER: Ay-eh! One! Two!

CABOT: *(Frightened.)* What air ye…?

PETER: Three!

>*(They both throw, the stones hitting the parlor window with a crash of glass, tearing the shade.)*

SIMEON: Whoop!

PETER: Whoop!

CABOT: *(In a fury now, rushing toward them.)* If I kin lay hands on ye— I'll break yer bones fur ye!

>*(But they beat a capering retreat before him, Simeon with the gate still under his arm. Cabot comes back panting with impotent rage.)*

SIMEON AND PETER: *(Their voices as they go off take up the song of the gold-seekers to the old tune of Oh, Susannah!)*

>"I jumped aboard the Liza ship,

And traveled on the sea,
And every time I thought of home
I wished it wasn't me!
Oh! Californi-a,
That's the land fur me!
I'm off to Californi-a!
With my wash bowl on my knee."
*(In the meantime, the window of the upper bedroom on right is raised and Abbie sticks her head out. She looks down at Cabot— with a sigh of relief.)*

ABBIE: Waal—that's the last o' them two, hain't it?
*(He doesn't answer.)*

ABBIE: *(Then in possessive tones.)* This here's a nice bedroom, Ephraim. It's a r'al nice bed. Is it my room, Ephraim?

CABOT: *(Grimly—without looking up.)* Our'n!
*(She cannot control a grimace of aversion and pulls back her head slowly and shuts the window. A sudden horrible thought seems to enter Cabot's head.)*

CABOT: They been up to somethin'! Mebbe—mebbe they've pizened the stock—'r somethin'! *(He almost runs off down toward the barn.)*
*(A moment later the kitchen door is slowly pushed open and Abbie enters. For a moment she stands looking at Eben. He does not notice her at first. Her eyes take him in penetratingly with a calculating appraisal of his strength as against hers. But under this her desire is dimly awakened by his youth and good looks. Suddenly be becomes conscious of her presence and looks up. Their eyes meet. He leaps to his feet, glowering at her speechlessly.)*

ABBIE: *(In her most seductive tones which she uses all through this scene.)* Be you—Eben? I'm Abbie— *(She laughs.)* I mean, I'm yer new Maw.

EBEN: *(Viciously.)* No, damn ye!

ABBIE: *(As if she hadn't heard—with a queer smile.)* Yer Paw's spoke a lot o' yew....

EBEN: Ha!

ABBIE: Ye mustn't mind him. He's an old man.
*(A long pause. They stare at each other.)*

ABBIE: I don't want t' pretend playin' Maw t' ye, Eben. *(Admiringly.)*

Ye're too big an' too strong fur that. I want t' be frens with ye. Mebbe with me fur a fren ye'd find ye'd like livin' here better. I kin make it easy fur ye with him, mebbe. *(With a scornful sense of power.)* I calc'late I kin git him t' do most anythin' fur me.

EBEN: *(With bitter scorn.)* Ha!

*(They stare again, Eben obscurely moved, physically attracted to her.)*

EBEN: *(In forced stilted tones.)* Yew kin go t' the devil!

ABBIE: *(Calmly.)* If cussin' me does ye good, cuss all ye've a mind t'. I'm all prepared t' have ye again me—at fust. I don't blame ye nuther. I'd feel the same at any stranger comin' t' take my Maw's place. *(He shudders.)*

ABBIE: *(She is watching him carefully.)* Yew must've cared a lot fur yewr Maw, didn't ye? My Maw died afore I'd growed. I don't remember her none. *(A pause.)* But yew won't hate me long, Eben. I'm not the wust in the world—an' yew an' me've got a lot in common. I kin tell that by lookin' at ye. Waal—I've had a hard life, too—oceans o' trouble an' nuthin' but wuk fur reward. I was a orphan early an' had t' wuk fur others in other folks' hums. Then I married an' he turned out a drunken spreer an' so he had to wuk fur others an' me too agen in other folks' hums, an' the baby died, an' my husband got sick an' died too, an' I was glad sayin' now I'm free fur once, on'y I diskivered right away all I was free fur was t' wuk agen in other folks' hums, doin' other folks' wuk till I'd most give up hope o' ever doin' my own wuk in my own hum, an' then your Paw come…

*(Cabot appears returning from the barn. He comes to the gate and looks down the road the brothers have gone. A faint strain of their retreating voices is heard: "Oh, Californi-a! That's the place for me." He stands glowering, his fists clenched, his face grim with rage.)*

EBEN: *(Fighting against his growing attraction and sympathy—harshly.)* An' bought yew—like a harlot!

*(She is stung and flushes angrily. She has been sincerely moved by the recital of her troubles.)*

EBEN: *(Adds furiously.)* An' the price he's payin' ye—this farm—was my Maw's, damn ye!—an' mine now!

ABBIE: *(With a cool laugh of confidence.)* Yewr'n? We'll see 'bout that!

(Then strongly.) Waal—what if I did need a hum? What else'd I marry an old man like him fur?

EBEN: (Maliciously.) I'll tell him ye said that!

ABBIE: (Smiling.) I'll say ye're lyin' a-purpose—an' he'll drive ye off the place!

EBEN: Ye devil!

ABBIE: (Defying him.) This be my farm—this be my hum—this be my kitchen—!

EBEN: (Furiously, as if he were going to attack her.) Shut up, damn ye!

ABBIE: (Walks up to him—a queer coarse expression of desire in her face and body—slowly.) An' upstairs—that be my bedroom—an' my bed!

(He stares into her eyes, terribly confused and torn.)

ABBIE: (She adds softly.) I hain't bad nor mean—'ceptin' fur an enemy—but I got t' fight fur what's due me out o' life, if I ever 'spect t' git it. (Then putting her hand on his arm—seductively.) Lets yew 'n' me be frens, Eben.

EBEN: (Stupidly—as if hypnotized.) Ay-eh. (Then furiously flinging off her arm.) No ye durned old witch! I hate ye! (He rushes out the door.)

ABBIE: (Looks after him smiling satisfiedly—then half to herself, mouthing the word.) Eben's nice. (She looks at the table proudly.) I'll wash up my dishes now.

(Eben appears outside, slamming the door behind him. He comes around corner, stops on seeing his father, and stands staring at him with hate.)

CABOT: (Raising his arms to heaven in the fury he can no longer control.) Lord God o' Hosts, smite the undutiful sons with Thy wust cuss!

EBEN: (Breaking in violently.) Yew 'n' yewr God! Allus cussin' folks—allus naggin' 'em!

CABOT: (Oblivious to him—summoningly.) God o' the old! God o' the lonesome!

EBEN: (Mockingly.) Naggin' His sheep t' sin! T' hell with yewr God! (Cabot turns. He and Eben glower at each other.)

CABOT: (Harshly.) So it's yew. I might've knowed it. (Shaking his finger threateningly at him.) Blasphemin' fool! (Then quickly.) Why hain't ye t' wuk?

EBEN: Why hain't yew? They've went. I can't wuk it all alone.

CABOT: *(Contemptuously.)* Nor noways! I'm wuth ten o' ye yit, old's I be! Ye'll never be more'n half a man! *(Then, matter-of-factly.)* Waal—let's git t' the barn.

*(They go. A last faint note of the "Californi-a" song is heard from the distance. Abbie is washing her dishes.)*

# Nocturnal

Balilla Pratella

**Dramatic**
**Scene:** a garret apartment—clean but poor. Night

The wife
The husband
Three thieves

WIFE: Looking at the stars doesn't fill one's stomach.
*(The husband doesn't respond, perhaps he hasn't heard.)*
WIFE: Ah! What a disgraceful life. I can stand no more of it, really no more! *(The wife cries.)*
*(The husband, as if dazed pulls himself away from the window approaches the table and blows on the candle stump putting it out. Then he returns and looks out into the darkness.)*
WIFE: Darkness too! *(She continues to cry.)*
*(The husband slowly opens the window. No noise. Above a grayish expanse of the snow-covered roof the sky is marvelously serene and flowery with stars.)*
WIFE: Darkness, cold! You want to make me die. Ah! I will leave here; I will leave you here alone. And then throw yourself out of the window as well, if it pleases you. *(Pause. The Wife, furious jumps to her feet and clings to the Husband's clothes shaking and tearing at him violently.)* But are you made of ice? Are you sleeping the dream of the dead!
HUSBAND: *(Turning slowly.)* I recognize ten million stars...red, yellow, green ones...
WIFE: *(Starting at a mysterious noise.)* Ah! What is that?
HUSBAND: How many millions of stars!...
WIFE: *(Trembling.)* They are outside the door! Who is it?
HUSBAND: *(Returning to his former position.)* To know all of them...all...
*(The door opens and three nocturnal Thieves enter: the last one closes the door. A Thief strikes a match and with it lights the candle stump; the other two place themselves in front of the Wife.)*
WIFE: *(Frightened.)* What do you want?
FIRST THIEF: We are thieves.

WIFE: *(Raising her hands.)* Hunger, cold, misery…

SECOND THIEF: *(Grabbing her.)* We steal women. Come with us.

WIFE: *(More tranquil.)* I will go with you.

FIRST THIEF: *(Threatening.)* And if you scream…

WIFE: *(Smiling.)* No, I won't scream…

THIRD THIEF: *(Discerning the Husband.)* There's a man…

*(All of them go toward the Husband. They drag him to the middle of the stage; he is impassive and doesn't see or feel anything.)*

WIFE: *(Happy.)* My husband. Leave him be; he counts stars…

FIRST THIEF: Ah! You count stars? Look, I am kissing your wife…

SECOND THIEF: Look, I am embracing your wife…

THIRD THIEF: Imbecile…go to hell…

*(A powerful blow; the Husband staggers he stumbles and falls without a movement or a cry.)*

THREE THIEVES AND WIFE: *(Laughing noisily.)* Ha ha ha ha ha ha ha! *(They flee embracing one another.)*

*(Silent pause. The Husband revives rises little by little goes to close the door and barricades it. He puts out the candle stump and then returns again to the window to contemplate the stars ecstatically.)*

# I Think It Would Be Correct To Do It This Way

Mario Dessy

**Dramatic**
**Scene:** an indefinable space

A Poet
A Philosopher
A Politician
Two Lovers

PHILOSOPHER: *(Glassy eyes, beard ninety-five centimeters long.)* That mass of rock that I see before me is the logic of life; one can no longer live without it, the desire to see profoundly of what it consists.

POET: *(Very young, with blue eyes.)* Ah! That enormous mass that I see in front of me! It is suffocating! It constricts my breath! I want to destroy it! Logic no longer has a reason to exist! Men would be able to live without it, only singing!

POLITICAL MAN: *(Black, penetrating eyes, a cubic meter of paunch.)* That enormous mass that I see before me is the state and society. In a furious battle, passions, sentiments, ideas clash within it. My mission is to amalgamate everything, to make everything adhere…to make everything fit.

*(Two lovers—kissing, smiling, murmuring sweet words.)*

SOMEONE: *(Enters from the back with a candle in one hand and a box of matches in the other. He looks around. He sees the five seated people, strikes a match and with it lights the candle, then repeats this two or three times.)* I think it would be correct to do it this way. *(Then he distributes to each one a candle and a box of matches.)* *(Everyone lights and extinguishes the candles five or six times, murmuring satisfied.)*

SOMEONE: It is correct, one must do it this way!

*(And they leave skipping about with the lit candles, preceded by Someone. Darkness.)*

# Café Crown
Hy Kraft
1942

**Comic**
**Scene:** a delicatessen frequented by theatrical folks, New York City

Rubin
Sam
Mendel Polan
Kaplan
Jacobsen
Mrs. Perlman
Hymie
Looie
Toplitz
A beggar

TOPLITZ: The gentleman wants to know why David Cole isn't acting any
    more?
MENDEL: *(Putting on his glasses and going at the matter academically.)*
    For two reasons, A and B.
WALTER: I didn't really mean to trouble you, I…
MENDEL: This is a subject in which I have made a thorough study. A, for
    thirty years, David Cole has already acted. B, our theater needs a
    great director who also knows a little something about acting.
TOPLITZ: Precisely.
MENDEL: Before they took up directing, Stanislavsky… *(Lowers head for
    a moment's silent adoration.)* …was once an actor, also David
    Belasco, also Max Reinhardt.
TOPLITZ: *(Very wistful.)* Once I wrote David Belasco a letter.
MENDEL: I have an article on this subject, "The New David Cole Transition
    Era." It was published twice, once in my paper, and in October,
    1935, The Theatre Arts Monthly asked my permission to repro-
    duce it.
WALTER: I should like very much to read it.
MENDEL: If you will come in tomorrow night, I will lend you a copy.
WALTER: Thank you very much.
MENDEL: Don't mention it.

*(Turns, walks back to game at Table 4, feeling very proud of himself, as Sam enters upstage center, carrying a plate and crosses to Walter.)*

SAM: *(As he deposits plate.)* Chopped herring!

WALTER: *(Plaintively.)* I ordered chopped liver.

SAM: When it's chopped so fine, even an expert couldn't tell the difference! *(Sam moves back to Table 4.)*

TOPLITZ: You are speaking with a foreign accent. You are not American, heh?

WALTER: I'm from Australia.

TOPLITZ: How's conditions there for the Jews?

*(Hymie deposits drinks on Table 2.)*

KAPLAN: *(Loud and angry.)* In Germany you should play pinochle.—He made it by two points.

RUBIN: How should I know you got all the trumps?

KAPLAN: *(Almost breaking a blood vessel.)* Why do I lead my king then? This is a sign.

JACOBSON: *(Simultaneously.)* Is it his fault?

WALTER: He wouldn't let me come in here, insisted I give him two hundred dollars.

HYMIE: It's a free country. He's got a right to ask.

WALTER: But two hundred dollars!

HYMIE: Did you give it to him?

WALTER: Of course not.

HYMIE: Well.

WALTER: *(To Beggar.)* Here's a dollar, old boy.

BEGGAR: A dollar has possibilities, but it's still not enough. Listen. *(Counting on his fingers.)* six months' room rent I owe, that's ninety dollars. My wife needs teeth, that's at least forty, forty-five dollars. Then there's food, shoes, incidentals, taxes. *(Firmly.)* So it's minimum two hundred dollars.

WALTER: My dear fellow.

BEGGAR: So show me how I can do it for less.

WALTER: *(To Hymie.)* Can't you get rid of this man?

BEGGAR: Two hundred dollars—take it or leave it.

*(Baffled and somewhat exhausted by the situation, Walter starts to sit at Table 2, but Hymie intercepts.)*

HYMIE: Excuse me, this table is reserved.

WALTER: *(Wearily.)* I don't see any people.

HYMIE: *(As to a child.)* If the people were sitting here, then naturally the table wouldn't be reserved any more.

WALTER: *(Indicating Table 1.)* How about that one?

HYMIE: Also.

WALTER: *(Noticing Sam at Table 4.)* Waiter!

SAM: *(Looking up.)* That is not my station.

HYMIE: I'm in charge.

WALTER: I say, I'd like to sit down.

HYMIE: So go in the back room, you can sit and eat all you like there.

WALTER: I'm looking for someone.

HYMIE: All over the world, there's ways and means.

WALTER: *(Slips Hymie a dollar bill.)* Now—is there a table here that's not reserved?

HYMIE: *(Indicating Table 2.)* What's the matter with this one?

WALTER: Thank you. *(Unwilling or unable to cope further with such maneuvers, Walter sits down.)*
*(Beggar shuffles up to him.)*

BEGGAR: Well? Have you decided?

RUBIN: *(As he hands Sam empty glass, saucer, spoon in glass.)* A glass tea.

SAM: *(Takes glass, etc., but continues to watch.)* If I played pinochle like you I'd drink iodine—not tea.

JACOBSON: *(Impatiently.)* Well, what do you say?

RUBIN: Three hundred, I've gotta say.

SAM: *(With biting irony.)* Are you a gambler! A real plunger!

KAPLAN: With a ten!
*(With a shrug of utter disgust Sam starts with glass for kitchen upstage center.)*

JACOBSON: *(Slightly sing-song, with a Talmudic analysis of the situation.)* You said three hundred. *(To Kaplan.)* And you said three-ten. *(Pauses, then.)* And I will say... *(Another pause.)* ...let it be three-fifty, what the hell!
*(At this Sam, who is almost off returns with heightened interest.)*

SAM: On what basis?

RUBIN: How about my tea?

SAM: *(Belligerently.)* What's the matter, you feel faint? Who else wants tea?

KAPLAN: Are you buying, by any chance, Rubin?

RUBIN: All right, so I'm buying.

KAPLAN: A glass tea I never refuse.

JACOBSON: *(Banging hand on table.)* What is this, a ladies' Auxiliary? Tea!

*(As Sam starts to go upstage.)*

JACOBSON: Bring me one, too.

*(Players begin to sort their cards. Mendel Polan leans forward and separates cards in the hand of Kaplan, the better to consider the possibilities.)*

KAPLAN: I beg you, Mendel, please don't touch my cards. Some people have a lucky touch but not you.

MENDEL: So sensitive suddenly. You can't even look.

KAPLAN: A person might just as well play in Union Square.

*(Phone rings.)*

MRS. PERLMAN: *(Calling into back room upstage center.)* Hymie!... Telephone!

*(Hymie enters from the back room right. He is a bus-boy who is more than a bus-boy, as we will presently discover. He is in his forties and such hair as he has is wispy. He wears a tuxedo—at least the coat has satin lapels and his bow tie is black, though closer inspection would reveal a couple of spots on the tie and the lapels. So the pants don't match—so what? With the weight of the Café only a small part of his burden, Hymie is a harassed man given to a great deal of audible muttering. Muttering now, he enters open phone booth.)*

HYMIE: *(Very cheerless, into phone.)* Café Crown speaking. Who? *(To the room.)* Kaplan, your wife!

KAPLAN: Take a message.

HYMIE: Kaplan's busy. *(Coming out of booth.)* She says you should come to her mother's house.

KAPLAN: Tell her as soon as I finish this hand.

HYMIE: *(On phone.)* He'll come soon as he finishes the hand. *(Listens for moment, then hangs up.)*

*(Looie, a stage hand, enters from kitchen, upstage center. Wears button-sweater and a cap, and he's middle-aged. But he's a man with a big nostalgia. He too yearns for the old days of the giants and comes into Café for a quick schnapps at regular intervals. In fact, just as kitchen door upstage center opens, and before the audience gets a full view of Looie, Mrs. Perlman reaches for whiskey bottle and the small glass, fills it, and without a word,*

*Looie gulps it down, simultaneously depositing a quarter on bar which Mrs. Perlman promptly rings up.)*

MRS. PERLMAN: What's happening on the stage now, Looie?

LOOIE: Ah—Second Act Curtain...The ship is now sailing for America and Madame Roberts is singing Au Revoir Poland, hello Broadway.

HYMIE: *(To Kaplan still seated at pinochle game, Table 4.)* She says if you come home late you should sleep on the couch. *(Walks upstage to Looie.)*

MRS. PERLMAN: It's such a nice song.

LOOIE: That's a nice song!...Ta ra ra rumm.

HYMIE: Never mind tarararumm...Where's my statement?

LOOIE: *(Takes statement from pocket.)* To make money from such a type is a crime.

HYMIE: A crime yet...If I didn't invest money in Lipsky's shows, where would you pull up and down a curtain?

LOOIE: So if it's your money which is making it possible for the people to hear such low grade music, so you go inside and listen to Lipsky's music every night.

HYMIE: A man gets paid sixty-seventy dollars a week to pull a curtain is also a critic.

LOOIE: To be a stage hand for a show like this a person has to be made of iron.

HYMIE: So be made of iron. Who cares? *(Hymie puts napkin over his shoulder and starts examining statement.)*
*(Sam, noticing Hymie's absorption, turns from pinochle game and moves over to Hymie above Table 2.)*

SAM: How was business tonight?

HYMIE: A benefit, what then?

SAM: So how does it stand?

HYMIE: Why should I complain? If I invest in a show and I break even, so its already a profit. Explain me something. Already for fifteen years in every statement is incidentals.

SAM: Why do you ask me?

HYMIE: Sometimes incidentals is making more than me or Lipsky.

SAM: So ask a certified public accountant.

HYMIE: How does an accountant come to show business? *(Moves away from Sam to Table 1.)*
*(Street door opens and Walter enters left, followed by the Beggar. Walter is a well-dressed young man. Beggar is in his fifties, his*

*overcoat is frayed, his hat crumpled, his neck covered with a muf-
fler.)*

WALTER: Is this the Café Crown?

SAM: The Rainbow Room it isn't.

*(Obviously Walter was braced outside the door by the Beggar, has
resisted his somewhat unreasonable demands, and now finds
himself inexplicably followed inside. And the Beggar is a leech. As
discussion progresses, Walter gets a wild feeling that he is in a
nightmare.)*

BEGGAR: So, are you going to give it to me?

WALTER: *(As he opens purse, handing Beggar a coin.)* Here—take it or
leave it.

BEGGAR: *(Contemptuously.)* A nickel! I'm not a nickel beggar.

WALTER: *(Impatiently, a slight English accent.)* It's not a nickel, it's a
quarter.

*(Mrs. Perlman looks up for an instant, goes on with her reading.)*

BEGGAR: It's not enough.

*(Walter, anxious for help, turns to Hymie.)*

WALTER: Excuse me, would you ask this man to leave me alone, please?

HYMIE: It's none of my affair.

WALTER: Look, my good man, I'm sure nobody's going to give you two
hundred dollars.

BEGGAR: How can you be so sure? How do you know the right man
won't come along some day?

WALTER: If you'll take my advice, you'll stop asking for it.

BEGGAR: *(Mildly.)* Are you a lawyer giving advice?

WALTER: *(With a sigh, pleading.)* Please leave me alone, or get out,
won't you?

HYMIE: *(With authority.)* Are you by any chance the proprietor here?
No? So don't be in such a hurry to tell people to get out.

*(Walter closes eyes and puts his head in his hand, licked. Hymie
gestures the beggar out.)*

BEGGAR: *(Retreating toward left door.)* He's still got no right to tell me
how to run my business. I'll keep out of his, let him keep out of
mine. That way we'll get along. *(Stops at Table 4, takes a look at
Kaplan's hand.)* My God! You got a hundred aces...

KAPLAN: I know. *(Kaplan is angry at his disclosure.)*

*(Beggar exits left.)*

WALTER: *(Not an unreasonable complaint.)* A persistent fellow, isn't he?

I shouldn't think a beggar molesting customers would be conducive to business.

HYMIE: Where should he stand? In the middle of the street and get run over? A man in his line of business must stand where people are coming and going, so you'll say if he wants two hundred dollars he should stand on Wall Street. But without security, bankers don't give money. So he stands here.

WALTER: I've been told this is where the actors eat.

HYMIE: If they're hungry, they eat.

WALTER: Are these people actors?

HYMIE: Actors, pinochle players, poets—on Second Avenue they're geniuses. Now what else can I do for you?

WALTER: I'd like something to eat.

HYMIE: Sam, the gentleman!

SAM: *(Over his shoulder.)* Coming! *(To Kaplan.)* Why do you bid? If you haven't got it in fifteen cards, why should it be in eighteen? *(Starts to go toward Walter.)*

RUBIN: Without a Queen of Spades, a person shouldn't be born.

SAM: *(At Table 2.)* What's your pleasure?

WALTER: What do you recommend?

SAM: *(Indifferently.)* It depends.

WALTER: How about some chopped herring?

SAM: If you like herring, you like herring. Personally, I recommend the chopped liver.

WALTER: I believe I'll have some chopped herring.

SAM: *(A sinister pause.)* It's your stomach, my friend.

WALTER: *(Hastily.)* Very well, make it chopped liver.

SAM: Okay, so it's chopped liver. *(Sam shuffles back upstage center but pauses at Table 4.)*

*(Sam is about to go on, when Mendel calls.)*

MENDEL: Sam, a split celery tonic.

SAM: What do you want from me? I only got two hands. *(Exits up center.)*

*(During last few lines, Toplitz has been eyeing Walter from afar. Now Toplitz rises, decides to investigate the phenomenon. He walks slowly, indifferently, past Walter, circles around him, then reverses the walk, stroking his beard. All this during above dialogue. When Sam goes out upstage center, Toplitz speaks.)*

TOPLITZ: *(Innocently.)* Do I know you from some place?

WALTER: I don't know.

TOPLITZ: *(Hopefully.)* My face is not familiar?

WALTER: I've never been here before.

TOPLITZ: This is obvious. My name is Aaron Toplitz.

WALTER: How do you do.

TOPLITZ: How do you do.

WALTER: Won't you sit down?

TOPLITZ: *(Sits at Table 2.)* Thank you. *(Wistfully.)* And you never heard of me?

WALTER: No, I haven't.

TOPLITZ: Such is fame. A man writes plays and the people don't know him. Actors they know, directors also—but authors, no.

WALTER: Now that you mention it, it's true.

TOPLITZ: Of course. Shakespeare wrote what—thirty-five plays; Gene O'Neil maybe fifteen. George Shaw maybe twenty-five minimum. Have you any conception how many plays I wrote?

WALTER: No.

TOPLITZ: Go ahead, take a guess.

WALTER: Thirty.

TOPLITZ: Thirty! You aren't even warm. Only yesterday I finished a new play called "Sirocco." Wonderful title, no? Would you believe it, "Sirocco" is my one hundred and third play—and you don't know me. You're not in the theatrical industry by any chance?

WALTER: No, I'm not.

TOPLITZ: Are you perhaps contemplating?

WALTER: *(Smiling.)* No.

TOPLITZ: For a minute I thought you might be looking around for a little investment.

WALTER: *(To Hymie, who is examining his accounts at Table 1.)* How's the chopped liver?

HYMIE: *(Rises.)* How should it be? Cocktail, highball, anything, something?

WALTER: *(Cheerfully.)* Yes, I think I'll have some schnapps.

HYMIE: *(Offended.)* What do you mean schnapps? I understand English. You want Scotch, or Rye?

WALTER: Have you any Bourbon?

HYMIE: Plain or with seltzer?

WALTER: Water on the side.

HYMIE: Water you got already.

*(As Mrs. Perlman gets off her chair to make drink.)*

WALTER: I say, Mr. Toplitz, would you join me?

TOPLITZ: As long as you're insisting, I'll have a wine and seltzer.

HYMIE: *(Again to Mrs. Perlman.)* Small spritzer—large. One Rye it should be Bourbon!
*(Hymie continues to arrange glasses at tables while Mrs. Perlman fills order.)*

WALTER: Do you happen to know David Cole?

TOPLITZ: Who doesn't know David Cole?

WALTER: I was told I might find him here. Is he appearing now?

TOPLITZ: For five years already Cole doesn't act any more.

WALTER: Has he retired?

TOPLITZ: He's now a director-producer. Why, you will ask?

WALTER: Yes, why?

TOPLITZ: *(Calls.)* Mendel!

MENDEL: Yes… *(Mendel takes a last look at the hand that's being played, freezes at the terrible play, and turns toward Toplitz.)*

TOPLITZ: *(To Walter.)* This is Mendel Polan, the critic.

MENDEL: *(To Walter.)* How do you do, sir.

WALTER: Will you have a drink?

MENDEL: I'm having a little celery tonic over there.

KAPLAN: Ask anyone if a man leads a king of trump—

RUBIN: Where does it stand that I should know?

JACOBSEN: Please—no post-mortems.

KAPLAN: Toplitz, come here and explain something.

TOPLITZ: *(To Walter.)* Excuse me. I'm needed. *(Toplitz goes to Table 4.)*
*(Walter nods and is about to lift his fork when his eyes begin to bulge at the he sight of Lester Freed, who enters through kitchen upstage center in the get-up of a typical Russian Jew of the Dybbuk period, skull cap, curled side-burns, fine looking beard and long satin garb. No one else pays any attention to him as he goes to Mrs. Perlman upstage right.)*

TOPLITZ: Please! First we will review the bidding. Who is dealing?
*(As this dies down, Freed has crossed to Mrs. Perlman's stand.)*

FREED: *(To Hymie at Table 1.)* Where's that message, Hymie?

HYMIE: *(Producing small piece of paper from pocket.)* Bryant 9-6200, no name.

FREED: *(Headed for phone booth.)* Man, or woman?

HYMIE: Maybe.

*(Freed goes towards phone booth. Walter watches him. Freed gives him a menacing look, enters booth, starts dialing, closes door.)*

WALTER: Pardon me, who is that venerable Jew?

HYMIE: Venerable Jew? That's Lester Freed, the actor. He's a young boy.

WALTER: Very impressive, isn't he?

HYMIE: That's impressive? Did you ever see David Cole play?

WALTER: No, I never did, but I'd like very much to see him. What's he like?

HYMIE: What's he like? Well—what's the use of trying to explain? Go explain a piece of boiled beef. It's all beef, cow—so what makes one piece better than the other?

WALTER: *(Trying to ingratiate himself.)* You've got a point there. If you build a better mouse-trap the world will beat a path to your door.

HYMIE: What mouse-traps? Who's talking about mouse-traps?

WALTER: David Cole has several children, hasn't he?

HYMIE: David Cole has everything. Wives, children—a basketful. Always trying to create another Cole, but you can't manufacture a David Cole.

# The Queen and the Rebels

Ugo Betti
1956

**Dramatic**
**Scene:** a large hall in the main public building of a hillside village

A Porter
A group of travellers, men, a few women
The Engineer
Raim

THE PORTER: You Can all wait in here for the time being.

ONE OF THE TRAVELLERS: *(Cautiously.)* We could wait just as well outside.

THE PORTER: Yes, but you can sit down in here. You'll find everything you want. This used to be the town-hall.

THE TRAVELLER: But we don't want to sit down. We want to get on. We're several hours late as it is.

THE PORTER: I m sorry, sir. But you'll be all right in here. There are plenty of rooms, even if you have to stay the night.

THE TRAVELLER: Well, let's hope we don't have to stay the night! They told us we'd only be here half an hour, while the engine was cooling down.

THE PORTER: Yes, it's a stiff climb up here. The roads up those hills are very steep.

THE TRAVELLER: This is the third time they've stopped us to look at our papers. *(After a pause.)* I'm a district engineer. I… *(Dropping his voice.)* Do you think they've some special reason for stopping us?

THE PORTER: No, no. They'll let you go on directly.

THE ENGINEER: Yes, but what are we waiting for?

THE PORTER: Sir, I…I really don't know what to say. I'm only the hall-porter here. That's to say, I *was* the hall-porter. Since the trouble began, I've been alone here. I have to look after everything. Anyway, will you all make yourselves comfortable?

THE ENGINEER: Is it possible to telegraph from here? Or telephone?

THE PORTER: All the lines are down. We're cut off from the world. And we're very out of the way here, in any case. I'll go and see if I can find you some blankets.
*(A pause.)*

THE ENGINEER: Look here: I can only speak for myself, of course, but I dare say these other ladies and gentlemen feel much the same as I do about this. You surely realize that nobody's going to travel about just now unless they have to. Every one of us here has some important business or other to attend to. We've all been given permits to travel. Otherwise we wouldn't have come up here at a time like this. We aren't political people; we're just ordinary peaceful travellers. We've all had to pay very large sums of money for a wretched little seat in that lorry out there. And we've all had to get permission from—

THE PORTER: *(Clearly unconvinced by his own words.)* But you'll see, sir: they'll let you go on directly.
*(A pause.)*

THE ENGINEER: Do you know who's in charge here?

THE PORTER: *I* don't, no, sir. I just take orders from everybody else.

THE ENGINEER: Is there anybody we can speak to?

THE PORTER: The trouble is they keep coming and going the whole time. They say there's a general expected here this evening; and a commissar.

THE ENGINEER: Then there's no one here now that we can speak to?

THE PORTER: The N.C.O.s are a bit rough-spoken, sir. The only one would be the interpreter. But no one takes much notice of him either, I'm afraid.

THE ENGINEER: Interpreter? What do they need an interpreter for?

THE PORTER: Oh, he's just an interpreter. He's an educated young man.

THE ENGINEER: Very well, then: fetch the interpreter.

THE PORTER: I'll get him, sir. *(He goes out.)*
*(Travellers sit down silently, here and there.)*

THE ENGINEER: I don't suppose it's anything to worry about. I saw some other people outside. They'd been held up too. It's obviously only another examination because we're so near the frontier. My own papers are all in order. But if there *is* anyone here who's…travelling irregularly…It might perhaps be as well if they had the courage to speak up straight away, and say so; before they get us all into trouble.

ANOTHER TRAVELLER: *(As though speaking to himself.)* The large number of spies about the place doesn't exactly inspire people with much desire to "speak up," as you call it. In any case, it's obvious no

.

one here is travelling irregularly. That would have been a little too simple-minded; or so I should have thought?

THE ENGINEER: Well if that's the case, we ought to be on our way again in half-an-hour or so.

THE TRAVELLER: I can't say I share your optimism. It's been rather an odd journey, all along. Why did they make us come round this way in the first place? This village wasn't on our route at all. And the engine didn't need to cool down either. And why do we have all these inspections anyway? The only reasonable explanation is that they're looking for someone.

THE ENGINEER: One of us?

THE TRAVELLER: Though it's just as likely that they're simply being stupid and awkward, as usual. That's about all nine-tenths of the revolution comes to.

THE ENGINEER: I...think we d better change the subject, if you don't mind. There's no point in...

THE TRAVELLER: In what?

THE ENGINEER: Well, after all, this upheaval has very great possibilities, when all's said and done.

THE TRAVELLER: You really think so?

THE ENGINEER: Yes. Yes, I do. Quite sincerely.

THE TRAVELLER: Couldn't you...spare yourself this extreme cautiousness? It looks rather as if the extremists aren't doing too well at the moment. You didn't notice, as we came along the road?

THE ENGINEER: Notice what?

THE TRAVELLER: Over towards the mountains. That faint crackling sound every now and then.

THE ENGINEER: What was it?

THE TRAVELLER: Rifle-fire. They're fighting near here, on the far slope. Everything's hanging by a thread at the moment. It's possible the Unitary Government won't last the week out.

THE ENGINEER: A week. It doesn't take a week to shoot anybody. *(He drops his voice.)* I didn't notice the noises; I was too busy noticing the smell. Did you...catch the smell every now and then?

THE TRAVELLER: It's the smell of history.

THE ENGINEER: They don't even take the trouble to bury them.

*(The Porter comes in. Raim, the interpreter, follows him, blustering and bombastic. He pretends not to deign to glance at the group of travellers.)*

THE PORTER: *(As he enters.)* The interpreter's just coming.

RAIM: *(Off.)* Where are they? Foreign slaves and spies, that's what they'll be. *(Entering.)* Where are the reactionary traitors?

THE ENGINEER: *(Amiably.)* You can see that we are not reactionaries. We are nothing of the kind.

RAIM: Then you must be filthy loyalists; a lot of monarchist swine.

THE ENGINEER: I assure you you're mistaken.

RAIM: You're enemies of the people. What have you come up here for? We fight and die, up here! Have you come up here to spy on us? Are you trying to smuggle currency across the frontier?

THE ENGINEER: We are ordinary peaceful travellers. Our papers have been inspected and stamped over and over again. I must ask you once again to rest assured that we are all sympathizers with the League of Councils.

RAIM: *(Satirically.)* Oh, yes, I knew you'd say that. You're a lot of exploiters, all of you. *(He drops his voice a little.)* And stuffed to the neck with money, I'll bet.

THE ENGINEER: No, sir.

RAIM: Poor little things. No money. We shall see about that.

THE ENGINEER: Not one of us has any money above the permitted amount.

RAIM: Gold, then? Valuables.

THE ENGINEER: No, sir. We all have permission to travel. We merely wish to be allowed to proceed On our way. On the lorry.

RAIM: I'm afraid you'll find that lorry's been requisitioned.

*(A silence.)*

THE ENGINEER: Shall we...be able to go on...by any other means?

RAIM: The road's blocked. In any case the bridges have all been blown up.

*(A silence.)*

THE ENGINEER: In that case, will you allow us to go back again to our families?

RAIM: Oh, yes, *I'm* sure! You people, you come up here, and poke your noses into everything, and then go back home and tell tales. I've a pretty shrewd suspicion you'll have to wait here.

THE TRAVELLER: And what shall we be waiting for?

RAIM: The requisite inspections.

THE TRAVELLER: Has anyone authorized you to speak in this way?

RAIM: Has anyone authorized you to poke your nose in?

THE TRAVELLER: On what precise powers do you base your right to interfere with our movements?

RAIM: My powers are my duties as a good citizen of the republic. I act for the republic. And you? What are you waiting for? Show me your hands. Come on.

*(The Traveller holds out his hands.)*

RAIM: Proper priest's hands, aren't they just? You've never worked for your living. A bishop at least, I should say.

THE TRAVELLER: Your own hands seem to be very well-kept ones too.

RAIM: Thanks, your reverence, very clever, aren't you? Yes: a great pianist's hands, mine are. A pity I can't play. *(He laughs, and turns to the Porter.)* Orazio, collect these people's documents.

*(The Porter begins to collect the documents.)*

THE TRAVELLER: Will *you* be examining them?

RAIM: They'll be inspected by Commissar Amos. We're expecting him any minute. Or better still, General Biante. He'll be here as well, very soon. Yes! Amos and Biante! Are those gigantic figures big enough for you?

THE TRAVELLER: Quite.

RAIM: In the meanwhile, let me hear you say very clearly the word: purchase.

THE TRAVELLER: Purchase.

RAIM: Center.

THE TRAVELLER: Center.

RAIM: Now say: January.

THE TRAVELLER: January.

RAIM: Can't say I like your accent very much. You wouldn't be a dirty refugee, by any chance?

THE TRAVELLER: Your own accent isn't particularly good either, if I may say so.

RAIM: Ah, but I'm the interpreter, your reverence. I'm unfortunately obliged to soil my lips with foreign expressions. See? Give me this man's papers, Orazio. *(After a pause.)* You claim to have been born in the High Redon, I see.

THE TRAVELLER: Yes.

RAIM: Are you a slav?

THE TRAVELLER: No.

RAIM: Your surname looks like all alien's to me. Are you a Catholic?

THE TRAVELLER: No.

RAIM: Orthodox? Protestant? Jew?

THE TRAVELLER: I haven't decided yet.

RAIM: Good: but I shouldn't take too long about it. Do you live on investments?

THE TRAVELLER: No.

RAIM: Do you own large estates?

THE TRAVELLER: No.

RAIM: Gold?

THE TRAVELLER: No.

# LARGE GROUP SCENES
# WITH A MAJORITY OF MEN

# Oedipus at Colonus

Sophocles
Translated by Carl R. Mueller

**Dramatic**
**Scene:** on the road to Colonus

Oedipus the King
Chorus
Antigone

CHORUS: Look for him!
Look,
look for the
man! Who can he
be? Where?
Where is he
hidden? Where?
Reckless man!
Shameless!
Look! Look for
him! Every
direction! A
wanderer, I hear!
Stranger, I hear!
Strange to this
place! Why
else has he
gone, why
else, into the
Holy Grove? The
Pathless
Grove? Sacred to the
Maidens! Furies!
Goddesses invincible!
Whose names we
fear to name,
tremble to name!

We pass with
    eyes cast
        down, voices
hushed, no word
    spoken, breathing
        pious thought only, in
veneration, in
    reverence!

LEADER:    Now one is come,
or so we hear,
    one has come who
        knows no reverence,
devotionless, impious man!
    Where is he to be
        found?
Where?

CHORUS: I look!
        I cannot tell!
Cannot find him!
    Where is he?
        Where?
Where? Where is the
    man?
        Where?

*(Oedipus, led by Antigonê, appears on the rocky ledge.)*

OEDIPUS: I am that man, that
    stranger. I see by
        sound, as the saying goes!

CHORUS: Oh!
    Oh! Terrible,
        terrible! Dreadful
sight! Dreadful to
    hear!

OEDIPUS:    I beg you, don't
see me as a
    lawless
        man.

CHORUS: Zeus protect us!
    Who is he, this

ancient man?

OEDIPUS:  Not one whose fate is
          enviable, o guardians of this
          land! Why else would I
move with other's
      eyes? You can
          see, here! Why
else would I lean my
      height on one so
          small? The weaker
on the stronger?

CHORUS:  Oh!
                  Oh! Blind!
Blind! Were you
      blind from birth? He is
              blind! Wretched,
wretched and
      long, wretched and
          long is your
life!

LEADER:  But if I can prevent it,
              you shall not add
this curse to your
      misery! You have
          gone too
far!

CHORUS:  Too far! Too
              far! Too
far!

LEADER:  Take care!

CHORUS:      Take care!
    care!

LEADER:  You mustn't intrude
              on the soft green
glade, the voiceless
      glade where the gentle
          hollow gathers softly flowing
streams; where swirling pure
      waters mix with the honey of

bees!

CHORUS: It is a sacred
        place! You mustn't
           set foot there, man of
grief! Come out!
        Come out!
          Don't delay!

LEADER: How far the distance is
        between us! Can you
          hear? Come down, miserable
wanderer, if you have any
        word for us here!
          Leave that place
forbidden to men! Come
        down where all are
          allowed to speak!
Till then, be silent!

*(The music changes character to a less frenzied mode.)*

OEDIPUS: What way does wisdom
        point, my child?

ANTIGONÊ: To obey them, father
        as custom demands;
          to give in and listen
to them, I think.

OEDIPUS: Give me your hand.

ANTIGONÊ:     It's here.
  Do you feel it?

OEDIPUS: Strangers, I must endure no
        wrong when I have
left my refuge. I
        trusted you.

LEADER:      Never, old man, we
will never force you to
        leave this refuge
          against your will.

*(Oedipus begins to move forward tentatively, supported but not led by Antigonê. He then pauses.)*

OEDIPUS: Farther still?

LEADER:    Yes; farther!

*(He takes another cautious step, then pauses again.)*

OEDIPUS:   Farther?

CHORUS: Yes; farther!

LEADER:   Led him, young woman.
            You see and
      may trust us.

ANTIGONÊ:   Come, let your
            blind steps follow.
      Follow where
          I'm leading.

LEADER:   Stranger in a strange land,
      be warned, poor wanderer!

CHORUS: Hate what we
            hate! Love what we
      love!

OEDIPUS: Lead me, then, child,
            to the place where we may
      speak and listen;
          to lawful ground. We
            must not fight Necessity.

*(He reaches the rocky outcropping at the edge of the Sacred Grove.)*

CHORUS: There!
          There!

LEADER:   No farther than the
      rocky platform.

OEDIPUS: Here, then?

LEADER:   Yes, as I have said.

OEDIPUS: May I sit?

LEADER:   Yes; a little to the
            side. Crouch down. Sit
      now—the edge of the
          rock.

ANTIGONÊ:   Father, let me help you.
      It's why I'm here.
          Careful now.
            Step by step.

*(He stumbles and is caught by Antigonê.)*

OEDIPUS: What—!
         Oh!

ANTIGONÊ:      Keep with me.
  Lean on my arm.
  *(She gently helps him down onto the seat of rock and moves*
  *away to the side.)*

OEDIPUS: Cruel misery of a darkened soul!

CHORUS:      Poor man, tell us,
  now you're at ease,
     who are you? Your
       parents? Why are you
  wandering in such terrible
     pain? Where are you
       from? What country?

OEDIPUS: Country?
     I have none.
       But don't ask me—

LEADER: Ask you?
     What? Why
       not, old man?

OEDIPUS: No, no! Don't
    ask! Don't ask who I
     am! Don't
  question!
     Please!

LEADER:      But why?

OEDIPUS: My birth was unspeakable—

LEADER:  Tell us.
  *(Oedipus gropes about for Antigonê's hand.)*

OEDIPUS:     Antigonê—
  child—
   what shall I
    say?
  *(Antigonê takes hold of his hand, trying to calm him.)*

LEADER: What is your
    family? Who was your
     father?

OEDIPUS: Child—
     child—what is to
      become of me—?

ANTIGONÊ: Answer them: you're
　　　　　driven to the edge.
OEDIPUS:　　　I will speak, then—
　　yes—no way
　　　　to hide it—
LEADER:　　　You have taken too long!
　　Hurry!
OEDIPUS: You have heard of the
　　　　　son of Laïos?
CHORUS: Ioo!
　　　Ioo!
　　　　　Ioo!
OEDIPUS: Born of the family
　　　　of Labdakos?
LEADER:　　　Dear god!
OEDIPUS: Of wretched
　　　　Oedipus?
LEADER:　　　You're that man?
OEDIPUS: Don't let what I
　　　　say frighten you!
(With a protracted shout of horror and loathing, the Chorus pulls
back and turns away, faces hidden behind folds of clothing, scat-
tering about the area as if to escape pollution.)
CHORUS:　　Ioo!
　Ooo!
　　　Ooo!
OEDIPUS:　　My destiny has
　been a misery!
CHORUS: Ooo!
　　　　Ooo!
OEDIPUS: My child, what
　　　　happens to us now?
LEADER:　　Go! Leave our land!
　　Leave us!
OEDIPUS: And what becomes of your
　　　　　promise?
LEADER: Fate doesn't punish
　　　a man who returns
　　　　　evil for evil! Deceit
　　invites deceit and brings

**418　SCENES FOR MEN**

pain, not reward!

CHORUS:　　　Leave this place!
　　At once! Go!
　　　　Go! Leave this land!
　　　　　　Hurry!

LEADER: Before pollution
　　　　falls on my
　　　　　　city!

ANTIGONÊ: Reverent men, whose
　　　　minds are just; you who
　　　　　　refuse to hear my agèd
　father's story because the
　　　　deeds done by him,
　　　　　　although unwilling, are
　too well known to you,
　　　　have pity, at least, on
　　　　　　me! On my unhappiness!
I appeal to you for my
　　　　father. Not with eyes
　　　　　　that have no sight, but as a
child of your own
　　　　blood might look, pleading
　　　　　　for care for the ancient
suppliant!
　　　　In our despair we
　　　　　　turn to you as to a
god! We ask you to
　　　　grant the unhoped-for
　　　　　　favor! I pray you by
what you love
　　　　most dearly: child,
　　　　　　wife, treasure,
gods! Search the world,
　　　　you will never find a
　　　　　　god-driven
man who
　　　　escapes his
　　　　　　fate!

*(The Chorus disburses variously around the orchestra as the Leader approaches Oedipus and the music fades out.)*

# The Frogs

Aristophanes
Translated by Dudley Fitts
405 B.C.

**Comic**
Dionysos
A large chorus of frogs

FROGS: Brekekekéx koáx koáx
    Brekekekéx koáx koáx!
    We are the swamp-children
    Greeny and tiny,
    Fluting our voices
    As all in time we
    Sing our koáx koáx
    Koáx koáx koáx
    For Dionysos
    Nysa-born
    On the Winey Festival
    When the throng
    Lurches in through his temple gate,
    Every man as drunk as a hake.
    Brekekekéx koáx koáx
    Brekekekéx koáx koáx!
DIONYSOS: My arse is sore, koáx koáx.
FROGS: Brekekekéx koáx koáx.
DIONYSOS: And you don't give a damn, koáx.
FROGS: Brekekekéx koáx koáx!
DIONYSOS: Go jump in the lake, koáx, koáx!
    Let's have a different tune, koáx!
FROGS: Different? What a
    Meddlesome fool!
    Pan and the Muses
    Love us, our whole
    Koáx koáx koáx
    Koáx koáx koáx
    Draws down Apollo
    Golden-lyred:

Ours are the marsh-reeds
God-inspired
That sing to his heavenly fingering
Their music with our own mingling
Brekekekéx koáx koáx!
DIONYSOS: My hands are ablaze, my bottom's a wreck!
In a minute or two you'll hear it speak.
FROGS: Brekekekéx koáx koáx!
DIONYSOS: Silence, you lily-pad lyrists, koáx!
FROGS: No, we must sing. The
Sunshine will bring the
Glint to the pools,
The shimmer of reeds,
And when Zeus descends
In rain on our heads
We'll leap with our friends
And pipe from our souls
Brekekekéx koáx koáx!
DIONYSOS: Brekekekéx koáx koáx!
Come, that's enough!
FROGS: We've hardly begun!
DIONYSOS: I suppose you think that rowing is fun?
*(A furious increase in volume and tempo to the end of the chorus.)*
FROGS: Brekekekéx koáx koáx!
DIONYSOS: Brekekekéx koáx koáx!
I wish you'd die!
FROGS: We'll swell up and cry
Brekekekéx koáx koáx!
Brekekekéx koáx koáx!
DIONYSOS: Brekekekéx koáx koáx!
I can beat you at that koáx koáx!
FROGS: The devil you can, koáx koáx!
DIONYSOS: I will, by God, if it takes all day!
*Brekekekéx koáx koáx!*
Go and koáx yourselves away!
KOAX KOAX *KOAX!*
*(He breaks wind hugely; the Frogs are silent.)*
DIONYSOS: There! That settles your damned koáx!
*(The boat has reached the opposite shore.)*

# The Merry Wives of Windsor

William Shakespeare

**Comic**
**Scene:** Windsor, in front of Page's house

Justice Shallow
Slender
Sir Hugh Evans
Page
Sir John Falstaff
Bardolph
Pistol
Nym
Anne Page
Mistress Page
Mistress Ford

SHALLOW: Sir Hugh, persuade me not; I will make a Star-Chamber matter of it: if he were twenty Sir John Falstaffs, he shall not abuse Robert Shallow, esquire.

SLENDER: In the county of Gloster, justice of peace and *coram.*

SHALLOW: Ay, cousin Slender, and *cust-alorum.*

SLENDER: Ay, and *rato-lorum* too; and a gentleman born, master parson; who writes himself *armigero,*—in any bill, warrant, quittance, or obligation, *armigero.*

SHALLOW: Ay, that I do; and have done any time these three hundred years.

SLENDER: All his successors gone before him hath done't; and all his ancestors that come after him may: they may give the dozen white luces in their coat.

SHALLOW: It is an old coat.

SIR HUGH EVANS: The dozen white louses do become an old coat well; it agrees well, passant; it is a familiar beast to man, and signifies— love.

SHALLOW: The luce is the fresh fish; the salt fish is an old coat.

SLENDER: I may quarter, coz?

SHALLOW: You may, by marrying.

SIR HUGH EVANS: It is marring indeed, if he quarter it.

SHALLOW: Not a whit.

SIR HUGH EVANS: Yes, py'r lady; if he has a quarter of your coat, there is but three skirts for yourself, in my simple conjectures: but that is all one. If Sir John Falstaff have committed disparagements unto you, I am of the church, and will be glad to do my benevolence to make atonements and compremises between you.

SHALLOW: The Council shall hear it; it is a riot.

SIR HUGH EVANS: It is not meet the Council hear a riot; there is no fear of Got in a riot: the Council, look you, shall desire to hear the fear of Got, and not to hear a riot; take your vizaments in that.

SHALLOW: Ha! o' my life, if I were young again, the sword should end it.

SIR HUGH EVANS: It is petter that friends is the sword, and end it: and there is also another device in my prain, which peradventure prings goot discretions with it:—there is Anne Page, which is daughter to Master George Page, which is pretty virginity.

SLENDER: Mistress Anne Page! She has brown hair, and speaks small like a woman.

SIR HUGH EVANS: It is that fery person for all the orld, as just as you will desire; and seven hundred pounds of moneys, and gold, and silver, is her grandsire upon his death's-bed (Got deliver to a joyful resurrections!) give, when she is able to overtake seventeen years old. It were a goot motion if we leave our pribbles and prabbles, and desire a marriage between Master Abraham and Mistress Anne Page.

SHALLOW: Did her grandsire leave her seven hundred pound?

SIR HUGH EVANS: Ay, and her father is make her a petter penny.

SHALLOW: I know the young gentlewoman; she has good gifts.

SIR HUGH EVANS: Seven hundred pounds and possibilities is goot gifts.

SHALLOW: Well, let us see honest Master Page. Is Falstaff there?

SIR HUGH EVANS: Shall I tell you a lie? I do despise a liar as I do despise one that is false, or as I despise one that is not true. The knight, Sir John, is there; and, I beseech you, be ruled by your well-willers. I will peat the door for Master Page. *(Knocks.)* What, ho! Got pless your house here!

PAGE: *(Within.)* Who's there?

SIR HUGH EVANS: Here is Got's plessing, and your friend, and Justice Shallow; and here young Master Slender, that peradventures shall tell you another tale, if matters grow to your likings.
*(Enter Page.)*

PAGE: I am glad to see your worships well. I thank you for my venison, Master Shallow.

SHALLOW: Master Page, I am glad to see you: much good do it your good heart! I wish'd your venison better; it was ill kill'd.—How doth good Mistress Page?— and I thank you always with my heart, la; with my heart.

PAGE: Sir, I thank you.

SHALLOW: Sir, I thank you; by yea and no, I do.

PAGE: I am glad to see you, good Master Slender.

SLENDER: How does your fallow greyhound, sir? I heard say he was out-run on Cotsall.

PAGE: It could not be judged, sir.

SLENDER: You'll not confess, you'll not confess.

SHALLOW: That he will not.—'Tis your fault, 'tis your fault:—'tis a good dog.

PAGE: A cur, sir.

SHALLOW: Sir, he's a good dog, and a fair dog: can there be more said? he is good and fair.—Is Sir John Falstaff here?

PAGE: Sir, he is within; and I would I could do a good office between you.

SIR HUGH EVANS: It is spoke as a Christians ought to speak.

SHALLOW: He hath wrong'd me, Master Page.

PAGE: Sir, he doth in some sort confess it.

SHALLOW: If it be confess'd, it is not redress'd: is not that so, Master Page? He hath wrong'd me; indeed he hath;—at a word, he hath;—believe me; Robert Shallow, esquire, saith he is wrong'd.

PAGE: Here comes Sir John.

*(Enter Sir John Falstaff, Bardolph, Nym, and Pistol.)*

SIR JOHN FALSTAFF: Now, Master Shallow,—you'll complain of me to the king?

SHALLOW: Knight, you have beaten my men, killed my deer, and broke open my lodge.

SIR JOHN FALSTAFF: But not kiss'd your keeper's daughter?

SHALLOW: Tut, a pin! this shall be answer'd.

SIR JOHN FALSTAFF: I will answer it straight; I have done all this:— that is now answer'd.

SHALLOW: The Council shall know this.

SIR JOHN FALSTAFF: 'Twere better for you if it were known in counsel: you'll be laugh'd at.

SIR HUGH EVANS: *Pauca verba,* Sir John, goot worts.

SIR JOHN FALSTAFF: Good worts! good cabbage—Slender, I broke your head: what matter have you against me?

SLENDER: Marry, sir, I have matter in my head against you: and against your cony-catching rascals, Bardolph, Nym, and Pistol; they carried me to the tavern and made me drunk, and afterward picked my pocket.

BARDOLPH: You Banbury cheese!

SLENDER: Ay, it is no matter.

PISTOL: How now, Mephostophilus!

SLENDER: Ay, it is no matter.

NYM: Slice, I say! *pauca, pauca;* slice! that's my humour.

SLENDER: Where's Simple, my man?—can you tell, cousin?

SIR HUGH EVANS: Peace, I pray you.—Now let us understand. There is three umpires in this matter, as I understand; that is, Master Page, *fidelicet* Master Page; and there is myself, *fidelicet* myself; and the three party is, lastly and finally, mine host of the Garter.

PAGE: We three, to hear it and end it between them.

SIR HUGH EVANS: Fery goot: I will make a prief of it in my notebook; and we will afterwards ork upon the cause with as great discreetly as we can.

SIR JOHN FALSTAFF: Pistol,—

PISTOL: He hears with ears.

SIR HUGH EVANS: The tevil and his tam! what phrase is this, 'He hears with ear'? why, it is affectations.

SIR JOHN FALSTAFF: Pistol, did you pick Master Slender's purse?

SLENDER: Ay, by these gloves, did he—or I would I might never come in mine own great chamber again else—of seven groats in mill-sixpences, and two Edward shovel-boards, that cost me two shilling and two pence a-piece of Yead Miller, by these gloves.

SIR JOHN FALSTAFF: Is this true, Pistol?

SIR HUGH EVANS: No; it is false, if it is a pick-purse.

PISTOL: Ha, thou mountain-foreigner!—Sir John and master mine, I combat challenge of this latten bilbo.—
Word of denial in thy labras here;
Word of denial:—froth and scum, thou liest!

SLENDER: By these gloves, then, 'twas he.

NYM: Be avised, sir, and pass good humours: I will say 'marry trap' with you, if you run the nuthook's humour on me; that is the very note of it.

SLENDER: By this hat, then, he in the red face had it; for though I cannot remember what I did when you made me drunk, yet I am not altogether an ass.

SIR JOHN FALSTAFF: What say you, Scarlet and John?

BARDOLPH: Why, sir, for my part, I say the gentleman had drunk himself out of his five sentences,—

SIR HUGH EVANS: It is his five senses: fie, what the ignorance is!

BARDOLPH: And being fap, sir, was, as they say, cashiered; and so conclusions passed the careires.

SLENDER: Ay, you spake in Latin then too; but 'tis no matter: I'll ne'er be drunk whilst I live again, but in honest, civil, godly company, for this trick: if I be drunk, I'll be drunk with those that have the fear of God, and not with drunken knaves.

SIR HUGH EVANS: So Got udge me, that is a virtuous mind.

SIR JOHN FALSTAFF: You hear all these matters denied, gentlemen; you hear it.

*(Enter Anne Page, with wine; Mistress Ford and Mistress Page.)*

PAGE: Nay, daughter, carry the wine in; we'll drink within. *(Exit Anne Page.)*

SLENDER: O heaven! this is Mistress Anne Page.

PAGE: How now, Mistress Ford!

SIR JOHN FALSTAFF: Mistress Ford, by my troth, you are very well met: by your leave, good mistress. *(Kisses her.)*

PAGE: Wife, bid these gentlemen welcome,—Come, we have a hot venison-pasty to dinner: come, gentlemen, I hope we shall drink down all unkindness.

*(Exeunt all except Shallow, Slender, and Evans.)*

SLENDER: I had rather than forty shillings I had my Book of Songs and Sonnets here.

*(Enter Simple.)*

SLENDER: How now, Simple! where have you been? I must wait on myself, must I? You have not the Book of Riddles about you, have you?

SIMPLE: Book of Riddles! why, did you not lend it to Alice Shortcake upon All-hallowmas last, a fortnight afore Michaelmas?

SHALLOW: Come, coz; come, coz; we stay for you. A word with you, coz; marry, this, coz;—there is, as 'twere, a tender, a kind of tender, made afar off by Sir Hugh here. Do you understand me?

SLENDER: Ay, sir, you shall find me reasonable; if it be so, I shall do that that is reason.

SHALLOW: Nay, but understand me.

SLENDER: So I do, sir.

SIR HUGH EVANS: Give ear to his motions, Master Slender: I will description the matter to you, if you be capacity of it.

SLENDER: Nay, I will do as my cousin Shallow says: I pray you, pardon me; he's a justice of peace in his country, simple though I stand here.

SIR HUGH EVANS: But that is not the question: the question is concerning your marriage.

SHALLOW: Ay, there's the point, sir.

SIR HUGH EVANS: Marry, is it; the very point of it; to Mistress Anne Page.

SLENDER: Why, if it be so, I will marry her upon any reasonable demands.

SIR HUGH EVANS: But can you affection the oman? Let us command to know that of your mouth or of your lips; for divers philosophers hold that the lips is parcel of the mouth. Therefore, precisely, can you carry your good will to the maid?

SHALLOW: Cousin Abraham Slender, can you love her?

SLENDER: I hope, sir, I will do as it shall become one that would do reason.

SIR HUGH EVANS: Nay, Got's lords and his ladies, you must speak positable, if you can carry her your desires towards her.

SHALLOW: That you must. Will you, upon good dowry, marry her?

SLENDER: I will do a greater thing than that, upon your request, cousin, in any reason.

SHALLOW: Nay, conceive me, conceive me, sweet coz: what I do is to pleasure you, coz. Can you love the maid?

SLENDER: I will marry her, sir, at your request: but if there be no great love in the beginning, yet heaven may decrease it upon better acquaintance, when we are married and have more occasion to know one another; I hope, upon familiarity will grow more contempt: but if you say, 'marry her,' I will marry her; that I am freely dissolved, and dissolutely.

SIR HUGH EVANS: It is a fery discretion answer; save the faul is in the ort 'dissolutely:' the ort is, according to our meaning, 'resolutely:'— his meaning is goot.

SHALLOW: Ay, I think my cousin meant well.

SLENDER: Ay, or else I would I might be hang'd, la.

SHALLOW: Here comes fair Mistress Anne.

*(Enter Anne Page.)*

SHALLOW: Would I were young for your sake, Mistress Anne!

ANNE PAGE: The dinner is on the table; my father desires your worships' company.

SHALLOW: I will wait on him, fair Mistress Anne.

SIR HUGH EVANS: Od's plessed will! I will not be absence at the grace.

*(Exeunt Shallow and Evans.)*

ANNE PAGE: Will't please your worship to come in, sir?

SLENDER: No, I thank you, forsooth, heartily; I am very well.

ANNE PAGE: The dinner attends you, sir.

SLENDER: I am not a-hungry, I thank you, forsooth.—Go, sirrah, for all you are my man, go wait upon my cousin Shallow.

*(Exit Simple.)*

SLENDER: A justice of peace sometime may be beholding to his friend for a man.—I keep but three men and a boy yet, till my mother be dead: but what though? yet I live like a poor gentleman born.

ANNE PAGE: I may not go in without your worship: they will not sit till you come.

SLENDER: I'faith, I'll eat nothing; I thank you as much as though I did.

ANNE PAGE: I pray you, sir, walk in.

SLENDER: I had rather walk here, I thank you. I bruised my shin th'other day with playing at sword and dagger with a master of fence,—three veneys for a dish of stew'd prunes; and, by my troth, I cannot abide the smell of hot meat since.—Why do your dogs bark so? be there bears i'th'town?

ANNE PAGE: I think there are, sir; I heard them talk'd of.

SLENDER: I love the sport well; but I shall as soon quarrel at it as any man in England. You are afraid, if you see the bear loose, are you not?

ANNE PAGE: Ay, indeed, sir.

SLENDER: That's meat and drink to me, now. I have seen Sackerson loose twenty times, and have taken him by the chain; but, I warrant you, the women have so cried and shriek'd at it, that it pass'd:— but women, indeed, cannot abide 'em; they are very ill-favour'd rough things.

*(Enter Page.)*

PAGE: Come, gentle Master Slender, come; we stay for you.

SLENDER: I'll eat nothing, I thank you, sir.

PAGE: By cock and pie, you shall not choose, sir: come, come.

SLENDER: Nay, pray you, lead the way.

PAGE: Come on, sir.

SLENDER: Mistress Anne, yourself shall go first.

ANNE PAGE: Not I, sir; pray you, keep on.

SLENDER: Truly, I will not go first; truly, la; I will not do you that wrong.

ANNE PAGE: I pray you, sir.

SLENDER: I'll rather be unmannerly than troublesome. You do yourself wrong, indeed, la. *(Exeuent.)*

# The Duchess of Malfi

John Webster
1614

**Dramatic**
Duchess
Cariola
Servant
Four Madmen
Four more madmen

    *(Enter Duchess and Cariola.)*
DUCHESS: What hideous noise was that?
CARIOLA: 'Tis the wild consort
    Of madmen, lady, which your tyrant brother
    Hath plac'd about your lodging. This tyranny,
    I think, was never practis'd till this hour.
DUCHESS: Indeed I thank him: nothing but noise, and folly
    Can keep me in my right wits, whereas reason
    And silence make me stark mad. Sit down,
    Discourse to me some dismal tragedy.
CARIOLA: O 'twill increase your melancholy.
DUCHESS: Thou art deceiv'd;
    To hear of greater grief would lessen mine.
    This is a prison?
CARIOLA: Yes, but you shall live
    To shake this durance off.
DUCHESS: Thou art a fool:
    The robin red-breast and the nightingale
    Never live long in cages.
CARIOLA: Pray dry your eyes.
    What think you of Madam?
DUCHESS: Of nothing:
    When I muse thus, I sleep.
CARIOLA: Like a madman, with your eyes open?
DUCHESS: Dost thou think we shall know one another
    In th'other world?
CARIOLA: Yes, out of question.
DUCHESS: O that it were possible we might

But hold some two days' conference with the dead,
From them I should learn somewhat, I am sure
I never shall know here. I'll tell thee a miracle,
I am not mad yet, to my cause of sorrow.
Th'heaven o'er my head seems made of molten brass,
The earth of flaming sulphur, yet I am not mad.
I am acquainted with sad misery,
As the tann'd galley-slave is with his oar.
Necessity makes me suffer constantly,
And custom makes it easy. Who do I look like now?

CARIOLA: Like to your picture in the gallery,
A deal of life in show, but none in practice:
Or rather like some reverend monument
Whose ruins are even pitied.

DUCHESS: Very proper:
And fortune seems only to have her eyesight,
To behold my tragedy.
How now! what noise is that?
(Enter Servant.)

SERVANT: I am come to tell you,
Your brother hath intended you some sport.
A great physician when the Pope was sick
Of a deep melancholy, presented him
With several sorts of madmen, which wild object,
Being full of change and sport, forc'd him to laugh,
And so th'imposthume broke: the selfsame cure
The Duke intends on you.

DUCHESS: Let them come in.

SERVANT: There's a mad lawyer, and a secular priest,
A doctor that hath forfeited his wits
By jealousy; an astrologian,
That in his works said such a day o'th' month
Should be the day of doom; and, failing of't,
Ran mad; an English tailor, craz'd i'th' brain
With the study of new fashion; a gentleman usher
Quite beside himself with care to keep in mind
The number of his lady's salutations,
Or 'How do you?' she employ'd him in each morning:
A farmer too, an excellent knave in grain,

Mad, 'cause he was hind'red transportation;
And let one broker, that's mad, loose to these,
You'd think the devil were among them.

DUCHESS: Sit Cariola: let them loose when you please,
For I am chain'd to endure all your tyranny.
*(Enter Madmen.)*

MADMEN: *Here, by a madman, this song is sung a dismal kind of music.*
*O let us howl, some heavy note,*
*Some deadly-dogged howl,*
*Sounding, as from the threat'ning throat,*
*Of beasts, and fatal fowl.*
*As ravens, screech-owls, bulls, and bears,*
*We'll bell, and bawl our parts,*
*Till yerksome noise, have cloy'd your ears,*
*And corrosiv'd your hearts.*
*At last when as our quire wants breath,*
*Our bodies being blest,*
*We'll sing like swans, to welcome death,*
*And die in love and rest.*

FIRST MADMAN: Doomsday not come yet? I'll draw it nearer by a perspective, or make a glass, that shall set all the world on fire upon an instant. I cannot sleep, my pillow is stuff'd with a litter of porcupines.

SECOND MADMAN: Hell is a mere glass-house, where the devils are continually blowing up women's souls on hollow irons, and the fire never goes out.

THIRD MADMAN: I will lie with every woman in my parish the tenth night: I will tithe them over like haycocks.

FOURTH MADMAN: Shall my pothecary outgo me, because I am a cuckold? I have found out his roguery: he makes alum of his wife's urine, and sells it to Puritans, that have sore throats with overstraining.

FIRST MADMAN: I have skill in heraldry.

SECOND MADMAN: Hast?

FIRST MADMAN: You do give for your crest a woodcock's head, with the brains pick't out on't. You are a very ancient gentleman.

THIRD MADMAN: Greek is turn'd Turk; we are only to be sav'd by the Helvetian translation.

FIRST MADMAN: Come on sir, I will lay the law to you.

SECOND MADMAN: O, rather lay a corrosive, the law will eat to the bone.

THIRD MADMAN: He that drinks but to satisfy nature is damn'd.

FOURTH MADMAN: If I had my glass here, I would show a sight should make all the women here call me mad doctor.

FIRST MADMAN: What's he, a rope-maker?

SECOND MADMAN: No, no, no, a snuffling knave, that while he shows the tombs, will have his hand in a wench's placket.

THIRD MADMAN: Woe to the caroche that brought home my wife from the masque, at three o'clock in the morning; it had a large feather bed in it.

FOURTH MADMAN: I have pared the devils nails forty times, roasted them in raven's eggs, and cur'd agues with them.

THIRD MADMAN: Get me three hundred milch bats, to make possets to procure sleep.

FOURTH MADMAN: All the college may throw their caps at me, I have made a soap-boiler costive: it was my masterpiece.

*(Here the dance consisting of eight madmen, with music answerable thereunto, after which Bosola, like an old man, enters.)*

DUCHESS: Is he mad too?

SERVANT: Pray question him; I'll leave you.

*(Exeunt Servant and Madmen.)*

# Leonce and Lena

Georg Buchner
Translated by Victor Price
1832

**Comic**
**Scene:** in King Peter's castle

Master of Ceremonies
First Servant
Second Servant
King Peter
Valerio
Leonce
Third Servant
Fourth Servant
President
Court Chaplain
Lena

MASTER OF CEREMONIES: What a shame! Everything's going to pot. The
roasts are drying up. Congratulations are going stale. Stand-up
collars are all bending over like melancholy pigs' ears. The peas-
ants' nails and beards are growing again. The soldiers' curls are
drooping. Among the twelve bridesmaids there is none who
wouldn't prefer a horizontal position to a vertical one. In their
white dresses they look like exhausted Angora rabbits, and the
Court Poet grunts around them like a distressed guinea pig. The
officers are going limp. *(To a servant.)* Go tell our private tutor to
let his boys make water.—The poor Court Chaplain! His coat is
hanging its tails most dejectedly. I think he has ideals and is
changing all the chamberlains into chamber stools. He's tired of
standing.

FIRST SERVANT: All meat spoils from standing. The Court Chaplain is at a
stale standstill too, after standing up this morning.

MASTER OF CEREMONIES: The ladies-in-waiting stand there like saltworks,
the salt crystallizes on their necklaces.

SECOND SERVANT: At least they're taking it easy. You can't accuse them of bearing a weight on their shoulders. If they aren't exactly openhearted, at least they're open down to the heart.

MASTER OF CEREMONIES: Yes, they're good maps of the Turkish Empire— you can see the Dardanelles and the Sea of Marmara. Out, you rascals! To the windows! Here comes His Majesty!

*(King Peter and the State Council enter.)*

KING PETER: So the Princess has disappeared as well? Has no trace been found of our beloved Crown Prince? Have my orders been carried out? Are the borders being watched?

MASTER OF CEREMONIES: Yes, Your Majesty. The view from this hall allows us the strictest surveillance. *(To the First Servant.)* What have you seen?

FIRST SERVANT: A dog ran through the kingdom looking for its master.

MASTER OF CEREMONIES: *(To another.)* And you?

SECOND SERVANT: Someone is taking a walk on the northern border, but it's not the Prince—I'd recognize him.

MASTER OF CEREMONIES: And you?

THIRD SERVANT: Begging your pardon, nothing.

MASTER OF CEREMONIES: That's very little. And you?

FOURTH SERVANT: Nothing either.

MASTER OF CEREMONIES: That's even less.

KING PETER: But Council, have I not resolved that My Royal Majesty shall rejoice today and that the wedding shall be celebrated? Was this not our most solemn resolution?

PRESIDENT: Yes, Your Majesty, it is so registered and recorded.

KING PETER: And would I not compromise myself, if I did not carry out my resolution?

PRESIDENT: If it were possible for Your Majesty to otherwise compromise yourself, this would be an instance in which this might be so.

KING PETER: Have I not given my Royal Word? Yes, I shall carry out my resolution immediately: I shall rejoice. *(He rubs his hands.)* Oh, I am exceptionally happy!

PRESIDENT: We join in sharing Your Majesty's emotion, insofar as it is possible and proper for subjects to do so.

KING PETER: Oh, I am beside myself with joy. I shall have red coats made for my chamberlains, I shall promote some cadets to lieutenants, I shall permit my subjects to…but…but, the wedding? Does not the other half of the resolution state that the wedding shall be celebrated?

PRESIDENT: Yes, Your Majesty.

KING PETER: Yes, but if the Prince does not come and neither does the Princess?

PRESIDENT: Yes, if the Prince does not come and neither does the Princess, then…then…

KING PETER: Then, then?

PRESIDENT: Then indeed they cannot get married.

KING PETER: Wait, is the conclusion logical? If…then.—Correct! But my Word, my Royal Word!

PRESIDENT: Take comfort, Your Majesty, with other majesties. A Royal Word is a thing…a thing…a thing…of nothing.

KING PETER: *(To the servants.)* Do you see anything yet?

SERVANTS: Nothing, Your Majesty, nothing at all.

KING PETER: And I had resolved to be so happy. I wanted to begin at the stroke of twelve and wanted to rejoice a full twelve hours. I am becoming quite melancholy.

PRESIDENT: All subjects are commanded to share the feelings of His Majesty.

MASTER OF CEREMONIES: For the sake of decorum, those who carry no handkerchiefs are forbidden to cry.

FIRST SERVANT: Wait! I see something! It's something like a projection, like a nose—the rest is not over the border yet—and now I see another man and two people of the opposite sex.

MASTER OF CEREMONIES: In which direction?

FIRST SERVANT: They're coming closer. They're approaching the palace. Here they are.

*(Valerio, Leonce, the Governess, and the Princess enter, masked.)*

KING PETER: Who are you?

VALERIO: Do I know? *(He slowly takes off several masks, one after another.)* Am I this? Or this? Or this? I'm truly afraid I could pare and peel myself away completely like this.

KING PETER: *(Confused.)* But…but you must be something, after all?

VALERIO: If Your Majesty commands it. But gentlemen, then turn the mirrors around and hide your shiny buttons somewhat and don't look at me so that I'm mirrored in your eyes, or I'll really no longer know who I actually am.

KING PETER: This man makes me confused, desperate. I am thoroughly mixed up.

VALERIO: But I actually wanted to announce to this exalted and honored company that the two world-famous automatons have arrived, and that I'm perhaps the third and most peculiar of them all, if only I really knew who I am, which by the way shouldn't surprise you, since I myself don't know what I'm talking about—in fact, I don't even know that I don't know it, so that it's highly probable that I'm merely being *allowed* to speak, and it's actually nothing but cylinders and air hoses that are saying all this. *(In a strident voice.)* Ladies and gentlemen, here you see two persons of opposite sexes, a little man and a little woman, a gentleman and a lady. Nothing but art and machinery, nothing but cardboard and watchsprings. Each one has a tiny, tiny ruby spring under the nail of the little toe of the right foot—press on it gently and the mechanism runs a full fifty years. These persons are so perfectly constructed that one couldn't distinguish them from other people if one didn't know that they're simply cardboard; you could actually make them members of human society. They are very noble: they speak the Queen's English. They are very moral: they get up punctually, eat lunch punctually, and go to bed punctually; they also have a good digestion, which proves they have a good conscience. They have a fine sense of propriety: the lady has no word for the concept "pants," and it is absolutely impossible for the gentleman to follow a lady going upstairs or to precede her downstairs. They are highly educated: the lady sings all the new operas and the gentleman wears cuffs. Take note, ladies and gentlemen: they are now in an interesting state. The mechanism of love is beginning to function—the gentleman has already carried the lady's shawl several times, the lady has turned her eyes up to heaven. Both have whispered more than once "Belief, love, hope!" Both already appear to be completely in accord; all that is lacking is the tiny word "amen."

KING PETER: *(Puts a finger next to his nose.)* In effigy? In effigy? President, if you hang a man in effigy, isn't that just as good as hanging him properly?

PRESIDENT: Begging Your Majesty's pardon, it's very much better, because no harm comes to him, yet he is hanged nevertheless.

KING PETER: Now I've got it. We shall celebrate the wedding in effigy. *(Pointing to Leonce and Lena.)* This is the Prince, this is the Princess. I shall carry out my resolution—I shall rejoice. Let the bells ring, prepare your congratulations! Quickly, Court Chaplain!

*(The Court Chaplain steps forward, clears his throat, looks toward heaven several times.)*

VALERIO: Begin! Leave thy damnable faces, and begin! Come on!

COURT CHAPLAIN: *(In the greatest confusion.)* When we…or…but…

VALERIO: Whereas and because…

COURT CHAPLAIN: For…

VALERIO: It was before the creation of the world…

COURT CHAPLAIN: That…

VALERIO: God was bored…

KING PETER: Just make it short, my good man.

COURT CHAPLAIN: *(Composing himself.)* May it please Your Highness Prince Leonce from the Kingdom of Popo and may it please Your Highness Princess Lena from the Kingdom of Peepee, and may it please Your Highnesses mutually to want each other respectively, then say a loud and audible yes.

LENA AND LEONCE: Yes.

COURT CHAPLAIN: Then I say amen.

VALERIO: Well done, short and to the point—thus man and woman are created and all the animals of paradise surround them.
*(Leonce takes off his mask.)*

ALL: The Prince!

KING PETER: The Prince! My son! I'm lost, I've been deceived! *(He runs over to the Princess.)* Who is this person? I shall declare everything invalid.

GOVERNESS: *(Takes off the Princess's mask, triumphantly.)* The Princess!

LEONCE: Lena?

LENA: Leonce?

LEONCE: Why Lena, I think that was an escape into paradise. I've been deceived.

LENA: I've been deceived.

LEONCE: Oh, Fortune!

LENA: Oh, Providence!

VALERIO: I can't help laughing, I can't help laughing. Fate has certainly been fortuitous for the two of you. I hope Your Highnesses will be so fortunate as to find favor with each other forthwith.

GOVERNESS: That my old eyes could see this! A wandering prince! Now I can die in peace.

KING PETER: My children, I am deeply moved, I am almost beside myself with emotion. I am the happiest of all men! I shall now, however, most solemnly place the kingdom in your hands, my son, and shall immediately begin to do nothing but think without interruption. My son, you will leave me these wise men, *(He points to the State Council.)*, so they can support me in my efforts. Come, gentlemen, we must think, think without interruption. *(He leaves with the State Council.)* That person confused me before—I must find my way out again.

LEONCE: *(To those present.)* Gentlemen, my wife and I are terribly sorry that you have had to attend us for so long today. Your deportment is so tenuous that we do not intend to test your tenacity any longer. Go home now, but don't forget your speeches, sermons, and verses, because tomorrow, in peace and leisure, we'll begin the game all over again. Good-bye!

*(All leave except Leonce, Lena, Valerio, and the Governess.)*

LEONCE: Well, Lena, now do you see how our pockets are full of dolls and toys? What shall we do with them? Shall we give them beards and hang swords on them? Or shall we dress them up in tails and let them play at protozoan polities and diplomacy and watch them through a microscope? Or would you prefer a barrel organ on which milk-white aesthetic shrews are scurrying about? Shall we build a theater?

*(Lena leans against him and shakes her head.)*

LEONCE: But I know what you really want: we'll have all the clocks smashed, all calendars prohibited, and we'll count hours and months only by flower-clocks, only by blossoms and fruit. And then we'll surround the country with heat reflectors so there'll be no more winter, and in the summer we'll distill ourselves up to Ischia and Capri, and we'll spend the whole year among roses and violets, among oranges and laurels.

VALERIO: And I'll be Minister of State, and it shall be decreed that whoever gets calluses on his hands shall be placed in custody, that whoever works himself sick shall be criminally prosecuted, that anyone who boasts of eating his bread in the sweat of his face shall be declared insane and dangerous to human society, and then we'll lie in the shade and ask God for macaroni, melons, and figs, for musical voices, classical bodies, and a comfortable religion!

# The Player Queen

William Butler Yeats

1922

**Dramatic**
**Scene:** an open space at the meeting of three streets

First old man
Second old man
Septimus
Old woman
First man
Second young man
A crowd of citizens, countrymen
Tapster

FIRST OLD MAN: Can you see the Queen's castle? You have better sight than I.

SECOND OLD MAN: I can just see it rising over the tops of the houses yonder on its great rocky hill.

FIRST OLD MAN: Is the dawn breaking? Is it touching the tower?

SECOND OLD MAN: It is beginning to break upon the tower, but these narrow streets will be dark for a long while. *(A pause.)* Do you hear anything? You have better hearing than I.

FIRST OLD MAN: No, all is quiet.

SECOND OLD MAN: At least fifty passed by an hour since, a crowd of fifty men walking rapidly.

FIRST OLD MAN: Last night was very quiet, not a sound, not a breath.

SECOND OLD MAN: And not a thing to be seen till the Tapster's old dog came down the street upon this very hour from Cooper Malachi's ash-pit.

FIRST OLD MAN: Hush, I hear feet, many feet. Perhaps they are coming this way. *(Pause.)* No, they are going the other way, they are gone now.

SECOND OLD MAN: The young are at some mischief,—the young and the middle-aged.

FIRST OLD MAN: Why can't they stay in their beds, and they can sleep too—seven hours, eight hours? I mind the time when I could sleep ten hours. They will know the value of sleep when they are near upon ninety years.

SECOND OLD MAN: They will never live so long. They have not the health and strength that we had. They wear themselves out. They are always in a passion about something or other.

FIRST OLD MAN: Hush! I hear a step now, and it is coming this way. We had best pull in our heads. The world has grown very wicked and there is no knowing what they might do to us or say to us.

SECOND OLD MAN: Yes, better shut the windows and pretend to be asleep.

*(They pull in their heads. One hears a knocker being struck in the distance, then a pause, and a knocker is struck close at hand. Another pause, and Septimus, a handsome man of thirty-five, staggers on to the stage. He is very drunk.)*

SEPTIMUS: An uncharitable place, and unchristian place. *(He begins banging at a knocker.)* Open there, open there. I want to come in and sleep.

*(A third old man puts his head from an upper window.)*

THIRD OLD MAN: Who are you? What do you want?

SEPTIMUS: I am Septimus. I have a bad wife. I want to come in and sleep.

THIRD OLD MAN: You are drunk.

SEPTIMUS: Drunk! So would you be if you had as bad a wife.

THIRD OLD MAN: Go away. *(He shuts the window.)*

SEPTIMUS: Is there not one Christian in this town? *(He begins hammering the knocker of First Old Man, but there is no answer.)* No one there? All dead or drunk maybe—bad wives! There must be one Christian man. *(He hammers a knocker at the other side of the stage.)*

*(An Old Woman puts her head out of the window above.)*

OLD WOMAN: *(In a shrill voice.)* Who's there? What do you want? Has something happened?

SEPTIMUS: Yes, that's it. Something has happened. My wife has hid herself, has run away, or has drowned herself.

OLD WOMAN: What do I care about your wife? You are drunk.

SEPTIMUS: Not care about my wife! But I tell you that my wife has to play by order of the Prime Minister before all the people in the great hall of the Castle precisely at noon, and she cannot be found.

OLD WOMAN: Go away, go away! I tell you, go away. *(She shuts the window.)*

SEPTIMUS: Treat Septimus, who has played before Kubla Khan, like this! Septimus, dramatist and poet!

*(The Old Woman opens the window again and empties a jug of water over him.)*

SEPTIMUS: Water! drenched to the skin—must sleep in the street. *(Lies down.)* Bad wife—others have had bad wives, but others were not left to lie down in the open street under the stars, drenched with cold water, a whole jug of cold water, shivering in the pale light of the dawn, to be run over, to be trampled upon, to be eaten by dogs, and all because their wives have hidden themselves.

*(Enter two Men a little older than Septimus. They stand still and gaze into the sky.)*

FIRST MAN: Ah, my friend, the little fair-haired one is a minx.

SECOND MAN: Never trust fair hair—I will have nothing but brown hair.

FIRST MAN: They have kept us too long—brown or fair.

SECOND MAN: What are you staring at?

FIRST MAN: At the first streak of the dawn on the Castle tower.

SECOND MAN: I would not have my wife find out for the world.

SEPTIMUS: *(Sitting up.)* Carry me, support me, drag me, roll me, pull me, or sidle me along, but bring me where I may sleep in comfort. Bring me to a stable—my Saviour was content with a stable.

FIRST MAN: Who are you? I don't know your face.

SEPTIMUS: I am Septimus, a player, a playwright, and the most famous poet in the world.

SECOND MAN: That name, sir, is unknown to me.

SEPTIMUS: Unknown?

SECOND MAN: But my name will not be unknown to you. I am called Peter of the Purple Pelican, after the best known of my poems, and my friend is called Happy Tom. He also is a poet.

SEPTIMUS: Bad, popular poets.

SECOND MAN: You would be a popular poet if you could.

SEPTIMUS: Bad, popular poets.

FIRST MAN: Lie where you are if you can't be civil.

SEPTIMUS: What do I care for any one now except Venus and Adonis and the other planets of heaven?

SECOND MAN: You can enjoy their company by yourself.

*(The two Men go out.)*

SEPTIMUS: Robbed, so to speak; naked, so to speak—bleeding, so to speak—and they pass by on the other side of the street.

*(A crowd of Citizens and Countrymen enter. At first only a few, and then more and more till the stage is filled by an excited crowd.)*

FIRST CITIZEN: There is a man lying here.

SECOND CITIZEN: Roll him over.

FIRST CITIZEN: He is one of those players who are housed at the Castle. They arrived yesterday.

SECOND CITIZEN: Drunk, I suppose. He'll be killed or maimed by the first milk-cart.

THIRD CITIZEN: Better roll him into the comer. If we are in for a bloody day's business, there is no need for him to be killed—an unnecessary death might bring a curse upon us.

FIRST CITIZEN: Give me a hand here.

*(They begin rolling Septimus.)*

SEPTIMUS: *(Muttering.)* Not allowed to sleep! Rolled off the street! Shoved into a stony place! Unchristian town!

*(He is left lying at the foot of the wall to one side of the stage.)*

THIRD CITIZEN: Are we all friends here, are we all agreed?

FIRST CITIZEN: These men are from the country. They came in last night. They know little of the business. They won't be against the people, but they want to know more.

FIRST COUNTRYMAN: Yes, that is it. We are with the people, but we want to know more.

SECOND COUNTRYMAN: We want to know all, but we are with the people.

*(Other voices take up the words, "We want to know all, but we are with the people," etc. There is a murmur of voices together.)*

THIRD COUNTRYMAN: Have you ever seen the Queen, countryman?

FIRST COUNTRYMAN: No.

THIRD CITIZEN: Our Queen is a witch, a bad evil-living witch, and we will have her no longer for Queen.

THIRD COUNTRYMAN: I would be slow to believe her father's daughter a witch.

THIRD CITIZEN: Have you ever seen the Queen, countryman?

THIRD COUNTRYMAN: No.

THIRD CITIZEN: Nor has any one else. Not a man here has set eyes on her.

For seven years she has been shut up in that great black house on the great rocky hill. From the day her father died she has been there with the doors shut on her, but we know now why she has hidden herself. She has no good companions in the dark night.

THIRD COUNTRYMAN: In my district they say that she is a holy woman and prays for us all.

THIRD CITIZEN: That story has been spread about by the Prime Minister. He has spies everywhere spreading stories. He is a crafty man.

FIRST COUNTRYMAN: It is true, they always deceive us country people. We are not educated like the people of the town.

A BIG COUNTRYMAN: The Bible says, Suffer not a witch to live. Last Candlemas twelvemonth I strangled a witch with my own hands.

THIRD CITIZEN: When she is dead we will make the Prime Minister King.

SECOND CITIZEN: No, no, he is not a king's son.

SECOND COUNTRYMAN: I'd send a bellman through the world. There are many kings in Arabia, they say.

THIRD COUNTRYMAN: The people must be talking. If you and I were to hide ourselves, or to be someway hard to understand, maybe they would put some bad name on us. I am not against the people, but I want testimony.

THIRD CITIZEN: Come, Tapster, stand up there on the stone and tell what you know.

(The Tapster climbs up on the mounting stone.)

TAPSTER: I live in the quarter where her Castle is. The garden of my house and the gardens of all the houses in my row run right up to the rocky hill that has her Castle on the top. There is a lad in my quarter that has a goat in his garden.

FIRST CITIZEN: That's Strolling Michael—I know him.

TAPSTER: That goat is always going astray. Strolling Michael got out of his bed early one morning to go snaring birds, and nowhere could he see that goat. So he began climbing up the rock, and up and up he went, till he was close under the wall, and there he found the goat and it shaking and sweating as though something had scared it. Presently he heard a thing neigh like a horse, and after that a something like a white horse ran by, but it was no horse, but a unicorn. He had his pistol, for he had thought to bring down a rabbit, and seeing it rushing at him as he imagined, he fired at the unicorn. It vanished all in a moment, but there was blood on a great stone.

THIRD CITIZEN: Seeing what company she keeps in the small hours, what wonder that she never sets foot out of doors!

THIRD COUNTRYMAN: I wouldn't believe all that night rambler says—boys are liars. All that we have against her for certain is that she won't put her foot out of doors. I knew a man once that when he was five-and-twenty refused to get out of his bed. He wasn't ill—no, not he, but he said life was a vale of tears, and for forty and four years till they carried him out to the churchyard he never left that bed. All tried him—parson tried him, priest tried him, doctor tried him, and all he'd say was, "Life is a vale of tears." It's too snug he was in his bed, and believe me, that ever since she has had no father to rout her out of a morning she has been in her bed, and small blame to her maybe.

THE BIG COUNTRYMAN: But that's the very sort that are witches. They know where to find their own friends in the lonely hours of the night. There was a witch in my own district that I strangled last Candlemas twelvemonth. She had an imp in the shape of a red cat, that sucked three drops of blood from her poll every night a little before the cock crew. It's with their blood they feed them; until they have been fed with the blood they are images and shadows; but when they have it drunk they can be for a while stronger than you or me.

THIRD COUNTRYMAN: The man I knew was no witch, he was no way active. "Life is a vale of tears," he said. Parson tried him, doctor tried him, priest tried him—but that was all he'd say.

FIRST CITIZEN: We'd have no man go beyond evidence and reason, but hear the Tapster out, and when you have you'll say that we cannot leave her alive this day—no, not for one day longer.

# The Troop Train

Mario Dessy

**Dramatic**
**Scene:** the interior of a military troop train going toward the front lines. Wartime

Up to thirty men, one woman
Soldiers

The interior of a carriage of a military troop train that is going toward the front.

Some thirty soldiers who laugh, sleep, talk, joke; everyone is happy and noisy.

A beautiful, very elegant and perfumed woman climbs on at a stop. Surprise and general amazement.

The woman is looking for someone. She makes a tour of the carriage looking at all the faces, then gets off again.

The train starts again, the perfume disappears. Smiles of those who are going toward the war.

# Galileo

Bertolt Brecht

**Dramatic**

Senators
Officials
Galileo
Virginia
Sagredo
Artisans
The Doge
Matti

CURATOR: *(Announcing.)* Senators, Artisans of the Great Arsenal of Venice; Mr. Galileo Galilei, professor of mathematics at your University of Padua.

*(Galileo steps forward and starts to speak.)*

GALILEO: Members of the High Senate! Gentlemen I have great pleasure, as director of this institute, in presenting for your approval and acceptance an entirely new instrument originating from this our great arsenal of the Republic of Venice. As professor of mathematics at your University of Padua, your obedient servant has always counted it his privilege to offer you such discoveries and inventions as might prove lucrative to the manufacturers and merchants of our Venetian Republic. Thus, in all humility, I tender you this, my optical tube, or telescope, constructed, I assure you, on the most scientific and Christian principles, the product of seventeen years patient research at your University of Padua.

*(Galileo steps back. The senators applaud.)*

SAGREDO: *(Aside to Galileo.)* Now you will be able to pay your bills.

GALILEO: Yes. It will make money for them. But you realize that it is more than a money-making gadget?—I turned it on the moon last night...

CURATOR: *(In his best chamber-of-commerce manner.)* Gentlemen: Our Republic is to be congratulated not only because this new acquisition will be one more feather in the cap of Venetian culture...

*(Polite applause.)*

CURATOR: ...not only because our own Mr. Galilei has generously handed this fresh product of his teeming brain entirely over to you, allowing you to manufacture as many of these highly saleable articles as you please…

*(Considerable applause.)*

CURATOR: But Gentlemen of the Senate, has it occurred to you that—with the help of this remarkably new instrument—the battlefleet of the enemy will be visible to us a full two hours before we are visible to him?

*(Tremendous applause.)*

GALILEO: *(Aside to Sagredo.)* We have been held up three generations for lack of a thing like this. I want to go home.

SAGREDO: What about the moon?

GALILEO: Well, for one thing, it doesn't give off its own light.

CURATOR: *(Continuing his oration.)* And now, Your Excellency, and Members of the Senate, Mr. Galilei entreats you to accept the instrument from the hands of his charming daughter Virginia.

*(Polite applause. He beckons to Virginia who steps forward and presents the telescope to the Doge.)*

CURATOR: *(During this.)* Mr. Galilei gives his invention entirely into your hands, Gentlemen, enjoining you to construct as many of these instruments as you may please.

*(More applause. The Senators gather round the telescope, examining it, and looking through it.)*

GALILEO: *(Aside to Sagredo.)* Do you know what the Milky Way is made of?

SAGREDO: No.

GALILEO: I do.

CURATOR: *(Interrupting.)* Congratulations, Mr. Galilei. Your extra five hundred scudi a year are safe.

GALILEO: Pardon? What? Of course, the five hundred scudi! Yes!

*(A prosperous man is standing beside the Curator.)*

CURATOR: Mr. Galilei, Mr. Matti of Florence.

MATTI: You're opening new fields, Mr. Galilei. We could do with you at Florence.

CURATOR: Now, Mr. Matti, leave something to us poor Venetians.

MATTI: It is a pity that a great republic has to seek an excuse to pay its great men their right and proper dues.

CURATOR: Even a great man has to have an incentive. *(He joins the Senators at the telescope.)*

MATTI: I am an iron founder.

GALILEO: Iron founder!

MATTI: With factories at Pisa and Florence. I wanted to talk to you about a machine you designed for a friend of mine in Padua.

GALILEO: I'll put you on to someone to copy it for you, I am not going to have the time.—How are things in Florence?

*(They wander away.)*

FIRST SENATOR: *(Peering.)* Extraordinary! They're having their lunch on that frigate. Lobsters! I'm hungry!

*(Laughter.)*

SECOND SENATOR: Oh, good heavens, look at her! I must tell my wife to stop bathing on the roof. When can I buy one of these things?

*(Laughter. Virginia has spotted Ludovico among the onlookers and drags him to Galileo.)*

VIRGINIA: *(To Ludovico.)* Did I do it nicely?

LUDOVICO: I thought so.

VIRGINIA: Here's Ludovico to congratulate you, father.

LUDOVICO: *(Embarrassed.)* Congratulations, sir.

GALILEO: I improved it.

LUDOVICO: Yes, sir. I am beginning to understand science.

*(Galileo is surrounded.)*

VIRGINIA: Isn't father a great man?

LUDOVICO: Yes.

VIRGINIA: Isn't that new thing father made pretty?

LUDOVICO: Yes, a pretty red. Where I saw it first it was covered in green.

VIRGINIA: What was?

LUDOVICO: Never mind. *(A short pause.)* Have you ever been to Holland?

*(They go. All Venice is congratulating Galileo, who wants to go home.)*

# The Devils

John Whiting
1961

**Dramatic**

Barré
Adam
Mannoury
De Cerisay
Mignon
Jeanne
Rangier
A Clerk

BARRÉ: Dear Sister in Christ, I must question you further.

JEANNE: Yes, Father.

BARRÉ: Do you remember the first time your thoughts were turned to these evil things?

JEANNE: Very well.

BARRÉ: Tell us.

JEANNE: I was walking in the garden. I stopped. Lying at my feet was a stick of hawthorn. I was sinfully possessed by anger, for that very morning I'd had cause to admonish two of the Sisters for neglecting their duties in the garden. I picked up the unsightly thing in rage. It must have been thorned, for blood ran from my body. Seeing the blood, I was filled with tenderness.

RANGIER: But this revelation may have come from a very different source.

BARRÉ: All the same— *(To the clerk.)* Are you getting this down?

JEANNE: There was another time.

BARRÉ: Tell us.

JEANNE: A day or two later. It was a beautiful morning. I'd had a night of dreamless sleep. On the threshold of my room lay a bunch of roses. I picked them up and tucked them into my belt. Suddenly, I was seized by a violent trembling in my right arm. And a great knowledge of love. This persisted throughout my orisons. I was unable to put my mind to anything. It was entirely filled with the representation of a man which had been deeply and inwardly impressed upon me.

BARRÉ: Do you know who sent those flowers?

JEANNE: *(Long silence: quietly.)* Grandier. Grandier.

BARRÉ: What is his rank?

JEANNE: Priest.

BARRÉ: Of what church?

JEANNE: Saint Peter's.

*(Barré turns to stare in silence at De Cerisay.)*

DE CERISAY: *(Quietly.)* This is nothing.

*(Barré turns back to Jeanne.)*

BARRÉ: We are unconvinced, my dear Sister. And if our conviction remains untouched I do not have to remind you that you face eternal damnation.

*(Jeanne suddenly throws herself across the bed: she utters grunts like a small pig: she grinds her teeth: she disorders the bed. The men draw back from her. Jeanne sits upright, staring at them.)*

BARRÉ: *(With great urgency.)* Speak! Speak!

JEANNE: It…was…night. Day's done!

BARRÉ: Yes?

JEANNE: I had tied back my hair, and scrubbed my face. Back to child-hood, eh? Poor Jane. Grown woman. Made for—for…

BARRÉ: Go on.

JEANNE: He came to me.

BARRÉ: Name him!

JEANNE: *(At once.)* Grandier! Grandier! The beautiful, golden lion entered my room, smiling.

BARRÉ: Was he alone?

JEANNE: No. Six of his creatures were with him.

BARRÉ: Then?

JEANNE: He took me gently in his arms and carried me to the chapel. His creatures each took one of my beloved sisters.

BARRÉ: What took place?

JEANNE: *(Smiling.)* Oh, my dear Father, think of our little chapel, so simple! so unadorned. That night it was a place of luxury and scented heat. Let me tell you. It was full of laughter and music. There were velvets, silks, metals, and the wood wasn't scrubbed, no, not at all. Yes, and there was food. High animal hesh, and wine, heavy, like the fruit from the East. I'd read about it all. How we stuffed ourselves.

DE CERISAY: This is an innocent vision of hell.

BARRÉ: Ssh! Go on.

JEANNE: I forgot. We were beautifully dressed. I wore my clothes as if they were part of my body. Later, when I was naked, I fell among the thorns. Yes, there were thorns strewn on the floor. I fell among them. Come here.
*(She beckons to Barré, who leans towards her. She whispers and then laughs.)*

BARRÉ: *(Bleakly.)* She says that she and her sisters were compelled to form themselves into an obscene altar, and were worshipped.

JEANNE: Again. *(Again she whispers: laughs.)*

BARRÉ: She says demons tended Grandier, and her beloved sisters incited her. You'll understand what I mean, gentlemen.
*(Jeanne again draws Barré to her. She whispers frantically, and gradually her words become audible.)*

JEANNE: ...and so we vanquished God from his house. He fled in horror at the senses fixed in men by another hand. Free of him, we celebrated His departure again and again. *(She lies back.)* To one who has known what I have known, God is dead. I have found peace.
*(Silence. Mignon has fallen on his knees and is praying. Barré takes De Cerisay by the arm. As they speak they will move far from Jeanne and the others.)*

BARRÉ: This was an innocent woman.

DE CERISAY: That was no devil. She spoke with her own voice. The voice of an unhappy woman, that's all.

BARRÉ: But the degraded imagination and filthy language she used in other depositions. These cannot spring unaided from a cloistered woman. She is a pupil.

DE CERISAY: Of Grandier?

BARRÉ: Yes.

DE CERISAY: But the man swears he's never been in the place.

BARRÉ: Not in his own person.

DE CERISAY: There must be some way of proving what she says. Will you let my people into the house? They will conduct an investigation on a police level.

BARRÉ: Proof? Three of the Sisters have made statements saying that they have undergone copulation with demons and been deflowered. Mannoury has examined them, and it's true that none of them is intact.

DE CERISAY: My dear Father, I don't want to offend your susceptibilities, but we all know about the sentimental attachments which go on between the young women in these places.

BARRÉ: You don't wish to be convinced.

DE CERISAY: I do. Very much. One way or another.

(De Cerisay goes. Barré turns. Mannoury and Adam are approaching.)

ADAM: Well, there, now.

MANNOURY: Fascinating.

ADAM: Unusual.

MANNOURY: Must say. Hell can't be as dull as some people make out. Haha! What?

ADAM: Such things.

MANNOURY: You know, I think a privately plinted testament of this case might have quite a sale. Shall we write it up?

ADAM: Let's.

(They have approached Barré.)

BARRÉ: Have you examined her?

MANNOURY: Yes. I'll let you have my report later.

BARRÉ: Can you give me anything to go on, meantime?

MANNOURY: As a professional man—

ADAM: He speaks for me.

MANNOURY: I don't like to commit myself.

BARRÉ: Even so—

MANNOURY: Well, let's put it this way. There's been hanky-panky.

BARRÉ: Don't mince words. There's been fornication!

MANNOURY: Rather!

BARRÉ: Lust! She's been had!

ADAM: I'll say.

BARRÉ: Thank you, gentlemen. That's all I need. Look.

(They are silent. Grandier is walking in the distance. Barré, Mannoury and Adam go. Grandier approaches. Phillipe comes quickly to him.)

PHILLIPE: They said you were at the Governor's house.

GRANDIER: I've just come from there. What's the matter?

PHILLIPE: I want to know. Was I restless last night? I had to leave you before it was light. I went as quietly as I could. Did I disturb you? It's important that I should know.

GRANDIER: I can't remember. Why is it important?

PHILLIPE: You can't remember. *(She gives a sudden, startling, harsh laugh.)*

GRANDIER: Walk to the church with me.

PHILLIPE: No.

GRANDIER: Very well.

PHILLIPE: There's no need to go into the confessional to say what I have to tell you. I'm pregnant.

*(Silence.)*

GRANDIER: So it ends.

PHILLIPE: I'm frightened.

GRANDIER: Of course. How can I own the child?

PHILLIPE: I'm very frightened.

GRANDIER: And there was such bravery in love, wasn't there, Phillipe? All through the summer nights. How unafraid we were each time we huddled down together. We laughed as we roused the animal. Remember? Now it has devoured us.

PHILLIPE: Help me.

GRANDIER: And we were to have been each other's salvation. Did I really believe it was possible?

PHILLIPE: I love you.

GRANDIER: Yes, I did believe it. I remember leaving you one day—you had been unusually adroit—

PHILLIPE: O God!

GRANDIER: I was filled with that indecent confidence which comes after perfect coupling. And as I went I thought—yes, solemnly I thought—the body can transcend its purpose. It can become a thing of such purity that it can be worshipped to the limits of imagination. Anything is allowed. All is right. And such perfection makes for an understanding of the hideous state of existence.

# Dance of the Wandering Souls

Huynh Quang Nhuong
1997

**Dramatic**

**Scene:** a battlefield. Fires of burning camps. Loud wailing sirens. Musket fire

A group of Vietnamese soldiers
A group of Co Hon, wandering souls
General Tran Can

    The Vietnamese soldiers suddenly fall down and sleep. Eerie wailing is heard. Co Hon appear and perform a ritual dance while continuing to wail, before systematically destroying the fort. When the construction is totally demolished, Co Hon disappear. Moments later the Vietnamese soldiers wake up. They look at the ruins of the construction, bewildered. General Tran Can appears and talks to the soldiers.

*(Blackout.)*

# PART THREE

# SCENES FOR
# MIXED GROUPS

# SMALL GROUP SCENES
# (5–10 ACTORS)

# Everyman

Anonymous
1500

**Dramatic**
**Scene:** Everyman on his journey. A road

Everyman
Good Deeds
Knowledge
Discretion
Beauty
Strength
Five Wits
An Angel

EVERYMAN: My body sore punished shall be.
   Take this, body, for the sin of the flesh! *(Scourges himself.)*
   Also thou delightest to go gay and fresh,
   And in the way of damnation thou did me bring;
   Therefore suffer now strokes of punishing.
   Now of penance I will wade the water clear,
   To save me from purgatory, that sharp fire.
   *(Good Deeds rises from the floor.)*
GOOD DEEDS: I thank God, now I can walk and go,
   And am delivered of my sickness and woe.
   Therefore with Everyman I will go, and not spare;
   His good works I will help him to declare.
KNOWLEDGE: Now, Everyman, be merry and glad!
   Your Good Deeds cometh now; ye may not be sad.
   Now is your Good Deeds whole and sound,
   Going upright upon the ground.
EVERYMAN: My heart is light, and shall be evermore;
   Now will I smite faster than I did before.
GOOD DEEDS: Everyman, pilgrim, my special friend,
   Blessed be thou without end;
   For thee is preparate the eternal glory.
   Ye have me made whole and sound,
   Therefore I will bide by thee in every stound.

EVERYMAN: Welcome, my Good Deeds! Now I hear thy voice,
    I weep for very sweetness of love.
KNOWLEDGE: Be no more sad, but ever rejoice;
    God seeth thy living in his throne above.
    Put on this garment to thy behove,
    Which is wet with your tears,
    Or else before God you may it miss,
    When ye to your journey's end come shall.
EVERYMAN: Gentle Knowledge, what do ye it call?
KNOWLEDGE: It is a garment of sorrow;
    From pain it will you borrow;
    Contrition it is,
    That getteth forgiveness;
    It pleaseth God passing well.
GOOD DEEDS: Everyman, will you wear it for your heal?
EVERYMAN: Now blessed be Jesu, Mary's Son,
    For now have I on true contrition.
    And let us go now without tarrying.
    Good Deeds, have we clear our reckoning?
GOOD DEEDS: Yea, indeed, I have here.
EVERYMAN: Then I trust we need not fear.
    Now, friends, let us not part in twain.
KNOWLEDGE: Nay, Everyman, that will we not, certain.
GOOD DEEDS: Yet must thou lead with thee
    Three persons of great might.
EVERYMAN: Who should they be?
GOOD DEEDS: Discretion and Strength they hight,
    And thy Beauty may not abide behind.
KNOWLEDGE: Also ye must call to mind
    Your Five Wits as for your counselors.
GOOD DEEDS: You must have them ready at all hours.
EVERYMAN: How shall I get them hither?
KNOWLEDGE: You must call them all together,
    And they will hear you incontinent.
EVERYMAN: My friends, come hither and be present,
    Discretion, Strength, my Five Wits, and Beauty.
    *(Enter Beauty, Strength, Discretion, and Five Wits.)*
BEAUTY: Here at your will we be all ready.
    What will ye that we should do?

GOOD DEEDS: That ye would with Everyman go,
   And help him in his pilgrimage.
   Advise you, will ye with him or not in that voyage?
STRENGTH: We will bring him all thither,
   To his help and comfort, ye may believe me.
DISCRETION: So will we go with him all together.
EVERYMAN: Almighty God, loved may thou be!
   I give thee laud that I have hither brought
   Strength, Discretion, Beauty, and Five Wits. Lack I nought.
   And my Good Deeds, with Knowledge clear,
   All be in my company at my will here.
   I desire no more to my business.
STRENGTH: And I, Strength, will by you stand in distress,
   Though thou would in battle fight on the ground.
FIVE WITS: And though it were through the world round,
   We will not depart for sweet ne sour.
BEAUTY: No more will I unto death's hour,
   Whatsoever thereof befall.
DISCRETION: Everyman, advise you first of all;
   Go with a good advisement and deliberation.
   We all give you virtuous monition
   That all shall be well.
EVERYMAN: My friends, harken what I will tell:
   I pray God reward you in his heavenly sphere.
   Now harken, all that be here,
   For I will make my testament
   Here before you all present:
   In alms half my good I will give with my hands twain
   In the way of charity with good intent,
   And the other half still shall remain
   In queth, to be returned there it ought to be.
   This I do in despite of the fiend of hell,
   To go quite out of his peril
   Ever after and this day.
KNOWLEDGE: Everyman, harken what I say:
   Go to Priesthood, I you advise,
   And receive of him in any wise
   The holy sacrament and ointment together.
   Then shortly see ye turn again hither;

We will all abide you here.

FIVE WITS: Yea, Everyman, hie you that ye ready were.
There is no emperor, king, duke, ne baron,
That of God hath commission
As hath the least priest in the world being;
For of the blessed sacraments pure and benign
He bareth the keys, and thereof hath the cure
For man's redemption—it is ever sure—
Which God for our soul's medicine
Gave us out of his heart with great pain
Here in this transitory life, for thee and me.
The blessed sacraments seven there be:
Baptism, confirmation, with priesthood good,
And the sacrament of God's precious flesh and blood,
Marriage, the holy extreme unction, and penance.
These seven be good to have in remembrance,
Gracious sacraments of high divinity.

EVERYMAN: Fain would I receive that holy body,
And meekly to my ghostly father I will go.

FIVE WITS: Everyman, that is the best that ye can do.
God will you to salvation bring,
For priesthood exceedeth all other thing:
To us Holy Scripture they do teach,
And converteth man from sin heaven to reach;
God hath to them more power given
Than to any angel that is in heaven.
With five words he may consecrate,
God's body in flesh and blood to make,
And handleth his Maker between his hands.
The priest bindeth and unbindeth all bands,
Both in earth and in heaven.
Thou ministers all the sacraments seven;
Though we kissed thy feet, thou were worthy;
Thou art surgeon that cureth sin deadly;
No remedy we find under God
But all only priesthood.
Everyman, God gave priests that dignity,
And setteth them in his stead among us to be.
Thus be they above angels in degree.

*(Exit Everyman to receive the last sacraments from the priest.)*

KNOWLEDGE: If priests be good, it is so, surely.
But when Jesus hanged on the cross with great smart,
There he gave out of his blessed heart
The same sacrament in great torment.
He sold them not to us, that Lord omnipotent.
Therefore Saint Peter the apostle doth say
That Jesu's curse hath all they
Which God their Savior do buy or sell,
Or they for any money do take or tell.
Sinful priests giveth the sinners example bad;
Their children sitteth by other men's fires, I have heard;
And some haunteth women's company
With unclean life, as lusts of lechery:
These be with sin made blind.

FIVE WITS: I trust to God no such may we find.
Therefore let us priesthood honor,
And follow their doctrine for our souls' succor.
We be their sheep, and they shepherds be,
By whom we all be kept in surety.
Peace, for yonder I see Everyman come,
Which hath made true satisfaction.

GOOD DEEDS: Methink it is he indeed.
*(Re-enter Everyman.)*

EVERYMAN: Now Jesu be your alder speed!
I have received the sacrament for my redemption,
And then mine extreme unction.
Blessed be all they that counseled me to take it!
And now, friends, let us go without longer respite;
I thank God that ye have tarried so long.
Now set each of you on this rod your hand,
And shortly follow me.
I go before there I would be; God be our guide!

STRENGTH: Everyman, we will not from you go
Till ye have done this voyage long.

DISCRETION: I, Discretion, will bide by you also.

KNOWLEDGE: And though this pilgrimage be never so strong,
I will never part you fro.

STRENGTH: Everyman, I will be as sure by thee

As ever I did by Judas Maccabee.
*(They go together to the grave.)*
EVERYMAN: Alas, I am so faint I may not stand;
    My limbs under me doth fold.
    Friends, let us not turn again to this land,
    Not for all the world's gold;
    For into this cave must I creep
    And turn to earth, and there to sleep.
BEAUTY: What, into this grave? Alas!
EVERYMAN: Yea, there shall ye consume, more and less.
BEAUTY: And what, should I smother here?
EVERYMAN: Yea, by my faith, and never more appear.
    In this world live no more we shall,
    But in heaven before the highest Lord of all.
BEAUTY: I cross out all this! Adieu, by Saint John!
    I take my cap in my lap, and am gone.
EVERYMAN: What, Beauty, whither will ye?
BEAUTY: Peace, I am deaf; I look not behind me,
    Not and thou wouldest give me all the gold in thy chest. *(Exit Beauty.)*
EVERYMAN: Alas, whereto may I trust?
    Beauty goeth fast away from me;
    She promised with me to live and die.
STRENGTH: Everyman, I will thee also forsake and deny;
    Thy game liketh me not at all.
EVERYMAN: Why, then, ye will forsake me all?
    Sweet Strength, tarry a little space.
STRENGTH: Nay, sir, by the rood of grace!
    I will hie me from thee fast,
    Though thou weep till thy heart to-brast.
EVERYMAN: Ye would ever bide by me, ye said.
STRENGTH: Yea, I have you far enough conveyed.
    Ye be old enough, I understand,
    Your pilgrimage to take on hand;
    I repent me that I hither came.
EVERYMAN: Strength, you to displease I am to blame;
    Yet promise is debt, this ye well wot.
STRENGTH: In faith, I care not.
    Thou art but a fool to complain;
    You spend your speech and waste your brain.

Go, thrust thee into the ground! *(Exit Strength.)*

EVERYMAN: I had wend surer I should you have found.
He that trusteth in his Strength
She him deceiveth at the length.
Both Strength and Beauty forsaketh me;
Yet they promised me fair and lovingly.

DISCRETION: Everyman, I will after Strength be gone;
As for me, I will leave you alone.

EVERYMAN: Why, Discretion, will ye forsake me?

DISCRETION: Yea, in faith, I will go from thee,
For when Strength goeth before
I follow after evermore.

EVERYMAN: Yet, I pray thee, for the love of the Trinity,
Look in my grave once piteously.

DISCRETION: Nay, so nigh will I not come;
Farewell, everyone! *(Exit Discretion.)*

EVERYMAN: O, all thing faileth, save God alone—
Beauty, Strength, and Discretion;
For when Death bloweth his blast,
They all run from me full fast.

FIVE WITS: Everyman, my leave now of thee I take;
I will follow the other, for here I thee forsake.

EVERYMAN: Alas, then may I wail and weep,
For I took you for my best friend.

FIVE WITS: I will no longer thee keep;
Now farewell, and there an end. *(Exit Five Wits.)*

EVERYMAN: O Jesu, help! All hath forsaken me.

GOOD DEEDS: Nay, Everyman; I will bide with thee.
I will not forsake thee indeed;
Thou shalt find me a good friend at need.

EVERYMAN: Gramercy, Good Deeds! Now may I true friends see.
They have forsaken me, every one;
I loved them better than my Good Deeds alone.
Knowledge, will ye forsake me also?

KNOWLEDGE: Yea, Everyman, when ye to Death shall go;
But not yet, for no manner of danger.

EVERYMAN: Gramercy, Knowledge, with all my heart.

KNOWLEDGE: Nay, yet I will not from hence depart
Till I see where ye shall be come.

EVERYMAN: Methink, alas, that I must be gone
  To make my reckoning and my debts pay,
  For I see my time is nigh spent away.
  Take example, all ye that this do hear or see,
  How they that I loved best do forsake me,
  Except my Good Deeds that bideth truly.
GOOD DEEDS: All earthly things is but vanity:
  Beauty, Strength, and Discretion do man forsake,
  Foolish friends, and kinsmen, that fair spake—
  All fleeth save Good Deeds, and that am I.
EVERYMAN: Have mercy on me, God most mighty;
  And stand by me, thou mother and maid, Holy Mary.
GOOD DEEDS: Fear not; I will speak for thee.
EVERYMAN: Here I cry God mercy.
GOOD DEEDS: Short our end, and minish our pain;
  Let us go and never come again.
EVERYMAN: Into thy hands, Lord, my soul I commend;
  Receive it, Lord, that it be not lost.
  As thou me boughtest, so me defend,
  And save me from the fiend's boast,
  That I may appear with that blessed host
  That shall be saved at the day of doom.
  *In manus tuas,* of might's most
  For ever, *commendo spiritum meum.*
  *(Everyman and Good Deeds descend into the grave.)*
KNOWLEDGE: Now hath he suffered that we all shall endure;
  The Good Deeds shall make all sure.
  Now hath he made ending.
  Methinketh that I hear angels sing,
  And make great joy and melody
  Where Everyman's soul received shall be.
ANGEL: Come, excellent elect spouse, to Jesu!
  Here above thou shalt go
  Because of thy singular virtue.
  Now the soul is taken the body fro,
  Thy reckoning is crystal clear.
  Now shalt thou in to the heavenly sphere,
  Unto the which all ye shall come
  That liveth well before the day of doom. *(Exit Knowledge.)*

# The School for Scandal

Richard Brinsley Sheridan
1777

**Comic**
**Scene:** Lady Sneerwell's dressing room

Lady Sneerwell
Snake
Servant
Sir Joseph Surface
Maria
Mrs. Candour
Mr. Crabtree
Sir Benjamin Backbite


LADY SNEER.: The paragraphs, you say, Mr. Snake, were all inserted?

SNAKE: They were, madam; and, as I copied them myself in a feigned hand, there can be no suspicion whence they came.

LADY SNEER.: Did you circulate the report of Lady Brittle's intrigue with Captain Boastall?

SNAKE: That's in as fine a train as your ladyship could wish. In the common course of things, I think it must reach Mrs. Clackitt's ears within four-and-twenty hours; and then, you know, the business is as good as done.

LADY SNEER.: Why, truly, Mrs. Clackitt has a very pretty talent, and a great deal of industry.

SNAKE: True, madam, and has been tolerably successful in her day. To my knowledge, she has been the cause of six matches being broken off, and three sons being disinherited; of four forced elopements, and as many close confinements; nine separate maintenances, and two divorces. Nay, I have more than once traced her causing a tête-à-tête in the "Town and Country Magazine," when the parties, perhaps, had never seen each other's face before in the course of their lives.

LADY SNEER.: She certainly has talents, but her manner is gross.

SNAKE: 'Tis very true. She generally designs well, has a free tongue and a bold invention; but her colouring is too dark, and her outlines often extravagant. She wants that delicacy of tint, and mellowness of sneer, which distinguish your ladyship's scandal.

LADY SNEER.: You are partial, Snake.

SNAKE: Not in the least; everybody allows that Lady Sneerwell can do more with a word or look than many can with the most laboured detail, even when they happen to have a little truth on their side to support it.

LADY SNEER.: Yes, my dear Snake; and I am no hypocrite to deny the satisfaction I reap from the success of my efforts. Wounded myself, in the early part of my life, by the envenomed tongue of slander, I confess I have since known no pleasure equal to the reducing others to the level of my own injured reputation.

SNAKE: Nothing can be more natural. But, Lady Sneerwell, there is one affair in which you have lately employed me, wherein, I confess, I am at a loss to guess your motives.

LADY SNEER.: I conceive you mean with respect to my neighbour, Sir Peter Teazle, and his family?

SNAKE: I do. Here are two young men, to whom Sir Peter has acted as a kind of guardian since their father's death; the eldest possessing the most amiable character, and universally well spoken of— the youngest, the most dissipated and extravagant young fellow in the kingdom, without friends or character: the former an avowed admirer of your ladyship, and apparently your favourite; the latter attached to Maria, Sir Peter's ward, and confessedly beloved by her. Now, on the face of these circumstances, it is utterly unaccountable to me, why you, the widow of a city knight, with a good jointure, should not close with the passion of a man of such character and expectations as Mr. Surface; and more so why you should be so uncommonly earnest to destroy the mutual attachment subsisting between his brother Charles and Maria.

LADY SNEER.: Then, at once to unravel this mystery, I must inform you that love has no share whatever in the intercourse between Mr. Surface and me.

SNAKE: No!

LADY SNEER.: His real attachment is to Maria or her fortune; but, finding in his brother a favoured rival, he has been obliged to mask his pretensions, and profit by my assistance.

SNAKE: Yet still I am more puzzled why you should interest yourself in his success.

LADY SNEER.: Heavens! how dull you are! Cannot you surmise the weakness which I hitherto, through shame, have concealed even from you? Must I confess that Charles—that libertine, that extravagant, that bankrupt in fortune and reputation—that he it is for whom I am thus anxious and malicious, and to gain whom I would sacrifice everything?

SNAKE: Now, indeed, your conduct appears consistent; but how came you and Mr. Surface so confidential?

LADY SNEER.: For our mutual interest. I have found him out a long time since I know him to be artful, selfish, and malicious—in short, a sentimental knave; while with Sir Peter, and indeed with all his acquaintance, he passes for a youthful miracle of prudence, good sense, and benevolence.

SNAKE: Yes, yet Sir Peter vows he has not his equal in England; and, above all, he praises him as a man of sentiment.

LADY SNEER.: True; and with the assistance of his sentiment and hypocrisy he has brought Sir Peter entirely into his interest with regard to Maria; while poor Charles has no friend in the house— though, I fear, he has a powerful one in Maria's heart, against whom we must direct our schemes.

*(Enter Servant.)*

SER.: Mr. Surface.

LADY SNEER.: Show him up. *(Exit Servant.)* He generally calls about this time. I don't wonder at people giving him to me for a lover.

*(Enter Joseph Surface.)*

JOS. SURFACE: My dear Lady Sneerwell, how do you do to-day? Mr. Snake, your most obedient.

LADY SNEER.: Snake has just been rallying me on our mutual attachment; but I have informed him of our real views. You know how useful he has been to us; and, believe me, the confidence is not ill-placed.

JOS. SURFACE: Madam, it is impossible for me to suspect a man of Mr. Snake's sensibility and discernment.

LADY SNEER.: Well, well, no compliments now; but tell me when you saw your mistress, Maria—or, what is more material to me, your brother.

JOS. SURFACE: I have not seen either since I left you; but I can inform you that they never meet. Some of your stories have taken a good efect on Maria.

LADY SNEER.: Ah, my dear Snake! the merit of this belongs to you. But do your brother's distresses increase?

JOS. SURFACE: Every hour. I am told he has had another execution in the house yesterday. In short, his dissipation and extravagance exceed anything I have ever heard of.

LADY SNEER.: Poor Charles!

JOS. SURFACE: True, madam; notwithstanding his vices, one can't help feeling for him. Poor Charles! I'm sure I wish it were in my power to be of any essential service to him; for the man who does not share in the distresses of a brother, even though merited by his own misconduct, deserves—

LADY SNEER.: O Lud! you are going to be moral, and forget that you are among friends.

JOS SURFACE: Egad, that's true! I'll keep that sentiment till I see Sir Peter. However, it is certainly a charity to rescue Maria from such a libertine, who, if he is to be reclaimed, can be so only by a person of your ladyship's superior accomplishments and understanding.

SNAKE: I believe, Lady Sneerwell, here's company coming; I'll go and copy the letter I mentioned to you. Mr. Surface, your most obedient.

JOS. SURFACE: I have lately detected him in frequent conference with old Rowley, who was formerly my father's steward, and has never, you know, been a friend of mine.

LADY SNEER.: And do you think he would betray us?

JOS. SURFACE: Nothing more likely: take my word for't, Lady Sneerwell, that fellow hasn't virtue enough to be faithful even to his own villany. Ah, Maria!
*(Enter Maria.)*

LADY SNEER.: Maria, my dear, how do you do? What's that matter?

MAR.: Oh! there's that disagreeable lover of mine, Sir Benjamin Backbite, has just called at my guardian's, with his odious uncle, Crabtree; so I slipped out, and ran hither to avoid them.

LADY SNEER.: Is that all?

JOS. SURFACE: If my brother Charles had been of the party, madam, perhaps you would not have been so much alarmed.

LADY SNEER.: Nay, now you are severe; for I dare swear the truth of the matter is, Maria heard you were here. But, my dear, what has Sir Benjamin done, that you should avoid him so?

MAR.: Oh, he has done nothing—but 'tis for what he has said: his conversation is a perpetual libel on all his acquaintance.

JOS. SURFACE: Ay, and the worst of it is, there is no advantage in not knowing him; for he'll abuse a stranger just as soon as his best friend: and his uncle's as bad.

LADY SNEER.: Nay, but we should make allowance; Sir Benjamin is a wit and a poet.

MAR.: For my part, I own, madam, wit loses its respect with me, when I see it in company with malice. What do you think, Mr. Surface?

JOS. SURFACE: Certainly, madam; to smile at the jest which plants a thorn in another's breast is to become a principal in the mischief.

LADY SNEER.: Psha! there's no possibility of being witty without a little ill-nature: the malice of a good thing is the barb that makes it stick. What's your opinion, Mr. Surface?

JOS. SURFACE: To be sure, madam; that conversation, where the spirit of raillery is suppressed, will ever appear tedious and insipid.

MAR.: Well, I'll not debate how far scandal may be allowable; but in a man, I am sure, it is always contemptible. We have pride, envy, rivalship, and a thousand motives to depreciate each other; but the male slanderer must have the cowardice of a woman before he can traduce one.

*(Re-enter Servant.)*

SER.: Madam, Mrs. Candour is below, and, if your ladyship's at leisure, will leave her carriage.

LADY SNEER.: Beg her to walk in. *(Exit Servant.)* Now, Maria, here is a character to your taste; for, though Mrs. Candour is a little talkative, everybody knows her to be the best-natured and best sort of woman.

MAR.: Yes, with a very gross affectation of good nature and benevolence, she does more mischief than the direct malice of old Crabtree.

JOS. SURFACE: I'faith that's true, Lady Sneerwell: whenever I hear the current running against the characters of my friends, I never think them in such danger as when Candour undertakes their defense.

LADY SNEER.: Hush! —here she is!

*(Enter Mrs. Candour.)*

MRS. CAN.: My dear Lady Sneerwell, how have you been this century?

—Mr. Surface, what news do you hear? —though indeed it is no matter, for I think one hears nothing else but scandal.

JOS. SURFACE: Just so, indeed, ma'am.

MRS. CAN.: Oh, Maria! child,—what, is the whole affair off between you and Charles? His extravagance, I presume—the whole town talks of nothing else.

MAR.: I am very sorry, ma'am, the town has so little to do.

MRS. CAN.: True, true, child: but there's no stopping people's tongues. I own I was hurt to hear it, as I indeed was to learn, from the same quarter, that your guardian, Sir Peter, and Lady Teazle have not agreed lately as well as could be wished.

MAR.: 'Tis strangely impertinent for people to busy themselves so.

MRS. CAN.: Very true, child; but what's to be done? People will talk—there's no preventing it. Why, it was but yesterday I was told that Miss Gadabout had eloped with Sir Filagree Flirt. But, Lord! there's no minding what one hears; though, to be sure, I had this from very good authority.

MAR.: Such reports are highly scandalous.

MRS. CAN.: So they are, child—shameful, shameful! But the world is so censorious, no character escapes. Lord, now who would have suspected your friend, Miss Prim, of an indiscretion? Yet such is the ill-nature of people, that they say her uncle stopped her last week, just as she was stepping into the York mail with her dancing-master.

MAR.: I'll answer for't there are no grounds for that report.

MRS. CAN.: Ah, no foundation in the world, I dare swear: no more, probably, than the story circulated last month, of Mrs. Festino's affair with Colonel Cassino—though, to be sure, that matter was never rightly cleared up.

JOS. SURFACE: The license of invention some people take is monstrous indeed.

MAR.: 'Tis so; but, in my opinion, those who report such things are equally culpable.

MRS. CAN.: To be sure they are; tale-bearers are as bad as the tale-makers —'tis an old observation, and a very true one: but what's to be done, as I said before? how will you prevent people from talking? To-day, Mrs. Clackitt assured me, Mr. and Mrs. Honeymoon were at last become mere man and wife, like the rest of their acquaintance. She likewise hinted that a certain widow, in the next street, had got rid of her dropsy and recovered her shape in a most surprising manner. And at the same time Miss Tattle, who was by, affirmed, that Lord Buffalo had discovered his lady at a house of no extraordinary fame; and that Sir Harry Bouquet and Tom Saunter were to measure swords on a similar provocation. But, Lord, do you think I would report these things! No, no! tale-bearers, as I said before, are just as bad as the tale-makers.

JOS. SURFACE: Ah! Mrs. Candour, if everybody had your forbearance and good nature!

MRS. CAN.: I confess, Mr. Surface, I cannot bear to hear people attacked behind their backs; and when ugly circumstances come out against our acquaintance I own I always love to think the best. By-the-by, I hope 'tis not true that your brother is absolutely ruined?

JOS. SURFACE: I am afraid his circumstances are very bad indeed, ma'am.

MRS. CAN.: Ah!—I heard so—but you must tell him to keep up his spirits; everybody almost is in the same way: Lord Spindle, Sir Thomas Splint, Captain Quinze, and Mr. Nickit—all up, I hear, within this week; so, if Charles is undone, he'll find half his acquaintance ruined too, and that, you know, is a consolation.

JOS. SURFACE: Doubtless, ma'am—a very great one.

*(Re-enter Servant.)*

SER.: Mr. Crabtree and Sir Benjamin Backbite. *(Exit Servant.)*

LADY SNEER.: So, Maria, you see your lover pursues you; positively you shan't escape.

*(Enter Crabtree and Sir Benjamin Backbite.)*

CRAB.: Lady Sneerwell, I kiss your hand. Mrs. Candour, I don't believe you are acquainted with my nephew, Sir Benjamin Backbite? Egad, ma'am, he has a pretty wit, and is a pretty poet too. Isn't he, Lady Sneerwell?

SIR BEN.: Oh, fie, uncle!

CRAB.: Nay, egad it's true: I back him at a rebus or a charade against the best rhymer in the kingdom. Has your ladyship heard the epigram he wrote last week on Lady Frizzle's feather catching fire? —Do, Benjamin, repeat it, or the charade you made last night extempore at Mrs. Drowzie's conversazione. Come now; your first is the name of a fish, your second a great naval commander, and—

SIR BEN.: Uncle, now—pr'ythee—

CRAB.: I'faith, ma'am, 'twould surprise you to hear how ready he is at all these sort of things.

LADY SNEER.: I wonder, Sir Benjamin, you never publish anything.

SIR BEN.: To say truth, ma'am, 'tis very vulgar to print; and, as my little productions are mostly satires and lampoons on particular people, I find they circulate more by giving copies in confidence to the friends of the parties. However, I have some elegies, which, when favoured with this lady's smiles, I mean to give the public. *(Pointing to Maria.)*

CRAB.: *(To Maria.)* 'Fore heaven, ma'am, they'll immortalize you—you will be handed down to posterity, like Petrarch's Laura, or Waller's Sacharissa.

SIR BEN.: *(To Maria.)* Yes, madam, I think you will like them, when you shall see them on a beautiful quarto page, where a neat rivulet of text shall meander through a meadow of margin. 'Fore Gad, they will be the most elegant things of their kind!

CRAB.: But, ladies, that's true—have you heard the news?

MRS. CAN.: What, sir, do you mean the report of—

CRAB.: No, ma'am, that's not it. —Miss Nicely is going to be married to her own footman.

MRS. CAN.: Impossible!

CRAB.: Ask Sir Benjamin.

SIR BEN.: 'Tis very true, ma'am: everything is fixed, and the wedding liveries bespoke.

CRAB.: Yes—and they do say there were pressing reasons for it.

LADY SNEER.: Why, I have heard something of this before.

MRS. CAN.: It can't be—and I wonder any one should believe such a story of so prudent a lady as Miss Nicely.

SIR BEN.: O Lud! ma'am, that's the very reason 'twas believed at once. She has always been so cautious and so reserved, that everybody was sure there was some reason for it at bottom.

MRS. CAN.: Why, to be sure, a tale of scandal is as fatal to the credit of a prudent lady of her stamp as a fever is generally to those of the strongest constitutions. but there is a sort of puny sickly reputation, that is always ailing, yet will outlive the robuster characters of a hundred prudes.

SIR BEN.: True, madam, there are valetudinarians in reputation as well as constitution, who, being conscious of their weak part, avoid the least breath of air, and supply their want of stamina by care and circumspection.

MRS. CAN.: Well, but this may be all a mistake. You know, Sir Benjamin, very trifling circumstances often give rise to the most injurious tales.

CRAB.: That they do, I'll be sworn, ma'am. Did you ever hear how Miss Piper came to lose her lover and her character last summer at Tunbridge? —Sir Benjamin, you remember it?

SIR BEN.: Oh, to be sure! —the most whimsical circumstance.

LADY SNEER.: How was it, pray?

CRAB.: Why, one evening, at Mrs. Ponto's assembly, the conversation happened to turn on the breeding Nova Scotia sheep in this country. Says a young lady in company, I have known instances of it; for Miss Letitia Piper, a first cousin of mine, had a Nova Scotia sheep that produced her twins. "What!" cries the Lady Dowager Dundizzy (who you know is as deaf as a post), "has Miss Piper had twins?" This mistake, as you may imagine, threw the whole company into a fit of laughter. However, 'twas the next morning everywhere reported, and in a few days believed by the whole town, that Miss Letitia Piper had atually been brought to bed of a fine boy and girl: and in less than a week there were some people who could name the father, and the farm-house where the babies were put to nurse.

LADY SNEER.: Strange, indeed!

CRAB.: Matter of fact, I assure you. O Lud! Mr. Surface, pray is it true that your uncle, Sir Oliver, is coming home?

JOS. SURFACE: Not that I know of, indeed, sir.

CRAB.: He has been in the East Indies a long time. You can scarcely remember him, I believe? Sad comfort, whenever he returns, to hear how your brother has gone on!

JOS. SURFACE: Charles has been imprudent, sir, to be sure; but I hope no busy people have already prejudiced Sir Oliver against him. He may reform.

SIR BEN.: To be sure he may; for my part I never believed him to be so utterly void of principle as people say; and though he has lost all his friends, I am told nobody is better spoken of by the Jews.

CRAB.: That's true, egad, nephew. If the old Jewry was a ward, I believe Charles would be an alderman: no man more popular there, 'fore Gad! I hear he pays as many annuities as the Irish tontine; and that, whenever he is sick, they have prayers for the recovery of his health in all the synagogues.

SIR BEN.: Yet no man lives in greater splendour. They tell me, when he entertains his friends he will sit down to dinner with a dozen of his own securities; have a score of tradesmen in the antechamber, and an officer behind every guest's chair.

JOS SURFACE: This may be entertainment to you, gentlemen, but you pay very little regard to the feelings of a brother.

MAR. *(Aside.)* Their malice is intolerable!— *(Aloud.)* Lady Sneerwell, I must wish you a good morning: I'm not very well. *(Exit.)*

# The Contrast

Royall Tyler
1787

**Comic**
**Scene:** Charlotte's apartment

Maria
Charlotte
Letitia
Dimple
Manly

MARIA: I don't know how it was,—I hope he did not think me indelicate,—but I asked him, I believe, to sit down, or pointed to a chair. He sat down, and, instead of having recourse to observations upon the weather, or hackneyed criticisms upon the theatre, he entered readily into a conversation worthy a man of sense to speak, and a lady of delicacy and sentiment to hear. He was not strictly handsome, but he spoke the language of sentiment, and his eyes looked tenderness and honour.

CHARLOTTE: Oh! *(Eagerly.)* you sentimental, grave girls, when your hearts are once touched, beat us rattles a bar's length. And so you are quite in love with this he-angel?

MARIA: In love with him! How can you rattle so, Charlotte? am I not going to be miserable? *(Sighs.)* In love with a gentleman I never saw but one hour in my life, and don't know his name! No; I only wished that the man I shall marry may look, and talk, and act, just like him. Besides, my dear, he is a married man.

CHARLOTTE: Why, that was good-natured—he told you so, I suppose, in mere charity, to prevent you falling in love with him?

MARIA: He didn't tell me so; *(Peevishly.)* he looked as if he was married.

CHARLOTTE: How, my dear; did he look sheepish?

MARIA: I am sure he has a susceptible heart, and the ladies of his acquaintance must be very stupid not to—

CHARLOTTE: Hush! I hear some person coming.
*(Enter Letitia.)*

LETITIA: My dear Maria, I am happy to see you. Lud! what a pity it is that you have purchased your wedding clothes.

MARIA: I think so. *(Sighing.)*

LETITIA: Why, my dear, there is the sweetest parcel of silks come over you ever saw! Nancy Brilliant has a full suit come; she sent over her measure, and it fits her to a hair; it is immensely dressy, and made for a court-hoop. I thought they said the large hoops were going out of fashion.

CHARLOTTE: Did you see the hat? Is it a fact that the deep laces round the border is still the fashion?

DIMPLE: *(Within.)* Upon my honour, Sir.

MARIA: Ha! Dimple's voice! My dear, I must take leave of you. There are some things necessary to be done at our house. Can't I go through the other room?

*(Enter Dimple and Manly.)*

DIMPLE: Ladies, your most obedient.

CHARLOTTE: Miss Van Rough, shall I present my brother Henry to you? Colonel Manly, Maria,—Miss Van Rough, brother.

MARIA: Her brother! *(Turns and sees Manly.)* Oh! my heart! the very gentleman I have been praising.

MANLY: The same amiable girl I saw this morning!

CHARLOTTE: Why, you look as if you were acquainted.

MANLY: I unintentionally intruded into this lady's presence this morning, for which she was so good as to promise me her forgiveness.

CHARLOTTE: Oh! ho! is that the case! Have these two penserosos been together? Were they Henry's eyes that looked so tenderly? *(Aside.)* And so you promised to pardon him? and could you be so good-natured? have you really forgiven him? I beg you would do it for my sake. *(Whispering loud to Maria.)* But, my dear, as you are in such haste, it would be cruel to detain you; I can show you the way through the other room.

MARIA: Spare me, my sprightly friend.

MANLY: The lady does not, I hope, intend to deprive us of the pleasure of her company so soon.

CHARLOTTE: She has only a mantua-maker who waits for her at home. But, as I am to give my opinion of the dress, I think she cannot go yet. We were talking of the fashions when you came in, but I suppose the subject must be changed to something of more importance now. Mr. Dimple, will you favour us with an account of the public entertainments?

DIMPLE: Why, really, Miss Manly, you could not have asked me a question more *mal-apropos*. For my part, I must confess that, to a man who has travelled, there is nothing that is worthy the name of amusement to be found in this city.

CHARLOTTE: Except visiting the ladies.

DIMPLE: Pardon me, Madam; that is the avocation of a man of taste. But for amusement, I positively know of nothing that can be called so, unless you dignify with that title the hopping once a fortnight to the sound of two or three squeaking fiddles, and the clattering of the old tavern windows, or sitting to see the miserable mummers, whom you call actors, murder comedy and make a farce of tragedy.

MANLY: Do you never attend the theatre, Sir?

DIMPLE: I was tortured there once.

CHARLOTTE: Pray, Mr. Dimple, was it a tragedy or a comedy?

DIMPLE: Faith, Madam, I cannot tell: for I sat with my back to the stage all the time admiring a much better actress than any there—a lady who played the fine woman to perfection; though, by the laugh of the horrid creatures round me, I suppose it was comedy. Yet, on second thoughts, it might be some hero in a tragedy, dying so comically as to set the whole house in an uproar. Colonel, I presume you have been in Europe?

MANLY: Indeed, Sir, I was never ten leagues from the continent.

DIMPLE: Believe me, Colonel, you have an immense pleasure to come; and when you shall have seen the brilliant exhibitions of Europe, you will learn to despise the amusements of this country as much as I do.

MANLY: Therefore I do not wish to see them; for I can never esteem that knowledge valuable which tends to give me a distaste for my native country.

DIMPLE: Well, Colonel, though you have not travelled, you have read.

MANLY: I have, a little; and by it have discovered that there is a laudable partiality which ignorant, untravelled men entertain for everything that belongs to their native country. I call it laudable; it injures no one; adds to their own happiness; and, when extended, becomes the noble principle of patriotism. Travelled gentlemen rise superior, in their own opinion, to this; but if the contempt which they contract for their country is the most valuable acquisition of their travels, I am far from thinking that their time and money are well spent.

MARIA: What noble sentiments!

CHARLOTTE: Let my brother set out where he will in the fields of conversation, he is sure to end his tour in the temple of gravity.

MANLY: Forgive me, my sister. I love my country, it has its foibles undoubtedly,—some foreigners will with pleasure remark them—but such remarks fall very ungracefully from the lips of her citizens.

DIMPLE: You are perfectly in the right, Colonel—America has her faults.

MANLY: Yes, Sir; and we, her children, should blush for them in private, and endeavour, as individuals, to reform them. But, if our country has its errors in common with other countries, I am proud to say America—I mean the United States—has displayed virtues and achievements which modern nations may admire, but of which they have seldom set us the example.

CHARLOTTE: But, brother, we must introduce you to some of our gay folks, and let you see the city, such as it is. Mr. Dimple is known to almost every family in town; he will doubtless take a pleasure in introducing you.

DIMPLE: I shall esteem every service I can render your brother an honour.

MANLY: I fear the business I am upon will take up all my time, and my family will be anxious to hear from me.

MARIA: His family! but what is it to me that he is married! *(Aside.)* Pray, how did you leave your lady, Sir?

CHARLOTTE: My brother is not married; *(Observing her anxiety.)* it is only an odd way he has of expressing himself. Pray, brother, is this business, which you make your continual excuse, a secret?

MANLY: No, sister; I came hither to solicit the honourable Congress, that a number of my brave old soldiers may be put upon the pension-list, who were, at first, not judged to be so materially wounded as to need the public assistance. My sister says true: *(To Maria.)* I call my late soldiers my family. Those who were not in the field in the late glorious contest, and those who were, have their respective merits; but, I confess, my old brother-soldiers are dearer to me than the former description. Friendships made in adversity are lasting; our countrymen may forget us, but that is no reason why we should forget one another. But I must leave you; my time of engagement approaches.

CHARLOTTE: Well, but, brother, if you will go, will you please to conduct my fair friend home? You live in the same street—I was to have gone with her myself.— *(Aside.)* A lucky thought.

MARIA: I am obliged to your sister, Sir, and was just intending to go. *(Going.)*

MANLY: I shall attend her with pleasure.

*(Exit with Maria, followed by Dimple and Charlotte.)*

MARIA: Now, pray, don't betray me to your brother.

CHARLOTTE: *(Just as she sees him make a motion to take his leave.)* One word with you, brother, if you please. *(Follows them out.)*

*(Manent, Dimple and Letitia.)*

DIMPLE: You received the billet I sent you, I presume?

LETITIA: Hush!—Yes.

DIMPLE: When shall I pay my respects to you?

LETITIA: At eight I shall be unengaged.

*(Reenter Charlotte.)*

DIMPLE: Did my lovely angel receive my billet? *(To Charlotte.)*

CHARLOTTE: Yes.

DIMPLE: What hour shall I expect with impatience?

CHARLOTTE: At eight I shall be at home unengaged.

DIMPLE: Unfortunate! I have a horrid engagement of business at that hour. Can't you finish your visit earlier and let six be the happy hour?

CHARLOTTE: You know your influence over me. *(Exeunt severally.)*

# Trifles

Susan Glaspell
1916

**Dramatic**
**Scene:** the kitchen of the now abandoned farmhouse of Mr. and Mrs.
John Wright

George Henderson, county attorney
Henry Peters, sheriff
Lewis Hale, a neighboring farmer
Mrs. Hale, his wife
Mrs. Peters, the sheriff's wife

COUNTY ATTORNEY: *(Rubbing his hands.)* This feels good. Come up to the
fire, ladies.

MRS. PETERS: *(After taking a step forward.)* I'm not—cold.

SHERIFF: *(Unbuttoning his overcoat and stepping away from the stove
as if to mark the beginning of official business.)* Now, Mr. Hale,
before we move things about, you explain to Mr. Henderson just
what you saw when you came here yesterday morning.

COUNTY ATTORNEY: By the way, has anything been moved? Are things
just as you left them yesterday?

SHERIFF: *(Looking about.)* It's just the same. When it dropped below
zero last night I thought I'd better send Frank out this morning to
make a fire for us—no use getting pneumonia with a big case on,
but I told him not to touch anything except the stove—and you
know Frank.

COUNTY ATTORNEY: Somebody should have been left here yesterday.

SHERIFF: Oh—yesterday. When I had to send Frank to Morris Center for
that man who went crazy—I want you to know I had my hands
full yesterday, I knew you could get back from Omaha by today
and as long as I went over everything here myself—

COUNTY ATTORNEY: Well, Mr. Hale, tell just what happened when you
came here yesterday morning.

HALE: Harry and I had started to town with a load of potatoes. We
came along the road from my place and as I got here I said, "I'm
going to see if I can't get John Wright to go in with me on a party
telephone." I spoke to Wright about it once before and he put

me off, saying folks talked too much anyway, and all he asked was peace and quiet—I guess you know about how much he talked himself; but I thought maybe if I went to the house and talked about it before his wife, though I said to Harry that I didn't know as what his wife wanted made much difference to John—

COUNTY ATTORNEY: Let's talk about that later, Mr. Hale. I do want to talk about that, but tell me now just what happened when you got to the house.

HALE: I didn't hear or see anything; I knocked at the door, and still it was all quiet inside. I knew they must be up, it was past eight o'clock. So I knocked again, and I thought I heard somebody say, "Come in." I wasn't sure, I'm not sure yet, but I opened the door—this door *(Indicating the door by which the two women are still standing.)* and there in that rocker— *(Pointing to it.)* sat Mrs. Wright.

*(They all look at the rocker.)*

COUNTY ATTORNEY: What—was she doing?

HALE: She was rockin' back and forth. She had her apron in her hand and was kind of—pleating it.

COUNTY ATTORNEY: And how did she—look?

HALE: Well, she looked queer.

COUNTY ATTORNEY: How do you mean—queer?

HALE: Well, as if she didn't know what she was going to do next. And kind of done up.

COUNTY ATTORNEY: How did she seem to feel about your coming?

HALE: Why, I don't think she minded—one way or other. She didn't pay much attention. I said, "How do, Mrs. Wright, it's cold ain't it?" And she said, "Is it?"—and went on kind of pleating at her apron. Well, I was surprised; she didn't ask me to come up to the stove, or to set down, but just sat there, not even looking at me, so I said, "I want to see John." And then she—laughed. I guess you would call it a laugh. I thought of Harry and the team outside, so I said a little sharp: "Can't I see John?" "No," she says, kind o' dull like. "Ain't he home?" says I. "Yes," says she, "he's home." "Then why can't I see him?" I asked her, out of patience. "'Cause he's dead," says she. *"Dead?"* says I. She just nodded her head, not getting a bit excited, but rockin' back and forth. "Why—where is he?" says I, not knowing what to say. She just pointed upstairs—like that *(Himself pointing to the room above.)*

I got up with the idea of going up there. I walked from there to here—then I says, "Why, what did he die of?" "He died of a rope round his neck," says she, and just went on pleatin' at her apron. Well, I went out and called Harry. I thought I might—need help. We went upstairs and there he was lyin'—

COUNTY ATTORNEY: I think I'd rather have you go into that upstairs, where you can point it all out. Just go on now with the rest of the story.

HALE: Well, my first thought was to get that rope off. It looked... *(Stops, his face twitches.)* ...but Harry, he went up to him, and he said, "No, he's dead all right, and we'd better not touch anything." So we went back down stairs. She was still sitting that same way, "Has anybody been notified?" I asked. "No," says she, unconcerned. "Who did this, Mrs. Wright?" said Harry. He said it businesslike—and she stopped pleatin' of her apron. "I don't know," she says. "You don't *know?*" says Harry. "No," says she. "Weren't you sleepin' in the bed with him?" says Harry. "Yes," says she, "but I was on the inside." "Somebody slipped a rope round his neck and strangled him and you didn't wake up?" says Harry. "I didn't wake up," she said after him. We must 'a looked as if we didn't see how that could be, for after a minute she said, "I sleep sound." Harry was going to ask her more questions but I said maybe we ought to let her tell her story first to the coroner, or the sheriff, so Harry went fast as he could to Rivers' place, where there's a telephone.

COUNTY ATTORNEY: And what did Mrs. Wright do when she knew that you had gone for the coroner?

HALE: She moved from that chair to this one over here *(Pointing to a small chair in the corner.)* and just sat there with her hands held together and looking down. I got a feeling that I ought to make some conversation, so I said I had come in to see if John wanted to put in a telephone, and at that she started to laugh, and then she stopped and looked at me—scared.

*(The County Attorney who has had his notebook out makes a note.)*

HALE: I dunno, maybe it wasn't scared. I wouldn't like to say it was. Soon Harry got back, and then Dr. Lloyd came, and you, Mr. Peters, and so I guess that's all I know that you don't.

COUNTY ATTORNEY: *(Looking around.)* I guess we'll go upstairs first—and then out to the barn and around there. *(To the Sheriff.)* You're convinced that there was nothing important here—nothing that would point to any motive.

SHERIFF: Nothing here but kitchen things.

*(The County Attorney after again looking around the kitchen, opens the door of a cupboard closet. He gets up on a chair and looks on a shelf. Pulls his hand away, sticky.)*

COUNTY ATTORNEY: Here's a nice mess.

*(The women draw nearer.)*

MRS. PETERS: *(To the other woman.)* Oh, her fruit; it did freeze. *(To the County Attorney.)* She worried about that when it turned so cold. She said the fire'd go out and her jars would break.

SHERIFF: Well, can you beat the woman! Held for murder and worryin' about her preserves.

COUNTY ATTORNEY: I guess before we're through she may have something more serious than preserves to worry about.

HALE: Well, women are used to worrying over trifles.

*(The two women move a little closer together.)*

COUNTY ATTORNEY: *(With the gallantry of a young politician.)* And yet, for all their worries, what would we do without the ladies?

*(The women do not unbend. He goes to the sink, takes a dipperful of water from the pail and pouring it into a basin, washes his hands. Starts to wipe them on the roller towel, turns it for a cleaner place.)*

COUNTY ATTORNEY: Dirty towels! *(Kicks his foot against the pans under the sink.)* Not much a housekeeper, would you say, ladies?

MRS. HALE: *(Stiffly.)* There's a great deal of work to be done on a farm.

COUNTY ATTORNEY: To be sure. And yet *(With a little bow to her.)* I know there are some Dickson county farmhouses which do not have such roller towels. *(He gives it a pull to expose its full length again.)*

MRS. HALE: Those towels get dirty awful quick. Men's hands aren't always as clean as they might be.

COUNTY ATTORNEY: Ah, loyal to your sex, I see. But you and Mrs. Wright were neighbors. I suppose you were friends, too.

MRS. HALE: *(Shaking her head.)* I've not seen much of her of late years. I've not been in this house—it's more than a year.

COUNTY ATTORNEY: And why was that? You didn't like her?

MRS. HALE: I liked her well enough. Farmers' wives have their hands full, Mr. Henderson. And then—

COUNTY ATTORNEY: Yes—?

MRS. HALE: *(Looking about.)* It never seemed a very cheerful place.

COUNTY ATTORNEY: No—it's not cheerful. I shouldn't say she had the homemaking instinct.

MRS. HALE: Well, I don't know as Wright had, either.

COUNTY ATTORNEY: You mean that they didn't get on very well?

MRS. HALE: No, I don't mean anything. But I don't think a place'd be any cheerfuller for John Wright's being in it.

COUNTY ATTORNEY: I'd like to talk more of that a little later. I want to get the lay of things upstairs now. *(He goes to the left, where three steps lead to a stair door.)*

SHERIFF: I suppose anything Mrs. Peters does'll be all right. She was to take in some clothes for her, you know, and a few little things. We left in such a hurry yesterday.

COUNTY ATTORNEY: Yes, but I would like to see what you take, Mrs. Peters, and keep an eye out for anything that might be of use to us.

MRS. PETERS: Yes, Mr. Henderson.

*(The women listen to the men's steps on the stairs, then look about the kitchen.)*

MRS. HALE: I'd hate to have men coming into my kitchen, snooping around and criticising. *(She arranges the pans under sink which the County Attorney had shoved out of place.)*

MRS. PETERS: Of course, it's no more than their duty.

MRS. HALE: Duty's all right, but I guess that deputy sheriff that came out to make the fire might have got a little of this on. *(Gives the roller towel a pull.)* Wish I'd thought of that sooner. Seems mean to talk about her for not having things slicked up when she had to come away in such a hurry.

MRS. PETERS: *(Who has gone to a small table in the left rear corner of the room, and lifted one end of a towel that covers a pan.)* She had bread set. *(Stands still.)*

MRS. HALE: *(Eyes fixed on a loaf of bread beside the breadbox, which is on a low shelf at the other side of the room. Moves slowly toward it.)* She was going to put this in there. *(Picks up loaf, then abruptly drops it. In a manner of returning to familiar things.)* It's a shame about her fruit. I wonder if it's all gone. *(Gets up on the chair and looks.)* I think there's some here that's all right, Mrs.

Peters. Yes—here; *(Holding it toward the window.)* this is cherries, too. *(Looking again.)* I declare I believe that's the only one. *(Gets down, bottle in her hand. Goes to the sink and wipes it off on the outside.)* She'll feel awful bad after all her hard work in the hot weather. I remember the afternoon I put up my cherries last summer. *(She puts the bottle on the big kitchen table, center of the room. With a sign, is about to sit down in the rocking chair. Before she is seated realizes what chair it is; with a slow look at it, steps back. The chair which she has touched rocks back and forth.)*

MRS. PETERS: Well, I must get those things from the front room closet. *(She goes to the door at the right, but after looking into the other room, steps back.)* You coming with me, Mrs. Hale? You could help me carry them.

*(They go in the other room; reappear, Mrs. Peters carrying a dress and skirt, Mrs. Hale following with a pair of shoes.)*

MRS. PETERS: My, it's cold in there. *(She puts the clothes on the big table, and hurries to the stove.)*

MRS. HALE: *(Examining the skirt.)* Wright was close. I think maybe that's why she kept so much to herself. She didn't even belong to the Ladies Aid. I suppose she felt she couldn't do her part, and then you don't enjoy things when you feel shabby. She used to wear pretty clothes and be lively, when she was Minnie Foster, one of the town girls singing in the choir. But that—oh, that was thirty years ago. This all you was to take in?

MRS. PETERS: She said she wanted an apron. Funny thing to want, for there isn't much to get you dirty in jail, goodness knows. But I suppose just to make her feel more natural. She said they was in the top drawer in this cupboard. Yes, here. And then her little shawl that always hung behind the door. *(Opens stair door and looks.)* Yes, here it is. *(Quickly shuts door leading upstairs.)*

MRS. HALE: *(Abruptly moving toward her.)* Mrs. Peters?

MRS. PETERS: Yes, Mrs. Hale?

MRS. HALE: Do you think she did it?

MRS. PETERS: *(In a frightened voice.)* Oh, I don't know.

MRS. HALE: Well, I don't think she did. Asking for an apron and her little shawl. Worrying about her fruit.

MRS. PETERS: *(Starts to speak, glances up, when footsteps are heard in the room above. In a low voice.)* Mr. Peters says it looks bad for her. Mr. Henderson is awful sarcastic in a speech and he'll make fun of her sayin' she didn't wake up.

MRS. HALE: Well, I guess John Wright didn't wake when they was slipping that rope under his neck.

MRS. PETERS: No, it's strange. It must have been done awful crafty and still. They say it was such a—funny way to kill a man, rigging it all up like that.

MRS. HALE: That's just what Mr. Hale said. There was a gun in the house. He says that's what he can't understand.

MRS. PETERS: Mr. Henderson said coming out that what was needed for the case was a motive, something to show anger, or—sudden feeling.

MRS. HALE: *(Who is standing by the table.)* Well, I don't see any signs of anger around here. *(She puts her hand on the dish towel which lies on the table, stands looking down at table, one half of which is clean, the other half is messy.)* It's wiped to here. *(Makes a move as if to finish work, then turns and looks at loaf of bread outside the breadbox. Drops towel. In that voice of coming back to familiar things.)* Wonder how they are finding things upstairs. I hope she had it a little more red-up up there. You know, it seems kind of *sneaking.* Locking her up in town and then coming out here and trying to get her own house to turn against her!

MRS. PETERS: But Mrs. Hale, the law is the law.

MRS. HALE: I s'pose 'tis. *(Unbuttoning her coat.)* Better loosen up your things, Mrs. Peters. You won't feel them when you go out.
*(Mrs. Peters takes off her fur tippet, goes to hang it on hook at back of room, stands looking at the under part of the small corner table.)*

MRS. PETERS: She was piecing a quilt.
*(She brings the large sewing basket and they look at the bright pieces.)*

MRS. HALE: It's log cabin pattern. Pretty, isn't it? I wonder if she was goin' to quilt it or just knot it?
*(Footsteps have been heard coming down the stairs. The Sheriff enters followed by Hale and the County Attorney.)*

SHERIFF: They wonder if she was going to quilt it or just knot it!
*(The men laugh; the women look abashed.)*

COUNTY ATTORNEY: *(Rubbing his hands over the stove.)* Frank's fire didn't do much up there, did it? Well, let's go out to the barn and get that cleared up.

*(The men go outside.)*

MRS. HALE: *(Resentfully.)* I don't know as there's anything so strange, our takin' up our time with little things while we're waiting for them to get the evidence. *(She sits down at the big table smoothing out a block with decision.)* I don't see as it's anything to laugh about.

MRS. PETERS: *(Apologetically.)* Of course they've got awful important things on their minds. *(Pulls up a chair and joins Mrs. Hale at the table.)*

# Friends

Kobo Abe
1967

**Dramatic**
**Scene:** at the door of Man's apartment

Man
Middle Daughter
Grandmother
Father
Mother
Younger Son
Elder Son
Eldest Daughter
Youngest Daughter

MAN: Well, that's about all for now. I'll call you later on to say good night…What? It has yellow spots? Sounds like an alley cat, doesn't it?…No, I'm sorry. I assure you, I have absolute confidence in your taste…Oh, just a second. *(He removes the receiver from his ear and listens.)* No, it wasn't anything. I can't imagine anyone would come visiting me now, at this hour of the night…Yes, isn't that what I've been saying all along? Next payday I'd like you to move in here for good. You should have your things packed and ready by then.

*(The eight members of the family approach slowly and hesitantly walking on tiptoe.)*

MAN: It sounds like rain? Yes, maybe it is raining. It couldn't be footsteps—it'd take too many people for that. You know, the insurance agent in the apartment below mine is a nut for poker…Of course the noise has nothing to do with me.

*(The footsteps suddenly grow louder. Man cocks his head and listens. The family enters from stage right and crosses stage front in a single line. Younger Son, who has in the meantime passed his guitar to Elder Son, goes past the entrance to Man's apartment then turns back; at which all the others stop in their tracks. Father and Younger Son stand on either side of the entrance. Father takes out a notebook and, after thumbing through the pages*

*compares what he finds with the name on the door. He nods and gives the signal to Middle Daughter, who is standing behind him. She comes forward and stands at the door then knocks gently.)*

MAN: Say, it's at my place! *(He glances hurriedly at his watch.)* Must be a telegram, at this hour of the night.

*(Middle Daughter knocks again and he calls to other side of the door.)*

MAN: I'll be with you in a minute!

*(The family is visibly relieved. He speaks into the telephone.)*

MAN: I'll go out and have a look. I'll call you later. Here's a kiss. *(He makes a noise with his lips and puts down the telephone.)*


Scene III

*(Grandmother, having slipped around from behind Middle Daughter, peeps through the keyhole. She sees Man coming to the door.)*

GRANDMOTHER: My goodness—what a handsome man!

FATHER: Shhh! *(He takes Grandmother by her sleeve and pulls her back.)*

MAN: Who is it? Who's there?

MIDDLE DAUGHTER: *(In a girlish voice.)* Excuse me, please. I'm sorry to bother you so late.

MAN: Who is it, please? *(He is disarmed to discover the visitor is a young woman, but is all the more suspicious.)*

MIDDLE DAUGHTER: I'm so sorry. I intended to come earlier.

*(Man shakes his head doubtfully, but eventually yields to curiosity and opens the door a little. Instantly Younger Son inserts his foot into the opening. Father takes the door knob and pulls the door open. The family, moving into action, assembles before the door. Man, dumfounded, stands rooted.)*

MIDDLE DAUGHTER: Oh, that's a relief! You hadn't gone to bed yet, had you?

FATHER: *(In the tone of an old friend.)* Of course not! The young folks these days are night owls, all of them.

MOTHER: *(Pushing Grandmother from behind.)* Shall we go inside, Grandma? The night air is bad for you.

MAN: *(His voice choked.)* Who are you, anyway?

GRANDMOTHER: *(Ignoring Man and starting to go in.)* Oh, dear, it's pretty bare, isn't it?

ELDEST DAUGHTER: *(Exhibiting strong curiosity.)* What do you expect? It's a bachelor apartment, after all.

MIDDLE DAUGHTER: That's right. And that's why it's so important somebody come and help him.

MAN: *(Baffled.)* Just a minute, please. I wonder if you haven't got the wrong party.

ELDER SON: *(With a melancholy smile.)* I used to work for a detective agency, you know.

MAN: But still—

YOUNGEST DAUGHTER: I'm cold.

MOTHER: Poor darling. You'll take an aspirin and get to bed early.
*(Mother, her arms around Youngest Daughter, propels Grandmother into the apartment. Man tries to prevent her, but Younger Son sees an opening and darts inside.)*

MAN: What do you mean, breaking in, without even taking off your shoes?

YOUNGER SON: Oh—sorry. *(He removes shoes.)*
*(The family takes advantage of Man's distraction to surge into the apartment in one wave. Father, the last in, shuts the door behind him, and turns the key. Man, in face of the concerted action of the eight of them, is powerless to resist. The members of the family scatter around the room with a kind of professional competence, neatly surrounding Man. They flash at him their usual bashful smiles. They seem to have got the better of him.)*

MAN: What's the big idea? It's enough to give a man the creeps.

FATHER: *(Unruffled.)* Please, I beg you, don't get so upset.

MAN: If you've got some business with me, how about explaining exactly what it is?

FATHER: It puts us in an awkward position if you're going to turn on us that way... *(He looks around from one to another of the family as if enlisting their support.)*

MAN: *(Excitedly.)* Puts you in an awkward position! You break in, without warning, on a total stranger, and you say it puts you in an awkward position! I'm the one who has something to complain about.

ELDER SON: *(Taps on the wall.)* Pretty good! The walls have been soundproofed.

ELDEST DAUGHTER: It's freezing in here. Doesn't he have an electric heater, I wonder.

MAN: *(Unable to take any more.)* Stop loitering around my apartment! All of you, get out of here! Now!

YOUNGER SON: *(Coolly.)* Why, I feel as if we weren't wanted.

MAN: That's not surprising, is it? Of all the crassness!

*(Youngest Daughter peeps into the back room.)*

YOUNGEST DAUGHTER: Look, there's another room here.

GRANDMOTHER: It won't be easy dividing the space with only two rooms for nine people. *(She goes up beside Youngest Daughter and examines the other room with her.)*

MIDDLE DAUGHTER: We can't be fussy, you know. We didn't come here for our amusement.

*(Man stands at the door to the back room, blocking it. He is bewildered and uneasy.)*

MAN: Out with all of you, and right now! If you refuse to go, I'll charge you with trespassing.

YOUNGEST DAUGHTER: *(With an exaggerated show of terror.)* Oh, he scares me!

MOTHER: *(Admonishingly.)* There's nothing for you to be afraid of. He's really a very nice man. There, just look at his face. He's just pretending to frighten you, that's all.

GRANDMOTHER: That's right. He's what I'd call a handsome man. If I were only ten years younger…

MAN: I've had all I can stand! *(He starts to lift the telephone.)*

FATHER: *(Quietly restraining him.)* Now calm yourself. You seem to be under some terrible misapprehension. You're making such a fuss anybody might think we intended to do you some harm.

MAN: What do you intend, if not to harm me?

FATHER: Why should you say such a thing?

MAN: You're in a stranger's house here.

FATHER: *(With all expression of dismay.)* A stranger's house?

ELDER SON: *(Contemptuously.)* A stranger's house! He certainly takes a very narrow view of things.

MAN: But, as a matter of fact, we are strangers aren't we?

FATHER: *(Soothing him.)* You mustn't get so worked up over each little thing. Have you never heard the saying that being brothers marks the first step on the way to being strangers? That means if you trace strangers back far enough you'll find they were once brothers. What difference does it make if we're strangers? A little thing like that shouldn't upset you.

MOTHER: Yes, when you get to know us better you'll see we're just so relaxed and easy-going it's positively funny. *(She laughs.)*

MAN: Don't act silly. Whatever you may think, the fact is, this is my apartment.

ELDEST DAUGHTER: That's obvious isn't it? If it weren't your apartment, you wouldn't be here.

YOUNGER SON: And if it weren't your apartment do you suppose we'd have listened in silence all this time to your bellyaching?

MIDDLE DAUGHTER: I thought I told you to lay off him.

YOUNGER SON: I apologize. The fact is, I have a wee bit of a hangover. Damn it!

*(Younger Son shadowboxes briefly to cover his confusion. Middle Daughter, acting as if she has suddenly noticed it, puts out her hand to remove a bit of wool fluff from Man's jacket. Eldest Daughter tries to beat her to it. But Man shrinks back from both of them, and neither is successful, Youngest Daughter chooses this moment to disappear into the kitchen.)*

ELDEST DAUGHTER: I'm going to take off my coat, if you don't mind.

FATHER: Yes, we can't go on standing around this way indefinitely. Why don't we sit down and discuss things in a more relaxed mood?
*(They all remove their coats and hats. Younger Son also removes his jacket. Eldest Daughter's dress rather emphasizes her physique. Man steps forward resolutely, pushes Father aside, and picks up the telephone and dials with an air of determination.)*

MAN: One, one, zero. *(He pauses, his finger inserted in the zero.)* Leave at once! Otherwise, I have only to release my finger and I'll be connected.

YOUNGER SON: To the police?

ELDEST DAUGHTER: Aren't you carrying things a bit too far?

FATHER: *(Perplexed.)* It's a misunderstanding…a complete misunderstanding.

MAN: I have no time to bandy words with you. I'll give you until I count ten, that's all. I advise you to start getting ready. *(He starts to count slowly.)*

*(Younger Son stands menacingly before Man. He looks at the family to see whether they want him to go ahead.)*

FATHER: *(Sharply.)* Stop! I forbid you to use violence.

MOTHER: Yes, we don't want people saying bad things about us. Stop it!

ELDER SON: How about, as a last resort, abiding by the will of the majority?

*(Man's attention is caught by the words "will of the majority." He slows down the speed of his counting.)*

ELDEST DAUGHTER: Even if we win a majority decision, it'd still be picking on someone weaker than us, wouldn't it?

ELDER SON: Don't be an idiot. The will of the majority means...

FATHER: Let's drop the whole matter. We know which side is going to win anyway. There aren't any thrills in this game.

GRANDMOTHER: Where might is master, justice is servant.

MIDDLE DAUGHTER: *(Somewhat uneasy.)* What do you intend to do, anyway?

MAN: That's what I'd like to know. When I count one more, that'll make ten.

FATHER: It can't be helped. If you think it's absolutely necessary, do whatever you think best. It won't be very pleasant, but who knows?—it may prove more effective in bringing you to your senses than repeating the same old arguments.

MAN: Don't try to intimidate me! You're prepared, I take it? I'm really phoning the police.

FATHER: Go right ahead.

MAN: *(Releasing his finger from the dial emphatically.)* Don't say I didn't warn you!

MOTHER: *(Sighs.)* It's true, just as they say, a child never knows its parent's love.

MIDDLE DAUGHTER: *(Sighs.)* This is the test run.

# Dollar Poem—from Mysteries and Smaller Pieces

Judith Malina and Julian Beck
1964

A voice/performance piece for any number of speakers

FIRST SPEAKER: One

SECOND SPEAKER: One

FIRST SPEAKER: One

SECOND SPEAKER: One

FIRST SPEAKER: One

FOURTH SPEAKER: One

SECOND SPEAKER: One

FIRST SPEAKER: One

THIRD SPEAKER: One

SECOND SPEAKER: One

FOURTH SPEAKER: One

SIXTH SPEAKER: One dollar

FIFTH SPEAKER: One dollar

FIRST SPEAKER: This certifies that there is

FIFTH SPEAKER: on deposit in the Treasury of

FOURTH SPEAKER: of the United States

FIFTH AND SIXTH SPEAKERS: United States of America

THIRD SPEAKER: One dollar

SECOND SPEAKER: A2

THIRD SPEAKER: S584

FOURTH SPEAKER: 1.4

FIRST SPEAKER: 558-A

FIFTH SPEAKER: One dollar

SECOND SPEAKER: One

FIRST SPEAKER: of the        SECOND AND THIRD SPEAKERS: the United States
                             of America

SECOND SPEAKER: of the

FIRST SPEAKER: One

FOURTH SPEAKER: One

FIRST SPEAKER: One

THIRD SPEAKER: One        FIFTH AND SIXTH SPEAKERS: United States of America

FIRST SPEAKER: S584        THIRD SPEAKER: One

SECOND SPEAKER: 1.4

THIRD SPEAKER: 558        FOURTH SPEAKER: One        FIFTH SPEAKER: A

SIXTH SPEAKER: A2

FIRST AND THIRD SPEAKERS: One

SECOND AND FOURTH SPEAKERS: One

SECOND AND THIRD SPEAKERS: One

FOURTH SPEAKER: One        FIFTH AND SIXTH SPEAKERS: The United States

ALL SPEAKERS: The United States of America

FIFTH SPEAKER: One

SIXTH SPEAKER: One

FIRST SPEAKER: This certifies that there is

SECOND SPEAKER: Washington

FOURTH SPEAKER: Washington D.C.

FIRST SPEAKER: on deposit        THIRD SPEAKER: One dollar

FIFTH SPEAKER: in the

FIRST SPEAKER: Treasury        SIXTH SPEAKER: An Eagle

SECOND SPEAKER: An eagle

FIRST SPEAKER: on deposit

SECOND SPEAKER: in the Treasury

THIRD AND FOURTH SPEAKERS: An eagle

FIFTH AND SIXTH SPEAKERS: The United States of America

FIRST SPEAKER: One

SECOND AND THIRD SPEAKERS: One

FOURTH AND SIXTH SPEAKERS: One

SECOND SPEAKER: One

FIRST AND THIRD SPEAKERS: One

FIFTH SPEAKER: One

SECOND SPEAKER: Washington

THIRD AND FOURTH SPEAKERS: Washington D.C.

FIFTH SPEAKER: An eagle

FIRST SPEAKER: Series 1957 B

SECOND AND THIRD SPEAKERS: An eagle

FOURTH SPEAKER: A2                SIXTH SPEAKER: S

FIFTH SPEAKER: 584

FIRST AND THIRD SPEAKERS: 1.4

SECOND AND FOURTH SPEAKERS: 558

FIRST AND SECOND SPEAKERS: One dollar

THIRD AND FOURTH SPEAKERS: One dollar

FIFTH AND SIXTH SPEAKERS: One dollar

SECOND AND FOURTH SPEAKERS: One dollar

FIFTH SPEAKER: On deposit     SIXTH SPEAKER: An eagle

FIRST SPEAKER: Thesaur

SECOND SPEAKER: Amer

THIRD SPEAKER: Septant

FOURTH SPEAKER: Sigil

FIFTH AND SIXTH SPEAKERS: E Pluribus Unum

FIRST AND SECOND SPEAKERS: An eagle

THIRD SPEAKER: One     SIXTH SPEAKER: Katherine O'Hay

SECOND SPEAKER: One     SIXTH SPEAKER: Granihan

FOURTH SPEAKER: One     FIFTH SPEAKER: Treasurer

FIRST AND SECOND SPEAKERS: of the United States

THIRD SPEAKER: C

FIFTH SPEAKER: Douglas     SIXTH SPEAKER: Dillon

FIRST SPEAKER: An eagle     THIRD SPEAKER: Secretary

FOURTH SPEAKER: of the Treasury     SIXTH SPEAKER: One

FIRST AND SECOND SPEAKERS: of the United States

THIRD SPEAKER: In God We Trust

FIFTH AND SIXTH SPEAKERS: In God We Trust

FIRST SPEAKER: C. Douglas Dillon

SECOND SPEAKER: One

FOURTH SPEAKER: Katherine O Hay Granihan

THIRD SPEAKER: An eagle

SECOND SPEAKER: One     FIFTH SPEAKER: One

FIRST SPEAKER: Washington

THIRD AND FOURTH SPEAKER: Washington D.C.

SIXTH SPEAKER: E Pluribus Unum

FIRST SPEAKER: Series 1957 B

FIFTH SPEAKER: Annuit Coeptis

SECOND AND THIRD SPEAKERS: In God We Trust

SECOND AND FOURTH SPEAKERS: The United States

FIRST AND THIRD SPEAKERS: One dollar

SIXTH SPEAKER: An eagle

FIRST SPEAKER: Novus     FOURTH SPEAKER: One

SECOND SPEAKER: Ordo

THIRD SPEAKER: Seclorum

SIXTH SPEAKER: 1776

SECOND AND FOURTH SPEAKERS: 1776

FIFTH SPEAKER: Washington

FIRST SPEAKER: Washington D.C.

SECOND AND FOURTH SPEAKERS: One

FIRST SPEAKER: One

FIRST SPEAKER: One

SECOND SPEAKER: in the Treasury

SIXTH SPEAKER: An eagle

FIRST SPEAKER: 1776

THIRD SPEAKER: One dollar

FOURTH SPEAKER: on deposit

SECOND SPEAKER: One

THIRD SPEAKER: One

FIFTH SPEAKER: One

FIRST, SECOND AND THIRD SPEAKERS: One

FOURTH SPEAKER: One

FOURTH SPEAKER: One dollar

FIRST SPEAKER: Katherine O'Hay Granihan

THIRD SPEAKER: on deposit

FOURTH SPEAKER: One

SECOND AND FIFTH SPEAKERS: One

FOURTH SPEAKER: One dollar

FIRST SPEAKER: Washington

THIRD AND FOURTH SPEAKERS: C. Douglas Dillon

FIFTH SPEAKER: One

SECOND SPEAKER: E Pluribus Unum

THIRD SPEAKER: Novus

FIRST SPEAKER: One

FOURTH SPEAKER: Ordo

FIRST SPEAKER: Seclorum

FOURTH SPEAKER: on deposit

FIFTH AND SIXTH SPEAKERS: In God We Trust

SECOND SPEAKER: One dollar

THIRD AND FOURTH SPEAKERS: An eagle

FIRST SPEAKER: A2

THIRD SPEAKER: S584

FOURTH SPEAKER: An eagle

FIRST AND SIXTH SPEAKERS: 1776

SECOND SPEAKER: on deposit

FOURTH SPEAKER: of the United States

ALL SPEAKERS: The United States of America

FOURTH SPEAKER: One dollar

FIRST SPEAKER: One dollar

SIXTH SPEAKER: One

# Sister Mary Ignatius Explains It All For You

Christopher Durang
1979

**Comic/Satiric**
**Scene:** at a school assembly, Christmas time

Sister Mary Ignatius
Gary
Diane
Philomena
Aloysius
Thomas

GARY: And then Mary and Joseph, realizing their lack of faith, thanked Misty and made a good act of contrition. And then Jesus came out from behind the tree where He was hiding, they spent forty days on earth enjoying themselves and setting the groundwork for the Catholic Church, and then Jesus, Mary, Joseph and Misty ascended into heaven and lived happily ever after.
*(Diane and Gary, holding the doll between them, stand in front of the camel. All sing the final jubilant phrase of "Angels We Have Heard on High" Christmas carol, as Diane and Gary mime ascension by waving their arms in a flying motion.)*
ALL: *(Singing.)* Glor-or-or-or-ia! In Excelsis Deo!
*(All four bow. Sister applauds enthusiastically. After their bow, the four quickly get out of their costumes, continuing to do so during some of Sister's next speech if necessary. Their "regular" clothes are indeed regular and not too noteworthy: Diane might wear slacks or jeans but with an attractive sweater or blouse and with a blazer; Gary might wear chinos, a nice shirt with even a tie, or a vest—casual but neat, pleasant; Philomena might wear a dress, Aloysius a shirt and slacks—or, if played as a bit formal, even a suit.)*
SISTER: Oh, thank you, children. That was lovely. Thank you. *(To audience.)* The old stories really are the best, aren't they? Mary Jean

Mahoney. What a good child. And what a nice reunion *we're* having. What year did you say you were in my class again?

GARY: 1959.

SISTER: 1959. Oh, those were happy years. Eisenhower, Pope Pius still alive, then the first Catholic president. And so now you've all grown up. Let's do some of the old questions, shall we? *(To Aloysius.)* Who made you?

ALOYSIUS: God made me.

SISTER: Quite correct. What is the seventh commandment?

PHILOMENA: The seventh commandment is thou shalt not steal.

SISTER: Very good. *(To Diane.)* What is contrition? You.

DIANE: Uh...being sorry for sin?

SISTER: *(Cheerfully chastising.)* That's not how we answer questions here, young lady. Thomas?

THOMAS: Contrition is sincere sorrow for having offended God, and hatred for the sins we have committed, with a firm purpose of sinning no more.

DIANE: Oh yes. Right.

SISTER: *(Still kindly.)* For someone who's just played the Virgin, you don't know your catechism responses very well. What grade are you in?

DIANE: I'm not in a grade. I'm in life.

SISTER: Oh yes, right. Well, cookies anyone? Thomas, go bring our nice guests some cookies.

*(Thomas exits.)*

SISTER: It's so nice to see you all again. You must all be married by now, I imagine. I hope you all have large families like we encouraged?

PHILOMENA: I have a little girl, age three.

SISTER: That's nice.

ALOYSIUS: I have two boys.

SISTER: I like boys. *(To Gary.)* And you?

GARY: I'm not married.

SISTER: Well, a nice-looking boy like you, it won't be long before some pretty girl snatches you up. *(To Diane.)* And you?

DIANE: I don't have any children. But I've had two abortions.

*(Sister is stunned. Enter Thomas with cookies.)*

SISTER: No cookies, Thomas. Take them away.

*(Thomas exits immediately.)*

SISTER: *(To Diane.)* You are in a state of mortal sin, young woman. What is the fifth commandment?

DIANE: Thou shalt not kill.

SISTER: You are a murderer.

DIANE: *(Unemotional.)* The first one was when I was raped when I was eighteen.

SISTER: Well I am sorry to hear that. But only God has power over life and death. God might have had very special plans for your baby. Are you sure I taught you?

DIANE: Yes you taught me.

SISTER: Did I give you good grades?

DIANE: Yes. Very good.

SISTER: Have you told these sins in confession?

DIANE: What sins?

SISTER: You know very well what I mean.

DIANE: I don't go to confession.

SISTER: Well, it looks pretty clear to me, we'll just add you to the list of people going to hell. *(Calling.)* Thomas!
*(Enter Thomas.)*

SISTER: We'll put her name right after Comden and Green.

THOMAS: All right. *(Exits.)*

SISTER: Now somebody change the subject. I don't want to hear any more about this.

GARY: *(Trying to oblige.)* Ummmm…it certainly is strange being able to chew the communion wafer now, isn't it?

SISTER: What?

GARY: Well, you used to tell us that because the communion wafer was really the body of Christ, if we chewed it, it might bleed.

SISTER: I was speaking metaphorically.

GARY: Oh.

SISTER: *(Pause.)* Well, I still feel shaken by that girl over there. Let's talk about something positive. *(Gestures to Philomena.)* You, with the little girl. Tell me about yourself.

PHILOMENA: Well my little girl is three, and her name is Wendy.

SISTER: There is no St. Wendy.

PHILOMENA: Her middle name is Mary.

SISTER: Wendy Mary. Too many y's. I'd change it. What does your husband do?

PHILOMENA: I don't have a husband.

*(Long pause.)*

SISTER: Did he die?

PHILOMENA: I don't think so. I didn't know him for very long.

SISTER: Do you sign your letters Mrs. or Miss?

PHILOMENA: I don't write letters.

SISTER: Did this person you lost track of *marry* you before he left?

PHILOMENA: *(Quiet.)* No.

SISTER: Children, you are making me very sad. *(To Philomena.)* Did you get good grades in my class?

PHILOMENA: No, Sister. You said I was stupid.

SISTER: Are you a prostitute?

PHILOMENA: Sister! Certainly not. I just get lonely.

SISTER: The Mother Superior of my own convent may get lonely, but does she have illegitimate children?

ALOYSIUS: There *was* that nun who stuffed her baby behind her dresser last year.

*(Sister stares at him.)*

ALOYSIUS: It was in the news.

SISTER: No one was addressing you, Aloysius. Philomena, my point is that loneliness does not excuse sin.

PHILOMENA: But there are worse sins. And I believe Jesus forgives me. After all, He didn't want them to stone the woman taken in adultery.

SISTER: That was merely a *political* gesture. In private Christ stoned *many* women taken in adultery.

DIANE: That's not in the Bible.

SISTER: *(Suddenly very angry.)* Not everything has to be in the Bible! *(To audience, trying to recoup.)* There's oral tradition within the Church. One priest tells another priest something, it gets passed down through the years.

PHILOMENA: *(Unhappy.)* But don't you believe Jesus forgives people who sin?

SISTER: Yes, of course, He forgives sin, but He's *tricky.* You have to be *truly* sorry, and you have to *truly* resolve not to sin again, or else He'll send you straight to hell just like the thief He was crucified next to.

PHILOMENA: Well, I think Jesus forgives me.

SISTER: Well I think you're going to hell. *(To Aloysius.)* And what about you? Is there anything the matter with you?

ALOYSIUS: Nothing. I'm fine.

SISTER: But are you living properly?

ALOYSIUS: Yes.

SISTER: And you're married?

ALOYSIUS: Yes.

SISTER: And you don't use birth control?

ALOYSIUS: No.

SISTER: But you only have two children. Why is that? You're not spilling your seed like Onan, are you? That's a sin, you know.

ALOYSIUS: No. It's just chance that we haven't had more.

SISTER: And you go to Mass once a week, and communion at least once a year, and confession at least once a year? Right?

ALOYSIUS: Yes.

SISTER: Well I'm very pleased then.

ALOYSIUS: *(Suddenly guilty, unhappy.)* I am an alcoholic, and recently I've started to hit my wife, and I keep thinking about suicide.

SISTER: Within bounds, all those things are venial sins. At least one of my students turned out well. Of course, I don't know how hard you're hitting your wife; but with prayer and God's grace…

ALOYSIUS: My wife is very unhappy.

SISTER: Yes, but eventually there's death. And then everlasting happiness in heaven. Some days I long for heaven. *(To Gary.)* And you? Have you turned out all right?

GARY: I'm okay.

SISTER: And you don't use birth control?

GARY: Definitely not.

SISTER: That's good. *(Looks at him.)* What do you mean, "definitely not"?

GARY: I don't use it.

SISTER: And you're not married. Have you not found the right girl?

GARY: *(Evasively.)* In a manner of speaking.

SISTER: *(Grim, not going to pursue it.)* Okay. *(Walks away, but then knows she has to pursue it.)* You do that thing that makes Jesus puke, don't you?

GARY: Pardon?

SISTER: Drop the polite boy manners, buster. When your mother looks at you, she turns into a pillar of salt, right?

GARY: What?

SISTER: Sodom and Gomorrah, stupid. You sleep with men, don't you?

GARY: Well…yes.

SISTER: Jesus, Mary, and Joseph! We have a regular cross section in here.

GARY: I got seduced when I was in the seminary. I mean, I guess I'd been denying it up to then.

SISTER: We don't want to hear about it.

GARY: And then when I left the seminary I was very upset, and then I went to New York and I slept with five hundred different people.

SISTER: Jesus is going to throw up.

GARY: But then I decided I was trashing my life, and so I only had sex with guys I had an emotional relationship with.

SISTER: That must have cut it down to about *three* hundred.

GARY: And now I'm living with this one guy who I'd gone to grade school with and only ran into again two years ago, and we're faithful with one another and stuff. He was in your class too. Jeff Hannigan.

SISTER: He was a bad boy. Some of them should be left on the side of a hill to die, and he was one.

GARY: You remember him?

SISTER: Not really. His type.

GARY: Anyway, when I met him again, he was still a practicing Catholic, and so now I am again too.

SISTER: I'd practice a little harder if I were you.

GARY: So I don't think I'm so bad.

SISTER: *(Vomit sound.)* Blah. You make me want to blah. Didn't any of you listen to me when I was teaching you? What were you all doing? *(Mad, trying to set the record straight again.)* There is the universe, created by God. Eve ate the apple, man got original sin, God sent down Jesus to redeem us. Jesus said to St. Peter, "Upon this rock," rock meaning Peter, "I build my Church," by which he meant that Peter was the first Pope and that he and the subsequent Popes would be infallible on matters of doctrine and morals. So your way is very clear: you have this infallible Church that tells you what is right and wrong, and you follow its teaching, and then you get to heaven. Didn't you all *hear* me say that? Did you all have wax in your ears? Did I speak in a foreign language? Or what? And you've all sinned against sex— *(To Aloysius.)* not you, you're just depressed, you probably need vitamins—but the rest of you. Why this obsession with sex? The Church has been very clear setting up the guidelines for you. *(To Philomena and Diane.)* For you two girls, why can't you simply marry one Catholic man and have as many babies as chance and the good Lord allows you to? Simple, easy to follow directions. *(To Gary.)* And for you, you can *force* yourself to marry and procreate with some nice Catholic girl—try it, it's not so hard—or you can be celibate for the rest of your life. Again, simple advice. *(Suddenly furious.)* Those are your options! No others. They are your direct paths to heaven and salvation, to everlasting happiness! Why aren't you following these paths? Are you insane?

DIANE: You're insane.

SISTER: You know, you're my least favorite person here today. I mean, the great big effeminate one over there *(Points to Gary.)* makes me want to blah, but I can tell he once was nice, and he might get better with shock treatments and aversion therapy. But I can tell shock treatments wouldn't help you. You're fresh as paint, and you're nasty. I can see it in your face.

DIANE: You shouldn't be teaching children. You should be locked up in a convent where you can't hurt anybody.

SISTER: Me hurt someone. You're the one who runs around killing babies at the drop of a hat.

DIANE: It's a medical procedure. And even the Church admits it can't pinpoint *when* life begins in the womb. Why should you decide that the minute the sperm touches the ovum that…

SISTER: Don't talk filth to me, I don't want to hear it. *(Suddenly very suspicious.)* Why did you all come here today? I don't remember asking you.

GARY: It was Diane's idea.

SISTER: What? What was?

PHILOMENA: We wanted to embarrass you.

ALOYSIUS: None of us ever liked you.

SISTER: What do you mean? My students always loved me. I was the favorite.

ALOYSIUS: No. We thought you were a bully.

SISTER: I was the *favorite.*

ALOYSIUS: You never let me go to the bathroom when I needed to.

SISTER: All you had to do was raise your hand.

ALOYSIUS: There were sixty children, and I sat in the back of the room; and I did raise my hand, but you never acknowledged me. Every afternoon my bladder became very full, and I always ended up wetting my pants.

SISTER: Big deal.

ALOYSIUS: I spoke to you about recognizing me sooner, and about my problem, but all you said then was "big deal."

SISTER: I remember you. You used to make a puddle in the last row every day.

ALOYSIUS: I have bladder problems to this day.

SISTER: What a baby. You flunked. I was giving you a lesson in life, and you flunked. It was up to you to solve the problem: don't drink your little carton of milk at lunch; bring a little container with you and urinate behind your desk; or simply hold it in and offer the discomfort up to Christ. He suffered three hours of agony on the cross, surely a full bladder pales by comparison. I talk about the universe and original sin and heaven and hell, and you complain to me about bathroom privileges. You're a ridiculous crybaby. *(Cuffs him on the head.)*

PHILOMENA: You used to hit me too.

SISTER: You probably said stupid things.

PHILOMENA: I did. I told you I was stupid. That was no reason to hit me.

SISTER: It seems a very good reason to hit you. Knock some sense into you.

PHILOMENA: You used to take the point of your pencil and poke it up and down on my head when I didn't do my homework.

SISTER: You should have done your homework.

PHILOMENA: And when I didn't know how to do long division, you slammed my head against the blackboard.

SISTER: Did I ever break a bone?

PHILOMENA: No.

SISTER: There, you see! *(To Gary.)* And what about you?

GARY: You didn't do anything to me in particular. I just found you scary.

SISTER: Well I am scary.

GARY: But my lover Jeff doesn't like you 'cause you made him wet his pants too.

SISTER: All this obsession with the bladder. *(To Diane.)* And you, the nasty one, why did you want to embarrass me?

DIANE: *(Said simply.)* Because I believed you. I believed how you said the world worked, and that God loved us and the story of the Good Shepherd and the lost sheep and I don't think you should lie to people.

# Never Tell Isobel

John Gruen
1981

**Comic**
**Scene:** a bare stage

Five couples, all in their thirties
Francesca and Douglas
Isobel and Sam
Melinda and Barnaby
Laura and Jacob
Tina and Roger
Claude, the observer

LAURA: Being a woman is difficult.

ISOBEL: So much is known about us.

FRANCESCA: So much is expected of us.

TINA: Women are the shadows of men.

MELINDA: Men are always terrified of women.

LAURA: A woman inspires both trust and fear.

ISOBEL: Oh, how glorious it is to be a woman!

FRANCESCA: How secretive!

TINA: And how strange!

MELINDA: Feel our arms—how soft they are!

LAURA: Let us cling to our womanhood.

ISOBEL: We are part flower.

FRANCESCA: And part magic.

TINA: A man's wounds never heal as quickly as a woman's.

MELINDA: The burdens of guilt lie less heavily upon a woman than upon
a man.

LAURA: A man always falls silent when we speak.

ISOBEL: Because he hears beyond our speech.

FRANCESCA: Let us vow to be women together.

TINA: For many centuries to come.

MELINDA: But let us acknowledge our enemy.

LAURA: Time.

ISOBEL: Time.

FRANCESCA: Time.

TINA: Time.

MELINDA: Time.

LAURA: Let us re-acknowledge our enemy.

ISOBEL: Time.

FRANCESCA: Time.

TINA: Time

MELINDA: Time.

LAURA: Time.

*(They move off.)*

JACOB: Will you play a death scene with me, Laura?

LAURA: Who will play the victim?

JACOB: I warn you—ask no questions.

LAURA: Will it be a heart-rending scene?

JACOB: It will be a scene of mixed emotions.

LAURA: Tell me how to begin.

JACOB: Sit down, Laura. Raise your arms in a beseeching gesture. Now, implore forgiveness.

LAURA: Dear God, forgive this sad, sad woman here. Yes, I have strayed, and have fallen upon other men. I, dear God, am surely the most inconstant of all women. But I am plagued by this need to injure my own man. What sustains me is the knowledge that the injury is, of itself, a call for help. Jacob, you would love me less if I did not injure you. I could not bear to lose your love. And so I beseech forgiveness. Will you forgive me?

JACOB: I will forgive you only if you promise to fall into another man's arms at once.

LAURA: I promise.

JACOB: Let the men come forward, then.

*(All the men stand facing Laura, including Jacob.)*

LAURA: Broaden your shoulders, men. Stand up straight, and show yourselves. Little Laura is here! First, she'll strut for you. Next, she'll stand still for you so that you may appraise her enticing and dazzling body. Now she will show you the subtle motions of seduction. Are you watching, Jacob? Prefer, if you will, the inner elbow. You, there, Roger—touch my left shoulder—pure silk, wouldn't you say? Come close, Barnaby—the back of my neck has a special sweetness—won't you discover it? A bone for you, dear Claude. Right here, Claude, is a hip bone. Feel it very gently, Claude, very gently. And for you, Douglas, the curve of my belly.

Place your head right here. The pressure must be delicate so that the shape of that exquisite curve is not disrupted. My breasts are for you, Sam. Place your head on my right breast—and place your hand on my left breast. Yours are the gestures of sanctity, Sam.

JACOB: There is an awkward logic to all this. I am moved by the spectacle of arms, hands, heads and lips upon the body of a woman. But I become ecstatic when the body happens to be Laura's. And yet, in that same instant of ecstasy, I become wracked with a rage that undoes me. The pain is physical—and quite logical.

LAURA: Now, go back, you men. We must discover even subtler places. The inner thigh. Who will place his lips on the inner thigh? You, Sam—come up. There, now. Like that. Who will place his hands on my buttocks? Douglas, you're the lucky one. Come close, Roger. You may nestle 'round my leg. And you may stroke and stroke…and stroke. Barnaby, put your arms around my waist. Encircle me. Grasp me tightly. Claude—I give you my lips. Don't be afraid, Claude. After all, no harm in a kiss.

JACOB: The time for dying comes nearer and nearer. Observe my death scene, Laura. First, death enters through my eyes. It moves slowly through my limbs. It makes its way carefully through my innards. It pauses to take effect. Now it spills into my blood stream. Oh, what a rush of death! Like a fierce gust of wind! Soon I will be drenched in death. Consider well this death scene, Laura. I grapple with it, but only passively. Paralysis of feeling now sets in. And with it comes something incredibly delicious. Pleasure inundates me. It steals softly through my paralyzed limbs. It lingers in unexpected places…it flows. It moves. It runs over me. Laura… Laura…I…am…dying…

*(All the women now come forward and surround Jacob. They grasp him, feel him, devour him with their hands. The men are doing similar things with Laura. Abruptly all action ceases. Blackout. When lights return couples are once more together, dancing as when play started. Claude stands to side. Then he beckons to Sam.)*

CLAUDE: Hello, Sam.

SAM: Hello, Claude.

CLAUDE: Would you care to dance?

SAM: No, thank you.

CLAUDE: Have I offended you?

SAM: No.

CLAUDE: Well, what is it, Sam?

SAM: I'm in pain.

CLAUDE: Where?

SAM: All over.

CLAUDE: When did it start?

SAM: I don't remember.

CLAUDE: Can you describe the pain?

SAM: Vaguely.

CLAUDE: Describe it vaguely, then.

SAM: What do you think of Isobel?

CLAUDE: I'd rather not say. Does she cause you pain?

SAM: All women cause me pain.

CLAUDE: Are you sure you don't want to dance?

SAM: Absolutely.

CLAUDE: I've not offended you, have I?

SAM: No.

CLAUDE: Well, go on. Why do all women cause you pain?

SAM: Walking on the beach one night, a young child came upon two shadows. They were the shadows of two women. The child explored further. He saw that the shadows were two women in a fierce embrace. The child ran from what he saw. But the image continued to haunt him. It haunts him still. On the beach, that night, the pain began. I cannot make it stop.

CLAUDE: How can I help you?

SAM: Never tell Isobel.

CLAUDE: Never tell Isobel.

SAM: Never tell Isobel.

EVERYONE: *(Chants.)* Never tell Isobel.

*(The chanting gets louder. Some mad music starts. The couples reunite. Claude leads them in the chant. He then turns to audience and motions it to chant "Never tell Isobel." The chant becomes a song.)*

EVERYONE: *(Singing.)* Never tell Isobel!

*(As everybody is singing the lights dim and the play is over.)*

# Cameras

Jon Jory
1980s

**Dramatic**
**Scene:** any place, a bare stage, a street

Six actors with cameras
A dancing couple in evening dress
Young man who strips down and models
Business man with briefcase
Pregnant woman

ACTOR ONE: There are people who love the technology. I have a friend who has fifty thousand dollars worth of lenses; thirty, forty cameras; a completely outfitted shop for his own repairs. Not me, For me, it's a point of honor, I don't care about the mechanism, the way it works, how you take it apart, put it together. Listen, I don't consider that the point. What I care about is the image, okay? Remember when there used to be F-stops? I lost a hundred pictures I couldn't afford to lose because I was fiddling with those F-stops. Ideally, I'd take the picture with my eyes, and the print would come out of my mouth. The rest of it just doesn't matter to me.

ACTOR TWO: High relief I can't get enough of it. I'm a junkie for high relief. Black blacks, white whites. Black on white. White on black. The kind of thing you see in the newspapers on a slow news day. Construction workers silhouetted against the sky twenty stories up. You've seen it. With these lacework cranes in the background. Low detail work, because the more detail the less sense you have of the image as a whole. I want to take it in like a breath or a swallow. I don't want you looking at this bit or that bit. I want you looking at the whole thing.

*(Someone comes out with three roses, tosses them casually onto the floor and exits. One photographer bends to rearrange them.)*

ACTOR THREE: No.

ACTOR FOUR: Why no?

ACTOR THREE: Shoot them like they are.

ACTOR FOUR: *(Reaching.)* Just this one.

ACTOR THREE: No. Let it be what it is. Leave the image alone. See what you get.

ACTOR FOUR: What I'll get will be no composition.

ACTOR THREE: Bingo. What I want is no composition. What I long for is no composition. It just drives me crazy. Control, control, control, control. I feel like I'll cash it in if I see one more indescribably manipulated, absolutely predictable, unbelievably arrogant, monumentally balanced composition.

ACTOR TWO: What you want is a rush. The composition's hidden inside the rush.

*(A couple in evening dress foxtrot on. Slick ballroom dancing. No music. Actor Five and a couple of others photograph them.)*

ACTOR FIVE: Good. Good. Better. Much better. You can't catch this stuff and think at the same time. You have to get your head out of your way if you want to do this. Great. Good. There is only one thing in this world a camera can do that the eye can't, and that is to stop movement. Bam! Bam! Think about it. If there was no movement you wouldn't need a photographer, you could bring people out on a bus to see it.

ACTOR THREE: Except for the light.

ACTOR SIX: Stopping the movement is commonplace. Stopping the movement is just what the camera does. Breaking down the image, lifting out part of the whole, making the selection. Choosing, as my post-modern friends might say, what isn't there...like the feet, love the feet, come here, feet. You may have seen dancing, but you ain't seen my feet.

ACTOR THREE: Freeze.

*(The dancers stop-action.)*

ACTOR THREE: You want to know how this works? This one right here? If you take an inanimate object...the roses...and you put a human being in the same frame, what happens? The viewer makes a story. Why did the dancers drop the flowers? Doomed love. They're dancing and one of them asks for a divorce! Really! The fact is, and this is a fact, that the viewer will either make a story out of the frame or they will reject the image. Reject it cold. You cannot, no matter how hard you try, make a meaningless picture. I'm telling you they will invent the meaning. You never have a picture, you have an interpretation of a picture.

*(The dancers dance off with photographers snapping and, at the*

*same time, a young man saunters on. He is stripped to the waist, wearing jeans. In slow motion he takes them off.)*

ACTOR TWO: Patterns. That's all it really it. Music has chords, a photograph has patterns. You know, you get right down to it, it's all just dots.

ACTOR ONE: *(Taking pictures of the strip.)* Well, it's not technology.

ACTOR FOUR: Engineering maybe.

ACTOR SIX: The hard sell.

ACTOR FOUR: How about two minutes of complete quiet to let me get off on this.

ACTOR FIVE: They don't see what you shoot anyway.

ACTOR TWO: Turn around…

ACTOR SIX: Slowwwwwwwwwwly.

ACTOR ONE: Over here.

ACTOR FIVE: They see ahead of the picture, or past it. The guy they see has no clothes on. The guy they see is touching them. They don't even see him, they feel him. They walk right through the picture into their own heads.

ACTOR SIX: End of a role.

ACTOR THREE: Got it.

ACTOR TWO: GOT IT.

ACTOR FOUR: Forget it.

*(The model walks off and is passed by a man in a business suit with dark glasses and a briefcase carrying a see-through plastic drop cloth still in its hardware store package.)*

ACTOR FOUR: The only thing left to do is get incredibly small, infinitesimally small.

*(The man opens the drop cloth and carefully spreads it out on the white floor covering.)*

ACTOR ONE: *(Looking at the man.)* No opportunity.

*(The man opens his briefcase, takes out a sheet and moves upstage where he hangs it over a wire stretched across the stage.)*

ACTOR SIX: Small is right. Smaller than small. Some part of a part of a part that can't be seen with the naked eye. Micro photography that's the only frontier. The only thing nobody's seen.

ACTOR TWO: The only image that isn't used up.

ACTOR SIX: We're talking hair follicles here, we're talking dust mote mites living on an elephant hide, blown up so they look like whatever scared the shit out of you while it ate the world in the fifties monster movies.

*(The man sits down on the drop cloth and opens the briefcase from which he takes a disassembled pistol. He professionally puts it together.)*

ACTOR SIX: See, I don't buy that storytelling stuff because there isn't a story left they haven't heard, not a variation of a story left. People are bored stiff with their minds, you haven't noticed? Mother, son, death, war, baby, redemption, love, separation. One giant, congealed, lump of a story. Rule one: you only want what you haven't seen before.

*(A pregnant women enters; she poses smelling a small spring bouquet.)*

ACTOR THREE: You have got to be kidding.

*(She exits. The man takes out a handful of cartridges and loads the pistol. Two photographers focus on him.)*

ACTOR FOUR: *(Casting a critical eye on him.)* I don't know, maybe.

ACTOR ONE: Stand over behind the guy.

ACTOR TWO: Why?

ACTOR ONE: Because it's a photo opportunity, okay?

*(The man on the drop cloth clicks the gun closed. Me sights along it. He puts it down. He takes a white apron out of the briefcase, stands up, and puts it on.)*

ACTOR TWO: The guy shooting the guy shooting, right?

ACTOR THREE: The guy shooting the guy shooting the guy shooting.

*(The photographers move in shooting each other and the guy. The man sits down again on the drop cloth.)*

ACTOR FIVE: So we've seen all the events but we haven't seen all the people seeing the events?

ACTOR ONE: There is no activity…you're in my way…no activity you can find or imagine…over here, please…that has any moral force or essential interest other than the emotion it contains. If it's passionate, you can see it a thousand times.

*(The man on the drop cloth puts the business end of the pistol in his mouth. The photographers shoot.)*

ACTOR THREE: All you've got is the act and the viewer. The act *and* the viewer.

ACTOR FIVE: Otherwise, it's a knife that doesn't cut.

# Kind Ness

Ping Chong

**Comic**
**Scene:** the second grade

Mr. Conklin
Mrs. Conklin
Dot
Buzz
Daphne
Alvin
Lulu
Rudy

MR. CONKLIN: Hello!
DOT: Hello!
MRS. CONKLIN: Hello!
DOT: Hello!
MR. CONKLIN: Hi Dot!
DOT: Hello!
MRS. CONKLIN: Hi Dot!
DOT: Hi!
MR. CONKLIN: Dot, we'd like you to meet Buzz.
DOT: Buzz!
MR. CONKLIN: Buzz, this is Dot.
DOT: *(Shyly.)* Dot.
MR. CONKLIN: Dot, this is Buzz.
DOT: Buzz.
MR. CONKLIN: You remember my wife Brenda, don't you Dot?
DOT: Brenda.
MRS. CONKLIN: You can call me Bunny.
DOT: Bunny.
MRS. CONKLIN: Hi, Dot!
DOT: Hi, Bunny.
MR. CONKLIN: Dot, Buzz has come all the way over here from Rwanda.
DOT: Rhode Island?
MRS. CONKLIN: In Africa, Dot.
DOT: Rhode Island in Africa?

MR. CONKLIN: *(Shouting.)* Rwanda in Africa, Dot!

MRS. CONKLIN: *(Disapproving.)* Daddy!

MR. CONKLIN: Buzz is over here to further his studies.

DOT: His studies, ohhh!

MRS. CONKLIN: *(Stroking Buzz.)* He's one of Mr. Conklin's best students, aren't cha, Buzzy!

MR. CONKLIN: *(Chuckling.)* Why don't you two get together?
*(The Conklins shove Buzz toward Dot.)*

MRS. CONKLIN: *(Nodding in approval.)* Get acquainted!

MR. CONKLIN: Have a little tête-à-tête.

MRS. CONKLIN: Aren't they cute, Daddy?! Bye, Dot!

MR. CONKLIN: Goodbye, Buzz!
*(The Conklins exit backwards on their upstage diagonal. Dot and Buzz join hands and run offstage on the downstage right diagonal. At the same time, Alvin runs in backwards, diagonally, from the upstage left wing, followed by Daphne. They arc around toward the audience. Buzz reenters from downstage right, also backwards, also on a diagonal. He too arcs around to face the audience. The Conklins reenter with an imaginary tray of snacks and candy.)*

MR. CONKLIN: Hey, kids!

DAPHNE AND ALVIN: Hi!

MRS. CONKLIN: We have some refreshments for you!

MR. CONKLIN: Hello Daphne.

DAPHNE: Mr. Conklin.

MR. CONKLIN: Hello again there, Buzz.

MRS. CONKLIN: Hello Alvin, good to see you.

ALVIN: Hi, Bunny.

MR. CONKLIN: Hey kids, help yourselves. There's Ding-Dongs, there's little Yoo-Hoos, there's Hum-Hums.

MRS. CONKLIN: There's Yo-Yos, and Snick-Snacks, and Doo-Doos and Cheeses.
*(Buzz reaches for one, but she pulls tray away from him.)*

MRS. CONKLIN: Your people don't eat cheese, do they?
*(Buzz shakes his head shyly.)*

MR. CONKLIN: Put that in your mouth, Daphne!

MRS. CONKLIN: Eat 'em up, Alvin.

MR. CONKLIN: Alvin, your father find any work yet?

*(Alvin is horrified and hurt by this question and turns away. Mrs. Conklin grabs Daphne and Buzz by the shoulders.)*

MRS. CONKLIN: Are you kids feeling relaxed?

DAPHNE: Totally relaxed.

MRS. CONKLIN: I'm so glad. I was saying to Daddy just the other day, Daddy—

MR. CONKLIN: *(Interrupting.)* Mother! Take your hands off the children!

MRS. CONKLIN: Good idea! *(She shoves them aside and joins Mr. Conklin.)*

MR. CONKLIN: Okay kids! You have a good time now.

MRS. CONKLIN: Enjoy yourselves, young people!

*(Buzz has one arm affectionately on Daphne's shoulder. Alvin, Daphne and Buzz wave.)*

MR. CONKLIN: Keep your hands to yourselves.

*(Buzz drops his arm from Daphne's shoulder.)*

MRS. CONKLIN: No hanky-panky!

*(The Conklins exit. At the same time Buzz exits backwards and Alvin hunches over downstage left, covering his face with his hands. Daphne touches Alvin's shoulders and he mimes being the werewolf again, growling at her. The next vignette is played on the diagonal from downstage left toward upstage right.)*

DAPHNE: *(Startled, but friendly.)* Hello—you must be Alvin. I'm Daphne. *(She start to head upstage very slowly as she speaks.)*

ALVIN: *(Shyly.)* Hi Daphne!

DAPHNE: I'm very, very—rich. You're very, very poor. *(Alvin turns away in shame for a second, then turns back toward her.)*

ALVIN: *(Following her upstage.)* Can we still be friends?

DAPHNE: Acquaintances—oh, yes—acquaintances.

*(Daphne quickly exits backwards, pursued by Alvin. Lulu enters from downstage right, heading diagonally toward upstage left.)*

LULU: *(Waving.)* Hello, hi there, hello, hi there, hello, hi there, hello. *(Dot and Buzz enter diagonally from upstage left.)*

DOT: Lulu, I'd like you to meet Buzz. Buzz this is Lulu!

LULU: Hi, Buzz. You can call me Lu! *(Rudy comes running in from behind Lulu on downstage right diagonal.)*

RUDY: Hi there!

DOT: Rudy, Buzz. Buzz, Rudy.

RUDY: Hi Buzz, you can call me Ru!

*(Rudy and Lulu pull Buzz by his hands and he falls forward onto the floor.)*

DOT: Buzz is a sparkling conversationalist.

*(Lulu and Rudy sigh audibly at this revelation.)*

RUDY: Buzz, I'm already fascinated by you.

DOT: Why don't you go have a chat?

LULU: Come on, Buzz.

*(She and Rudy grab Buzz, head back down diagonal toward downstage right.)*

LULU: Let's go have some fun!

*(Dot has been skipping backwards back up her diagonal. She comes forward quickly to say her line.)*

DOT: Have a chitchat!

*(Dot exits backwards up her entrance diagonal. Rudy and Lulu exit with Buzz. All four reenter choreographically, crisscrossing the stage in various configurations, sometimes backwards, sometimes forwards, heading on and off the stage. All this action is in counterpoint to the music.)*

ALVIN: Hi, Lulu!

LULU: Hi, Alvin!

RUDY: Hi, Dot!

DOT: Hi, Rudy!

*(More choreographic patterns before the next speech.)*

LULU: This summer I went to Rainbow Lake. Boy was it fun, tomato sauce and everything.

*(More choreographic patterns.)*

DAPHNE: My family took me to Africa to look at the wild animals. It was very boring.

*(Choreographic patterns are at their most complex.)*

ALVIN: I made five dollars...mowing the lawns. One time, I couldn't sleep all night...guess I'll never be a priest.

*(All join hands upstage center facing audience, swaying and singing their summer song.)*

ALL: In autumn time come quiet days
The mountain wears a golden haze
The vale is closer to the hill
The autumn brings a warning chill
Good-bye! Good-bye!

The summer days are gone
Good-bye! Good-bye!
The summer days are gone
The summer days are gone.

RUDY: Hey Buzz, let's go get some pop!

ALVIN: Did he say pop?! Oh, boy!

*(Alvin runs off, followed by everyone else, except Dot. In their excitement, she's been left behind.)*

DOT: I'd love some pop! And some hot dogs, and some ice cream, and some candy, and some Juju-Bees, and some Hum-Hums, and some Tic-Tacs, and some Snoo-Snoos, and some Yo-Yos and some Bim-Bums...

*(Halfway through Dot's speech, Daphne enters running and takes her off. Blackout.)*

# The Colored Museum

George C. Wolfe
1988

**Comic/Satiric**
**Scene:** Mama's living room

Narrator
Mama
Walter-Lee-Beau-Willie-Jones
Lady in Plaid
Medea Jones

The Last Mama-on-the-Couch Play

>   (*A Narrator, dressed in a black tuxedo, enters through the audience and stands center stage. He is totally solemn.*)

NARRATOR: We are pleased to bring you yet another Mama-on-the-Couch play. A searing domestic drama that tears at the very fabric of racist America. (*He crosses upstage center, sits on a stool and reads from a playscript.*) Act One. Scene One.
>   (*Mama revolves on stage left, sitting on a couch reading an oversized Bible. There is a window stage right. Mama's dress, the couch and drapes are made from the same material. A doormat lies down center.*)

NARRATOR: Lights up on a dreary, depressing but with middle-class aspirations tenement slum. There is a couch, with a Mama on it. Both are well worn. There is a picture of Jesus on the wall...
>   (*A picture of Jesus is instantly revealed.*)

NARRATOR: and a window which looks onto an abandoned tenement. It is late spring. Enter Walter-Lee-Beau-Willie-Jones.
>   (*Son enters through the audience.*)

NARRATOR: He is Mama's thirty-year-old son. His brow is heavy from three hundred years of oppression.

MAMA: (*Looking up from her Bible, speaking in a slow manner.*) Son, did you wipe your feet?

SON: (*An ever-erupting volcano.*) No, Mama, I didn't wipe me feet! Out there, every day, Mama, is the Man. The Man, Mama. Mr. Charlie! Mr. Bossman! And he's wipin' his feet on me. On me,

Mama, every damn day of my life. Ain't that enough for me to deal with? Ain't that enough?

MAMA: Son, wipe your feet.

SON: I wanna dream. I wanna be somebody. I wanna take charge of my life.

MAMA: You can do all of that, but first you got to wipe your feet.

SON: *(As he crosses to the mat, mumbling and wiping his feet.)* Wipe my feet...wipe my feet...wipe my feet...

MAMA: That's a good boy.

SON: *(Exploding.)* Boy! Boy! I don't wanna be nobody's good boy, Mama. I wanna be my own man!

MAMA: I know son, I know. God will show the way.

SON: God, Mama! Since when did your God ever do a damn thing for the black man. Huh, Mama, huh? You tell me. When did your God ever help me?

MAMA: *(Removing her wire-rim glasses.)* Son, come here.
*(Son crosses to Mama, who slowly stands and with an exaggerated stage slap, backhands Son clear across the stage. The Narrator claps his hands to create the sound for the slap. Mama then lifts her clenched fists to the heavens.)*

MAMA: Not in my house, my house, will you ever talk that way again!
*(The Narrator, so moved by her performance, erupts in applause and encourages the audience to do so.)*

NARRATOR: Beautiful. Just stunning.
*(He reaches into one of the secret compartments of the set and gets an award which he ceremoniously gives to Mama for her performance. She bows and then returns to the couch.)*

NARRATOR: Enter Walter-Lee-Beau-Willie's wife, the Lady in Plaid.
*(Music from nowhere is heard, a jazzy pseudo-abstract intro as the Lady in Plaid dances in through the audience, wipes her feet and then twirls about.)*

LADY IN PLAID: She was a creature of regal beauty
who in ancient time graced the temples of the Nile
with her womanliness.
But here she was, stuck being colored
and a woman in a world that valued neither.

SON: You cooked my dinner!

LADY IN PLAID: *(Oblivious to son.)* Feet flat, back broke,
she looked at the man who, though he be thirty,

still ain't got his own apartment.
Yeah, he's still livin' with his Mama!
And she asked herself, was this the life
for a Princess Colored, who by the
translucence of her skin, knew the
universe was her sister. *(The Lady in Plaid twirls and dances.)*

SON: *(Becoming irate.)* I've had a hard day of dealin' with the Man.
Where's my damn dinner? Woman, stand still when I'm talkin' to
you!

LADY IN PLAID: And she cried for her sisters in Detroit
who knew, as she, that their souls belonged
in ancient temples on the Nile.
And she cried for her sisters in Chicago
who, like her, their life has become
one colored hell.

SON: There's only one thing gonna get through to you.

LADY IN PLAID: And she cried for her sisters in New Orleans
and her sisters in Trenton and Birmingham,
and
Poughkeepsie and Orlando and Miami Beach
and
Las Vegas, Palm Springs.
*(As she continues to call out cities, he crosses offstage, returns
with two black dolls, then crosses to the window.)*

SON: Now are you gonna cook me dinner?

LADY IN PLAID: Walter-Lee-Beau-Willie-Jones, no! Not my babies.
*(Son throws them out the window. She lets out a primal scream.)*

LADY IN PLAID: He dropped them!!!!
*(The Narrator breaks into applause.)*

NARRATOR: Just splendid. Shattering.
*(The Narrator crosses to Mama and after an intense struggle with
her, takes the award from her and gives it to the Lady in Plaid,
who is still suffering primal pain.)*

LADY IN PLAID: Not my babies...not my... *(Upon receiving the award,
she instantly recovers.)* Help me up, sugar. *(She bows and crosses
to stand behind the couch.)*

NARRATOR: Enter Medea Jones, Walter-Lee-Beau-Willie's sister.
*(Medea moves very ceremoniously, wiping her feet, then speak-
ing and gesturing as if she just escaped from a Greek tragedy.)*

MEDEA: Ah, see how the sun kneels to speak
her evening vespers, exalting all
in her vision, even lowly tenement
long abandoned.

Mother, wife of brother, I trust
the approaching darkness finds you
safe in Hestia's bosom.

Brother, why wear the face of a man
in anguish. Can the garment of thine
feelings cause the shape of your
countenance to disfigure so?

SON: *(At the end of his rope.)* Leave me alone, Medea.

MEDEA: *(To Mama.)* Is good brother still going on and on and on
about He and the Man.

MAMA AND LADY IN PLAID: What else?

MEDEA: Ah brother, if with our thoughts and
words we could cast thine oppressors
into the lowest bowels of wretched
hell, would that make us more like the
gods or more like our oppressors.

No, brother, no, do not let thy rage
choke the blood which anoints thy
heart with love. Forgo thine darkened
humor and let love shine on your
soul, like a jewel on a young maiden's hand.
*(Dropping to her knees.)*
I beseech thee, forgo thine
anger and leave wrath to the gods!

SON: Girl, what has gotten into you.

MEDEA: Julliard, good brother. For I am no
longer bound by rhythms of race or
region. Oh, no. My speech, like my
pain and suffering, have become
classical and therefore universal.

LADY IN PLAID: I didn't understand a damn thing she said, but girl you
usin' them words.

(*Lady in Plaid crosses and gives Medea the award. Everyone applauds.*)

SON: (*Trying to stop the applause.*) Wait one damn minute! This my play. It's about me and the Man. It ain't got nuthin' to do with no ancient temples on the Nile and it ain't got nuthin' to do with Hestia's bosom. And it ain't got nuthin' to do with you slappin' me across no room. (*His gut-wrenching best.*) It's about me. Me and my pain! My pain!

THE VOICE OF THE MAN: Walter-Lee-Beau-Willie, this is the Man. You have been convicted of overacting. Come out with your hands up.

(*Son starts to cross to the window.*)

SON: Well now that does it.

MAMA: Son, no, don't go near that window. Son, no!

(*Gunshots ring out and son falls dead.*)

MAMA: (*Crossing to the body, too emotional for words.*) My son, he was a good boy. Confused. Angry. Just like his father. And his father's father. And his father's father's father. And now he's dead.

(*Seeing she's about to drop to her knees, the Narrator rushes and places a pillow underneath her just in time.*)

MAMA: If only he had been born into a world better than this. A world where there are no well-worn couches and no well-worn Mamas and nobody overemotes. If only he had been born into an all-black musical.

(*A song intro begins.*)

MAMA: Nobody ever dies in an all-black musical.

(*Medea and Lady in Plaid pull out church fans and begin to fan themselves. Mama sings a soul-stirring gospel.*)

MAMA: Oh why couldn't he
Be born
Into a show with lots of singing
And dancing

I say why
Couldn't he
Be born

LADY IN PLAID: Go ahead hunny. Take your time.

MAMA: Into a show where everybody
Is happy

NARRATOR AND MEDEA: Preach! Preach!

MAMA: Oh why couldn't he be born with the chance
　　To smile a lot and sing and dance
　　Oh why
　　Oh why

　　Oh why
　　Couldn't he
　　Be born
　　Into an all-black show
　　Woah-woah
　　*(The Cast joins in, singing doo-wop gospel background to Mama's lament.)*

MAMA: Oh why
　　Couldn't he
　　Be born
　　(He be born)
　　Into a show where everybody
　　Is happy

　　Why couldn't he be born with the chance
　　To smile a lot and sing and dance
　　Wanna know why
　　Wanna know why

　　Oh why
　　Couldn't he
　　Be born
　　Into an all-black show
　　A-men
　　*(A singing/dancing, spirit-raising revival begins.)*

MAMA: Oh, son, get up
　　Get up and dance
　　We say get up
　　This is your second chance

　　Don't shake a fist
　　Just shake a leg
　　And do the twist

Don't scream and beg
Son Son Son
Get up and dance

Get
Get up
Get up and
Get up and dance—All right!
Get up and dance—All right!
Get up and dance!
*(Walter-Lee-Beau-Willie springs to life and joins in the dancing. A foot-stomping, hand-clapping production number takes off, which encompasses a myriad of black Broadwayesque dancing styles—shifting speeds and styles with exuberant abandonment.)*
MAMA: *(Bluesy.)* Why couldn't he be born into an all-black show
CAST: With singing and dancing
MAMA: Black show
*(Mama scats and the dancing becomes manic and just a little too desperate to please.)*
CAST: We gotta dance
We gotta dance
Get up get up get up and dance
We gotta dance
We gotta dance
Gotta dance!
*(Just at the point the dancing is about to become violent, the Cast freezes and pointedly, simply sings.)*
CAST: If we want to live
We have got to
We have got to
Dance…and dance…and dance…
*(As they continue to dance with zombie-like frozen smiles and faces, around them images of coon performers flash as the lights slowly fade.)*

# Vera Takes Her Seat

Julie Eble
1998

**Comic**
**Scene:** the dining room of the family home

Vera
Herb
Lyle
Susie
Becky

HERB: The kids will be here pretty soon. *(Pause. Herb looks out over the paper.)* I said the kids will be here pretty soon. *(Pause.)* Aren't you going to finish setting the table? Are you tired? Sit down. Take it easy. Susie will help you when she gets here.

VERA: I am sitting down.

HERB: Do you want ME to help you? All you have to do is ask. Ah, here they are.

*(Susie, Lyle and Becky enter from stage right.)*

LYLE: What's for dinner, Mom? I'm starving. Susie didn't make any lunch. Hmm. Smells good.

*(Lyle looks at Vera who remains silent.)*

LYLE: Mom?

HERB: Your mother is tired. She needs help setting the table.

LYLE: Becky, help your grandmother set the table.

*(Becky rolls her eyes.)*

SUSIE: I'll finish the table, Mom. *(Susie exits upstage.)*

LYLE: Are your legs broken?

*(Becky exits to kitchen as Susie returns with a relish tray. Lyle immediately grabs some veggies and starts eating.)*

LYLE: Boys, that's all she thinks about.

SUSIE: He's a nice boy.

LYLE: That's what they said about Ted Bundy.

HERB: What's his name again?

SUSIE: Phil. He is a nice boy. *(To Vera.)* I turned off the peas. Everything else is ready.

*(Becky returns and mimes setting the table.)*

LYLE: Phil gets his term paper typed for him, doesn't he, Becky?

SUSIE: Lyle, please. Grammy, you just keep sitting. Becky and I will serve dinner.

BECKY: Great.

LYLE: So the typist is too important to serve dinner to her own family, huh?

SUSIE: Your grandmother is tired, Becky. It'll only take a minute.

VERA: I'm not tired.

SUSIE: Of course you are. Come on, everyone, come take a seat. *(Susie returns to kitchen.)*

BECKY: *(Mimes setting the place in front of Vera.)* Grammy, it's time to eat.

*(Vera looks at her.)*

BECKY: You're in Pop-pop's spot.

*(Herb comes to the table and stands beside her.)*

HERB: Vera, it's time for dinner.

VERA: I'm not moving.

HERB: You're in my spot.

*(Silence.)*

LYLE: Mom, you're in Dad's spot.

*(Susie returns with imaginary bottle of soda.)*

VERA: I'm sitting here.

HERB: Vera, stop being silly. It's dinnertime and the kids are hungry.

VERA: I'm not moving.

LYLE: Mom, don't you feel well?

BECKY: Whoa, Grammy.

LYLE: Be quiet!

HERB: Vera, you're making a scene. Move to your own chair.

VERA: I'm not moving.

LYLE: What's going on here? Did you two have a fight?

SUSIE: I don't understand.

LYLE: Sue, sit down!

*(Susie sits in Vera's usual seat.)*

LYLE: Not there! That's my mother's seat!

*(Susie sits in a different seat.)*

HERB: We did not have fight. In fact I just finished telling her that I'd be happy to help her out. She just needed to ask.

LYLE: You must have had a fight. Mom, give Dad his chair. You can sit in your normal seat.

VERA: I'm not moving.

HERB: Vera, what's the matter with you!

LYLE: You must have had a fight. Here, Mom, do you want my seat? Have my seat.

BECKY: This is too weird.

LYLE: *(To Becky.)* Your grandmother is not weird! *(To Vera.)* Mother, this is weird. What's gotten into you? Dad needs his seat.

HERB: Vera, do I have to move you myself!

LYLE: Dad!

HERB: She doesn't have to move. I'll move her myself.

SUSIE: Dad, remember your heart.

HERB: Is this what you want, Vera?

LYLE: Calm down, Dad.

HERB: I don't get it. What does she want? All of a sudden she stops setting the table and she sits in my chair! I told her I'd help. I can't believe we're having this discussion. This is absurd.

BECKY: I agree with that.

HERB: Who asked you, young lady? You want me to physically move you? Is that it?

SUSIE: Now, Dad.

HERB: You want me to have a heart attack and die just after I retire? *(Silence.)*

HERB: That's it. I'm moving her.

LYLE: *(Grabbing the arm of the chair.)* Dad, don't be crazy.

SUSIE: Dad. Sit, Lyle and I will do it.

LYLE: We will?

SUSIE: *(Grabs the other arm of the chair.)* We can't let HIM do it.

LYLE: All right on the count of three. One. Two. Three.
*(Susie and Lyle try to lift the chair but Vera mimes holding onto the table.)*

HERB: She's doing this on purpose! What's the matter with you, woman! Have you gone senile?

LYLE: Shush, Dad! *(More calmly.)* Mother. *(More excited.)* What are you doing?

VERA: I'm sitting.

SUSIE: She is right about that.
*(Lyle and Herb glare at Susie.)*

LYLE: Why are you sitting in Dad's seat?

VERA: I told him years ago. I should sit by the kitchen because I'm always jumping up to get things. But he insisted on having this seat. He insisted and I let him.

LYLE: Mom. He's had that seat for more than thirty years.

VERA: Forty one.

LYLE: There you go. Forty one.

HERB: I insisted, did I? This is ridiculous, Vera. GET OUT OF MY CHAIR!

LYLE: Dad, sit here.

HERB: That's not my seat. Vera!

*(Vera looks at Herb.)*

HERB: I'm warning you.

VERA: Are you going to beat me?

LYLE: Mother!

SUSIE: Mom!

BECKY: Grammy!

*(Herb grabs Vera's arm and tries to pull her out of the chair while Vera clings on tightly to the arms.)*

LYLE: *(Getting hold of Herb.)* Dad! Dad! Come on now. My God. You go sit in the living room. Go ahead now.

*(Herb goes to the stuffed chair.)*

LYLE: Mom, what the hell is going on around here?

VERA: For forty one years, I've run around this chair to get food out the kitchen. To get soda. And ketchup. And napkins. And every other thing that anybody wanted. I'm not running around this chair anymore. I am sitting in it.

LYLE: But, Mom. If you've run around it for forty years why…

VERA: Forty one!

LYLE: Okay. Forty one. If you've run around it for forty one years, why make a fuss now?

VERA: I deserve it.

HERB: I'm the man of the house, Vera!

VERA: And what's that get me!

HERB: How about a pension!

VERA: I've got my own pension coming, Herb.

HERB: You want the lawn mowed!

VERA: I'll mow it myself, thanks. I want this chair and I'm not moving.

HERB: *(Coming out to the dining room.)* It's my GOD-DAMN CHAIR!

VERA: I'm sitting in it! Be a man, Herb. Take another seat.

BECKY: Pop-pop. *(Hands him a celery stalk.)* Have a celery stalk.

SUSIE: *(Intervening before Herb can react.)* Here, Pop-pop. Now you sit right here. There you go. Now, how about some soda?
*(Herb sits reluctantly and Susie mimes pouring him a soda.)*

BECKY: Grammy? I understand this seat is closer to the kitchen. That makes sense. But, Grammy, Pop-pop's been sitting there for forty…
*(Vera looks at her.)*

BECKY: Forty-one years. Why change now? I thought you liked where you sat.

VERA: Did you think that?

LYLE: We all thought you liked your seat.

VERA: And you thought I liked to set the table, I bet.

LYLE: Don't you? Susie does. She loves that stuff.

SUSIE: No, I don't.

HERB: Come on. Women love to take care of people. It's just in your nature.

VERA: Don't tell me what's in my nature, Herb.

HERB: You're not going to sit there and deny that you liked raising the kids.

VERA: I liked raising the kids. I don't like raising you! You're a grown man. Set your own place at the table.

HERB: If I knew it was an issue, I would. Like it's such a big deal. A dish and some silverware. And, Vera, don't you sit there and say I haven't helped raise this family.

LYLE: Come on, Mom. Dad coached little league. He taught us to play ball. He took us fishing.

VERA: And what was I doing?

LYLE: I don't know. What were you doing?

VERA: Scrubbing the toilets. Mending your clothes. Cooking your meals.

HERB: That's all done now, Vera. And I don't believe you didn't enjoy it.

SUSIE: Gee, I just love scrubbing toilets.

LYLE: This doesn't concern you!

VERA: Don't you yell at your wife.

HERB: Look what you're doing, Vera. You've got the kids yelling at each other. Are you happy now? I don't understand. Haven't I always been good to you? Have I ever forgotten an anniversary? Didn't I buy you pearls for your fiftieth birthday?

VERA: I am sitting in this chair.

HERB: Fine. Sit in that chair. It's only a chair. I can sit anywhere.

VERA: You can't sit here.

HERB: Vera, that has always been my chair. Why all of a sudden do you want my chair?

VERA: It isn't your chair. I never gave it to you.

HERB: I always sat there. That makes it mine.

VERA: You always took it. I didn't give it to you. Now I'm taking it and you can't make me give it back.

HERB: I could if I wanted to but that's not the point.

VERA: No you couldn't.

HERB: Don't think I couldn't.

LYLE: Dad, this is silly.

HERB: Of course it's silly. It's very silly.

VERA: So just sit somewhere else.

HERB: Don't think I'm going to let you boss me around just because my heart's not so good anymore. I'm not falling apart. I'm still a man. I could move you if I wanted.

VERA: Go ahead.

LYLE: Mother!

HERB: By God, I will in a minute.

VERA: It comes down to that in the end, doesn't it?

HERB: I could still move you if I wanted to.

LYLE: That's not why he sat there all those years. It was just his place at the head of the table.

HERB: I could move you, Vera.

(Herb and Vera look at each other.)

HERB: You know I could.

BECKY: Pop-pop, wait. Wait. Grammy, I understand. You want to be equal. But why that chair and why now.

VERA: (Looking at Becky.) Mostly because...Because I just decided. But there's a second reason, you.

BECKY: Me? What's this got to do with me, Grammy?

VERA: You're dating this Phil now, right?

(Becky nods.)

VERA: Guess you think he's pretty important. But, you know what? You're important, too.

BECKY: I know that, Grammy.

VERA: Do you? Do you know you don't have to type his papers?

BECKY: Sure, I know.

VERA: Do you really? Who showed you? Did I ever show you? Did your Mom? Think about it next time he wants you to type a paper, or he tells you to "sit here" or "get me something to eat." Next thing you know you'll be scrubbing his toilet and he'll be sitting at the head of the table.

HERB: So this is about our granddaughter. I should have known it wasn't about me. Women!

SUSIE: Well, I say let's eat.

LYLE: I'm starved. Hey, Mom. Now that you showed Becky, why don't you move back to your chair?

VERA: No.

LYLE: But you've shown her how. She gets the point. Let Dad have his seat back.

VERA: Showing her how to sit in the chair was only part of it. Showing her how to keep sitting in it, that's the rest of it. Besides, this is my seat now.

*(Herb jumps up shouting. Lyle, Susie, and Becky jump up to contain him. Commotion continues till curtain closes.)*

# LARGE GROUP SCENES
## (11+ ACTORS)

# Lysistrata

Aristophanes
Translated by Carl R. Mueller

**Comic**
**Scene:** the Akropolis

Chorus of Old Men
Leader of the Chorus of Old Men
Chorus of Old Women
Leader of the Chorus of Old Women
A Magistrate
Four Scythian Policemen
Two Slaves

>   *(Enter a Chorus of Old Men, poorly dressed, exhausted by their
>   load, coughing, wheezing. Each carries two logs, a torch and a
>   bucket of live coals. The Chorus's sentences are spoken individually.)*

MEN'S LEADER: Onward, Drakës!
    Onward and upward, old friend!
    Watch your shoulders, don't skin them
    With those infernal big olive-tree branches.
    Ah, what a life!

OLD MEN'S CHORUS: Onward and upward, old cockers! Oooo!
    The awful things age does to you!
    You, Strymodoros, who would have thought it?
    Right where it hurts, that's where we've caught it—
    And from women what's more!
    The shameless whores!
    The wives we wed,
    The wives we fed,
    The wives we dragged off to bed have fled!
    They've taken the Akropolis of my favorite metropolis!
    And why? I ask why?
    They've barred the gates and bolted the doors!
    The ladies from Hades!
    The devious whores!

MEN'S LEADER: That's right, Philourgos!
    When we get up there we'll pile our branches

Next to the wall in a heaven-high pyre!
We'll burn the bitches, traitors to Athens,
Burn them to cinders and rout the conspiracy!
And the first one will be that Lysistrata!
No one gets the better of us!

OLD MEN'S CHORUS: Not even that Spartan,
The great Kleomenês, all stuffed full of pride
And riding his high-horse,
Got the better of us.
Six hundred men he marched up here,
Six hundred Spartans.
They stayed six years.
The swell and the swagger,
The puff and the pride of those
Six hundred men was doomed to subside.
We slept at the gate.
Sixteen ranks deep.
That sealed their fate.
We protected our state!

MEN'S LEADER: He came out a wreck,
Old King Kleomenês, with
Scarcely a rag to cover his penis.
Starved and unshaved and unwashed for six years!
I remember his smell!

OLD MEN'S CHORUS: We remember it well.

MEN'S LEADER: But he learned his lesson.

OLD MEN'S CHORUS: He learned it well.

MEN'S LEADER: And now these women, these
Pests out of Hades!
These frivolous ladies!
These whores out of Hell!
Have taken the Akropolis of my favorite metropolis!
Down with these ladies!
These pests out of Hades!
All the world hates them!
The gods and Euripides!

OLD MEN'S CHORUS: We fought the Medes at Marathon.
So we will not be put upon.
We won it there!

We'll win it here!

MEN'S LEADER: But first let's haul these logs on up there!

OLD MEN'S CHORUS: My legs are wobbly.
My knees a bit quaky.
A good stiff drink would make them less shaky.
A team of oxen would lighten this load,
Steady on, men, it's right up the road,

MEN'S LEADER: Careful there!
Don't drop your pots.
They hold the only fire we've got.
So blow on the embers!
Blow as you go!

OLD MEN'S CHORUS: Hoo! Hoo!
What a stench!
The smoke makes me choke!
This smoke is a wench that tears at my eyes!
Hoo! Hoo!
How fiercely it flies!
Flies straight to my eyes!
This fire is a bitch to make my eyes itch!

MEN'S LEADER: Steady on, men!
We've almost arrived!
Another few steps and we'll get there alive!

OLD MEN'S CHORUS: One more step.
Another step onward.
Courage, men, we're almost there.
Just short of despair.
We're almost there.
At the cost of our lives
We'll rescue the goddess from our miscreant wives.

MEN'S LEADER: We're here, men! Halt!
Lower your loads!
Pile them about!
We'll make us a pyre
To fire the fools out!

OLD MEN'S CHORUS: Ah, my old back!
What a misery I'm in!
My shoulders are slack with that weight off my back.
My arms are undone.

My fingers are numb.
What a misery I'm in!
What a misery we're in!

MEN'S LEADER: Blow on your embers!
Let's make them glow bright.

OLD MEN'S CHORUS: Miserable smoke!
Came right off of Lemnos!
Hoo! Hoo!
Miserable stench!

MEN'S LEADER: Bring the pots over.
Set them down here.
Now dip in your torches.
Let them catch fire.
Then straight to the pyre.

OLD MEN'S CHORUS: Hoo! Hoo!
Miserable stench!
Attacking my eyes like a rabid bitch!
Hoo! Hoo!
How fiercely it flies!
Straight to my eyes!

MEN'S LEADER: There! They're burning!
And now we're ready!
Steady there, steady!
We've set them alight!
And now we'll charge the gates like rams!
If that doesn't teach these women what's right,
We'll fire the doors and smoke them to Hades,
The miscreant ladies!
What we really need is that famous general
Who sits on his duff all day on Samos.

Lady Luck! Help us! We need it!
We'll kick the living shit from these bitches,
Or die trying!
Down with women!
Up with men!
Onward to victory!

(While the Men are preparing the logs and branches on one side
of the stage, there enters on the other side a Chorus of Old

*Women, nicely dressed and carrying jugs and jars of water on their heads. At first they do not see each other. The Chorus' sentences are spoken individually.)*

WOMEN'S LEADER: Fire, girls! I smell smoke!
    Hurry! We have to save our friends!
    Run, Nikodikê, run, before
    Kalykê's done to a turn!
    And Kritylla's buns are
    Burned to a crisp!
    Winds are gusting and fanning the flames!
    The rickety codgers and their hateful ways,
    These bags of bones will do them in!
    I hope we're not late!

OLD WOMEN'S CHORUS: I went to the well
    At dawn this morning to fill my jug.
    The crowd was frantic.
    Shoving and jostling.
    Housewives and slaves.
    Waves of people everywhere.
    Elbows right in the gut, but
    I filled it and set it square on my head.
    Then sped up here to save my friends.
    They're coming, they say!
    To get at the women and turn them to cinders!
    Screaming, howling!
    Shouting terrible threats to destroy them!
    Bitches of Hell is what they call them.
    The farting old codgers are making their way here
    To force the Akropolis
    Of our favorite metropolis,
    Or burn it down!

WOMEN'S LEADER: I pray to the goddess
    I may never see them
    In flames, these women!
    These noble women!
    They have a mission!
    To rescue Greece and all her citizens
    From the madness of war!
    Let them succeed!

Goddess, help them!
There's no other reason
They've taken your temple!
And let us help to put out the flames
With the water we've brought—
If water is needed!
Goddess of the Golden Crest!
Faithful Guardian of the Citadel!
Hear us!
*(The Chorus of Old Women becomes aware of the Chorus of Old Men.)*

WOMEN'S LEADER: Ah, and what do we have here!

OLD WOMAN ONE: Men! Foul, ugly men!
No, gentlemen. No self-respecting man
Would be caught doing such things.

MEN'S LEADER: Ah! A fly in the ointment!

OLD MAN ONE: Trouble, boys! Who'd have thought it!

OLD MAN TWO: A gaggle of old crones on the Akropolis
To help the damn bitches inside!

WOMEN'S LEADER: You haven't seen the half of us yet.

OLD WOMAN THREE: There's more on the road.

OLD WOMAN FOUR: Swarms of us coming.

WOMEN'S LEADER: So tremble away.

MEN'S LEADER: Phaidrias! Get over here!
I need help with these jawing females!
Bust them over the head with a log!

WOMEN'S LEADER: Pots on the ground, girls.
If these antique specimens
Who claim to be men attack us
We'll have both hands to fight with.

OLD MAN THREE: 1 think this one wants her face smashed!

OLD WOMAN TWO: Take a swing. I can take it.
Just be ready for a death grip on your balls!

OLD WAN FOUR: I'll get you, bitch!

OLD MAN TWO: Here's a stick! Watch out!

WOMEN'S LEADER: Put a finger on Stratyllis,
And you'll have more than the stick in your hand
To worry about!

OLD MAN FOUR: Drop dead, you old broad!

OLD WOMAN ONE: I'll eat your guts raw, old windbag!

OLD MAN ONE: Ah, Euripides! How well you knew women!

OLD WOMAN ONE: Up with the pots, Rhodippê!

MEN'S LEADER: Pots?

OLD MAN TWO: For what?

OLD MAN THREE: Water?

OLD MAN FOUR: Witch!

WOMEN'S LEADER: Why did you bring *fire,*
    You refugee from the grave?
    To burn yourself up?

MEN'S LEADER: To build a pyre and barbecue your friends!

WOMEN'S LEADER: In that case, we'll put it out with this!

MEN'S LEADER: Put out *my* fire, with *that?*

OLD WOMAN TWO: Stay around long enough and you'll see.

MEN'S LEADER: I might just roast you for dinner with this torch!

OLD WOMAN THREE: I hope you've brought soap
    For the bath you'll be getting.

MEN'S LEADER: *Me,* a *bath,* from *you,* you doddering crone?

WOMEN'S LEADER: A bath fit for a senile bridegroom.

MEN'S LEADER: Senile!

OLD MAN TWO: Bitch!

OLD MAN FOUR: Shut your hole!

WOMEN'S LEADER: I'm not a slave, you know!

MEN'S LEADER: I'll stop this jabbering!

WOMEN'S LEADER: Well, you're not a juror now!

MEN'S LEADER: Set her hair on fire, men!

WOMEN'S LEADER: God of Rivers, do your duty!

    *(The old Women empty their pots on the Old Men.)*

MEN'S LEADER: Fucking shit!

OLD MAN ONE: Offff!

OLD WAN FOUR: Argh!

OLD MAN THREE: Damn the old hags!

WOMEN'S LEADER: How's the temperature?

MEN'S LEADER: Temperature!

OLD MAN TWO: Hell!

OLD MAN THREE: Stop!

OLD MAN FOUR: What are you doing?!

OLD WOMAN THREE: We're watering you to help you bloom.

MEN'S LEADER: I'm cold as a witch's tit!

WOMEN'S LEADER: Then sit by your fire-pots and warm up.
  (Enter an Old Magistrate, more interested in airing his own views
  than in taking charge of the situation, along with four Scythian
  Policemen with bows and quivers, and two Slaves with crowbars.)
OLD MAGISTRATE: Women! Degenerate bunch!
  Women's depravity bursting into flame again!
  Drums and eternal yapping for Adonis!
  Boom-boom-boom-boom!
  Drives you out of your mind! Cavorting
  On rooftops! Drunken orgies! It's like
  The time in the Assembly when that fool Demostatos—
  Out of order, of course, as usual—
  Was plugging we send an armada to Sicily
  At the same time his wife was dancing around in circles,
  Bellowing at the top of her lungs:
  "Alas for Adonis!" and all that rot!
  Then that ox-brained demagogue of a husband of hers
  Insists we sign up every Zakynthian male
  Who can walk, while his wife is up on the roof,
  Drunk as a skunk, hooting away in some
  Ecstatic state: "Weep for Adonis!
  Weep, weep, oh weep! Beat your breast!"
  But no stopping him! On he goes,
  The old blight on the earth's surface,
  Ramrodding his program through with the
  Subtlety of a cattleprod—all the while
  Putting up with this riotous *female*-business!
  So there it is! Woman's gift to the world!
  Moral chaos!
MEN'S LEADER: Save your breath
  Till you've heard the atrocities
  They've done to *us* here today!
  The nerve of these godforsaken bitches!
  Doused us with water from their pitchers
  So we, look like kids who've pissed our tunics!
OLD MAGISTRATE: By the god of the salty sea,
  We deserve what we get! Whose fault is it
  That women get out of hand?
  Ours, gentlemen, ours!

We pamper them, we instruct them in prurience,
Lead them down the primrose path to depravity!
We go into a goldsmith's shop and say:
"Ah, goldsmith, you remember that necklace
You made for my wife, I'm sure.
Well, last night she was at a dance
And the screw came loose that holds the clasp.
I'm off to Salamis on business,
So I wonder if you could stop by the house this evening
And give her another screw."
Or off we go to the shoemaker,
A lusty lad with a cock that won't quit,
And say: "My wife's having some trouble with her sandal,
It rubs her little pinkie that's awfully tender.
Could you take a long lunch break,
Drop by the house and stretch it out for her—
Give it a little more play?"
Well, we reap what we sow!
And this is what it's come to!
Here am I, a Public Servant, a Magistrate,
Who have lined up a source of timber for oars,
And have come to the Treasury for the necessary funds
To pay the dealer, and what do I find?
What I find is myself, standing at the gate, locked out—
Which is bad enough—but locked out by *women!*
But I'm not about to stand around. Not me.
*(To the two Slaves.)*
You, slaves, bring the crowbars!
It's time we put a stop to this women's arrogance.
*(To the Scythian Policemen.)*
What are *you* gawking at?
Keep your mind on the job and stop
Daydreaming about an escape to the pubs!
*(To the Slaves.)*
Get those crowbars under the gates
And start heaving! I'll do a little
Heaving over here myself.

# Noah

Anonymous—The Wakefield Mystery Cycle
15th century

**Dramatic**
**Scene:** on Noah's land

Noah
God
Noah's Wife
First Son
Second Son
Third Son
First Son's Wife
Second Son's Wife
Third Son's Wife

GOD: Into the ship with thee;
Thy sons of good fame,
Ham, Japhet, and Shem,
On board must remain,
With their wives three.

For all shall be destroyed, that lives on land, but ye,
With floods that fill the void, and falling in plenty;
The heavens shall be employed to rain incessantly,
When days seven have cloyed, it shall last days forty,

Without fail.
Take in thy ship also
Two beasts of each kind, so,
Male and female, see they go,
Before thou raise thy sail.

So thou may thee avail when all these things are wrought,
Stuff thy ship with victual for hunger that ye lack nought;
For beasts, fowl, and cattle keep them in your thought
For them is my counsel, that some succour be sought,

Uppermost;
They must have corn and hay,
And meat enough alway;
Do now, as I thee say,
In the name of the holy ghost.

NOAH: Ah! Benedicite! What art thou thus,
That tells before what shall be? Thou art full marvellous!
Tell me for charity thy name so gracious.

GOD: My name is of dignity and also full glorious
To know.
I am God most mighty,
One God in trinity,
Made thee and each man to be;
Love to me thou should show.

NOAH: I thank thee, Lord, so dear, that would vouchsafe
Thus low to appear to a simple knave;
Bless us, Lord, here for charity I it crave,
The better may we steer the ship that we have,
Certain.

GOD: Noah, to thee and to thy fry
My blessing grant I;
Ye shall work and multiply,
And fill the earth again,
When all these floods are past and fully gone away.

NOAH: Lord, homeward will I fast in haste as that I may;
(Exit God.)

NOAH: My wife will I ask what she will say,
And I am all aghast lest there be some fray
Between us both;
For she is full tetchy,
For little oft angry,
If anything wrong be,
Soon is she wroth.
(He goes to his wife.)
God speed thee, wife, how fare ye?

WIFE: Now, as ever might I thrive, the worse to see thee;
Tell me, on your life, where thus long could thou be?
To death may we drive, because of thee,
Alack.

When work weary we sink,
Thou dost what thou think,
Yet of meat and drink
Have we great lack.

NOAH: Wife, we are hard pressed with tidings new.
WIFE: But thou ought to be dressed in stafford blue;
For thou art always depressed, be it false or true;
God knows I am oppressed, and that may I rue,
Full ill;
All I hear is thy crow,
From even till morrow,
Screeching ever of sorrow;
God send thee once thy fill.

We women may harry all ill husbands;
I have one, by Mary! That loosed me of my bands;
If he twits I must tarry, however so it stands,
And seem to be full sorry, wringing both my hands

For dread.
But in a little while,
What with game and guile,
I shall smite and smile
And pay him back instead.

NOAH: Hush! Hold thy tongue, ramshit, or I shall thee still.
WIFE: As I thrive, if thou smite, I shall pay back with skill.
NOAH: We shall see who is right, have at thee, Gill!
Upon the bone shall it bite!
WIFE: Ah, by Mary! Thou smitest ill!
But I suppose
I shall not in thy debt
Leave this place yet!
This strap is what you get
To tie up thy hose!
NOAH: Ah! Wilt thou so? Mary, that is mine.
WIFE: Have thou three for two, I swear, by God divine,
NOAH: I shall requite each blow, your skin will bear my sign.
WIFE: Out upon thee, ho!
NOAH: Thou can both bite and whine

For all thou art worth.
For though she will strike,
Her shrieks my ears spike,
There is not her like
On all this earth.

WIFE: But I will keep charity in this to-do
Here shall no man tarry thee; I pray thee go to!
Full well may we miss thee, as peace is our due;
To spin will I address me.

NOAH: Farewell, then, to you;
But wife,
Pray for me busily,
Till again I come to thee.

WIFE: Even as thou prayst for me,
As ever might I thrive.

NOAH: I tarry full long, to my work I must go;
My gear take along and watch the work grow;
I may go all wrong, in truth, I it know;
If God's help is not strong I may sit in sorrow,
I ken;
Now assay will I
Something of carpentry,
*In nomine patris, et filii,*
*Et spiritus sancti,* Amen.
To begin with this tree, my bones will I bend,
I trust that the trinity succour will send;
The work prospers fairly to a fitting end;
Now blessed be he that this did commend.
Lo, here the length,
Three hundred cubits evenly,
Of breadth lo is it fifty,
The height is even thirty
Cubits full strength.
Now my gown will I cast and work in my coat
Make will I the mast to set in the boat,
Ah! My back breaks fast! This is a sorry note!
It is wonder that I last, so weak that I dote,
Behold,
To begin this affair!

My bones are so bare,
No wonder they despair,
For I am full old.

The top and the sail both will I make,
The helm and the castle also will I take,
To drive in each a nail without a mistake,
This way will never fail, that dare I undertake
Right soon.
This was a noble plan,
These nails so swiftly ran
Through more or less the span
Of these boards each one.

Window and door even as he said
Three cabins more, they are well made,
Pitch and tar full sure upon them have been laid,
This will ever endure, I count myself well paid;
And why?
It is better wrought
Than I could have thought;
Him, that made all of nought,
I thank only.

Now will I hie me despite the ill weather
My wife and my family, to bring even hither.
Listen here carefully, wife, and consider,
Hence must we flee all together
Right fast.
WIFE: Why, sir, what ails you?
Who is it assails you?
To flee it avails you,
Yet ye be aghast.
NOAH: The yarn on the reel is otherwise, dame.
WIFE: Tell me more and less, else ye be to blame.
NOAH: He can cure our distress, blessed be his name.
Our dole he will redress to shield us from shame
And said,
All this world about

With fierce floods so stout,
That shall run in a rout,
Shall be overspread.

He said all shall be slain save only we,
Our bairns shall remain and their wives three;
A ship he bad me ordain to save our company,
Therefore with all our maill that Lord thank we,
Saviour of our blood;
Get along fast, go thither.

WIFE: I know not whither,
I daze and I dither,
For fear of that flood.

NOAH: Be not afraid, have done, truss up our gear,
Lest we be undone, without more fear.

FIRST SON: Full soon it shall be done, brothers help me here.

SECOND SON: My part I shall not shun, no matter how severe,
My brother.

THIRD SON: Without any yelp
With my might shall I help.

WIFE: I've a blow for each whelp,
If you help not your mother.

NOAH: Now are we there, as we should be;
Go, get in our gear, cattle and company,
Into this vessel here, my children free.

WIFE: Shut up was I never, so God save me,
In such an oyster as this.
In faith I cannot find
Which is before, which is behind;
Shall we here be confined,
Noah, as have thou bliss?

NOAH: Dame, peace and still, we must abide grace;
Therefore, wife, with good will, come into this place.

WIFE: Sir, for Jack nor for Gill, will I turn my face,
Till I have on this hill, spun a space
On my distaff;
Woe to him who moves me,
Now will I down set me,
And let no man prevent me,

For him will I strafe.

NOAH: Behold in the heaven, the cataracts all
   That are open full even, both great and small
   And the planets seven, left have their stall,
   The thunder downdriven, and lightnings now fall

   Full stout,
   On halls and bowers,
   Castles and towers;
   Full sharp are these showers,
   That deluge about.

   Therefore, wife have done, come in the ship fast.

WIFE: Patch your shoes and run, the better they will last.

FIRST WIFE: Come, good mother, come, for all is overcast,
   Both the moon and the sun.

SECOND WIFE: And many winds blast
   Full sharp;
   These floods may drown our kin,
   Therefore, mother, come in.

WIFE: In faith, still will I spin;
   All in vain ye carp.

THIRD WIFE: If ye like, ye may spin, mother, in the ship.

NOAH: Ye be twice bidden in, dame, in all friendship.

WIFE: Whether I lose or win,
   in faith, thy fellowship,
   Set I not at a pin, this spindle will I slip
   Upon this hill.
   Ere one foot I stir.

NOAH: By Peter, but ye err;
   Without further spur
   Come in if ye will.

WIFE: Yea, the water nighs so near that I sit not dry,
   Into the ship for fear quickly will I hie
   For dread that I drown here.

NOAH: Dame, but surely,
   Paid ye have full dear, ye stayed so long by,
   Out of the ship.

WIFE: I will not at thy bidding,

Go from door to dunghill gadding.

NOAH: In faith and for your long tarrying,
Ye shall taste of the whip.

WIFE: Spare me not, I pray thee, do even as thou think,
These great words shall not flay me.

NOAH: Abide dame and drink,
For beaten shalt thou be with this staff till thou stink;
Are these strokes good, say ye.

WIFE: What say ye? Go sink!

NOAH: Now quake!
Cry me mercy, I say!

WIFE: To that say I nay.

NOAH: If not, by this day,
Thy head shall I break.

WIFE: Lord, I were at ease and heartily hale
With a pottage of pease and my widow's kale;
For thy soul it would please me to pay penny bail,
So would more than these I see in this dale,
Of the wives that here stir,
For the dance they are led,
Wish their husbands were dead,
For, as ever eat I bread,
So, would I our sire were.

NOAH: Ye men that have wives, while they are young,
If ye love your lives, chastise their tongue:
Methinks my heart rives, both liver and lung,
To see such a strife, wedded men among;
But I,
As have I bliss,
Shall chastise this.

WIFE: Yet may ye miss,
Nichol needy!

NOAH: I shall make thee still as stone, beginner of blunder!
I shall beat thee, back and bone, and break all in sunder.
(They fight.)

WIFE: Out, alas, I am overthrown! Out upon thee, man's wonder!

NOAH: See how she can groan, and I lie under;
But wife,
Haste we, without ado,

For my back is near in two.

WIFE: And I am beaten so blue
And wish for no more strife.

*(They enter the Ark.)*

FIRST SON: Ah! Why fare ye thus? father and mother, both!

SECOND SON: Your spite would scarce free us from such sin as wroth.

THIRD SON: These scenes are so hideous, I swear on my oath.

NOAH: We will do as ye bid us, and that with no sloth.
Sons dear!
At the helm now I am bent
To steer the ship as is meant.

WIFE: I see in the firmament
The seven stars here.

NOAH: This is a great flood, wife, take heed.

WIFE: So methought as I stood we are in great need;
That these waves be withstood.

NOAH: Now God help us, we plead!
As thou art helmsman good, and best may succeed
Of all;
Rule us in this race,
Thy word we embrace.

# Dr. Faustus

Christopher Marlowe
circa 1590

**Dramatic**
**Scene:** Faust's study

Faust
Lucifer
Belzebub
Mephostophilis
A piper
The seven deadly sins:
>Pride
>Covetousness
>Wrath
>Gluttony
>Sloth
>Letchery

FAUSTUS: O Christ, my savior, my savior!
>Help to save distressèd Faustus' soul.
>*(Enter Lucifer, Belzebub, and Mephostophilis.)*

LUCIFER: Christ cannot save thy soul, for He is just.
>There's none but I have interest in the same.

FAUSTUS: O, what art thou that look'st so terribly?

LUCIFER: I am Lucifer
>And this is my companion prince in hell.

FAUSTUS: O Faustus, they are come to fetch thy soul!

BELZEBUB: We are come to tell thee thou dost injure us.

LUCIFER: Thou call'st on Christ contrary to thy promise.

BELZEBUB: Thou should'st not think on God.

LUCIFER: Think on the Devil.

BELZEBUB: And his dam too.

FAUSTUS: Nor will Faustus henceforth. Pardon him for this,
>And Faustus vows never to look to heaven!
>Never to name God or to pray to Him,
>To burn His Scriptures, slay His ministers,
>And make my spirits pull His churches down.

LUCIFER: So shalt thou show thyself an obedient servant,
   And we will highly gratify thee for it.

BELZEBUB: Faustus, we are come from hell in person to show thee some pastime. Sit down and thou shalt behold the Seven Deadly Sins appear to thee in their own proper shapes and likeness.

FAUSTUS: That sight will be as pleasant to me as Paradise was to Adam the first day of his creation.

LUCIFER: Talk not of Paradise or creation but mark the show. Go Mephostophilis, fetch them in.

*(Enter the Seven Deadly Sins [led by a Piper].)*

BELZEBUB: Now Faustus, question them of their names and dispositions.

FAUSTUS: That shall I soon. What art thou, the first?

PRIDE: I am Pride. I disdain to have any parents. I am like to Ovid's flea, I can creep into every corner of a wench: sometimes, like a periwig I sit upon her brow; next, like a necklace I hang about her neck; then, like a fan of feathers I kiss her; and then, turning myself to a wrought smock, do what I list—But fie, what a smell is here! I'll not speak a word more for a king's ransom unless the ground be perfumed and covered with cloth of arras.

FAUSTUS: Thou art a proud knave indeed. What art thou, the second?

COVETOUSNESS: I am Covetousness, begotten of an old churl in a leather bag; and might I now obtain my wish, this house, you and all, should turn to gold that I might lock you safe into my chest. O my sweet gold!

FAUSTUS: And what art thou, the third?

FAUSTUS: I am Envy, begotten of a chimney-sweeper and an oyster-wife. I cannot read and therefore wish all books burned. I am lean with seeing others eat. O, that there would come a famine over all the world that all might die and I live alone! Then thou shouldst see how fat I'd be. But must thou sit and I stand? Come down, with a vengeance!

FAUSTUS: Out, envious wretch! But what art thou, the fourth?

WRATH: I am Wrath. I had neither father nor mother. I leapt out of a lion's mouth when I was scarce an hour old and ever since have run up and down the world with these case of rapiers, wounding myself when I could get none to fight withal. I was born in hell! And look to it, for some of you shall be my father.

FAUSTUS: And what art thou, the fifth?

GLUTTONY: I am Gluttony. My parents are all dead, and the devil a penny they have left me, but a small pension: and that buys me thirty meals a day and ten bevers, a small trifle to suffice nature. I come of a royal pedigree. My father was a gammon of bacon, and my mother was a hogshead of claret wine. My godfathers were these: Peter Pickled herring and Martin Martlemas-beef. But my god mother, O, she was an ancient gentlewoman: her name was Margery March-beer. Now Faustus, thou hast heard all my progeny, wilt thou bid me to supper?

FAUSTUS: Not I.

GLUTTONY: Then the devil choke thee!

FAUSTUS: Choke thyself, glutton! What art thou, the sixth?

SLOTH: Heigh-ho! I am Sloth. I was begotten on a sunny bank. Heigh-ho, I'll not speak a word more for a king's ransom.

FAUSTUS: And what are you, Mistress Minx, the seventh and last?

LECHERY: Who, I, I sir? I am one that loves an inch of raw mutton better than an ell of fried stockfish, and the first letter of my name begins with Lechery.

LUCIFER: Away to hell, away! On, piper!

*(Exeunt the Seven Sins.)*

FAUSTUS: O, how this sight doth delight my soul!

LUCIFER: But Faustus, in hell is all manner of delight

FAUSTUS: O, might I see hell and return again safe, how happy were I then!

LUCIFER: Faustus, thou shalt. At midnight I will send for thee.
Meanwhile peruse this book and view it thoroughly,
And thou shalt turn thyself into what shape thou wilt.

FAUSTUS: Thanks mighty Lucifer. This will I keep as chary as my life.

LUCIFER: Now Faustus, farewell.

FAUSTUS: Farewell great Lucifer. Come Mephostophilis.

*(Exeunt omnes several ways.)*

# Woyzeck

Georg Buchner
Translated by Victor Price
1836

**Dramatic**
**Scene:** a local dance. Woyzeck, is outside peeking in

Apprentices
First Apprentice
Marie
The Drum Major
Woyzeck
Dancing couples

FIRST APPRENTICE: *This shirt I've got, I don't know whose,*
*My soul it stinks like booze.*
SECOND APPRENTICE: Brother, shall I in friendship bore a hole in your
nature? Dammit, I want to bore a hole in your nature. I'm quite
a guy, too, you know—I'm going to kill all the fleas on his body.
FIRST APPRENTICE: My soul, my soul it stinks like booze.—Even money
eventually decays. Forget-me-not! Oh, how beautiful this world
is. Brother, I could cry a rain barrel full of tears. I wish our noses
were two bottles and we could pour them down each other's
throats.
OTHERS: *(In chorus.)* A hunter from the west
Once went riding through the woods.
Hip-hip, hooray! A hunter has a merry life,
O'er meadow and o'er stream,
Oh, hunting is my dream!
*(Woyzeck stands at the window. Marie and the Drum Major*
*dance past without seeing him.)*
MARIE: *(Dancing by.)* On! and on, on and on!
WOYZECK: *(Chokes.)* On and on—on and on! *(Jumps up violently and*
*sinks back on the bench.)* On and on, on and on. *(Beats his hands*
*together.)* Spin around, roll around. Why doesn't God blow out
the sun so that everything can roll around in lust, man and
woman, man and beast. Do it in broad daylight, do it on our
hands, like flies.—Woman!—That woman is hot, hot! On and on,

on and on. *(Jumps up.)* The bastard! Look how he's grabbing her, grabbing her body! He—he's got her now, like I used to have her.

FIRST APPRENTICE: *(Preaches on the table.)* Yet when a wanderer stands leaning against the stream of time or gives answer for the wisdom of God, asking himself: Why does man exist? Why does man exist.?—But verily I say unto you: how could the farmer, the cooper, the shoemaker, the doctor exist if God hadn't created man? How could the tailor exist if God hadn't given man a feeling of shame? How could the soldier exist, if men didn't feel the necessity of killing one another? Therefore, do not ye despair, yes, yes, it is good and pleasant, yet all that is earthly is passing, even money eventually decays.

# Spreading the News

Lady Gregory
1906

**Serio-comic**
**Scene:** an apple stall at the outskirts of the fair

Policeman
Magistrate
Mrs. Tarpey
James Ryan
Bartley Fallon
Mrs. Fallon
Jack Smith
Tim Casey
Mrs. Tully
Shawn Early

*(Mrs. Tarpey sitting at it. Magistrate and Policeman enter.)*

MAGISTRATE: So that is the Fair Green. Cattle and sheep and mud. No system. What a repulsive sight!

POLICEMAN: That is so, indeed.

MAGISTRATE: I suppose there is a good deal of disorder in this place?

POLICEMAN: There is.

MAGISTRATE: Common assault.

POLICEMAN: It's common enough.

MAGISTRATE: Agrarian crime, no doubt?

POLICEMAN: That is so.

MAGISTRATE: Boycotting? Maiming of cattle? Firing into houses?

POLICEMAN: There was one time, and there might be again.

MAGISTRATE: That is bad. Does it go any farther than that?

POLICEMAN: Far enough, indeed.

MAGISTRATE: Homicide, then! This district has been shamefully neglected! I will change all that. When I was in the Andaman Islands, my system never failed. Yes, yes, I will change all that. What has that woman on her stall?

POLICEMAN: Apples mostly—and sweets.

MAGISTRATE: Just see if there are any unlicensed goods underneath—

spirits or the like. We had evasions of the salt tax in the Andaman Islands.

POLICEMAN: *(Sniffing cautiously and upsetting a heap of apples.)* I see no spirits here—or salt.

MAGISTRATE: *(To Mrs. Tarpey.)* Do you know this town well, my good woman?

POLICEMAN: *(Shouting.)* The gentleman is asking do you know the town? He's the new magistrate!

MRS. TARPEY: *(Rising and ducking.)* Do I know the town? I do, to be sure.

MAGISTRATE: *(Shouting.)* What is its chief business?

MRS. TARPEY: Business, is it? What business would the people here have but to be minding one another's business?

MAGISTRATE: I mean what trade have they?

MRS. TARPEY: Not a trade. No trade at all but to be talking.

MAGISTRATE: I shall learn nothing here.

*(James Ryan comes in, pipe in mouth. Seeing Magistrate he retreats quickly, taking pipe from mouth.)*

MAGISTRATE: The smoke from that man's pipe had a greenish look; he may be growing unlicensed tobacco at home. I wish I had brought my telescope to this district. Come to the post-office, I will telegraph for it. I found it very useful in the Andaman Islands. *(Magistrate and Policeman go out left.)*

MRS. TARPEY: Bad luck to Jo Muldoon, knocking my apples this way and that way. *(Begins arranging them.)* Showing off he was to the new magistrate.

*(Enter Bartley Fallon and Mrs. Fallon.)*

BARTLEY: Indeed it's a poor country and a scarce country to be living in. But I'm thinking if I went to America it's long ago the day I'd be dead!

MRS. FALLON: So you might, indeed. *(She puts her basket on a barrel and begins putting parcels in it, taking them from under her cloak.)*

BARTLEY: And it's a great expense for a poor man to be buried in America.

MRS. FALLON: Never fear, Bartley Fallon, but I'll give you a good burying the day you'll die.

BARTLEY: Maybe it's yourself will be buried in the graveyard of Cloonmara before me, Mary Fallon, and I myself that will be dying unbeknownst some night, and no one a-near me. And the cat itself may be gone straying through the country, and the mice squealing over the quilt.

MRS. FALLON: Leave off talking of dying. It might be twenty years you'll be living yet.

BARTLEY: *(With a deep sigh.)* I'm thinking if I'll be living at the end of twenty years, it's a very old man I'll be then!

MRS. TARPEY: *(Turns and sees them.)* Good morrow, Bartley Fallon; good morrow, Mrs. Fallon. Well, Bartley, you'll find no cause for complaining today; they are all saying it was a good fair.

BARTLEY: *(Raising his voice.)* It was not a good fair, Mrs. Tarpey. It was a scattered sort of a fair. If we didn't expect more, we got less. That's the way with me always; whatever I have to sell goes down and whatever I have to buy goes up. If there's ever any misfortune coming to this world, it's on myself it pitches, like a flock of crows on seed potatoes.

MRS. FALLON: Leave off talking of misfortunes, and listen to Jack Smith that is coming the way, and he singing.

VOICE OF JACK SMITH: *(Heard singing.)* I thought, my first love,
There'd be but one house between you and me,
And I thought I would find
Yourself coaxing my child on your knee.
Over the tide
I would leap with the leap of a swan,
Till I came to the side
Of the wife of the red-haired man!
*(Jack Smith comes in; he is a red-haired man and is carrying a hayfork.)*

MRS. TARPEY: That should be a good song if I had my hearing.

MRS. FALLON: *(Shouting.)* It's "The Red-haired Man's Wife."

MRS. TARPEY: I know it well. That's the song that has a skin on it! *(She turns her back to them and goes on arranging her apples.)*

MRS. FALLON: Where's herself, Jack Smith?

JACK SMITH: She was delayed with her washing; bleaching the clothes on the hedge she is, and she daren't leave them, with all the tinkers that do be passing to the fair. It isn't to the fair I came myself, but up to the Five Acre Meadow I'm going, where I have a contract for the hay. We'll get a share of it into tramps today. *(He lays down hayfork and lights his pipe.)*

BARTLEY: You will not get it into tramps today. The rain will be down on it by evening, and on myself too. It's seldom I ever started on a journey but the rain would come down on me before I'd find any place of shelter.

JACK SMITH: If it didn't itself, Bartley, it is my belief you would carry a leaky pail on your head in place of a hat, the way you'd not be without some cause for complaining.

*(A voice heard, "Go on, now, go on out o' that. Go on I say.")*

JACK SMITH: Look at that young mare of Pat Ryan's that is backing into Shaughnessy's bullocks with the dint of the crowd! Don't be daunted, Pat, I'll give you a hand with her. *(He goes out, leaving his hayfork.)*

MRS. FALLON: It's time for ourselves to be going home. I have all I bought put in the basket. Look at there, Jack Smith's hayfork he left after him! He'll be wanting it. *(Calls.)* Jack Smith! Jack Smith!—He's gone through the crowd—hurry after him, Bartley, he'll be wanting it.

BARTLEY: I'll do that. This is no safe place to be leaving it. *(He takes up fork awkwardly and upsets the basket.)* Look at that now! If there is any basket in the fair upset, it must be our own basket! *(He goes out to right.)*

MRS. FALLON: Get out of that! It is your own fault, it is. Talk of misfortunes and misfortunes will come. Glory be! Look at my new eggcups rolling in every part—and my two pound of sugar with the paper broke—

MRS. TARPEY: *(Turning from stall.)* God help us, Mrs. Fallon, what happened to your basket?

MRS. FALLON: It's himself that knocked it down, bad manners to him. *(Putting things up.)* My grand sugar that's destroyed, and he'll not drink his tea without it. I had best go back to the shop for more, much good may it do him!

*(Enter Tim Casey.)*

TIM CASEY: Where is Bartley Fallon, Mrs. Fallon? I want a word with him before he'll leave the fair. I was afraid he might have gone home by this, for he's a temperate man.

MRS. FALLON: I wish he did go home! It'd be best for me if he went home straight from the fair green, or if he never came with me at all! Where is he, is it? He's gone up the road *(Jerks elbow.)* following Jack Smith with a hayfork. *(She goes out to left.)*

TIM CASEY: Following Jack Smith with a hayfork! Did ever any one hear the like of that. *(Shouts.)* Did you hear that news, Mrs. Tarpey?

MRS. TARPEY: I heard no news at all.

TIM CASEY: Some dispute I suppose it was that rose between Jack Smith and Bartley Fallon, and it seems Jack made off, and Bartley is following him with a hayfork!

MRS. TARPEY: Is he now? Well, that was quick work! It's not ten minutes since the two of them were here, Bartley going home and Jack going to the Five Acre Meadow; and I had my apples to settle up, that Jo Muldoon of the police had scattered, and when I looked round again Jack Smith was gone, and Bartley Fallon was gone, and Mrs. Fallon's basket upset, and all in it strewed upon the ground—the tea here—the two pound of sugar there—the eggcups there—Look, now, what a great hardship the deafness puts upon me, that I didn't hear the commencement of the fight! Wait till I tell James Ryan that I see below; he is a neighbour of Bartley's, it would be a pity if he wouldn't hear the news! *(She goes out.)*

*(Enter Shawn Early and Mrs. Tully.)*

TIM CASEY: Listen, Shawn Early! Listen, Mrs. Tully, to the news! Jack Smith and Bartley Fallon had a falling out, and Jack knocked Mrs. Fallon's basket into the road, and Bartley made an attack on him with a hayfork, and away with Jack, and Bartley after him. Look at the sugar here yet on the road!

SHAWN EARLY: Do you tell me so? Well, that's a queer thing, and Bartley Fallon so quiet a man!

MRS. TULLY: I wouldn't wonder at all. I would never think well of a man that would have that sort of a mouldering look. It's likely he has overtaken Jack by this.

*(Enter James Ryan and Mrs. Tarpey.)*

JAMES RYAN: That is great news Mrs. Tarpey was telling me! I suppose that's what brought the police and the magistrate up this way. I was wondering to see them in it a while ago.

SHAWN EARLY: The police after them? Bartley Fallon must have injured Jack so. They wouldn't meddle in a fight that was only for show!

MRS. TULLY: Why wouldn't he injure him? There was many a man killed with no more of a weapon than a hayfork.

JAMES RYAN: Wait till I run north as far as Kelly's bar to spread the news! *(He goes out.)*

TIM CASEY: I'll go tell Jack Smith's first cousin that is standing there south of the church after selling his lambs. (Goes out.)

MRS. TULLY: I'll go telling a few of the neighbours I see beyond to the west. (Goes out.)

SHAWN EARLY: I'll give word of it beyond at the east of the green.
(Is going out when Mrs. Tarpey seizes hold of him.)

MRS. TARPEY: Stop a minute, Shawn Early, and tell me did you see red Jack Smith's wife, Kitty Keary, in any place?

SHAWN EARLY: I did. At her own house she was, drying clothes on the hedge as I passed.

MRS. TARPEY: What did you say she was doing?

SHAWN EARLY: (Breaking away.) Laying out a sheet on the hedge. (He goes.)

MRS. TARPEY: Laying out a sheet for the dead! The Lord have mercy on us! Jack Smith dead, and his wife laying out a sheet for his burying! (Calls out.) Why didn't you tell me that before, Shawn Early? Isn't the deafness the great hardship? Half the world might be dead without me knowing of it or getting word of it at all! (She sits down and rocks herself.) O my poor Jack Smith! To be going to his work so nice and so hearty, and to be left stretched on the ground in the full light of the day!
(Enter Tim Casey.)

TIM CASEY: What is it, Mrs. Tarpey? What happened since?

MRS. TARPEY: O my poor Jack Smith!

TIM CASEY: Did Bartley overtake him?

MRS. TARPEY: O the poor man!

TIM CASEY: Is it killed he is?

MRS. TARPEY: Stretched in the Five Acre Meadow!

TIM CASEY: The Lord have mercy on us! Is that a fact?

MRS. TARPEY: Without the rites of the Church or a ha'porth!

TIM CASEY: Who was telling you?

MRS. TARPEY: And the wife laying out a sheet for his corpse. (Sits up and wipes her eyes.) I suppose they'll wake him the same as another?
(Enter Mrs. Tully, Shawn Early, and James Ryan.)

MRS. TULLY: There is great talk about this work in every quarter of the fair.

MRS. TARPEY: Ochone! cold and dead. And myself maybe the last he was speaking to!

JAMES RYAN: The Lord save us! Is it dead he is?

TIM CASEY: Dead surely, and his wife getting provision for the wake.

SHAWN EARLY: Well, now, hadn't Bartley Fallon great venom in him?

MRS. TULLY: You may be sure he had some cause. Why would he have made an end of him if he had not? *(To Mrs. Tarpey, raising her voice.)* What was it rose the dispute at all, Mrs. Tarpey?

MRS. TARPEY: Not a one of me knows. The last I saw of them, Jack Smith was standing there, and Bartley Fallon was standing there, quiet and easy, and he listening to "The Red-haired Man's Wife."

# Murderer the Women's Hope

Oskar Kokoschka
Translated by Michael Hamburger
1907

**Dramatic**
**Scene:** a tower. Night. Torches flaming

The man in blue armor
Men
The woman in red
Women attendants
First
Second
First Girl
Second girl
First man
Second man
Third man
Chorus and three masked men

> (*The man in blue armor, white face, kerchief covering a wound, with a crowd of men—savage in appearance, gray-and-red kerchiefs, white-black-and-brown clothes, signs on their clothes, bare legs, long-handled torches, bells, din—creeping up with handles of torches extended and lights; wearily, reluctantly try to hold back the adventurer, pull his horse to the ground; he walks on, they open up the circle around him, crying out in a slow crescendo.*)

MEN: We were the flaming wheel around him,
> We were the flaming wheel around you, assailant of locked fortresses!
> (*Hesitantly follow him again in chain formation; he, with the torch bearer in front of him, heads the procession.*)

MEN: Lead us, pale one!
> (*While they are about to pull his horse to the ground, women with their leader ascend steps on the left. Woman, red clothes, loose yellow hair, tall.*)

WOMEN: (*Loud.*) With my breath I fall the yellow disc of the sun, my eye collects the jubilation of the men, their stammering lust prowls around me like a beast.

*(Female Attendants separate themselves from her, only now catch sight of the stranger.)*

FIRST FEMALE ATTENDANT: His breath attaches itself to the virgin!

FIRST MAN: *(To the others.)* Our master is like the moon that rises in the East.

SECOND GIRL: *(Quiet, her face averted.)* When will she be enfolded joyfully?

*(Listening, alert, the chorus walks round the whole stage, dispersed in groups; the man and the woman meet in front of the gate. Pause.)*

WOMAN: *(Observes him spellbound, then to herself.)* Who is the stranger that has looked on me?

*(Girls press to the fore.)*

FIRST GIRL: *(Recognizes him, cries out.)* His sister died of love.

SECOND GIRL: O the singing of Time, flowers never seen.

THE MAN: *(Astonished; his procession halts.)* Am I real? What did the shadows say? *(Raising his face to her.)* Did you look at me, did I look at you?

WOMAN: *(Filled with fear and longing.)* Who is the pallid man? Hold him back.

FIRST GIRL: *(With a piercing scream, runs back.)* Do you let him in? It is he who strangles my little sister praying in the temple.

FIRST MAN: *(To the girl.)* We saw him stride through the fire, his feet unharmed.

SECOND MAN: He tortured animals to death, killed neighing mares by the pressure of his thighs.

THIRD MAN: Birds that ran before us he made blind, stifled red fishes in the sand.

THE MAN: *(Angry, heated.)* Who is she that like an animal proudly grazes amidst her kin?

FIRST MAN: She divines what none has understood.

SECOND MAN: She perceives what none has seen or heard.

THIRD MAN: They say shy birds approach her and let themselves be seized.

*(Girls in time with the men.)*

FIRST GIRL: Lady, let us flee. Extinguish the flares of the leader.

SECOND GIRL: Mistress, escape!

THIRD GIRL: He shall not be our guest or breathe our air. Let him not lodge with us, he frightens me.

*(Men, hesitant, walk on, Women crowd together anxiously. The Woman goes up to the Man, prowling, cautious.)*

FIRST GIRL: He has no luck.

FIRST MAN: She has no shame.

WOMAN: Why do you bind me, man, with your gaze? Ravening light, you confound my flame! Devouring life overpowers me. O take away my terrible hope—and may torment overpower you.

THE MAN: *(Enraged.)* My men, now brand her with my sign, hot iron into her red flesh.

*(Men carry out his order. First the Chorus, with their lights, struggle with her, then the Old Man with the iron; he rips open her dress and brands her.)*

WOMAN: *(Crying out in terrible pain.)* Beat back those men, the devouring corpses.

*(She leaps at him with a knife and strikes a wound in his side. The Man falls.)*

MEN: Free this man possessed, strike down the devil. Alas for us innocents, bury the conqueror. We do not know him.

THE MAN: *(In convulsions, singing with a bleeding, visible wound.)* Senseless craving from horror to horror, unappeasable rotation in the void. Birth pangs without birth, hurtling down of the sun, quaking of space. The end of those who praised me. Oh, your unmerciful word.

MEN: We do not know him; spare us. Come, you singing girls, let us celebrate our nuptials on his bed of affliction.

GIRLS: He frightens us; you we loved even before you came.

*(Three masked men on the wall lower a coffin on ropes; the wounded man, hardly stirring now, is placed inside the tower. Women retire with the men. The Old Man rises and locks the door, all is dark, a torch, quiet, blue light above in the cage.)*

WOMAN: *(Moaning and revengeful.)* He cannot live, nor die; how white he is! *(She creeps round the cage like a panther. She crawls up to the cage inquisitively, grips the bars lasciviously, inscribes a large white cross on the tower, cries out.)* Open the gate; I must be with him. *(Shakes the bars in despair.)*

MEN AND WOMEN: *(Enjoying themselves in the shadows, confused.)* We have lost the key—we shall find it—have you got it?—haven't you seen it?—we are not guilty of your plight, we do not how you—

*(They go back again. A cock crows, a pale light rises in the background.)*

WOMAN: *(Slides her arm through the bars and prods his wound, hissing maliciously, like an adder.)* Pale one, do you recoil? Do you know fear? Are you only asleep? Are you awake? Can you hear me?

THE MAN: *(Inside, breathing heavily, raises his head with difficulty; later, moves one hand; then slowly rises, singing higher and higher, soaring.)*

Wind that wanders, time repeating time, solitude, repose and hunger confuse me.

Worlds that circle past, no air, it grows long as evening.

WOMAN: *(Incipient fear.)* So much light is flowing from the gap, so much strength from the pale as a corpse he's turned. *(Once more creeps up the steps, her body trembling, triumphant once more and crying out with a high voice.)*

*(The Man has slowly risen, leans against the grille, slowly grows.)*

WOMAN: *(Weakening, furious.)* A wild beast I tame in this cage; is it with hunger your song barks?

THE MAN: Am I the real one, you the dead ensnared? Why are you turning pale?

*(Crowing of cocks.)*

WOMAN: *(Trembling.)* Do you insult me, corpse?

THE MAN: *(Powerfully.)* Stars and moon! Woman! In dream or awake, I saw a singing creature brightly shine. Breathing, dark things become clear to me. Who nourishes me?

*(Woman covers him entirely with her body; separated by the grille, to which she clings high up in the air like a monkey.)*

THE MAN: Who suckles me with blood? I devour your melting flesh.

WOMAN: I will not let you live, you vampire, piecemeal you feed on me, weaken me, woe to you, I shall kill you—you fetter me—you I caught and caged—and you are holding me—let go of me. Your love imprisons me—grips me as with iron chains—throttles me— let go—help! I lost the key that kept you prisoner. *(Lets go the grille, writhes on the steps like a dying animal, her thighs and muscles convulsed.)*

*(The Man stands upright now, pulls open the gate, touches the*

woman who rears up stiffly, dead white—with his fingers. She feels that her end is near, highest tension, released in a slowly diminishing scream; she collapses and, as she falls, tears away the torch from the hands of the rising leader. The torch goes out and covers everything in a shower of sparks. He stands on the highest step; men and women who attempt to flee from him run into his way, screaming.)

CHORUS: The devil! Tame him, save yourselves, save yourselves if you can—all is lost!

(He walks straight towards them. Kills them like mosquitoes and leaves red behind. From very far away, crowing of cocks.)

# The Weavers

Gerhart Hauptmann
Translated by Carl Mueller
1892

**Dramatic**
**Scene:** Dreissinger's home, A room where the weavers deliver their
finished work

Neumann
First Weaver Woman
Pfeifer
Apprentice
Baecker
First Man Weaver
Old Baumert
Men and Women Weavers
Dreissinger

CASHIER NEUMANN: *(Counting out money.)* That leaves sixteen silver
groschen and two pfenning.

FIRST WEAVER WOMAN: *(About thirty, very emaciated. She puts away the
money with trembling fingers.)* Thank you.

NEUMANN: *(When the woman fails to move on.)* Well? Something
wrong again?

FIRST WEAVER WOMAN: *(Excitedly, begging.)* I was wondering, could I
have a few pfennig in advance, I need it awful bad.

NEUMANN: And I need a couple hundred thalers. Nice if all we had to
do is need it—! *(Already busy counting out money to another
weaver, curtly.)* Herr Dreissiger's the one who takes care of
advance payments.

FIRST WEAVER WOMAN: Then maybe I could talk with Herr Dreissiger for a
minute?

MANAGER PFEIFER: *(Formerly a weaver himself, his type is unmistakable,
except that he is well fed, well groomed, cleanly shaven, and a
heavy user of snuff. He calls across brusquely.)* God knows, Herr
Dreissiger'd have enough to do if he had to worry about every
petty request. That's what *we're* here for. *(He measures and then
inspects with the magnifying glass.)* Damn! There's a draft! *(He*

*wraps a heavy scarf around his neck.)* Close the door when you come in.

APPRENTICE: *(Loudly to Pfeifer.)* Might as well talk to a stone wall.

PFEIFER: All right, that's done! Weigh it!

*(The weaver places his web on the scale.)*

PFEIFER: Why don't you learn to do your work better? It's full of lumps again. I don't even have to look at it. A good weaver doesn't put off the winding for God knows how long.

*(Baecker enters. He is a young and exceptionally strong weaver whose unconstrained deportment is almost impudent. Pfeifer, Neumann and the Apprentice exchange knowing glances at his entrance.)*

BAECKER: Damn! Sweating like a dog again!

FIRST WEAVER: *(In a low voice.)* This heat means rain.

OLD BAUMERT: *(Pushes through the glass door at the right. On the other side of the door one can see the weavers waiting, crowded together, shoulder to shoulder. Old Baumert has hobbled his way forward and laid down his pack on the bench near Baecker's. He sits down beside it and wipes the perspiration from his face.)* I can use a rest after that.

BAECKER: Rest's better than money anytime.

OLD BAUMERT: I could use a little money too. Good day to you, Baecker!

BAECKER: Good day to you, Father Baumert! Looks like another long wait here, uh?

FIRST WEAVER: What's the difference? A weaver can wait an hour or a day. He don't count.

PFEIFER: Quiet back there! How can I hear myself think?

BAECKER: *(Softly.)* One of his bad days again.

PFEIFER: *(To the weaver in front of him.)* How many times do we have to tell you to clean up your webs better! What do you call a mess like that? Clots of dirt in here long as my finger, and straw and all kinds of muck.

WEAVER REIMANN: But there's always a pound waste figured in.

PFEIFER: I haven't got time. That's done with.—What have *you* got?

*(Weaver Heiber puts down his web. While Pfeifer examines it he steps up to him and talks to him in a low and eager voice.)*

WEAVER HEIBER: Beg pardon, Herr Pfeifer, sir, I wanted to ask you a favor, sir, if maybe you'd be so kind and wanted to do me a good turn, sir, and not have my advance pay come off my salary this time.

PFEIFER: *(Measuring and inspecting, scornfully.)* Well, now! Very well done. Looks like half of the woof was left on the spool again.

WEAVER HEIBER: *(Continues in his own way.)* I'll be sure to make it up this week, sir. Last week I had to work two days on the estate. And then my wife's home sick too…

PFEIFER: *(Placing the web on the scales.)* Here's another fine piece of sloppy work. *(Already beginning to inspect a new web.)* You call this a selvage? Broad here, narrow there! In one place the woof's all drawn together. God knows how much, and then here the reed's been pulled apart. And you've hardly got seventy threads to the inch. Where's the rest of it? You call this honest work? Whoever heard of such a thing?

*(Weaver Heiber, suppressing his tears, stands there humiliated and helpless.)*

BAECKER: *(In a low voice, to Baumert.)* Looks like those bastards would like to make us pay for our own yarn too.

FIRST WEAVER WOMAN: *(Who has stepped back only a few paces from the cashier's table and has looked staringly about her from time to time, seeking help, without moving from the place. She now takes heart and turns again beseechingly toward the cashier.)* I can hardly…I just don't know if you don't give me any advance…O Jesus, Lord Jesus…

PFEIFER: *(Calls across.)* What's all this calling the Lord Jesus! Let Him in peace for a while! you never bothered much about your Lord Jesus up to now. Give a little more mind to your husband, you'd be better off, so we don't see him sitting at a tavern window all day long. We can't give any advances. We have to account here for every pfenning. Besides that, it's not our money. They'd be after *us* for it later. People who work hard and understand their business and do their work in the fear of the Lord don't need advances. So that's the end of that.

NEUMANN: And if a weaver from Bielau got paid four times as much, he'd waste just four times as much and still be in debt.

FIRST WEAVER WOMAN: *(Loudly as if appealing to everyone's sense of justice.)* There's nobody can say I'm lazy, but I can't go on like this anymore. Two time I had a miscarriage. And for my husband, he can do only half his part too. He even went to the shepherd at Zerlau but he couldn't help him with his trouble either…there's nobody can do more than he's able. We do our work here, all right, we do all we can. I've not had much sleep these past weeks, but everything'll be all right soon if only I can get some strength back into my bones. But you must have a little bit of consideration then. *(Beseeching him fawningly.)* You'll be good enough, won't you sir, and allow me a few groschen this time.

PFEIFER: *(Without interrupting himself.)* Fiedler: eleven silver groschen.

FIRST WEAVER WOMAN: Just a few groschen to buy our bread. The farmer, he won't give no more credit. And then there's all our children…

NEUMANN: *(In a low voice, with comic earnestness, to the Apprentice.)* Every year the line-weaver has another kid, lálalala, lálalala, lá, lá, lá!

APPRENTICE: *(Takes it up.)* And the little brat is as blind as a lid, lálalala, lálalala, lá, lá, lá!

WEAVER REIMANN: *(Not touching the money which the cashier has counted out for him.)* We always used to get thirteen and a half groschen for a web.

PFEIFER: *(Calling over.)* If it don't suit you, Reimann, all you got to do is say so. There's enough weavers around. Especially your kind. You get full pay when your web's full weight.

WEAVER REIMANN: How could anything be wrong with the weight…

PFEIFER: Bring us a flawless piece of cotton sometime and your pay'll be all right, too.

WEAVER REIMANN: I don't understand how there are any mistakes in it.

PFEIFER: *(As he inspects.)* Weave well, live well.

WEAVER HEIBER: *(Has stayed near Pfeifer, looking for another favorable opportunity. He smiled together with the others over Pfeifer's witticism, and now he starts toward him again and addresses him as before.)* What I wanted to ask you, Herr Pfeifer, sir, is if perhaps you'd be so kind as not to take the five groschen advance off this week's pay. My wife she's been a-bed since Shrove Tuesday. There's nothing she can do to help me. So I have to pay the girl to tend the spools. So you see…

PFEIFER: *(Taking snuff.)* Heiber, you're not the only one I've got to take care of here. The others want their turn too.

WEAVER REIMANN: This is how I got the warp—so this is how I wound it up and took it off again. I can't bring back better yarn than I got.

PFEIFER: If you don't like it then don't bother picking up anymore. We got enough around here who'd run their soles off for it.

NEUMANN: *(To Reimann.)* Do you want the money or not?

WEAVER REIMANN: How could I feel right if I took that money?

NEUMANN: *(No longer troubling himself with Reimann.)* Heiber: ten silver groschen. Take off five for advance, that leaves five silver groschen.

WEAVER HEIBER: *(Steps forward, looks at the money, shakes his head as though there were something he can't believe, then puts the money slowly and carefully into his pocket.)* My God, my God— *(Sighs.)* Well—

OLD BAUMERT: *(Looking Heiber in the face.)* Yes, yes, Franz! There's cause enough for sighing.

WEAVER HEIBER: *(Speaking with difficulty.)* Then, you see, I got a sick girl at home too. She needs a bottle of medicine.

OLD BAUMERT: What's she got?

WEAVER HEIBER: Well, you see, she's been a sick one from when she was born. I don't know…well, I can tell you this much: she's brought it with her into the world. All kinds of troubles break out over and over on her. It's in the blood.

OLD BAUMERT: There's trouble all over. Wherever there's poor people there's bad luck after bad luck. There's no end to it and no saving us.

WEAVER HEIBER: What's that there in the bundle?

OLD BAUMERT: We had nothing at all to eat at home. And so I had our little dog killed. There's not much on him, he was half-starved away. He was a nice little dog. I didn't want to kill him myself. I couldn't find the heart for that.

PFEIFER: *(Has inspected Baecker's web, calls.)* Baecker: thirteen and a half silver groschen.

BAECKER: That's a shabby piece of charity, not pay.

PFEIFER: Whoever's been taken care of has to leave. We can't even move around for all the crowd.

BAECKER: *(To the people standing about, not lowering his voice.)* This is a shabby tip, that's all it is. And for this we're supposed to work our treddle from early morning to late at night. And when you've worked eighteen days over the loom, night after night, worn out, half dizzy with the dust and the burning heat, then you're lucky if you made thirteen and a half silver groschen.

PFEIFER: We don't allow back-talk here.

BAECKER: You don't tell *me* what not to say!

PFEIFER: *(Jumps up shouting.)* We'll see about that! *(Goes to the glass door and calls into the office.)* Herr Dreissiger, Herr Dreissiger, if you'd be so kind, sir!

DREISSIGER: *(Enters. He is in his early forties, fat, asthmatic, with a severe look.)* What is it, Pfeifer?

PFEIFER: *(Angrily.)* Baecker here says he won't keep his mouth shut.

DREISSIGER: *(Draws himself up, throws back his head, stares at Baecker with quivering nostrils.)* Yes, of course—Baecker! *(To Pfeifer.)* Is this the one?

*(The clerk nods.)*

BAECKER: *(Impudently.)* Right enough, Herr Dreissiger! *(Pointing to himself.)* This is *this* one— *(Pointing to Dreissiger.)* and that's *that* one.

DREISSIGER: *(With indignation.)* Who does he think he's talking to?

PFEIFER: He's too well off, that's what! He'll skate on thin ice just once too often.

BAECKER: *(Roughly.)* You shut your mouth, you stinking toad. Your mother must have rode a broomstick with Satan himself to get a devil like you!

DREISSIGER: *(Bellowing in sudden anger.)* Hold your tongue! Hold your tongue this minute or I'll... *(He trembles, come forward a few steps.)*

BAECKER: *(Awaiting him with determination.)* I'm not deaf. My hearing's all right.

DREISSIGER: *(Controls himself and asks with apparent business-like calm.)* Isn't this one of those who...

PFEIFER: He's a weaver from Bielau. You find them wherever there's trouble.

DREISSIGER: *(Trembling.)* Just let me warn you of one thing: if ever it happens again like it did yesterday evening that a horde of half-drunken wet-nosed young louts passes my house again—and singing that vile song...

BAECKER: I guess it's *The Song of Bloody Justice* you mean, uh?

DREISSIGER: You know which one I mean. You just let me warn you: if I ever hear it again, I'll get hold of one of you and—I promise you this on my word of honor, I'm not joking—he will be turned over to the state's attorney. And if I ever find out who's responsible for that vile thing you call a song...

BAECKER: It's a beautiful song!

DREISSIGER: One more word out of you and I'll send for the police—and at once. I don't fool around. We know how to take care of young louts like you. I've taken care of people a lot different from you.

BAECKER: I take your word for it. Sure, a factory owner like you can take care of two or three hundred weavers before a man can turn around, and not even a bone left over. A man like that's got four bellies like a cow and the jaws of a wolf. For him it's nothing, nothing!

DREISSIGER: *(To the clerk.)* This one gets no more work from us.

BAECKER: What do I care whether I go hungry over a loom or at the side of a road!

DREISSIGER: Get out of here! Get out!

BAECKER: *(Firmly.)* First I'll take my pay.

DREISSIGER: What's he got coming, Neumann?

NEUMANN: Thirteen silver groschen, five pfenning.

DREISSIGER: *(Takes the money overhastily from the cashier and tosses it onto the counter so that some of the coins roll onto the floor.)* There you are! Now—get out of my sight!

BAECKER: First I'll get my pay.

DREISSIGER: There's your pay; and unless you get out of here, and quick…It's exactly twelve…My dyers are just now taking off for lunch…

BAECKER: I get my pay in my hand. My pay belongs here. *(He touches the palm of his left hand with the fingers of his right hand.)*

DREISSIGER: *(To the Apprentice.)* Pick it up, Tilgner.
*(The Apprentice does so and places the money in Baecker's hand.)*

BAECKER: Everything done proper. *(Without hurrying he places the money in an old purse.)*

DREISSIGER: Well? *(Impatiently, since Baecker does not leave.)* Shall I *help* you out?
*(Agitation has risen among the crowd of weavers. A long, deep sigh is heard. Then someone falls. All interest is turned towards the new event.)*

DREISSIGER: What's the matter here?

VARIOUS WEAVERS AND WEAVER WOMEN: Someone fainted—It's a sick little boy.—Is it the falling sickness, or what?

DREISSIGER: What…what's that? Fainted, you say? *(He goes nearer.)*

AN OLD WEAVER: He just lays there.
*(Room is made. An eight-year-old boy is seen lying on the ground as if dead.)*

DREISSIGER: Does anybody know the boy?

THE OLD WEAVER: Not from our village.

OLD BAUMERT: He looks like one of the Heinrichs. *(Looks at him more closely.)* Yes, yes! It's Heinrich's boy Gustav.

DREISSIGER: Where do these people live?

OLD BAUMERT: Up around us, in Kasbach, Herr Dreissiger. He goes around playing music, and in the daytime he works at his loom. They have nine children, the tenth on the way.

VARIOUS WEAVERS AND WEAVER WOMEN: They've got a lot of trouble, those people.—It rains through their roof.—The wife can't get two shirts for all the nine children.

OLD BAUMERT: *(Grabbing hold of the boy.)* Hey there, boy, what's the matter with you? Wake up now!

DREISSIGER: Get hold of him there, we'll pick him up. Whoever heard of such foolishness, letting a child weak as him make such a long trip! Pfeifer, bring some water!

WEAVER WOMAN: *(Helps him sit up.)* You're not going to go and die on us now, boy, are you?

DREISSIGER: Or some cognac, Pfeifer, cognac's better.

BAECKER: *(Forgotten by everyone, he has stood there watching. Now, with one hand on the doorknob, he calls across loud and mockingly.)* Give him something to eat, too, and he'll come round all right. *(Off.)*

DREISSIGER: That one'll come to no good end.—Grab him under the arms, Neumann. Slowly, slowly...there...there...we'll take him into my office. What is it?

NEUMANN: He said something, Herr Dreissiger! He moved his lips.

DREISSIGER: What do you want, boy?

THE BOY: *(Whispering.)* I'm hungry!

DREISSIGER: *(Turning pale.)* I can't understand him.

WEAVER WOMAN: I think he wants...

DREISSIGER: We'll see what it is. Just don't hold us up.—He can lie down on my sofa. We'll hear what the doctor has to say.

*(Dreissiger, Neumann and the Weaver Woman take the boy into the office. Excited agitation arises among the weavers as though they were school children whose teacher had just left the room. They stretch their limbs, they whisper, they shift from one foot to another, and within a few seconds their conversation is loud and general.)*

OLD BAUMERT: I do believe Baecker was right.

SEVERAL WEAVERS AND WEAVER WOMEN: The boy said something that sounded like that.—It's nothing new around here, people fainting with hunger.—And what'll happen with us this winter if this cutting our wages keeps up?—And with the potatoes like they are, it'll be a bad year.—They won't do anything here until they find us all laying flat on our backs.

OLD BAUMERT: The best thing to do is what the weaver in Nentwich did, put a rope around your neck and hang yourself to your loom.

# The Devil and Daniel Webster

Stephen Vincent Benet
1938

**Dramatic**

**Scene:** a wedding party is in progress in Jabez Stone's New Hampshire Farmhouse, 1841

Townspeople, many men and women, lines divided
A Fiddler
Jabez Stone
Mary, his bride
Daniel Webster

FIRST WOMAN: Right nice wedding.

FIRST MAN: Handsome couple.

SECOND WOMAN: *(Passing through crowd with dish of oyster stew.)* Oysters for supper!

SECOND MAN: *(Passing cake.)* And layer cake—layer cake—

AN OLD MAN: *(Hobbling toward cider barrel.)* Makes me feel young again! Oh, by jingo!

AN OLD WOMAN: *(Pursuing him.)* Henry, Henry, you've been drinking cider!

FIDDLER: Set to your partners! Dosy-do!

WOMEN: Mary and Jabez.

MEN: Jabez and Mary.

A WOMAN: Where's the State Senator?

A MAN: Where's the lucky bride?

> *(With cries of "Mary—Jabez—strike it up, fiddler—make room for the bride and groom," the crowd drags Mary and Jabez, pleased but embarrassed, into the center of the room, and Mary and Jabez do a little solo dance, while the crowd claps, applauds, and makes various remarks.)*

A MAN: Handsome steppers!

A WOMAN: She's pretty as a picture.

A SECOND MAN: Cut your pigeon wing, Jabez!

THE OLD MAN: Young again, young again, that's the way I feel! *(He tries to cut a pigeon wing himself.)*

THE OLD WOMAN: Henry, Henry, careful of your rheumatiz!

A THIRD WOMAN: Makes me feel all teary, seeing them so happy.

*(The solo dance ends, the music stops for a moment.)*

THE OLD MAN: *(Gossiping to a neighbor.)* Wonder where he got it all. Stones was always poor.

HIS NEIGHBOR: Ain't poor now. Makes you wonder just a mite.

A THIRD MAN: Don't begrudge it to him—but I wonder where he got it.

THE OLD MAN: *(Starting to whisper.)* Let me tell you something—

THE OLD WOMAN: *(Quickly.)* Henry, Henry, don't you start to gossip. *(She drags him away.)*

FIDDLER: *(Cutting in.)* Set to your partners! Scratch for corn!

*(The dance resumes, but as it does so, the crowd chants back and forth.)*

WOMEN: Gossip's got a sharp tooth.

MEN: Gossip's got a mean tooth.

WOMEN: She's a lucky woman. They're a lucky pair.

MEN: That's true as gospel. But I wonder where he got it.

WOMEN: Money, land, and riches.

MEN: Just came out of nowhere.

WOMEN AND MEN: *(Together.)* Wonder where he got it all. But that's his business.

FIDDLER: Left and right—grand chain!

*(The dance rises to a pitch of ecstasy with the final figure. The fiddle squeaks and stops. The dancers mop their brows.)*

FIRST MAN: Whew! Ain't danced like that since I was knee high to a grasshopper!

SECOND MAN: Play us "The Portland Fancy," fiddler!

THIRD MAN: No, wait a minute, neighbor. Let's hear from the happy pair! Hey, Jabez!

FOURTH MAN: Let's hear from the State Senator!

*(They crowd around Jabez and push him up on the settle.)*

OLD MAN: Might as well. It's the last time he'll have the last word!

OLD WOMAN: Now, Henry Banks, you ought to be ashamed of yourself!

OLD MAN: Told you so, Jabez!

THE CROWD: Speech!

JABEZ: *(Embarrassed.)* Neighbors, friends—I'm not much of a speaker, spite of your 'lecting me to State Senate—

THE CROWD: That's the ticket, Jabez. Smart man, Jabez. I voted for ye. Go ahead, Senator, you're doing fine.

JABEZ: But we're certainly glad to have you here—me and Mary. And we want to thank you for coming and—

A VOICE: Vote the Whig ticket!

ANOTHER VOICE: Hurray for Daniel Webster!

JABEZ: And I'm glad Hi Foster said that, for those are my sentiments, too. Mr. Webster has promised to honor us with his presence here tonight.

THE CROWD: Hurray for Dan'l! Hurray for the greatest man in the U.S.!

JABEZ: And when he comes, I know we'll give him a real New Hampshire welcome.

THE CROWD: Sure we will—Webster forever—and to hell with Henry Clay!

JABEZ: And meanwhile—well, there's Mary and me *(Takes her hand.)* and, if you folks don't have a good time, well, we won't feel right about getting married at all. Because I know I've been lucky—and I hope she feels that way, too. And, well, we're going to be happy or bust a trace!

*(He wipes his brow to terrific applause. He and Mary look at each other.)*

A WOMAN: *(In kitchen doorway.)* Come and get the cider, folks! *(The crowd begins to drift away—a few to the kitchen, a few toward the door that leads to the outside. They furnish a shifting background to the next little scene, where Mary and Jabez are left alone by the fireplace.)*

JABEZ: Mary.

MARY: Mr. Stone.

JABEZ: Mary.

MARY: My husband.

JABEZ: That's a big word, husband.

MARY: It's a good word.

JABEZ: Are you happy, Mary?

MARY: Yes. So happy I'm afraid.

JABEZ: Afraid?

MARY: I suppose it happens to every girl just for a minute. It's like spring turning into summer. You want it to be summer. But the spring was sweet. *(Dismissing the mood.)* I'm sorry. Forgive me. It just came and went, like something cold. As if we'd been too lucky.

JABEZ: We can't be too lucky, Mary. Not you and me.

MARY: *(Rather mischievously.)* If you say so, Mr. Stone. But you don't even know what sort of housekeeper I am. And Aunt Hepsy says—

JABEZ: Bother your Aunt Hepsy! There's just you and me and that's all that matters in the world.

MARY: And you don't know something else—

JABEZ: What's that?

MARY: How proud I am of you. Ever since I was a little girl. Ever since you carried my books. Oh, I'm sorry for women who can't be proud of their men. It must be a lonely feeling.

JABEZ: *(Uncomfortably.)* A man can't always be proud of everything, Mary. There's some things a man does, or might do, when he has to make his way.

MARY: *(Laughing.)* I know—terrible things—like being the best farmer in the county and the best State Senator—

JABEZ: *(Quietly.)* And a few things besides. But you remember one thing, Mary, whatever happens. It was all for you. And nothing's going to happen. Because he hasn't come yet—and he would have come if it was wrong.

MARY: But it's wonderful to have Mr. Webster come to us.

JABEZ: I wasn't thinking about Mr. Webster. *(He takes both her hands.)* Mary, I've got something to tell you. I should have told you before, but I couldn't seem to bear it. Only, now that it's all right, I can. Ten years ago—

A VOICE: *(From off stage.)* Dan'l! Dan'l Webster!

*(Jabez drops Mary's hands and looks around. The crowd begins to mill and gather toward the door. Others rush in from the kitchen.)*

ANOTHER VOICE: Black Dan'l! He's come!

ANOTHER VOICE: Three cheers for the greatest man in the U.S.!

ANOTHER VOICE: Three cheers for Daniel Webster!

*(And, to the cheering and applause of the crowd, Daniel Webster enters and stands for a moment upstage, in the familiar pose, his head thrown back, his attitude leonine. He stops the cheering of the crowd with a gesture.)*

WEBSTER: Neighbors, old friends—it does me good to hear you. But don't cheer me—I'm not running for President this summer. *(A laugh from the crowd.)*

WEBSTER: I'm here on a better errand—to pay my humble respects to a most charming lady and her very fortunate spouse.

*(There is the twang of a fiddle string breaking.)*

FIDDLER: 'Tarnation! Busted a string!

A VOICE: He's always bustin' strings.

*(Webster blinks at the interruption but goes on.)*

WEBSTER: We're proud of State Senator Stone in these parts—we know what he's done. Ten years ago he started out with a patch of land that was mostly rocks and mortgages and now—well, you've only to look around you. I don't know that I've ever seen a like-lier farm, not even at Marshfield, and I hope, before I die, I'll have the privilege of shaking his hand as Governor of this state. I don't know how he's done it—I couldn't have done it myself. But I know this—Jabez Stone wears no man's collar.

*(At this statement there is a discordant squeak from the fiddle and Jabez looks embarrassed. Webster knits his brows.)*

WEBSTER: And what's more, if I know Jabez, he never will. But I didn't come here to talk politics—I came to kiss the bride.

*(He does so amid great applause. He shakes hands with Jabez.)*

WEBSTER: Congratulations, Stone—you're a lucky man. And now, if our friend in the corner will give us a tune on his fiddle—

*(The crowd presses forward to meet the great man. He shakes hands with several.)*

# The Adding Machine

Elmer Rice
1923

**Serio-comic**
**Scene:** the dining room of the Zero home. Mrs. Zero is watching the
   clock. She is dressed up for company

Mrs. Zero
Mr. Zero
Mr. and Mrs. One
Mr. and Mrs. Two
Mr. and Mrs. Three
Mr. and Mrs. Four
Mr. and Mrs. Five
Mr. and Mrs. Six
Policeman

MRS. ZERO: There's the door-bell. The company's here already. And we
   ain't hardly finished supper. *(She rises.)* But I'm goin' to clear off
   the table whether you're finished or not. If you want your supper,
   you got a right to be home on time. Not standin' around lookin'
   at scoreboards.
   *(As she piles up the dishes, Zero rises and goes toward the
   entrance door.)*
MRS. ZERO: Wait a minute! Don't open the door yet. Do you want the
   company to see all the mess? An' go an' put on a clean collar.
   You got red ink all over it.
   *(Zero goes toward bedroom door.)*
MRS. ZERO: I should think after pushin' a pen for twenty-five years,
   you'd learn how to do it without gettin' ink on your collar.
   *(Zero exits to bedroom. Mrs. Zero takes dishes to kitchen talking
   as she goes.)*
MRS. ZERO: I guess I can stay up all night now washin' dishes. You
   should worry! That's what a man's got a wife for, ain't it? Don't
   he buy her her clothes an' let her eat with him at the same table?
   An' all she's gotta do is cook the meals an' do the washin' an'
   scrub the floor, an' wash the dishes, when the company goes.

But, believe me, you're goin' to sling a mean dish-towel when the company goes to-night!

*(While she is talking Zero enters from bedroom. He wears a clean collar and is cramming the soiled one furtively into his pocket. Mrs. Zero enters from kitchen. She has removed her apron and carries a table cover which she spreads hastily over the table. The clicking noise is heard again.)*

MRS. ZERO: There's the bell again. Open the door, cancha?

*(Zero goes to the entrance door and opens it. Six men and six women file into the room in a double column. The men are all shapes and sizes, but their dress is identical with that of Zero in every detail. Each, however, wears a wig of a different color. The women are all dressed alike, too, except that the dress of each is of a different color.)*

MRS. ZERO: *(Taking the first woman's hand.)* How de do, Mrs. One.

MRS. ONE: How de do, Mrs. Zero.

*(Mrs. Zero repeats this formula with each woman in turn. Zero does the same with the men except that he is silent throughout. The files now separate, each man taking a chair from the right wall and each woman one from the left wall. Each sex forms a circle with the chairs very close together. The men—all except Zero—smoke cigars. The women munch chocolates.)*

SIX: Some rain we're havin'.

FIVE: Never saw the like of it.

FOUR: Worst in fourteen years, paper says.

THREE: Y'can't always go by the papers.

TWO: No, that's right, too.

ONE: We're liable to forget from year to year.

SIX: Yeh, come t' think, last year was pretty bad, too.

FIVE: An' how about two years ago?

FOUR: Still this year's pretty bad.

THREE: Yeh, no gettin' away from that.

TWO: Might be a whole lot worse.

ONE: Yeh, it's all the way you look at it. Some rain, though.

MRS. SIX: I like them little organdie dresses.

MRS. FIVE: Yeh, with a little lace trimmin' on the sleeves.

MRS. FOUR: Well, I like 'em plain myself.

MRS. THREE: Yeh, what I always say is the plainer the more refined.

MRS. TWO: Well, I don't think a little lace does any harm.

MRS. ONE: No, it kinda dresses it up.

MRS. ZERO: Well, I always say it's all a matter of taste.

MRS. SIX: I saw you at the Rosebud Movie Thursday night, Mr. One.

ONE: Pretty punk show, I'll say.

TWO: They're gettin' worse all the time.

MRS. SIX: But who was the charming lady, Mr. One?

ONE: Now don't you go makin' trouble for me. That was my sister.

MRS. FIVE: Oho! That's what they all say.

MRS. FOUR: Never mind! I'll bet Mrs. One knows what's what, all right.

MRS. ONE: Oh, well, he can do what he likes—'slong as he behaves himself.

THREE: You're in luck at that, One. Fat chance I got of gettin' away from the frau even with my sister.

MRS. THREE: You oughta be glad you got a good wife to look after you.

THE OTHER WOMEN: *(In unison.)* That's right, Mrs. Three.

FIVE: I guess I know who wears the pants in your house, Three.

MRS. ZERO: Never mind. I saw them holdin' hands at the movie the other night.

THREE: She musta been tryin' to get some money away from me.

MRS. THREE: Swell chance anybody'd have of gettin' any money away from you.

*(General laughter.)*

FOUR: They sure are a loving couple.

MRS. TWO: Well, I think we oughta change the subject.

MRS. ONE: Yes, let's change the subject.

SIX: *(Sotto voce.)* Did you hear the one about the travellin' salesman?

FIVE: It seems this guy was in a sleeper.

FOUR: Goin' from Albany to San Diego.

THREE: And in the next berth was an old maid.

TWO: With a wooden leg.

ONE: Well, along about midnight—

*(They all put their heads together and whisper.)*

MRS. SIX: *(Sotto voce.)* Did you hear about the Sevens?

MRS. FIVE: They're gettin' a divorce.

MRS. FOUR: It's the second time for him.

MRS. THREE: They're two of a kind, if you ask me.

MRS. TWO: One's as bad as the other.

MRS. ONE: Worse.

MRS. ZERO: They say that she—

*(They all put their heads together and whisper.)*

SIX: I think this woman suffrage is the bunk.

FIVE: It sure is! Politics is a man's business.

FOUR: Woman's place is in the home.

THREE: That's it! Lookin' after the kids, 'stead of hangin' around the streets.

TWO: You hit the nail on the head that time.

ONE: The trouble is they don't know what they want.

MRS. SIX: Men sure get me tired.

MRS. FIVE: They sure are a lazy lot.

MRS. FOUR: And dirty.

MRS. THREE: Always grumblin' about somethin'.

MRS. TWO: When they're not lyin'!

MRS. ONE: Or messin' up the house.

MRS. ZERO: Well, believe me, I tell mine where he gets off.

SIX: Business conditions are sure bad.

FIVE: Never been worse.

FOUR: I don't know what we're comin' to.

THREE: I look for a big smash-up in about three months.

TWO: Wouldn't surprise me a bit.

ONE: We're sure headin' for trouble.

MRS. SIX: My aunt has gall-stones.

MRS. FIVE: My husband has bunions.

MRS. FOUR: My sister expects next month.

MRS. THREE: My cousin's husband has erysipelas.

MRS. TWO: My niece has St. Vitus's dance.

MRS. ONE: My boy has fits.

MRS. ZERO: I never felt better in my life. Knock wood!

SIX: Too damn much agitation, that's at the bottom of it.

FIVE: That's it! too damn many strikes.

FOUR: Foreign agitators, that's what it is.

THREE: They ought be run outa the country.

TWO: What the hell do they want, anyhow?

ONE: They don't know what they want, if you ask me.

SIX: America for the Americans is what I say!

ALL: *(In unison.)* That's it! Damn foreigners! Damn dagoes! Damn Catholics! Damn sheenies! Damn niggers! Jail 'em! shoot 'em! hang 'em! lynch 'em! burn 'em! *(They all rise. Sing in unison.)* "My country 'tis of thee, Sweet land of liberty!"

MRS. FOUR: Why so pensive, Mr. Zero?

ZERO: *(Speaking for the first time.)* I'm thinkin'.

MRS. FOUR: Well, be careful not to sprain your mind.
*(Laughter.)*

MRS. ZERO: Look at the poor men all by themselves. We ain't very sociable.

ONE: Looks like we're neglectin' the ladies.
*(The women cross the room and join the men, all chattering loudly. The doorbell rings.)*

MRS. ZERO: Sh! The doorbell!
*(The volume of sound slowly diminishes. Again the doorbell.)*

ZERO: *(Quietly.)* I'll go. It's for me.
*(They watch curiously as Zero goes to the door and opens it, admitting a policeman. There is a murmur of surprise and excitement.)*

POLICEMAN: I'm lookin for Mr. Zero.
*(They all point to Zero.)*

ZERO: I've been expectin' you.

POLICEMAN: Come along!

ZERO: Just a minute. *(He puts his hand in his pocket.)*

POLICEMAN: What's he tryin' to pull? *(He draws a revolver.)* I got you covered.

ZERO: Sure, that's all right. I just want to give you somethin'. *(He takes the collar from his pocket and gives it to the policeman.)*

POLICEMAN: *(Suspiciously.)* What's that?

ZERO: The collar I wore.

POLICEMAN: What do I want it for?

ZERO: It's got blood-stains on it.

POLICEMAN: *(Pocketing it.)* All right, come along!

ZERO: *(Turning to Mrs. Zero.)* I gotta go with him. You'll have to dry the dishes yourself.

MRS. ZERO: *(Rushing forward.)* What are they takin' you for?

ZERO: *(Calmly.)* I killed the boss this afternoon.
*(Quick curtain as the policeman takes him off.)*

# From the Window

Arnaldo Corradini and Emilio Settimelli
1915

**Scene:** a crowd of spectators to the action on the wall of a castle

All the spectators, many men and women
Sleepwalking Father
Sleepwalking Daughter

First Moment (First Night)
> At the rise of the curtain one sees the very high wall of a castle looming in a moonlit night. Gusts of wind. Midnight strikes on a monotonous clock nearby. A completely dressed man appears from the left on the castle wall, a sleepwalker who moves against the wind (which makes his cloak flutter) with mechanical and secure steps. He disappears. Every spectator hypnotizes himself into believing that the man is his father.
> *(Curtain.)*

Second Moment (Second Night)
> Same scene, same wind, same clock, same time. A young woman comes from the right with her clothes on and her loose hair blowing in the wind. She crosses the stage with the same sleepwalking steps, walking on the same very high castle wall. Every spectator hypnotizes himself into believing she is his sister.
> *(Curtain.)*

Third Moment (Third Night)
> Same scene, same wind, same clock, same time. At the same time the two sleepwalkers, Father and Daughter, appear on the wall, one from the right, one from the left, moving toward each other in the wind. They approach each other, collide, and fall into the void uttering a horrible scream.
> *(Curtain.)*

# The Lottery

Shirley Jackson
Adapted by Bainerd Duffield
1953

**Dramatic**
**Scene:** a village square on June 27th

A village full of people
Joe
Mrs. Dunbar
Mrs. Watson
Tessie
Hutchison
Martin
Warner
Delacroix
Miss Bessom
Belva

JOE: *(Raising voice.)* Now, folks, I'm just about ready to declare this Lottery open. But you know how I always got this last-minute fussin' to do. Want to make sure the list is accurate—with all the heads of families and members of each household in each family.

MRS. DUNBAR: You go right ahead, Mr. Summers.

MRS. WATSON: Joe never made a mistake yet.

*(Tessie Hutchison, wearing an apron over her house dress, enters.)*

MRS. DUNBAR: Why, Tessie! Where you been?

TESSIE: Clean forgot what day it was.

*(Other women close by laugh softly.)*

TESSIE: *(She is drying her hands on her apron as she speaks.)* Thought Bill was out back stackin' wood. But I looked out the window and seen little Davy was gone. Then I remembered it was the twenty-seventh—and come a-runnin'.

MRS. DUNBAR: You made it all right, though. Joe is still checkin' his list.

TESSIE: Seems like there's no time at all between Lotteries any more. Seems like we barely got through with the last one.

MRS. DUNBAR: Time sure goes fast.

TESSIE: *(Glancing around.)* Where's Bill at? Oh, I see him. 'Scuse me, Janey.

*(Villagers make way for her as she moves to join Hutchison.)*

VILLAGERS: Hey, Hutchison! Here she comes! Here's your missus, Bill! Look, Bill! She made it after all!

TESSIE: *(Bending down, to Davy.)* Give Mama a kiss.

*(Davy kisses her.)*

TESSIE: That's my good boy.

*(Looks at Hutchison for a moment. He smiles faintly and takes her hand.)*

HUTCHISON: So you got here, did you?

JOE: *(Calling amiably.)* Thought we were goin' to have to get on without you, Tessie.

TESSIE: *(With forced pleasantness.)* Wouldn't have me leave my dishes in the sink, would you, Joe?

JOE: No, ma'am.

*(General ripple of laughter from Villagers.)*

HUTCHISON: You stay put, Dave, while I talk with your mother.

*(Davy joins other children, as Hutchison brings Tessie to a spot where they talk somewhat apart from other Villagers. He is not angry, but seems deeply concerned and worried.)*

HUTCHISON: What ever kept you?

TESSIE: I don't know, Bill. I just wasn't thinkin', I guess.

HUTCHISON: That story's all right for the women. I know better. You knew the Lottery was today.

TESSIE: Well, it don't matter now. So long as I'm here.

HUTCHISON: What about Davy? Why'd you try to hide him?

TESSIE: Hide him? I didn't hide him. What makes you say that?

HUTCHISON: I found him in the stable loft. He said you told him to wait there—

TESSIE: Yes, but I was goin' to get him, Bill. I was goin' to bring him— honest.

HUTCHISON: What reason did you have to put him there?

TESSIE: Oh, Bill, he's such a little boy! And his birthday just last month. I hate to see the children takin' part in grownup ructions before they've even put aside their toys.

HUTCHISON: I went through it when I was little.

TESSIE: I know, Bill. I guess I was born and brought up with it, same as yourself.

HUTCHISON: Then how did you think you could get away with such a thing? You know Davy's name has to be there along with ours. And you know how careful Joe Summers is. Why, we'd have been a laughing' stock in front of everybody.

TESSIE: But I told you I intended to bring him. You got to believe me, Bill.

HUTCHISON: Talkin' a lot of sentimental tommyrot. I always gave you credit for more sense than some of these other females. What's come over you lately, anyway?

TESSIE: I told you—nothin'.

HUTCHISON: Next thing you'll be sayin' we ought to give up Lotteries altogether—like poor Joe Summers' sister.

TESSIE: Well, I've not come to that yet. But some places have given them up. Lots of little towns up to the north—

HUTCHISON: No good'll come of it, either. You wait and see.

TESSIE: I don't say it will. No, I reckon the Lottery serves its useful purpose. When a custom's been handed down from generation to generation, there must be good in it.

HUTCHISON: (Wagging head, grinning.) Then you shouldn't be so cussed busy, findin' fault.

JOE: (Clearing throat.) Well, now, guess we better get started—get this over with—so's we can get back to work. Anybody ain't here?

VILLAGERS: Dunbar! Clyde Dunbar! Dunbar ain't here!

JOE: (Glancing at list.) Clyde Dunbar—that's right. He's broke his leg, hasn't he? Who's drawin' for him?

MRS. DUNBAR: Me, I guess.

JOE: Wife draws for husband. Don't have a grown boy to do it for you, Janey?

MRS. DUNBAR: Ralph's not but sixteen yet. Guess I got to fill in for the old man this year.
*(Mild chuckle from Villagers.)*

JOE: (Making note.) Right. Jack Wilkins, you're drawin' this year?

JACK: (Blinking nervously.) Yessir. I'm drawin' for my mother and me.

MARTIN: Good fellow, Jack. Glad to see your mother's got a man to do it.

JOE: Well, I guess that's everyone. (With a wink.) Old Man Warner make it?

WARNER: (Raising hand.) Here!

JOE: (Nodding.) Knew you would. (Raps on box.) All ready?

*(Whisper runs through villagers; then a hush follows. Everyone is quite serious now. There is no more laughter.)*

JOE: Now, I'll read off the names—heads of families first—and the men come up and take a paper out of the box. Keep the paper folded in your hand without lookin' at it until everyone has had a turn. Everything clear?

*(Villagers are silent, but nervous, wetting their lips, not looking around or moving.)*

JOE: *(Reads from list.)* Adams.

*(A man disengages himself from crowd, comes forward, reaches into black box and takes out a folded paper.)*

JOE: *(Greets him.)* Hi, Steve.

*(Holding paper firmly, the man goes back to his place and stands, not looking down at his hand.)*

JOE: *(Calls next name.)* Allen.

*(Another man comes to box, repeating same business.)*

JOE: How are you, Mr. Allen?

*(Now, as scene continues, Joe continues to call out names. Each time, someone comes forward, reaches into box, takes out folded piece of paper and returns to his place, not looking down at hand holding paper. As dialogue of villagers breaks into scene, overlapping Joe's voice, calling of the names becomes less distinct, becoming sort of a muted background to villagers' dialogue.)*

JOE: Appleby...Barrows...Burgess...Caswell...Collins...

DELACROIX: They do say that over in the north village, they're talkin' of givin' up the Lottery.

WARNER: Pack of crazy fools! Listenin' to the young folks—nothin's good enough for them. Next thing you know, they'll want to go back to livin' in caves—nobody work any more—live *that* way for a while.

DELACROIX: That's right, Mr. Warner.

WARNER: First thing you know we'd all be eatin' stewed chickweed and acorns. There's *always* been a Lottery.

JOE: Dunbar...

MRS. WATSON: Go on, Janey. That's you.

MISS BESSOM: *(As Mrs. Dunbar crosses to draw.)* There she goes...

JOE: Foster...Graves...Hutchison...

MRS. WATSON: Where do they keep the black box in between times?

MISS BESSOM: It varies. Sometimes one place—sometimes another.

MRS. WATSON: I heard it spent one whole winter in Mr. Graves's barn.

MISS BESSOM: Another year, Clem Martin put it on a shelf in his grocery and left it set there.

MRS. WATSON: Yep. I recall that time.

JOE: Tatum...Townsend...Tuttle...Vincent...

MRS. DUNBAR: *(To Tommy.)* I wish they'd hurry.

TOMMY: They're almost through, Ma.

MRS. DUNBAR: You get ready to run and tell Dad.

JOE: Warner...Howdy, Mr. Warner.

*(Warner takes slip and returns to his place.)*

WARNER: Got mine. Seventy-seventh year I been in the Lottery.

JOE: Watson...Hi, Stella.

MRS. WATSON: *(Drawing.)* Hi, Joe.

JOE: Wilkins...

MISS BESSOM: *(As Jack crosses to draw.)* Don't be nervous, Jack.

JOE: *(Kindly.)* Take your time, son.

JACK: *(Drawing.)* Thanks, Mr. Summers.

JOE: *(Checking off list.)* Now, that's all. *(A breathless pause. Joe draws and holds up his hand with his slip of paper in it.)* All right, fellows. *(For a moment, no one moves; then there is a rustle as all the slips are opened.)*

VILLAGERS: *(Whispering.)* Who is it? Who's got it? Is it the Dunbars? Is it the Watsons? *(Then, louder ad libs are heard, building to an excited climax.)* It's Hutchison! It's Bill! Bill Hutchison's got it! Hutchison!

*(The Hutchisons break away from others and form a small group.)*

MRS. DUNBAR: *(Excitedly.)* Go tell your father!

*(Tommy takes a last awestruck look at Bill Hutchison, where he stands quietly flanked by Tessie and Davy, then Tommy runs out. Hutchison is staring at bit of paper in his hand. villagers are silent again, all eyes on Hutchison family.)*

TESSIE: *(Shouting suddenly.)* Joe Summers! You didn't give him time enough to take any paper he wanted. I saw you. It wasn't fair!

MRS. WATSON: Be a good sport, Tessie.

MISS BESSOM: All of us took the same chance.

HUTCHISON: You hush up, Tessie.

JOE: Well, everyone, that was done pretty fast, and now we've got to be hurryin' a little more to get done in time. *(Consulting list.)* Bill, you draw for the Hutchison family. You got any other households in the Hutchisons?

TESSIE: *(Shrilly.)* There's Don and Eva! Make *them* take their chance!

JOE: *(Gently.)* Daughters draw with their husbands' families. You know that as well as anyone, Tessie.

TESSIE: It wasn't fair!

HUTCHISON: I guess there's just the three of us, Joe. Eva draws with her husband. That's only as it should be.

JOE: Then, as far as drawin' for families is concerned, it's you, and, as far as drawin' for households is concerned, that's you, too. Right?

HUTCHISON: Right.

JOE: How many kids, Bill?

HUTCHISON: Just the one. Little Davy here. Bill, Jr., he died when he was a baby.

JOE: All right, then. Jack, you got some blank tickets back?
*(Jack holds up two blank slips of paper which he has taken from some of the villagers.)*

JOE: Put them in the box, then. Take Bill's and put it in.
*(Jack does so.)*

TESSIE: *(Out of the ensuing silence.)* I think we ought to start over. *(As quietly as she can.)* I tell you, it wasn't fair! You didn't give him time enough to choose. Everybody saw that. *(Appealing.)* Listen, everybody!
*(Jack has stepped back from box. Other villagers have crumpled their own slips and let them drop to ground.)*

JOE: Ready, Bill?
*(Hutchison takes a quick glance at his wife and son and then nods.)*

JOE: Remember, take the slips and keep them folded until each of you has taken one. Jack, you help little Davy.
*(Jack takes Davy's hand and leads him to box.)*

JOE: Take a paper out of the box, Dave. Take just *one* paper.
*(Davy does so.)*

JOE: That's right. Jack, you hold it for him.
*(Jack takes paper and holds it carefully.)*

JOE: Tessie next.
*(Tessie hesitates for a moment, looking around defiantly, then she sets her lips and goes to box. She snatches out a paper and holds it behind her.)*

JOE: Bill…

*(Hutchison reaches into box and brings out last slip of paper. The villagers are silent and tense.)*

MISS BESSOM: *(Breaking silence.)* I hope it isn't little Dave.

*(Villagers begin to whisper.)*

WARNER: *(Clearly.)* It's not the way it used to be. People ain't the same way they used to be.

JOE: All right. Open the papers. Jack, you open little Dave's.

*(Jack opens paper, holds it up, and a sigh of relief goes through villagers as they see that it is blank.)*

JOE: *(Turns to Tessie.)* Tessie…

*(There is a pause. Tessie does not move to open her slip of paper. Joe turns to Hutchison, who unfolds his paper and shows it. It is blank.)*

JOE: *(Speaks to Tessie in a hushed voice.)* It's Tessie. Show us her paper, Bill.

*(Hutchison turns to Tessie and forces her slip of paper out of her hand. It has a black spot on it. He holds it up. A murmur goes through villagers.)*

JOE: *(Comes forward.)* All right, folks. Let's finish quickly. *(Jack carries black box, paddle, and stool off and presently returns to rejoin villagers.)*

MRS. WATSON: *(Excitedly.)* Come on, Janey. Hurry up! Come on, Miss Bessom.

MISS BESSOM: I can't move as fast as I used to.

*(Villagers move toward front of stage, some of them picking up stones as they come. Dickie gives little Davy a fistful of stones. As villagers shift about, Tessie backs away, like a trapped animal, until she is alone at the center of a cleared space at rear. Villagers are grouped at both sides of stage. Now Tessie holds out her hands in a desperate appeal, as villagers turn to face her and begin slowly to close in.)*

TESSIE: It isn't fair! It wasn't done fair!

HUTCHISON: Be quiet, Tess. We got to do this.

*(Throws a stone, and Tessie flinches, putting her hand to her brow.)*

HUTCHISON: Come on. Come on, everyone.

*(Davy throws his fistful of stones. Tessie utters a cry and sinks to her knees. Villagers throw stones.)*

TESSIE: It isn't fair! It isn't right!

(Shields her face as villagers continue to throw stones at her.)

(Belva has crossed the stage, thrusting Joe aside in passing. She goes out without looking at spectacle on stage. By now, villagers have hemmed in their victim, cutting her off from view. The clamor of voices builds, as does the ferocity of the stone-throwing.)

VILLAGERS: Come on! Get it over with! Hit her! That's the way! Hit her, everybody! Get it over!

(Lights dim out, and with darkness comes a low rumble of thunder. Voices of the villagers stop abruptly. Silence.)

# Thunder on Sycamore Street

Reginald Rose
1954

**Dramatic**
**Scene:** inside the Blake house

Anna
Joe
Mrs. Blake
Charlie Denton
First Man
Second Man
Frank Morrison
First Woman
Clarice
Phyllis
Arthur
Christopher, unseen small boy
Whole neighborhood full of angry people

ANNA: What've we done to hurt them? What've we done? I don't understand.

JOE: *(Softly.)* Well, I guess maybe they think we've destroyed the dignity of their neighborhood, darling. That's why they've thrown garbage on our lawn.

ANNA: Dignity! Throwing garbage. Getting together a mob. Those are dignified things to do. Joe, how can you want to stay? How can you want to live on the same street with them? Don't you see what they are?

JOE: They're people, Anna. And I guess they're afraid, just like we are. That's why they've become a mob. It's why people always do.
*(The bedroom door opens and Joe's mother enters. She goes to her rocker and sits in it and begins to rock.)*

ANNA: What are they afraid of?

JOE: Living next door to someone they think is beneath them. An ex-convict. Me.
*(Anna runs to Joe and grips him excitedly.)*

ANNA: What do they think you did? They must think you're a thief or a murderer.

JOE: Maybe they do.

ANNA: Well, they can't. You'll tell them. You'll tell them, Joe.

JOE: Anna, listen…

ANNA: It could've happened to any one of them. Tell them you're not a common criminal. You were in an accident, and that's all it was. An accident. Joe, they'll listen. I know they will.

JOE: No, Anna…

ANNA: *(Eagerly.)* All you have to do is tell them and they'll go away. It's not like you committed a crime or anything. You were speeding. Everybody speeds. You hit an old man, and he died. He walked right in front.

JOE: They're not asking what I did, Anna.

ANNA: *(Pleading.)* Joe, please. Look at me. I'm so frightened…You have to tell them.

JOE: Anna, we have our freedom. If we beg for it, then it's gone. Don't you see that?

ANNA: *(Shouting.)* No!

*(He come to her and grips her, and speaks to her with his face inches from hers.)*

JOE: How can I tell it to you? Listen, Anna, we're only little people, but we have certain rights. Judy's gonna learn about them in school in a couple of years…and they'll tell her that no one can take them away from her. She's got to be able to believe that. They include the right to be different. Well, a group of our neighbors have decided that we have to get out of here because they think we're different. They think we're not nice. *(Strongly.)* Do we have to smile in their faces and tell them we are nice? We don't have to win the right to be free! It's the same as running away, Anna. It's staying on their terms, and if we can't stay here on our terms, then there are no more places to stay anywhere. For you—for me—for Judy—for anyone, Anna.

*(See sees it now and she almost smiles, but the tears are running down her cheeks and it's difficult to smile. Joe kisses her forehead.)*

JOE: *(Quietly.)* Now we'll wait for them.

*(Anna goes slowly to a chair and sits in it. Mrs. Blake rocks rhythmically on her rocking chair. Joe stands firm at one side of the*

room and they wait in silence. Suddenly the ticking of the clock on the mantelpiece thunders in our ears and the monotonous beat of it is all we hear. They wait. Anna looks at Joe and then speaks softly.)

ANNA: Joe. My hands are shaking. I don't want them to shake.

(Joe walks over to her, stands over her strongly and clasps both her hands together. Then he holds them in his till they are still. The clock ticks on, and now we cut to it. It reads ten after seven. Dissolve to a duplicate of the clock which now reads quarter after seven. Cut to long shot of room as we begin to hear the tramping of the feet down the street. They wait. The rocker rocks. The clock ticks. The tramping grows louder. Joe stands in the center of the room, hard and firm. Then he turns to his mother and speaks gently and softly.)

JOE: Go inside, Mother.

MRS. BLAKE: (Slowly.) No, Joe. I'm staying here. I want to watch you. I want to hear you. I want to be proud.

(She continues to rock and now the tramping noise reaches a crescendo and then stops. For a moment there is silence, absolute silence, and then we hear a single angry voice.)

CHARLIE DENTON: (Shouting.) Joseph Blake!

(There is a chorus of shouts and a swelling of noise.)

CHARLIE DENTON: Joseph Blake...come out here!

(The noise from outside grows in volume. Inside only the rocking chair moves.)

FIRST MAN: (Shouting.) Come out of that house!

(The noise, the yelling of the crowd, continues to grow. Inside the room no one gives a signal that they have heard.)

SECOND MAN: (Shouting.) Come out—or we'll drag you out!

(The yelling continues, grows louder. Still the Blakes do not move. Then suddenly a rock smashes through the window. Glass sprays to the floor. The pitch of the noise outside rises even more. Joe begins to walk firmly to the door.)

ANNA: (Softly.) Joe...

(But he doesn't hear her. He gets to the door and flings it open violently and steps outside. As he does, the shouting, which has reached its highest pitch, stops instantly and from deafening noise we plunge into absolute silence, broken only by the steady creaking of the rocking chair inside. Joe stands there in front of *his house like a rock. Now for the first time we see the crowd. The camera plays over the silent faces watching him—the faces of the men and women and children. The Morrisons are directly in front, Charlie Denton is further back. Mrs. Carson is there. And far to the rear we see Arthur Hayes and Phyllis. Still the silence holds. Then, little by little, the people begin to speak. At first we only hear single voices from different parts of the crowd.)*

FIRST MAN: *(Shouting.)* Look at him, standing there like he owns the block!

*(There is a chorus of ad-lib approvals.)*

SECOND MAN: *(Shouting.)* Who do you think you are busting in where decent people live?

*(Another chorus of approvals. Joe stands like a fierce and powerful statue.)*

FIRST WOMAN: *(Shouting.)* Why don't you go live with your own kind…in a gutter somewhere?

*(Another chorus of approvals. The camera moves about catching the eagerness, the mounting temper of the crowd, then the shame and anguish of Arthur Hayes, then the giant strength of Joe.)*

FIRST MAN: *(Shouting.)* Your limousine is waiting, Mr. Blake. You're taking a one-way trip!

*(There a few laughs at this, and now the crowd, although not moving forward, is a shouting mass again. Joe still waits quietly.)*

CHARLIE DENTON: *(Shouting.)* Well, what are we waiting for? let's get him!

*(The intensity of the noise grows and the mob begins to move forward. Then, with a tremendous roar, Frank Morrison stops them.)*

FRANK: *(Roaring.)* Quiet! Everybody shut up.

*(The noise dies down gradually.)*

FRANK: *(To crowd.)* Now listen to me! This whole thing is gonna be handled the way we planned at the meeting.

*(Roger, standing next to Frank, looks at him adoringly. Chris holds Clarice's hand and looks around calmly.)*

CLARICE: *(Loud.)* That's right! It's what we agreed on.

FRANK: *(Shouting.)* This man here is gonna be asked politely and quietly to pack his things and get his family out of here. We don't have to tell him why. He knows that. He's gonna be given a chance to leave right now. If he's got any brains in his head he'll be out in one hour—and nobody'll touch him or his house. If he hasn't—

*(There is a loud-throated, ominous murmur from the crowd.)*

FRANK: Right! This thing is gonna be done fair and square. *(Turning to Joe.)* What d'ya say, Mr. Blake?

*(Joe looks at him for a long time. The crowd waits silently. Arthur Hayes lowers his head and clenches his fists, and looks as if he wants to be sick. The crowd waits. When Joe speaks, it is with a controlled fury that these people have never heard before. He speaks directly to Frank.)*

JOE: I spit on your fairness!

*(The crowd gasps. Joe waits, then he thunders out.)*

JOE: I own this house and God gave me the right to live in it. The man who tries to take it away from me is going to have to climb over a pile of my bones to do it. You good people of Sycamore Street are going to have to kill me tonight! Are you ready, Mr. Morrison? Don't bother to be fair. You're the head man here. Be first!

*(The crowd, rocked back on its heels, doesn't know what to do. Behind Joe, in the house, we see framed in the doorway the rocking chair moving steadily, and Anna standing next to it. Frank is stunned by this outburst. He calls for action. But not with the force he displayed earlier.)*

FRANK: You heard him, everybody…Let's get him.

JOE: I asked for you first, Mr. Morrison!

FRANK: *(Shouting.)* Listen to me! Let's go, men!

*(But the crowd is no longer moving as a whole. Some of them are still strongly with Frank, including Charlie, the first man, the second man, and several of the others. But others are not so sure of themselves now.)*

CHARLIE: *(Roaring.)* Don't let him throw you, Frank! he asked for it. Let's give it to him!

*(Joe looks only at Frank. Waits calmly for him.)*

FRANK: *(Roaring.)* Come on!

*(He takes a step forward, but the people behind him don't follow. He turns to them.)*

FRANK: What's the matter with you people?

JOE: They're waiting for you, Mr. Morrison.

*(Frank whirls and faces him and they look long and hard at each*

*other. Cut to Charlie Denton at rear of crowd. He has a stone in his hand.)*

CHARLIE: *(Shouting.)* Let's start it off, Frankie boy. *(He flings the stone.)* *(We hear it hit and drop to the ground. The crowd gasps. Cut to Joe. There is blood running down the side of his head. He stands there firmly. Cut to Arthur Hayes. He looks up in horror, and then a transformation comes over him. He seems to grow taller and broader. His face sets strongly and he begins to stride forward, elbowing people aside. Phyllis knows. She clings to him, trying to pull him back.)*

PHYLLIS: *(Screaming.)* Artie…Artie…don't…

*(But he breaks loose from her and pushes forward. Whoever is in his way is knocked aside, and finally he reaches Joe. He looks up at Joe. Then he turns and stands next to him. He takes off his eyeglasses and flings them into the crowd.)*

ARTHUR: *(Strong.)* Throw the next stone at me, neighbors. I live here too! *(The crowd is uncertain as the two men stand together and the blood runs down Joe's face. Frank tries to rally them. During his next lines we shoot through the open door into the living room. Mrs. Blake gets up from her rocking chair and takes Anna's hand. Together they walk to the front door, come outside and stand proudly behind Joe and Arthur.)*

FRANK: Listen to me! Pay attention, you people. Let's remember what we came here to do…and why! This man is garbage! He's cluttering up our street. He's wrecking our neighborhood. We don't want him here. We agreed, every last man and woman of us…we agreed to throw him out! Are we gonna let him stop us? If we do—you know what'll happen.

*(Mrs. Blake and Anna are out of the house now. They wait, along with Joe and Arthur. The crowd listens. Frank shouts on, running from person to person as the crowd begins ashamedly to drift away. Christopher clings to Frank's jacket, and begins to sob.)*

FRANK: You know what Sycamore Street'll be like. I don't have to tell you. How do we know who we'll be rubbing elbows with next? Listen, where are you going? We're all together in this! What about our kids? Listen to me, people. Our kids'll be playing and going to school with his. How do you like that, neighbors? Makes you a little sick, doesn't it? Come back here! I'm telling you we've got to do this! Come back here!

*(But the crowd continues to drift away. Finally only the Morrisons and Phyllis Hayes are left in the street. Joe and his family, and Arthur, watch them proudly. Roger looks at his bewildered father and then he turns away, takes Clarice's hand, and his father is no longer the greatest guy in the world. Frank looks down at the sobbing Christopher, and picks him up and walks slowly off. Clarice and Roger follow. The Blakes turn and go into their house, leaving Arthur on the porch. And standing alone, starkly in the middle of the street, is Phyllis. Arthur looks at her as she stands, heartbreakingly alone, for a long time.)*

ARTHUR: *(Sadly.)* Well, what are you standing there for? My neighbor's head is bleeding!

*(And then, slowly, knowing that Arthur is no longer a grown-up child, Phyllis moves forward into Joseph Blake's house. Fade out.)*

# Syndrome

Dale Allias
1995

**Dramatic**
**Scene:** a bare stage

Large mixed cast, all types

    In the darkness, a well-modulated, unseen female voice is heard. She reads a list of American names, prominently male. The off-stage reader continues to read the names, in a metronome-like rhythm throughout the piece. Her voice shows neither compassion nor any other emotion; rather her voice is relentless. Music can accompany the voice if it is atonal with unexpected rhythm and made by unexpected instrumentation.

    Lights up to reveal a large bare stage. On stage left is a long, long single file line of actors. The line is so long that it must snake back and forth several times. The actors are cheery, good natured, and smiling. They do not speak, but they do touch the person in front of them, in a friendly way, on the shoulder, hair, back, buttocks. The touching is slightly sexual, definitely comforting and pleasurable. There are soft sounds from the actors, "Ah" "Mmmm." Sighs. Several minutes pass. No one seems impatient with the wait.

    Two-thirds down the line, one of the actors collapses into the arms of the actor behind him. All look as the actor behind and the actor in front carry the limp body of the fallen actor to the empty stage-right side of the stage. The others look confused, but the touching continues. Another actor falls, then another. Each time the limp actor is carried to the other side of the stage. The fallen actors' limp unmoving bodies are lined up side by side, in an orderly row on the stage right side. Those who carried fallen actors return to their places in line.

    The voice continues reading names at the same pace, and it does not necessarily match the rate actors are falling on the stage. As more actors fall into the arms of the people behind them, the gentle touching stops. The standing actors look concerned. The posture of the standing actors becomes rigid. Arms are folded tightly across chest. Muscles taut.

Soon there are more fallen actors than standing actors. The standing actors move close together to catch one another, but they do not, in any way, connect otherwise.

The falling seems to slow down for a few moments; although the voice continues. The standing actors look around; "is it over?" is the expression on their faces. No one falls for a few moments more, and the standing actors begin to smile. A few tentatively touch. Then, one falls. And another. And another. Many fall in quick succession. There are so many fallen actors, that there is no time to carry them to the orderly row on stage right. They are caught, dropped to the ground and left where they began. Only three are left standing. The three stand in a triangle, then walk in a circle watching the each other to see who will fall next. Two of the three fall almost simultaneously, first to fall without being caught.

There is only one actor left; he steps over the fallen, in an aimless cross across the stage toward the stage-eft wing. After he has reached the far side of the stage, he too collapses. Blackout. The voice continues reading three more names. She stops in the middle of a name.

Every effort has been made to locate the proper copyright holder for each excerpt published in this anthology. Any discrepancies or exclusions are unintentional.

**610**